THE GLENN MILLER ARMY AIR FORCE BAND:

Sustineo Alas / I Sustain the Wings

volume two

by
EDWARD F. POLIC

studies in jazz, no. 8

1989

The Scarecrow Press, Inc.
Metuchen, N.J., & London Institute of Jazz Studies
Rutgers University

TABLE OF CONTENTS

APPENDIX I

GLENN MILLER ARMY AIR FORCE BAND

SCRIPTS

This section is comprised of a sampling of scripts of various broadcasts, recordings, a bond rally and a concert that were done by the Glenn Miller Army Air Force Band and its various subunits.

An indented name of a speaker signifies that the speaking was taking place while the music listed before it was being played. Some of the script material that follows was transcribed from recordings. Material within [ ] was taken from written scripts; material that was taken totally from scripts is noted by the designation "Script." In those cases the actual dialogue may have varied slightly from the written script. Air dates for recordings signify the first air dates of those recordings.

SCRIPTS

05Jun43	I Sustain the Wings	
12Jun43	I Sustain the Wings	Excerpts
19Jun43	I Sustain the Wings	Excerpts
26Jun43	I Sustain the Wings	Excerpts
10Jul43	I Sustain the Wings	Excerpts
17Jul43	I Sustain the Wings	
24Jul43	I Sustain the Wings	
31Jul43	I Sustain the Wings	
07Aug43	I Sustain the Wings	
14Aug43	I Sustain the Wings	
21Aug43	I Sustain the Wings	
28Aug43	I Sustain the Wings	
04Sep43	I Sustain the Wings	
11Sep43	I Sustain the Wings	
18Sep43	Uncle Sam Presents	
18Sep43	I Sustain the Wings	
25Sep43	I Sustain the Wings	
02Oct43	Uncle Sam Presents	
02Oct43	6:00PM I Sustain the Wings	
02Oct43	11:30PM I Sustain the Wings	
09Oct43	Uncle Sam Presents	
09Oct43	6:00PM I Sustain the Wings	
09Oct43	11:30PM I Sustain the Wings	
16Oct43	6:00PM I Sustain the Wings	
16Oct43	11:30PM I Sustain the Wings	
23Oct43	6:00PM I Sustain the Wings	
23Oct43	11:30PM I Sustain the Wings	
29Oct43	V-Disc Recording Session	
30Oct43	6:00PM I Sustain the Wings	
30Oct43	11:30PM I Sustain the Wings	
04Nov43	March of Time	
06Nov43	Uncle Sam Presents	Excerpt
06Nov43	6:00PM I Sustain the Wings	
06Nov43	11:30PM I Sustain the Wings	
12Nov43	Treasury Star Parade Program 309 (G-6685-P1)	
12Nov43	Treasury Star Parade Program 314 (G-6686-P2)	
13Nov43	Uncle Sam Presents	Excerpt
13Nov43	I Sustain the Wings	
20Nov43	Uncle Sam Presents	
20Nov43	6:00PM I Sustain the Wings	
20Nov43	11:30PM I Sustain the Wings	
27Nov43	Uncle Sam Presents	
27Nov43	6:00PM I Sustain the Wings	
04Dec43	Uncle Sam Presents	
04Dec43	6:00PM I Sustain the Wings	
11Dec43	Uncle Sam Presents	

11Dec43	6:00PM	I Sustain the Wings	
11Dec43	11:30PM	I Sustain the Wings	
18Dec43	Hello Latin-America		
18Dec43	6:00PM	I Sustain the Wings	
18Dec43	11:30PM	I Sustain the Wings	
25Dec43	6:00PM	I Sustain the Wings	
25Dec43	11:30PM	I Sustain the Wings	Excerpts
01Jan44	I Sustain the Wings		Excerpts
08Jan44	Uncle Sam Presents		
08Jan44	6:00PM	I Sustain the Wings	Excerpt
08Jan44	11:30PM	I Sustain the Wings	Excerpts
15Jan44	Uncle Sam Presents		
15Jan44	6:00PM	I Sustain the Wings	Excerpt
15Jan44	11:30PM	I Sustain the Wings	Excerpts
17Jan44	Let's Back the Attack		Excerpt
22Jan44	Uncle Sam Presents		
22Jan44	6:00PM	I Sustain the Wings	
22Jan44	11:30PM	I Sustain the Wings	Excerpts
29Jan44	Uncle Sam Presents		Excerpts
29Jan44	I Sustain the Wings		Excerpts
05Feb44	Uncle Sam Presents		
05Feb44	6:00PM	I Sustain the Wings	
05Feb44	11:30PM	I Sustain the Wings	Excerpts
11Feb44	Treasury Star Parade 1st show		
11Feb44	Treasury Star Parade 2nd show		
12Feb44	Uncle Sam Presents		
12Feb44	6:00PM	I Sustain the Wings	
12Feb44	11:30PM	I Sustain the Wings	Excerpts
19Feb44	Uncle Sam Presents		Excerpt
19Feb44	6:00PM	I Sustain the Wings	
19Feb44	11:30PM	I Sustain the Wings	Excerpts
26Feb44	Uncle Sam Presents		
26Feb44	6:00PM	I Sustain the Wings	
26Feb44	11:30PM	I Sustain the Wings	Excerpts
04Mar44	Uncle Sam Presents		
04Mar44	6:00PM	I Sustain the Wings	
04Mar44	11:30PM	I Sustain the Wings	Excerpts
11Mar44	Uncle Sam Presents		Excerpt
11Mar44	6:00PM	I Sustain the Wings	
11Mar44	11:30PM	I Sustain the Wings	Excerpts
18Mar44	Uncle Sam Presents		
18Mar44	6:00PM	I Sustain the Wings	Excerpts
18Mar44	11:30PM	I Sustain the Wings	Excerpts
25Mar44	Uncle Sam Presents		Excerpt
25Mar44	6:00PM	I Sustain the Wings	
25Mar44	11:30PM	I Sustain the Wings	Excerpts
01Apr44	Uncle Sam Presents		
01Apr44	6:00PM	I Sustain the Wings	
01Apr44	11:30PM	I Sustain the Wings	Excerpts
06Apr44	Home Base		
08Apr44	6:00PM	I Sustain the Wings	Excerpt
08Apr44	11:30PM	I Sustain the Wings	Excerpts
15Apr44	6:00PM	I Sustain the Wings	
15Apr44	11:30PM	I Sustain the Wings	Excerpts
22Apr44	Uncle Sam Presents		Excerpt
22Apr44	6:00PM	I Sustain the Wings	
22Apr44	11:30PM	I Sustain the Wings	Excerpts
29Apr44	Uncle Sam Presents		
29Apr44	6:00PM	I Sustain the Wings	
29Apr44	11:30PM	I Sustain the Wings	Excerpts

06May44	6:00PM	I Sustain the Wings			Excerpt
06May44	11:30PM	I Sustain the Wings			Excerpts
13May44	6:00PM	I Sustain the Wings			Excerpts
13May44	11:30PM	I Sustain the Wings			Excerpts
20May44	6:00PM	I Sustain the Wings			
20May44	11:30PM	I Sustain the Wings			Excerpts
27May44	6:00PM	I Sustain the Wings			Excerpt
27May44	11:30PM	I Sustain the Wings			Excerpts
03Jun44	6:00PM	I Sustain the Wings			
03Jun44	11:30PM	I Sustain the Wings			
10Jun44	6:00PM	I Sustain the Wings			
10Jun44	11:30PM	I Sustain the Wings			
09Jul44		Welcome to American Band		SWN-18891	
20Jul44		American Band of the Supreme Allied Command		SWN-18901	
22Jul44		The Swing Shift		SWN-18971	Excerpts
23Jul44		American Band of the Supreme Allied Command		SWN-18908	
27Jul44		American Eagle in Britain		DOX-36114	
28Jul44	11:00AM	The Uptown Hall		SLO-59930	
Jul-Dec44		Corporal Paul Dubov dialogue			
29Jul44		V-8 Bond Rally			Excerpt
03Aug44		American Band of the AEF		SWN-18951	
03Aug44	9:00PM	The Uptown Hall		31214/31217	Excerpts
07Aug44, or 06Sep44	7:45PM	Strings with Wings			Excerpt
09Aug44		The Uptown Hall		SOX-36628	Excerpts
10Aug44		American Eagle in Britain		DOX-36727	
10Aug44		American Band of the AEF		SWN-18986	Excerpts
12Aug44	2:35PM	The Uptown Hall		SLO-60537/A	Excerpts
12Aug44	2:55PM	The Uptown Hall		SLO-60537/B	
18Aug44		The Swing Shift		SLO-60496	Excerpt
22Aug44	11:15AM	The Uptown Hall		SLO-61066	Excerpts
24Aug44		American Band of the AEF		SWN-19041	Excerpt
27Aug44		Variety Bandbox		DLO-60978	Excerpt
27Aug44		Special Show			Excerpt
31Aug44		American Eagle in Britain		DOX-37918	
31Aug44		American Band of the AEF		SWN-19136	
02Sep44		Atlantic Spotlight		FWN-19139	
06Sep44	c. 3:00PM	The Uptown Hall		SWN-19244	Excerpt
06Sep44	c. 3:30PM	The Uptown Hall		SWN-19245	Excerpt
07Sep44		American Band of the AEF		SWN-19167	Excerpts
08Sep44	7:30PM	The Uptown Hall			
09Sep44		Strings with Wings		SLO-61673	
13Sep44	8:15PM	Strings with Wings		SLO-61750	
14Sep44		Here's Wishing You Well			
23Sep44	10:45AM	The Uptown Hall		SAL-16667	
26Sep44	8:45PM	The Uptown Hall		SLO-62523	
28Sep44		American Eagle in Britain	DOX-39135/DLO-62311/DLO-62354A		Excerpt
29Sep44		The Swing Shift		SLO-62604	
30Sep44	11:00AM	The Uptown Hall		SAL-16706	
05Oct44		American Band of the AEF		SWN-19353	Excerpt
08Oct44		The Swing Shift		SLO-63029A	
12Oct44		American Band of the AEF		SLO-63391	Excerpt
17Oct44		The Swing Shift			Excerpt
30Oct44		OWI Recording Session for ABSIE			
01Nov44		The Uptown Hall			Excerpts
01Nov44		Strings with Wings			
02Nov44		American Band of the AEF		SWN-19498	Excerpts
04Nov44		Piano Parade			
04Nov44		The Swing Shift			
04Nov44		The Uptown Hall			
05Nov44		Songs By Sgt. Johnny Desmond			

06Nov44	OWI Recording Session for ABSIE		
06Nov44	Strings with Wings		
08Nov44	The Uptown Hall		
08Nov44	Strings with Wings		
10Nov44	The Uptown Hall		
11Nov44	Piano Parade		
11Nov44	The Uptown Hall		
13Nov44	Songs by Sgt. Johnny Desmond		
13Nov44	Strings with Wings		
14Nov44	Moonlight Serenade	SWN-19601	Excerpts
15Nov44	Strings with Wings		
17Nov44	Moonlight Serenade	SLO-65370	Excerpts
18Nov44	The Swing Shift	SLO-65292	
20Nov44	OWI Recording Session for ABSIE		
20Nov44	Strings with Wings		
24Nov44	Moonlight Serenade	SLO-65321	
25Nov44	5:15PM Strings with Wings	SLO-65810	
25Nov44	5:45PM Strings with Wings	SLO-65811	
25Nov44	The Uptown Hall		Excerpts
25Nov44	9:00PM Moonlight Serenade	SLO-65813	
25Nov44	11:00PM Moonlight Serenade	SLO-65911	
26Nov44	3:50PM Songs by Sgt. Johnny Desmond	SLO-65815	Excerpts
26Nov44	4:10PM Songs by Sgt. Johnny Desmond	SLO-65816	
26Nov44	4:25PM Songs by Sgt. Johnny Desmond	SLO-65914	Excerpt
26Nov44	4:40PM Songs by Sgt. Johnny Desmond	SLO-65915	
27Nov44	OWI Recording Session for ABSIE		
27Nov44	3:30PM Moonlight Serenade	SLO-65817	
27Nov44	7:15PM Strings with Wings		
28Nov44	11:00AM Moonlight Serenade	SLO-65820	
28Nov44	8:30PM American Band of the AEF	SLO-64971	
29Nov44	7:45PM Strings with Wings		
30Nov44	5:55PM The Swing Shift	SLO-66424	
01Dec44	10:00AM Moonlight Serenade	DLO-66425A	
01Dec44	10:40AM Moonlight Serenade	DLO-65918A	Excerpts
01Dec44	8:30PM Moonlight Serenade	SLO-65322	
01Dec44	Moonlight Serenade	SLO-65831A	
02Dec44	Piano Parade		
02Dec44	5:45PM Strings with Wings	SLO-65835	
02Dec44	6:35PM Strings with Wings	SLO-66436	
03Dec44	3:30PM Songs by Sgt. Johnny Desmond	SLO-65840	
03Dec44	4:00PM Songs by Sgt. Johnny Desmond	SLO-65841 or	
8Oct44	12:45PM A Soldier and a Song		Excerpt
03Dec44	4:30PM Songs by Sgt. Johnny Desmond	SLO-65842	
03Dec44	10:20PM The Uptown Hall	SLO-65844	
04Dec44	3:30PM The Swing Shift	SLO-66381	
04Dec44	Songs by Sgt. Johnny Desmond		
04Dec44	7:15PM Strings with Wings		
06Dec44	Christmas Greetings from Don Haynes		
06Dec44	Christmas Greetings from Glenn Miller		
06Dec44	6:15PM The Uptown Hall		
06Dec44	Strings with Wings		
06Dec44	11:00PM The Uptown Hall	SLO-65855	
06Dec44	11:50PM The Uptown Hall	SLO-65857	
07Dec44	12:15AM The Uptown Hall	SLO-65858	
07Dec44	1:05AM The Uptown Hall	SLO-65860	
07Dec44	1:30AM The Uptown Hall	SLO-66654	
07Dec44	5:50PM The Swing Shift	SLO-66555	
07Dec44	7:30PM The Swing Shift	SLO-64996	
07Dec44	9:15PM The Uptown Hall		Excerpt
08Dec44	Songs by Sgt. Johnny Desmond	SAL-17833	

08Dec44	11:30PM	The Swing Shift	SLO-66682	
09Dec44		Piano Parade		
09Dec44		The Uptown Hall	SLO-65867	
09Dec44		The Uptown Hall	SLO-65868	Excerpts
09Dec44	7:45PM	Strings with Wings	SLO-65864	
11Dec44		Songs by Sgt. Johnny Desmond		
11Dec44		Strings with Wings		
12Dec44	4:00PM	Moonlight Serenade	SLO-65879	
12Dec44	8:30PM	Moonlight Serenade	SLO-65569	
c.23-31Dec44		Corporal Paul Dubov dialogue		
24Dec44		News announcements		
25Dec44		War World News Roundup		
25Dec44		Grand Roundup	SLO-67216	
15Jan45	3:30PM	American Band of the AEF	SLO-68223	Excerpts
15Jan45	8:30PM	American Band of the AEF	SLO-67959	Excerpt
22Jan45	5:30PM	American Band of the AEF	SLO-67948	Excerpts
29Jan45	5:30PM	American Band of the AEF	SLO-69208	Excerpts
05Feb45	5:30PM	American Band of the AEF	SLO-68716	Excerpts
05Feb45	8:30PM	American Band of the AEF	SLO-69094	Excerpts
06Feb45		The Swing Shift	SLO-68994	Excerpts
12Feb45	6:30PM	American Band of the AEF	SBU-59233	Excerpts
15Feb45	11:20PM	The Swing Shift	SLO-69668	Excerpt
18Feb45	Concert	Paris Opera House		
19Feb45	3:15PM	American Band of the AEF	SLO-69971	Excerpts
20Feb45		The Swing Shift	SLO-69784/SLO-69974	Excerpts
26Feb45	3:15PM	American Band of the AEF	SLO-69690	Excerpts
26Feb45	8:30PM	American Band of the AEF	SLO-69194	Excerpts
27Feb45		The Swing Shift	SLO-69691	Excerpts
06Mar45		The Swing Shift	SLO-70421	Excerpts
08Mar45		The Swing Shift	SLO-70422	
12Mar45	8:30PM	American Band of the AEF	SLO-70222	Excerpts
13Mar45		The Swing Shift	SLO-70336	Excerpts
15Mar45	10:40PM	The Swing Shift	SLO-70268	Excerpts
19Mar45	3:15PM	American Band of the AEF	SLO-70285	Excerpts
26Mar45	2:40PM	American Band of the AEF	SLO-70759	Excerpt
02Apr45	3:20PM	American Band of the AEF	SLO-71948	Excerpt
03Apr45		American Band of the AEF	SAL-19920	Excerpt
05Apr45	10:35PM	The Swing Shift	SAL-20115	
05Apr45	11:10PM	The Swing Shift	SAL-20116	
09Apr45	2:45PM	American Band of the AEF	SLO-71256	
09Apr45	3:20PM	American Band of the AEF	SLO-71954	
10Apr45		The Swing Shift	SLO-71510	Excerpt
11Apr45		The Swing Shift	SLO-71956	Excerpts
16Apr45	8:30PM	American Band of the AEF	SLO-71881	Excerpt
20Apr45	10:30PM	The Swing Shift	SLO-72005	Excerpts
07May45	8:45PM	American Band of the AEF	SLO-73128	Excerpts
10May45	10:30PM	The Swing Shift	SLO-74256	Excerpt
14May45	2:45PM	American Band of the AEF	SLO-74270	Excerpts
14May45	3:20PM	American Band of the AEF	SLO-74365	Excerpt
15May45	10:40PM	Strings with Wings	SLO-74541	
21May45		The Swing Shift	SLO-74073	Excerpt
21May45	8:50PM	American Band of the AEF	SLO-74075	Excerpt
24May45	10:30PM	The Swing Shift	SLO-74785	Excerpt
28May45	2:50PM	American Band of the AEF	SLO-74528	Excerpts
28May45	3:35PM	American Band of the AEF	SLO-75136	Excerpt
31May45	10:30PM	Strings with Wings	SLO-74642	
04Jun45	8:45PM	American Band of the AEF	SLO-75684	Excerpt
21Jul45	Concert			
29Sep45		I Sustain the Wings		
06Oct45		I Sustain the Wings dress rehearsal		

13Oct45 I Sustain the Wings dress rehearsal
20Oct45 I Sustain the Wings dress rehearsal
03Nov45 I Sustain the Wings
10Nov45 I Sustain the Wings dress rehearsal
17Nov45 I Sustain the Wings

Unknown dates Alphabetically by tune titles   Excerpts

05Jun43 (Sat) 6:15-6:45PM Woolsey Hall, Yale University, New Haven, Connecticut
  I SUSTAIN THE WINGS broadcast WEEI (CBS), Boston, Massachusetts   Audience

I SUSTAIN THE WINGS (opening theme)
  Pfc. Broderick Crawford: "I Sustain the Wings." "I Sustain the Wings," a program of
    music and entertainment brought to you by the Technical Training Command of the Army
    Air Forces, the men who keep 'em flying. The program features the Technical Training
    Command Orchestra, the Glee Club ...
  Vocal refrain by Private First Class Tony Martin and the Glee Club
  Pfc. Broderick Crawford: ... and Captain Glenn Miller.
Captain Glenn Miller: Good evening, everybody. Here we are again, all your friends,
    Broderick Crawford, Tony Martin, Damian O'Flynn, Mel Powell, Zeke Zarchy, Hank Freeman,
    and all the other boys in a program of music for your listenin' pleasure. The boys
    start marchin' with the "American Patrol," so, Corporal McKinley, roll off.
AMERICAN PATROL
MOONLIGHT BECOMES YOU
  Captain Glenn Miller: The band plays and Private Bob Houston sings "Moonlight Becomes
    You."
  Vocal refrain by Private Bob Houston
DRINK TO ME ONLY WITH THINE EYES (Old tune)
  Captain Glenn Miller: And now something old, something new, something borrowed and
    something blue, the old song, "Drink to Me Only with Thine Eyes."
  Captain Glenn Miller: For the new tune Private Arthur Malvin and the orchestra give 'em
    "Don't Get Around Much Anymore."
DON'T GET AROUND MUCH ANYMORE (New tune)
  Vocal refrain by Private Artie Malvin
  Captain Glenn Miller: We borrow Chief Petty Officer Artie Shaw's beautiful theme,
    "Begin the Beguine," Private Tony Martin doin' the singin'.
BEGIN THE BEGUINE (Borrowed tune)
  Vocal refrain by Private First Class Tony Martin
  Captain Glenn Miller: Last in our medley is something blue, "Blue Moon."
BLUE MOON (Blue tune)
Announcer: Did you ever hear a 50-caliber machine gun? The sound of a gun turret
    spinning? The whining whistle of a block buster falling? A crash of a bomb? The
    rainfall of shrapnel? These are magic sounds. A huge symphony from the instruments of
    victory. On December the 7th, 1941 this strange song began with a somber theme, words
    like Wake Island, Guam, Bataan, Corregidor; they became vows to avenge. Then came words
    like Coral Sea, Midway, Doolittle, MacArthur, Montgomery, Eisenhower, North Africa,
    Tunis and Beserta. Magic words.
Incidental music
  Announcer: They've changed the music of the spheres. Magic words, they give their
    thanks to the men whose deeds go unsung, the soldiers of the Technical Training
    Command. To a band of men, the men who place the bombs in the racks, fix the
    cartridge belts in the machine guns, service the turrets, use the explosives, set the
    gun sights. They're in New Guinea, secret bases in China, hopping off points in
    Africa. You'll find them wherever you see an American plane. They're making history.
    They're Uncle Sam's Armorers.
Pfc. Broderick Crawford (as Sgt. Abe Miller): I got bombs that "Jingle, Jangle, Jingle,"
    as they go flyin' merrily along. And they sing of ain't you bad o'jingle.
Private Damian F. O'Flynn (as Pvt. Tim Wiggins): Uh, uh. Hello, Sarge.
Pfc. Broderick Crawford: Oh, pull up a window and sit down. I got bomb... Hey, I don't
    know you, do I?
Private Damian F. O'Flynn: No, Sarge. I came in last night on the transport. The C.O.
    told me to report to you for duty.
Pfc. Broderick Crawford: Yeah? What's your handle?
Private Damian F. O'Flynn: My what?
Pfc. Broderick Crawford: Your handle, John Hancock, moniker, your name.
Private Damian F. O'Flynn: Oh, oh. Tim Wiggins, Sarge.
Pfc. Broderick Crawford: Oh, glad to know you, Tim. My name's Abe. Just call me Abe.
Private Damian F. O'Flynn: O.K., Abe.

Pfc. Broderick Crawford: Yeah, it's about time they give me a helper here. Say, you're gonna like it on this post, kid. It's a cinch. You got no reveille and no roll call and you're only on duty for 24 hours a day. You'll like it fine. How was your trip comin' in?

Private Damian F. O'Flynn: Aw, terrific. We ran into a pack of FW-190s but the Lightnings on our escort beat 'em up somethin' fierce.

Pfc. Broderick Crawford: Yeah, solid job those Lightnings, but don't worry, Tim, nothing like that happens here. This is a very quiet field, nothing happens, just like in Grand Hotel, very quiet.

Private Damian F. O'Flynn: No kiddin'?

Pfc. Broderick Crawford: May I never live to see Ebbets Field if I'm lyin'. This job is too easy.

Private Damian F. O'Flynn: Hey, that's an air raid signal. Let's beat it.

Pfc. Broderick Crawford: Hey, wait a minute, kid. Are you forgettin' we're Armorers? We got work to do out there. Come on, on the double. Here, make yourself a necklace with these cartridges and take 'em over to Shirley.

Private Damian F. O'Flynn: Shirley?

Pfc. Broderick Crawford: Yeah, the B-17 with the lifted nose. Here, I'll help you.

Private Damian F. O'Flynn: Hey, I thought you said this was a quiet field.

Pfc. Broderick Crawford: Yeah, yeah, yeah. Come on, let's go. Oh, oh, here comes the visitin' team, Stucker Sonjas and some Italian escorts.

Flyer: Right here, men. Hand those belts up. We got to get this plane off the ground. Everything else all set?

Pfc. Broderick Crawford: Yes, sir. All the guns are serviced. Here you are. You ready, Tim?

Private Damian F. O'Flynn: Yep.

Pfc. Broderick Crawford: Come on, kid. Let's get out of the way. Now you'll get to see a real show, kid.

Private Damian F. O'Flynn: Look, there goes a Stucker.

Pfc. Broderick Crawford: Yeah, don't it look pretty all lit up like that?

Private Damian F. O'Flynn: And look at those P-38s whip into those formations.

Pfc. Broderick Crawford: Aw, solid job those Lightnings, solid. Look there goes another Heine and another one. Boy, what they don't know about this business of shooting and bombing would fill a book.

Private Damian F. O'Flynn: Look, look. They hit the hanger. I thought you said they didn't know much about bombin'.

Pfc. Broderick Crawford: Aw, the lucky bums. I bet you that son of a Nazi was aimin' at somethin' else, that lucky ...

Private Damian F. O'Flynn: Hey, look over there, two more Stuckers out of the picture.

Pfc. Broderick Crawford: Yeah, it's a double play, Herman to Vandrick to Milly. Well, that's another war bond to my collection.

Private Damian F. O'Flynn: Another war bond? I don't get it.

Pfc. Broderick Crawford: My own little deal with Uncle Sam. Every time I see five enemy planes hit the dirt I buy me a war bond. And I got a terrific collection. By the time the war's over I hope to be a millionaire.

(I Got Spurs) Jingle Jangle Jingle (Incidental music)

Announcer: Ha. Good for you, Abe. A bond for every five enemy planes shot down. Our planes return. Some are bullet riddled and all are safe. The construction squads are on the job, bomb craters are filled, leveled off, the hanger is rebuilt, the planes are patched. It's a race against time. Orders have come through for an attack on a strategic port somewhere in Italy.

Pfc. Broderick Crawford: Hand me that socket wrench, Tim. My, this turret's still a little shaky.

Private Damian F. O'Flynn: Here you are, Abe. Boy, won't I like to be up in this kite when she sails over Italy.

Pfc. Broderick Crawford: Yeah, yeah, yeah. I tried my hand in it but I washed out. We can't all be pilots, you know. Then I wanted to be a turret gunner but they told me I was too big to squeeze into a turret. I know all about planes and guns and stuff so they made me an armorer. But it's a solid job, a quiet job.

Private Damian F. O'Flynn: Head up, Sarge. Here comes the C.O.

Commanding Officer (Major): As you were, men. Sergeant Miller.
Pfc. Broderick Crawford: Yes, sir.
Commanding Officer: Private Wiggins.
Private Damian F. O'Flynn: Yes, sir.
Commanding Officer: Men, we're sending some bombers over Italy tonight, more than I'd
  expected and I'm short on gunners. I see by your records that you men have had
  train-training in gunnery.
Pfc. Broderick Crawford and Private Damian F. O'Flynn: Yes, sir.
Commanding Officer: You two will report to Captain Ainley. He needs two waist gunners
  for tonight's operation.
Pfc. Broderick Crawford: Solid, sir, solid.
Commanding Officer: That's all and good luck to you.
Private Damian F. O'Flynn: Gee, that's great, that's terrific. Oh, Boy, I always wanted
  to see Italy.
Pfc. Broderick Crawford: I told you, kid. This is a solid job.
Private Damian F. O'Flynn: Yeah, yeah, I know, a quiet job.
Incidental music
Announcer: The pilot sits at the controls checking the switches, the mechanics the
  engines, the fuel tanks. Abe and Tim check the bomb racks, the fuses, the cannon, the
  machine gun.
Pilot: Shirley 5 to control. Shirley 5 to control. Ready to taxi. We're ready to taxi.
  Go ahead.
Control: Control to Shirley 5. Control to Shirley 5. All clear. Good luck.
Pilot: Check stations. Check stations. Bombardier.
Bombardier: Everything O.K., sir.
Pilot: Tail gunner.
Tail gunner: Swell, Captain.
Pilot: Left waist gunner.
Pfc. Broderick Crawford: In the groove, boss.
Pilot: Right waist gunner.
Private Damian F. O'Flynn: Everything fine, sir.
Pilot: Navigator.
Pfc. Broderick Crawford: How do you feel, kid? Nervous?
Private Damian F. O'Flynn: Oh, heck no. But it doesn't look as though I'll get to see
  Italy after all.
Pfc. Broderick Crawford: What do you mean?
Private Damian F. O'Flynn: Well, it's so dark.
Pfc. Broderick Crawford: Did you check them bomb fuses?
Private Damian F. O'Flynn: Why sure, you were with me, Abe.
Pfc. Broderick Crawford: Did you get a load of those incendiaries those Mitchells carry?
Private Damian F. O'Flynn: Yeah, but ...
Pfc. Broderick Crawford: Then relax, Tim. You'll see Italy all right.
Announcer: Thirty miles from the target, twenty miles, fifteen miles. Look, Tim. You
  see those fireworks? The twin-motored Mitchells have already set a thousand spotlights
  on the objective. Eight miles from the target, seven miles, six miles.
Navigator (Jack): Navigator to pilot. Navigator to pilot. Three miles to target, due
  north beyond mountain ridge, sir.
Pilot: On the beam, Jack.
Private Damian F. O'Flynn: This is it, Abe.
Pilot: Bomb Bay open.
Bombardier: Bombardier to pilot. Altitude twenty thousand.
Pilot: Altitude twenty thousand.
Bombardier: Right fifteen degrees.
Pilot: Right fifteen degrees.
Bombardier: Level off. Steady. Steady.
Incidental music
  Bombardier: First rack gone.
Private Damian F. O'Flynn: Wow, bull's eye.
Pfc. Broderick Crawford: Is it light enough for you?
Private Damian F. O'Flynn: Looks like Coney Island.

Pfc. Broderick Crawford: Aw, aw, here comes the flak.
Pilot: Enemy planes at three o'clock.
Pfc. Broderick Crawford: That's for you, kid. Give 'em the works.
Private Damian F. O'Flynn: Take it, Abe. They're flyin' under.
Pfc. Broderick Crawford: Right.
Private Damian F. O'Flynn: You got him, Abe. You got him.
Pfc. Broderick Crawford: Nothin' to it, nothin'.
Private Damian F. O'Flynn: Abe, you're hurt.
Pfc. Broderick Crawford: Where? What are you talkin' about?
Private Damian F. O'Flynn: It's your shoulder. It's bleeding.
Pfc. Broderick Crawford: Hey, that's where I got Mamie tattooed.
Private Damian F. O'Flynn: Here, let me help you.
Pfc. Broderick Crawford: Why that dirty, no good, they hit Mamie right in the
  ...
Pilot: Pilot to bombardier. How 'bout that last bomb rack?
Bombardier: She's stuck, sir. Can't shake it loose.
Pilot: We need that stick for the central pier.
Pfc. Broderick Crawford: Left waist gunner to pilot. I'll fix it. Take this baby up so
  we can lose the flak and I'll do it.
Pilot: O.K.
Pfc. Broderick Crawford: Tim, that fuse wire's gummin' up the works. I'm too heavy to
  hang down but if I hold you by the feet you might be able to reach that wire and clip it
  back.
Private Damian F. O'Flynn: Let's go.
Pfc. Broderick Crawford: It's a pretty ticklish situation if them fuses get clipped.
Private Damian F. O'Flynn: Yeah, I know. Come on, Abe. Time's a'wastin'.
Pfc. Broderick Crawford: You're gonna have to hang upside down, kid.
Private Damian F. O'Flynn: Well, can you hold me? That shoulder of your's
  ...
Pfc. Broderick Crawford: Don't make me laugh, will you?
Private Damian F. O'Flynn: What are we waitin' for?
Pfc. Broderick Crawford: O.K., kid, let's go.
Private Damian F. O'Flynn: Got a good hold, Abe?
Pfc. Broderick Crawford: Solid, Timmy.
Private Damian F. O'Flynn: Then here we go.
Pfc. Broderick Crawford: How is it, kid?
Private Damian F. O'Flynn: I don't know if I can make it.
Pfc. Broderick Crawford: You gotta, kid. How's it goin', Tim?
Private Damian F. O'Flynn: I-I think I got it now.
Pilot: Pilot to left waist gunner. Can't wait much longer, fuel running low.
Pfc. Broderick Crawford: Just a couple of seconds, sir.
Private Damian F. O'Flynn: O.K., Abe, help me up.
Pfc. Broderick Crawford: In the bag. You can drop that last stick whenever you're ready.
  Easy, Tim. Easy, boy, you're comin' up. There you are, Tim. How you feel, boy?
Private Damian F. O'Flynn: A little dizzy, Abe. I feel solid, Abe.
Pfc. Broderick Crawford: Atta boy, Tim.
Pilot: Pilot to bombardier. Last rack ready. Just say when.
Bombardier: Five degrees left.
Pilot: Five degrees left.
Bombardier: Level off. Steady. Bombs away.
Incidental music
Commanding Officer: Sgt. Miller.
Pfc. Broderick Crawford: Yo.
Commanding Officer: Private Wiggins.
Private Damian F. O'Flynn: Hip.
Commanding Officer: Front and center. You men are to be commended for valor and bravery
  beyond the line of duty. We're proud of you and proud to present you both with the Army
  Air Corps Flying Medal.

Pfc. Broderick Crawford: Well, thank you, Major. But medals ain't important to me. See, I'm a technician, an armorer, and anything I do is my duty. But, Major, I would like to ask a favor, a big favor, that is if you won't mind my askin'.
Commanding Officer: What's on your mind, Miller?
Pfc. Broderick Crawford: Well, I'd like to be transferred to another base. It's too quiet here.
Commanding Officer: What was that, Miller?
Pfc. Broderick Crawford: I said it's too quiet here.
Commanding Officer: Yes, ah, you were saying?
Pfc. Broderick Crawford: Aw, forget it, Major. I guess it's O.K. here after all.
Incidental music
THE CAISSONS GO ROLLING ALONG
  Vocal refrain by the Ensemble
  Captain Glenn Miller: The Technical Training Command pays tribute to its comrades in arms. We salute the United States Field Artillery.
I SUSTAIN THE WINGS (closing theme)
  Pfc. Broderick Crawford: "I Sustain the Wings" is prepared and produced entirely by soldiers of the Technical Training Command of the Army Air Forces, Major General Walter R. Weaver, Commanding General. This program came to you from the Army Air Forces Technical School at Yale University. This is CBS, the Columbia Broadcasting System.
THE TECHNICAL TRAINING COMMAND (closing theme)
  Vocal refrain by the Glee Club

12Jun43 (Sat) 6:15-6:45PM Woolsey Hall, Yale University, New Haven, Connecticut
   I SUSTAIN THE WINGS broadcast WEEI (CBS), Boston, Massachusetts   Audience

I SUSTAIN THE WINGS (opening theme)
   Pfc. Broderick Crawford: "I Sustain the Wings." "I Sustain the Wings," a program of
     music and entertainment brought to you (by the Technical Training) Command of the Army
     Air Forces, the men who keep 'em flying. The program features the Technical Training
     Command Orchestra, the Glee Club, ...
   Vocal refrain by Private First Class Tony Martin and the Glee Club
   Pfc. Broderick Crawford: ... and Captain Glenn Miller.
Captain Glenn Miller: Thank you, Private Broderick Crawford, and good evening, everybody.
   Here we are with more music for your listenin' pleasure and the Technical Training
   Command Orchestra starts jumpin' with "Sun Valley Jump."
SUN VALLEY JUMP
EV'RYTHING I LOVE
   Vocal refrain by Private Bob Houston and the Glee Club
   Captain Glenn Miller: Private Bob Houston and Glee Club, the orchestra and "Ev'rything
     I Love."
Announcer: Listen to that, America. Isn't that a lovely sound? It's the music of
   victory.
Beethoven's 5th Symphony (Incidental music)
Announcer: There are big bombers bound on a mission, a mission of destruction. The
   bombardiers are doing a grand job, paving the road to victory with their bombs. But
   before they take off, someone has to tell them where to drop those bombs to do the most
   good, to locate the target for them. That someone is the aerial photographer.
Incidental music
   Announcer: A product of the Technical Training Command, the aerial photographer, the
     bombardier's bloodhound, is a peculiar sort of soldier. He does his fighting with a
     camera instead of a gun. A camera isn't much good when a Zero or a Messerschmitt
     comes zooming at you from out of the clouds. But we've got to have those pictures.
     Our entire aerial campaign depends tremendously on photographic reconnaissance.
     Corporal Johnny Rutgers is an aerial photographer stationed at an advanced air base
     somewhere in Burma.
Felix Daly: Hand me that bottle of hypo, will you, Johnny?
Pfc. Broderick Crawford (as Cpl. Johnny Rutgers): Aw, get it yourself. Your arm ain't
   broken.
Felix Daly: Say, what's eating you? All week you've been as nervous as a guy waiting for
   his induction papers.
Pfc. Broderick Crawford: I'm sorry, Daly. I'm just an unhappy character, that's all.
Felix Daly: Unhappy?
Pfc. Broderick Crawford: Why not? I enlisted in this man's army, in the Air Force, to
   get a crack at the Japs and what happened? The only time I draw a bead on one it's
   through a camera finder.
Felix Daly: Aw, don't let that worry you. Those photographs of yours are plenty
   important.
Pfc. Broderick Crawford: Aw, let someone else take the pretty pictures. I just want to
   get on the business end of a machine gun. You know why I ...
Colonel Spiro (CO): Attention. As you were. Corporal, let's take a look at that map of
   Valachio area.
Pfc. Broderick Crawford: Yes, sir. Here it is.
Colonel Spiro (CO): Let's see. Uh huh. Yeah, right here. Somewhere in this section we
   lost another eight bombers this morning. They were attacked by Zeros.
Pfc. Broderick Crawford: Zeros? But there isn't a Jap base anywhere near there.
Colonel Spiro (CO): There has to be. Their planes can't take off from a cloud. We've
   got to find that base.
Pfc. Broderick Crawford: Aw, here we go again. Another job for me and Betsy.
Colonel Spiro (CO): Betsy?
Felix Daly: That's what he calls his camera, sir.
Pfc. Broderick Crawford: Yes, sir. And I wish I had her eyesight. She can pick out
   things on the ground that my 20-20 vision can't see for sour apples.

Colonel Spiro (CO): Well, just to make sure Betsy sees what we're looking for, I'll pilot the plane myself.
Pfc. Broderick Crawford: Yes, sir.
Incidental music
Colonel Spiro (CO): We've been out for two hours, Corporal. Betsy should have picked up something by this time.
Pfc. Broderick Crawford: She's certainly been busy taking it all in, sir.
Colonel Spiro (CO): See anything that might be this Japanese Shangri-La?
Pfc. Broderick Crawford: No, sir. Nothing but jungle. Hey, Colonel, wait a minute. What's that over there? Are those planes?
Colonel Spiro (CO): Where? Where?
Pfc. Broderick Crawford: Right over there, sir.
Colonel Spiro (CO): Yeah. Yeah, they look like it. Swell job of camouflage. Looks just like a part of the jungle. I think that's the field we're looking for, Johnny.
Pfc. Broderick Crawford: Well, no wonder we couldn't find it. Look, they're coming up after us.
Colonel Spiro (CO): I'm going over the field. Get your camera ready.
Pfc. Broderick Crawford: Don't worry. I'll get the pictures.
Colonel Spiro (CO): Here they come.
Pfc. Broderick Crawford: Nice goin'. You sure plastered him, two down. Look - look out, sir. There's another one divin' from eight o'clock.
Incidental music
  Pfc. Broderick Crawford: Colonel! Colonel! Colonel!
Pfc. Broderick Crawford: Come on, Betsy. Let's bail out o' here. Well, we made it just in time, Betsy. It's too bad about the Colonel. Let's go, Betsy. The boys'll want those pictures. They'll need 'em to even up the score for the Colonel.
Incidental music
Pfc. Broderick Crawford: You're gettin' heavy, Betsy. Too heavy. I can't carry you any further. I'm gonna leave you here. I'll have to take your films though. Felix said pictures were important. So long, Betsy. I'll be back for you.
Incidental music
Pfc. Broderick Crawford: Oh, these darn bugs are drivin' me nuts.
Incidental music
Voice: Be careful, Johnny. Their bite means fever.
Pfc. Broderick Crawford: Get off my neck. Oh, that one got me good.
Incidental music
  Pfc. Broderick Crawford: I gotta have water. Oh, boy, I'm thirsty. I need water. I'm burnin' up.
  Voice: No wonder. That little bug gave you the fever. You're a sick man, Johnny.
Pfc. Broderick Crawford: What? What? What am I thinkin' about, I'm goin' crazy. No, no, no, I'm all right. I just need water. Yeah, I need water.
Incidental music
  Voice: You're tired, too. Why don't you give up? Let someone else worry about the pictures. You're through. Why don't you lie down and rest, Johnny?
Pfc. Broderick Crawford: Yeah, yeah, that's right. I need rest. Naw, naw, I - I gotta keep goin', keep marchin'. The Drill Sergeant said march in cadence. Hut, two, three, four. Hut, two, three, shhh. Do you think the Japs'll hear me? I can't let 'em catch me. I gotta get pictures to the base for the Colonel's funeral. Gotta develop 'em quick. Hand me that hypo, Daly. Your arm ain't broke. Oh, look at the pretty pictures, Japanese Shangri-La. Give me that hypo, Daly, and the developer. I'll get the pictures. Give me a gun, a gun to kill Japs. Give me a gun. A gun. A gun. A gun, somebody's shootin' at me. He's tryin' to kill me.
Incidental music
  Voice: Nice goin', Johnny. Let him think he got you. He's looking for you. He sees you, Johnny. He's coming closer with a bayonet. He's coming closer, closer, closer. Roll, Johnny, roll.
Pfc. Broderick Crawford: No you don't. You can't stop me. I got pictures, important pictures, pictures for a funeral. Your funeral.
Incidental music

Voice: Watch out, Johnny. Watch out now. You know Judo. Knee him, Johnny, knee him. Now the strangle hold. Break his neck, go on.
Pfc. Broderick Crawford: I gotta keep movin'. I can't let 'em find me. I gotta get pictures to the base. I'll take your gun, it might come in handy.
Incidental music
   Pfc. Broderick Crawford: Get out of my way. You can't stop me. I've got a message to Garcia. I got films to deliver, important pictures. Let go of my shirt, let go. I told you you couldn't stop me.
   Voice: Watch out, Johnny. Over there. It's a Jap sentry. He's seen you. Trick him, Johnny, trick him. Make him think you're a raiding party.
Pfc. Broderick Crawford: Yeah. All right, men. Get a bullet, find - get a leg, go ahead. Ha, ha. Look at 'em run. They're scared to death.
Incidental music
   Voice: Now you can deliver the pictures, Johnny. But wait. You're hungry. You need food. Maybe they left some.
Pfc. Broderick Crawford: Yeah. That's a good idea. I'll take a look. Here it is, rice and fish. Well, it's better than nothin'.
Incidental music
   Voice: Eat fast, Johnny. Or, better yet, take it with you. They might come back and then you couldn't get home those pictures, those important pictures.
Pfc. Broderick Crawford: Yeah, that's right. I'll take 'em with me. I gotta keep movin' with the film. I gotta keep movin'.
Incidental music
   Pfc. Broderick Crawford: Aw, I'm tired. I'm awful tired.
   Voice: We know you're tired, Johnny. Why don't you give up? You'll never get to the base. Forget about the pictures, Johnny.
Pfc. Broderick Crawford: No, no. I'll get there if I have to crawl.
Incidental music
   Voice: All right, crawl. You can't walk any further. You're crawling, Johnny. Crawling.
Pfc. Broderick Crawford: Sure I'm crawlin', but I'm movin'. I'm still movin', do you hear me? I'm still movin'.
Incidental music
   Pfc. Broderick Crawford: Moving. Moving. Moving.
   Voice: What's that ahead? Soldiers? Wait, don't shoot, Johnny. They're your own men. Let 'em know you're here. You can get up now.
Pfc. Broderick Crawford: Hey, don't shoot. I'm an American, do you hear, an American.
Soldier: Hold you fire, men, it's a Yank.
Pfc. Broderick Crawford: I got pictures, pretty pictures to take to the base. I got pictures for Colonel Spiro. Show what's happening in Shangri-La. Pictures important, important pictures.
Incidental music
   Announcer: And so Johnny Rutgers became a hero, a hero without benefit of guns, one of the heroes behind the gun. His pictures located the Japanese base and our own Air Force bombed it out of existence. Thus we moved one step nearer our goal, nearer because the man of the Technical Training Command delivered the goods. His own personal message to Garcia.

   ...

SWANEE RIVER (Old tune)
   Captain Glenn Miller: With the new tune, Private Tony Martin sings "Let's Get Lost."
LET'S GET LOST (New tune)
   Vocal refrain by Private First Class Tony Martin
   Captain Glenn Miller: We borrow Bob Crosby's theme song, "Summertime."
SUMMERTIME (Borrowed tune)
   Vocal refrain by the Glee Club
   Captain Glenn Miller: Last in our medley it's something blue, "Blue Champagne."
BLUE CHAMPAGNE (Blue tune)

Pfc. Broderick Crawford: Soldiers in coveralls, that's another name for the men of the Technical Training Command. Every man is a trained fighter as well as an accomplished technician. For in doing his job he must be able to fight to defend his posts, the lives of his comrades, and the planes he loves. Every mechanic, photographer, welder, metal worker, radio man, armorer and parachute rigger can be depended upon to give an excellent account of himself in combat. These are our soldiers in coveralls.

I Sustain the Wings (Incidental music)
Pfc. Broderick Crawford: The men who must keep our planes flying in spite of the hail of enemy fire, who are taught to do their particular jobs blind-folded, who can drop their wrenches, files and other working equipment to handle a rifle or a machine gun with deadly accuracy and perfection, whose ability and resourcefulness have saved planes so badly damaged that their own pilots had given them up for lost, they are the men of the Technical Training Command whose credo is "Sustineo Alas," "I Sustain the Wings."

THE ARMY AIR CORPS
Vocal refrain by Private First Class Tony Martin and the Glee Club
Captain Glenn Miller: The Technical Training Command pays tribute to its comrades in arms. We salute all the other Commands of the Army Air Forces.

I SUSTAIN THE WINGS (closing theme)
Pfc. Broderick Crawford: "I Sustain the Wings" is prepared and produced entirely by soldiers of the Technical Training Command of the Army Air Forces, Major General Walter R. Weaver, commanding general. This program came to you from the Air Force Technical Schools at Yale University. This is C.B.S., the Columbia Broadcasting System.

THE TECHNICAL TRAINING COMMAND (closing theme)
Vocal refrain by the Glee Club

The parts of Announcer, Felix Daly, Colonel Spiro (CO), Voice and Soldier were played by Cpl. Tom Stanmetz, Pvt. Damian F. Flynn (O'Flynn), Pfc. Franklin Cook and Pfc. Joseph Shulman.

19Jun43 (Sat) 6:15-6:45PM Woolsey Hall, Yale University, New Haven, Connecticut
  I SUSTAIN THE WINGS broadcast WEEI (CBS), Boston, Massachusetts   Audience

I SUSTAIN THE WINGS (opening theme)
  Pfc. Broderick Crawford: "I Sustain the Wings." "I Sustain the Wings," the program of
  music and entertainment brought to you by the Technical Training Command of the Army
  Air Forces, the men who keep 'em flying. The program features the Technical Training
  Command Orchestra, Private Tony Martin, Corporal Ray McKinley, and many of your old
  friends. And now Captain Glenn Miller.
Captain Glenn Miller: Thank you, Private Broderick Crawford, and good evening, everybody.
  Here we are again with music and entertainment for your listenin' pleasure, and the
  Technical Training Command Orchestra stomps off with the "Anvil Chorus."
ANVIL CHORUS
DEARLY BELOVED
  Captain Glenn Miller: The orchestra plays, Private Tony Martin with the Glee Club sings
  "Dearly Beloved."
DEARLY BELOVED
  Vocal refrain by Private First Class Tony Martin and the Glee Club
Incidental music
Pfc. Broderick Crawford (as Sgt. Frank McConnell): I'm Sergeant Frank McConnell, first
  radio operator on a B-24 Liberator bomber. I'm a graduate of the Technical Training
  Command Radio School at Chanute Field. I've helped to blast Zeros out of the Aleutian
  skies and I've watched my plane bop - bomb Jap transports off Kiska. But I didn't do it
  for any medals or bows. You see, the slanty-eyed sons of heaven were just a little too
  close to California for their own good and for my peace of mind. I've got a wife in
  California, swell gal. She's about five-feet-two, she's big enough to hold down an
  important spot on an assembly line turning out bombers, and she manages to find time to
  take care of our home in the Valley and to write to me every day. We named our plane
  after her. Her name's Lillian and she's 24 years old, so we christened our kite the
  Lillian 24. Our base was somewhere between Dutch Harbor and Kiska, a lot of snow, fog,
  high peaks, and a couple of Eskimos. That country was never built for flying but we had
  to fly and bomb and fight. Lots of us went out and some of us never came back. Our
  morale was usually pretty low and all on account of salmon. We had salmon three times a
  day, seven days a week, and too many weeks in a row. Things were getting mighty tough
  until Johnson came to the post. Johnson was a good looking guy and about the best
  navigator in the business. We never suspected that he'd been a chef at the Waldorf
  until he started whipping up sauces to camouflage our diet of salmon. He spent most of
  his spare time in the kitchen, and before we knew it, he had salmon tasting like
  chicken, fresh veal, and sometimes it even looked and tasted like a thick, juicy steak.
  We began to like salmon, and what's more, we began to like Norman Johnson. I'd been
  living in that forsaken strip of nowhere for eight months when the C.O. told me that my
  application for furlough had been approved. Just one more flight and then three weeks
  in California with the little lady. And that flight came on March 29th, 1943. Our
  plane took off at zero-eight-hundred.
Pfc. Broderick Crawford: Quite a fog. With that sun tryin' to come through it's like
  flying in a white soup.
Pvt. Damian O'Flynn (as Norman Johnson): Vichyssoise.
Pfc. Broderick Crawford: Vichy what?
Pvt. Damian O'Flynn: Vichyssoise, a white and very delicious soup.
Pfc. Broderick Crawford: Where'd you dig up such a fancy name for chowder?
Pvt. Damian O'Flynn: Switzerland, Frankie. Went to a hotel school there.
Pfc. Broderick Crawford: Oh, hey, Norm. We're flying awful close to the water, aren't
  we?
Pvt. Damian O'Flynn: Can't help it, Frank. Can't take a chance on getting lost in this
  fog.
Pfc. Broderick Crawford: Yeah, well listen. My furlough starts tomorrow and I want you
  to know that my fate is in your hands with a song with the same name.
Pvt. Damian O'Flynn: Don't worry, Frankie. As far as I'm concerned you're as good as on
  your way home right now.

Pfc. Broderick Crawford: Well, I hope so. It's going to be swell to be with Lillian
    again, even if it is only for a few hours each day. She's not going to take any time
    off from her job while I'm on furlough, and that's the way it should be. This business
    of absenteeism is strictly for people who don't care how long this war lasts. Lillian's
    sticking to the assembly line just as long as she's needed.
Pvt. Damian O'Flynn: Yeah, there ought to be more like her.
Pfc. Broderick Crawford: Yeah, that's why I won't mind staying at home waitin' for her,
    just like she used to wait for me. I'll do the housecleaning and gardening. You know,
    I might even do a little cooking.
Pvt. Damian O'Flynn: Ah, can you cook?
Pfc. Broderick Crawford: A little. I'm pretty good at scrambled eggs and steak, French
    fried potatoes and, well, scrambled eggs and steak and ...
Pvt. Damian O'Flynn: Ha, ha, ha.
Pfc. Broderick Crawford: Say, Norm, you could do me a big favor.
Pvt. Damian O'Flynn: Yeah? Like what?
Pfc. Broderick Crawford: Well, like giving me some of your recipes. Boy, can you imagine
    how surprised Lillian would be if I made some fillet of sole with that special sauce of
    your's, you know, that Remo ... ah, "Remoulaid."
Pvt. Damian O'Flynn: Ah, yes, you mean Sauce Remoulade.
Pfc. Broderick Crawford: Yeah, that's the one. Gee, I wish I could make it.
Pvt. Damian O'Flynn: Ah, there's nothing to it. First you take six hard-boiled eggs.
Pfc. Broderick Crawford: Yeah?
Pvt. Damian O'Flynn: Chop the eggs and mix with a cup of mayonnaise.
Pfc. Broderick Crawford: Ah, that sounds pretty easy.
Pvt. Damian O'Flynn: Well, the rest of it is even easier. Take six stuffed olives, add
    some chopped parsley, four sweet gherkins, three anchovy filets and ...
Pfc. Broderick Crawford: Wait a minute, wait a minute, wait a minute. I'm gonna write
    this down now. What was that, six eggs and what?
Pvt. Damian O'Flynn: No, no, no, no. A little later, Frankie. We're getting close to
    the target. Navigator to pilot. Navigator to pilot.
Pilot: Go ahead, Johnson.
Pvt. Damian O'Flynn: We're eighteen miles from target, due Northeast. Course
    two-one-eight.
Pilot: Good. All right, men, checking stations. Stand by. Report.
Harry: Tail gunner O.K., sir.
Left Wait Gunner: Left waist gunner O.K., sir.
Pfc. Broderick Crawford: Radio fine. Well, the soup's gettin' thinner now.
Pvt. Damian O'Flynn: Navigator to pilot. Three miles from objective. Due North over
    that mountain on the left, sir.
Pilot: Bomb bay doors open. Heh, what a beautiful runway, so nice and smooth. Let's do
    something about it, boys. Any time you're ready, Charlie.
Pfc. Joseph Shulman (as Charlie): Any minute now. Altitude 3000.
Pilot: Altitude 3000.
Pfc. Joseph Shulman: Left seven degrees.
Pilot: Left seven degrees.
Pfc. Joseph Shulman: Steady now, level off, steady.
Incidental music
  Pfc. Joseph Shulman: First strike gone.
Pfc. Broderick Crawford: Here comes the flak.
Pfc. Joseph Shulman: Now ...

   ...

Pilot: You all right, Charlie?
Pfc. Joseph Shulman: Gotta hang on to last me, sir.
Pfc. Broderick Crawford: Gunner to pilot. Zero coming in at nine o'clock.
Pvt. Damian O'Flynn: Frankie got a Zero! Frankie got a Zero!
Pfc. Broderick Crawford: Ah, come on, Norm, cut it out. Say, this flight's gettin'
    thicker than Mulligan stew now.

Pfc. Joseph Shulman: Bombardier to pilot. I'm ready with that last rack. Steady now, easy, easy. Bombs away.
Pilot: Good work, men. Let's go home.
Incidental music
Pfc. Broderick Crawford: Boy, what a shellackin' those Japs took. You know, Norm, I thought for a minute that ...
Incidental music
  Pfc. Broderick Crawford: Johnson, Norm, are you hurt?
  Pvt. Damian O'Flynn: No, no, it's nothing, it's just a little scratch.
  Pfc. Broderick Crawford: A scratch? Here, let me help you.
  Pvt. Damian O'Flynn: Go on, get back to your gun turret.
  Pfc. Broderick Crawford: It's all over now, Norm, we're on our way home. Where'd you get it?
  Pvt. Damian O'Flynn: Here. My right shoulder. Help. Think it's anything to ...
  Pfc. Broderick Crawford: All right, I put sulfa powder in it now.
  Pvt. Damian O'Flynn: Frankie.
  Pfc. Broderick Crawford: Now look, just rest. Take it easy, will you?
  Pvt. Damian O'Flynn: Frankie, I got to tell you about the fish.
  Pfc. Broderick Crawford: Relax, Norm, relax. Now move a little this way.
  Pvt. Damian O'Flynn: Aft - after you make the sauce, ...
  Pfc. Broderick Crawford: Look, forget about that "Remoulode" sauce for a minute, will yeah?
  Pvt. Damian O'Flynn: Remoulade.
  Pfc. Broderick Crawford: All right, it's Remoulade, so what?
  Pvt. Damian O'Flynn: Get a buttered hot pan. Are you listening?
  Pfc. Broderick Crawford: Yeah, yeah. Now come on, lift your arm a minute.   I gotta slide this tape under it.
  Pvt. Damian O'Flynn: Sprinkle some mixed onion and ...
  Pfc. Broderick Crawford: Feel any better now?
  Pvt. Damian O'Flynn: Hold the filets. Put - put the pan ...
  Pfc. Broderick Crawford: Easy now, Johnson. Take it easy.
  Pvt. Damian O'Flynn: Let it simmer five minutes.
Pfc. Broderick Crawford: Johnson! Norm! Hey, somebody give me a hand here.
Pfc. Broderick Crawford: Yeah, I thought Johnson was a goner. He lost more blood than he could spare and he wasn't the only one who got hurt. Harry, the tail gunner, well he got it in a spot they couldn't miss. That kid had a heart as big as they come. One of our engines conked out and the flak ripped out a big chunk of the left wing. The fuel lines were clipped and the floor of our plane was flooded with gasoline. One stray spark and we'd all be dead pigeons. To make matters worse, the radio's gone dead and the fog whipped in on us. Whipped in heavier than I'd ever seen it. The pilot ...
Pilot: Pilot to radio. How you comin' along, Frank?
Pfc. Broderick Crawford: I can't get a thing out of it.
Pilot: Have you tried switching the tubes?
Pfc. Broderick Crawford: I've checked every possible connection.
Pilot: Well, keep trying. You just got to get that receiver working.
Pfc. Broderick Crawford: Yeah, yeah, I know.
Pilot: We can't possibly land this crate unless you can get us on the beam. And the gas is way down.
Pfc. Broderick Crawford: I'm doin' all I can.
Pilot: We can't last more than half an hour.
Pfc. Broderick Crawford: Yeah, looks like one of the resistors popped out when we got that last load of flak. Look, I need some help back here. Johnson's having a tough time, bleeding like mad. I'm all out of bandages and adhesive.
Pilot: I'll send Charlie back to you. And keep tryin', Frank, keep tryin'.
Pfc. Broderick Crawford: Right.
Pfc. Joseph Shulman: Frankie, hey, Frankie.
Pfc. Broderick Crawford: Hurry up, will you?
Pfc. Joseph Shulman: Here's the bandage, but we're all out of adhesive. You'll have to use some friction tape.
Pfc. Broderick Crawford: There's some in that kit. Hand it over.

Pfc. Joseph Shulman: O.K.
Pfc. Broderick Crawford: Come on. Come on. Hurry up. Hurry up.
Pfc. Joseph Shulman: Hold your horses, Frank. I gotta get this tin foil off it.
Pfc. Broderick Crawford: Johnson's gonna need a transfusion as soon as we get in, if we
  get in. Hey, wait a minute. Don't throw that tin foil away.
Pfc. Joseph Shulman: What's the matter with you? You gone nuts?
Pfc. Broderick Crawford: Give me that tin foil. I got an idea.
Pfc. Joseph Shulman: Man, you're takin' a screwy time to cut out paper dolls.
Pfc. Broderick Crawford: I think I can make a resistor out of this. My screwdriver.
  Hey, where's my screwdriver?
Pfc. Joseph Shulman: In the tool kit. But what about Johnson?
Pfc. Broderick Crawford: You're gonna have to change his bandages. Tape him up real
  tight. I got work to do.
Pilot: Pilot to radio. How's it comin', Frank?
Pfc. Broderick Crawford: I think I can fix it now.
Pilot: The gas is almost gone, maybe ten minutes, maybe less.
Pfc. Broderick Crawford: Well, if this works we'll be home with time to spare.
Pilot: Well, it's got to work. Let me know how you make out, and in a hurry.
Pfc. Broderick Crawford: Yes, sir. Well, I gotta loosen this nut here, now the tin foil,
  twist it around. Where are my pliers? Hey, Charlie, where are my - oh, never mind,
  Charlie, I got 'em, here they are. Twist it, put it right in between here, right in
  there, tighten it up. Well, cross your fingers, here goes nothing. The tubes. Yeah.
  Hey, Charlie, look, the tubes are lit. Radio to pilot. Radio to pilot. The radio's
  workin'.
Pilot: Good boy, Frankie.
Pfc. Broderick Crawford: Lillian 24 calling base 77. Go ahead. Lillian 24 calling base
  77. Go ahead.
Base 77: Hello, Lillian 24. Lillian 24, base 77 receiving. Go ahead.
Pfc. Broderick Crawford: Lillian 24 lost in fog, asking for beam. Go ahead.
Base 77: O.K. How's that?
Pfc. Broderick Crawford: Oh, it's the most beautiful thing I ever heard.
Incidental music
  Jimmy: Is that you, Frankie?
  Pfc. Broderick Crawford: Yeah, Jimmy?
  Jimmy: Right. Frankie, there's a cargo plane waiting to take off for California. If
    you can get in by 9:30 you'll be able to catch it.
  Pfc. Broderick Crawford: Don't you worry, Jimmy, I'm as good as there. Radio to pilot.
    Radio to pilot. Radio to pilot.
Pfc. Broderick Crawford: Well, thanks to a little piece of tin foil we made it all right.
  If I hadn't a been for what I learned from the Technical Training Command I wouldn't
  have been able to fix that radio with makeshift materials. They taught me and a lot of
  other guys; mechanics, armorers, photographers; they taught us our jobs, to work under
  pressure, to keep a clear head when the going's toughest. That's why the pilots admit
  they owe a lot to the men of the Technical Training Command, the boys of the ground
  grew, because they really keep 'em flying.
Incidental music
DANNY BOY (Old tune)
  Captain Glenn Miller: Now it's medley time with something old, something new, something
    borrowed and something blue. The old song, the orchestra plays "Danny Boy."
  Captain Glenn Miller: Private Arthur Malvin sings the new tune, "Takin' a Chance on
    Love."
TAKING A CHANCE ON LOVE (New tune)
  Vocal refrain by Private Artie Malvin
  Captain Glenn Miller: We borrow the theme song of Captain Wayne King as the orchestra
    plays "The Waltz You Saved for Me."
THE WALTZ YOU SAVED FOR ME (Borrowed tune)
  Captain Glenn Miller: And for something blue, the "Serenade in Blue."
SERENADE IN BLUE (Blue tune)

Pfc. Broderick Crawford: The Technical Training Command is the biggest university in the world, turning out a victory parade of men who really keep our planes flying. Not satisfied to stick to the letter and take principles for granted, the men of the Technical Training Command are always on the alert, seeking methods to improve present conditions and solve problems on the basis of past performances. One of the latest innovations stressed in the training of these men is the Weights and Balance Control course. A plane flying with an off balance load has been one of our airmen's worst problems. The plane, taking off with great difficulty, flies at reduced speed, follows an erratic course and stands a better than even chance of cracking up when it comes in to land. To cure this evil, ...

I Sustain the Wings (Incidental music)
Pfc. Broderick Crawford: ... the Technical Training Command made use of a slide rule known as the Load Adjuster. It tells the flight control officers every detail in the balance of the plane, and if the plane is overloaded and unbalanced, it tells them exactly where the correction must be made. Armed with this magic wand, pilots know that they will be able to fly their planes evenly and smoothly and reach their destinations safely. The men of the Technical Training Command can truthfully say "I Sustain the Wings."

(Hail to the) KINGS OF THE HIGHWAY
Captain Glenn Miller: The Technical Training Command pays tribute to its comrades in arms, and this week a 21-gun musical salute to the Infantry.
Vocal refrain by the Glee Club

I SUSTAIN THE WINGS (closing theme)
Pfc. Broderick Crawford: "I Sustain the Wings," is prepared and produced entirely by soldiers of the Technical Training Command of the Army Air Forces, Major General Walter R. Weaver, commanding general. This program came to you from the Army Air Forces Technical Training School at Yale University. This is C.B.S., the Columbia Broadcasting System.

THE TECHNICAL TRAINING COMMAND (closing theme)
Vocal refrain by the Glee Club

26Jun43 (Sat) 6:15-6:45PM TTC School at Pawling, New York
 I SUSTAIN THE WINGS broadcast WEEI (CBS), Boston, Massachusetts   Audience

I SUSTAIN THE WINGS (opening theme)
  Pfc. Broderick Crawford: "I Sustain the Wings." "I Sustain the Wings," the program of
   music and entertainment brought to you by the Technical Training Command of the Army
   Air Forces, the men who keep 'em flying. The program features the Technical Training
   Command Orchestra, Private Tony Martin, Corporal Ray McKinley and many of your old
   friends. And now Captain Glenn Miller.
  Captain Glenn Miller: Thank you, Private Broderick Crawford, and good evening, everyone.
   Time for some music now. The Technical Training Command Orchestra starts off with
   "American Patrol." Corporal McKinley, roll off.
AMERICAN PATROL
THAT OLD BLACK MAGIC
  Captain Glenn Miller: Private Tony Martin and the Glee Club sing "That Old Black
   Magic."
  Vocal refrain by Private First Class Tony Martin and the Glee Club
Incidental music
  Pfc. Broderick Crawford (as Sgt. Bud Hawkins): How do you like that piano? It's pretty
   nice, isn't it? That's my buddy Denny, Sergeant Denny Adam. Remember him? Before
   the war he had one of the biggest dance bands in the country and that piano style was
   his trade mark. Still sounds pretty much the same, doesn't it? You wouldn't think he
   was playing with only one hand. No, no, I'm not kiddin'. He lost his left arm
   someplace in the South Pacific. How'd it happen? Well, it's kind of a long story but
   if you'll bear with me, here goes. I knew Denny before we both joined up. Once in a
   while we used to both play the same night spots. What? Me? Oh, my name's Hawkins,
   Bud Hawkins. I used to be a dancer, you know, tap and the rest of that. Well, to get
   on with Denny's story, we were sent to the same basic training center, we were room
   mates. Denny's sense of rhythm made him a natural for communications work, so the
   Technical Training Command sent him to a radio school for specialized training. That
   split us up because, well, they decided I'd make a good mechanic. That meant another
   type of school for me, a school where they taught me everything there is to know about
   airplane engines. Not to pat myself on the back, but I was a good mechanic when I got
   out of that school, and because the Technical Training Command knows how to train men,
   knows how to tell them to keep 'em flying. And believe me, they do a good job. And
   don't get the idea that we're just radio operators, mechanics and armorers and the
   like. We're not. We're soldiers, too, soldiers in coveralls. They taught us to
   fight, to use a gun, to toss grenades. They taught us everything we needed to know.
   Ho, ho, so we could take care of ourselves when the going got tough. Well, I better
   get on with Denny's story. We met again on a transport bound for Australia. We were
   assigned to a ground crew at one of the regular bases. For a couple of months we
   serviced bombers. You know, just sort of routine work. Then all of a sudden we were
   ordered to occupy a small island somewhere North of New Guinea. What made the order
   tough was that the Japs already had a base on the island and they were stubborn about
   giving it up. But our bombers softened them up and then the ground forces moved in
   and took over. They cleared the Japs out of the airfield and drove them into the
   interior. But the fighting ... when we landed. Our first job after we got ashore was
   ...
Joe: Man, what a drag. First we're soldiers, and then mechanics, and now ditch diggers.
Pfc. Broderick Crawford: Aw, quit your beefin'. We're lucky it didn't take longer to fix
 this field up than it did, the way our bombers messed it up.
Joe: Yeah, well it ain't my idea of the South Seas. Anyway, not the way I read about it
 in the travel folders.
Pfc. Broderick Crawford: Yeah, yeah, I know. Dancing girls and the calm of the blue
 Pacific.
Joe: Yeah, well how about that? You must have been reading the same magazine.
Pfc. Broderick Crawford: Hey look, here comes our first customer.
Joe: Hey, he's got troubles.
Pfc. Broderick Crawford: He's gotta bail. He's out of control now.
Joe: Look at that plane burn.

Pfc. Broderick Crawford: That poor guy, he's a goner.
Joe: Yeah. Hey, somebody's runnin' for the plane.
Pfc. Broderick Crawford: It's Denny, the crazy fool, look. Get away from that plane,
  it'll blow up. Denny, Denny, get away from that plane. Denny, Denny, where are you?
Joe: Get back, boys. You can't do any good. There's no use of both of you goin' in
  there.
Pvt. Damian O'Flynn (as Denny Adam): Hey, you guys, give me a lift. Give me a lift, will
  you?
Pfc. Broderick Crawford: Denny, you O.K.?
Pvt. Damian O'Flynn: Sure, sure. I'm O.K. What did you expect?
Pfc. Broderick Crawford: Look at your hands, they're burned.
Pvt. Damian O'Flynn: Forget about my hands. We've got to get this pilot to the hospital
  tent.
Pfc. Broderick Crawford: Here, let me take him.
Pvt. Damian O'Flynn: Joey and I can manage. You stay here and put that fire out. Maybe
  you can salvage some of the plane for spare parts.
Pfc. Broderick Crawford: Joey, make him get his hands fixed, will you?
Pvt. Damian O'Flynn: I'll take care of my hands. You see what you can do about that
  plane.
Incidental music
  Pfc. Broderick Crawford: Yeah, that was typical of Denny. The only thing he thought
    about was saving the plane. He knew our job was to keep 'em flying and the job came
    first with him. The Japs resented our taking over the island and the airfield and
    they tried desperately to get it back. They made a feeble attempt to copy our 'round
    the clock bombings and their loses were terrific. But they kept coming and that meant
    we were on duty, and I mean duty, brother, thirty-six hours out of twenty-four. Sleep
    was just one of those things you dream about, if you had a chance to dream. We all
    did double duty, but Denny really delivered the goods. He'd do his regular work on
    the radio, then hurry over to the hangars and shops. He'd help us tune up the motors,
    refuel the planes.
Pfc. Broderick Crawford: Boy, it seems to me I've refueled and serviced a jillion planes
  this month.
Pvt. Damian O'Flynn: Aw, you won't be servicing any if the Japs keep comin'.
Pfc. Broderick Crawford: Yeah, it looks like they're playin' for keeps, don't it?
Sir: I think they're landing on the North beach. Barges, tanks, the whole works.
Pfc. Broderick Crawford: Well, we're really in a spot.
Sir: Check number 88.
Pfc. Broderick Crawford: Yes, sir. Right away, sir. Well, let's see. Ah. Ignition's
  O.K., oil lines look all right, fuel, awp, here's the trouble.
Joe: Hey, what gives?
Pfc. Broderick Crawford: Fuel pump's shot.
Joe: Can you fix it?
Pfc. Broderick Crawford: Not a chance. Looked like it stopped a bullet. Get me a new
  one from supply, Joe.
Joe: Aw, no dice. We al - used that last one yesterday.
Pvt. Damian O'Flynn: I'll get the pump from that P-38 that crashed last week.
Pfc. Broderick Crawford: Nice goin', Denny. Joe and I'll get this one off. Hand me that
  wrench, Joe.
Joe: Hey, that's a Jap machine gun.
Pfc. Broderick Crawford: Yeah, they spotted Denny. Look out, Denny, look out! Man that
  machine gun and cover him, Joe, cover him! Keep goin', Denny.
Joe: Come back here, Bud, you can't do him any good.
Pfc. Broderick Crawford: Denny! Denny, you hurt bad?
Pvt. Damian O'Flynn: No, not bad. Just my arm.
Pfc. Broderick Crawford: I'll help you back.
Pvt. Damian O'Flynn: I can take care of myself. You get that fuel pump.
Pfc. Broderick Crawford: Look, you can't get back alone.
Pvt. Damian O'Flynn: Get that fuel pump.
Incidental music

Pfc. Broderick Crawford: Well, that's news. She ought to perk all right now. Joe, give those engines a try.
Joe: Yeah, workin' like a charm.
Pfc. Broderick Crawford: Number 88's ready, sir.
Sir: O.K., Sergeant. I'll take over now.
Pfc. Broderick Crawford: O.K., Joe, pull those blocks.
C: Sergeant Hawkins.
Pfc. Broderick Crawford: Yes, sir.
C: Japs have broken through. Get those planes off the ground as quickly as you can and dig in. We've got to hold this field at all costs.
Pfc. Broderick Crawford: Well, get movin', Joe. We'll get those planes out of the way.
Joe: I'm with you, Bud.
Pvt. Damian O'Flynn: What do you want from me, Sarge?
Pfc. Broderick Crawford: De - look, Denny, the first thing I want you to do is go to the hospital and have that arm fixed.
Pvt. Damian O'Flynn: I still have one good arm and I'm gonna use it.
Pfc. Broderick Crawford: O.K. You win. Use that machine gun and make those Japs keep their distance. Come on, Joe. Let's get busy on these planes.
Incidental music
   Pfc. Broderick Crawford: Yeah, the Japs kept movin' closer all the time. We were under a constant hail of enemy fire. But we kept working and got all those planes in the air. Denny, with that bum arm, kept burning lead with that shadow box and was still right with us when we dug in for that last ditch fight, his arm was giving plenty of trouble but he ...
Pfc. Broderick Crawford: I'll take over now, Denny.
Pvt. Damian O'Flynn: You'll take over nothin'. I'm doin' all right.
Pfc. Broderick Crawford: But your arm.
Pvt. Damian O'Flynn: My arm's O.K. I tell you.
Pfc. Broderick Crawford: You're being stupid.
Pvt. Damian O'Flynn: So I'm stupid. Now get out of here and grab another gun before I turn this one on you.
Joe: Hey, hey, look what's comin'. Tanks, Jap tanks, a whole flock of 'em.
Pfc. Broderick Crawford: They're headin' for that narrow pass in the hills behind us.
Pvt. Damian O'Flynn: If they get through there it's curtains for us. We can't stop them with machine guns.
Pfc. Broderick Crawford: They won't get through. I can stop them. Joe, get that jeep and drive it over here.
Joe: Right away, Sarge.
Pvt. Damian O'Flynn: Now, what's on your mind, Bud?
Pfc. Broderick Crawford: I'm gonna load a two hundred pounder in that jeep and explode it in the pass. Then let 'em try and get through.
Pvt. Damian O'Flynn: You're takin' an awful chance.
Pfc. Broderick Crawford: Better than havin' 'em get all of us, isn't it?
Joe: There she is, Bud.
Pfc. Broderick Crawford: O.K., Joe, give me a hand with this bomb.
Joe: Are you out of your mind? This ain't no bomb rack.
Pfc. Broderick Crawford: Stop squawkin' and heave.
Pvt. Damian O'Flynn: Come on now, over here, over here, Joe.
Pfc. Broderick Crawford: All right, easy. There it is, boys.
Pvt. Damian O'Flynn: Hurry up, they're starting into the pass.
Pfc. Broderick Crawford: I'm all ready. Where do you think you're goin'?
Pvt. Damian O'Flynn: With you.
Pfc. Broderick Crawford: Look, this is a one-man job.
Pvt. Damian O'Flynn: Not quite. You'll need somebody to set the fuse.
Pfc. Broderick Crawford: I can handle this alone. Now get out of here.
Pvt. Damian O'Flynn: We haven't much time, Bud.
Pfc. Broderick Crawford: O.K., Junior, it's your funeral.
Pvt. Damian O'Flynn: First tank's almost through the pass.
Pfc. Broderick Crawford: O.K., Denny, set that fuse.
Pvt. Damian O'Flynn: All set.

Pfc. Broderick Crawford: All right, now jump, Denny, jump!
Incidental music
  Pfc. Broderick Crawford: That explosion blew up the mouth of the pass and took the
    leading tank along with it. Denny and I managed to jump clear before the crash, so
    we're alive to tell the story. Well, can you imagine a guy like Denny takin' that
    suicide ride just to make sure the bomb fuse'd be set right? That's the kind of
    soldiers the Technical Training Command turns out. They not only service the planes
    and repair the motors and load the guns and fix the radios, ...
Pfc. Broderick Crawford: ... but they fight, they fight for the privilege of keeping 'em
  flying. Well, you see, mister, my buddy's really a hero.
Pvt. Damian O'Flynn: Here's the news for you, Bud.
Pfc. Broderick Crawford: Thanks a lot, Denny. Well, so long, mister. Come again, will
  you? Is the doctor coming today, nurse?
Incidental music
  Pvt. Damian O'Flynn: What a guy. He probably told you all about my being a hero.
  Well, he's the real hero. Sure, I lost an arm but I still have both my eyes, haven't
  I? And Bud, well, Bud will never see again.
OLD BLACK JOE (Old tune)
  Captain Glenn Miller: And now medley time and that means something old, something new,
    something borrowed and something blue. The old tune, "Old Black Joe."
  Vocal refrain by Private First Class Tony Martin and the Glee Club
  Captain Glenn Miller: For the new tune, the orchestra plays "As Time Goes By."
AS TIME GOES BY (New tune)
  Captain Glenn Miller: We borrow the favorite song of the boys in the R.A.F. Private
    Arthur Malvin sings and the orchestra plays "I've Got Sixpence."
I'VE GOT SIXPENCE (As We Go Rolling Home) (Borrowed tune)
  Vocal refrain by Private Artie Malvin
  Captain Glenn Miller: Last in our medley is something blue, George Gershwin's "Rhapsody
    in Blue."
RHAPSODY IN BLUE (Blue tune)

  ...

I Sustain the Wings (Incidental music)
  Pfc. Broderick Crawford: ... they too are called upon to perform heroic deeds. These
    men of the Technical Training Command are truly soldiers in coveralls, the heroes
    behind the heroes, the men who really "Sustain the Wings."
THE ARMY AIR CORPS
  Captain Glenn Miller: The Technical Training Command pays tribute to its comrades in
    arms, a 21-gun musical salute to all the other Commands of the Army Air Forces.
  Vocal refrain by Private First Class Tony Martin and the Glee Club
I SUSTAIN THE WINGS (closing theme)
  Pfc. Broderick Crawford: "I Sustain the Wings," is prepared and produced entirely by
    soldiers of the Technical Training Command of the Army Air Forces, Major General
    Walter R. Weaver, commanding general. This program came to you from the Technical
    Training Command School at Pawling, New York. This is C.B.S., the Columbia
    Broadcasting System.
THE TECHNICAL TRAINING COMMAND (closing theme)
  Vocal refrain by the Glee Club

10Jul43 (Sat) 2:05-2:30PM EWT CBS Playhouse No. 2, New York, New York
  I SUSTAIN THE WINGS broadcast First coast-to-coast airing scheduled but canceled at
  last minute. The show was played for the studio audience.

  ...

Captain Glenn Miller: ... Corporals Mel Powell and Jimmy Priddy and many others. And
  now, just to get you in the mood, here's "In the Mood."
IN THE MOOD
DEARLY BELOVED
  Captain Glenn Miller: The orchestra plays and Corporal Tony Martin sings "Dearly
    Beloved."
  Vocal refrain by Corporal Tony Martin and the Glee Club

  ...

OLD BLACK JOE (Old tune)
  Captain Glenn Miller: ... blue. The old tune, "Old Black Joe."
  Captain Glenn Miller: For the new tune, Corporal Tony Martin sings "As Time Goes By."
AS TIME GOES BY (New tune)
  Vocal refrain by Corporal Tony Martin
  Captain Glenn Miller: We borrow the favorite song of the boys in the R.A.F. Private
    Art Malvin sings and the orchestra plays "I've Got Sixpence."
I'VE GOT SIXPENCE (As We Go Rolling Home) (Borrowed tune)
  Vocal refrain by Private First Class Artie Malvin

17Jul43 (Sat) 2:05-2:30PM EWT WABC, CBS Playhouse No. 4, New York, New York
  I SUSTAIN THE WINGS broadcast First coast-to-coast airing   Audience

Station announcer: [WAB]C, New York
I SUSTAIN THE WINGS (opening theme)
  Corporal Broderick Crawford: "I Sustain the Wings." "I Sustain the Wings," brought to
    you by the Training Command of the Army Air Forces, the men who keep 'em flying. The
    program features the Army Air Forces Training Command Band, a story of our men in
    action and many of your old friends who, in addition to their regular duties as
    soldiers, bring you this program of music and entertainment. And now Captain Glenn
    Miller.
Captain Glenn Miller: Thank you, Corporal Brod Crawford, and good afternoon, everybody.
  Welcome to a brand new radio show by the men who really keep 'em flyin'. And now, just
  to get you in the mood, here's "In the Mood."
IN THE MOOD
DEARLY BELOVED
  Captain Glenn Miller: Corporal Tony Martin, with the Glee Club, sings "Dearly Beloved."
  Vocal refrain by Corporal Tony Martin and the Glee Club
Corporal Broderick Crawford (as Captain Paul Walker): You hear those planes, America?
  Those planes right over your head? They're carrying men and supplies to one of our
  distant outposts so we'll be there firstest with mostest. Sure, you know all about
  those planes and planes like the Suzy Q and her heroic sisters. So do I. I ought to,
  I'm a pilot and I fly one of them. My name's Paul Walker, Captain Paul Walker. I was
  taught to fly by the Army Air Forces Training Command and they sure put me through the
  paces before they gave me my silver wings. After that I was sent to the South Pacific.
  There's plenty of action there and plenty of Japs. They gave me a medal for what I did
  but it wouldn't have been possible if it hadn't a been for the men of the ground crew,
  the men that serve the planes and repair them and treat them with such tender care.
  They learned their jobs in the Training Command just like I did and believe me, they
  know their stuff. They're a lot of swell guys these soldiers in coveralls and we pilots
  think a lot of 'em. It's kind of hard to explain the relationship between the air crew
  and the ground crew of a plane but there's something awfully close between us. We work
  together like a team. We're, well, maybe you'll understand what I'm driving at if I
  tell you about Master Sergeant Jim Brennan.
Incidental music
  Corporal Broderick Crawford: Jim was a cracker-jack mechanic, a ground crew chief
    stationed with me in an air base in the heart of the New Guinea jungle. He had one
    plane, a B-17, his particular pet. He called her Pee-Gee after his girl friend and he
    spent more hours taking care of that plane. We used to kid him a lot. We used to say
    he was in love with the plane. Well, one day Pee-Gee and five other beautifully slick
    flying fortresses sailed off into the wild blue yonder to bomb a concentration of Jap
    ships in Rabul harbor. Right on schedule came the terse radio message "mission
    accomplished" when only five fortresses returned and Pee-Gee was not one of those
    five. Anxious hours passed with no word of the missing plane. She had only enough
    gas to last until two o'clock in the afternoon. Jim really started to worry when we
    heard nothing by noon. We haunted the radio room. It was after four when suddenly we
    heard ...
  Pfc. Joseph Shulman: Hello, Sunday night. Hello, hello. This is Pee-Gee calling
    Sunday night. Hello, this is Pee-Gee calling Sunday night.
  Corporal Broderick Crawford: Yeah, it was Pee-Gee all right and she'd run into real
    trouble in the form of a flock of Jap Zeros. Her radio reported that she'd done all
    right until a stray bullet conked out one of her engines and a couple of propellers
    were shattered. The badly wounded pilot was forced to put the plane down the best way
    he could and the spot selected wasn't exactly a landing field, just a small jungle
    clearing about fifty miles from home base. There was no chance at a takeoff with the
    plane in her present condition. The inevitable conclusion was that it was curtains
    for Pee-Gee but Jim refused to accept the inevitable.
Pvt. Damian F. O'Flynn (as M/Sgt. Jim Brennan): But look, Captain Walker, I tell you
  again I can put Pee-Gee in flying condition.

Corporal Broderick Crawford: I know you can, Jim. You're a swell mechanic but you can't
   get to her. It's fifty miles through some of the worst jungle in the world.
Pvt. Damian F. O'Flynn: But we can get through. Our scout report ...
Corporal Broderick Crawford: Oh, Jim, even if you did you'd probably run into trouble.
   The plane's only a couple of miles from the main Jap lines and they're patrolling that
   area.
Pvt. Damian F. O'Flynn: If I can get to Pee-Gee, sir, I'll risk running into a dozen Jap
   patrols.
Corporal Broderick Crawford: No, Jim, it can't be done. You know as well as I do it's
   impassible country.
Pvt. Damian F. O'Flynn: Not to a plane, sir.
Corporal Broderick Crawford: Use your head, Sergeant. I've scouted that country myself.
   It's impossible to set a ship down any place near Pee-Gee.
Pvt. Damian F. O'Flynn: Well, maybe not a plane, sir. But how about a man with a
   parachute?
Incidental music
Pfc. Joseph Shulman (as Jack): This is the spot, Captain, right above Pee-Gee.
Corporal Broderick Crawford: O.K., Jack, take over. Circle around a couple of times
   while we bail out.
Pfc. Joseph Shulman: Right, sir.
Corporal Broderick Crawford: O.K., boys, this is the end of the line.
Pfc. Joseph Shulman (as Eddie Jones): Gee, I never thought I'd be a human bomb going
   through these bomb doors.
Pvt. Damian F. O'Flynn: Give me a hand, Eddie, to unload these tools and props.
Pfc. Joseph Shulman: Man, look at 'em drop.
Pvt. Damian F. O'Flynn: Sure gettin' dark down there.
Corporal Broderick Crawford: Good. The job's got to be done before dawn.
Pfc. Joseph Shulman: What's the hurry, sir?
Pvt. Damian F. O'Flynn: If we're still here in the morning the Japs'll be down on us like
   a flock of vultures.
Pfc. Joseph Shulman: Then let's get goin'.
Corporal Broderick Crawford: O.K., Jonesy, I'll hit the silk first.
Pvt. Damian F. O'Flynn: But you're not going, sir. This is a job for mechanics.
Corporal Broderick Crawford: And a pilot. Somebody's got to fly Pee-Gee out of there.
Pvt. Damian F. O'Flynn: You're taking an awful risk, sir.
Corporal Broderick Crawford: See you downstairs, men. Wooooo.
Incidental music
Pfc. Joseph Shulman: Now I know why the Training Command made us work on these planes
   blindfolded, that's so we could fix 'em in the dark.
Pvt. Damian F. O'Flynn: Yeah.
Corporal Broderick Crawford: How are you men comin' with that prop?
Pvt. Damian F. O'Flynn: Through in a minute, Captain.
Corporal Broderick Crawford: Hurry it up, it's gettin' light. Snipers, hit the dirt.
Pfc. Joseph Shulman: There he is.
Pvt. Damian F. O'Flynn: He's too far away for our automatics.
Corporal Broderick Crawford: I'll try to make for the plane. I can get him with that
   right waist gun.
Pvt. Damian F. O'Flynn: Don't do it, sir. Don't, don't do it, sir, you'll be ...
Pfc. Joseph Shulman: Oh, the Captain. He got the Captain.
Pvt. Damian F. O'Flynn: Use your automatic to draw the sniper's fire. I'm gonna help the
   Captain.
Pfc. Joseph Shulman: Come back here, Jim. You crazy ...
Pvt. Damian F. O'Flynn: You hurt bad, Captain?
Corporal Broderick Crawford: No, not too bad. It's just my arm.
Pvt. Damian F. O'Flynn: I'll help you to cover.
Corporal Broderick Crawford: I can take care of myself. You get to that machine gun.
Pvt. Damian F. O'Flynn: You're in a bad spot.
Corporal Broderick Crawford: Don't argue, get to that machine gun. Keep goin', Sergeant,
   keep goin'. Don't let it stop you. Keep goin'. Nice shootin', Brennan. You got him.

Pvt. Damian F. O'Flynn: Yeah. We gotta move out of here fast. That Jap's friends will
   want to know what all the shooting's all about.
Corporal Broderick Crawford: Get busy on that prop right away.
Pvt. Damian F. O'Flynn: Eddie's already workin' on it. I'll take care of your arm.
Corporal Broderick Crawford: My arm's all right, Sergeant. You help Jonesy.
Pfc. Joseph Shulman: Plane's O.K. now, Captain.
Pvt. Damian F. O'Flynn: Good work, Eddie.
Pfc. Joseph Shulman: Aw, she'll have to be a "heliocopter" to get off this postage stamp.
Pvt. Damian F. O'Flynn: What are you talkin' about? That's easy. Now look, we'll chop
   down those trees over there and move a couple of them boulders.
Pfc. Joseph Shulman: Yeah, yeah, but the Captain's hurt. Who are we going to use for a
   pilot?
Corporal Broderick Crawford: Well, the Sergeant.
Pfc. Joseph Shulman: The Sergeant? Can you fly, Jim?
Pvt. Damian F. O'Flynn: I don't know. I never tried.
Pfc. Joseph Shulman: That's all, brother. I'm walkin'.
Corporal Broderick Crawford: Now wait a minute, Jonesy. Won't be so bad. You make, men
   can fix me up in my seat. I'm not so badly hurt I can't tell the Sergeant what to do.
Incidental music
[Corporal Broderick Crawford: Are you up to air speed?
Pvt. Damian F. O'Flynn: Right!
Corporal Broderick Crawford: O.K., release the brake and give her the gun! All right,
   now pull your stick back. Easy, not too far, you'll turn her over.
Incidental music
   Corporal Broderick Crawford: She's coming up, Jim. She's ... Look out for that tree!
      You made it, Jim. We're flying. Who said Pee-Gee was a goner?
Corporal Broderick Crawford: We got Pee-Gee back to the base all right. And Jim and I
   were given a couple of nice shiny medals. But the medals aren't the point of my story.
   What I'm trying to show you is the teamwork that exists between men on the ground and
   the men in the air. We're all trained by the Training Command of the Army Air Forces
   and one of the things they taught us was co-operation. How to work together to keep the
   planes in the air, to "keep 'em flying!", so that we can do our share in winning
   ultimate Victory.
Incidental music
OLD BLACK JOE (Old tune)
   Captain Glenn Miller: And now comes medley time, and that means something old,
      something new, something borrowed and something blue. The old tune is "Old Black
      Joe."]
   Captain Glenn Miller: Our new tune, Corporal Tony Martin sings "As Time Goes By."
AS TIME GOES BY (New tune)
   Vocal refrain by Corporal Tony Martin
   Captain Glenn Miller: We borrow the favorite song of the boys in the R.A.F. and Private
      Art Malvin sings and the orchestra plays "I Got Sixpence."
I'VE GOT SIXPENCE (As We Go Rolling Home) (Borrowed tune)
   Vocal refrain by Private First Class Artie Malvin
   Captain Glenn Miller: Last in our medley's something blue, George Gershwin's famous
      "Rhapsody in Blue."
RHAPSODY IN BLUE (Blue tune)
THE ARMY AIR CORPS
   Captain Glenn Miller: The Training Command plays tribute to its comrades in arms.
      Here's a 21-gun musical salute to all the other commands of the Army Air Forces.
   Vocal refrain by Corporal Tony Martin and the Glee Club
I SUSTAIN THE WINGS (closing theme)
   Corporal Broderick Crawford: "I Sustain the Wings" is prepared and produced entirely by
      soldiers of the Technical Command of the Army Air Forces, Major General [Barton K.
      Yount, Commanding General.
   CBS Announcer: This program came to you from New York City. This is C.B.S., the
      Columbia Broadcasting System.
THE TECHNICAL TRAINING COMMAND (closing theme)
   Vocal refrain by the Glee Club]

24Jul43 (Sat) 2:05-2:30PM EWT WABC, CBS Playhouse No. 4, New York, New York
  I SUSTAIN THE WINGS broadcast   Audience

[**I SUSTAIN THE WINGS** (opening theme)
  Corporal Broderick Crawford: "I Sustain the Wings." "I Sustain the Wings," brought to
    you by the Army Air Forces, the men who "Keep 'Em Flying." The program features the
    band from the Army Air Forces School at Yale University and many of your old friends
    who, in addition to their regular duties as soldiers, bring you this program of music
    and entertainment. And now Captain Glenn Miller.]
Captain Glenn Miller: Thank you Corporal Brod Crawford and good afternoon, everybody.
  I'm glad to have you with us again and here are the boys ready to start marchin' with
  the "American Patrol." Corporal McKinley, roll off.
AMERICAN PATROL
Captain Glenn Miller: Corporal Tony Martin sings and the orchestra plays "Oklahoma's" big
  musical hit, "People Will Say We're in Love."
PEOPLE WILL SAY WE'RE IN LOVE
  Vocal refrain by Corporal Tony Martin
[**I Sustain the Wings** (Incidental music)
  Vocal refrain by Corporal Tony Martin and the Glee Club:
    "I Sustain the Wings" 'til we reach the goal." (Vocalists hum from this point.)
  Captain Glenn Miller: "'Til we reach the goal," our goal of victory! And freedom for
    the whole world! In every theater of operations, in the South Pacific, the Aleutians,
    in Burma, Sicily, and over Germany, our fighting forces are proving their
    determination to win this war with superhuman courage!
Captain Glenn Miller: No little part of our current success is due to the awe-inspiring
  display of superior air power. Protective umbrellas of fighting planes that permit
  otherwise impossible landings, 'round the clock bombings to destroy the industrial heart
  of the enemy, wave upon wave of bombers blasting an island into submission. Thousands
  of planes completing their missions at every hour of the day and night! But it takes
  more than just numerical superiority of fighters and bombers. There must be men of
  skill and courage to "Keep 'Em Flying!" And we have just such men, millions of 'em!
  Their courage is an American heritage! Their skill is the result of a long course of
  intensive instruction by the Training Command of the Army Air Forces. Every man of
  every crew, no matter what his previous occupation, has attended one or more of a vast
  network of schools maintained by the Army Air Forces Training Command. Meet the crew.
Pilot: I'm the pilot. The Air Forces taught me to fly, and they took a lot of time and
  trouble to see that I knew how to handle a plane. After twelve months' training they
  handed me my silver sings and said I was ready for combat. Flying had become second
  nature with me. But that's not all. We have the best equipment in the world, and the
  Training Command furnishes the men that keep it the best, the men of the ground crew,
  the mechanics. When I take off I know that it's in perfect condition because the
  mechanic has done his job the way it should be done. I know I can depend on the
  engines, the controls, the oxygen system. I know that plane will fly under all
  conditions.
Bombardier: I'm the bombardier, a graduate of the world's biggest university, the A.A.F.
  Training Command. My job depends a lot on one of America's most remarkable fighting
  weapons, the secret bombsight. It insures our lethal blockbusters falling where they'll
  do the most good. Its accuracy has to be checked and re-checked after every mission.
  That's the work of another member of the ground crew, the precision instrument man.
  When he tells me my bombsight's O.K., I can take his word for it. I know I'm going to
  hit the target. You can bet I'm glad he's on the job.
Gunner: I'm the aerial gunner. I went to a Training Command School along with the rest
  of the boys. Me, who thought my school days was over. But man! - am I glad they taught
  me what they did. It's wonderful to know how to handle a gun when a Zero or a
  Messerschmitt comes diving at you from out of the clouds. But it's more wonderful to
  know those guns are gonna work. That's where the armorer comes in. He's the guy that
  checks my guns, cleans 'em, oils 'em, loads 'em with ammunition. He's the man I depend
  on. He's my buddy.

Navigator: I'm the navigator. I'm the eyes when we're flying blind. It's my job to get our bomber to the target. Like the bombardier, my work demands precision instruments which must be more accurate than the finest watch. I, too, depend upon the instrument man.

Corporal Broderick Crawford: I'm the technician. That's where I come in. I am the Air Force technician. I make it possible for flyers to be heroes and heroes to be flyers. I drill and work and fight. I work that others may fly and fight. I fight that I may work to keep them flying. I am the mechanic, the machinist, the armorer, the weather observer, the instrument man, the radio man. I'm a technician but I fight like a commando. I am one of an unbeatable trio, the plane, the air crew, the ground crew, each indispensable to the other two. Without me the plane would be a motionless machine, the pilot a helpless gladiator. When I trained, I beefed at the constant stream of repetition, of routine. But now I realize I was learning to act on instinct. I griped at scrubbing and shining and cleaning, but now I realize neatness means a clean job of every task. An unbuttoned pocket seemed trivial, but now I know a forgotten button might be a forgotten cotter key and that key might mean a plane destroyed and a crew lost. Because of strict training I am good and I know I'm good. The folks at home may never know how important I am; the public may never see my name in print. I am the plodding lineman of modern football. I make long runs possible for All-Americans. I am the blocker that never carries the ball.

Incidental music

Corporal Broderick Crawford: But that pilot there knows me. He knows that when he climbs aboard, the plane is ready. He knows those engines are perfect; the radio, his ears; the instrument, his eyes. That bombardier knows his hits are going to be perfect. And when they come back there is something in their handshake no newspaper could describe, no medal could equal. It is the grip of men whose lives depend on me. "I Sustain the Wings!"

DRINK TO ME ONLY WITH THINE EYES (Old tune)

Captain Glenn Miller: And now it's medley time with something old, something new, something borrowed and something blue. The old tune is "Drink to Me Only with Thine Eyes."

Captain Glenn Miller: Corporal Tony Martin sings the new tune, "You'll Never Know."

YOU'LL NEVER KNOW (New tune)

Vocal refrain by Corporal Tony Martin

Captain Glenn Miller: We borrow Bob Crosby's beautiful theme song, "Summertime."

SUMMERTIME (Borrowed tune)

Captain Glenn Miller: And for something blue, it's Irving Berlin's "Blue Skies."

BLUE SKIES (Blue tune)

Phil Goulding (CBS announcer): Attention, you young Americans! If you have reached your seventeenth birthday you may be eligible to join the Air Corps Enlisted Reserve and wear the silver propeller and wings of the Army Air Forces. Go at once to your nearest Army Recruiting Agency, Aviation Cadet Board or post office and learn how you may be assigned to the Air Corps Enlisted Reserve while you are still seventeen. This is an invitation to America's bravest and best to fly with the Army Air Forces. And, now, back to the music.

Captain Glenn Miller: Thank you, Phil Goulding. The Army Air Forces pays tribute to its comrades in arms. A 21-gun musical salute to our fliers all over the world.

COMIN' IN ON A WING AND A PRAYER

Vocal refrain by Corporal Tony Martin and the Glee Club

I SUSTAIN THE WINGS (closing theme)

Corporal Broderick Crawford: "I Sustain the Wings" is written and produced by the Army Air Forces. We'll be seeing you again next week at the same time.

Phil Goulding: This program came to you from New York City. This is C.B.S., the Columbia Broadcasting System.]

31Jul43 (Sat) 2:05-2:30PM EWT   WABC, CBS Playhouse No. 4, New York, New York
I SUSTAIN THE WINGS broadcast   Audience

[I SUSTAIN THE WINGS (opening theme)
  Corporal Broderick Crawford: "I Sustain the Wings." "I Sustain the Wings," brought to
    you by the Army Air Forces, the men who "Keep 'Em Flying." The program features the
    band from the Army Air Forces School at Yale University, and many of your old friends
    who, in addition to their regular duties as soldiers, bring you this program of music
    and entertainment. And now Captain Glenn Miller.
Captain Glenn Miller: Thank you, Corporal Broderick Crawford, and good evening,
  everybody. Opening our program is a tune that should jump right fancy, so here's
  Corporal Ray McKinley rollin' off for the "Anvil Chorus."
ANVIL CHORUS
I NEVER MENTION YOUR NAME (Oh, No!)
  Captain Glenn Miller: One of the season's better tunes sung by Corporal Tony Martin and
    the Glee Club, "I Never Mention Your Name."
  Vocal refrain by Corporal Tony Martin and the Glee Club
Captain Glenn Miller: Listen to that, America! Isn't it a lovely sound? The music of
  victory!
Victory Theme from Beethoven's Fifth Symphony (Incidental music)
Captain Glenn Miller: Victory music interpreted by the roar of engines from the finest
  planes in the world, terrific planes carrying America's answer to a treacherous message
  received at Pearl Harbor. But a plane that won't fly is the most useless thing in the
  world. So these planes must have thousands of young men of skill and daring to fly
  them, and thousands more to keep 'em flying! It is the job of the Army Air Forces
  Training Command, the world's biggest university, to furnish these men of the air and
  ground crews. They come from every walk of life to be trained as soldiers as well as
  specialists. Each man, when he graduates, must fight like a ranger and work on a plane
  blind-folded like a magician. He can. Well, let's have the crew speak for themselves.
Pvt. Damian O'Flynn: Who, me? I am the photographer. My pictures locate the target for
  the bombardier, the guy who is paving the road to victory with his bombs. The Training
  Command taught me to do my fighting with a camera instead of a gun, and sometimes I get
  the jitters, thinking that a camera won't shoot down an enemy plane. But those pictures
  of mine are plenty important. We've got to have them. And if you come right down to
  it, I probably have a lot of planes to my credit. Our entire campaign, on the ground
  and in the air, depends on photographic reconnaissance.
Pfc. Paul Huston: I'm the armorer. It's my job, the job taught me by the Army Air Forces
  Training Command, to see that the power turrets are operating, that the guns are in
  working order. It's up to the aerial gunner to protect the planes in the air with the
  guns I've serviced and loaded. So, you see, the pilot and his crew really depend on me
  to give them the necessary protection. You can bet I'm gonna keep those guns firing.
Pfc. Joseph Shulman: I'm the mechanic, the guy that works on the engines and makes 'em
  perk, gives 'em a real goin' over after every flight. I gotta check the spark plugs,
  an' the ignition, the fuel line, everything that helps the engines give with the
  necessary horsepower. That's some job for a guy that used to jerk sodas like I did, but
  the Training Command sent me to school and taught me all the answers about engines. Now
  I can fix 'em with one hand tied behind my back. Sure the goin' is tough once in a
  while, an' I get awful beat, you know, tired out, especially on this round-the-clock
  bombing deal. Sometimes the job seems like a terrific drag, but I'm not gonna let that
  pilot down, not when he's dependin' on me to see that his engines are a hundred per cent
  O.K. He's gotta fly the plane, and I'm gonna keep him flying!
Corporal Broderick Crawford: I'm the man in the plane, the man who wears the silver
  wings. I'm the pilot ...
Pvt. Damian O'Flynn: ... the bombardier ...
Pfc. Paul Huston: ... the navigator ...
Pfc. Paul Huston: ... the aerial gunner.

Corporal Broderick Crawford: I am the air crew that flies the plane and keeps it flying. I am the eyes of the plane, its ears, its brain and heart. I give it life, and strength, and purpose. Without me the ship would be a lifeless machine, an inanimate mass of modern design and material, a helpless monster whose wings are clipped and its sting removed. I guide the plane to its destination. Together we carry the fight to the enemy, stopping the beat of his industrial pulse with our bombs, clearing the sky of his aircraft with our guns. I am another of that unbeatable trio, the plane, the air crew and the ground crew, the modern d'Artàgnan of the three musketeers. Like that deathless hero, I, too, must duel, but my weapon is the plane instead of the sword. I must parry the deadly thrusts of the enemy, dodging, twisting, turning, side-stepping, to maneuver him into position for the kill, so that I may be the victor in this duel between slavery and freedom. Months of strict training have made me good, better than anything the enemy has to offer, good enough to carry the hopes and prayers of one-hundred and forty million Americans whose eyes are upon me whenever I take off.

The Army Air Corps (Incidental music)

Corporal Broderick Crawford: I am one of America's heroes! And, to justify their faith, I must continue to fly and fight. They have given me skill through intensive training, and entrusted me with the finest weapons money can buy. I'm going to use that skill and those weapons to the best of my ability, and more. I'm going to keep on flying and fighting until the heart and spirit of all mankind, a free mankind, can enjoy the god-given benefits of a free world. I am the wings of freedom!

CARRY ME BACK TO OLD VIRGINNY (Old tune)

Captain Glenn Miller: And now it's medley time with something old, something new, something borrowed and something blue. The old tune is] "Carry Me Back to Old Virginny."

Captain Glenn Miller: Something new, a brand new tune, first time on the air. Corporal Tony Martin sings "Mister Lucky Me."

MISTER LUCKY ME (New tune)

Vocal refrain by Corporal Tony Martin

[Captain Glenn Miller: We borrow the favorite song of our Canadian good neighbors, Private Malvin and the Glee Club singing "Alouette."

ALOUETTE (Borrowed tune)

Vocal refrain by Private First Class Artie Malvin the the Glee Club

Captain Glenn Miller: Last on our medley is something blue, "Blue Moon."

BLUE MOON (Blue tune)

Corporal Broderick Crawford: Attention, you young Americans! If you have reached your seventeenth birthday you may be eligible to join the Air Corps Enlisted Reserve and wear the silver propeller and wings of the Army Air Forces. Go at once to your nearest Army Recruiting Agency, Aviation Cadet Board or post office and learn how you may be assigned to the Air Corps Enlisted Reserve while you are still seventeen. This is an invitation to America's bravest and best to fly with the Army Air Forces. And, now, back to the music.

OVER THERE!

Captain Glenn Miller: The Army Air Forces pays tribute to all our comrades in the Air Force who are doing such a wonderful job, "Over There!"

Vocal refrain by the Glee Club

I SUSTAIN THE WINGS (closing theme)

Corporal Broderick Crawford: "I Sustain the Wings" is written and produced by the Army Air Forces. We'll be seeing you again next week at the same time. So long.

CBS announcer: This program came to you from New York City. This is C.B.S., the Columbia Broadcasting System.]

07Aug43 (Sat) 2:05-2:30PM EWT WABC, CBS Playhouse No. 4, New York, New York
I SUSTAIN THE WINGS broadcast   Audience

[THE ARMY AIR CORPS (opening fanfare)
2nd Lt. Donald P. Briggs: "I Sustain the Wings!"
I SUSTAIN THE WINGS (opening theme)
  2nd Lt. Donald P. Briggs: "I Sustain the Wings," presented by the Army Air Forces.
    Each week the program will feature the band from the Army Air Forces Technical School
    at Yale University, Corporal Broderick Crawford, Johnnie, the kid next door, and many
    of your old friends. And now Captain Glenn Miller.
Captain Glenn Miller: Thank you, Lieutenant Don Briggs, and good afternoon, everybody.
  This afternoon's program salutes the Army Air Forces Technical School at Yale
  University. We start with the tune that has the cadets jumpin' every noon in the mess
  hall, the "Sun Valley Jump."
SUN VALLEY JUMP
NOW WE KNOW
  Captain Glenn Miller: Corporal Tony Martin sings and the band plays "Now We Know."
  Vocal refrain by Corporal Tony Martin
Corporal Broderick Crawford: You remember Johnnie, Johnnie, the kid next door. The boy
  that broke your parlor window when he played baseball in the vacant lot, the one that
  used to mow your lawn for a quarter so he could go to the Saturday afternoon movies.
  Once in a while he'd get in your hair and you'd wonder if he'd ever amount to anything.
  You needn't have worried because right now Johnnie is a pretty important character.
  He's one guy in a million, and a million guys in one! He's Mr. Johnnie Know-how,
  Johnnie Technician, but most important, he's Johnnie American! He's every mother's son
  that joined the Air Force. He's been taught to fly and to keep 'em flying, by the Army
  Air Forces Training Command. Yes, Johnnie is a lot of different young men from
  different parts of these United States, but this afternoon he's one in particular.
  Aviation Cadet Theodore C. Hossfeld, Army serial number 11082406, represents Johnnie
  today. Cadet Hossfeld has permitted Private Damian O'Flynn to speak for him, and this
  typical American boy is learning to be a laboratory commander in the photographic
  section, one of the four different divisions of the Army Air Forces Technical School at
  Yale University. When he graduates he'll know everything there is to know about a
  camera. He'll --- but Johnnie knows his own job better than I and he's right here to
  tell us about it. Johnnie, meet the folks.
Pvt. Damian O'Flynn (as Aviation Cadet Theodore C. Hossfeld): Hello, folks.
Corporal Broderick Crawford: Johnnie, suppose you tell us a little about yourself.
Pvt. Damian O'Flynn: There isn't much to tell. I received my basic at ...
Corporal Broderick Crawford: No, let's begin at the beginning. Where are you from?
Pvt. Damian O'Flynn: Washington, D.C.
Corporal Broderick Crawford: And I'll bet you were a photographer before you joined the
  Air Force.
Pvt. Damian O'Flynn: I'll take that bet. I was a salesman and surveyor, but I'm sure
  going to make photography my business when we've finished taking care of Herr Hitler and
  his playmates.
Corporal Broderick Crawford: Your record shows that you've been in the Army fourteen
  months and that you received your basic training at Boca Raton, Florida.
Pvt. Damian O'Flynn: Right.
Corporal Broderick Crawford: And from there you came to the Technical School at Yale.
Pvt. Damian O'Flynn: Keep it up, Brod, you're batting a thousand.
Corporal Broderick Crawford: I've heard a lot about the camera magic you cadets are being
  taught at Yale. I didn't know the Training Command was turning out magicians.
Pvt. Damian O'Flynn: Not exactly magicians, but they sure teach us a lot. They seem to
  think our job's pretty important.

Corporal Broderick Crawford: It is, Johnnie, I happen to know that the aerial photographer is called the bombardier's bloodhound, because he smells out the target for him. Your photographs detect flaws in camouflage, locate the targets, expose the movements of enemy troops and transports, show the extent of the damage done in bombing raids, keep a pictorial record of enemy planes, tanks and ships destroyed in combat. Commanding generals use those pictures to plan their campaigns, and a lot of planning depends on good photography.

Pvt. Damian O'Flynn: You make it sound like a mighty big job.

Corporal Broderick Crawford: Well, they don't furnish you with those fine cameras and modern laboratory equipment just so you can give the boys pictures of pin-up girls.

Pvt. Damian O'Flynn: Don't give me away, but I do manage a glamour portrait once in a while.

Corporal Broderick Crawford: I see, just to make your work interesting.

Pvt. Damian O'Flynn: That's an angle, but photography is pretty interesting, even without the girls.

Corporal Broderick Crawford: You talk like you're taking those "never had it so good" pills. Can you tell us what's so intriguing, or is it a military secret?

Pvt. Damian O'Flynn: Some of it is, but there's a lot I can talk about. For instance, last month two of the cadets, working as a team, snapped a picture, developed the film, printed it and turned the finished product over to the instructor in one minute and seventeen seconds.

Corporal Broderick Crawford: One minute and seventeen seconds! That's some sort of a record, isn't it?

Pvt. Damian O'Flynn: The fastest it's ever been done.

Corporal Broderick Crawford: And you said they weren't turning out magicians.

Pvt. Damian O'Flynn: I suppose you could call it magic, especially when we take pictures without a camera.

Corporal Broderick Crawford: Pictures without a camera! I've heard everything now.

Pvt. Damian O'Flynn: No, Brod, I'm on the level. It's a regular part of our instruction. It all started one evening when Sergeant Greene, the instructor, was giving a class of cadets a lecture demonstration on emergency photography methods in the field. ...

Sergeant Greene: ... The Air Force has given you the best equipment possible. If you follow approved methods in using that equipment, you can't fail to turn out good pictures.

Cadet Hopkins: Sergeant Greene.

Sergeant Greene: Yes, Cadet Hopkins?

Cadet Hopkins: Suppose we're in a photo mobile trailer and shrapnel smashes our cameras? How could we make hurry-up pictures of a new type gun found in a destroyed enemy plane?

Sergeant Greene: Then, mister, you'd make your own camera

Corporal Broderick Crawford: How d'ya like that? That's really laying it in your lap. Make your own camera. Sounds like a man-sized job to me.

Pvt. Damian O'Flynn: It's not so tough. All you need is a cardboard box, a piece of dark celluloid and a pin.

Corporal Broderick Crawford: Then what?

Pvt. Damian O'Flynn: You make the cardboard box light proof. Cut a hole in one end and paste the celluloid over it and then make a small pin-hole in the celluloid. Another piece of cardboard is used for a shutter. The film is placed at one end of the box and exposed from thirty to sixty seconds by sliding back the shutter.

Corporal Broderick Crawford: Sounds all right, but what if you haven't any film?

Pvt. Damian O'Flynn: We'd substitute sensitized paper instead.

Corporal Broderick Crawford: Pictures without a camera or film, that really takes know-how. And next you'll be telling me you can develop those films without the proper chemicals.

Pvt. Damian O'Flynn: Hey! You're getting ahead of me.

Corporal Broderick Crawford: You mean you can do it?

Pvt. Damian O'Flynn: Of course. Captain Bradford, Sergeant Greene and Staff Sergeant
  Rolston searched until they found substitutes for many of the chemicals ordinarily
  needed to develop film. Common table salt will take the place of potassium bromide,
  naphtha-smelling G.I. soap does the job for sodium carbonate, granulated sugar will in
  some cases do the work of sodium sulphate, and acetic acid can be replaced by water
  treated with carbon dioxide gas from the exhaust of a jeep.
Corporal Broderick Crawford: Developing films by using the exhaust of a jeep, that's a
  new job for a jeep.
Pvt. Damian O'Flynn: That's right, but the Air Forces teach us to handle any emergency
  with materials at hand.
Corporal Broderick Crawford: I still say it's magic. And thanks a lot, Johnnie, for
  telling us about it.
Corporal Broderick Crawford: That was Johnnie, folks, Johnnie, the kid next door. He's
  one of the many thousands of young men being trained by the Army Air Forces Training
  Command to fly our planes and to keep 'em flying. When Johnnie graduates as a Second
  Lieutenant, he will be thoroughly familiar with all phases of photography. His
  intensive training has prepared him to meet any emergency so that he can deliver
  important photographs, whenever and wherever they are needed. So you see, you needn't
  worry about Johnnie. He's contributing his share, a big share, toward our ultimate
  victory!
CAPRICE VIENNOIS (Old tune)
  Captain Glenn Miller: And now something for the gals. For the wives and sweethearts of
    the cadets at Yale University we play something old, something new, something borrowed
    and something blue. A famous melody from the pen of Fritz Kreisler.]
  Captain Glenn Miller: Something new, Corporal Tony Martin sings "Sunday, Monday, or
    Always."
SUNDAY, MONDAY, OR ALWAYS (New tune)
  Vocal refrain by Corporal Tony Martin
  [Captain Glenn Miller: We borrow Phil Spitalny's lovely theme, the "Isle of Golden
    Dreams."
MY ISLE OF GOLDEN DREAMS (Borrowed tune)
  Captain Glenn Miller: Last in our medley is something blue, the "Birth of the Blues."
BIRTH OF THE BLUES (Blue tune)
2nd Lt. Donald P. Briggs: Young Americans! How would you like to wear the silver
  propeller and wings of the Army Air Forces? If you have reached your seventeenth
  birthday the Air Forces invite you to join the Air Corps Enlisted Reserve. Choose how
  you may best serve your country while you are still seventeen. Go at once to your
  nearest Army Recruiting Agency, Aviation Cadet Board or post office. This is your
  chance to fly with the finest, the Army Air Forces. Now, back to the music, Captain.
Captain Glenn Miller: Thank you, Lieutenant. And now, the top tune of the week as chosen
  by the cadets at Yale University. A song written by Private Frank Loesser of the Army
  Air Forces, "In My Arms."
IN MY ARMS
  Vocal refrain by the Glee Club
I SUSTAIN THE WINGS (closing theme)
  2nd Lt. Donald P. Briggs: "I Sustain the Wings" has presented the band from the Army
    Air Forces Technical School at Yale University, Captain Glenn Miller, Corporal
    Broderick Crawford, and Johnnie, the kid next door. Next week you'll learn more about
    Johnnie at the Army Air Forces Training School at Farmingdale, Long Island. We'll be
    seeing you again next Saturday, same time, same station.
  CBS announcer: This program is written and produced entirely by soldiers of the Army
    Air Forces. It came to you from New York City. This is C.B.S., the Columbia
    Broadcasting System.]

14Aug43 (Sat) 2:05-2:30PM EWT WABC, CBS Playhouse No. 4, New York, New York
  I SUSTAIN THE WINGS broadcast   Audience

THE ARMY AIR CORPS (opening fanfare)
2nd Lt. Donald P. Briggs: "I Sustain the Wings."
I SUSTAIN THE WINGS (opening theme)
  2nd Lt. Donald P. Briggs: "I Sustain the Wings," presented by the Army Air Forces.
    Each week the program features the band from the Army Air Forces Technical School at
    Yale University, Corporal Broderick Crawford, Johnnie, the kid next door, and many of
    your old friends. And now Captain Glenn Miller.
Captain Glenn Miller: Thank you, Lieutenant Don Briggs, and good afternoon, everybody.
  Today's program salutes the Army Air Forces Technical School at Farmingdale, Long
  Island, where the Training Command, in cooperation with the Republic Aviation
  Corporation, trains mechanics to keep Thunderbolts flyin'. And speakin' of flyin',
  here's the band on board the "Caribbean Clipper."
CARIBBEAN CLIPPER
IF YOU PLEASE
  Captain Glenn Miller: Corporal Tony Martin sings and the band plays "If You Please."
  Vocal refrain by Corporal Tony Martin and the Glee Club
[Corporal Broderick Crawford: Faster than the speed of sound! That's the world's fastest
  plane, America, traveling more than fifteen miles a minute! While you were listening,
  that plane dove more than four miles. That's a lot of space to cover in a matter of
  seconds, an awful lot! And those machine guns, they're spitting out over eight hundred
  bullets a minute, eight hundred separate little messages of death for the Axis. Yeah,
  that's the Thunderbolt, a plane that's giving the Axis plenty of trouble, today, and
  every day. That wonderful plane would be just a bunch of useless gadgets if it weren't
  for Johnnie, Johnnie, the kid next door. The kid that used to drive you nuts tinkering
  with jalopy motors, that filled the vacant lot with junked cars he brought home for
  salvage. You often wondered if he'd ever amount to much. Well, you can rest easy on
  that score because right now Johnnie amounts to a lot. He's made good. But he isn't
  just one guy, he's thousands of America's finest young men. He's Johnnie Pilot, Johnnie
  Crew-chief, Johnnie Mechanic, yeah, he's young Mr. Johnnie Know-how. And he's getting
  his know-how through training received in the many schools maintained by the Army Air
  Forces Training Command. This afternoon Johnnie is one of the boys that "Keep 'Em
  Flying." He's working on a P-47 at the Farmingdale Technical School, which is operated
  by the Army Air Forces Training Command in cooperation with the Republic Aviation
  Corporation, the firm that builds the famed P-47, the Thunderbolt. He's busy actually
  servicing a plane at the school's flying field. Johnnie! Johnnie! Hey! You over
  there!
Pvt. Damian O'Flynn: Want something, soldier?
Corporal Broderick Crawford: Yeah, I wanted to talk to you a minute, if you can spare the
  time.
Pvt. Damian O'Flynn: I'm pretty busy, but talk ahead.
Corporal Broderick Crawford: It won't take very long, Johnnie, just a few ...
Pvt. Damian O'Flynn: Wait a minute, soldier, you're talking to the wrong guy. My name
  isn't Johnnie, I'm Corporal Arthur C. Tribley.
Corporal Broderick Crawford: I know, Corporal, that's the way it is on the Army records.
  But today you've got a new name. You're Johnnie, Johnnie Ground-crew.
Pvt. Damian O'Flynn: My mother won't like the change, Arthur's her favorite name.
Corporal Broderick Crawford: I don't think she'll mind this once. What kind of a kite is
  that you're working on?
Pvt. Damian O'Flynn: She's a Thunderbolt, and we're being trained here at Farmingdale to
  take care of just this one type of plane.
Corporal Broderick Crawford: I don't get it. I had an idea that if you knew about one
  fighter plane, you'd know about the others. They're all pretty much alike to me.
Pvt. Damian O'Flynn: You're wrong there, soldier. There are different planes for
  different purposes. Some are better at high altitudes, others at low. Take the P-47,
  for instance. She handles like a dream at forty thousand feet.
Corporal Broderick Crawford: Forty thousand feet! That's really getting up there!

Pvt. Damian O'Flynn: You're not fooling, and the Thunderbolt makes the grade because of the turbosupercharger.
Corporal Broderick Crawford: Turbosupercharger? What's that?
Pvt. Damian O'Flynn: It's a special kind of device that keeps the same atmospheric pressure in the carburetor at all altitudes.
Corporal Broderick Crawford: What kind of talk is that?
Pvt. Damian O'Flynn: In other words, the engine always gets the same mixture of gasoline and air.
Corporal Broderick Crawford: Still sounds pretty complicated to me.
Pvt. Damian O'Flynn: It is, and it's a big part of the plane. Taking care of the turbo's a job in itself.
Corporal Broderick Crawford: How did you get to know so much about it?
Pvt. Damian O'Flynn: I had plenty of time, ten months training in the Air Forces. And before I joined the Army, I worked two and half years for an aircraft factory in San Diego.
Corporal Broderick Crawford: Is San Diego your home town?
Pvt. Damian O'Flynn: No, my home's in Hubbard, Ohio, that's where my family lives.
Corporal Broderick Crawford: I suppose with your plane factory experience you were sent right to this school.
Pvt. Damian O'Flynn: It wasn't that easy. First I went to Victorville, California, for my basic training and some primary mechanic's training. I stayed there about four months then went to an airplane mechanic's school in Lincoln, Nebraska, where I spent another five months.
Corporal Broderick Crawford: Next stop, Farmingdale.
Pvt. Damian O'Flynn: You guessed it that time. And you can take it from me, I'm learning a lot here. This is really a school.
Corporal Broderick Crawford: Looks to me more like an operational hangar to me. Are those planes over there being checked for flight?
Pvt. Damian O'Flynn: Yup! It's part of our training to get those planes ready to fly. They're used to give pilots their final training just before being sent overseas.
Corporal Broderick Crawford: Do you spend all your time in the hangar here?
Pvt. Damian O'Flynn: Not by a long shot. This is only one phase of our schooling. Before we come out here, they teach us practically everything there is to know about servicing a Thunderbolt and keeping it in condition. Over two-thirds of our time at school is taken up with class room instruction.
Corporal Broderick Crawford: Class room instruction. That could be pretty boring.
Pvt. Damian O'Flynn: Not the way they handle it at Farmingdale. Our civilian instructors are especially trained by Republic to teach us the know-how of taking care of a Thunderbolt. They don't talk at us, they work with us. They do most of their teaching on full-sized models, we call them "mock-ups," of the various sections of the plane.
Corporal Broderick Crawford: Who makes these mock-ups?
Pvt. Damian O'Flynn: They're usually parts of real planes that have washed out. These ships can no longer be used for flying, so they're salvaged by the school for teaching models. We get actual experience repairing these damaged planes.
Corporal Broderick Crawford: Sounds like a pretty thorough course of instruction. You should know all about taking care of a P-47 when you finish here.
Pvt. Damian O'Flynn: We do, or we don't get our certificates. I've got to go now, soldier. That plane's due for a fifty-hour check-up, and I'm helping. Be seeing you.
Corporal Broderick Crawford: O.K., Johnnie, and thanks a lot for your time, and good luck. We've just talked to Johnnie, folks, Johnnie, the kid next door. Today Johnnie was represented by Corporal Arthur C. Tribley, who gave his permission for Private Damian O'Flynn to speak for him. Corporal Tribley, as Johnnie, is one of the many young men being trained by the Army Air Forces Training Command to keep our planes flying. When he finishes his course of training at Farmingdale, he'll know everything there is about the Thunderbolt. He'll send his P-47 into the air knowing that it won't fail the pilot. No, Johnnie won't fail the pilot. Johnnie won't fail America, because Johnnie is America.]
Captain Glenn Miller: And now something for the gals. And for the wives and sweethearts of the trainees at Farmindale we play something old, something new, something borrowed and something blue. The old song, "Silver Threads among the Gold."

SILVER THREADS AMONG THE GOLD (Old tune)
  Captain Glenn Miller: For something new, Private Lynn Allison sings "Wait for Me Mary."
WAIT FOR ME MARY (New tune)
  Vocal refrain by Private Lynn Allison
  Captain Glenn Miller: We borrow the familiar theme of Glen Gray and the Casa Loma
    Orchestra, "Smoke Rings."
SMOKE RINGS (Borrowed tune)
  Captain Glenn Miller: Last in our medley something blue with the old time "Saint Louis
    Blues."
THE SAINT LOUIS BLUES (Blue tune)
[2nd Lt. Donald P. Briggs: Young Americans of seventeen, this is your chance to be
  Johnnie, Johnnie, the kid next door, and sit behind the controls of a Thunderbolt. You
  are invited to win your wings, to fly with the finest. Join the Air Corps Enlisted
  Reserve. You may enroll while you are still seventeen, so go immediately to your
  nearest post office, Aviation Cadet Board or Army Recruiting Agency for full
  particulars. Wear the silver propeller and wings of the Army Air Forces, and join the
  mighty victory parade over Rome, Berlin and Tokyo! Captain.
Captain Glenn Miller: Here is the top tune of the week as chosen by the soldiers at the
  Army Air Forces Technical School at Farmingdale, Long Island, "Comin' in on a Wing and a
  Prayer."
COMIN' IN ON A WING AND A PRAYER
  Vocal refrain by Corporal Tony Martin and the Glee Club
I SUSTAIN THE WINGS (closing theme)
  2nd Lt. Donald P. Briggs: "I Sustain the Wings" has presented the band from the Army
    Air Forces Technical School at Yale University, Captain Glenn Miller, Corporal
    Broderick Crawford, and Johnnie, the kid next door. Next week you'll learn more about
    Johnnie at the Meteorological School at New York University. We'll be seeing you
    again next Saturday, same time, same station.
  CBS Announcer: This program is written and produced entirely by soldiers of the Army
    Air Forces and came to you from New York City. This is C.B.S., the Columbia
    Broadcasting System.]

21Aug43 (Sat) 2:05-2:30PM EWT WABC, CBS Playhouse No. 4, New York, New York
 I SUSTAIN THE WINGS broadcast   Audience

THE ARMY AIR CORPS (opening fanfare)
2nd Lt. Donald P. Briggs: "I Sustain the Wings."
I SUSTAIN THE WINGS (opening theme)
  2nd Lt. Donald P. Briggs: "I Sustain the Wings," presented by the Army Air Forces.
   Each week the program features the band from the Army Air Forces Technical School at
   Yale University; Corporal Broderick Crawford; Johnnie, the kid next door, and many of
   your old friends. And now Captain Glenn Miller.
Captain Glenn Miller: Thank you, Lieutenant Don Briggs, and good afternoon, everybody.
   Today we salute the Army Air Forces Meteorological School at New York University right
   here in New York City. And now we get goin' with some music. You figure out the
   connection with the weather as the band plays "I Hear You Screamin'."
I HEAR YOU SCREAMIN'
PEOPLE WILL SAY WE'RE IN LOVE
  Captain Glenn Miller: Corporal Tony Martin sings "People Will Say We're in Love."
  Vocal refrain by Corporal Tony Martin
Corporal Broderick Crawford: Weather is a weapon of war! [Wind! Howling across Arctic
   wastes, sweeping everything from its path! Winds that drive ships from their course,
   and toss heavy four-motored bombers around in the sky! Rain! Sheets of water pouring
   from the skies. Rain that turns the earth beneath it into a quagmire, and prevents the
   use of mechanized weapons. Pouring rain that blinds the pilot and grounds his plane!
   Fog! Snow! Ice and sleet! Elements over which man has no control, elements that can
   help or hinder in the prosecution of the war. Yes, America, weather is a weapon of war!
   Everybody talks about the weather, but no one does anything about it, except Johnnie,
   Johnnie, the kid next door. You remember Johnnie. He's the kid that drove you crazy
   with those peculiar odors from his woodshed chemical lab, that made you run away when
   you saw him coming because he could always stump you with the sixty-four dollar
   question, then made it worse by supplying the answer. Well, Johnnie's experiments and
   his thirst for knowledge are helping us right now, helping us to win this war. He's the
   modern version of "All for one, and one for all." He's the thousands of our country's
   finest young men that are being trained by the Army Air Forces Training Command, the
   Command that makes him Mr. Johnnie Know-how by teaching him to fly and to "Keep 'em
   flying." This afternoon we'll find Johnnie learning about the weather in the
   Meteorological School operated by the Army Air Forces Training Command at New York
   University. At the moment Johnnie is making observations at a weather station located
   on the roof of one of the school buildings. Let's go up and see him. Aren't you a
   little old to be playing with balloons?
Pvt. Damian O'Flynn (as Cadet Frank W. McIntosh): What? Playing with balloons? Yeah,
   yeah, I suppose I am. But it isn't exactly play, it's part of my job. You see, I send
   ...
Corporal Broderick Crawford: What are you trying to give me? I thought only clowns and
   bubble-dancers used balloons in their work.
Pvt. Damian O'Flynn: Well, we're not bubble-dancers ...
Corporal Broderick Crawford: No, you don't look the type.
Pvt. Damian O'Flynn: ... but we are meteorologists and we do need balloons.
Corporal Broderick Crawford: Meteorologist? That's a fancy name for a weather man, isn't
   it?
Pvt. Damian O'Flynn: That's about it, and we use balloons to make weather observations.
Corporal Broderick Crawford: Weather observations? All right, mister, explain yourself.
Pvt. Damian O'Flynn: We fill the balloon with hydrogen and send it aloft. Then we watch
   its ascent through the theodolite ...
Corporal Broderick Crawford: Theodolite? Oh, you mean that gadget over there that looks
   like a telescope.
Pvt. Damian O'Flynn: That's the one. We make readings with it at one minute intervals,
   and then we're able to calculate the speed and direction of the wind at different
   levels.
Corporal Broderick Crawford: Sounds great, but what's it for?

Pvt. Damian O'Flynn: It helps us figure out changes in the weather, and we can tell a
  pilot at what level to fly to get the benefit of a good, strong tail-wind.
Corporal Broderick Crawford: And a good tail-wind saves gasoline.
Pvt. Damian O'Flynn: Right.
Corporal Broderick Crawford: Another thing, Johnnie, you are Johnnie, aren't you?
Pvt. Damian O'Flynn: That's what everybody calls me, but my real name is Frank W.
  McIntosh. I'm an aviation cadet.
Corporal Broderick Crawford: And you'll be a Second Lieutenant and a full-fledged
  meteorologist when you graduate the sixth of next month.
Pvt. Damian O'Flynn: I hope.
Corporal Broderick Crawford: Your C.O., Major Edward G. Hanson, said that farmers with a
  scientific education made the best meteorologists. You weren't a farmer by any chance?
Pvt. Damian O'Flynn: I was raised on a farm, and my home is Farmville, Virginia.
Corporal Broderick Crawford: That's really pouring it on. And you graduated from a
  technical school, of course.
Pvt. Damian O'Flynn: Right, Virginia Polytechnic Institute.
Corporal Broderick Crawford: You're a farmer-technician. Any brothers or sisters?
Pvt. Damian O'Flynn: Five. And five of the six of us are in service. One of my brothers
  is in Sicily, two are training for the Air Forces, and my sister's a nurse in Africa.
  She's a Lieutenant.
Corporal Broderick Crawford: Your sister's the only officer in the family. Does she pull
  her rank on you?
Pvt. Damian O'Flynn: Why do you think I'm so anxious for that Lieutenant's commission
  next month?
Pfc. Joseph Shulman (as Eddie): Hey, Johnnie. We got our clearance. We can send her up
  in five minutes.
Corporal Broderick Crawford: Clearance? For a weather balloon?
Pvt. Damian O'Flynn: You bet. In war time everything we send into the sky has to be
  O.K.ed by the Air Command.
Corporal Broderick Crawford: Good idea. Say, what's that box you're carrying, your
  lunch?
Pfc. Joseph Shulman: Hardly. That's radiosonde.
Corporal Broderick Crawford: Radiosonde? Come on, give me the answers without the
  questions.
Pvt. Damian O'Flynn: That little box holds a thermometer, a hygrometer and a barometer
  ...
Corporal Broderick Crawford: Barometer, that's that ingenious little instrument that
  tells us what kind of weather we're having.
Pvt. Damian O'Flynn: It's a lot more than that, Brod. It gives us important data for
  weather forecasts. There's also a radio in the box ...
Corporal Broderick Crawford: A radio? That box isn't big enough to hold four such
  complicated instruments.
Pfc. Joseph Shulman: Sure it is, and it operates automatically.
Corporal Broderick Crawford: I'm all ears.
Pvt. Damian O'Flynn: We tie it to a hydrogen-filled balloon and send it aloft. The
  instruments are adjusted so that the radio sends back signals. We pick up these signals
  on a set here and decode them. They tell us the temperature, atmospheric pressure and
  humidity at any level up to twenty-five miles.
Corporal Broderick Crawford: Sounds wonderful. What do you do with the information?
Pvt. Damian O'Flynn: It's sent to a Weather Central ...
Pfc. Joseph Shulman: That's a clearing house for weather observations.
Pvt. Damian O'Flynn: The Central receives similar information from different observation
  stations. This data is compared with known conditions of previous years and we're able
  to make a pretty accurate forecast of the weather.
Corporal Broderick Crawford: Seems to me the pilot depends on you a lot.
Pvt. Damian O'Flynn: He does. We supply him with charts that plot his "roadway through
  the skies." He knows how high to fly to get the best tail-winds, to avoid ice, snow,
  clouds and fog. He knows when the target is visible, when he will have a bomber's moon.
  The pilot can ...

Pfc. Joseph Shulman: It's not only the pilot. Other services depend on our forecasts. A meteorologist stuck his neck way out by predicting perfect weather conditions for the invasion of Sicily, and he made his forecast right in the middle of a big storm.

Corporal Broderick Crawford: After what happened at Messina it looks like he was right.

Pvt. Damian O'Flynn: You bet he was right. He had to be. If our predictions aren't accurate it may mean that a whole campaign may go haywire.

Corporal Broderick Crawford: Yes, Johnnie, the meteorologist must be right. A lot depends on his work, a modern science in this modern war. And you, Johnnie, Johnnie, the kid next door, will soon be a meteorologist. Well, thanks a lot, Johnnie. Be seeing you. Today Johnnie was represented by Aviation Cadet Frank W. McIntosh who permitted Private Damian O'Flynn to speak for him. Cadet McIntosh, as Johnnie, is just one of the many young men being trained by the Army Air Forces Training Command to keep our planes flying. When he graduates next month as a Second Lieutenant, he'll be a finished meteorologist, he'll be able to make accurate forecasts of the weather, to tell Johnnie Pilot about flying conditions all over the world. Johnnie's work will insure the success of our campaigns, he'll save the waste of planes, ships, tanks, and men. He'll be doing a big part in helping us toward victory, because Johnnie has learned to make use of the weather as a weapon of war.

Incidental music

Captain Glenn Miller: And now] here's something for the gals at New York University who are taking the government sponsored aeronautical drawing course. We play something old, something new, something borrowed and something blue. The old song, "Sweet and Low."

SWEET AND LOW (Old tune)

Captain Glenn Miller: Something new, Corporal Tony Martin sings "In the Blue of Evening."

IN THE BLUE OF EVENING (New tune)

Vocal refrain by Corporal Tony Martin

Captain Glenn Miller: We borrow a swell tune from our old friend Duke Ellington, "Things Ain't What They Used to Be."

THINGS AIN'T WHAT THEY USED TO BE (Borrowed tune)

Captain Glenn Miller: Last in our medley, something blue, "A Blues Serenade."

A BLUES SERENADE (Blue tune)

2nd Lt. Donald P. Briggs: Attention, young Americans! How would you like to wear the silver propeller and wings of the Army Air Forces? How would you like to win your wings and fly with the world's mightiest air armada? For full particulars go immediately to your nearest post office, Aviation Cadet Board or Army Recruiting Office. You may enroll while you're still seventeen. Do your part in the fight for freedom, fight for ultimate victory with the Army Air Forces!

WITH MY HEAD IN THE CLOUDS

Captain Glenn Miller: Now a song written by Irving Berlin for the all soldier hit picture "This Is the Army." The Training Command Band from Yale University plays "With My Head in the Clouds." The song is written for and dedicated to the Commanding General of the United States Army Air Forces, General H. H. Arnold.

Vocal refrain by Corporal Tony Martin and the Glee Club

I SUSTAIN THE WINGS (closing theme)

2nd Lt. Donald P. Briggs: "I Sustain the Wings" has presented the band from the Army Air Forces Technical School at Yale University, Captain Glenn Miller, Corporal Broderick Crawford and Johnnie, the kid next door. Next week you'll learn more about Johnnie at the Airplane Mechanic's School at Seymour Johnson Field, Goldsboro, North Carolina. We'll be seeing you again next Saturday, same time, same station.

CBS announcer: This program is written and produced entirely by soldiers of the Army Air Forces and came to you from New York City. This is C.B.S., the Columbia Broadcasting System.

28Aug43 (Sat) 2:05-2:30PM EWT WABC, CBS Playhouse No. 4, New York, New York
  I SUSTAIN THE WINGS broadcast   Audience

THE ARMY AIR CORPS (opening fanfare)
2nd Lt. Donald P. Briggs: "I Sustain the Wings."
I SUSTAIN THE WINGS (opening theme)
  2nd Lt. Donald P. Briggs: "I Sustain the Wings," presented by the Army Air Forces.
    Each week the program features the band from the Army Air Forces Technical School at
    Yale University; Corporal Broderick Crawford; Corporal Tony Martin; Johnnie, the kid
    next door, and many of your old friends. And now Captain Glenn Miller.
Captain Glenn Miller: Thank you, Lieutenant Don Briggs, and good afternoon, everybody.
  Today's program salutes the Army Air Forces Technical School at Seymour Johnson Field,
  Goldsboro, North Carolina. Colonel Dona-Donald B. Smith is the commanding officer. The
  band plays the first number for the boys at Singin' Garden at P.X. Number One. Here's
  one for the road, boys, "Here We Go Again."
HERE WE GO AGAIN
I NEVER MENTION YOUR NAME (Oh, No!)
  Captain Glenn Miller: Corporal Tony Martin to sing ...
  Vocal refrain by Corporal Tony Martin and the Tail End Charlies
Corporal Broderick Crawford: These are the sounds of victory! [The sound of America's
  mechanical wizardry! The truculent tune of America's might being forged into metal!
  These are the sounds you hear as you move through a new kind of medical school, a school
  where plastic surgeons graft aluminum instead of skin and use acetylene torches for
  scalpels, they do their stitching with rivets, whose M.D. are the sturdy initials
  "A.M.," Aviation Mechanic! These are the men who take the planes that come in "on a
  wing and a prayer," they do for the wounded planes what medics do for wounded men, using
  pliers instead of plasma, bolts and screws instead of plaster casts, breathing new life
  into planes that are almost human, the Suzy Q, the Memphis Belle, the fighting queens of
  the flak-black skies! These mechanical medics are Johnnie; Johnnie, the kid next door.
  The kid who tossed the morning paper with unerring aim from his bicycle to your front
  porch, that put the front gate on your roof on Halloween night. Yes, it's the same
  Johnnie today, only grimmer and more purposeful. He's Johnnie Can-do, the kid with the
  know-how that every pilot salutes. Today we meet Johnnie at the Aviation Mechanics
  School, Seymour Johnson Field, North Carolina. The school is maintained by the Army Air
  Forces Training Command to teach thousands of young Johnnie Americans to "Keep 'Em
  Flying." Here Johnnie gets his first initiation into the mysteries of the aircraft
  "physician-magician." Like a medical student studying anatomy, he learns the bones of a
  plane, its nerves, its muscles and heart, Johnnie is just graduating as an aviation
  mechanic. Let's stop in and congratulate him. Congratulations, Johnnie, on your
  graduation from a new kind of war-time college, a college in coveralls.
Pvt. Damian O'Flynn: Huh? Were you talking to me?
Corporal Broderick Crawford: Yeah, you're the one.
Pvt. Damian O'Flynn: Oh, well, thanks a lot, I didn't know ...
Corporal Broderick Crawford: Just a minute, Johnnie. Say, what is your name?
Pvt. Damian O'Flynn: James W. Vipond. Private First Class.
Corporal Broderick Crawford: Well, you're still Johnnie to us. Where are you from?
Pvt. Damian O'Flynn: Detroit, I live on Brooklyn Avenue.
Corporal Broderick Crawford: Even in Detroit you can't get away from Brooklyn.
Pvt. Damian O'Flynn: Seems that way, but I still prefer the Tigers.
Corporal Broderick Crawford: Not much time for ball-playing here, is there, Johnnie?
Pvt. Damian O'Flynn: No, it's a pretty stiff school. They believe in thorough training,
  but if you pay attention you won't have any trouble.
Corporal Broderick Crawford: Been in the Air Force long?
Pvt. Damian O'Flynn: Since last February. I came in by way of Fort Custer, Michigan. I
  stayed there long enough for some aptitude tests, then I went to St. Petersburgh,
  Florida, where they gave me more tests. After that, I guess they figured I was a
  natural for this.
Corporal Broderick Crawford: Tell me more.

Pvt. Damian O'Flynn: Well, to me it was a new version of an old job. I was an apprentice
   at the Ford plant when I was drafted. Before that I monkeyed around a lot with dad's
   car. Believe me, that's learning the hard way.
Corporal Broderick Crawford: That must have given you a pretty hot background.
Pvt. Damian O'Flynn: It did, but not the way you mean.
Corporal Broderick Crawford: I suppose most of the boys here had mechanical skill to
   start with.
Pvt. Damian O'Flynn: Skill, but not training. We've had newspapermen, accountants,
   lawyers. Hey, Sherm!
Sherman Carll: Yeah!
Pvt. Damian O'Flynn: This is my buddy, Sherman Carll. He developed his mechanical
   aptitude milking cows.
Sherman Carll: That's right. I used to be a bossy-puller on my dad's farm near Commack,
   New York, where we raise cows, corn and beautiful women.
Corporal Broderick Crawford: How did you find the change to beautiful planes?
Sherman Carll: Man, you can fall in love with them, too, thanks to what we learn here.
   The course is nobody's vacation. We have swell instructors, and when you're through
   here, you really know about planes.
Pvt. Damian O'Flynn: They start out by teaching us all about the tools we'll have to use,
   then we go through twelve other phases, all the way from the structure of an airplane to
   making our own tools.
Sherman Carll: And we wind up our training by living outdoors under actual battle
   conditions, dodging air raids, creating camouflage, making battle repairs and all that.
Pvt. Damian O'Flynn: That's the part we get the most kick out of, using the know-how we
   get here in the school.
Corporal Broderick Crawford: Do you specialize in any particular plane here at Seymour
   Johnson?
Pvt. Damian O'Flynn: No, that comes later. Here we get the solid foundations. We work
   on all types of planes, including those made in this country for Great Britain.
Corporal Broderick Crawford: Say, I see a sign over on that hangar that reads, "You fixed
   it, would you fly it?"
Pvt. Damian O'Flynn: That's the standard we go by around here.
Corporal Broderick Crawford: And would you?
Sherman Carll: I'll say we would.
Corporal Broderick Crawford: I guess that's why they call you boys the "Gremlin
   Exterminators."
Pvt. Damian O'Flynn: That's us, all right. Of course, we've got a lot of training to
   pick up even after we leave here.
Sherman Carll: But most of us want to end up as a crew chief.
Pvt. Damian O'Flynn: Yeah, he's quite a guy. The crew chief takes care of the plane, and
   whatever he says goes. They say of the crew chief that he owns the plane, and only
   lends it to the pilot on occasions. He's the guy that puts the final stamp on the
   plane, the O.K. for the K.O.
Corporal Broderick Crawford: You're right, Johnnie, he's quite a guy. And
   congratulations again on your graduation from Aviation Mechanics' School, your first
   step toward becoming a crew chief yourself.
Pvt. Damian O'Flynn: Thanks.
Corporal Broderick Crawford: We've just visited Johnnie, Johnnie, the kid next door.
   This afternoon Johnnie was represented by Private First Class James W. Vipond who
   permitted Private Damian O'Flynn to speak for him. Private Vipond as Johnnie is just
   one of the many thousands of America's young men who our commanding general, Major
   General Barton K. Yount, is talking about when he says:
Voice (as Major General Barton K. Yount): There's a natural affinity between an American
   boy and an American plane.
Incidental music
   Corporal Broderick Crawford: And Johnnie has that affinity. When he graduated today as
      an aviation mechanic, he was wearing the finest graduation garb that it has ever been
      any man's privilege to wear, the American uniform.
BRAHMS' LULLABY (Old tune)

Captain Glenn Miller: And now, a serenade for the mothers, wives and sweethearts of the
   soldiers at Seymour] Johnson Field. Here's something old, something new, something
   borrowed and something blue. The old song, Corporal Tony Martin and the Glee Club
   sing "Brahms' Lullaby."
Vocal refrain by Corporal Tony Martin and the Glee Club
Captain Glenn Miller: For something new, Private Art Malvin sings "Johnny Zero."
JOHNNY ZERO (New tune)
Vocal refrain by Private First Class Artie Malvin
Captain Glenn Miller: We borrow Claude Thornhill's beautiful theme, "Snowfall."
SNOWFALL (Borrowed tune)
Captain Glenn Miller: Last in our medley, something blue, "Serenade in Blue."
SERENADE IN BLUE (Blue tune)
[2nd Lt. Donald P. Briggs: Attention, young Americans! How would you like to sit behind
   the controls of the fastest, most powerful planes in the world? How would you like to
   press the magic button that sends blockbusters screaming into the heart of the Axis?
   How would you like to become a part of the mightiest air armada of all time? Go at once
   to your nearest Aviation Cadet Board and learn how you may be assigned to the Air Corps
   Enlisted Reserve while you are still seventeen. You may find the Aviation Cadet Board
   by asking any recruiting officer or by inquiring at any Army Air Forces field. Wear the
   silver propeller and wings of the Army Air Forces! See the Aviation Cadet Board today!
   And fly with America to freedom, and victory!]
PUT YOUR ARMS AROUND ME, HONEY
Captain Glenn Miller: Here's the top tune of the week as chosen by the soldiers of
   Seymour Johnson Field, the one they jump to when Sergeant Norm Leyden and the 28th
   Army Air Forces Band beat it out at those Saturday night dances, "Put Your Arms Around
   Me, Honey, Hold Me Tight."
Vocal refrain by Corporal Tony Martin and the Glee Club
I SUSTAIN THE WINGS (closing theme)
2nd Lt. Donald P. Briggs: "I Sustain the Wings" has presented the band from the Army
   Air Forces Technical School at Yale University, Captain Glenn Miller, Corporal
   Broderick Crawford and Johnnie, the kid next door. Next week you'll learn more about
   Johnnie at Stewart Field, West Point, New York. We'll be seeing you again next
   Saturday, same time, same station.
CBS announcer: This program is written and produced entirely by soldiers of the Army
   Air Forces and came to you from New York City. This is C.B.S., the Columbia
   Broadcasting System.

The parts of Sherman Carll and Voice were played by Pfc. Joe Shulman and 2nd Lt. Donald P.
Briggs. Most probably Sherman Carll was played by Pfc. Joe Shulman and Voice was played
by 2nd Lt. Donald P. Briggs.

04Sep43 (Sat) 2:00-2:30PM EWT WABC, CBS Playhouse No. 4, New York, New York
  I SUSTAIN THE WINGS broadcast   Audience

THE ARMY AIR CORPS (opening fanfare)
2nd Lt. Donald P. Briggs: "I Sustain the Wings."
I SUSTAIN THE WINGS (opening theme)
  2nd Lt. Donald P. Briggs: "I Sustain the Wings," presented by the Army Air Forces.
    Each week the program features the band from the Army Air Forces Technical School at
    Yale University; Captain Glenn Miller; Corporal Broderick Crawford; Corporal Tony
    Martin; Corporal Ray McKinley; Johnnie, the kid next door, and many of your old
    friends. And now Captain Glenn Miller.
Captain Glenn Miller: Thank you, Lieutenant Don Briggs, and good afternoon, everybody.
    Today's program salutes the Army Air Forces School at Stewart Field, West Point, New
    York, Colonel George F. Schlatter, commanding officer. The band starts off with a
    number we played a few weeks back, and according to the mailman the cash customers must
    have liked it because they asked for another go around on it, "In the Mood."
IN THE MOOD
Captain Glenn Miller: Now here's a song that's tops with everybody around these parts.
    Corporal Tony Martin and our quartet, the Crew Chiefs, sing "It's Always You."
IT'S ALWAYS YOU
  Vocal refrain by Corporal Tony Martin and the Crew Chiefs
Captain Glenn Miller: Now we'd like you to meet the "Tail End Charlies," four of the boys
    in our band, Sergeant Trigger Alpert, bass; Corporal Ray McKinley, drums; Corporal Mel
    Powell, piano; and Private Carmen Mastren, guitar. The strings just sort of string
    along and the song is "I Want to Be Happy."
I WANT TO BE HAPPY
Pfc. Artie Malvin (as co-pilot): Johnnie, can you see anything at all?
Pfc. Joe Shulman (as pilot): No, this fog is [thicker than Hitler's head.
Pfc. Artie Malvin: Pilot to bombardier, pilot to bombardier.
Corporal Tony Martin (as bombardier Tom): Bombardier to pilot. Go ahead, Johnnie.
Pfc. Joe Shulman: Can you see anything out of that fish bowl, Tom?
Corporal Tony Martin: Not even the wing-tips, much less the Brenner Pass.
Pfc. Joe Shulman: O.K., Tom. Navigator says we're only ten minutes away. I guess we'll
    have to take her in by instrument and hope we find a hole.
Corporal Tony Martin: Right. But, hey, don't get into an argument with any mountain
    tops.
Pfc. Joe Shulman: After all the hours I spent in a Link trainer? Are you kidding?
Corporal Tony Martin: Maybe I am, but those mountains aren't.
Pfc. Joe Shulman: Pilot to bombardier. I'll drop her another five hundred feet, but if
    we go any lower than that, we won't have to bomb 'em, we can slap 'em.
Corporal Tony Martin: I'm game. Hey, Johnnie, we've broken through! Look at that
    bridge.
Pfc. Joe Shulman: P.D.I. on.
Corporal Tony Martin: Steady, steady, a little to the left, hold it there. Come to
    pappy, Nazi. Bombs Away!
Pfc. Joe Shulman: Wow! Look at that flak! I'm hiking for the fog again.
Corporal Broderick Crawford: Yes, it's a new kind of blind man's buff our pilots are
    playing all over the world, blasting objectives through blackest storm and thickest fog,
    a new kind of blind man's buff without which Attu and Kiska, sheltered in the world's
    foulest weather belt, might never have fallen, blind man's buff with instruments instead
    of eyes, taught to kids you know by kids you know. Yes, taught by Johnnie; Johnnie, the
    kid next door; the kid whose cheerful whistle you used to hear when he delivered the
    groceries from old man Fuller's store, the kid you used to see on the river bank fishing
    right under the "No Fishing" sign. Well, it's the same Johnnie today, but now he's
    Johnnie Know-how, Johnnie Teacher, instructing other Johnnies in the superb skills
    developed through the teaching he, himself, received in the many schools maintained by
    the Army Air Forces Training Command. Today we meet Johnnie at Stewart Field, West
    Point, New York, where cadets of the United States Military Academy get their flying
    training, where Johnnie, a Link trainer specialist, helps to teach our future air
    generals in the difficult art of flying blind. We find Johnnie in a long hall full of

Link trainers, miniature planes with penguin wings and blue bodies not much bigger than a good sized trunk. Each is mounted on a small black pedestal, connected electrically to the control desk directly behind it. At the desk sits Johnnie, checking the actions of the student in the blacked-out cockpit.

Pvt. Damian O'Flynn (as Sergeant John S. Thornton): Hi there, looking for me?

Corporal Broderick Crawford: Yeah, mind if I interrupt?

Pvt. Damian O'Flynn: It's O.K. Right now my student is ten thousand feet up, somewhere over Tokyo. He'll be all right for a while. I'm sure he's enjoying it.

Corporal Broderick Crawford: Who wouldn't? Say, Johnnie, where are you from?

Pvt. Damian O'Flynn: How did you know my name?

Corporal Broderick Crawford: With us every boy is Johnnie, Johnnie American.

Pvt. Damian O'Flynn: Oh, I see. Well, I'm really Johnnie, Sergeant John S. Thornton, from Wappinger Falls, New York.

Corporal Broderick Crawford: That Link trainer must be quite a gadget. From here it looks like something invented by Rube Goldberg.

Pvt. Damian O'Flynn: Don't let it fool you, Mister, that thing can do almost anything except make coffee and answer the telephone. The boys call it "The Whirling Dervish."

Corporal Broderick Crawford: I told you it looked dizzy.

Pvt. Damian O'Flynn: Well, it can spin you dizzy if you don't watch your instruments. In fact, with that trainer we can create almost all actual operating conditions, rough air that makes a ship hard to handle, strong winds that blow a plane off its course, we can even simulate icing conditions.

Corporal Broderick Crawford: And yet the student never gets any higher off the ground than that pedestal.

Pvt. Damian O'Flynn: That's right. But with the cockpit cover closed down, it makes no difference to the student. He's in a cockpit that contains all the main basic instruments of a regular plane, and they respond exactly as if he were in the air. Just a second, he's calling. If you want to listen in, just pick up those earphones.

Corporal Broderick Crawford: Thanks.

2nd Lt. Donald P. Briggs (as student): Shangri-La. This is Army 21811. Over.

Pvt. Damian O'Flynn: Army 21811 from Shangri-La. Go ahead.

2nd Lt. Donald P. Briggs: Shangri-La, this is Army 21811. Request permission to make instrument letdown Shangri-La Field. Coming in on North-east leg over Chungking, at 14:15, air speed 150. Estimated over Shangri-La 14:25. Out.

Pvt. Damian O'Flynn: Permission granted. But you left out something.

2nd Lt. Donald P. Briggs: What's that?

Pvt. Damian O'Flynn: Your altitude.

2nd Lt. Donald P. Briggs: That's right. Altimeter setting three thousand. Shall I say it?

Pvt. Damian O'Flynn: No, just remember. Out.

Corporal Broderick Crawford: Do the boys put in much time on these trainers, Johnnie?

Pvt. Damian O'Flynn: Yes, indeed. This is a vital part of all flying training. You'll find whole batteries of these "Whirling Dervishes" at every training field. Here at Stewart Field the cadets have put in a total of twenty-five hours on the trainer alone. And they're darned glad to have it.

Corporal Broderick Crawford: Well, from all you say, that gahinkus must be a life-saver.

Pvt. Damian O'Flynn: It has been, literally. Some of the stuff the students do in it would be pretty dangerous for a beginner if he were in the air. That's one reason we get such a kick out of this job, we figure we're saving lives and planes every day.

Corporal Broderick Crawford: That's quite a load of responsibility you carry there, Johnnie.

Pvt. Damian O'Flynn: Oh, we take it in our stride. It's a pretty thorough course they give us before we graduate as instructors from the Link Trainer School at Chanute Field, Illinois. We get stiff training in the air traffic laws, radio procedure, meteorology, and, of course, basic and advanced instrument flying. Then, whenever we have any spare time around here, we climb into the trainers and fly problems ourselves, taking turns instructing one another.

Corporal Broderick Crawford: I understand you do a little genuine flying, too. That right?

Pvt. Damian O'Flynn: Oh, yes, we all have time in the air to give us the real feel of it.

Corporal Broderick Crawford: Do you ever get nervous teaching West Point cadets who might
  some day be generals and all?
Pvt. Damian O'Flynn: Oh, they're a great bunch of boys. They give us a lot of respect,
  and that's mutual. Of course, it's a little embarrassing sometimes when you have to
  remind a future general that for the last two minutes, according to the instruments,
  he's been flying four hundred feet underground.
Corporal Broderick Crawford: I don't suppose that happens very often.
Pvt. Damian O'Flynn: Only when a student tries to fly by instinct instead of by
  instrument.
Corporal Broderick Crawford: By instinct?
Pvt. Damian O'Flynn: Yeah, by feel. In the old days they called it "flying by the seat
  of his pants." But we've got a little trick to discourage that.
Corporal Broderick Crawford: What's the trick?
Pvt. Damian O'Flynn: The seat in every one of these trainers is permanently tilted just
  enough to make trouble for anybody who trusts his pants more than his instruments.
Corporal Broderick Crawford: Well, that's one way of keeping on the beam.
Pvt. Damian O'Flynn: We do that, too.
Corporal Broderick Crawford: Huh?
Pvt. Damian O'Flynn: Teach them how to ride the radio beam that guides planes into
  friendly airports. That's where the expression comes from.
Corporal Broderick Crawford: Oh, I thought it came from "On the button."
Pvt. Damian O'Flynn: No, that's where we hit 'em.
Corporal Broderick Crawford: Well, thanks a lot, Johnnie. We know you're all on the
  beam. We've just talked to Johnnie again, folks, Johnnie, the kid next door. Today he
  was represented by Sergeant John S. Thornton, who gave his permission for Private Damian
  O'Flynn to speak for him.
Incidental music
  Corporal Broderick Crawford: Thanks to Johnnie, Link trainer operator, Johnnie Pilot
    receives instruction that enables him to keep on the beam. Neither ice nor snow nor
    fog nor sleet, not even the blackness of night, will stay the air man from the
    completion of his flight. Instruments are his eyes, the radio his ears, and he knows
    how to use them, knows well enough to play on the winning side in this new game of
    blind man's buff, blind flying. It matters not that the weather is clear or foul,
    because Johnnie is on the beam. And he'll stay on the beam whether he is in the air
    or on the ground helping to keep them in the air, because that beam leads him straight
    over the heart of Berlin and Tokyo!]
Captain Glenn Miller: And now it's medley time, a serenade for the mothers, wives and
  sweethearts of the soldiers at Stewart Field. Here's something old, something new,
  something borrowed and something blue. The old song, "Goin' Home."
GOIN' HOME (Old tune)
  Captain Glenn Miller: For something new, our quartet to sing "Paper Doll."
PAPER DOLL (New tune)
  Vocal refrain by the Crew Chiefs
  Captain Glenn Miller: From the hit show "Very Warm for May" we borrow one of Jerome
    Kern's most beautiful melodies. Corporal Tony Martin sings "All the Things You Are."
ALL THE THINGS YOU ARE (Borrowed tune)
  Vocal refrain by Corporal Tony Martin
  Captain Glenn Miller: Last in our medley is something blue, "Blue Heaven."
MY BLUE HEAVEN (blue tune)
CALL TO THE COLORS
2nd Lt. Donald P. Briggs: The "Call to the Colors." Yes, calling every young man, every
  wide-awake young American who hears it, to the service of his country and the Army Air
  Forces. Fellows, if you've ever thought even once that you'd be proud to wear the
  silver propeller and wings of the Army Air Forces, that flying a fast, hard-hitting
  fighter plane is the job you'd like best of all, well, do something about it right now.
  You may volunteer for Aviation Cadet Training on a reserve basis, even while you're
  still seventeen. No high school or college credits required. Full information is
  simple and easy to get at your nearest post office, Aviation Cadet Board or Army
  Recruiting Office. Think it over, fellows. This is your chance to fly. Your chance to

fight. Your chance to help keep America free with the flyingest, fightingest men in the world, the Army Air Forces.

THE ARMY AIR CORPS

Captain Glenn Miller: Here's the top tune of the week as chosen by special ballot among the soldiers of Stewart Field. The number one song on the Brenner Pass Hit Parade, "The Army Air Corps" song.

Vocal refrain by Corporal Tony Martin and the Glee Club

I SUSTAIN THE WINGS (closing theme)

2nd Lt. Donald P. Briggs: "I Sustain the Wings" has presented the band from the Army Air Forces Technical School at Yale University; Captain Glenn Miller; Corporal Broderick Crawford; Corporal Tony Martin; and Johnnie, the kid next door. Next week you'll learn more about Johnnie at the Army Air Forces Training Command School, Wright Aeronautical Factory, Paterson, New Jersey. We'll be seeing you again next Saturday, same time, same station.

CBS announcer: This program is written and produced entirely by soldiers of the Army Air Forces and came to you from New York City. This is C.B.S., the Columbia Broadcasting System.

11Sep43 (Sat) 2:00-2:30PM EWT WABC, CBS Playhouse No. 4, New York, New York
  I SUSTAIN THE WINGS broadcast   Audience

[THE ARMY AIR CORPS (opening fanfare)
2nd Lt. Donald P. Briggs: "I Sustain the Wings."
I SUSTAIN THE WINGS (opening theme)
  2nd Lt. Donald P. Briggs: "I Sustain the Wings," presented by the Army Air Forces. The
    program features the band from the Army Air Forces Technical School at Yale
    University; Captain Glenn Miller; Corporal Broderick Crawford; Corporal Tony Martin;
    Corporal Ray McKinley; Johnnie, the kid next door, and many of your old friends. And
    now Captain Glenn Miller.]
Captain Glenn Miller: Thank you, Lieutenant Don Briggs, and good afternoon, everybody.
  Today's program salutes the Army Air Forces Technical Command School at the Wright
  Aeronautical Factory, Paterson, New Jersey. With this week's number one headline news
  makin' it one down and two to go, we lead off with Private Jerry Gray's latest tune,
  "Bums Away." All right, boys, this is it.
BUMS AWAY (Enlisted Men's Mess)
Captain Glenn Miller: This being Corporal Tony Martin's last go around on our program, we
  asked Tony what he'd like to sing for you folks before he leaves for Officer Candidate
  School Monday. Tony picked his favorite tune, "Begin the Beguine."
BEGIN THE BEGUINE
  Vocal refrain by Corporal Tony Martin
Captain Glenn Miller: Now here's a tune for all you lads that deposit your nickels in the
  juke boxes for safe keepin', "A String of Pearls."
A STRING OF PEARLS
Corporal Broderick Crawford: Listen to that, America, listen closely and be proud! It's
  our new national anthem, the smashing, dashing song of horsepower! Thousands of
  horsepower crammed into a few cubic feet of space, crammed into the precision smooth
  walls of modern aircraft engine. The aircraft engine's a piece of mechanical magic.
  It's the symbol of speed and power and American manufacturing ingenuity, American
  know-how, the know-how that is the heritage of Johnnie; Johnnie, the kid next door. You
  remember Johnnie, well, you ought to. He's the kid that almost broke your ear drums
  with his loud yells as he played war games with the other boys in the neighborhood.
  Well, war isn't a game with Johnnie any more, it's a serious business. He's a soldier,
  he's a lot of soldiers, he's a legion of young Americans being trained by the Army Air
  Forces Training Command to fly our planes, and "Keep 'Em Flying." Today Johnnie's a
  soldier-student at the Army Air Forces Technical School. The school is maintained by
  the Training Command in co-operation with Wright Aeronautical Corporation. They're the
  makers of the famed Cyclone and Whirlwind engines. Let's go downstairs and talk to him.
  He's in a basement class room working on a section ... Say, that looks like a job for a
  welder.
Pvt. Damian O'Flynn (as Lt. C. E. Allesina): A welder?
Corporal Broderick Crawford: Yeah, the way that housing's broken away.
Pvt. Damian O'Flynn: It isn't broken, it's deliberately cut that way.
Corporal Broderick Crawford: Now, wait a minute. Nobody's going around cutting up
  expensive airplane engines just for fun.
Pvt. Damian O'Flynn: But it isn't for fun, it's to show us just how the internal
  supercharger works. A practical demonstration like this is a lot easier and faster than
  trying to get the stuff out of books.
Corporal Broderick Crawford: Aw, I know what you mean.
Pvt. Damian O'Flynn: Our instructors have "cut-away" models of practically every
  individual section of the Wright Cyclone engine, that way it doesn't take us long to
  learn enough to become specialists.
Corporal Broderick Crawford: Well, sounds like a thorough way of teaching.
Pvt. Damian O'Flynn: It is that, and we get the same thing in six phases, each phase
  covering a different section of the engine.
Corporal Broderick Crawford: Yeah? What's the next phase, Johnnie?
Pvt. Damian O'Flynn: Well, that all depends. Ah, maybe we'll go into crankshaft. Well,
  I can explain this better in the test cells. Come on.

Corporal Broderick Crawford: Say, Johnnie, I just noticed something. Do those gold bars on your coveralls mean anything?

Pvt. Damian O'Flynn: Why sure, I'm a Lieutenant.

Corporal Broderick Crawford: A Lieutenant! I thought this school was for enlisted men.

Pvt. Damian O'Flynn: Well, most of the students are E.M.s, but we engineering officers have to know our engines, too, so they've been sending us here.

Corporal Broderick Crawford: How do you like that. I'm a smart guy, here I've been calling you Johnnie and I should have ...

Pvt. Damian O'Flynn: Yeah, I wondered where you got the Johnnie. My name's really C. E. Allesina.

Corporal Broderick Crawford: Well, do you mind if I ask you a couple of questions, sir?

Pvt. Damian O'Flynn: Skip the "sir" and call me Johnnie, I like it better.

Corporal Broderick Crawford: Thank you, sir, er, I mean, Johnnie, er. Do you live around here?

Pvt. Damian O'Flynn: No. My home's in Portland, Oregon, that's were my wife and family are.

Corporal Broderick Crawford: Family?

Pvt. Damian O'Flynn: Yeah. I've got two kids, a boy, five, and a girl, three. Ah, here are their pictures.

Corporal Broderick Crawford: You don't usually carry these. You just happen to have them with you today.

Pvt. Damian O'Flynn: Yeah.

Corporal Broderick Crawford: Say, they're plenty cute, at that.

Pvt. Damian O'Flynn: Yeah, I think so.

Corporal Broderick Crawford: It looks like Selective Service jumped the gun in your case, doesn't it?

Pvt. Damian O'Flynn: Oh, I wasn't inducted. I was in the Air Force in 1934, stationed at Nicholls Field in Manila.

Corporal Broderick Crawford: You must have had a lovely time on December 8th.

Pvt. Damian O'Flynn: I wasn't there then. They sent me home in 1935 and transferred me to the Air Corps Reserve because of a tropical fever.

Corporal Broderick Crawford: Oh, but you stuck with aviation, huh?

Pvt. Damian O'Flynn: You bet, I helped organize the Oregon National Guard Air Corps. My civilian job was to take care of the planes we used.

Corporal Broderick Crawford: Well, you're certainly a natural for Johnnie Technician. You were called up from the Reserves when war broke out, I suppose.

Pvt. Damian O'Flynn: Yeah, that's right. I spent eight months with the 123rd Observation Squadron. Anti-submarine patrol on the Pacific coast.

Corporal Broderick Crawford: That's nice goin'. When did you get your commission, Johnnie?

Pvt. Damian O'Flynn: About six months ago. I graduated from Officers' Candidate School at Miami Beach, Florida, then I was assigned as engineering officer to the 34th Bombardment Group at Blythe, California, and from there I came here to learn more about what makes the Cyclone engine tick.

Corporal Broderick Crawford: Uh, huh. Hey, that one's certainly tickin'.

Pvt. Damian O'Flynn: Well, it ought to be. Those men have been working on it and checking it all day.

Corporal Broderick Crawford: Ah, so these are the test cells, huh?

Pvt. Damian O'Flynn: Yeah, that's right. Notice those engines mounted on concrete?

Corporal Broderick Crawford: Yeah.

Pvt. Damian O'Flynn: They're the same engines used in various types of planes, the, ah, B-17, for instance.

Corporal Broderick Crawford: Uh, huh.

Pvt. Damian O'Flynn: Here's where we put into practice all the things we've learned during our course of instruction.

Corporal Broderick Crawford: In other words, you get practical experience.

Pvt. Damian O'Flynn: That's right. It's just like working on a plane, except the controls are in this glass-enclosed booth instead of the cockpit. This way we learn how to operate the engine controls, adjust them, start the engine, and all that.

Corporal Broderick Crawford: I see. Ah, is this particular engine working?

Pvt. Damian O'Flynn: Well, it is, unless one of the instructors has crossed us up. They often do that by removing a spark plug, loosening a nut, cutting the gas supply, or any of a number of things. Then we have to trace the trouble and fix it. Here, I'll try it. This is the starter button.
Corporal Broderick Crawford: Uh, huh.
Pvt. Damian O'Flynn: Ah, this engine's running O.K.
Corporal Broderick Crawford: Yes, that engine's running O.K. and all those engines will be O.K. as long as Johnnie is on the job. You've just seen Johnnie at work; Johnnie, the kid next door. Today Johnnie was represented by Lieutenant C. E. Allesina, who gave his permission for Private Damian O'Flynn to speak for him.
Incidental music
  Corporal Broderick Crawford: American engineering skill has given our pilots the finest aircraft engines in the world, and that same skill, as demonstrated by Johnnie Specialist, will keep them the finest. When the pilot climbs into the cockpit of his plane, he knows he'll be flying with more than "A Wing and a Prayer," He knows that, because of Johnnie, his engines will keep perking under [any conditions, he knows he'll have] plenty of horsepower to deliver firepower to the Axis. [And Johnnie;] Johnnie, the kid next door, is gonna make sure those engines are operating because Johnnie knows they'll furnish the horsepower to speed us along the road to victory!
Captain Glenn Miller: And now, medley time. A serenade] for the mothers, wives and sweethearts of the enlisted men at Wright Aeronautical Factory School. Here's something old, something new, something borrowed and something blue. The old song, "Long, Long Ago."
LONG, LONG AGO (Old tune)
  Captain Glenn Miller: For something new here's Corporal Tony Martin to sing.
I HEARD YOU CRIED LAST NIGHT (And So Did I) (New tune)
  Vocal refrain by Corporal Tony Martin
  Corporal Broderick Crawford: For something borrowed the band plays Captain Glenn Miller's beautiful theme. I think you'll remember "Moonlight Serenade."
MOONLIGHT SERENADE (Borrowed tune)
  Captain Glenn Miller: Last in our medley something blue, the band plays "Blues in My Heart."
BLUES IN MY HEART (Blue tune)
2nd Lt. Donald P. Briggs: America's modern combat planes need tough, skillful, aggressive pilots, bombardiers and navigators! Young Americans! Right here is where you come in! Right now there's a chance waiting for you to join those thousands of other young men in the Army Air Forces, who are sweeping the skies clean of America's enemies! Even while you are still seventeen, you may volunteer for Aviation Cadet Training on a reserve basis. Just ask for full details at your nearest post office, Aviation Cadet Board, or Army Recruiting Office. Join hands with those heroes of the sky who wear the silver propeller and wings of the Army Air Forces, by enrolling in the Army Air Corps Enlisted Reserve! And do it today, this very afternoon while you're thinking about it. And now, back to the music.
Captain Glenn Miller: Thank you, Lieutenant. Here's the top tune of the week as chosen by the guys and gals at Wright Aeronautical. The band and Glee Club get together, we hope, on "In My Arms."
IN MY ARMS
  Vocal refrain by the Glee Club
I SUSTAIN THE WINGS (closing theme)
  2nd Lt. Donald P. Briggs: "I Sustain the Wings" has presented the band from the Army Air Forces Technical School at Yale University, Captain Glenn Miller, Corporal Broderick Crawford, Corporal Tony Martin, Corporal Ray McKinley, and Johnnie, the kid next door. This program is the last in a series over the Columbia network. The Army Air Forces wishes to take this opportunity to thank all their friends at C.B.S. for their splendid and unqualified co-operation. Beginning next week "I Sustain the Wings" will be heard over another network. For the exact time and stations please consult your local newspaper. See you then.
  CBS announcer: This program has been written and produced entirely by soldiers of the Army Air Forces and came to you from New York City. This is C.B.S., the Columbia Broadcasting System.

18Sep43 (Sat) 9:15AM NBC, New York, New York
UNCLE SAM PRESENTS recording

I SUSTAIN THE WINGS (opening theme)
2nd Lt. Donald P. Briggs: From the United States of America, to the other united nations of the world, "Uncle Sam Presents," the band of the Training Command of the Army Air Forces, under the direction of Captain Glenn Miller, with Corporal Ray McKinley, and many of your old friends.
2nd Lt. Donald P. Briggs: And here is Captain Glenn Miller.
Captain Glenn Miller: Thank you, Lieutenant Briggs, and hello, everybody. Corporal Ray McKinley's waitin', sticks in hand, to roll off for "American Patrol." So, two beats and we'll hit it, Mac. One, two.
AMERICAN PATROL
Captain Glenn Miller: When the book of this century is written, listing America's contributions to the world, the job you fellows are doing will be topic number one, and if that book happens to have a music section here's a piece of music that will be right up there on top too. George Gershwin's "Rhapsody in Blue."
RHAPSODY IN BLUE
Captain Glenn Miller: And now the band and a tune that hit the jackbox on every juke box from Natchez to Mobile and Memphis to Saint Joe. You may not recognize it at first, as Private Jerry Gray made a pretty rough arrangement of it, but stick with us. It's "Pistol Packin' Mama."
PISTOL PACKIN' MAMA
Vocal refrain by Private Carmen Mastren, Corporal Ray McKinley and the Glee   Club
I SUSTAIN THE WINGS (closing theme)
Captain Glenn Miller: There it is. That's all for now. We'll be back next week at the same time and we hope you'll all be with us. Thanks for the swell letters you fellows been writing and don't forget to let us know what tunes you want to hear. We'll be glad to play them. Now for Lieutenant Don Briggs, Corporal Ray McKinley and all the rest of us, thanks a lot for listenin'. So long for now.
2nd Lt. Donald P. Briggs: The Army Air Forces Training Command Band, under the direction of Captain Glenn Miller, has come to you from New York City. Don't forget tomorrow, same time, same station, "Uncle Sam Presents" another famous service band with music from us to you.
TUXEDO JUNCTION (fade-out tune)
2nd Lt. Donald P. Briggs: This is the United States of America, one of the united nations.
Captain Glenn Miller: All right, Zeke, ...

18Sep43 (Sat) 6:00-6:30PM EWT WEAF, NBC Vanderbilt Theatre, New York, New York
  I SUSTAIN THE WINGS broadcast   Audience

THE ARMY AIR CORPS (opening fanfare)
2nd Lieutenant Donald P. Briggs: "I Sustain the Wings!"
I SUSTAIN THE WINGS (opening theme)
  2nd Lieutenant Donald P. Briggs: "I Sustain the Wings," presented by the   Army Air
    Forces. Each week this program will feature the band from the Army Air Forces
    Technical School at Yale University; Captain Glenn Miller; Corporal Ray McKinley;
    Johnnie, the kid next door; and many of your old friends. And now Captain Glenn
    Miller.
Captain Glenn Miller: Thank you, Lieutenant Don Briggs, and good evening, everybody.
  Welcome to the first in a series of radio programs by the men who really keep 'em
  flyin'. Tonight's program salutes the Headquarters of the Army Air Forces Training
  Command at Fort Worth, Texas. The band passes in review. The tune, "American Patrol."
  Corporal McKinley, roll off.
AMERICAN PATROL
Captain Glenn Miller: And now for those of you who like their music on the pretty side we
  play one of George Gershwin's greatest, "Rhapsody in Blue."
RHAPSODY IN BLUE
2nd Lieutenant Donald P. Briggs: Radio, bringing you headlines of victory,   headlines
  from all corners of the war torn world. Headlines like:
Pfc. Franklin Cook: Italy surrenders unconditionally.
2nd Lieutenant Donald P. Briggs: Teletype machines pounding out the news, bringing
  stories of our growing military strength to the news rooms of America, telling the
  country of victories in the air. Just listen to the headlines of air power those wires
  have carried in the past few weeks:
Voice 1: Pantelleria bombed into submission.
Sgt. Victor Young: Three hundred and sixteen Jap planes destroyed on the   ground.
Pvt. Damian F. O'Flynn: Allied planes win complete air control of Messina   Straights.
Sgt. Victor Young: 50 tons of bombs a minute dropped on Berlin.
Voice 5: Two thousand sorties by Allied planes over Salerno battlefields.
Captain Glenn Miller: Yes, those are the headlines of air power, the power that is paving
  our road to certain victory. We Americans have the planes and the weapons. We've got
  the mechanical mind, all right, but it would be worthless if it weren't properly handled
  by thousands of young Americans af our ... of our Army Air Forces, the boys that General
  H. H. Arnold, Commanding General of the Army Air Forces is talking about when he says:
Voice (as General H. H. Arnold): In no other nation does the average young man have the
  natural ability and temperament so essential to aviation students. It is the heritage
  of all American boys.
Captain Glenn Miller: Yes, it is the heritage of all American boys. The heritage of
  Johnnie, Johnnie, the kid next door. You remember Johnnie, the boy that broke your
  parlor window when he played baseball in the vacant lot, the kid that drove you nuts
  tinkerin' with jalopy motors. Once in a while he'd get in your hair and you'd wonder if
  he'd ever amount to much. Well, you needn't have worried 'cause right now he's a pretty
  important character. He's one guy in a million and a million guys in one. He's Mister
  Johnnie Know-how, Johnnie Technician. But most important he's Johnnie American. He's
  every mother's son that joined the Army Air Forces. He's been taught to fly and to keep
  'em flying by the Army Air Forces Training Command. Last year Johnnie was playing
  All-American football to the accompaniment of cheering crowds. But today the roar of
  the crowd has become a more ominous sound. It is the roar of plane engines, planes
  bound on deadly missions of destruction with Johnnie at the controls. He's still an
  All-American team but he's engaged in a serious business, the business of winning this
  war. He's ... well, let's have Johnnie speak for himself.
Pvt. Damian F. O'Flynn: I'm Johnnie Pilot. My job to carry the ball. By that I mean
  that I guide the plane to its destination, to the goal, but instead of side-stepping
  friendly tacklers I've got to dodge enemy planes. And if I miss it means curtains for
  me and the rest of the team, the crew. Of course, I don't do the job all alone.
  There's lots of guys helping me, swell guys that know the meaning of teamwork and how
  important it is. Take the navigator, for instance.

Pvt. George O'Hanlon: I'm Johnnie Navigator. You might call me the quarterback of this modern day All-American team. I figure out the plays and call them. It's up to me to calculate the shortest and safest route to the target, to find holes in the home team's defenses and lead the ball carrier, the pilot, toward the goal. Once in a while the enemy pulls a fast one. Then we're in for real trouble. That's where another guy on the team comes in. A guy we can all depend on.

Pfc. Joseph Shulman: Ah, that's me he's talking about, Johnnie Aerial Gunner. I run interference for the rest of the team and when those enemy tacklers, you know, those Zeros and Messerschmitts, when they try and stop us it's up to me to take them on and get rid of them. Man, it sure is a pleasure to see them fade away when I block them out by throwing lead at them with my machine gun. But if I miss, man!!!

Sgt. Victor Young: I'm Johnnie Bombardier, the guy that makes the touchdowns on this All-American team. The rest of the team gets the ball to the one yard line and then they let me carry it over the goal for the score. And when we all work together as a team I know that pulling the bomb release means a direct hit, a touchdown for our side. But we'll never get that ball across the goal line, deliver the bombs to target if it weren't for some of the members of the team, the boys on the line, Johnnie Ground Crew.

Pvt. Martin Ritt: That's me, Johnnie Ground Crew. I'm the Air Force technician. I make it possible for flyers to be heroes and heroes to be flyers. I drill and work and fight. I work that others may fly and fight. I fight that I may work to keep 'em flying. I'm the mechanic, the machinist, the armorer, the weather observer, the instrument man, the radio man. I'm a technician but I fight like a commando. I'm one of an unbeatable trio: the plane, the air crew, the ground crew; each indispensable to the other two. Without me the plane would be a motionless machine, the pilot a helpless gladiator. When I trained I beefed at the constant stream of repetition of routine. But now I realize that I was learning to act on instinct. I griped at scrubbing and shining and cleaning but now I realize neatness means a clean job of every task. An unbuttoned pocket seemed trivial, but now I know a forgotten button might be a forgotten cotter key and that key might mean a plane destroyed and a crew lost. Because of strict training I'm good and I know I'm good. The folks at home may never know how important I am, the public may never see my name in print. But I'm the plodding linesman of modern football. I make long runs possible for All-Americans. I'm the blocker that never carries the ball.

Incidental music

Pvt. Martin Ritt: But that pilot there knows me. He knows that when he climbs aboard, the plane's ready. He knows those engines are perfect. The radio his ears, the instruments his eyes. That bombardier knows his hits are going to be perfect. And when they come back there's something in their handshake no newspaper could describe, no medal could equal. It's the grip of men whose lives depend on me. I Sustain the Wings!

Captain Glenn Miller: And now medley time, a serenade for the mothers, wives and sweethearts of the officers and enlisted men at Training Command Headquarters in Fort Worth. Here's something old, something new, something borrowed and something blue. The old song, "Caprice Viennois."

CAPRICE VIENNOIS (Old tune)

Captain Glenn Miller: For something new, Private Art Malvin sings "Sunday, Monday, or Always."

SUNDAY, MONDAY, OR ALWAYS (New tune)

Vocal refrain by Private First Class Artie Malvin

Captain Glenn Miller: We borrow the lovely theme of Phil Spitalny and his lovely gals, "The Isle of Golden Dreams."

MY ISLE OF GOLDEN DREAMS (Borrowed tune)

Captain Glenn Miller: Last in our medley, something blue, "The Birth of the Blues."

THE BIRTH OF THE BLUES (Blue tune)

2nd Lieutenant Donald P. Briggs: Mister, can you think of any bigger thrill than being at the stick of one of America's fast fighter planes? It's an opportunity that's open to any young, healthy, stout-hearted American. Even while you're still seventeen you can volunteer for aviation cadet training by enrolling in the Army Air Corps Enlisted Reserve. Full details are waiting for you at your nearest post office, Aviation Cadet Board, or Army recruiting office. Decide today. Write now to find out how you can join hands with the thousands of young Americans who are blasting and bombing the Axis into oblivion in the Army Air Forces. Now, Captain Miller.

Captain Glenn Miller: Thank you, Lieutenant. We've received many requests to attempt something musically more serious with our orchestra. It's in answer to these requests that we play a symphonic composition from the pen of the eminent young American composer Alfred Dexter. After the introduction the main theme is stated by the strings, followed in true symphonic form by the development, transition, recapitulation and finale. Here it is, specially arranged and broadcast for the first time on this program.

PISTOL PACKIN' MAMA

Vocal refrain by Private Carmen Mastren, Corporal Ray McKinley and the Crew Chiefs

I SUSTAIN THE WINGS (closing theme)

2nd Lieutenant Donald P. Briggs: "I Sustain the Wings" has presented the band from the Army Air Forces Technical School at Yale University; Captain Glenn Miller; Corporal Ray McKinley; Johnnie, the kid next door; and many of your old friends. Next week you'll learn more about Johnnie at Lowry Field, Denver, Colorado. Be with us again next Saturday, same time, same station. This program is written and produced entirely by soldiers of the Army Air Forces and came to you from New York City.

2nd Lieutenant Donald P. Briggs: This is the National Broadcasting Company.

NBC chimes

Voice 1, Voice 5 and Voice are unidentified. Pfc. Franklin Cook performed one or more of those parts.

25Sep43 (Sat) 6:00-6:30PM EWT WEAF, NBC Vanderbilt Theatre, New York, New York
I SUSTAIN THE WINGS broadcast   Audience

THE ARMY AIR CORPS (opening fanfare)
2nd Lieutenant Donald P. Briggs: "I Sustain the Wings!"
I SUSTAIN THE WINGS (opening theme)
   2nd Lieutenant Donald P. Briggs: "I Sustain the Wings," presented by the   Army Air
      Forces. Each week this program features the band from the Army Air Forces Technical
      School at Yale University; Captain Glenn Miller; Corporal Ray McKinley; Johnnie, the
      kid next door; and many of your old friends. And now Captain Glenn Miller.
Captain Glenn Miller: Thank you, Lieutenant Don Briggs, and good afternoon, everybody.
   Today's program salutes the Army Air Forces Technical School at Lowry Field, Denver,
   Colorado, Brigadier General Albert L. Sneed, commanding general. And just to get things
   started now, the band plays "Caribbean Clipper."
CARIBBEAN CLIPPER
Captain Glenn Miller: And now medley time, a serenade for the mothers, wives and
   sweethearts of the officers and enlisted men at Lowry Field out in Denver. Here's
   something old, something new, something borrowed and something blue. The old song,
   "Drink to Me Only with Thine Eyes."
DRINK TO ME ONLY WITH THINE EYES (Old tune)
   Captain Glenn Miller: For something new, Private Art Malvin sings ...
YOU'LL NEVER KNOW (New tune)
   Vocal refrain by Private First Class Artie Malvin
   Captain Glenn Miller: We borrow a beautiful theme from George Gershwin's opera "Porgy
      and Bess," "Summertime."
SUMMERTIME (Borrowed tune)
   Captain Glenn Miller: Last in our medley, something blue, the band plays "Blue Skies."
BLUE SKIES (Blue tune)
2nd Lt. Donald P. Briggs: Machine guns and bombs, the weapons of America's fighting Air
   Forces, the armament that signifies our ever-increasing aerial power, the armament which
   is making itself felt on every fighting front. But before those weapons can do their
   jobs, those bombs have to be fused and placed in the bomb racks, machine guns must be
   checked and loaded, and that's the work of the armorer, one of the unbeatable trio, the
   plane, the air crew and the ground crew, each indispensable to the other. You've
   probably met the armorer because he's Johnnie; Johnnie, the kid next door. You know
   him, you know him well. Why, he's the kid that pestered you to death to subscribe to
   some magazine or other so he could get a B-B gun free. He's the kid that later wangled
   a 22 rifle out of his dad and used it to go squirrel hunting in the fall. Well,
   Johnnie's traded that squirrel rifle for a caliber fifty machine gun and don't get the
   idea that Johnnie's just one guy, because he isn't. Naw, he's a lot of people, he's a
   team. He's every last man that has been or is being trained by the Army Air Forces
   Training Command to fly and to "Keep 'Em Flying." He's the pilot, the mechanic, the
   navigator, the machinist, the aerial gunner, the weather observer, the bombardier, and
   the armorer. And as an armorer he's being trained at the Bombardment Armament School of
   the Army Air Forces Technical Command situated at Lowry Field, Denver, Colorado. There
   Johnnie's learning all the intricacies of armament maintenance, earning the coveted
   degree of J.K., Mr. Johnnie Know-how. If you'd like to meet Johnnie again you'll find
   him working on a power-operated gun turret in one of the armament school hangars. Hey,
   Hey, Johnnie, Johnnie, is that a new kind of merry-go-round you've got there?
Cpl. Don Richards (as Pvt. John W. Skinner): Ha, ha, ha. Hardly at all. It's a
   Consolidated tail turret.
2nd Lt. Donald P. Briggs: Sounds like there's something awful wrong with it.
Cpl. Don Richards: Oh, no. You mean that noise like a wail of a banshee?
2nd Lt. Donald P. Briggs: That's it.
Cpl. Don Richards: Ho, ho, ho, don't worry about that. As long as it keeps up that
   wailing it means trouble for the Axis.
2nd Lt. Donald P. Briggs: The - the Consolidated, that's the turret used by the tail
   gunner on a B-24 Liberator.
Cpl. Don Richards: That's the one.

2nd Lt. Donald P. Briggs: Heh, it's pretty small, looks like only a midget could get into it.
Cpl. Don Richards: Well, it does take a pretty small man, but he's small only in size.
2nd Lt. Donald P. Briggs: Hum.
Cpl. Don Richards: He packs plenty o' wallop with those two caliber fifty machine guns stickin' out of that turret there.
2nd Lt. Donald P. Briggs: I see what you mean. Say, Johnnie, how come you're working on turrets. I - I thought your job was taking care of guns and bombs and ammunition and stuff like that.
Cpl. Don Richards: That's just part of it. Anything that has to do with armament is the armorer's job and you might call this, ah, turret a gun mount.
2nd Lt. Donald P. Briggs: I get it, but it's sort of a new part of the armorer's work, isn't it?
Cpl. Don Richards: It's strictly A.D., After Dunkirk. The first ones were used there by the R.A.F., they were hand-operated. The gunner cranked them around. But all the present turrets are power-operated.
2nd Lt. Donald P. Briggs: Something new has been added, huh?
Cpl. Don Richards: Right.
2nd Lt. Donald P. Briggs: Say, Johnnie, you --- I hope you don't mind the "Johnnie."
Cpl. Don Richards: Not at all, but if you want to be strictly on the beam, mister, I usually answer to the name of "Jack."
2nd Lt. Donald P. Briggs: "Jack," well, that's just another version of Johnnie.
Cpl. Don Richards: Well, you've got me there. The Army records carry me as Private John W. Skinner.
2nd Lt. Donald P. Briggs: O.K., then, we'll stick to "Johnnie," Johnnie.
Cpl. Don Richards: Ho, ho. O.K. Have it your own way. Say, you were going to ask me something.
2nd Lt. Donald P. Briggs: Yeah, yeah. What else do they teach you here in Lowry Field besides taking care of turrets?
Cpl. Don Richards: They teach us armament, every angle of it.
2nd Lt. Donald P. Briggs: I suppose there's a lot of theory connected with your instruction?
Cpl. Don Richards: Enough. But we learn mostly by doing.
2nd Lt. Donald P. Briggs: Ah, ha, the - the practical experience routine, huh?
Cpl. Don Richards: Right. For instance, we start out by learning all the parts of the machine gun. Then we tear it apart, reassemble it, but blindfolded.
2nd Lt. Donald P. Briggs: That's to teach you to work in the dark?
Cpl. Don Richards: And fast. After that [they take us to the malfunction range there.
2nd Lt. Donald P. Briggs: Malfunction range?
Cpl. Don Richards: Uh-huh,] that's right, that's where the instructor fouls up a machine gun, then tells us [to find out what's wrong with it by firing, or trying to fire] a short burst.
2nd Lt. Donald P. Briggs: Well, that sounds intriguing.
[Cpl. Don Richards: It is. I'm going over there now. Want to come along?
2nd Lt. Donald P. Briggs: Lead the way. By the way, Johnnie, you said] you worked with bombs. Any particular type?
Cpl. Don Richards: No, [study 'em all,] from small incendiaries to two-ton blockbusters. We go into the theory of explosives and do the actual [work of fusing bombs and loading them] into every different type of bomb rack made.
2nd Lt. Donald P. Briggs: Well, that could be dangerous.
Cpl. Don Richards: It [would if we didn't use practice bombs or] empty cases.
2nd Lt. Donald P. Briggs: I see, I think.
Cpl. Don Richards: Here's the range. Say, let's try this machine gun here.
2nd Lt. Donald P. Briggs: Huh, sure something wrong with it.
Cpl. Don Richards: Yeah. Looks like failure to feed. Yeah, that's it. Won't take a second to fix. You see, it's caused by one of the cartridges being out of line. Ah, there she is. She's firing O.K. now.

2nd Lt. Donald P. Briggs: Yes, you bet that machine gun's firing O.K., and it'll keep on firing as long as Johnnie Armorer is on the job. We've just been to Lowry Field where we renewed our acquaintance with Johnnie; Johnnie, the kid next door. Today Johnnie was represented by Private John W. Skinner, who permitted Corporal Don Richards to speak for him. Private Skinner, as Johnnie, is a "soldier in coveralls," one of the thousands of young men being trained by the Army Air Forces Training Command to "Keep our planes flying." As an armorer, ...

I Sustain the Wings (Incidental music)
2nd Lt. Donald P. Briggs: ... Johnnie's doing a man-sized job. He's got to keep our machine guns firing, he's got to fuse the bombs and load the bomb racks and see that the gun turrets and other mechanical gadgets are operating smoothly. Yes, and it's a big job, but Johnnie's the boy to handle it, and, like every one of America's fighting sons, Johnnie'll go right on doing his best and better than his best, living up to the Air Forces' rightful boast, "The difficult we accomplish immediately, the impossible takes a little longer!"

Captain Glenn Miller: And now, just for old time's sake, here's "Tuxedo Junction."

TUXEDO JUNCTION
Captain Glenn Miller: For the next tune we've picked an All-American all-time favorite. The band plays "Star Dust."

STAR DUST
Voice A: Squadron, attention. Count off.
Voice B: One.
Voice C: Two.
Voice D: Three.
Voice E: Four.
Voice F: Five.
Voice G: Six.
Voice H: Seven

2nd Lt. Donald P. Briggs: Yes, in numbers almost too many to count, young Americans are lining up in defense of their country, by joining the ranks of the Army Air Forces! Perhaps you've already seen many of your own buddies enlist as Aviation Cadets in the Army Air Forces. And today many of them proudly wear the silver wings of full-fledged fighting pilots! Now, the same chance can you yours, too! And it's one you shouldn't miss! Even while you're seventeen, you may volunteer for training as an Aviation Cadet, on a reserve basis. Just ask at any post office, Aviation Cadet Board, or Army Recruiting Office. They'll be glad to give you full information. Ask about it today! A life of action, new experiences, a training you can't beat anywhere, and a chance to slug it out with America's enemies, are waiting for you now, in the Army Air Forces! Now back to music.

PUT YOUR ARMS AROUND ME, HONEY
Captain Glenn Miller: Now Private Jerry Gray's arrangement of "Put Your Arms Around Me, Honey, Hold Me Tight."
Vocal refrain by the Crew Chiefs and the Glee Club

I SUSTAIN THE WINGS (closing theme)
2nd Lt. Donald P. Briggs: "I Sustain the Wings" has presented the band from the Army Air Forces Technical School at Yale University; Captain Glenn Miller; Corporal Ray McKinley; Johnnie, the kid next door; and many of your old friends. Next week you'll learn more about Johnnie at the Army Air Forces Officer Candidate School, in Miami Beach, Florida. Be with us again next Saturday, same time, same station. This program is written and produced entirely by soldiers of the Army Air Forces, and came to you from New York City. This is the National Broadcasting Company.

NBC chimes

02Oct43 (Sat) 1:15PM   NBC, New York, New York
UNCLE SAM PRESENTS recording

I SUSTAIN THE WINGS (opening theme)
   2nd Lt. Donald P. Briggs: From the United States of America, to the other united
      nations of the world, "Uncle Sam Presents," the Band of the Training Command of the
      Army Air Forces, under the direction of Captain Glenn Miller, with Corporal Ray
      McKinley, and many of your old friends.
   2nd Lt. Donald P. Briggs: And here is Captain Glenn Miller.
   Captain Glenn Miller: Thank you, Lieutenant Don Briggs, and hello, everybody. The
      bandwagon is loaded with plenty of music, so here's Corporal Ray McKinley with the big
      hammers all warmed up for "Anvil Chorus."
ANVIL CHORUS
   Captain Glenn Miller: Nice going, boys. Now here's an All-American favorite which you
      boys out there ask for frequently. It's been arranged especially for all of you, it's
      "Stormy Weather." Sergeant Zarchy, you got those boys ready up there? Here's the down
      beat.
STORMY WEATHER (Keeps Rainin' All the Time)
   Captain Glenn Miller: Now for something in the vocal department. Here are the Crew
      Chiefs and "Juke Box Saturday Night."
JUKE BOX SATURDAY NIGHT
   Vocal refrain by the Crew Chiefs
I SUSTAIN THE WINGS (closing theme)
   Captain Glenn Miller: That wraps it up for today. On behalf of the band, many thanks
      for your swell letters. As long as you keep writing, we'll keep playing your favorite
      tunes. You can always reach us in care of this station. And so now for Lieutenant
      Don Briggs, Corporal Ray McKinley and all the rest of us, so long 'til next week same
      time.
   2nd Lt. Donald P. Briggs: The Army Air Forces Training Command Band, under the
      direction of Captain Glenn Miller, has come to you from New York City. Don't forget
      tomorrow, same time, same station, "Uncle Sam Presents" another famous service band
      with music from us to you.
EVERYBODY LOVES MY BABY (But My Baby Don't Love Nobody but Me (fade-out tune)
   2nd Lt. Donald P. Briggs: This is the United States of America, one of the united
      nations.

02Oct43 (Sat) 6:00-6:30PM EWT WEAF, NBC Vanderbilt Theatre, New York, New York
  I SUSTAIN THE WINGS broadcast   Audience

[**THE ARMY AIR CORPS** (opening fanfare)
2nd Lieutenant Donald P. Briggs: "I Sustain the Wings!"
I SUSTAIN THE WINGS (opening theme)
  2nd Lieutenant Donald P. Briggs: "I Sustain the Wings," presented by the Army Air
    Forces. Each week this program features the band from the Army Air Forces Technical
    School at Yale University; Captain Glenn Miller; Corporal Ray McKinley; Johnnie, the
    kid next door; and many of your old friends. And now Captain Glenn Miller.
Captain Glenn Miller: Thank you, Lieutenant Don Briggs, and good afternoon, everybody.
  Today's program salutes the Army Air Forces Officers' Candidate School at Miami Beach,
  Florida, Lieutenant Colonel Donald G. Storck, commanding officer. For the future
  Lieutenants and all the gang at Miami Beach, we play the "Anvil Chorus."
ANVIL CHORUS
2nd Lt. Donald P. Briggs: Someday the last block-buster will fall! And someday the last
  burst of American tracers will find their mark. But until that happy day comes, there's
  a mighty big job to be done! A job for young men who can take it, yes, and dish it out,
  too! A job that you yourself may be able to help do, as a pilot in the Army Air Forces!
  You may only be seventeen, but you can still volunteer for Aviation Cadet training right
  now, on a reserve basis. Drop in at your nearest post office, Aviation Cadet Board, or
  Army Recruiting Office, and ask how you can enroll in the Army Air Forces Enlisted
  Reserve. Do it today, and join those thousands of other young American eagles who are
  helping to free the world of tyranny and terror. Find your place in the sky, in the
  Army Air Forces! And now, Captain Miller.]
Captain Glenn Miller: Thank you, Lieutenant. It's medley time now and a serenade for the
  mothers, wives and sweethearts of the officers and officer candidates at Miami Beach.
  Here's something old, something new, something borrowed and something blue. The old
  song, "Loch Lomond."
LOCH LOMOND (By Yon Bonnie Banks) (Old tune)
  Captain Glenn Miller: Something new, the Crew Chiefs sing "If That's the Way You Want
    It, Baby."
IF THAT'S THE WAY YOU WANT IT, BABY (New tune)
  Vocal refrain by the Crew Chiefs
  Captain Glenn Miller: Something borrowed, the band plays one of the beautiful songs
    from Jerome Kern's "Show Boat," only "Make-Believe."
MAKE-BELIEVE (Borrowed tune)
  Captain Glenn Miller: Last in our medley, something really blue, the band plays "Mood
    Indigo."
MOOD INDIGO (Blue tune)
[Voice 1: Hut, two, three, four! Hut, two, three, four!
I've Got Sixpence (As We Go Rolling Home) (Incidental music)
  Vocal refrain by the Glee Club
  2nd Lt. Donald P. Briggs: Singing as they march! Swinging down the street,
    rhythmically, in perfect step, lines beautifully straight, eyes steadfastly to the
    front! The men of the Army Air Forces Officers' Candidate School! The marching men
    of the Officers' Candidate School! To this "streamlined West Point" come soldiers
    from every branch of the Army Air Forces, men selected for their leadership,
    intelligence and initiative, the top twenty-three men of every one thousand enlistees.
  2nd Lt. Donald P. Briggs: Here they receive training that qualifies them to lead
    their fellow-soldiers in the business of war! While they are marching, study their
    eager faces, clean-cut, healthy, alert! The face of America's youth at its best! The
    face of Johnnie; Johnnie, the kid next door! He's the kid who was always organizing
    some affair in the neighborhood, the backyard circus for which he charged two pins
    admission, the local Boy Scout troop, the annual berry-picking hike. And he was
    always the leader, captain of the football team, manager of the high school cafeteria,
    president of his graduating class. Those things seemed pretty important to Johnnie at
    the time, but they're small-time stuff compared to the job Johnnie has now, the job of
    helping to win this war, of leading his comrades in dangerous missions on the field of
    combat. He's that broad-shouldered, husky young man in the front rank, or that

shorter boy leading the second flight, or that serious looking young fellow passing us now, that one, I mean, the tall, straight boy in the third rank. And Johnnie's working hard these days. He's got a lot to learn and a lot to do in a short space of time. He has to study map reading, military courtesy, base and staff functions, military law, chemical warfare, well, suppose we follow Johnnie through a typical day and see just what he has to do.

Voice 2: Hit the deck, mister! Get it out of bed!

2nd Lt. Donald P. Briggs: It's five-thirty, mister, time to get up, time to start a long day. Remember, mister, you have five minutes, only five minutes, to get yourself dressed, in full uniform, mind you, and to "fall in" downstairs for reveille roll-call. Comb your hair, mister, and remember your dog-tags and pay book, and don't forget your garters! Better hurry it up, mister, those seconds are ticking by awful fast. Time's almost up, mister, better make it on the double!

Voice 2: Fall in! Flight, attention! Dress right, dress!

2nd Lt. Donald P. Briggs: All right, mister, dress right! Turn your head and eyes forty-five degrees to the right, keep arm's length from the next fellow in line, forty inches from the man in front of you, straighten up those lines!

Voice 2: Ready, front! Anderson.

Voice 3: Here, sir.

Voice 2: Batchellor.

Voice 4: Here, sir.

Voice 2: Campbell.

Voice 5. Here, sir.

2nd Lt. Donald P. Briggs: Now it's six A.M., mister, you have half an hour, or less, to get your room and yourself ready for inspection. Make every minute of those thirty count. You'll have to work fast, mister. Make that bed tight enough to bounce a coin, mister, sweep and mop that floor so it won't dirty the inspecting officer's white gloves, dust the furniture and woodwork, and don't forget the picture moulding, they'll climb up on the bed and inspect there, too, and polish up those bathroom fixtures. Make 'em bright enough to use for a mirror. And then there's your own belt buckle and shoes. They've got to glisten in the light. That whistle means breakfast formation. Hurry it up, mister, get downstairs on the double.

Voice 2: All right, fall in!

2nd Lt. Donald P. Briggs: Yes, mister, fall in! Fall in to march to breakfast. Then fall in again to march back to your barracks. Maybe you'll have a few minutes to finish tidying up your room before you "fall in" for another formation to march to class, classes where a whole year of ordinary college is crammed into four short months. Better not drop your pencil, mister, you'll miss a semester of algebra. It'll be eleven o'clock, mister, after those classes.

Alouette (Incidental music, male chorus, no band)

2nd Lt. Donald P. Briggs: And you'll be marching back for your noon meal. Yes, mister, you'll be marching all day long ..

Vocal refrain by the Glee Club

2nd Lt. Donald P. Briggs: ... but you'll be singing as you march, singing because you're eager to do your part in America's mighty war effort! And after lunch, you'll march to the beach for calisthenics, to the field for extended order drill, to Bayshore Golf Club for the stirring ceremony of Retreat.

Retreat (Bugle)

2nd Lt. Donald P. Briggs: But after supper, mister, you'll have some time, some of that very precious time, to yourself. That is, you can use it to study, to prepare for your next day's lessons, to brush up for those examinations, twenty-six of them in two weeks! Make good use of those swiftly passing seconds, mister, time's a'wastin'!

Voice 2: Lights out!

2nd Lt. Donald P. Briggs: It's ten-thirty, mister, time to hit the hay. Time to douse those lights and crawl into bed. And, boy, does that bed feel good! You've had a long, hard day, but sleep tight, mister, there'll be another longer day tomorrow.

Taps (Bugle, echoed by the string section)

2nd Lt. Donald P. Briggs: It's "lights out" for tonight, Johnnie, but you're just at the beginning of a big job, a responsible job, the job of leading men in the flame and fury of combat! The Officers' Candidate School has given you a lot, Johnnie, but it made you earn what it gave you, and you came through with flying colors.

Incidental music

2nd Lt. Donald P. Briggs: The discipline of O.C.S. has not killed your spirit. It has enriched it, molded your character, inspired in you a pride that makes you not only demand the best of your men, but expect more of yourself! So, at last, when your long training is done, you can repeat with pride ...

Cast: I do solemnly swear that I will support and defend the Constitution of the United States of America against all enemies, foreign and domestic, that I will bear true faith and allegiance to the same, that I will take this obligation freely, without any mental reservation or purpose of evasion, and that I will well and faithfully discharge the duties of the office, upon which I am about to enter! So help me God.

Incidental music

Captain Glenn Miller: Now for something a little special from our "Hot Club," Sergeant Trigger Alpert on the bass, Corporal Ray McKinley on the drums, Corporal Mel Powell at the piano and Private Carmen Mastren, guitar. We call on the "Tail End Charlies" and they're going to play "I Want to Be Happy."

I WANT TO BE HAPPY

Captain Glenn Miller: A couple of weeks ago we pulled a swindle on you and told you we were going to play something serious, but it turned out to be "Pistol Packin' Mama." In answer to many requests, we're going to play it again in all its fancy dress. See if you can pick out the melody in the first part, we know you won't have any trouble later on. Here it is, "Pistol Packin' Mama."

PISTOL PACKIN' MAMA

Vocal refrain by Corporal Ray McKinley, Private Carmen Mastren and the Glee   Club

I SUSTAIN THE WINGS (closing theme)

2nd Lt. Donald P. Briggs: "I Sustain the Wings" has presented the band from the Army Air Forces Technical School at Yale University; Captain Glenn Miller; Corporal Ray McKinley; Johnnie, the kid next door; and many of your old friends. Next week you'll learn more about Johnnie when we salute the Army Air Forces' Technical School at Westerly, Rhode Island. Be with us again next Saturday, same time, same station. This program is written and produced entirely by soldiers of the Army Air Forces and came to you from New York City.

2nd Lt. Donald P. Briggs: This is the National Broadcasting Company.]

The part of Voice 1, Voice 2, Voice 3, Voice 4, Voice 5 and Cast were played by Pfc. Joseph Shulman, Pfc. Paul Huston, Pvt. Cutler and Pvt. Stone.

02Oct43 (Sat) 11:30PM-Midnight EWT   WEAF, NBC Vanderbilt Theatre, New York, New York
  I SUSTAIN THE WINGS broadcast   Audience

THE ARMY AIR CORPS (opening fanfare)
2nd Lieutenant Donald P. Briggs: "I Sustain the Wings!"
I SUSTAIN THE WINGS (opening theme)
  2nd Lieutenant Donald P. Briggs: "I Sustain the Wings," presented by the   Army Air
    Forces. Each week this program features the band from the Army Air Forces Technical
    School at Yale University; Captain Glenn Miller; Corporal Ray McKinley; Johnnie, the
    kid next door; and many of your old friends. And now Captain Glenn Miller.
Captain Glenn Miller: Thank you, Lieutenant Don Briggs, and good afternoon, good evening,
  everybody. Today's program salutes the Army Air Forces Officers' Candidate School at
  Miami Beach, Florida, Lieutenant Colonel Donald G. Storck, commanding officer. The
  bandwagon tonight is loaded with plenty of music and here's Corporal Ray McKinley with
  the big hammers all warmed up for "Anvil Chorus."
ANVIL CHORUS
[2nd Lt. Donald P. Briggs: Someday the last block-buster will fall! And someday the last
  burst of American tracers will find their mark. But until that happy day comes, there's
  a mighty big job to be done! A job for young men who can take it, yes, and dish it out,
  too! A job that you yourself may be able to help do, as a pilot in the Army Air Forces!
  You may only be seventeen, but you can still volunteer for Aviation Cadet training right
  now, on a reserve basis. Drop in at your nearest post office, Aviation Cadet Board, or
  Army Recruiting Office, and ask how you can enroll in the Army Air Forces Enlisted
  Reserve. Do it today, and join those thousands of other young American eagles who are
  helping to free the world of tyranny and terror. Find your place in the sky, in the
  Army Air Forces! And now, Captain Miller.]
Captain Glenn Miller: Thank you, Lieutenant.] It's medley time and a serenade for the
  mothers, wives and sweethearts of the officers and officer candidates at Miami Beach.
  Here's something old, something new, something borrowed and something blue. The old
  song, "Loch Lomond."
LOCH LOMOND (By Yon Bonnie Banks) (Old tune)
  Captain Glenn Miller: Something new, the Crew Chiefs sing "If That's the Way You Want
    It, Baby."
IF THAT'S THE WAY YOU WANT IT, BABY (New tune)
  Vocal refrain by the Crew Chiefs
  Captain Glenn Miller: Something borrowed, the band plays one of the beautiful songs
    from Jerome Kern's "Show Boat," only "Make-Believe."
MAKE-BELIEVE (Borrowed tune)
  Captain Glenn Miller: Last in our medley, somethin' really blue, the boys plays "Mood
    Indigo."
MOOD INDIGO (Blue tune)
[Voice 1: Hut, two, three, four! Hut, two, three, four!
I've Got Sixpence (As We Go Rolling Home) (Incidental music)
  Vocal refrain by the Glee Club
  2nd Lt. Donald P. Briggs: Singing as they march! Swinging down the street,
    rhythmically, in perfect step, lines beautifully straight, eyes steadfastly to the
    front! The men of the Army Air Forces Officers' Candidate School! The marching men
    of the Officers' Candidate School! To this "streamlined West Point" come soldiers
    from every branch of the Army Air Forces, men selected for their leadership,
    intelligence and initiative, the top twenty-three men of every one thousand enlistees.
  2nd Lt. Donald P. Briggs: Here they receive training that qualifies them to lead
    their fellow-soldiers in the business of war! While they are marching, study their
    eager faces, clean-cut, healthy, alert! The face of America's youth at its best! The
    face of Johnnie; Johnnie, the kid next door! He's the kid who was always organizing
    some affair in the neighborhood, the backyard circus for which he charged two pins
    admission, the local Boy Scout troop, the annual berry-picking hike. And he was
    always the leader,] captain of the football team, manager of the high school
    cafeteria, heh, president of his graduating class. Huh, those things seemed pretty
    important to Johnnie at the time, but they're small-time stuff compared to the job
    Johnnie has now, the job of helping to win this war, of leading his comrades in

dangerous missions on the field of combat. He's that, ah, broad-shouldered, husky young man in the front rank, or that, ah, shorter boy leading the second flight, or that, ah, serious looking young fellow passing us now, that, that one, I mean, the tall, straight boy in the third rank. Yeah, and Johnnie's working hard these days. He's got a lot to learn and a lot to do in a short space of time. He's got to study map reading, military courtesy, base and staff functions, military law, chemical warfare and, well, suppose we follow Johnnie through a typical day and see just what he has to do.

Voice 2: Hit the deck, mister! Get it out of bed!

Voices: Oh, brother, is it always 5:30? Gee ...

2nd Lt. Donald P. Briggs: It's five-thirty, mister, time to get up, time to start a long day. Remember, mister, you have five minutes, only five minutes, to get yourself dressed, in full uniform, mind you, and to "fall in" downstairs for reveille roll-call. Ah, comb your hair, mister. Remember your dog-tags and pay book, and don't forget your garters! Yeah, better hurry it up, mister, those seconds are ticking by awful fast. Time's almost up, mister, better make it on the double!

Voice 2: Fall in! Flight, attention! Dress right, ...

2nd Lt. Donald P. Briggs: All right, mister, dress right! Turn your head and eyes forty-five degrees to the right, keep and arm's length to the next fellow in line, forty inches from the man in front of you and straighten up those lines!

Voice 2: Ready, front! Anderson.

Voice 3: Here, sir.

Voice 2: Batchellor.

Voice 4: Here, sir.

Voice 2: Campbell.

Voice 5. Here, sir.

2nd Lt. Donald P. Briggs: Now it's six o'clock, mister, you have half an hour, or less, to get your room and yourself ready for inspection. Make every minute of those thirty count. Gotta work fast, mister. Yeah, make that bed tight enough to bounce a coin, mister, sweep and mop that floor so it won't dirty the inspecting officer's white gloves. Ah, dust the furniture and woodwork, and don't forget the picture moulding, eh, eh. Climb up on the bed and inspect there, too, and polish up those bathroom fixtures. Make 'em bright enough to use for a mirror. And then there's your own belt buckle and shoes. They've got to glitter. That whistle means breakfast formation. Hurry up, mister, get downstairs on the double.

Voice 2: All right, fall in!

2nd Lt. Donald P. Briggs: Yes, mister, fall in! Fall in to march to breakfast. Then fall in again to march back to your barracks. Maybe you'll have a few minutes to finish tidying up your room before you "fall in" again for another formation to march to class, classes where a whole year of ordinary college is crammed into four short months. Heh, better not drop your pencil, mister, you'll miss a semester of algebra.

Alouette (Incidental music, male chorus, no band)

2nd Lt. Donald P. Briggs: Yeah, and after those classes you'll be marching back to your noon meal. Yes, mister, you'll be marching all day long ..

Vocal refrain by the Glee Club

2nd Lt. Donald P. Briggs: ... but you'll be singing as you march, because you're eager to do your part in America's mighty war effort! And after lunch, you'll march to the beach for calisthenics, to the field for extended order drill, to Bayshore Golf Club ...

2nd Lt. Donald P. Briggs: ... for the stirring ceremony of Retreat.

Retreat (Bugle)

2nd Lt. Donald P. Briggs: But after supper, mister, you'll have some time, some of that very precious time, to your own self. That is, you'll have time for study, to prepare for your next day's lessons, to brush up for those examinations, twenty-six of them in two weeks! Huh, make good use of those swiftly passing seconds, mister, time's a'wastin'!

Voice 2: Lights out!

Taps (Bugle, echoed by the string section)
  2nd Lt. Donald P. Briggs: It's ten-thirty, mister, time to hit the hay. Time to douse those lights and crawl into bed. And, boy, does that bed feel good! You've had a long, hard day, but sleep tight, mister, there'll be another longer day tomorrow.
2nd Lt. Donald P. Briggs: It's "lights out," mister. Good night.
Incidental music
2nd Lt. Donald P. Briggs: Yes, it's "lights out" for tonight, Johnnie, but you're just at the beginning of a big job, a big responsible job. A job of leading men in the flame and fury of combat! The Officers' Candidate School's given you a lot, Johnnie, but it made you earn what it gave you, and you came through with flying colors.
Incidental music
  2nd Lt. Donald P. Briggs: The discipline of O.C.S. has not killed your spirit. No, no, indeed, it - it's enriched it. It's, it's molded your character. It's inspired in you a pride that makes you not only demand the best of your men, but expect more of yourself! So, at last, when your long training is done, you can repeat ...
2nd Lt. Donald P. Briggs: with pride ...
Cast: I do solemnly swear that I will support and defend the Constitution of the United States of America against all enemies, foreign and domestic, that I will bear true faith and allegiance to the same, that I will take this obligation freely, without any mental reservation or purpose of evasion, and that I will well and faithfully discharge the duties of the office, upon which I am about to enter! So help me God.
Incidental music
Captain Glenn Miller: And now for something a little on the special side from our "Hot Club," Sergeant Trigger Alpert on the bass, Corporal Ray McKinley on the drums, Corporal Mel Powell at the piano and Private Carmen Mastren at the guitar. We call on the "Tail End Charlies" and they're gonna play "I Want to Be Happy."
I WANT TO BE HAPPY
Captain Glenn Miller: A couple of weeks ago we pulled a swindle on you folks and told you we were going to play something a little bit on the serious side, but it finally turned out to be "Pistol Packin' Mama." In answer to many requests, now we're going to play it again in all its fancy dress to see if you can pick out the melody in the first part. I know you won't have too much trouble later on. Here it is, "Pistol Packin' Mama."
PISTOL PACKIN' MAMA
  Vocal refrain by Corporal Ray McKinley, Private Carmen Mastren and the Glee   Club
I SUSTAIN THE WINGS (closing theme)
  2nd Lt. Donald P. Briggs: "I Sustain the Wings" has presented the band from the Army Air Forces Technical School at Yale University; Captain Glenn Miller; Corporal Ray McKinley; Johnnie, the kid next door; and many of your old friends. Next week you'll learn more about Johnnie when we salute the Army Air Forces' Technical School at Westerly, Rhode Island. Be with us again next Saturday, same time, same station. This program is written and produced entirely by soldiers of the Army Air Forces and came to you from New York City. This is the National Broadcasting Company.
NBC chimes

The part of Voice 1, Voice 2, Voice 3, Voice 4, Voice 5 and Cast were played by Pfc. Joseph Shulman, Pfc. Paul Huston, Pvt. Cutler and Pvt. Stone.

09Oct43 (Sat) NBC, New York, New York
  UNCLE SAM PRESENTS recording

I SUSTAIN THE WINGS (opening theme)
  2nd Lt. Donald P. Briggs: From the United States of America, to the other united
    nations of the world, "Uncle Sam Presents" the Band of the Training Command of the
    Army Air Forces, under the direction of Captain Glenn Miller, with Corporal Ray
    McKinley, and many of your old friends.
  2nd Lt. Donald P. Briggs: And here is Captain Glenn Miller.
  Captain Glenn Miller: Thank you, Lieutenant Donald Briggs, and hello, everybody. First
    off the band plays a new tune by Private Jerry Gray, the "Jeep Jockey Jump."
JEEP JOCKEY JUMP
ALL THE THINGS YOU ARE
  Captain Glenn Miller: And now to all fighting men of the united nations in all corners
    of the world we dedicate our next song. We think that you'll recognize it, "All the
    Things You Are."
  Captain Glenn Miller: Now here's an old timer that fits the picture pretty well these
    days, especially with our Russian friends beating it out like they are, "The Volga
    Boatmen."
SONG OF THE VOLGA BOATMEN
  Vocal chant by the Ensemble
WITH MY HEAD IN THE CLOUDS
  2nd Lt. Donald P. Briggs: And now a song written by Irving Berlin for the all soldier
    hit picture "This Is the Army." The Training Command Band from Yale University plays
    "With My Head in the Clouds." The song is written for and dedicated to the commanding
    general of the United States Army Air Forces, General H. H. Arnold.
  Vocal refrain by the Glee Club
I SUSTAIN THE WINGS (closing theme)
  Captain Glenn Miller: Well, that winds things up for today. On behalf of the band,
    thanks for all the swell letters you've been sending. Keep 'em coming. Write and ask
    us to play your favorite tunes and we'll be glad to. You can reach us in care of this
    station. And now for Lieutenant Don Briggs, Corporal Ray McKinley, and all the rest
    of us, so long until next week, same time. We'll be seeing you.
  2nd Lt. Donald P. Briggs: The Army Air Forces Training Command Band, under the
    direction of Captain Glenn Miller, has come to you from New York City. Don't forget
    tomorrow, same time, same station, "Uncle Sam Presents" another famous service band
    with music from us to you.
7-0-5 (fade-out tune)
  2nd Lt. Donald P. Briggs: This is the United States of America, one of the united
    nations.

09Oct43 (Sat) 6:00-6:30PM EWT WEAF, NBC Vanderbilt Theatre, New York, New York
  I SUSTAIN THE WINGS broadcast   Audience

THE ARMY AIR CORPS (opening fanfare)
2nd Lt. Donald P. Briggs: "I Sustain the Wings."
I SUSTAIN THE WINGS (opening theme)
  2nd Lt. Donald P. Briggs: "I Sustain the Wings," presented by the Army Air Forces
    Training Command. Each week this program features the band from the Army Air Forces
    Technical School at Yale University; Captain Glenn Miller; Corporal Ray McKinley;
    Johnnie, the kid next door; and many of your old friends. And now Captain Glenn
    Miller.
Captain Glenn Miller: Thank you, Lieutenant Don Briggs, and good evening, everybody.
  Today's program salutes the Army Air Forces Technical School at the Hamilton Standard
  Propellers plant in Westerly, Rhode Island, Captain Julius T. Ames, commanding officer.
  First off though, a new tune by Private Jerry Gray, "Jeep Jockey Jump."
JEEP JOCKEY JUMP
2nd Lt. Donald P. Briggs: Do you hear that machine gun chattering away? Well, believe
  me, that's not idle chatter. It's America speaking in the only language that the Axis
  understands. Behind that gun sits a young fighter pilot saying it with lead. And in
  the skies beside him are thousands of other young Americans just like you, helping to
  win this war in the Army Air Forces. There's a chance for you to join them too. Even
  if you're still only seventeen, you can volunteer for Aviation Cadet Training on a
  reserve basis. No school or college credits are required. If you're not employed in
  war production, visit any post office, Aviation Cadet Board, or Army Recruiting Office
  and find out how you can enroll now in the Army Air Forces Enlisted Reserve. If
  accepted you're immediately entitled to wear a pair of silver Army Air Forces Reserve
  wings with a good chance that one day you'll be wearing the famous silver wings of a
  full-fledged Army pilot, bombardier or navigator. Get in the fight today, fellows, and
  say it with lead in the Army Air Forces.
GOIN' HOME (Old tune)
  Captain Glenn Miller: Now medley time, a serenade for the mothers and wives and
    sweethearts of the officers and enlisted men of Hamilton Standard Propellers in
    Westerly, Rhode Island. Here's something old, something new, something borrowed and
    something blue. The old song, the beautiful "Largo" from Dvorak's "New World
    Symphony," "Goin' Home."
  Captain Glenn Miller: For something new, the Crew Chiefs sing "Paper Doll."
PAPER DOLL (New tune)
  Vocal refrain by the Crew Chiefs
  Captain Glenn Miller: We borrow the hit song from Jerome Kern's "Very Warm for May,"
    "All the Things You Are."
ALL THE THINGS YOU ARE (Borrowed tune)
  Captain Glenn Miller: Last in our medley, something blue, the band plays "My Blue
    Heaven."
MY BLUE HEAVEN (Blue tune)
2nd Lt. Donald P. Briggs: Power and more power. Aw, it's a comforting sound when sung by
  America's modern aircraft engines. But all that power those engines boast about would
  be useless if it weren't converted into motion, motion to speed the planes along the
  runway and into the air, motion to carry them to their targets and return. Yes, the
  magic of turning power into motion and it's done by a simple twist of a propeller. Yes,
  the propeller, another miracle of modern design. Into its design and manufacture have
  gone years of painstaking research, hours and hours of the finest precision workmanship.
  The propeller is to the plane what wheels are to an automobile, so you can see it's
  plenty important. So important that the Army Air Forces Training Command especially
  prepares a man just for the job of taking care of them and he's called the propeller
  specialist. And as a propeller specialist he's a member of the ground crew, one of that
  unbeatable trio, the plane, the air crew and the ground crew, each indispensable to the
  other. Well, that's what our Johnnie is doing today, learning to take care of
  propellers. You remember Johnnie; Johnnie, the kid next door. Why sure, he's that, ah,
  freckle-faced, grinning youngster that was always whittling, yeah, carving his initials
  in odd places, fashioning a boomerang, or a propeller for his model plane, from a block

of wood and leaving a trail of shavings all over the neighborhood. Well, today Johnnie's a man. Yes, sir, he's a lot of men. In fact he's all the men trained by the Army Air Forces Training Command to fly our planes and to "Keep 'Em Flying." And he's studying to become a specialist at the Army Air Forces Technical School located in the Westerly, Rhode Island plant of Hamilton Standard propellers, makers of the famed Hydromatic propellers. What do you say we go over and talk to Johnnie, huh? Maybe he can tell us more about propellers and what makes 'em tick. The, ah, school's right upstairs here in this converted cotton mill. Hey, ah, hey, Johnnie, Johnnie, what are you doing with that propeller?

Johnnie: Why, I'm learning to balance it.

2nd Lt. Donald P. Briggs: Balance it? Well, is balance so important?

Sergeant Experience: That's right, go on, Johnnie, tell him. Is it important? You bet it's important. Plenty important. Lieutenant, a propeller is so delicately balanced that a lead pencil mark, just a mark, mind you, on a tip of one of the blades will set it movin'. So don't go writing any greetings to Hitler or Tojo on those propeller blades, the mark of your pencil'll throw if off balance. And it isn't silly to worry about such a seemingly small item because a propeller is more than a stick whittled out of wood, a great deal more. Ninety-nine out of a hundred it won't be wood, it'll be metal, usually aluminum. What's more, it's an efficient piece of machinery made with all the care and precision of a fine watch. Why, a plane can't fly without a propeller, it just isn't a plane. Oh, ah, excuse me a minute, Lieutenant. Ah, I'm needed over there.

2nd Lt. Donald P. Briggs: Hey, hey, Johnnie, who's your friend?

Johnnie: Who, him?

2nd Lt. Donald P. Briggs: Yeah.

Johnnie: Oh, that's Sergeant Experience, you meet him a lot around here. He's a swell guy and, man, does he know his stuff.

2nd Lt. Donald P. Briggs: Yeah, especially about propellers. Hey, look, Johnnie, I - I - I know a propeller makes a plane move, but tell me, just how does it operate?

Sergeant Experience: If you'll step over to this bench, Lieutenant, I'll show you with this brace and bit. Now you see [when I turn the bit, it digs] itself into the wood, biting chunks out of it and shoving them back out of the way as it moves forward. Well the - the propeller does the same thing to air, in other words, it bites into the air, pulls itself and the plane forward and pushes the air back over the wing. Well, you can see, Lieutenant, that the modern propeller has a man-sized job to do and it does it to perfection, especially the Hydromatic. Ha, ha, ha, ha. I can see by your expression that "Hydromatic's" a puzzle to you. Well, there's a model of it over there. It's cut away so you can see how it works. Now you might call this Hydromatic propeller the - the gear shift of the air. It automatically adjusts itself to get the most out of any given engine speed. You know, it's like one of those automatic gear shifts on a car. The Hydromatic propeller, through engine oil pressure, automatically changes the pitch of its blades to compensate for the change in load. In other words, it, ah, it shifts gears for the pilots. Oh, oh. Ah, somebody else needs my help, ah, I'll be right back, Lieutenant.

2nd Lt. Donald P. Briggs: Eh, you're right, Johnnie, he does know his stuff. That Hydromatic propeller's really something.

Johnnie: Eh - eh. But even then he didn't tell you all about it.

2nd Lt. Donald P. Briggs: Well, what else?

Johnnie: Well, you see, in case an engine fails, the pilot can "feather his prop" merely by pressing a switch.

2nd Lt. Donald P. Briggs: Well, now, now, now, "feathering the prop," what does that mean?

Sergeant Experience: If you don't mind, Johnnie, I'll answer that. Lieutenant, "feathering" means setting the blades so that the propeller won't revolve and turn the conked-out engine. It stops the dangerous counter-vibration that - well, it might tear the engine loose and cause a plane to crash. Now over here on the test blocks the boys are running a series of tests. Look, Lieutenant, look at that propeller spin. Brother, that means plenty of speed and plenty of power. Oh, ha, ha, now don't get nervous, Lieutenant. That propeller isn't going to let go. Not as long as Johnnie here is on the job to keep it in perfect running condition.

2nd Lt. Donald P. Briggs: No, folks, that propeller isn't going to let go, not with Johnnie as the propeller specialist. Johnnie, as the thousands of young men trained by the Army Air Forces Training Command to keep our planes flying, knows his job and he knows it well.

Incidental music

  2nd Lt. Donald P. Briggs: And as a propeller specialist Johnnie'll be handling a big responsibility, because without a propeller, well, then a plane's grounded. And when a pilot hops into a plane for a fast takeoff in that quick, vertical climb to intercept the enemy, he's gonna "hang it on the prop." And a lot hangs on that all-important propeller, the lives of the plane and the crew. And you can bet that Johnnie, knowing that, is going to have those propellers in top shape, that he's gonna keep on working and fighting, and that he'll make good his proud motto "I Sustain the Wings."

Captain Glenn Miller: A nickel in the slot'll give you a lot of strange things these days. Listen to the Crew Chiefs and they'll tell you all about a "Juke Box Saturday Night."

JUKE BOX SATURDAY NIGHT

  Vocal refrain by the Crew Chiefs

Captain Glenn Miller: One of the hit tunes of yesterday and I think still one of your favorites. The band plays our new arrangement of "Stormy Weather."

STORMY WEATHER (Keeps Rainin' All the Time)

WITH MY HEAD IN THE CLOUDS

  2nd Lt. Donald P. Briggs: And now a song written by Irving Berlin for the all-soldier hit picture "This Is the Army." The Training Command Band from Yale University plays "With My Head in the Clouds." The song is written for and dedicated to the commanding general of the United States Army Air Forces, General H. H. Arnold.

  Vocal refrain by the Glee Club

I SUSTAIN THE WINGS (closing theme)

  2nd Lt. Donald P. Briggs: "I Sustain the wings" has presented the band from the Army Air Forces Technical School at Yale University; Captain Glenn Miller; Corporal Ray McKinley; Johnnie, the kid next door; and many of your old friends. Next week you'll learn more about Johnnie at the Army Air Forces Air Service Command at Patterson Field, Dayton, Ohio. Be with us again next Saturday, same time, same station. This program is produced by Major Frank Healey, directed by Sergeant George Voutsas, written by Private First Class Paul Huston and came to you from New York City.

2nd Lt. Donald P. Briggs: This is the National Broadcasting Company.

The parts of Johnnie and Sergeant Experience were played by Pfc. Joseph Shulman and Don Douglas.

09Oct43 (Sat) 11:30PM-Midnight EWT WEAF, NBC Vanderbilt Theatre, New York, New York
   I SUSTAIN THE WINGS broadcast   Audience

THE ARMY AIR CORPS (opening fanfare)
2nd Lt. Donald P. Briggs: "I Sustain the Wings."
I SUSTAIN THE WINGS (opening theme)
   2nd Lt. Donald P. Briggs: "I Sustain the Wings," presented by the Army Air Forces
      Training Command. Each week this program features the band from the Army Air Forces
      Technical School at Yale University; Captain Glenn Miller; Corporal Ray McKinley;
      Johnnie, the kid next door; and many of your old friends. And now Captain Glenn
      Miller.
Captain Glenn Miller: Thank you, Lieutenant Don Briggs, and good evening, everybody.
   Today's program salutes the Army Air Forces Technical School at the Hamilton Standard
   Propellers plant in Westerly, Rhode Island, Captain Julius T. Ames, commanding officer.
   First off in the musicville, a new tune by Private Jerry Gray, "Jeep Jockey Jump."
JEEP JOCKEY JUMP
2nd Lt. Donald P. Briggs: Do you hear that machine gun chattering away? Well, believe
   me, that's not idle chatter. It's America speaking in the only language that the Axis
   understands. Behind that gun sits a young fighter pilot saying it with lead. And in
   the skies beside him are thousands of other young Americans just like you, helping to
   win this war in the Army Air Forces. There's a chance for you to join them too. Even
   if you're still only seventeen, you can volunteer for Aviation Cadet Training on a
   reserve basis. No school or college credits are required. If you're not employed in
   war production, visit any post office, Aviation Cadet Board, or Army Recruiting Office
   and find out how you can enroll now in the Army Air Forces Enlisted Reserve. If
   accepted you're immediately entitled to wear a pair of silver Army Air Forces Reserve
   wings with a good chance that one day you'll be wearing the famous silver wings of a
   full-fledged Army pilot, bombardier or navigator. Get in the fight today, fellows, and
   say it with lead in the Army Air Forces.
GOIN' HOME (Old tune)
   Captain Glenn Miller: And now it's medley time, a serenade for the mothers and wives
      and sweethearts of the officers and enlisted men of Hamilton Standard Propellers in
      Westerly, Rhode Island. Here's something old, something new, something borrowed and
      something blue. The old song, the beautiful "Largo" from Dvorak's "New World
      Symphony," "Goin' Home."
   Captain Glenn Miller: For something new, the Crew Chiefs sing "Paper Doll."
PAPER DOLL (New tune)
   Vocal refrain by the Crew Chiefs
   Captain Glenn Miller: We borrow the hit song from Jerome Kern's "Very Warm for May,"
      "All the Things You Are."
ALL THE THINGS YOU ARE (Borrowed tune)
   Captain Glenn Miller: Last in our medley, something blue, the band plays "My Blue
      Heaven."
MY BLUE HEAVEN (Blue tune)
[2nd Lt. Donald P. Briggs: Power and more power! It's a comforting sound when sung by
   America's modern aircraft engines. But all that power those engines boast about would
   be useless if it weren't converted into motion, motion to speed the planes along the
   runway and into the air, motion to carry them to their targets and return. Yes, the
   magic of turning power into motion and it's done by a simple twist of the propeller!
   Yes, the propeller, another miracle of modern design. Into its design and manufacture
   have gone years of painstaking research, hours and hours of the finest precision
   workmanship. The propeller is to the plane what wheels are to an automobile, so you can
   see it's plenty important. So important that the Army Air Forces Training Command
   especially prepares a man just for the job of taking care of it. He's called the
   propeller specialist. And as a propeller specialist he's a member of the ground crew,
   one of that unbeatable trio, the plane, the air crew, the ground crew, each
   indispensable to the other. That's what Johnnie's doing today, learning to take care of
   propellers. You remember Johnnie; Johnnie, the kid next door. He's that freckle-faced,
   grinning youngster that was always whittling, carving his initials in odd places,
   fashioning a boomerang, or a propeller for his model plane, from a block of wood,

leaving a trail of shavings all over the neighborhood. Well, today Johnnie's a man.
He's a lot of men. In fact he's all the men trained by the Army Air Forces Training
Command to fly our planes and to "Keep 'Em Flying." And he's studying to become a
specialist at the Army Air Forces Technical School located in the Westerly, Rhode Island
plant of Hamilton Standard propellers, makers of the famed Hydromatic propellers. Let's
go over and talk to Johnnie. Maybe he can tell us more about propellers and what makes
'em tick. The school's right upstairs in that converted cotton mill. Say there,
Johnnie, what are you doing with that propeller?
Johnnie: Learning to balance it.
2nd Lt. Donald P. Briggs: Balance it? Is balance so important?
Sergeant Experience: Go on, Johnnie, tell him. Is it important? You bet it's important.
    Plenty important. Listen, Lieutenant, a propeller is so delicately balanced that a lead
    pencil mark, just a mark, mind you, on the tip of one of the blades will set it moving.
    So don't go writing any greetings to Hitler or Tojo on those propeller blades, the mark
    of your pencil will throw if off balance. And it isn't silly to worry about such a
    seemingly small item because a propeller is more than a stick whittled out of wood, a
    great deal more. Ninety-nine out of a hundred it won't be wood, it'll be metal, usually
    aluminum. And what's more, it's an efficient piece of machinery made with all the care
    and precision of a fine watch. A plane can't fly without a propeller, it just isn't a
    plane. Excuse me a minute, Lieutenant. I'm needed over there.
2nd Lt. Donald P. Briggs: Say, Johnnie, who's your friend?
Johnnie: Him?
Johnnie: Oh, that's Sergeant Experience, you meet him a lot around here. He's a swell
    guy and, man, does he know his stuff.
2nd Lt. Donald P. Briggs: Especially about propellers. Look, Johnnie, I know a propeller
    makes a plane move, but just how does it operate?
Sergeant Experience: If you'll step over to this bench I'll show you with this brace and
    bit. Now when I turn the bit, it digs itself into the wood, biting chunks out of it and
    shoving them back out of the way as it moves forward. Well the propeller does the same
    thing to air, in other words, it bites into the air, pulls itself and the plane forward
    and pushes the air back over the wings. Lieutenant, the modern propeller has a
    man-sized job to do and it does it to perfection, especially the Hydromatic. Ha, ha,
    ha, ha. I can see by your expression that "Hydromatic" is a puzzle to you. Well,
    there's a model of it over there. It's cut away so you can see how it works. You might
    call this Hydromatic propeller the gear shift of the air. It automatically adjusts
    itself to get the most out of any given engine speed. You know, it's like one of those
    automatic gear shifts on a car. The Hydromatic propeller, through engine oil pressure,
    automatically changes the pitch of its blades to compensate for the change in load. It
    shifts gears for the pilots. Oh, oh. Somebody else needs my help. I'll be right back.
2nd Lt. Donald P. Briggs: You're right, Johnnie, he does know his stuff. And that
    Hydromatic propeller really is something.
Johnnie: Even then he didn't tell you all about it.
2nd Lt. Donald P. Briggs: What else?
Johnnie: In case an engine fails, the pilot can "feather the prop" merely by pressing a
    switch.
2nd Lt. Donald P. Briggs: "Feathering the prop," what does that mean?
Sergeant Experience: If you don't mind, Johnnie, I'll answer that. "Feathering" means
    setting the blades so that the propeller won't revolve and turn the conked-out engine.
    It stops the dangerous counter-vibration that might tear the engine loose and cause a
    plane to crash. Over there on the test blocks the boys are running a series of tests.
    Look, Lieutenant, look at that propeller spin. That means plenty of speed and plenty of
    power. Oh, ha, ha, don't get nervous, Lieutenant. That propeller isn't going to let
    go. Not as long as Johnnie here is on the job to keep it in perfect running condition.
2nd Lt. Donald P. Briggs: No, folks, that propeller isn't going to let go, not with
    Johnnie as the propeller specialist. Johnnie, as the thousands of young men trained by
    the Army Air Forces Training Command to keep our planes flying, knows his job and he
    knows it well.

Incidental music

    2nd Lt. Donald P. Briggs: As a propeller specialist Johnnie will be handling a big responsibility, because without a propeller, a plane is grounded. When a pilot hops into a plane for a fast takeoff and that quick, vertical climb to intercept the enemy, he's going to "hang it on the prop." And a lot hangs on that all-important propeller, the lives of the plane and the crew. You can bet that Johnnie, knowing that, is going to have those propellers in top shape, that he's going to keep on working and fighting, and that he'll make good his proud motto "I Sustain the Wings."]

Captain Glenn Miller: A nickel in the slot'll get you a lot of strange things these days. Listen to the Crew Chiefs and they'll tell you all about a "Juke Box Saturday Night."

JUKE BOX SATURDAY NIGHT

    Vocal refrain by the Crew Chiefs

Captain Glenn Miller: One of the hit tunes of yesterday now and I think still one of your favorites. The band plays our new arrangement of "Stormy Weather."

STORMY WEATHER (Keeps Rainin' All the Time)

WITH MY HEAD IN THE CLOUDS

    2nd Lt. Donald P. Briggs: And now a song written by Irving Berlin for the all-soldier hit picture "This Is the Army." The Training Command Band from Yale University plays "With My Head in the Clouds." The song is written for and dedicated to the commanding general of the United States Army Air Forces, General H. H. Arnold.

    Vocal refrain by the Glee Club

I SUSTAIN THE WINGS (closing theme)

    2nd Lt. Donald P. Briggs: "I Sustain the wings" has presented the band from the Army Air Forces Technical School at Yale University; Captain Glenn Miller; Corporal Ray McKinley; Johnnie, the kid next door; and many of your old friends. Next week you'll learn more about Johnnie at the Army Air Forces Air Service Command at Patterson Field, Dayton, Ohio. Be with us again next Saturday, same time, same station. This program is produced by Major Frank Healey, directed by Sergeant George Voutsas, written by Private First Class Paul Huston and came to you from New York City. This is the National Broadcasting Company.

The parts of Johnnie and Sergeant Experience were played by Pfc. Joseph Shulman and Don Douglas.

16Oct43 (Sat) 6:00-6:30PM EWT WEAF, NBC Vanderbilt Theatre, New York, New York
I SUSTAIN THE WINGS broadcast   Audience

THE ARMY AIR CORPS (opening fanfare)
2nd Lt. Donald P. Briggs: "I Sustain the Wings."
I SUSTAIN THE WINGS (opening theme)
  2nd Lt. Donald P. Briggs: "I Sustain the Wings," presented by the Army Air Forces
    Training Command. Each week this program features the band from the Army Air Forces
    School at Yale University; Captain Glenn Miller; Corporal Ray McKinley; Johnnie, the
    kid next door; and many of your old friends. And now Captain Glenn Miller.
Captain Glenn Miller: Thank you, Lieutenant Don Briggs, and good evening, everybody.
  Tonight's program salutes the Army Air Forces Air Service Command at Patterson Field,
  Dayton, Ohio, Major General Walter H. Frank, commanding general. Well, now the boys in
  the band are ready and waitin', so first off "It Must Be Jelly 'cause Jam Don't Shake
  Like That."
IT MUST BE JELLY ('Cause Jam Don't Shake Like That)
  Chant by the Ensemble
HOW SWEET YOU ARE
  Captain Glenn Miller: And now a newcomer to our program, a lad with a swell voice, we
    think. Private First Class Johnny Desmond sings the currently popular "How Sweet You
    Are."
  Vocal refrain by Private First Class Johnny Desmond
2nd Lt. Donald P. Briggs: Our footsteps echo back from the walls of this giant warehouse
  as we walk down its main corridor together, Johnnie and I. You know Johnnie. Yeah, I
  thought so. Sure, he's the kid that used to live next door to you, the kid who used to
  deliver your groceries from the corner store and made you wait while he stopped to play
  marbles with the other kids. Yeah, well, today he's not stopping for marbles or
  anything else. He's delivering far more important things than groceries. He's one of
  the huge organization of men and women, soldiers and civilians, known as the Air Service
  Command of the Army Air Forces. A soldier in coveralls whose job it is to supply
  America's planes with everything they need to keep flying and to keep fighting.
  This vast warehouse we're walking through is Johnnie's workshop here at Patterson Field,
  Dayton, Ohio, headquarters of the Air Service Command. Stretching off on every side of
  us as we walk along are rows upon rows of shelves, jam-packed clear to the high roof,
  with rivets, ah, engine parts, instruments, maintenance equipment of every description,
  for servicing and repairing all the one hundred and forty-three types of aircraft made
  in this country. Ah, let - let's stop here a minute, the shelf on the left. Ah, ah,
  hand me that box, Johnnie. Yeah, thanks. Here's a cotter key no more than an inch in
  length. Now come on over here. Yeah, come right along. Yeah, right here. Take a look
  at these. Heh, they're bigger, aren't they? Yes, sir, brake assemblies for America's
  giant B-24s, so big they need a two-foot shelf for each one. Yes, there's everything
  here and that's only a sample of all the different parts handled by the Air Service
  Command. Over 400,000 pieces of equipment, ten times the number of items you'll find in
  the largest mail order catalog.
  Now where do you suppose all this material comes from? Well, Johnnie can tell you. It
  comes from everywhere. It's the product of American ingenuity and toil. It comes from
  the busy assembly lines of our great war factories with their whirring motors and
  pounding machines by the thousands. Yes, and it comes, too, from the little shops in
  every corner of the land, where a handful of workers bend over one or two machines.
  From the little garage on the outskirts of town, now converted into a miniature factory
  where dad works the lathe, mom sorts the rivets, sis keeps the books and Bud handles the
  metal press after he gets home from high school each day.
  Yes, from everywhere they come, thousands of plane parts, a mighty river of material
  flowing into this mighty warehouse of Johnnie's to be distributed by the Air Service
  Command to its network of depots and sub-depots all over the world as replacement parts
  for America's fighters and bombers. Their destination? Huh, anywhere and everywhere.
  Wherever Uncle Sam's planes sweep the skies. Over the frozen islands of the Aleutians
  an American bomber comes limping home to its base, its motors coughing like a wounded
  sea lion. Over the green hills of central Italy four German fighters tear the tail
  assembly of a P-47 to shreds. Over an American base in New Guinea Japan bombers blast a

hangar, ripping the wing from a Flying Fortress. From every battlefront calls for help come back to Johnnie and his fellow workers in the Air Service Command.

Voice: Plane grounded. Must have spare parts immediately. Send at once. Urgent.

2nd Lt. Donald P. Briggs: Instantly the tremendous organization of the Air Service Command moves into action. There's not a second to be wasted. At top speed the needed supplies are collected at the warehouse, where trucks are waiting to take them on their way. Faster, driver, faster. Somewhere the air crew of a bomber is waiting for those parts, counting the minutes until they arrive. No time to stop for a cup of coffee this trip. Keep 'em rolling, mister. A train's waiting for you at the station.

Pour on the steam, engineer. Pour it on. You're routed straight through, war department orders. Yes, and there's a ship waiting for you at the dock, waiting for that precious freight that you've got aboard.

Hurry it up, Captain. More speed. Over on the other shore of that ocean there's a transport plane waiting for you, it's engines idling, ready to carry to their destination those big boxes marked "Rush -- Air Service Command." Full speed ahead, Captain.

At a foreign port the equipment is quickly unloaded with an Air Service Command officer supervising the job. Then it's rushed to an airfield where it's loaded on the transport plane and an hour or so later at a bomber base it's being fitted on to the wounded bomber by the ground crew and Air Service Command technicians. Tomorrow or the next day those parts that we saw in Johnnie's warehouse may be flying in a bomber over enemy territory, dealing destruction to Nazis or Japs and helping to win the war of the air, thanks to the Air Service Command.

We're back in the warehouse. Johnnie works on, delivering the goods and proud of the fact that he, he is a vital cog in the biggest supply and maintenance organization in the world. Ha, it's a big organization, it has to be, for the Air Service Command furnishes supplies for all Army Air Force planes everywhere. It repairs, overhauls and rebuilds these same planes here and overseas. It trains the personnel needed for its specialized supply and maintenance jobs. It prepares American and Lend-Lease planes for shipment overseas and it operates the new 39th Air Freight Wing, which handles all Air Service Command freight as well as air shipments for all agencies of the war department within the continent, carrying millions of pounds of air freight monthly.

Incidental music

2nd Lt. Donald P. Briggs: No obstacle is too great for the Air Service Command to overcome. No job is too big for Johnnie. Whether it's warm jackets for our airmen in the Arctic, propellers for a grounded plane in Burma, jungle kits for a bomber squadron in the South Pacific, Johnnie'll get 'em there, yes, sir, keeping always in mind the slogan of the Air Service Command, "the right part, in the right place, at the right time."

Captain Glenn Miller: And now here are the "Tail End Charlies" to play "Hallelujah!"

HALLELUJAH! (quartet: Powell, Mastren, Alpert, McKinley and string section)

Captain Glenn Miller: And now it's medley time, a serenade for the mothers, wives and sweethearts of the officers and enlisted men at Air Service Command headquarters in Dayton, Ohio. Here's something old, something new, something borrowed and something blue. The old song, Kreisler's "Old Refrain."

THE OLD REFRAIN (Old tune)

Captain Glenn Miller: Something new, Private First Class Johnny Desmond sings "Blue Rain."

BLUE RAIN (New tune)

Vocal refrain by Private First Class Johnny Desmond

Captain Glenn Miller: The song we borrow is one of Jerome Kern's best, from the hit show "Roberta," "Smoke Gets in Your Eyes."

(When Your Heart's on Fire) SMOKE GETS IN YOUR EYES (Borrowed tune)

Captain Glenn Miller: Last in our medley, something blue, "Blue Again."

BLUE AGAIN (Blue tune)

2nd Lt. Donald P. Briggs: Are you a young man of seventeen? Then this message is for you. Today it's possible [for young men of seventeen to volunteer] in the Army Air Forces Enlisted Reserve. Fellows, listen to this. By enrolling now you have ...

Young man: Hey, Joe. Did you hear that?

Joe: Yeah, say, I didn't know a fellow like you or me, only seventeen, could get in the Air Forces.

Young man: Why sure, I read about it just the other day. You just enlist in the Army Air Forces Enlisted Reserve and if they accept you you get to wear a silver wings insignia on your lapel. And after you're eighteen you're called for regular cadet training as a pilot, navigator or bombardier.

Joe: That's what I've always wanted to do, get in the Air Forces. I'm going to ask my folks about it tonight.

Young man: Yeah, me too. Hey, turn that radio up a little, will you?

2nd Lt. Donald P. Briggs: Remember, the Army Air Forces Enlisted Reserve gives you a chance to do your share in winning the war. It gives you training for a future in aviation, training you might otherwise not be able to afford. So, if you're not employed in war production, visit any post office, Aviation Cadet Board or Army Recruiting Office and find out how you can enroll now in the Army Air Forces Enlisted Reserve. Do it today.

THE ARMY AIR CORPS

Captain Glenn Miller: Tomorrow, October 17th, is the second anniversary of the activation of the Air Service Command as a separate command of the Army Air Forces. So today we of the Army Air Forces Training Command salute this important division of the service and we extend our congratulations to its commanding general, Major General Walter H. Frank, for 300,000 civilian employees of the Air Service Command. And for its tens of thousands of officers and enlisted men delivering supplies for P-40s in China, repairing Fortresses in England, servicing our Army Air Force planes everywhere in the world, we play "The Air Corps" song.

Vocal refrain by the Glee Club

I SUSTAIN THE WINGS (closing theme)

2nd Lt. Donald P. Briggs: "I Sustain the Wings" has presented the band from the Army Air Forces Technical School at Yale University; Captain Glenn Miller; Corporal Ray McKinley; Johnnie, the kid next door; and many of your old friends. Next week you'll learn more about Johnnie at the Army Air Forces Training School at Chanute Field, Illinois. Be with us again next Saturday, same time, same station. This program is written and produced entirely by soldiers of the Army Air Forces and came to you from New York City.

2nd Lt. Donald P. Briggs: This is the National Broadcasting Company

The parts of Voice, Joe and Young man were played by Pfc. Joseph Shulman and another member of the band.

16Oct43 (Sat) 11:30PM-Midnight EWT WEAF, NBC Vanderbilt Theatre, New York, New York
I SUSTAIN THE WINGS broadcast   Audience

THE ARMY AIR CORPS (opening fanfare)
2nd Lt. Donald P. Briggs: "I Sustain the Wings."
I SUSTAIN THE WINGS (opening theme)
  2nd Lt. Donald P. Briggs: "I Sustain the Wings," presented by the Army Air Forces
    Training Command. Each week this program features the band from the Army Air Forces
    School at Yale University; Captain Glenn Miller; Corporal Ray McKinley; Johnnie, the
    kid next door; and many of your old friends. And now Captain Glenn Miller.
Captain Glenn Miller: Thank you, Lieutenant Don Briggs, and good evening, everybody.
  Tonight's program salutes the Army Air Forces Air Service Command at Patterson Field,
  Dayton, Ohio, Major General Walter H. Frank, commanding general. Well, now the boys in
  the band are ready and waitin', so first off "It Must Be Jelly 'cause Jam Don't Shake
  Like That."
IT MUST BE JELLY ('Cause Jam Don't Shake Like That)
  Chant by the Ensemble
HOW SWEET YOU ARE
  Captain Glenn Miller: And now a newcomer to our program, a lad with a swell voice, we
    think. Private First Class Johnny Desmond sings the currently popular "How Sweet You
    Are."
  Vocal refrain by Private First Class Johnny Desmond
2nd Lt. Donald P. Briggs: Our footsteps echo back from the walls of this giant warehouse
  as we walk down its main corridor together, Johnnie and I. You know Johnnie. Yeah, I
  thought so. Sure, he's the kid that used to live next door to you, the kid who used to
  deliver your groceries from the corner store and made you wait while he stopped to play
  marbles with the other kids. But today he's not stopping for marbles or anything else,
  no, sir. He's delivering far more important things than groceries. He's one of the
  huge organization of men and women, soldiers and civilians, known as the Air Service
  Command of the Army [Air Forces. A soldier in coveralls whose job it is to supply
  America's planes with everything they need to keep flying and to keep fighting.
  This vast warehouse we're walking through is Johnnie's workshop here at Patterson Field,
  Dayton, Ohio, headquarters of the Air Service Command. Stretching off on every side of
  us as we walk along are rows upon rows of shelves, jam-packed clear to the high roof,
  with rivets, engine parts, instruments, maintenance equipment of every description, for
  servicing and repairing all the one hundred and forty-three types of aircraft made in
  this country. Stop here a minute, at this shelf on the left. Hand me that box,
  Johnnie. Here's a cotter key no more than an inch in length. And now come over here.
  Look at these. A bit bigger, aren't they? Brake assemblies for America's giant B-24s,
  so big they need a two-foot shelf for each one. Yes, there's everything here and that's
  only a sample of all the different parts handled by the Air Service Command. Over
  400,000 pieces of equipment, ten times the number of items you'll find in the largest
  mail order catalog.
  Now where do you suppose all this material comes from? Well, Johnnie can tell you. It
  comes from everywhere. It's the product of American ingenuity and toil. It comes from
  the busy assembly lines of our great war factories with their whirring motors and
  pounding machines by the thousands. And it comes, too, from the little shops in every
  corner of the land, where a handful of workers bend over one or two machines. From the
  little garage on the outskirts of town, now converted into a miniature factory where dad
  works the lathe, mom sorts rivets, sis keeps the books and Bud handles the metal press
  after he gets home from high school each day.
  From everywhere they come, thousands of plane parts, a mighty river of material flowing
  into this mighty warehouse of Johnnie's to be distributed by the Air Service Command to
  its network of depots and sub-depots all over the world as replacement parts for
  America's fighters and bombers. Their destination? Anywhere and everywhere. Wherever
  Uncle Sam's planes sweep the skies. Over the frozen islands of the Aleutians an
  American bomber comes limping home to its base, its motors coughing like a wounded sea
  lion. Over the green hills of central Italy four German fighters tear the tail assembly
  of a P-47 to shreds. Over an American base in New Guinea Jap bombers blast a hangar,

ripping the wing from a Flying Fortress. From every battlefront calls for help come
back to Johnnie and his fellow workers in the Air Service Command.
Voice: Plane grounded. Must have spare parts at once. Send immediately. Urgent.
2nd Lt. Donald P. Briggs: Instantly the tremendous organization of the Air Service
  Command moves into action. There's not a second to be wasted. At top speed the needed
  supplies are collected at the warehouse, where trucks are waiting to take them on their
  way. Faster, driver. Somewhere the air crew of a bomber is waiting for those parts,
  counting the minutes 'til they arrive. No time to stop for a cup of coffee this trip.
  Keep 'em rolling. The train is waiting for you at the station.
  Pour on the steam, engineer. Pour it on. You're routed straight through, war
  department orders. There's a ship waiting for you at the dock, waiting for that
  precious freight that you've got aboard.
  Hurry it up, Captain. More speed. Over on the other shore of that ocean there's a
  transport plane waiting for you, it's engines idling, ready to carry to their
  destination those big boxes marked "Rush -- Air Service Command." Full speed ahead,
  Captain.
  At a foreign port the equipment is quickly unloaded with an Air Service Command officer
  supervising the job. Then it's rushed to an airfield where it's loaded on the transport
  plane and an hour or so later at a bomber base it's being fitted on to the wounded
  bomber by the ground crew and Air Service Command technicians. Tomorrow or the next day
  those parts that we saw in Johnnie's warehouse may be flying in a bomber over enemy
  territory, dealing destruction to Nazis or Japs and helping to win the war of the air,
  thanks to the Air Service Command.
  Back in the warehouse, Johnnie works on, delivering the goods, proud of the fact that he
  is a vital cog in the biggest supply and maintenance organization in the world. It's a
  big organization, it has to be, for the Air Service Command furnishes supplies for all
  Army Air Force planes everywhere. It repairs, overhauls and rebuilds these same planes
  here and overseas. It trains the personnel needed for its specialized supply and
  maintenance jobs. It prepares American and Lend-Lease planes for shipment overseas and
  it operates the new 39th Air Freight Wing, which handles all Air Service Command freight
  as well as air shipments for all agencies of the war department within the continent,
  carrying millions of pounds of air freight monthly.
Incidental music
  2nd Lt. Donald P. Briggs: No obstacle is too great for the Air Service Command to
    overcome. No job is too big for Johnnie. Whether it's warm jackets for our airmen in
    the Arctic, propellers for a grounded plane in Burma, jungle kits for a bomb squadron
    in the South Pacific, Johnnie will get them there, keeping always in mind the slogan
    of the Air Service Command, "the right part, in the right place, at the right time."
Captain Glenn Miller: And now here's the "Tail End Charlies" with "Hallelujah!"]
HALLELUJAH! (quartet: Powell, Mastren, Alpert, McKinley and string section)
Captain Glenn Miller: And now it's medley time, and that means a serenade for the
  mothers, wives and sweethearts of the officers and enlisted men at Air Service Command
  headquarters in Dayton, Ohio. Here's something old, something new, something borrowed
  and something blue. The old song, Kreisler's "Old Refrain."
THE OLD REFRAIN (Old tune)
  Captain Glenn Miller: For something new, Private First Class Johnny Desmond sings "Blue
    Rain."
BLUE RAIN (New tune)
  Vocal refrain by Private First Class Johnny Desmond
  Captain Glenn Miller: The song we borrow is one of Jerome Kern's best, from the hit
    show "Roberta," "Smoke Gets in Your Eyes."
(When Your Heart's on Fire) SMOKE GETS IN YOUR EYES (Borrowed tune)
  Captain Glenn Miller: Last in our medley, something blue, "Blue Again."
BLUE AGAIN (Blue tune)
2nd Lt. Donald P. Briggs: Are you a young man of seventeen? Then this message is for
  you. Today it's possible for young men of seventeen to volunteer in the Army Air Forces
  Enlisted Reserve. Fellows, listen to this. By enrolling now you have ...
Young man: Hey, Joe. Did you hear that?
Joe: Yeah, say, I didn't know a fellow like you or me, only seventeen, could get in the
  Air Forces.

Young man: Sure, I read about it just the other day. You just enlist in the Army Air
  Forces Enlisted [Reserve. Then if they accept you you get to wear a silver wings
  insignia on your lapel. And after eighteen you're called for regular cadet training as
  a pilot, navigator or bombardier.
Joe: Boy! That's something! Just what I've always wanted to do, get in the Air Force.
  I'm going to ask my folks about it tonight.
Young man: Me too. Hey, turn up the radio a little!
2nd Lt. Donald P. Briggs: So remember, the Army Air Forces Enlisted Reserve gives you a
  chance to do your share in winning the war. It gives you training for a future in
  aviation, training you might otherwise never be able to afford. So, if you're not
  employed in war production, visit any post office, Aviation Cadet Board or Army
  Recruiting Office and find out how you can enroll now in the Army Air Forces Enlisted
  Reserve. Do it today.]

THE ARMY AIR CORPS
  Captain Glenn Miller: Tomorrow, October 17th, is the second anniversary of the
  activation of the Air Service Command as a separate command of the Army Air Forces.
  So today we of the Army Air Forces Technical Command salute this important division of
  the service and we extend our congratulations to its commanding general, Major General
  Walter H. Frank, for 300,000 civilian employees of the Air Service Command. And for
  its tens of thousands of officers and enlisted men delivering supplies for the P-40s
  in China, repairing Fortresses in England, servicing our Army Air Force planes
  everywhere in the world, we play "The Air Corps" song.
  Vocal refrain by the Glee Club

I SUSTAIN THE WINGS (closing theme)
  2nd Lt. Donald P. Briggs: "I Sustain the Wings" has presented the band from the Army
  Air Forces Technical School at Yale University; Captain Glenn Miller; Corporal Ray
  McKinley; Johnnie, the kid next door; and many of your old friends. Next week you'll
  learn more about Johnnie at the Army Air Forces Training School at Chanute Field,
  Illinois. Be with us again next Saturday, same time, same station. This program is
  written and produced entirely by soldiers of the Army Air Forces and came to you from
  New York City.
2nd Lt. Donald P. Briggs: This is the National Broadcasting Company

The parts of Voice, Joe and Young man were played by Pfc. Joseph Shulman and another
member of the band.

23Oct43 (Sat) 6:00-6:30PM EWT WEAF, NBC Vanderbilt Theatre, New York, New York
  I SUSTAIN THE WINGS broadcast   Audience

THE ARMY AIR CORPS (opening fanfare)
2nd Lt. Donald P. Briggs: "I Sustain the Wings."
I SUSTAIN THE WINGS (opening theme)
  2nd Lt. Donald P. Briggs: "I Sustain the Wings," presented by the Army Air Forces
    Training Command. Each week this program features the band from the Army Air Forces
    Technical School at Yale University; Captain Glenn Miller; Corporal Ray McKinley;
    Johnnie, the kid next door; and many of your old friends. And now Captain Glenn
    Miller.
Captain Glenn Miller: Thank you, Lieutenant Don Briggs, and good evening, everybody.
    Tonight's program salutes the Army Air Forces Technical School at Chanute Field out in
    Rantoul, Illinois, Brigadier General R. E. O'Neill, commanding general. Now, musically
    the big guns in the brass section open up with "I Hear You Screamin'."
I HEAR YOU SCREAMIN'
MY HEART TELLS ME (Should I Believe My Heart?)
  [Captain Glenn Miller: Next, a new tune sung by Private First Class Johnny Desmond, "My
    Heart Tells Me."
  Vocal refrain by Private First Class Johnny Desmond
Pfc. Joseph Shulman: Skipper! Jerries! A whole flock of 'em at eight o'clock!
Pvt. Murray Kane (as Pilot 1): This is it, boys! I'm climbing to stay on top of 'em.
  Nice going, Charlie. That's one less to worry ...
Pfc. Joseph Shulman: Skipper! The other side, another formation, waiting for us!
Pvt. Murray Kane: Chalk one up for Jerry, men, we're afire! Prepare to abandon ship.
  Hit the silk! O.K., boys, here we go.
2nd Lt. Donald P. Briggs: Yes, there they go! Their lives hanging on a silken thread, a
    silken thread fashioned from the equivalent of four hundred and forty-four pairs of silk
    stockings, fashioned into a parachute! "Parachute," that's a nice sounding word, but it
    has a much nicer sound to the pilot that has to use it when he is forced to abandon his
    stricken ship. To him it means "another chance," another chance to fly and fight! And
    many an American eagle is living to fly again, and to fight again, because a parachute
    bit the air and brought him safely to earth, a parachute rigged by calm and steady
    hands, hands that belong to Johnnie; Johnnie, the kid next door. You remember him.
    He's the boy who cut your grass a couple of years ago so he could earn enough money to
    take your daughter, Dorothy, to the senior prom. You got a kick out of the way he
    finagled that ticket out of you, and you wondered then what he'd be like when he grew
    up. Well, he's grown up now. He's a man doing a man-sized job. He's thousands of men
    doing thousands of different important jobs. He's every man being trained by the Army
    Air Forces Training Command to keep our planes in the air, flying them or fixing them.
    Yes, Johnnie's one of that unbeatable trio, the plane, the air crew, the ground crew,
    each indispensable to the other. As one of the ground crew, Johnnie's rigging the
    parachutes and testing life rafts, learning to make good his slogan:
Sgt. David Ross (as Johnnie): We bring 'em back!
2nd Lt. Donald P. Briggs: And Johnnie will bring them back with his trade that has meant
    the difference between life and death to thousands of airmen. He's learning the fine
    points of parachute rigging in the oldest Training Command school in the country, the
    grand-daddy of them all, Chanute Field, Illinois! Let's go see Johnnie and try to pick
    up a few of his tricks of the trade. We'll find him in the packing room.
Sgt. David Ross: ... 22, 23, 24. O.K. on all shroud lines.
2nd Lt. Donald P. Briggs: This is the packing room and over there in the far corner are
    the sewing machines. Notice those big tables. I'll bet they're the longest, smoothest
    tables you've ever seen. What a place for a banquet! But wait a minute, nobody'll be
    eating off those tables, they're for something much more important. That's where they
    pack the parachutes. The tables are each forty feet long so the 'chute can be stretched
    out to its full length. And that high wax polish, glistening like a cadet's belt
    buckle, is to make sure they're absolutely free of any splinters or rough spots that
    would cause even the slightest rip, a rip or a tear that might spill wind and make the
    parachute useless. And look at those great big parachutes in the corner. Aren't they
    huge? Well, those are the cargo and ammunition 'chutes, made out of heavy rayon.

They'll float down a load of hundreds of pounds. But Johnnie can tell you more about parachutes than I can. Let's get over and talk to him.

Pfc. Joseph Shulman (as pilot 2): Hey, where is he? Where is that guy?

2nd Lt. Donald P. Briggs: Oh, oh. Looks like someone else has the same idea.

Sgt. David Ross: Where is who?

Pfc. Joseph Shulman: The man who packed 'chute number 389-81.

Sgt. David Ross: 389- ? I guess I'm the guy you're looking for. What's wrong?

Pfc. Joseph Shulman: Nothing's wrong, but this is for you!

Sgt. David Ross: A box of cigars! What's the idea?

Pfc. Joseph Shulman: Brother! I just had to use that 'chute!

2nd Lt. Donald P. Briggs: Go on, Johnnie, take the cigars! They're yours. You deserve them.

Incidental music

2nd Lt. Donald P. Briggs: And you've earned more than that, you've earned the thanks of every pilot and crew member that ever had to "hit the silk." They're not kidding when one of them says, "My life is in your hands." Those boys call you and the other parachute riggers the "last chance" department, but they really mean "another chance," because you, Johnnie, give them that other chance when they can use it most, when the going is toughest. They're all depending on you, Johnnie, so pack that 'chute carefully. See that each fold is in its proper place, that each shroud line is folded just right. Packing is delicate work, Johnnie, almost like sleight of hand. You've got to be steady. You can't force that tremendous mass of silk into that little pack, you've got to fit it in, just so! Carelessness would be criminal in your job, Johnnie, because if you made one mistake it would be the last mistake for another man! You've got to ...

2nd Lt. Donald P. Briggs: ... know your job, to do your part in keeping alive Chanute Field's proudest record:

Sgt. David Ross: Of all the thousands of parachutes handled by men from Chanute Field, no failure has ever been traced to a bad pack!

2nd Lt. Donald P. Briggs: A fine record, Johnnie. But remember this, packing parachutes isn't your only job, you're going to have to sew them. And besides parachutes, you'll be packing emergency kits for the air crew, kits that contain all the necessities for an air man forced down in any part of the world, whether it be the jungles of Burma, the icy floes of Alaska, or the hot desert of Africa. Yes, Johnnie, you'll be taking care of everything that "brings 'em back," Mae Wests, rubber life rafts, flares that burn for forty seconds even after they hit the water! These and other things like them make your job an important one, Johnnie. They may call you a "parachute rigger," but you're really an "aerial life-saver."

Incidental music

2nd Lt. Donald P. Briggs: So, you see, Johnnie, a lot depends on you, an awful lot. Your work is going to save the most precious cargoes ever carried in the air, Uncle Sam's pilots and crew men! You'll be making every effort, day after day, to see that your kind of life insurance pays off, any time it's needed. Yes, Johnnie, with you on the job, hundreds of fallen eagles will live to soar again and smash their way straight to the heart of the enemy, wherever he may be found! They're counting on you, Johnnie, counting on you to "bring 'em back!"

Captain Glenn Miller: Here's an old-timer that hits the war picture very well these days, especially with our Russian friends beating it out as they are. The tune, "The Volga Boatmen."

SONG OF THE VOLGA BOATMEN]

Captain Glenn Miller: And now it's medley time, a serenade for the mothers, wives and sweethearts of the officers and enlisted men out at Chanute Field. Here's something old, something new, something borrowed, something blue. The old song, "Sweet and Low."

SWEET AND LOW (Old tune)

Captain Glenn Miller: Something new, P.F.C. Johnny Desmond sings "In the Blue of Evening."

IN THE BLUE OF EVENING (New tune)

Vocal refrain by Private First Class Johnny Desmond

Captain Glenn Miller: We borrow a swell tune from our old friend Duke Ellington, "Things Ain't What They Used to Be."

THINGS AIN'T WHAT THEY USED TO BE (Borrowed tune)
    Captain Glenn Miller: Last in our medley something blue, "A Blues Serenade."
A BLUES SERENADE (Blue tune)
[2nd Lt. Donald P. Briggs: "Keeping 'Em Flying," is not just a "man's job" these days,
    it's a job that many women are helping with, too, in the Air WACs, the Army Air Forces
    branch of the Women's Army Corps! Why don't you join them? The Army Air Forces offer
    you over a hundred specialized jobs to choose from, all of them interesting, and all of
    them indispensable, such jobs as stenographers, control tower operators, clerks, and
    photographers. You can get full information at your nearest Army Recruiting Station.
    Talk to the WAC officer there. She'll be glad to help you select the job you feel best
    qualified to fill. Do it now! The opportunities are many, the need is great! Help
    "Keep 'Em Flying" as an Air WAC, in the Army Air Forces! And now here's Captain Miller.
Captain Glenn Miller: There's a popular song going the rounds today, all about what a
    foot-soldier does in the Army. We've changed the words around in a few spots to make it
    fit the Air Corps. The Crew Chiefs and "What Do You Do in the Infantry."
WHAT DO YOU DO IN THE INFANTRY
    Vocal refrain by the Crew Chiefs
I SUSTAIN THE WINGS (closing theme)
    2nd Lt. Donald P. Briggs: "I Sustain the Wings" has presented the band from the Army
        Air Forces Technical School at Yale University; Captain Glenn Miller; Corporal Ray
        McKinley; Johnnie, the kid next door; and many of your old friends. Next week you'll
        learn more about Johnnie at the Army Air Forces Training Command Gunnery School at
        Tyndall Field, Panama City, Florida. Be with us again next Saturday, same time, same
        station. This program is written and produced entirely by soldiers of the Army Air
        Forces, and came to you from New York City.
2nd Lt. Donald P. Briggs: This is the National Broadcasting Company.]

23Oct43 (Sat) 11:30PM-Midnight EWT WEAF, NBC Vanderbilt Theatre, New York, New York
  I SUSTAIN THE WINGS broadcast   Audience

THE ARMY AIR CORPS (opening fanfare)
2nd Lt. Donald P. Briggs: "I Sustain the Wings."
I SUSTAIN THE WINGS (opening theme)
  2nd Lt. Donald P. Briggs: "I Sustain the Wings," presented by the Army Air Forces
    Training Command. Each week this program features the band from the Army Air Forces
    Technical School at Yale University; Captain Glenn Miller; Corporal Ray McKinley;
    Johnnie, the kid next door; and many of your old friends. And now Captain Glenn
    Miller.
Captain Glenn Miller: Thank you, Lieutenant Don Briggs, and good evening, everybody.
  This evening's program salutes the Army Air Forces Technical School at Chanute Field,
  Rantoul, Ill - Illinois, Brigadier General R. E. O'Neill is the commanding general. And
  now, musically the big guns in the brass section open up with "I Hear You Screamin'."
I HEAR YOU SCREAMIN'
MY HEART TELLS ME (Should I Believe My Heart?)
  Captain Glenn Miller: Next, a new tune sung by Private First Class Johnny Desmond, "My
    Heart Tells Me."
  Vocal refrain by Private First Class Johnny Desmond
[Pfc. Joseph Shulman: Skipper! Jerries! A whole flock of 'em at eight o'clock!
Pvt. Murray Kane (as Pilot 1): This is it, boys! I'm climbing to stay on top of 'em.
  Nice going, Charlie. That's one less to worry ...
Pfc. Joseph Shulman: Skipper! The other side, another formation, waiting for us!
Pvt. Murray Kane: Chalk one up for Jerry, men, we're afire! Prepare to abandon ship.
  Hit the silk! O.K., boys, here we go.
2nd Lt. Donald P. Briggs: Yes, there they go! Their lives hanging on a silken thread, a
  silken thread fashioned from the equivalent of four hundred and forty-four pairs of silk
  stockings, fashioned into a parachute! "Parachute," that's a nice sounding word, but it
  has a much nicer sound to the pilot that has to use it when he is forced to abandon his
  stricken ship. To him it means "another chance," another chance to fly and fight! And
  many an American eagle is living to fly again, and to fight again, because a parachute
  bit the air and brought him safely to earth, a parachute rigged by calm and steady
  hands, hands that belong to Johnnie; Johnnie, the kid next door. You remember him.
  He's the boy who cut your grass a couple of years ago so he could earn enough money to
  take your daughter, Dorothy, to the senior prom. You got a kick out of the way he
  finagled that ticket out of you, and you wondered then what he'd be like when he grew
  up. Well, he's grown up now. He's a man doing a man-sized job. He's thousands of men
  doing thousands of different important jobs. He's every man being trained by the Army
  Air Forces Training Command to keep our planes in the air, flying them or fixing them.
  Yes, Johnnie's one of that unbeatable trio, the plane, the air crew, the ground crew,
  each indispensable to the other. As one of the ground crew, Johnnie's rigging the
  parachutes and testing life rafts, learning to make good his slogan:
Sgt. David Ross (as Johnnie): We bring 'em back!
2nd Lt. Donald P. Briggs: And Johnnie will bring them back with his trade that has meant
  the difference between life and death to thousands of airmen. He's learning the fine
  points of parachute rigging in the oldest Training Command school in the country, the
  grand-daddy of them all, Chanute Field, Illinois! Let's go see Johnnie and try to pick
  up a few of his tricks of the trade. We'll find him in the packing room.
Sgt. David Ross: ... 22, 23, 24. O.K. on all shroud lines.
2nd Lt. Donald P. Briggs: This is the packing room and over there in the far corner are
  the sewing machines. Notice those big tables. I'll bet they're the longest, smoothest
  tables you've ever seen. What a place for a banquet! But wait a minute, nobody'll be
  eating off those tables, they're for something much more important. That's where they
  pack the parachutes. The tables are each forty feet long so the 'chute can be stretched
  out to its full length. And that high wax polish, glistening like a cadet's belt
  buckle, is to make sure they're absolutely free of any splinters or rough spots that
  would cause even the slightest rip, a rip or a tear that might spill wind and make the
  parachute useless. And look at those great big parachutes in the corner. Aren't they
  huge? Well, those are the cargo and ammunition 'chutes, made out of heavy rayon.

They'll float down a load of hundreds of pounds. But Johnnie can tell you more about parachutes than I can. Let's get over and talk to him.

Pfc. Joseph Shulman (as pilot 2): Hey, where is he? Where is that guy?

2nd Lt. Donald P. Briggs: Oh, oh. Looks like someone else has the same idea.

Sgt. David Ross: Where is who?

Pfc. Joseph Shulman: The man who packed 'chute number 389-81.

Sgt. David Ross: 389- ? I guess I'm the guy you're looking for. What's wrong?

Pfc. Joseph Shulman: Nothing's wrong, but this is for you!

Sgt. David Ross: A box of cigars! What's the idea?

Pfc. Joseph Shulman: Brother! I just had to use that 'chute!

2nd Lt. Donald P. Briggs: Go on, Johnnie, take the cigars! They're yours. You deserve them.

Incidental music

  2nd Lt. Donald P. Briggs: And you've earned more than that, you've earned the thanks of every pilot and crew member that ever had to "hit the silk." They're not kidding when one of them says, "My life is in your hands." Those boys call you and the other parachute riggers the "last chance" department, but they really mean "another chance," because you, Johnnie, give them that other chance when they can use it most, when the going is toughest. They're all depending on you, Johnnie, so pack that 'chute carefully. See that each fold is in its proper place, that each shroud line is folded just right. Packing is delicate work, Johnnie, almost like sleight of hand. You've got to be steady. You can't force that tremendous mass of silk into that little pack, you've got to fit it in, just so! Carelessness would be criminal in your job, Johnnie, because if you made one mistake it would be the last mistake for another man! You've got to ...

2nd Lt. Donald P. Briggs: ... know your job, to do your part in keeping alive Chanute Field's proudest record:

Sgt. David Ross: Of all the thousands of parachutes handled by men from Chanute Field, no failure has ever been traced to a bad pack!

2nd Lt. Donald P. Briggs: A fine record, Johnnie. But remember this, packing parachutes isn't your only job, you're going to have to sew them. And besides parachutes, you'll be packing emergency kits for the air crew, kits that contain all the necessities for an air man forced down in any part of the world, whether it be the jungles of Burma, the icy floes of Alaska, or the hot desert of Africa. Yes, Johnnie, you'll be taking care of everything that "brings 'em back," Mae Wests, rubber life rafts, flares that burn for forty seconds even after they hit the water! These and other things like them make your job an important one, Johnnie. They may call you a "parachute rigger," but you're really an "aerial life-saver."

Incidental music

  2nd Lt. Donald P. Briggs: So, you see, Johnnie, a lot depends on you, an awful lot. Your work is going to save the most precious cargoes ever carried in the air, Uncle Sam's pilots and crew men! You'll be making every effort, day after day, to see that your kind of life insurance pays off, any time it's needed. Yes, Johnnie, with you on the job, hundreds of fallen eagles will live to soar again and smash their way straight to the heart of the enemy, wherever he may be found! They're counting on you, Johnnie, counting on you to "bring 'em back!"

Captain Glenn Miller: Here's an old-timer that hits the war picture very well these days, especially with our Russian friends beating it out as they are.] The tune, "The Volga Boatmen."

SONG OF THE VOLGA BOATMEN

Captain Glenn Miller: And now it's medley time. That means a serenade for the mothers, wives and sweethearts of the officers and enlisted men at Chanute Field out in Rantoul, Illinois. Here's something old, something new, something borrowed, something blue. The old song, "Sweet and Low."

SWEET AND LOW (Old tune)

  Captain Glenn Miller: Something new, Private First Class Johnny Desmond sings "In the Blue of Evening."

IN THE BLUE OF EVENING (New tune)

  Vocal refrain by Private First Class Johnny Desmond

Captain Glenn Miller: We borrow a swell tune from our old friend Duke Ellington,
  "Things Ain't What They Used to Be."
THINGS AIN'T WHAT THEY USED TO BE (Borrowed tune)
  Captain Glenn Miller: Last in our medley something blue, "A Blues Serenade."
A BLUES SERENADE (Blue tune)
2nd Lt. Donald P. Briggs: "Keeping 'Em Flying," is not just a "man's job" these days.
  No, sir, it's a job that many women are helping with, too, in the [Air WACs, the Army
  Air Forces branch of the Women's Army Corps! Why don't you join them? The Army Air
  Forces offer you over a hundred specialized jobs to choose from, all of them
  interesting, and all of them indispensable, such jobs as stenographers, control tower
  operators, clerks, and photographers. You can get full information at your nearest Army
  Recruiting Station. Talk to the WAC officer there. She'll be glad to help you select
  the job you feel best qualified to fill. Do it now! The opportunities are many, the
  need is great! Help "Keep 'Em Flying" as an Air WAC, in the Army Air Forces! And now
  here's Captain Miller.
Captain Glenn Miller: There's a popular song going the rounds today, all about what a
  foot-soldier does in the Army.] So we've changed the words around in a few spots to
  make it fit the Air Corps, too. The Crew Chiefs and "What Do You Do in the Infantry."
WHAT DO YOU DO IN THE INFANTRY
  Vocal refrain by the Crew Chiefs
I SUSTAIN THE WINGS (closing theme)
  2nd Lt. Donald P. Briggs: "I Sustain the Wings" presented the band from the Army Air
    Forces Technical School at Yale University; Captain Glenn Miller; Johnnie, the kid
    next door; and many of your old friends. Next week you'll learn more about Johnnie at
    the Army Air Forces Training Command Gunnery School at Tyndall Field, Panama City,
    Florida. Be with us again next Saturday, same time, same station. This program is
    written and produced entirely by soldiers of the Army Air Forces, and came to you from
    New York City.
  2nd Lt. Donald P. Briggs: This is the National Broadcasting Company.]

29Oct43 (Fri) 2:00-6:00PM Victor Recording Studio, New York, New York
  V-DISC RECORDING SESSION

VP-264   Breakdown   **SPEECH by Captain Glenn Miller**

            This is Captain Glenn Miller speakin' for the Army Air Forces
            Training Command Orchestra and we hope --- Jesus Christ, what ...

            (Breakdown was caused by something dropping in the background.)

VP-264   D3-MC-286   **SPEECH by Captain Glenn Miller**

            This is Captain Glenn Miller speakin' for the Army Air Forces
            Training Command Orchestra and we hope that you soldiers of the
            Allied Forces enjoy these V-Discs that we're making for you.

30Oct43 (Sat) 6:00-6:30PM EWT WEAF, NBC Vanderbilt Theatre, New York, New York
I SUSTAIN THE WINGS broadcast   Audience

THE ARMY AIR CORPS (opening fanfare)
2nd Lt. Donald P. Briggs: "I Sustain the Wings."
I SUSTAIN THE WINGS (opening theme)
    2nd Lt. Donald P. Briggs: "I Sustain the Wings," presented by the Army Air Forces
        Training Command. Each week this program features the band from the Army Air Forces
        Technical School at Yale University; Captain Glenn Miller; Corporal Ray McKinley;
        Johnnie, the kid next door; and many of your old friends. And now Captain Glenn
        Miller.
Captain Glenn Miller: Thank you, Lieutenant Don Briggs, and good evening, everybody. Men
    who serve in the Army Air Forces Training Command wear a distinctive insignia inscribed
    with the Latin words "Sustineo Alas," meaning "I Sustain the Wings." And that's the
    proud motto of those who keep America's planes in the air and train the men who fly
    them. To these men of the Army Air Forces Training Command, this series of programs is
    dedicated. Today we salute the Army Air Forces Aerial Gunnery School at Tyndall Field,
    Panama City, Florida, Colonel Leland S. Stranathon, commanding officer. This band here,
    being an Air Force outfit, we thought all of you folks might like our arrangement of
    "Keep 'Em Flying." Well, fasten that safety belt, we're takin' off.
KEEP 'EM FLYING
Captain Glenn Miller: And now it's medley time. That means a serenade for the mothers,
    wives and sweethearts of the officers and enlisted men at Tyndall Field. Here's
    something old, something new, something borrowed, something blue. The old song,
    "Londonderry Air."
LONDONDERRY AIR (Old tune)
    Captain Glenn Miller: For something new, the Crew Chiefs sing "Shoo-Shoo Baby."
SHOO-SHOO BABY (New tune)
    Vocal refrain by the Crew Chiefs
    Captain Glenn Miller: We borrow a tune from Jerome Kern's "Swing Time," just "The Way
        You Look To-night."
THE WAY YOU LOOK TO-NIGHT (Borrowed tune)
    Captain Glenn Miller: Last in our medley something blue, "Blue Danube."
BEAUTIFUL BLUE DANUBE (Blue tune)
[2nd Lt. Donald P. Briggs: Ever wonder how it feels like to be a tail gunner in a B-17?
    Twenty thousand feet above good old terra firma? Sitting out there in the tail of a
    plane, like a crow on a limb, with nothing to do but watch the world go by! Well,
    that's Johnnie's job today! Johnnie, the kid next door, the kid who used to knock tin
    cans off the fence with his sling-shot, 'til he broke your kitchen window! Yes, today
    Johnnie's an aerial gunner, one of that unbeatable trio, the plane, the air crew, and
    the ground crew, each indispensable to the other. In fact, he's every young man who has
    been taught to fly, or to "Keep 'Em Flying," by the Army Air Forces Training Command.
    Today as an Aerial Gunner Johnnie's after much bigger game than tin cans on a fence
    post! His targets for today, and tonight, are Zeros and Messerschmitts! Along with
    thousands of other Johnnies in the Army Air Forces, he's bagging plenty of them from his
    perch in the tail of a Flying Fortress! Pretty dull, though, up there for Johnnie right
    now, when the target lies behind him, and the nose of old "Kalamazoo Katie" is pointed
    back toward England. He gets to thinking maybe the rest of the crew up front have gone
    home and left him to bring the tail in alone. So he calls the pilot on the interphone,
    just to hear his own voice.
Johnnie (as Johnnie): Tail gunner to pilot, all clear at this end, sir. You can take
    Johnnie home now.
2nd Lt. Donald P. Briggs: Home! The word home makes you think of a lot of things,
    doesn't it, Johnnie? The folks back in Kansas, for one thing. That girl whose picture
    you carry in your breast pocket, the day you went downtown and joined the Army! The
    morning you arrived at the induction camp! And remember Tyndall? Say, there was a
    field! Right on the edge of the Gulf, it was, near Panama City in Florida. That's
    where you got those silver gunner's wings you wear so proudly! Tyndall Field. Kneeling
    there in the tail of that old B-17, I'll bet you think of those days a lot, that you're
    thinking of them right now.

Johnnie: Good old Tyndall! It seems like only yesterday we climbed off that train at
   Panama City. They put us in the receiving pool. And, man, was it rugged!
2nd Lt. Donald P. Briggs: Oh, it was rugged, Johnnie! No doubt about that! But this
   aerial gunner business is for "men only." Those caliber 50s aren't popguns! No, sir!
   Yes, it was plenty tough those first few days, and it got even tougher when you started
   to school ...
Johnnie: First off, we studied machine guns, then power-operated turrets. And we got
   plenty of practice in learning to sight a gun. Then range work, with skeet guns.
   First, on a regular skeet range, then on a "moving base" range where we fired at clay
   pigeons while riding in the back of an Army truck. No kidding, brother, that moving
   base range had me scared stiff!
2nd Lt. Donald P. Briggs: Scared, Johnnie? No, you were never scared of anything. Just
   worried a little, that's all. As you said, it felt like two fellows shaking hands in
   your stomach when you climbed into the back of that truck, and somebody handed you a
   shotgun. But that was nothing compared to the way you felt when you came to that
   machine gun range! But you managed that all right, everything was going O.K. And what
   a thrill the day you first went up for air-to-air firing out over the Gulf of Mexico,
   the water a million miles below you. The bright sunlight glistening along the barrel of
   the machine gun, in the rear cockpit of the plane you'd been assigned to. And up in the
   front cockpit, you could see the pilot grinning at you in his rear view mirror. Off to
   one side, you could see the target plane, towing a long, white target behind it on a six
   hundred foot cable. Two or three follows in other planes fired first. Then your turn
   came. You fired. Came down, went up again. Fired. Came down. It seemed sort of
   automatic now, didn't it? All at once you felt strangely confident, not nervous
   anymore. Sure of yourself!
Johnnie: Yeah, I was a gunner at last, and they assigned me to "Kalamazoo Katie." What a
   swell bunch of fellas. Hey, what's that? Messerschmitts! Hello, tail gunner to pilot,
   four Messerschmitts coming down on us from behind. I got one! Part of his wing came
   off! Here they come again! Another one down! The others are leaving. All clear, sir.
   Yes, all clear again, and nothing to do but sit out here on the end of nothing, like a
   crow on a limb, watching the world go by. Say, I wonder what the guys back at Tyndall
   are doing?
2nd Lt. Donald P. Briggs: "What are the guys back at Tyndall doing?" Well, Johnnie,
   they're doing just what you did. They're busy learning to be the best aerial gunners
   that ever squeezed a trigger!
I Sustain the Wings (Incidental music)
   2nd Lt. Donald P. Briggs: Yes, Johnnie, the Training Command is making sure that your
      pals and comrades-in-arms, the other Johnnie Aerial Gunners, are getting the know-how
      to make them the quickest and deadliest marksmen in the world. Those Johnnies are
      getting ready for a big job, the job of protecting Uncle Sam's planes and their
      precious crews. And the pilot and the rest of the crew are grateful, Johnnie,
      grateful for your skill and training, because they know that it's the gunner with the
      straightest aim who brings his plane back to fight again! And so, Johnnie, keep those
      guns firing, blast those Zeros and Messerschmitts out of the sky. You're clearing an
      important roadway, Johnnie, a road that leads straight to victory!
Captain Glenn Miller: That was Lieutenant Donald Briggs telling the story for the aerial
   gunnery boys, and right fancy I thought, Lieutenant.
2nd Lt. Donald P. Briggs: Thank you, Captain.
Captain Glenn Miller: And now, the title of the next tune is just what it ain't. Because
   the violins and other stringed instruments have anything but a holiday. It's called
   "Holiday for Strings."
HOLIDAY FOR STRINGS
2nd Lt. Donald P. Briggs: Visit almost any Army Air Base these days, either here or
   overseas, and you'll find women performing many vitally important jobs! Yes, these
   women are Air WACs, that is, they're members of the Women's Army Corps of the Army Air
   Forces. And the work they're doing is mighty valuable. Now, chances are one of the
   jobs they handle is a job that you women can do, too. Maybe you're qualified as a clerk
   or stenographer. Or, then again, maybe you can help operate a control tower, or do
   photographic work. The Air WACs offer you more than a hundred specialized jobs to
   choose from, all of them interesting, and every single one of them indispensable. So

why not visit your nearest Army Recruiting Office, and talk it over with the WAC officer there? She'll tell you how you can play a real part in winning the war, in the Army Air Forces. Join now, and help "Keep 'Em Flying" as an Air WAC! And now Captain Miller.

Captain Glenn Miller: You probably all know by now that "Oklahoma" is the big Broadway show, and here's one of the main reasons, "Oh, What a Beautiful Mornin'" with Private First Class Johnny Desmond to sing it for you.

OH, WHAT A BEAUTIFUL MORNIN'
  Vocal refrain by Private First Class Johnny Desmond

Captain Glenn Miller: And now, here's one for all the "Johnnie Aerial Gunners." To all those kids up in the sky who "Keep 'Em Firin'" we dedicate this next tune, "Guns in the Sky."

GUNS IN THE SKY
  Vocal refrain by Private First Class Johnny Desmond and the Crew Chiefs]

I SUSTAIN THE WINGS (closing theme)
  2nd Lt. Donald P. Briggs: "I Sustain the Wings" has presented the band from the Army Air Forces Technical School at Yale University; Captain Glenn Miller; Corporal Ray McKinley; Johnnie, the kid next door; and many of your old friends. Next week you'll learn more about Johnnie at the Army Air Forces Training Command School at Truax Field, Madison, Wisconsin. Be with us again next Saturday, same time, same station. This program is written and produced entirely by soldiers of the Army Air Forces and came to you from New York City.
[2nd Lt. Donald P. Briggs: This is the National Broadcasting Company.]

The part of Johnnie was played by Sgt. David Ross or Pfc. Joseph Shulman.

30Oct43 (Sat) 11:30PM-Midnight EWT WEAF, NBC Vanderbilt Theatre, New York, New York
  I SUSTAIN THE WINGS broadcast   Audience

THE ARMY AIR CORPS (opening fanfare)
2nd Lt. Donald P. Briggs: "I Sustain the Wings."
I SUSTAIN THE WINGS (opening theme)
  2nd Lt. Donald P. Briggs: "I Sustain the Wings," presented by the Army Air Forces
    Training Command. Each week this program features the band from the Army Air Forces
    Technical School at Yale University; Captain Glenn Miller; Corporal Ray McKinley;
    Johnnie, the kid next door; and many of your old friends. And now Captain Glenn
    Miller.
Captain Glenn Miller: Thank you, Lieutenant Don Briggs, and good evening, everybody. Men
  who serve in the Army Air Forces Training Command wear a distinctive insignia inscribed
  with the Latin words "Sustineo Alas," meaning "I Sustain the Wings." And that's the
  proud motto of those who keep America's planes in the air and train the men who fly
  them. To these men of the Army Air Forces Training Command, this series of programs is
  dedicated. And today we salute the Army Air Forces Aerial Gunnery School at Tyndall
  Field, Panama City, Florida, Colonel Leland S. Stranathon, commanding officer. Now this
  band being an Air Force outfit, we thought all of you folks might like to hear our
  arrangement of "Keep 'Em Flying." Well, fasten on that safety belt, we're takin' off.
KEEP 'EM FLYING
Captain Glenn Miller: And now medley time, a serenade for the mothers, wives and
  sweethearts of the officers and enlisted men at Tyndall Field. [Here's something old,
  something new, something borrowed, something blue. The old song, "Londonderry Air."
LONDONDERRY AIR (Old tune)
  Captain Glenn Miller: For something new, the Crew Chiefs sing "Shoo-Shoo Baby."
SHOO-SHOO BABY (New tune)
  Vocal refrain by the Crew Chiefs
  Captain Glenn Miller: We borrow a tune from Jerome Kern's "Swing Time," just "The Way
    You Look To-night."]
THE WAY YOU LOOK TO-NIGHT (Borrowed tune)
  Captain Glenn Miller: Last in our medley something blue, "Blue Danube."
BEAUTIFUL BLUE DANUBE (Blue tune)
2nd Lt. Donald P. Briggs: Did you ever wonder what it feels like to be a tail gunner on a
  B-17? Twenty thousand feet above good old terra firma? Just sitting out there in the
  tail of the plane, like a crow on a limb, with nothing to do but watch the world go by!
  Well, that's Johnnie's job today! Johnnie, the kid next door, the, the, the, the kid
  who used to knock tin cans off the fence with his sling-shot, ['til he broke your
  kitchen window! Yes, today Johnnie's an aerial gunner, one of that unbeatable trio, the
  plane, the air crew, and the ground crew, each indispensable to the other. In fact,
  he's every young man who has been taught to fly, or to "Keep 'Em Flying," by the Army
  Air Forces Training Command. Today as an Aerial Gunner Johnnie's after much bigger game
  than tin cans on a fence post! His targets for today, and tonight, are Zeros and
  Messerschmitts! Along with thousands of other Johnnies in the Army Air Forces, he's
  bagging plenty of them from his perch in the tail of a Flying Fortress! Pretty dull,
  though, up there for Johnnie right now, when the target lies behind him, and the nose of
  old "Kalamazoo Katie" is pointed back toward England. He gets to thinking maybe the
  rest of the crew up front have gone home and left him to bring the tail in alone. So he
  calls the pilot on the interphone, just to hear his own voice.
Johnnie (as Johnnie): Tail gunner to pilot, all clear at this end, sir. You can take
  Johnnie home now.
2nd Lt. Donald P. Briggs: Home! The word home makes you think of a lot of things,
  doesn't it, Johnnie? The folks back in Kansas, for one thing. That girl whose picture
  you carry in your breast pocket, the day you went downtown and joined the Army! The
  morning you arrived at the induction camp! And remember Tyndall? Say, there was a
  field! Right on the edge of the Gulf, it was, near Panama City in Florida. That's
  where you got those silver gunner's wings you wear so proudly! Tyndall Field. Kneeling
  there in the tail of that old B-17, I'll bet you think of those days a lot, that you're
  thinking of them right now.

Johnnie: Good old Tyndall! It seems like only yesterday we climbed off that train at
   Panama City. They put us in the receiving pool. And, man, was it rugged!
2nd Lt. Donald P. Briggs: Oh, it was rugged, Johnnie! No doubt about that! But this
   aerial gunner business is for "men only." Those caliber 50s aren't popguns! No, sir!
   Yes, it was plenty tough those first few days, and it got even tougher when you started
   to school ...
Johnnie: First off, we studied machine guns, then power-operated turrets. And we got
   plenty of practice in learning to sight a gun. Then range work, with skeet guns.
   First, on a regular skeet range, then on a "moving base" range where we fired at clay
   pigeons while riding in the back of an Army truck. No kidding, brother, that moving
   base range had me scared stiff!
2nd Lt. Donald P. Briggs: Scared, Johnnie? No, you were never scared of anything. Just
   worried a little, that's all. As you said, it felt like two fellows shaking hands in
   your stomach when you climbed into the back of that truck, and somebody handed you a
   shotgun. But that was nothing compared to the way you felt when you came to that
   machine gun range! But you managed that all right, everything was going O.K. And what
   a thrill the day you first went up for air-to-air firing out over the Gulf of Mexico,
   the water a million miles below you. The bright sunlight glistening along the barrel of
   the machine gun, in the rear cockpit of the plane you'd been assigned to. And up in the
   front cockpit, you could see the pilot grinning at you in his rear view mirror. Off to
   one side, you could see the target plane, towing a long, white target behind it on a six
   hundred foot cable. Two or three follows in other planes fired first. Then your turn
   came. You fired. Came down, went up again. Fired. Came down. It seemed sort of
   automatic now, didn't it? All at once you felt strangely confident, not nervous
   anymore. Sure of yourself!
Johnnie: Yeah, I was a gunner at last, and they assigned me to "Kalamazoo Katie." What a
   swell bunch of fellas. Hey, what's that? Messerschmitts! Hello, tail gunner to pilot,
   four Messerschmitts coming down on us from behind. I got one! Part of his wing came
   off! Here they come again! Another one down! The others are leaving. All clear, sir.
   Yes, all clear again, and nothing to do but sit out here on the end of nothing, like a
   crow on a limb, watching the world go by. Say, I wonder what the guys back at Tyndall
   are doing?
2nd Lt. Donald P. Briggs: "What are the guys back at Tyndall doing?" Well, Johnnie,
   they're doing just what you did. They're busy learning to be the best aerial gunners
   that ever squeezed a trigger!
I Sustain the Wings (Incidental music)
   2nd Lt. Donald P. Briggs: Yes, Johnnie, the Training Command is making sure that your
   pals and comrades-in-arms, the other Johnnie Aerial Gunners, are getting the know-how
   to make them the quickest and deadliest marksmen in the world. Those Johnnies are
   getting ready for a big job, the job of protecting Uncle Sam's planes and their
   precious crews. And the pilot and the rest of the crew are grateful, Johnnie,
   grateful for your skill and training, because they know that it's the gunner with the
   straightest aim who brings his plane back to fight again! And so, Johnnie, keep those
   guns firing, blast those Zeros and Messerschmitts out of the sky. You're clearing an
   important roadway, Johnnie, a road that leads straight to victory!
Captain Glenn Miller: That was Lieutenant Donald Briggs telling the story for the aerial
   gunnery boys, and right fancy I thought, Lieutenant.
2nd Lt. Donald P. Briggs: Thank you, Captain.
Captain Glenn Miller: And now, the title of the next tune is just what it ain't. Because
   the violins and other stringed instruments have anything but a holiday. It's called
   "Holiday for Strings."
HOLIDAY FOR STRINGS
2nd Lt. Donald P. Briggs: Visit almost any Army Air Base these days, either here or
   overseas, and you'll find women performing many vitally important jobs! Yes, these
   women are Air WACs, that is, they're members of the Women's Army Corps of the Army Air
   Forces. And the work they're doing is mighty valuable. Now, chances are one of the
   jobs they handle is a job that you women can do, too. Maybe you're qualified as a clerk
   or stenographer. Or, then again, maybe you can help operate a control tower, or do
   photographic work. The Air WACs offer you more than a hundred specialized jobs to
   choose from, all of them interesting, and every single one of them indispensable. So

why not visit your nearest Army Recruiting Office, and talk it over with the WAC officer there? She'll tell you how you can play a real part in winning the war, in the Army Air Forces. Join now, and help "Keep 'Em Flying" as an Air WAC! And now Captain Miller.]
Captain Glenn Miller: Most of you probably know that "Oklahoma" is the big Broadway show, and here's one of the main reasons, "Oh, What a Beautiful Mornin'" with P.F.C. Johnny Desmond to sing it for you.

OH, WHAT A BEAUTIFUL MORNIN'
Vocal refrain by Private First Class Johnny Desmond
Captain Glenn Miller: And now, here's one for all the "Johnnie Aerial Gunners." To all those kids up in the sky who "Keep 'Em Firin'" we dedicate this next tune, it's "Guns in the Sky."

GUNS IN THE SKY
Vocal refrain by Private First Class Johnny Desmond and the Crew Chiefs]
I SUSTAIN THE WINGS (closing theme)
2nd Lt. Donald P. Briggs: "I Sustain the Wings" has presented the band from the Army Air Forces Technical School at Yale University; Captain Glenn Miller; Corporal Ray McKinley; Johnnie, the kid next door; and many of your old friends. Next week you'll learn more about Johnnie at the Army Air Forces Training Command School at Truax Field, Madison, Wisconsin. Be with us again next Saturday, same time, same station. This program is written and produced entirely by soldiers of the Army Air Forces and came to you from New York City. This is the National Broadcasting Company.

The part of Johnnie was played by Sgt. David Ross or Pfc. Joseph Shulman.

04Nov43 (Thu) Yale University, New Haven, Connecticut
  MARCH OF TIME newsreel shots

BLUES IN THE NIGHT MARCH (My Mama Done Tol' Me)
  Captain Glenn Miller: Lieutenant, would you say your men march better to that type of
    music?
  Lieutenant: I certainly would, sir.
  Captain Glenn Miller: What do you think, Briggs?
  2nd Lt. Donald P. Briggs: Well, they're really on the ball today, sir.
  Captain Glenn Miller: And they look good to me, too.

06Nov43 (Sat) NBC, New York, New York
  UNCLE SAM PRESENTS recording

  ...

AMERICAN PATROL
Captain Glenn Miller: Nice goin', boys. And now one of the most popular tunes of any
  season. I'm sure you'll think it's one of your favorites, "Star Dust."
STAR DUST
Captain Glenn Miller: And the last item on this program and I'm afraid you're gonna have
  to guess the title.
PISTOL PACKIN' MAMA
  Vocal refrain by Corporal Ray McKinley and the Crew Chiefs
I SUSTAIN THE WINGS (closing theme)
  Captain Glenn Miller: Well, sir, that winds things up for today. Speaking for the
    band, thanks for all the swell letters you've been sending us and keep 'em comin'.
    When you write ask us for your favorite tunes, we'll be more than glad to play 'em for
    you. You can reach us in care of this station. And now for Lieutenant Don Briggs,
    Corporal Ray McKinley, all the rest of us, so long until next week at the same time.
  2nd Lt. Donald P. Briggs: The Army Air Forces Training Command Band, under the
    direction of Captain Glenn Miller, has come to you from New York City. Don't forget
    tomorrow, same time, same station, "Uncle Sam Presents" another famous service band
    with music from us to you.
HERE WE GO AGAIN (fade-out tune)
  2nd Lt. Donald P. Briggs: This is the United States of America, one of the united
    nations.

06Nov43 (Sat) 6:00-6:30PM EWT WEAF, NBC Vanderbilt Theatre, New York, New York
 I SUSTAIN THE WINGS broadcast   Audience

THE ARMY AIR CORPS (opening fanfare)
2nd Lt. Donald P. Briggs: "I Sustain the Wings."
I SUSTAIN THE WINGS (opening theme)
  2nd Lt. Donald P. Briggs: "I Sustain the Wings," presented by the Army Air Forces
    Training Command Band. Each week this program features the band from the Army Air
    Forces Technical School at Yale University; Corporal Ray McKinley; Captain Glenn
    Miller; Johnnie, the kid next door; and many of your old friends. And now Captain
    Glenn Miller.
Captain Glenn Miller: Thank you, Lieutenant Don Briggs, and good evening, everybody. Men
    who serve in the Army Air Forces Training Command wear a distinctive insignia inscribed
    with the Latin words "Sustineo Alas," meaning "I Sustain the Wings." Now, that's the
    proud motto of those who keep America's planes in the air and train the men who fly
    them. To these men of the A.A.F. Training Command, this series of programs is
    dedicated. And tonight we salute the A.A.F. Technical School at Truax Field, Madison,
    Wisconsin, Brigadier General S. W. Fitzgerald, commanding general. Now in the music
    department Corporal Ray McKinley's waitin' with the big sticks back there to roll off
    for "American Patrol."
AMERICAN PATROL
CAPRICE VIENNOIS (Old tune)
  Captain Glenn Miller: And now it's medley time and that means a serenade for the
    mothers, wives and sweethearts of the officers and enlisted men at Truax Field.
    Here's something old, something new, something borrowed and something blue. The old
    song, Fritz Kreisler's "Caprice Viennois."
  Captain Glenn Miller: Something new, Private Art Malvin sings "Sunday, Monday, or
    Always."
SUNDAY, MONDAY, OR ALWAYS (New tune)
  Vocal refrain by Private First Class Artie Malvin
  Captain Glenn Miller: We borrow Phil Spitalny's theme, "Isle of Golden Dreams."
MY ISLE OF GOLDEN DREAMS (Borrowed tune)
  Captain Glenn Miller: Last in our medley, something blue, the "Birth of the Blues."
BIRTH OF THE BLUES (Blue tune)
Pvt. Murray Kane: Amber Tower, this is Army 5-5-0-7, over.
Sgt. David Ross: Amber Tower, this is Army 7-8-1-0, over.
Voice 3: Amber Tower, this is Army 1-1-3-9, over.
Pfc. Joseph Shulman (as Johnnie): Army 5-5-0-7, this is Amber Tower, over. Army 7-8-1-0,
  wait. Army 1-1-3-9, wait.
Pvt. Murray Kane: Amber tower, this is 5-5-0-7. Seven miles west of your field at four
  thousand feet. Request landing instructions, over.
Pfc. Joseph Shulman: 5-5-0-7, this is Amber Tower. Seven miles west at four thousand,
  traffic to the left at one thousand, land on runway 2-7. Call tower on base leg.
2nd Lt. Donald P. Briggs: That, ah, lingo may not make much sense to you but it sure
  makes sense to a pilot coming into an air field for a landing. Yes, sir, it tells him
  whether or not a runway is clear so that he can come in without crashing into another
  plane. Yeah, those pilots know the meaning of that special control tower language. And
  so does Johnnie. He's the guy who talks their language; Johnnie, the kid next door.
  You remember him. The kid that had put on his Scout uniform and spent the afternoon
  helping the cops untangle a traffic jam. Well, Johnnie's changed that Boy Scout uniform
  for the khaki of Uncle Sam's A.A.F. And Johnnie's a mighty important character. He's
  all the men trained by the Army Air Forces Training Command. And today, as a control
  tower operator, he's one of that unbeatable trio, the plane, the air crew, and the
  ground crew, each indispensable to the other. Well, Johnnie's still directing traffic,
  but it isn't on the ground, no, sir, it's in the air. And that makes the job a lot
  tougher because Johnny has to think in three dimensions instead of two. And in the sky
  every direction of the compass is a roadway. Yes, air traffic over a - a busy landing
  field would be a hopeless mess, a series of accidents, if it weren't for Johnnie sitting
  up there in the control tower, that glassed-in birdcage high up on stilts at the edge of

the airfield, just sitting there cool and competent, looking constantly at the sky and
talking in the ...

Pfc. Joseph Shulman: 5-5-0-7, this is Amber Tower. Seven miles west at four thousand,
traffic to the left at one thousand, land on runway 2-7. Call tower on base leg, over.

Pvt. Murray Kane: Amber Tower, this is 5-5-0-7, wilco.

Pfc. Joseph Shulman: 7-8-1-0, this is Amber Tower. Send your message, over.

Sgt. David Ross: Amber Tower, this is 7-8-1-0, twelve miles east.

Pfc. Paul Huston: Amber Tower, Army 9-9-5-9, port engine on fire, request emergency
landing instructions. I'm six miles east of your field flying at 8-1-8, over.

2nd Lt. Donald P. Briggs: An emergency. But Johnny'll be able to handle it, believe me.
But don't take anything for granted, listen to the facts, with the training he's
received at the A.A.F. Technical School at Truax Field, and judge for yourself. First,
the physical requirements.

Sgt. David Ross: Vision, hearing and speech.

2nd Lt. Donald P. Briggs: They must all be perfect. He must be able to spot planes
quickly and identify them instantly. He's got to be able to hear important details like
height, speed and distance. And his instructions must be spoken clearly and quickly.

Sgt. David Ross: Nerves.

2nd Lt. Donald P. Briggs: Huh, he can't have any. He must remain calm and confident in
any and all emergencies. [Yes, physically and mentally, Johnnie's got to be "right on
the beam." And his course of instruction at Truax Field is plenty tough, too. He got
most of it around a big table, laid out as a miniature air field, complete in every
detail, with planes, floodlights, obstruction lights, boundary markers, buildings in the
area, everything that would meet the eye at a full-scale air field. Around this large
table, each with his individual radio, sit twenty students impersonating arriving
planes, until it comes their turn to man the control tower overlooking the table. This
method is a safety measure, safe because it gives Johnnie plenty of practice without
endangering planes or pilots. And he spends at least ten hours in a Link trainer. He
studies hydraulic landing gears, radio aids to navigation, weather, air traffic
regulations, everything to help the pilot make a safe landing. Yes, Johnnie knows all
about these things, and plenty more besides. And what's more, he's got to have all this
information in his head. He hasn't time to look it up, because, in this 300
mile-an-hour flying game, things happen in a hurry. He must think and act quickly in an
emergency, like the one confronting him now, a plane on fire coming in for a landing,
other planes stacked up at all levels on all legs.

Pfc. Paul Huston: My port engine is on fire! Request emergency landing instructions. Am
six miles east of your field, flying an A-20. Over.

Pfc. Joseph Shulman: All ships in vicinity of Amber Tower traffic pattern, emergency
landing, emergency landing! Clear traffic pattern! Over. Army 9-9-5-9, this is Amber
Tower. Roger. You are cleared to make straight-in approach. Land on runway 2-7.
Over. Press that crash button, Eddie. Now the crash phone. All stations. Emergency
landing on runway twenty-seven. An A-20 with port engine on fire. Emergency landing on
runway twenty-seven. An A-20 with port engine on fire. There she is, Eddie. She's
comin' in mighty fast. Oh - oh! Hello, 9-9-5-9. Your wheels aren't down. Your wheels
aren't down! Over.

Pfc. Paul Huston: Amber Tower, this is 9-9-5-9. Thanks. Roger.

Pfc. Joseph Shulman: That's got it. He's O.K. now. Everything's under control! All
ships in vicinity of Amber Tower, resume your positions. Call tower on base leg. All
ships in ...

2nd Lt. Donald P. Briggs: Everything's under control! And it'll stay that way, Johnnie,
as long as you're there in the control tower, scanning the skies for Uncle Sam's air men
and guiding them to a safe landing.

I Sustain the Wings (Incidental music)

2nd Lt. Donald P. Briggs: It's a big job, Johnnie, one that permits no mistakes.
You've got to bring our planes and their crews safely to Earth on the long landing
strips. You've got to stay on your toes, Johnnie, because if you fall asleep, even
for one second, some other fellow may sleep for a very long time. But you know that,
and the pilot knows that you know it. He know, too, that when he climbs into his
plane to fly to his "target for tonight" that the runway will be clear for a safe
takeoff, a takeoff that will hurtle him into the air for one more sledge-hammer blow

at Hitler's "Fortress Europe." This constant pounding will cause that fortress to crumble, clear it out of the way, so that nothing, nothing the enemy can do, will stop our victorious march to Berlin!

Captain Glenn Miller: Most popular tune of any season and I'm sure you'll say it's one of your favorites, "Star Dust."]

STAR DUST

2nd Lt. Donald P. Briggs: The next time you see an Army Air Forces plane, just think of this. [Part of the credit for keeping that plane in the air belongs to women, members of the Women's Army Corps serving in the Army Air Forces, known as Air WACs! There are many serving already, but more are constantly needed. So if you are a woman between the ages of twenty and fifty, with no dependents and no children under fourteen, why not see about joining the WACs for assignment with the A.A.F.? The Army Air Forces offer you over a hundred specialized jobs, such as clerks, stenographers, control tower operators, and photographers. And each one is a vital, important job, work that must be done now, to give your fighting men the help they need and speed them on the road to victory! Visit your nearest Army Recruiting Station right away, and talk with the WAC officer there. She'll help you select the special job that you can do best, and explain how you, as an Air WAC, can help "Keep 'Em Flying!" And now Captain Miller.

Captain Glenn Miller: And now for the last time on this program and] I'm afraid you'll just have to the guess the title.

PISTOL PACKIN' MAMA

Vocal refrain by Corporal Ray McKinley and the Crew Chiefs

I SUSTAIN THE WINGS (closing theme)

[2nd Lt. Donald P. Briggs: "I Sustain the Wings" has presented the band from the Army Air Forces Technical School at Yale University; Captain Glenn Miller; Corporal Ray McKinley; Johnnie, the kid next door; and many of your old friends. Next week Johnnie will tell you about the Air WACs, members of the Women's Army Corps of the Army Air Forces, who are helping Johnnie to "Keep 'Em Flying!" Be with us again next Saturday, same time, same station. This program is written and produced entirely by soldiers of the Army Air Forces and came to you from New York City.

2nd Lt. Donald P. Briggs: This is the National Broadcasting Company.]

06Nov43 (Sat) 11:30PM-Midnight EWT WEAF, NBC Vanderbilt Theatre, New York, New York
  I SUSTAIN THE WINGS broadcast   Audience

[**THE ARMY AIR CORPS** (opening fanfare)
2nd Lt. Donald P. Briggs: "I Sustain the Wings."
I SUSTAIN THE WINGS (opening theme)
  2nd Lt. Donald P. Briggs: "I Sustain the Wings," presented by the Army Air Forces
    Training Command Band. Each week this program features the band from the Army Air
    Forces Technical School at Yale University; Captain Glenn Miller; Corporal Ray
    McKinley; Johnnie, the kid next door; and many of your old friends. And now Captain
    Glenn Miller.
Captain Glenn Miller: Thank you, Lieutenant Don Briggs, and good evening, everybody. Men
  who serve in the Army Air Forces Training Command wear a distinctive insignia inscribed
  with the Latin words "Sustineo Alas," meaning "I Sustain the Wings," the proud motto of
  those who keep America's planes in the air and train the men who fly them. To these men
  of the Army Air Forces Training Command, this series of programs is dedicated. Tonight
  we salute the Army Air Forces Technical School at Truax Field, Madison, Wisconsin,
  Brigadier General S. W. Fitzgerald, commanding general. And now I see Corporal McKinley
  waitin' to roll off with "American Patrol."]
AMERICAN PATROL
CAPRICE VIENNOIS (Old tune)
  Captain Glenn Miller: And now it's medley time, a serenade for the mothers, wives and
    sweethearts of the officers and enlisted men at Truax Field. Here's something old,
    something new, something borrowed and something blue. The old song, Fritz Kreisler's
    "Caprice Viennois."
  Captain Glenn Miller: For something new, Private Art Malvin sings "Sunday, Monday, or
    Always."
SUNDAY, MONDAY, OR ALWAYS (New tune)
  Vocal refrain by Private First Class Artie Malvin
  Captain Glenn Miller: We borrow Phil Spitalny's theme, "Isle of Golden Dreams."
MY ISLE OF GOLDEN DREAMS (Borrowed tune)
  [Captain Glenn Miller: Last in our medley, something blue, the "Birth of the Blues."
BIRTH OF THE BLUES (Blue tune)
Pvt. Murray Kane: Amber Tower, this is Army 5-5-0-7, over.
Sgt. David Ross: Amber Tower, this is Army 7-8-1-0, over.
Voice 3: Amber Tower, this is Army 1-1-3-9, over.
Pfc. Joseph Shulman (as Johnnie): Army 5-5-0-7, this is Amber Tower, over. Army 7-8-1-0,
  wait. Army 1-1-3-9, wait.
Pvt. Murray Kane: Amber tower, this is 5-5-0-7. Seven miles west of your field at four
  thousand feet. Request landing instructions, over.
Pfc. Joseph Shulman: 5-5-0-7, this is Amber Tower. Seven miles west at four thousand,
  traffic to the left at one thousand, land on runway 2-7. Call tower on base leg.
2nd Lt. Donald P. Briggs: That, ah, lingo may not make much sense to you but it sure
  makes sense to a pilot coming into an air field for a landing. Yes, sir, it tells him
  whether or not a runway is clear so that he can come in without crashing into another
  plane. Yeah, those pilots know the meaning of that special control tower language. And
  so does Johnnie. He's the guy who talks their language; Johnnie, the kid next door.
  You remember him. The kid that had put on his Scout uniform and spent the afternoon
  helping the cops untangle a traffic jam. Well, Johnnie's changed that Boy Scout uniform
  for the khaki of Uncle Sam's A.A.F. And Johnnie's a mighty important character. He's
  all the men trained by the Army Air Forces Training Command. And today, as a control
  tower operator, he's one of that unbeatable trio, the plane, the air crew, and the
  ground crew, each indispensable to the other. Well, Johnnie's still directing traffic,
  but it isn't on the ground, no, sir, it's in the air. And that makes the job a lot
  tougher because Johnny has to think in three dimensions instead of two. And in the sky
  every direction of the compass is a roadway. Yes, air traffic over a - a busy landing
  field would be a hopeless mess, a series of accidents, if it weren't for Johnnie sitting
  up there in the control tower, that glassed-in birdcage high up on stilts at the edge of
  the airfield, just sitting there cool and competent, looking constantly at the sky and
  talking in the ...

Pfc. Joseph Shulman: 5-5-0-7, this is Amber Tower. Seven miles west at four thousand, traffic to the left at one thousand, land on runway 2-7. Call tower on base leg, over.

Pvt. Murray Kane: Amber Tower, this is 5-5-0-7, wilco.

Pfc. Joseph Shulman: 7-8-1-0, this is Amber Tower. Send your message, over.

Sgt. David Ross: Amber Tower, this is 7-8-1-0, twelve miles east.

Pfc. Paul Huston: Amber Tower, Army 9-9-5-9, port engine on fire, request emergency landing instructions. I'm six miles east of your field flying at 8-1-8, over.

2nd Lt. Donald P. Briggs: An emergency. But Johnny'll be able to handle it, believe me. But don't take anything for granted, listen to the facts, with the training he's received at the A.A.F. Technical School at Truax Field, and judge for yourself. First, the physical requirements.

Sgt. David Ross: Vision, hearing and speech.

2nd Lt. Donald P. Briggs: They must all be perfect. He must be able to spot planes quickly and identify them instantly. He's got to be able to hear important details like height, speed and distance. And his instructions must be spoken clearly and quickly.

Sgt. David Ross: Nerves.

2nd Lt. Donald P. Briggs: Huh, he can't have any. He must remain calm and confident in any and all emergencies. Yes, physically and mentally, Johnnie's got to be "right on the beam." And his course of instruction at Truax Field is plenty tough, too. He got most of it around a big table, laid out as a miniature air field, complete in every detail, with planes, floodlights, obstruction lights, boundary markers, buildings in the area, everything that would meet the eye at a full-scale air field. Around this large table, each with his individual radio, sit twenty students impersonating arriving planes, until it comes their turn to man the control tower overlooking the table. This method is a safety measure, safe because it gives Johnnie plenty of practice without endangering planes or pilots. And he spends at least ten hours in a Link trainer. He studies hydraulic landing gears, radio aids to navigation, weather, air traffic regulations, everything to help the pilot make a safe landing. Yes, Johnnie knows all about these things, and plenty more besides. And what's more, he's got to have all this information in his head. He hasn't time to look it up, because, in this 300 mile-an-hour flying game, things happen in a hurry. He must think and act quickly in an emergency, like the one confronting him now, a plane on fire coming in for a landing, other planes stacked up at all levels on all legs.

Pfc. Paul Huston: My port engine is on fire! Request emergency landing instructions. Am six miles east of your field, flying an A-20. Over.

Pfc. Joseph Shulman: All ships in vicinity of Amber Tower traffic pattern, emergency landing, emergency landing! Clear traffic pattern! Over. Army 9-9-5-9, this is Amber Tower. Roger. You are cleared to make straight-in approach. Land on runway 2-7. Over. Press that crash button, Eddie. Now the crash phone. All stations. Emergency landing on runway twenty-seven. An A-20 with port engine on fire. Emergency landing on runway twenty-seven. An A-20 with port engine on fire. There she is, Eddie. She's comin' in mighty fast. Oh - oh! Hello, 9-9-5-9. Your wheels aren't down. Your wheels aren't down! Over.

Pfc. Paul Huston: Amber Tower, this is 9-9-5-9. Thanks. Roger.

Pfc. Joseph Shulman: That's got it. He's O.K. now. Everything's under control! All ships in vicinity of Amber Tower, resume your positions. Call tower on base leg. All ships in ...

2nd Lt. Donald P. Briggs: Everything's under control! And it'll stay that way, Johnnie, as long as you're there in the control tower, scanning the skies for Uncle Sam's air men and guiding them to a safe landing.

I Sustain the Wings (Incidental music)

2nd Lt. Donald P. Briggs: It's a big job, Johnnie, one that permits no mistakes. You've got to bring our planes and their crews safely to Earth on the long landing strips. You've got to stay on your toes, Johnnie, because if you fall asleep, even for one second, some other fellow may sleep for a very long time. But you know that, and the pilot knows that you know it. He know, too, that when he climbs into his plane to fly to his "target for tonight" that the runway will be clear for a safe takeoff, a takeoff that will hurtle him into the air for one more sledge-hammer blow at Hitler's "Fortress Europe." This constant pounding will cause that fortress to crumble, clear it out of the way, so that nothing, nothing the enemy can do, will stop our victorious march to Berlin!

Captain Glenn Miller: Most popular tune of any season and I'm sure you'll say it's one of your favorites,] "Star Dust."

STAR DUST

[2nd Lt. Donald P. Briggs: The next time you see an Army Air Forces plane, just think of this. Part of the credit for keeping that plane in the air belongs to women, members of the Women's Army Corps serving in the Army Air Forces, known as Air WACs! There are many serving already, but more are constantly needed. So if you are a woman between the ages of twenty and fifty, with no dependents and no children under fourteen, why not see about joining the WACs for assignment with the A.A.F.? The Army Air Forces offer you over a hundred specialized jobs, such as clerks, stenographers, control tower operators, and photographers. And each one is a vital, important job, work that must be done now, to give your fighting men the help they need and speed them on the road to victory! Visit your nearest Army Recruiting Station right away, and talk with the WAC officer there. She'll help you select the special job that you can do best, and explain how you, as an Air WAC, can help "Keep 'Em Flying!" And now Captain Miller.

Captain Glenn Miller: And now for the last time on this program and I'm afraid you'll just have to the guess the title.

PISTOL PACKIN' MAMA

Vocal refrain by Corporal Ray McKinley and the Crew Chiefs

I SUSTAIN THE WINGS (closing theme)

2nd Lt. Donald P. Briggs: "I Sustain the Wings" has presented the band from the Army Air Forces Technical School at Yale University; Captain Glenn Miller; Corporal Ray McKinley; Johnnie, the kid next door; and many of your old friends. Next week Johnnie will tell you about the Air WACs, members of the Women's Army Corps of the Army Air Forces, who are helping Johnnie to "Keep 'Em Flying!" Be with us again next Saturday, same time, same station. This program is written and produced entirely by soldiers of the Army Air Forces and came to you from New York City.

2nd Lt. Donald P. Briggs: This is the National Broadcasting Company.]

12Nov43 (Fri) New York, New York
  TREASURY STAR PARADE recording Program 309 (G-6685-P1) For broadcast 22Dec43

Treasury Star Parade Theme
  Played by David Brockman and the Treasury Orchestra
  Larry Elliot: This is a program of the United States Treasury. The "Treasury Star
    Parade" brings you the Army Air Forces Training Command Band under the direction of
    Captain Glenn Miller.
  Larry Elliot: Friends, this is no time to let down on our War Bond buying. The most
    decisive battles of the war are still ahead of us. We're waging a war of invasion and
    it's costing us more than ten million dollars every single hour. So buy War Bonds and
    buy more bonds. It's a way to help win faster. It's a way to help get our boys back
    home sooner. Enlist now in the Payroll Savings Plan. If you already belong, then do
    your best to boost your allotment for War Bonds. You help to bring about a speedier
    victory, to help prevent inflation, when you invest in War Bonds every dollar of the
    difference between what comes in and what you need to live. Protect your own future and
    the future of those you love, buy more bonds and buy them right away.
I SUSTAIN THE WINGS (opening theme)
  Larry Elliot: Now here is Captain Glenn Miller.
  Captain Glenn Miller: Thank you, Larry Elliot, and hello, everybody. In the music
    department here's Corporal Ray McKinley waitin' with the big sticks to roll off for
    "American Patrol."
AMERICAN PATROL
HOW SWEET YOU ARE
  Captain Glenn Miller: Now here's Private First Class Johnny Desmond with a song
    especially for you gals, "How Sweet You Are."
  Vocal refrain by Private First Class Johnny Desmond
  Captain Glenn Miller: Now, with a nickel you can get a lot of strange things providin'
    you've got a juke box. Listen to the Crew Chiefs and "Juke Box Saturday Night."
JUKE BOX SATURDAY NIGHT
  Vocal refrain by the Crew Chiefs
  Captain Glenn Miller: Now, what does a foot soldier do in the Army? Well, here's the
    answer in one of the war's top tunes, "What Do You Do in the Infantry."
WHAT DO YOU DO IN THE INFANTRY
  Vocal refrain by the Crew Chiefs
  Captain Glenn Miller: Folks, this is Captain Glenn Miller. And I want to ...
I SUSTAIN THE WINGS (closing theme)
  Captain Glenn Miller: ... ask you a question. Do you know how much it costs to train
    an aviation cadet, to make him into a skilled pilot, a navigator, a bombardier in the
    Army Air Forces? Well, you probably think around five or ten thousand dollars. Well,
    that's entirely wrong. It costs thirty thousand dollars for the training alone and as
    often as much as a quarter of a million dollars for the plane he flies. That's one
    reason, I think one mighty good reason, why we've got to buy more and more War Bonds.
  Larry Elliot: Yes, it costs big money to win a war. But, after all, money is the lesser
    sacrifice. So let's dig down and keep on digging to back up our fighting men, to get
    this war over and done with faster. Put every extra dollar you can scrape together into
    War Bonds. Every bond you buy is an investment, an investment in victory, in freedom,
    in security for your own future. The easiest way to buy bonds is through the Payroll
    Savings Plan. If you're already enrolled, go to your employer tomorrow and boost your
    buying. Think of that thirty thousand ...
Treasury Star Parade Theme
  Played by David Brockman and the Treasury Orchestra
  Larry Elliot: ... dollars it costs to train just one flyer. Think of that quarter
    million dollars it takes to build just one plane. Yes, think it over, friends, and
    then buy more War Bonds. The United States Treasury Department thanks Captain Glenn
    Miller and the boys of the Army Air Forces Training Command Band, also this station
    for the use of its facilities. Special material was written by Thelma Ritter and
    Joseph Moran. This especially transcribed program was produced by Henry P. Hayward.
    This is Larry Elliot suggesting that you check the radio column of your local
    newspaper and tune in the "Treasury Star Parade."

12Nov43 (Fri) New York, New York
  TREASURY STAR PARADE recording Program 314 (G-6686-P2) For broadcast 03Jan44

Treasury Star Parade Theme
  Played by David Brockman and the Treasury Orchestra
  Larry Elliot: This is a program of the United States Treasury. The "Treasury Star
    Parade" brings you the Army Air Forces Training Command Band under the direction of
    Captain Glenn Miller.
  Larry Elliot: Folks, if any of you have a son, a brother, a sweetheart who's in the Army
    Air Forces, maybe he's told you just a little bit of what it feels like to be up there
    fighting it out with the enemy. Or maybe not, because our boys don't do very much
    talking about those things. But, of course, all of us can imagine something of what
    it's like. And we know that our fighting boys deserve to be, must be, backed up with
    our fighting dollars. So invest in more War Bonds. Don't let down for one minute. The
    most important battles are still ahead of us, and the costliest ones. Your country
    needs to borrow your money now to win faster. You'll need your money in the future.
    It'll come back to you four dollars for every three you invest in War Bonds when those
    War Bonds mature. Let's every one of us put more dollars to work in the finest
    investment in the world, more United States War Bonds.
I SUSTAIN THE WINGS (opening theme)
  Larry Elliot: Now here is Captain Glenn Miller.
  Captain Glenn Miller: Thank you and hello, everybody. We start our "Treasury Star
    Parade" as the band beats it out with an old favorite, "In the Mood."
IN THE MOOD
MY HEART TELLS ME (Should I Believe My Heart?)
  Captain Glenn Miller: Here's Private First Class Johnny Desmond to sing.
  Vocal refrain by Private First Class Johnny Desmond
  Captain Glenn Miller: Now for something in the easy-to-take department, our violin
    section and "Holiday for Strings."
HOLIDAY FOR STRINGS (String section only)
  Captain Glenn Miller: Nice goin', boys. Now here's the gang playin' and singin' a song
    we all want to hear, the "Vict'ry Polka."
VICT'RY POLKA
  Vocal refrain by Private First Class Johnny Desmond, the Crew Chiefs and Glee Club
  Captain Glenn Miller: Folks, this is Captain Glenn Miller again with a thought for your
    memory book. Never has aviation played such a part in any war. With the bombing of
    Sicily, of Italy, the constant bombing of Berlin, those attacks spell quicker victory,
    but those attacks cost money and ...
I SUSTAIN THE WINGS (closing theme)
  Captain Glenn Miller: ... big money. Just one single raid of five hundred Flying
    Fortresses over the Rhineland costs almost three-quarters of a million dollars for
    gasoline and bombs alone. Now multiply that by hundreds of raids and you can see why
    it's up to all of us to buy more War Bonds, not just one extra bond now and then when
    you feel you can spare the money, but more bonds regularly to help pay the high cost
    of this war for freedom and to win this war and win it faster.
  Larry Elliot: Yes, victory does come high, but there's not one living American who'd say
    it isn't worth the price. We've seen what's happened in other countries. And we know
    that no price is too great to pay for victory and the perpetuation of our democracy. No
    sacrifice is too great. So dig down and dig down deep to buy more War Bonds. The
    Payroll Savings Plan is the easiest way for most of us to do it. If you're already
    enrolled in this plan, then try your level best to boost your buying. Make a sacrifice.
    Give up something. You'll find it's more than worth it in the future.
Treasury Star Parade Theme
  Played by David Brockman and the Treasury Orchestra
  Larry Elliot: Back up our fighting boys to the hilt. Help them to win this war for us
    and win it faster. Help them to get home to you. The United States Treasury
    Department thanks Captain Glenn Miller and the boys of the Army Air Forces Training
    Command Band, also this station for the use of its facilities. Special material was
    written by Thelma Ritter and Joseph Moran. This especially transcribed program was

produced by Henry P. Hayward. This is Larry Elliot suggesting that you check the radio column of your local newspaper and tune in the "Treasury Star Parade."

13Nov43 (Sat) NBC, New York, New York
UNCLE SAM PRESENTS recording

I SUSTAIN THE WINGS (opening theme)
  2nd Lt. Donald P. Briggs: From the United States of America, to the other united nations of the world, "Uncle Sam Presents" the Band of the Training Command of the Army Air Forces, under the direction of Captain Glenn Miller, with Corporal Ray McKinley, and many of your old friends.
2nd Lt. Donald P. Briggs: And here is Captain Glenn Miller.
Captain Glenn Miller: Thank you, Lieutenant Donald Briggs, and hello, everybody. First off in the music department an old favorite. We thought you might like "In the Mood."
IN THE MOOD
Captain Glenn Miller: Nice going, boys. That incidental talk was by Corporal Ray McKinley, incidentally. Next, one of the top romantic tunes of today, it's from the Broadway show "Oklahoma," which is really the top show along the street. Private First Class Johnny Desmond sings "People Will Say We're in Love."
PEOPLE WILL SAY WE'RE IN LOVE
  Vocal refrain by Private First Class Johnny Desmond
Captain Glenn Miller: Now a beautiful old melody in some fancy clothes, "In the Gloaming."
IN THE GLOAMING
Captain Glenn Miller: Now a tune that pretty well describes time that everybody's waiting anxiously for, the "Vict'ry Polka."
VICT'RY POLKA
  Vocal refrain by Private First Class Johnny Desmond, the Crew Chiefs and the Ensemble
I SUSTAIN THE WINGS (closing theme)
  Captain Glenn Miller: Well, that winds things up for today, folks. Speaking for the band, thanks for all the swell letters you've been sending us and keep 'em comin'. When you write, ask for your favorite ...

  ...

13Nov43 (Sat) 11:30PM-Midnight EWT WEAF, NBC Vanderbilt Theatre, New York, New York
  I SUSTAIN THE WINGS broadcast   Audience

THE ARMY AIR CORPS (opening fanfare)
2nd Lt. Donald P. Briggs: "I Sustain the Wings."
I SUSTAIN THE WINGS (opening theme)
  2nd Lt. Donald P. Briggs: "I Sustain the Wings." The Army Air Forces Training Command
    presents the Band of the Training Command; Captain Glenn Miller; Corporal Ray
    McKinley; Johnnie, the kid next door; and many of your old friends. And now Captain
    Glenn Miller.
Captain Glenn Miller: Thank you, Lieutenant Briggs, and good evening, everybody. Men who
    serve in the A.A.F. Training Command wear a distinctive insignia inscribed with the
    Latin words "Sustineo Alas," and that means "I Sustain the Wings," that's the proud
    motto of those who keep America's planes in the air and train the men who fly them. To
    these men of the A.A.F. Training Command, this series of programs is dedicated. And
    tonight we salute the A.A.F. Technical School at Yale University, New Haven,
    Connecticut, Colonel Raymond J. Reeves, commanding officer. Now gettin' into the music
    department here's an old favorite we thought you'd enjoy hearing again, "In the Mood."
IN THE MOOD
Captain Glenn Miller: And now medley time, a serenade for the mothers, wives and
    sweethearts of the officers, cadets and enlisted men at the A.A.F. Technical School at
    Yale University. Something old, something new, something borrowed and something blue.
    The old song, "In the Gloaming."
IN THE GLOAMING (Old tune)
  Captain Glenn Miller: For something new, here's P.F.C. Johnny Desmond to sing.
FOR THE FIRST TIME (I've Fallen in Love) (New tune)
  Vocal refrain by Private First Class Johnny Desmond
  Captain Glenn Miller: From our good friend Benny Goodman we borrow "Stompin' at the
    Savoy."
STOMPIN' AT THE SAVOY (Borrowed tune)
  Captain Glenn Miller: Last in our medley something a shade darker than blue, "Deep
    Purple."
DEEP PURPLE (Blue tune)
2nd Lt. Donald P. Briggs: Just listen to that, America. Isn't it a lovely sound? The
  music of Victory.
Victory Theme from Beethoven's Fifth Symphony (Incidental music)
  2nd Lt. Donald P. Briggs: Those are our big bombers on a mission, a mission of
    destruction. The bombardiers are doing a wonderful job paving the road to victory
    with their bombs, but before they take off, someone has to tell them where to drop
    those bombs to do the most good, to locate the target for them.
2nd Lt. Donald P. Briggs: And that someone is the aerial photographer. Just like the
  pilots, the mechanics, [bombardiers, gunners, armorers, navigators, the aerial
  photographer is a product of the A.A.F. Training Command. And Johnnie is all these
  guys! You remember Johnnie; Johnnie, the kid next door, the boy that broke your parlor
  window when he played baseball in the vacant lot, the one that did odd jobs around your
  place to earn a quarter to go to the Saturday afternoon movies so he wouldn't miss a
  chapter of the current serial. Once in a while he'd get into your hair, and you'd
  wonder if he'd ever amount to anything. You needn't have worried, because right now
  Johnnie is a pretty important character. He's one guy in a million, and a million guys
  in one. He's Mr. Johnnie Know-how, Johnnie Technician, but most important, he's Johnnie
  American! He's every mother's son that's being trained to fly and to keep 'em flying by
  the A.A.F. Training Command. Yes, Johnnie is a lot of different young men from a lot of
  different parts of these United States, but today he's one guy in particular. Johnnie's
  that aerial photographer we were talking about, one of that unbeatable trio, the plane,
  the air crew and the ground crew, each indispensable to the other. And Johnnie, as an
  aerial photographer, is really indispensable.
Pfc. Joseph Shulman (as bombardier): I'll say he is! I'm the bombardier, and I ought to
  know. More than once his "purty" pictures have fixed it so I could drop those
  blockbusting eggs right in Hitler's basket. And, you know, I call Johnnie the
  "bombardier's bloodhound" because he smells out my targets for me.

Cpl. Paul A. Dubov (as tactical officer): Is Johnnie indispensable? You can take it from
   me he is! I'm the tactical officer, a member of the general's staff, and I help to plan
   our campaigns. We couldn't do our job nearly so well nor so fast if it weren't for
   Johnnie.
2nd Lt. Donald P. Briggs: "If it weren't for Johnnie," Johnnie, the aerial photographer,
   and his photographs. Those photographs, hundreds of them, are fitted into a huge map,
   called a "mosaic," like pieces of a jig-saw puzzle, and this map shows all the important
   topographical details of a given area. And what's more, Johnnie can furnish such a map
   in a hurry. He and his camera can cover more territory in a day than a surveyor, using
   the old methods, can in months. But his photographs are more than maps. They detect
   flaws in camouflage, pick out factories, dams, railroad junctions and other important
   targets, expose the movements of enemy troops and transports, show the extent of damage
   done in bombing raids. Yes, keep a pictorial record of enemy planes, tanks and ships
   destroyed in combat. So you see, the importance of Johnnie's pictures can't be
   overestimated. But Johnnie isn't only a photographer, he's a soldier.
Pvt. Murray Kane (as pilot): You bet he's a soldier. As a pilot I've met Johnnie plenty
   of times. I've flown planes with him on reconnaissance flights and watched him keep
   working with his camera under the hottest kind of fire, when any minute might be the
   last. He's a real soldier.
2nd Lt. Donald P. Briggs: A real soldier, but a special kind. He does his fighting with
   a camera instead of a gun. And, brother, a camera isn't much good when a Zero or a
   Messerschmitt comes diving at you from out of the clouds. But Johnnie knows those
   pictures are important, and he keeps clicking that shutter until he gets them, Zeros or
   no Zeros. But not all of Johnnie's work is done in the air. There's plenty to be done
   on the ground, in the laboratory. Yes, when Johnnie returns from a flight, his films
   must be developed, and prints made. And he can handle that job, too. He's been
   thoroughly trained as a laboratory technician. Why, one day not so long ago, Johnnie
   snapped a picture, developed the film, printed it and had the finished product in one
   minute and seventeen seconds, and that's plenty fast. But there are times when Johnnie
   finds himself in a spot where modern laboratory equipment and chemicals aren't
   available, so he's been taught to meet just such an emergency. He's learned that
   ordinary every day things like table salt, G.I. soap, granulated sugar, carbon monoxide
   gas from a jeep exhaust pipe, shoe polish, will take the place of chemicals ordinarily
   required in photography. It's sort of modern chemical magic with Johnnie as the
   magician, but the most magical thing of all is taking pictures without a camera. Sounds
   a little on the impossible side, doesn't it? But just listen how it's done.
Cpl. Paul A. Dubov (as instructor): All that is needed is a cardboard box, a piece of
   dark celluloid and a pin. The box is made light-tight, a hole is cut in one end and the
   celluloid pasted over it and a pin-hole is then made in the celluloid. Another piece of
   cardboard is used for a shutter. The film is placed at one end of the box and exposed
   from thirty to sixty seconds by sliding back the shutter.
2nd Lt. Donald P. Briggs: Sounds simple, doesn't it? It is, but you've got to know how,
   and Johnnie has that "know-how." He got it from an A.A.F. Technical School, the school
   that taught him everything there is to know about cameras and photography.
I Sustain the Wings (Incidental music)
   2nd Lt. Donald P. Briggs: Johnnie's using that hard-earned knowledge every minute of
      every day and night to help put the finishing touches on Hitler and the Axis. As an
      aerial photographer, Johnnie's blazing the trail, the trail that leads our bombers
      straight to the target. Forewarned by Johnnie's picture-maps, our navigators can
      guide their planes to the weaknesses in the enemy's chain of defenses, and, by
      ceaselessly hammering with tons of lethal destruction, smash these weakest links in
      the enemy's chain of defenses to shorten the time until our ultimate victory.
Captain Glenn Miller: There's a swell tune kicking around in the juke boxes these days,
   Benny Goodman's record of] "Mission to Moscow." Benny features the composer of the tune
   at the piano, Mel Powell. Well, Mel is now Corporal Powell and he's our pianist and
   he's arranged "Mission to Moscow" for our band to feature his piano and the clarinet of
   Corporal Hucko. Here's "Mission to Moscow."
MISSION TO MOSCOW
Captain Glenn Miller: In the romance department one of today's top tunes. P.F.C. Johnny
   Desmond sings "People Will Say We're in Love."

PEOPLE WILL SAY WE'RE IN LOVE
   Vocal refrain by Private First Class Johnny Desmond
2nd Lt. Donald P. Briggs: Women, you know, are not allowed to serve in the front lines.
   Yet, as a patriotic woman, you're not content to sit quietly on the sidelines either and
   that's one reason why so many women today are enlisting as Air WACs, as members of the
   Women's Army Corps serving in the A.A.F. Because Air WACs have a chance to help win the
   war in a big way, they're taking over vital jobs in the Army Air Forces that women can
   do as skillfully as men, releasing men for other duties that only men can handle.
   That's a worthy job, a job that you'd be proud to do. The Air WACs offer you a choice
   of over one hundred specialized jobs, such as clerks, stenographers, control tower
   operators, photographers, personnel experts, and weather observers. So, if you're not
   engaged in essential war work, visit your nearest Army Recruiting Station and ask about
   joining the Air WACs. Yes, join the Air WACs and help give your fighting men the
   backing up they need to speed them on the road to victory. And now, back to the music.
Captain Glenn Miller: Thank you, Lieutenant. Now a tune that describes pretty well the
   time that everybody's waitin' for, the "Vict'ry Polka."
VICT'RY POLKA
   Vocal refrain by Private First Class Johnny Desmond, the Crew Chiefs and Glee Club
I SUSTAIN THE WINGS (closing theme)
   2nd Lt. Donald P. Briggs: "I Sustain the Wings" has presented the Band of the A.A.F.
      Training Command; Captain Glenn Miller; Corporal Ray McKinley; Johnnie, the kid next
      door; and many of your old friends. Next week we'll tell you about the Air WACs,
      members of the Women's Army Corps serving in the A.A.F. at the Fort Worth Army Air
      Base in Fort Worth, Texas. Be with us again next Saturday, same time, same station.
      This program is written and produced entirely by soldiers of the A.A.F. and came to
      you from New York City.
Announcer: This is the National Broadcasting Company.

20Nov43 (Sat) 9:15-9:30AM   NBC, New York, New York
UNCLE SAM PRESENTS recording

I SUSTAIN THE WINGS (opening theme)
   2nd Lt. Donald P. Briggs: From the United States of America, to the other united
      nations of the world, "Uncle Sam Presents" the Band of the Training Command of the
      Army Air Forces, under the direction of Captain Glenn Miller, with Corporal Ray
      McKinley, and many of your old friends.
2nd Lt. Donald P. Briggs: Here is Captain Glenn Miller.
Captain Glenn Miller: Thank you, Lieutenant Donald Briggs, and hello, everybody. First
   off in the music department, "Here We Go Again."
HERE WE GO AGAIN
Captain Glenn Miller: And there they went again. Now here's Private First Class Johnny
   Desmond to sing one of today's top tunes, "Star Eyes."
STAR EYES
   Vocal refrain by Private First Class Johnny Desmond
Captain Glenn Miller: Comes now a tune that's on everyone's lists of old-time favorites,
   "The End of a Perfect Day."
THE END OF A PERFECT DAY
Captain Glenn Miller: No greater story will come out of this war than the story of those
   men of the A.A.F. who today are making history in the sky. The band and the Crew Chiefs
   offer a musical tribute to their courage and skill, "The Squadron Song."
THE SQUADRON SONG
   Vocal refrain by Private First Class Johnny Desmond, the Crew Chiefs and the Glee Club
I SUSTAIN THE WINGS (closing theme)
   Captain Glenn Miller: Well, that winds things up for today, folks. Speaking for the
      band, thanks for all the swell letters you've been sending us. Keep 'em coming. And
      when you write, ask for your favorite tunes. We'll be su --- more than glad to play
      'em for you. You can reach us in care of this station. Now for Lieutenant Don
      Briggs, Corporal Ray McKinley and all the rest of us, so long until next week at the
      same time. See you then.
   2nd Lt. Donald P. Briggs: The Army Air Forces Training Command Band, under the
      direction of Captain Glenn Miller, has come to you from New York City. Don't forget
      tomorrow, same time, same station, "Uncle Sam Presents" another famous service band
      with music from us to you.
TAIL END CHARLIE (fade-out tune)
   2nd Lt. Donald P. Briggs: This is the United States of America, one of the united
      nations.

20Nov43 (Sat) 6:00-6:30PM EWT WEAF, NBC Vanderbilt Theatre, New York, New York
  I SUSTAIN THE WINGS broadcast   Audience

THE ARMY AIR CORPS (opening fanfare)
2nd Lt. Donald P. Briggs: "I Sustain the Wings."
I SUSTAIN THE WINGS (opening theme)
  2nd Lt. Donald P. Briggs: "I Sustain the Wings." The Army Air Forces Training Command
    presents the Band of the Training Command; Captain Glenn Miller; Corporal Ray
    McKinley; Johnnie, the kid next door; and many of your old friends. And now Captain
    Glenn Miller.
Captain Glenn Miller: Thank you, Lieutenant Don Briggs, and good evening, everybody. Men
  who serve in the A.A.F. Training Command wear a distinctive insignia. On it are three
  white plumes representing that unbeatable trio, the plane, the air crew, and the ground
  crew, each indispensable to the other. Under these plumes are the Latin words "Sustineo
  Alas," meaning "I Sustain the Wings," and that's the proud motto of those who keep
  America's planes in the air and train the men who fly them. To these men of the
  Training Command, this series of programs is dedicated. And tonight we salute the WACs
  stationed at the Army Air Field, Fort Worth, Texas, Colonel Carlye I. Ferris, commanding
  officer. We pay special tribute to all members of the Women's Army Corps serving the
  A.A.F. And now in the music department, "Here We Go Again."
HERE WE GO AGAIN
Captain Glenn Miller: And now it's medley time, a serenade for all the WACs serving in
  the A.A.F. Here's something old, something new, something borrowed, something blue.
  The old song, "Perfect Day."
THE END OF A PERFECT DAY (Old tune)
  Captain Glenn Miller: For something new, P.F.C. Johnny Desmond sings "Do You Know."
DO YOU KNOW (New tune)
  Vocal refrain by Private First Class Johnny Desmond
  Captain Glenn Miller: We borrow Beethoven's "Moonlight Sonata."
MOONLIGHT SONATA (Borrowed tune)
  Captain Glenn Miller: Last in our medley, something blue, "Blue Room."
THE BLUE ROOM (Blue tune)
Johnnie: Ah, Johnnie's my name. Remember me? Yeah, I thought you would. I'm Johnnie,
  the kid next door. That's right, the same kid who used to repair a broken light switch
  for the neighbors or mend a leaky water pipe in the basement. Mr. Fix-It they called
  me, you remember? Well, I'm still Mr. Fit-It but only I'm fixing much bigger and
  important things, yes, sir, the fighter planes of Uncle Sam's Army Air Forces here in
  Italy. Yeah, I'm all the guys trained by the A.A.F. Training Command and I'm over here
  helping to teach those Nazis a lesson they won't forget, doing just the kind of work I
  wanted to do. There were times though when I didn't think I'd get a chance at active
  service. But you know what made it possible? Well, I'll tell you. It was a woman.
  Heh, now wait a minute, don't laugh. I really mean it, seriously. You see, after I
  joined the Army I was sent to a technical school and taught to be a first class airplane
  mechanic. All of us fellows were hankering to get into action. We wanted to be right
  up in the front lines fighting and doing the job we've been trained to do. But the
  field I was sent to after I graduated was short on men so I had to take a job helping in
  the engineering office there, doing paper work. Oh, brother, was I discouraged. It -
  it - it looked like I'd never get overseas because the work there was important and
  somebody had to do it. Heh, and I was "it." Well, then one day, one day they told us
  that WACs were being assigned to our field. Didn't mean much to us at the time. A - a
  couple of the fellows were talking about it and what they said then sort of went for all
  of us.
Soldier 1: Aw, this WAC business won't amount to anything. There's no place for women in
  the Army. Man, all they'll be able to do is just stand out and look sharp in a uniform.
Solder 2: Yeah, WACs or no WACs we'll be stuck here in the States for the duration plus.

Johnnie: Well, that just goes to show you how wrong a fellow can be. The same week the WACs arrived we were put on shipment and sent overseas. Huh, it happened so fast my head's still spinning. And when I heard the news I was the happiest guy on Earth, believe me, yeah. Here was a chance to get over here where the action's goin' on, to do a real man's job. The WAC who took my place, no - no, I never got a chance to meet her. I don't even know whether she's dark or blond, short or tall, but I can tell you one thing, I'm plenty grateful to her. And I know she's doing a swell job. When I was in Africa I - I - I saw the work WACs were doing there in General Eisenhower's headquarters. Yeah. And some of the fellows who left the States after I did, say the WACs have practically taken over the field where I was stationed. You know, if you went back there now you'd probably find WACs doing all kinds of jobs, like, for instance, ah, ah, teaching the cadets instrument flying in the Link trainer.

Cadet: This is Army plane 2-2-4. Request permission to make instrument landing at your field, northeast leg of pattern, airspeed 1-5-0.

WAC: Permission granted, come on in. That was all right, mister, but don't forget to give your altitude next time. Now try again.

Johnnie: And because she's there on the job, another guy like me has been released for service over here. You know, at that same field you'll probably find a WAC in the weather station, too, handling reports on the Teletype.

WAC: Overcast. Low scattered rain. Light blowing dust. Barometric pressure 1-0-1-5 point 2 millibars. Wind shifting south at 1-6-1-8.

Johnnie: Yep and one more guy can be over here with with me, because that WAC is on the job. Or maybe she's working there as a motor vehicle dispatcher.

WAC: Deliver the crates to the supply depot. Then pick up these tools for Squadron A. Got it?

Soldier: Crates to Supply, tools for Squadron A. I gotcha. So long.

Johnnie: Yep, you'll find WACs all through the A.A.F. today, checking supplies, learning how to run commissaries, ah, working in photographic laboratories, figuring up payrolls, doing personnel work, handling public relations and acting as recreational directors and, aw, doing a lot of other things, things that women can do just as well or even better than men. Wonderful? Ha, ha, brother, you said it. Those WACs are wonderful. And if you don't think us guys in the service are for 'em 100 per cent then you don't know your Army. Fact is though I've thought once or twice of writing a letter of thanks to that WAC who took my place back in the States even if I don't know her. But, well, you know how it is. We've been been pretty busy over here and anyway I think I already know what her letter'd say. Yeah, she - she'd probably write something like this, "Yes, Johnny, I do understand when you say you're grateful to me. I appreciate your thanks,
...

WAC and Johnnie together: I really do. But honestly, just a chance to be a WAC is reward enough!

WAC: It's not easy work, this job we WACs are doing. When we joined, we gave up a lot of the things that most of us were used to. But it's useful work and interesting work, and when it's over each day, there's plenty of chance to enjoy ourselves. We have homey, attractive day rooms here, comfortable barracks and excellent food. Yes, and just as much chance for fun and recreation as we ever had, maybe more. Then, too, we get an opportunity to make new friends and learn how to work with others and how to get along on our own. But there's more to it than just that, Johnnie, many of us have husbands,
...

I Sustain the Wings (Incidental music)

WAC: ... brothers or sweethearts in this war and those of us in the WACs have this satisfaction, we know that we're backing up those men of ours personally, really doing something to help bring them home sooner. Every one of us has a stake in this war, Johnnie, I know I do. After it's all over I want a home, I want my children to have a free country to live in, to have all the opportunities and privileges that I've had. I don't want them to live in a world where the truth has to be whispered, where decency has to be disguised, where tyranny can put the lights out all over the world. I want them to live without fear, to be able to worship as they please, and go and come as they choose in a world where the only dictator is your own conscience. I want a world where we can enjoy in peace and liberty the big things and the little things, too, that make life precious to us all. I want a world, ah, but, ah, well, I - I guess you know what I'm trying to say, Johnnie, because as Americans we're all working and striving for the same thing. So across the thousands of miles that separate us as you read this letter, I reach out tonight and shake hands with you. This is our war and come what may we'll win it, Johnnie, together."

Captain Glenn Miller: Now here's Private First Class Johnny Desmond to sing one of today's top tunes, "Star Eyes."

STAR EYES

Vocal refrain by Private First Class Johnny Desmond

Captain Glenn Miller: No greater story will come out of this war than the story of those men of the A.A.F. who today are making history in the sky. The band and the Crew Chiefs offer a musical tribute to their courage and skill. Here it is, "The Squadron Song."

THE SQUADRON SONG

Vocal refrain by Private First Class Johnny Desmond, the Crew Chiefs and the Glee Club

AMERICAN PRAYER

Captain Glenn Miller: On Thanksgiving, next Thursday, Americans will give thanks as they do every day for all the good things, great and small, that make America worth fighting for. We've come a long way since last Thanksgiving. You remember the headlines, "U-Boats Take Heavy Toll of Allied Shipping," "Russians Face Defeat at Stalingrad," "Rommel Sends British Reeling Back to El Alemein." Today the tide has turned. More hard work will make victory certain. So, with thanks for the past year, and for the hope with which we face the future, we offer this "American Prayer."

Prayer by 2nd Lt. Donald P. Briggs

Vocal refrain by the Crew Chiefs and the Glee Club

I SUSTAIN THE WINGS (closing theme)

2nd Lt. Donald P. Briggs: "I Sustain the Wings: has presented the Band from the A.A.F. Training Command; Captain Glenn Miller; Corporal Ray McKinley; Johnnie, the kid next door; and many of your old friends. Next week you'll learn more about Johnnie at the A.A.F. Radio School at Scott Field, Belleville, Illinois. Be with us again next Saturday, same time, same station. This program is produced and written entirely by soldiers of the A.A.F. and came to you from New York City.

NBC announcer: This is the National [Broadcasting Company.]

The parts of Johnnie, Soldier one, Soldier two, Cadet and Soldier were played by Cpl. Paul A. Dubov, Pfc. Joseph Shulman and one or more other members of the band.

20Nov43 (Sat) 11:30PM-Midnight EWT WEAF, NBC Vanderbilt Theatre, New York, New York
 I SUSTAIN THE WINGS broadcast   Audience

THE ARMY AIR CORPS (opening fanfare)
2nd Lt. Donald P. Briggs: "I Sustain the Wings."
I SUSTAIN THE WINGS (opening theme)
  2nd Lt. Donald P. Briggs: "I Sustain the Wings." The Army Air Forces Training Command
    presents the Band of the Training Command; Captain Glenn Miller; Corporal Ray
    McKinley; Johnnie, the kid next door; and many of your old friends. And now Captain
    Glenn Miller.
Captain Glenn Miller: Thank you, Lieutenant Don Briggs, and good evening, everybody. Men
  who serve in the A.A.F. Training Command wear a distinctive insignia. On it are three
  white plumes representing that unbeatable trio, the plane, the air crew, and the ground
  crew, each indispensable to the other. Under these plumes are the Latin words "Sustineo
  Alas," which mean "I Sustain the Wings," and that's the proud motto of those who keep
  America's planes in the air and train the men who fly them. To these men of the
  Training Command, this series of programs is dedicated. Tonight we salute the WACs
  stationed at the Army Air Field, Fort Worth, Texas, Colonel Carlye I. Ferris, commanding
  officer. We pay special tribute to all members of the Women's Army Corps serving in the
  A.A.F. And now in the music department, "Here We Go Again."
HERE WE GO AGAIN
Captain Glenn Miller: And now it's medley time, a serenade for all the WACs serving in
  the A.A.F. Here's something old, something new, something borrowed and something blue.
  The old song, "Perfect Day."
THE END OF A PERFECT DAY (Old tune)
  Captain Glenn Miller: For something new, P.F.C. Johnny Desmond sings "Do You Know."
DO YOU KNOW (New tune)
  Vocal refrain by Private First Class Johnny Desmond
  Captain Glenn Miller: Tonight we borrow Beethoven's "Moonlight Sonata."
MOONLIGHT SONATA (Borrowed tune)
  Captain Glenn Miller: Last in our medley, something blue, "Blue Room."
THE BLUE ROOM (Blue tune)
Johnnie: Ah, Johnnie's my name. Remember me? Yeah, I thought you would. [I'm Johnnie,
  the kid next door. That's right, the same kid who used to repair a broken light switch
  for the neighbors or mend a leaky water pipe in the basement. Mr. Fix-It they called
  me, remember? Well, I'm still Mr. Fit-It, only I'm fixing much bigger and important
  things, the fighter planes of Uncle Sam's Army Air Forces here in Italy. Yes, I'm all
  the guys trained by the A.A.F. Training Command and I'm over here helping to teach these
  Nazis a lesson they won't forget, doing just the kind of work I wanted to do. There
  were times though when I didn't think I'd get a chance, didn't think I'd get a chance at
  active service. But you know what made it possible? Well, I'll tell you. It was a
  woman. No, don't laugh. I really mean it, seriously. You see, after I joined the Army
  I was sent to a technical school and taught to be a first class airplane mechanic. All
  of us fellows were hankering to get into action. We wanted to be right up on the front
  line, fighting and doing the job we've been trained to do. But the field I was sent to
  after I graduated was short on men. And so I had to take a job helping in the
  engineering office there, doing paper work. Brother, was I discouraged. It looked like
  I'd never get overseas because the work there was important and somebody had to do it.
  I was "it." Then one day they told us that WACs were being assigned to our field. But
  it didn't mean much to us at the time. A couple of the fellows were talking about it
  and what they said then sort of went for all of us.
Soldier 1: Aw, this WAC business won't amount to anything. There's no place for women in
  the Army. All they'll be able to do is just stand around and look pretty in a smart
  uniform.
Solder 2: Yeah, WACs or no WACs we'll be stuck here in the States for the duration plus.
Johnnie: Well, that just shows you how wrong a fellow can be. The same week the WACs
  arrived we were put on shipment and sent overseas. It happened so fast my head's still
  spinning. And when I heard the news I was the happiest guy on Earth, believe me. Here
  was a chance to get over here where the action's goin' on, to do a real man's job. The
  WAC who took my place, no - no, I never got a chance to meet her. I don't even know

whether she's dark or blond, short or tall, but I can tell you one thing, I'm plenty grateful to her. And I know she's doing a swell job. When I was in Africa I saw the work WACs were doing there in General Eisenhower's headquarters. And some of the fellows who left the States after I did, say the WACs have practically taken over the field where I was stationed. Why, if you went back there now you'd probably find WACs doing all kinds of jobs, like, for instance, teaching the cadets instrument flying in the Link trainers.

Cadet: This is Army plane 2-2-4. Request permission to make instrument landing at your field, on northeast leg of pattern, airspeed 1-5-0.

WAC: Permission granted, come on in. That was all right, mister, but don't forget to give your altitude next time. Now try again.

Johnnie: And because she's there on the job, another guy like me has been released for service over here. At that same field you'll probably find a WAC in the weather station, too, handling reports on the Teletype.

WAC: Ceiling estimated three thousand feet. Overcast. Low scattered rain. Light blowing dust. Barometric pressure 1-0-1-5 point 2 millibars. Temperature, 62 Fahrenheit. Wind shift from south at 1-6-1-8, Eastern War Time.

Johnnie: And one more guy can be over here with me, because that WAC is on the job. Or maybe she's working there as a motor vehicle dispatcher.

WAC: All right, driver, it all checks. Deliver the crates to the supply depot. Then pick up these tools for Squadron A. Got it?

Soldier: Crates to Supply, tools for Squadron A. I gotcha. So long.

Johnnie: Yes, you'll find WACs all through the A.A.F. today, checking supplies, learning how to run commissaries, ah, working in photographic laboratories, figuring up payrolls, doing personnel work, handling public relations, acting as recreational directors and doing a lot of other things, things that women can do just as well or even better than men. Wonderful? Brother, you said it. Those WACs are wonderful. And if you don't think us guys in the service are for them 100 per cent, well, you don't know your Army. Fact is though I've thought once or twice of writing a letter of thanks to that WAC who took my place back in the States even if I don't know her. But, well, you know how it is. We've been been pretty busy over here and anyway I think I already know what her letter would say. She'd probably write something like this, "Yes, Johnny, I do understand when you say you're grateful to me. I appreciate your thanks, ...

WAC and Johnnie together: I really do. But honestly, just the chance to be a WAC is reward enough!

WAC: It's not easy work, this job we WACs are doing. When we joined, we gave up a lot of the things that most of us were used to. But it's useful work and interesting work, and when it's over each day, there's plenty of chance to enjoy ourselves. We have homey, attractive day rooms here, comfortable barracks and excellent food. Yes, and just as much chance for fun and recreation as we ever had, maybe more. Then, too, we get an opportunity to make new friends and learn how to work with others and how to get along on our own. But there's more to it than just that, Johnnie, ...

I **Sustain the Wings** (Incidental music)

WAC: ... many of us have husbands, brothers or sweethearts in this war and those of us in the WACs have this satisfaction, we know that we're backing up those men of ours personally, really doing something to help bring them home sooner. Every one of us has a stake in this war, Johnnie, I know I do. After it's all over I want a home, I want my children to have a free country to live in, to have all the opportunities and privileges that I've had. I don't want them to live in a world where the truth has to be whispered, where decency has to be disguised, where tyranny can put the lights out all over the world. I want them to live without fear, to be able to worship as they please, and go and come as they choose in a world where the only dictator is your own conscience. I want a world where we can enjoy in peace and liberty the big things and the little things, too, that make life precious to us all. I want a world, but, well, I guess you know what I'm trying to say, Johnnie, because as Americans we're all working and striving for the same things. So across the thousands of miles that separate us as you read this letter, I reach out tonight and shake hands with you. This is our war. Yes, mine and yours. And come what may we'll win it, Johnnie, together."

Captain Glenn Miller: Here's Private First Class Johnny Desmond again to sing one of]
   today's top tunes, "Star Eyes."
STAR EYES
   Vocal refrain by Private First Class Johnny Desmond
Captain Glenn Miller: No greater story will come out of this war than the story of those
   men of the A.A.F. who today are making history in the sky. The band and the Crew Chiefs
   offer a musical tribute to their courage and skill, "The Squadron Song."
THE SQUADRON SONG
   Vocal refrain by Private First Class Johnny Desmond, the Crew Chiefs and the Glee Club
AMERICAN PRAYER
   Captain Glenn Miller: On Thanksgiving, next Thursday, Americans will give thanks as
      they do every day for all the good things, great and small, that make America worth
      fighting for. We've come a long way since last Thanksgiving. You remember the
      headlines, "U-Boats Take Heavy Toll of Allied Shipping," "Russians Face Defeat at
      Stalingrad," "Rommel Sends British Reeling Back to El Alemein." But today the tide
      has turned. More hard work will make victory certain. So, with thanks for the past
      year, and for the hope with which we face the future, we offer this "American Prayer."
   Prayer by 2nd Lt. Donald P. Briggs
   Vocal refrain by the Crew Chiefs and the Glee Club
I SUSTAIN THE WINGS (closing theme)
   2nd Lt. Donald P. Briggs: "I Sustain the Wings: has presented the Band from the A.A.F.
      Training Command; Captain Glenn Miller; Corporal Ray McKinley; Johnnie, the kid next
      door; and many of your old friends. Next week you'll learn more about Johnnie at the
      A.A.F. Radio School at Scott Field, Belleville, Illinois. Be with us again next
      Saturday, same time, same station. This program is produced and written entirely by
      soldiers of the A.A.F. and came to you from New York City.

The parts of Johnnie, Soldier one, Soldier two, Cadet and Soldier were played by Cpl. Paul
A. Dubov, Pfc. Joseph Shulman and one or more other members of the band.

27Nov43 (Sat) NBC, New York, New York
  UNCLE SAM PRESENTS recording

I SUSTAIN THE WINGS (opening theme)
  2nd Lt. Donald P. Briggs: (From the United States of America, to the other united
    nations of the world,) "Uncle Sam Presents" the Band of the Training Command of the
    Army Air Forces, under the direction of Captain Glenn Miller, with Corporal Ray
    McKinley and many of your old friends.
  2nd Lt. Donald P. Briggs: And here is Captain Glenn Miller.
  Captain Glenn Miller: Thank you, Lieutenant Don Briggs, and hello, everybody. The boys
    in the band are all settin' here looking very eager and the first tune is "Sun Valley
    Jump."
SUN VALLEY JUMP
HOW SWEET YOU ARE
  Captain Glenn Miller: P.F.C. Johnny Desmond sings.
  Vocal refrain by Private First Class Johnny Desmond
  Captain Glenn Miller: Nice going, Johnny. Now an old favorite from the musical pen of
    Private Jerry Gray, "String of Pearls."
A STRING OF PEARLS
  Captain Glenn Miller: Nice goin', boys. Now here's the whole gang playin' and singin'
    "Put Your Arms Around Me." Ready, Zeke?
PUT YOU ARMS AROUND ME, HONEY
  Vocal refrain by Private First Class Johnny Desmond, the Crew Chiefs and the Glee Club
I SUSTAIN THE WINGS (closing theme)
  Captain Glenn Miller: Well, that winds things up for today, folks. Speaking for the
    band, thanks for all the swell letters you've been sending us and keep 'em comin'.
    When you write, ask for your favorite tunes, we'll be more than glad to play them for
    you. You can reach us in care of this station. Now for Lieutenant Don Briggs,
    Corporal Ray McKinley, and all the rest of us, so long until next week same time.
  2nd Lt. Donald P. Briggs: The Army Air Forces Training Command Band, under the
    direction of Captain Glenn Miller, has come to you from New York City. Don't forget
    tomorrow, same time, same station, "Uncle Sam Presents" another famous service band
    with music from us to you.
SWING LOW, SWEET CHARIOT (fade-out tune)
  2nd Lt. Donald P. Briggs: This is the United States of America, one of the united
    nations.

27Nov43 (Sat) 6:00-6:30PM EWT WEAF, NBC Vanderbilt Theatre, New York, New York
  I SUSTAIN THE WINGS broadcast   Audience

[**THE ARMY AIR CORPS** (opening fanfare)
2nd Lt. Donald P. Briggs: "I Sustain the Wings."
I SUSTAIN THE WINGS (opening theme)
  2nd Lt. Donald P. Briggs: "I Sustain the Wings." The Army Air Forces Training Command
    presents the Band of the Training Command; Captain Glenn Miller; Corporal Ray
    McKinley; Johnnie, the kid next door; and many of your old friends.] And now Captain
    Glenn Miller.
Captain Glenn Miller: Thank you, Lieutenant Don Briggs, and good evening, everybody. Men
  who serve in the A.A.F. Training Command wear a distinctive insignia and on it are the
  Latin words "Sustineo Alas," which mean "I Sustain the Wings." That's the proud motto
  of those who keep America's planes in the air and train the men who fly them. And it's
  to these men of the Training Command, this series of programs is dedicated. Tonight we
  salute the A.A.F. Training Command Radio School, Scott Field, Belleville, Illinois,
  Brigadier General Wolcott P. Hayes, commanding general. Now in the music department the
  boys in the band are all settin' here looking very eager and the first tune is "Sun
  Valley Jump."
SUN VALLEY JUMP
HOW SWEET YOU ARE
  Captain Glenn Miller: Now here's P.F.C. Johnny Desmond to sing.
  Vocal refrain by Private First Class Johnny Desmond
2nd Lt. Donald P. Briggs: Enemy fighters attacking one of our giant Liberators on its way
  back from a raid on Hitler's Europe.
Pilot: Pilot to radio. Two engines out, Johnnie. Landing gear's smashed. We've shaken
  'em off. Radio control station for our position. We're off the course. Hurry.
Johnnie: Radio to pilot. Sorry, sir, transmitter got a dose of lead poisoning. It's out
  of operation.
Pilot: We've got to get our position by radio. Try to fix the transmitter. We're low on
  gas. It's up to you, Johnnie.
2nd Lt. Donald P. Briggs: Yes, it's up to Johnnie now and not a second to lose. As he
  bends over the bomber's crippled transmitter, an anxious look on his face, he's no
  longer the kid you used to know. Aw, you might not even recognize him as Johnnie, the
  kid next door, the kid who used to scare the daylights out of you when he climbed on the
  roof to build an aerial for his first crystal set. Naw, naw, he - he's older now, no
  longer a kid but a man and doing a man's job as a member of Uncle Sam's fighting A.A.F.
  Today Johnnie's one of that unbeatable trio, the plane, the air crew and the ground
  crew, each indispensable to the other. And he's the fellow who joins them all together,
  the radio operator. And he - he learned a lot at Scott Field, he learned radio from "A
  to Z" and, for one thing, he learned code. Yeah, Johnnie, you - you certainly got
  plenty of that at Scott. You ate code, you slept code, you lived code all the time you
  were there. You sat in classrooms while instructors tapped letters and words into your
  earphones. Hour after hour was filled with those maddening di-das and di-da-dits. Ah -
  ha, they even flashed them at you with blinker lights from miniature planes set in the
  classroom walls. Yeah, but what good is code now with no transmitter? It's got to be
  fixed and fixed in a hurry. They're depending on you. The - the pilot, the navigator
  and the bombardier and the others. They're waiting on you, counting on you. How 'bout
  it?
Johnnie: Radio to pilot. Checked transmitter. It's in bad shape. One tube gone
  completely. Spare's gone. One resister's broken. I'll do my best, sir.
2nd Lt. Donald P. Briggs: Yeah, we know you'll do your best, Johnnie, but this is a tough
  one. This is gonna take all the skill you ever learned back there at Scott. Huh,
  funny, you used to wonder then if it was all necessary, wondered if you'd ever use all
  that information and knowledge. Well, you know now it was all pointed toward this.
  This is why you spent long hours learning all about electrical fundamentals and the
  various types of aircraft radios and a million other things like rheostats and
  condensers and tubes and a ... Hey, wait a minute. Wasn't there something you learned
  back there at Scott about replacing broken tubes by - by shifting them around in a

certain way? That's right. Sure. This one goes here and that one there and ... Say, maybe that'll work after all. But hold on, there's the pilot calling.

Pilot: Pilot to radio. How's it coming, Johnnie? We're losing altitude on two engines. Anything you can do?

Johnnie: I think I've got the tube replaced, sir, but there's still a resister. Haven't got another. I'll do my best.

2nd Lt. Donald P. Briggs: Yeah, but what can you do, Johnnie? For a resister you need something like, eh, like, eh, tinfoil, the tinfoil on that roll of friction tape. Maybe that might do it. It's worth a try. Yeah, off it comes, quick. Twist it into shape. Then into the transmitter in place of the broken resister. There, now, now test it.

Johnnie: Radio to pilot. It's working. It's working, sir. We're going to be all right. Signals are going out O.K.

Pilot: Good boy, Johnnie. Good boy. Get the control station in a hurry. About thirty minutes of gas left, maybe less. Hurry.

Johnnie: P-3-D from plane K-9-Y-A. P-3-D from plane K-9-Y-A. Give position fix. Where are we? Where are we?

P-3-D: Plane K-9-Y-A from station P-3-D. Send a series of dashes so we can give fix. Plane K-9-Y-A from station P-3-D. Your position is 5-3 degrees, 2-5 minutes, 2-0 seconds north latitude. 1 degree, 5-0 minutes, 4-0 seconds east longitude.

Johnnie: This is plane K-9-Y-A. Position received. O.K. Thanks. Number one and four engines knocked out by cannon fire. Give nearest field. Landing gear smashed. Must crash land.

P-3-D: Go to Brentwood Field. Go to Brentwood Field. Brentwood notified to prepare for crash landing. Come on in. Good luck.

2nd Lt. Donald P. Briggs: A few minutes later at Brentwood Field the big bomber circles, levels off for a landing and then comes gliding in. The belly of the plane skids along the dirt, plowing up the ground and then in a great cloud of dust and smoke, comes to a stop, flak-torn and bullet-riddled, but safe at last. Yes, safe because Johnnie was on the job, Johnnie, the radio operator. On his quick knowledge and on his cool, rapid skill hang the lives of men and the fate of countless bombers and the success of every mission. For his is the job of bringing Uncle Sam's planes home safely. In his capable hands, radio becomes a life line, often the difference between safety and disaster. Yeah, he - he's an important man, Johnnie is, an important part of a great fighting outfit, the A.A.F., the A.A.F. that's smashing Hitler and his power-hungry partners into a well deserved oblivion.

I Sustain the Wings (Incidental music)

2nd Lt. Donald P. Briggs: He's one of thousands of men who are helping to drive home to our enemies the lesson that treachery does not pay. That those who live by the sword shall perish by the sword. And wherever he may be today, sparking from his busy radio is the message of victory, a message that will someday swell into one final hallelujah of triumph, mission accomplished.

Captain Glenn Miller: And now it's medley time, a serenade for the mothers, wives and sweethearts of the officers and enlisted men at Scott Field. Something old, something new, something borrowed, something blue. The old song, "Silver Threads among the Gold."

SILVER THREADS AMONG THE GOLD (Old tune)

Captain Glenn Miller: For something new, Private First Class Johnny Desmond sings "Absent Minded."

ABSENT MINDED (New tune)

Vocal refrain by Private First Class Johnny Desmond

2nd Lt. Donald P. Briggs: The Captain turns to the back of the book and borrows his version of "String of Pearls."

A STRING OF PEARLS (Borrowed tune)

Captain Glenn Miller: Last in our medley something blue, "The Saint Louis Blues."

THE SAINT LOUIS BLUES (Blue tune)

Cpl. Paul A Dubov: When a Jap sniper levels his rifle at an American soldier in the jungles of New Guinea, tell me, who do you think he's aiming at? The soldier? Huh, huh. Don't kid yourself. He's aiming at all Americans. Consider this carefully, women of America, then do something about it by enlisting in the Women's Army Corps. Answer this challenge of our enemies by helping to win the war as a WAC. In the A.A.F. alone, WACs are handling over a hundred different specialized jobs formerly done by men, men who can now be freed for active service. Join them and have the satisfaction of doing a job that's not only interesting but vital to victory. Remember, you may now choose the branch of the Army you prefer, the Air Forces, the Ground Forces, or the Service Forces. So, if you're not engaged in essential war work, visit your nearest Army Recruiting Station and have a talk with the WAC officer there. Find out how you, as an Air WAC, can give our fighting men the help they need to speed them on the road to victory. And now back to the music.

PUT YOUR ARMS AROUND ME, HONEY
Captain Glenn Miller: The Crew Chiefs and the band playin' and singin' "Put Your Arms Around Me."
Vocal refrain by the Crew Chiefs

I SUSTAIN THE WINGS (closing theme)
2nd Lt. Donald P. Briggs: "I Sustain the Wings" has presented the Band of the Training Command of the A.A.F.; Captain Glenn Miller; Corporal Ray McKinley; Johnnie, the kid next door; and many of your old friends. Next week you'll learn more about Johnnie at the A.A.F. Training Command School at the Sperry Gyroscope Corporation in Brooklyn, New York. Be with us again next Saturday, same time, same station. This program is produced and written entirely by soldiers of the A.A.F. and came to you from New York City.
NBC announcer: This (is the National Broadcasting Company.)

The parts of Pilot, Johnnie and P-3-D were played by Cpl. Paul A. Dubov, Pfc. Joseph Shulman and another member of the band.

04Dec43 (Sat) 2:15PM   NBC, New York, New York
  UNCLE SAM PRESENTS recording

I SUSTAIN THE WINGS (opening theme)
  2nd Lt. Donald P. Briggs: From the United States of America, to the other united
    nations of the world, "Uncle Sam Presents" the Band of the Training Command of the
    Army Air Forces, under the direction of Captain Glenn Miller, with Corporal Ray
    McKinley, Corporal Mel Powell, and many of your old friends.
  2nd Lt. Donald P. Briggs: And here is Captain Glenn Miller
  Captain Glenn Miller: Thank you, Lieutenant Donald Briggs, and hello, everybody.
    Starting off we salute those rugged lads that man the tail guns in the last planes in
    our bomber formations, the "Tail End Charlies."
TAIL END CHARLIE
  Captain Glenn Miller: Yes, sir, that's pretty. One of yesteryear's fine melodies now
    enjoying the well deserved current popularity. The lyrics by Private First Class Johnny
    Desmond, the tune, "My Ideal."
MY IDEAL
  Vocal refrain by Private First Class Johnny Desmond
  Captain Glenn Miller: "Fats" Waller wrote it, Corporal Mel Powell arranged it and he's
    gonna play it on the piano, "Honeysuckle Rose." Two beats, boys, one, two.
HONEYSUCKLE ROSE
  Captain Glenn Miller: "What Do You in the Infantry?" You march, you march, you march.
    Well, brother, all ain't flyin' in the Air Force, too. Listen to the Crew Chiefs and
    the band and you'll know what I'm talking about.
WHAT DO YOU DO IN THE INFANTRY
  Vocal refrain by Private First Class Artie Malvin and the Crew Chiefs
I SUSTAIN THE WINGS (closing theme)
  Captain Glenn Miller: Well, that winds things up for today. Speakin' for the band,
    thanks for all the swell letters you've been sending to us. Keep 'em comin', and when
    you write ask for your favorite tunes, we'll be more than glad to play 'em for you.
    You can reach us in care of this station. Now for Lieutenant Don Briggs, Corporal Ray
    McKinley, Corporal Mel Powell and all the rest of us, so long 'til next week same
    time.
  2nd Lt. Donald P. Briggs: The Army Air Forces Band of the Training Command, under the
    direction of Captain Glenn Miller, has come to you from New York City. Don't forget
    tomorrow, same time, same station, "Uncle Sam Presents" another famous service band
    with music from us to you.
7-0-5 (fade-out tune)
  2nd Lt. Donald P. Briggs: This is the United States of America, one of the united
    nations.

04Dec43 (Sat) 6:00-6:30PM EWT WEAF, NBC, Vanderbilt Theatre, New York, New York
I SUSTAIN THE WINGS broadcast   Audience

THE ARMY AIR CORPS (opening fanfare)
2nd Lt. Donald P. Briggs: "I Sustain the Wings."
I SUSTAIN THE WINGS (opening theme)
  2nd Lt. Donald P. Briggs: "I Sustain the Wings." The Army Air Forces Training Command
    presents the Band of the Training Command; Captain Glenn Miller; Corporal Ray
    McKinley; Corporal Mel Powell; Johnnie, the kid next door; and many of your old
    friends. And now Captain Glenn Miller.
Captain Glenn Miller: Thank you, Lieutenant Don Briggs, and good evening, everybody.
  Tonight's program, one of a series dedicated to the men of the A.A.F. Training Command,
  salutes the A.A.F. Technical School at the Sperry Gyroscope Factory in Brooklyn, New
  York, Captain Robert Wardrop, commanding officer. And startin' off we salute those
  rugged lads that man the tail guns in the last planes in our bomber formations, the
  "Tail End Charlies."
TAIL END CHARLIE
Captain Glenn Miller: Now one of yesteryear's fine melodies enjoying a well deserved
  current popularity. The lyrics sung by P.F.C. Johnny Desmond, the tune, "My Ideal."
MY IDEAL
  Vocal refrain by Private First Class Johnny Desmond
2nd Lt. Donald P. Briggs: Ah, do you recognize that sound? Yeah, probably not, because
  it's louder than usual and you don't hear it very often. Heh, heh, no - no, it - it
  isn't an angry hornet, nor a humming-bird in flight. It - it's the hum of a spinning
  top. Just watch it as it moves slowly across the floor, spinning, spinning, always
  upright. Oh - oh, it - it's bumping into the wall. It - it bounces back, but it
  doesn't go over. It - it moves back into its upright position. And that top will stay
  upright as long as it continues to spin. That's what scientists call rigidity. Huh,
  know it - it may seem a little on the silly side to be talking about spinning tops. You
  may think it's a game or something, but it isn't a game and it isn't silly. And Johnnie
  doesn't think so either. He knows that that principle of rigidity is plenty important.
  Ah, you remember Johnnie; Johnnie, the kid next door. Sure, he's the youngster that
  always used to be first with all the seasonal games and kids' sports like, ah, marbles
  and model planes, kites and especially tops. Yeah, those brightly painted pear-shaped
  blocks of wood held a particular fascination for Johnnie, a fascination that stands him
  in good stead today as a bomb-sight maintenance mechanic. A job for which he was
  trained by the A.A.F. Training Command at the Sperry Technical School in Brooklyn, New
  York. Now, ah, spinning tops don't actually have anything to do with a bomb-sight but
  that same principle of rigidity is the operating basis for the Sperry gyroscope, an
  integral part of the Sperry bomb-sight, one of America's most remarkable fighting
  weapons. Huh, the - the Sperry bomb-sight. Ah, there - there it is right there in that
  canvas case that the bombardier is carrying toward his waiting plane. Just look how
  proudly he walks. Yeah, he - he's got a right to be proud. He's been entrusted with
  one of our country's most priceless secrets, a secret he's sworn to protect with his
  life. In a few minutes they'll be ready to take off, the bombardier, his pal the
  bomb-sight, and the rest of the air crew, ready to take off on a mission that will
  demonstrate the A.A.F.'s most valued piece of air strategy, precision bombing. They're
  ready now. The engines are revving up. What do you say we go along with them?
Here we are, out over the Channel riding in one of hundreds of big four-engined bombers.
Our destination is a military secret but we can tell you that it's headed for the heart
of Hitler's Reich. This mighty air armada, which we're a part, is a thrilling sight,
stretching almost as far as the eye can see. Above and below, in front and behind, and
on either side of us, are our fighter planes, ever ready to protect us from enemy
attacks.
Pilot Tom: Pilot to bombardier. Pilot to bombardier.
Bombardier: Bombardier to pilot. Go ahead, Tom.
Pilot Tom: Hey, how's everything up there in that fish bowl of yours?
Bombardier: Everything's O.K., Tom. Right on the beam.
Pilot Tom: Good, we're only 58 minutes from the target. Pilot to bombardier.
  Approaching target.

Bombardier: Bombardier to pilot. Roger. Huh - ha, it won't be a target when we get
  through with it.
2nd Lt. Donald P. Briggs: Say, ah, tell me, Mister Bombardier, what makes you so sure the
  bomb-sight'll do the job?
Bombardier: What makes me so sure? Well, it's because I know Johnnie back there at the
  base can be depended upon to do his work. Johnnie's a sort of walking encyclopedia when
  it comes to bomb-sights. He knows the bomb-sight is a complicated system of gears,
  cams, automatic computing devices, even radio tubes. He knows there are ten separate
  major units with more than three thousand different parts. He knows how to adjust it,
  how to take it apart and put it back together again, how to maintain its accuracy.
  Yeah, and Johnnie knows that if he didn't do his job as a bomb-sight maintenance
  technician I couldn't do mine, and there wouldn't be any precision bombing. So all of
  us together, Johnnie and I, along with the bomb-sight, put those bombs where they'll do
  the most good --- right on the target.
Pilot Tom: Pilot to bombardier. Target dead ahead.
Bombardier: Bombardier to pilot. Roger. O.K., Tom, I'll take over.
2nd Lt. Donald P. Briggs: Here we go into the bombing run. Our target is that munitions
  factory straight ahead of us there. Oh, e-e-e-exploding flak is rocking our plane but
  the - the pilot rights her again and pulls her back on course. Enemy planes are
  attacking from all sides but our fighters are on the job. We're getting closer to the
  target, closer, closer ...
Bombardier: A little to the right. There it is. Bombs away.
2nd Lt. Donald P. Briggs: Bombs away, the A.A.F.'s new battle cry. A cry of triumph that
  strikes terror into the hearts of the Nazis as they in Berlin are feeling a hundred
  times over the weight of the destruction that they released upon the world. Bombs that
  hit their targets right on the nose because Johnnie is on the job keeping those bomb-
  sights accurate, checking them for the slightest variation to make sure that they're at
  the peak of efficiency.
I Sustain the Wings (Incidental music)
  2nd Lt. Donald P. Briggs: When the bombardier takes over for that dangerous bombing run
    through flak-blacked skies, he knows he can depend on his bomb-sight because Johnnie
    has done his work well and he and his training stand as a guarantee of the
    instrument's accuracy. So, when the bombardier, with his delicate, highly-trained
    fingers, adjusts the controls of the bomb-sight, he knows the bombs will smash into
    the target and blast away one more obstacle to final and complete victory.
Captain Glenn Miller: The Band of the Training Command and the tune, "Sleepy Town Train."
SLEEPY TOWN TRAIN
Captain Glenn Miller: And now it's medley time. A serenade for the mothers, wives and
  sweethearts of the officers and enlisted men at the A.A.F. Technical School in the
  Sperry Gyroscope Factory. Here's something old, something new, something borrowed and
  something blue. The old song, the "Largo" from Dvorak's "New World Symphony," "Goin'
  Home."
GOIN' HOME (Old tune)
  Captain Glenn Miller: For something new, the Crew Chiefs sing "Paper Doll."
PAPER DOLL (New tune)
  Vocal refrain by the Crew Chiefs
  Captain Glenn Miller: Corporal Mel Powell borrows a page from "Fats" Waller's piano
    book, "Honeysuckle Rose."
HONEYSUCKLE ROSE (Borrowed tune)
  Captain Glenn Miller: Last in our medley something blue, "My Blue Heaven."
MY BLUE HEAVEN (Blue tune)
Cpl. Paul A Dubov: If you're at a dance and you're a little tired, you can say, "I guess
  I'll sit this one out." But not in war. No one can sit this war out. It calls for
  help from everybody because it's a treat to everybody. You women of America know this
  and one way you're answering this challenge is by enlisting in the Women's Army Corps,
  because you know that as a WAC you can really help. Air WACs serving in the A.A.F. are
  doing a tremendous job. You'll find them driving jeeps, doing stenographic work,
  directing traffic in control towers, doing skilled technical work in photographic
  laboratories and many other jobs. And the job they're doing is invaluable. Today you
  may choose the branch of service you're best fitted for whether it's the Air Forces, the

Ground Forces, or the Service Forces. So, if you're not engaged in essential war work, decide now to take a personal part in this war. Visit your nearest Army Recruiting Station right away. Talk with the WAC officer there and start now to do your share toward victory as an Air WAC. And now back to Captain Miller.

Captain Glenn Miller: Thank you, Corporal. "What Do You Do in the Infantry?" You march, you march, you march. Well, brother, all ain't flying in the Air Force, too. Listen to the Crew Chiefs and the band and I think you'll know what I'm talkin' about.

WHAT DO YOU DO IN THE INFANTRY
Vocal refrain by the Crew Chiefs

I SUSTAIN THE WINGS (closing theme)

Captain Glenn Miller: And that's all for now. Speakin' for the Band of the Training Command, thanks to all you folks listening for your swell letters. You guys and gals in the service let us know your favorite tunes because this program is dedicated to you.

2nd Lt. Donald P. Briggs: "I Sustain the Wings" has presented the Band of the Training Command of the A.A.F.; Captain Glenn Miller; Corporal Ray McKinley; Corporal Mel Powell; Johnnie, the kid next door; and many of your old friends. Next week you'll learn more about Johnnie as an instrument maintenance man at Randolph Field, Texas. Be with us again next Saturday, same time, same station. [This program is produced and written entirely by soldiers of the A.A.F., and came to you from New York City.]

The parts of Pilot Tom and Bombardier were played by Cpl. Paul A Dubov and Pfc. Joseph Shulman.

11Dec43 (Sat) NBC, New York, New York
UNCLE SAM PRESENTS recording

I SUSTAIN THE WINGS (opening theme)
  2nd Lt. Donald P. Briggs: From the United States of America, to the other united
    nations of the world, "Uncle Sam Presents" the Band of the Training Command of the
    Army Air Forces, under the direction of Captain Glenn Miller, with Corporal Ray
    McKinley, Corporal Mel Powell, and many of your old friends.
  2nd Lt. Donald P. Briggs: And here is Captain Glenn Miller.
  Captain Glenn Miller: Thank you, Lieutenant Donald Briggs, and hello, everybody. This
    year the yuletide greeting reads "An American Christmas" and the first tune for the top
    of the tree is a tune you'll all remember from the old days, "Don't Be That Way."
DON'T BE THAT WAY
  Captain Glenn Miller: Now here's a dedication to all those gallant lads of Uncle Sam's
    Armed Forces who are spending a red, white and blue Christmas overseas. P.F.C. Johnny
    Desmond sings "White Christmas."
WHITE CHRISTMAS
  Vocal refrain by Private First Class Johnny Desmond
  Captain Glenn Miller: Time now for the Crew Chiefs to come out swingin' and they're
    swingin' "Shoo-Shoo Baby."
SHOO-SHOO BABY
  Vocal refrain by the Crew Chiefs
  Captain Glenn Miller: Nice going, Crew Chiefs. And we're all rooting for this next song
    to need new words by Christmas 1944. We hope by then we'll be singing about the past
    instead of the future and the tune will be the "Vict'ry Polka."
VICT'RY POLKA
  Vocal refrain by the Glee Club
I SUSTAIN THE WINGS (closing theme)
  Captain Glenn Miller: No more time left for this week but there's plenty more music
    left for next week. So now, speaking for Lieutenant Don Briggs, Corporal Ray
    McKinley, Corporal Mel Powell, P.F.C. Johnny Desmond, and all the rest of the gang,
    thanks a million for your letters. Keep 'em flying at us. Ask for your favorite
    tunes and if you like 'em we'll play 'em for you. So long for now, see you next week,
    and a Merry Christmas.
  2nd Lt. Donald P. Briggs: The Band of the Training Command of the Army Air Forces,
    under the direction of Captain Glenn Miller, has come to you from New York City.
    Don't forget tomorrow, same time, same station, "Uncle Sam Presents" another famous
    service band with music from us to you.
SNAFU JUMP (fade-out tune)
  2nd Lt. Donald P. Briggs: This is the United States of America, one of the united
    nations.

11Dec43 (Sat) 6:00-6:30PM EWT WEAF, NBC Vanderbilt Theatre, New York, New York
  I SUSTAIN THE WINGS broadcast   Audience

THE ARMY AIR CORPS (opening fanfare)
2nd Lt. Donald P. Briggs: "I Sustain the Wings."
I SUSTAIN THE WINGS (opening theme)
  2nd Lt. Donald P. Briggs: "I Sustain the Wings." The Army Air Forces Training Command
    presents the Band of the Training Command; Captain Glenn Miller; Corporal Ray
    McKinley; Corporal Mel Powell; P.F.C. Johnny Desmond; Johnnie, the kid next door; and
    many of your old friends. And now Captain Glenn Miller.
Captain Glenn Miller: Thank you, Lieutenant Don Briggs, and good evening, everybody.
  Tonight's program, one of a series dedicated to the men of the A.A.F. Training Command,
  salutes the A.A.F. instrument maintenance men at Randolph Field, Texas, Colonel Walter
  C. White, commanding officer. Now the boys in the band are all set to go with "Snafu
  Jump."
SNAFU JUMP
Captain Glenn Miller: And now it's medley time, a serenade to the mothers, wives and
  sweethearts of the officers and enlisted men at Randolph Field. Here's something old,
  something new, something borrowed and something blue. The old song, "Flow Gently, Sweet
  Afton."
FLOW GENTLY, SWEET AFTON (Old tune)
  Captain Glenn Miller: For something new, Johnny Desmond, the Crew Chiefs sing "Later
    Tonight."
LATER TONIGHT (New tune)
  Vocal refrain by Private First Class Johnny Desmond and the Crew Chiefs
  Captain Glenn Miller: We borrow one of Benny Goodman's old timers, "Don't Be That Way."
DON'T BE THAT WAY (Borrowed tune)
  Captain Glenn Miller: Last in our medley, something blue, "Blue Champagne."
BLUE CHAMPAGNE (Blue tune)
2nd Lt. Donald P. Briggs: Bombs away. An American bomber unloads its "eggs" on an enemy
  target, then turns and roars homeward. As the giant bomber heads for home the pilot
  puts the plane into a steep dive to pick up speed, then takes a quick glance at his
  panel, checking the instruments to make sure everything is set for the trip back. Each
  one has a message for him. The altimeter tells him ...
Cpl. Paul A. Dubov: Altitude is ten thousand feet.
2nd Lt. Donald P. Briggs: Air speed.
Cpl. Paul A. Dubov: Air speed is one sixty-five.
2nd Lt. Donald P. Briggs: Engine speed.
Cpl. Paul A. Dubov: Engine speed is two thousand revolutions per minute.
2nd Lt. Donald P. Briggs: Manifold pressure.
Cpl. Paul A. Dubov: Manifold pressure is twenty-nine inches.
2nd Lt. Donald P. Briggs: To the pilot each instrument tells some vital fact, reports to
  him on the position of the plane, its speed and the condition of its engines. It's just
  as though Johnnie himself were there at the pilot's elbow, an unseen member of the crew
  speaking to him through those instruments. But Johnnie is the man behind these
  instruments, the instrument maintenance man in the plane's ground crew, the fellow who
  takes care of the instruments and makes 'em accurate. You remember Johnnie. Sure,
  Johnnie, the kid next door. He's the same kid who made you laugh when he wrecked the
  family phonograph trying to see what made it work. Yeah, today he's still seeing what
  make things work, and seeing that they work right, as an instrument specialist in Uncle
  Sam's fighting A.A.F. He learned his job in the A.A.F. Training Command and, believe
  me, he learned it well. He learned all about, ah, altimeters, rate-of-climb indicators,
  fuel gauges, and all the, eh, complex tubes and wires and electrical gadgets that make
  'em tick. His knowledge is vital to every mission. The bombardier, as he unloaded his
  bombs on that enemy base, counted on the altimeter to do his job. The slightest flaw in
  this delicate instrument would have sent his bombs wide of the target. Yes, and the
  navigator counted on instruments to set the course for home. And now, as the pilot
  glances at the instruments in front of him, he too counts on them for an accurate
  report.

Cpl. Paul A. Dubov: Danger, the oil pressure on engines one and four is only 45 and 50
  pounds. The cylinder head temperatures are 2-50 and 2-63 centigrade.
Pilot Bill: Pilot to navigator. Engines one and four overheating. Oil lines acting up.
  Cutting two engines.
Navigator Ed: Navigator to pilot. Mountain range ahead. Map says ninety-five hundred
  feet. Can we clear on two engines?
Pilot Bill: Pilot to navigator. Can't say, Ed. Still over enemy territory. Losing
  altitude. Shall we try to clear mountains? Come in, everybody.
Navigator Ed: Navigator. Don't think we'll make it, Bill, but I'm game.
Bombardier: Bombardier. O.K. by me, Bill.
Radio: Radio. Let's go.
Tail gunner: Tail gunner. Shoot the works, but keep her tail up.
Pilot Bill: Pilot to crew. Thanks, gang. It's one chance in a million. Still losing
  altitude.
Cpl. Paul A. Dubov: Your altitude is ninety-seven hundred feet. Your altitude is
  ninety-six hundred and fifty feet. Your altitude is ninety-six hundred feet.
Pilot Bill: Pilot to navigator. Altimeter reads ninety-six hundred feet. Running into
  heavy clouds. Can't see mountains. Have to go over them blind. Can have hundred feet
  clearance if altimeter correct.
2nd Lt. Donald P. Briggs: And if it isn't correct, Johnnie? If you made the slightest
  error in checking it before the flight, a bomber and its crew will never get home. In
  just about a minute they'll be a tangle of smoking wreckage on a mountain peak. They're
  betting their lives that you were right, Johnnie. If that altimeter of yours is wrong
  even by so much as a quiver ...
Cpl. Paul A. Dubov: Your altitude is ninety-five hundred and fifty feet. Ninety-five
  hundred and fifty feet.
Pilot Bill: Pilot to crew. Only fifty feet clearance left. Throw out everything to
  lighten plane. Pilot to crew. Take crash stations. Take crash stations. [It's now or
  never, fellows. Here we go.
Navigator Ed: How about it, Bill? Bill, come in, Bill.
Pilot Bill: O.K., Ed. That's it. We're over!
2nd Lt. Donald P. Briggs: And another plane comes home safe, another crew comes back
  alive, because Johnnie was on the job! Because Johnnie knew his job! Johnnie, the
  instrument maintenance man, upon whose skill and knowledge hang the lives of men, the
  fate of every mission! For without instruments, no plane could get off the ground, or
  get back to Earth safely. Navigation instruments alone are essential to ninety per cent
  of all missions flown by the A.A.F. And these instruments must be correct, accurate to
  the last degree. If they're not, everything else counts for nothing, the pilot's skill,
  the navigator's precise calculations, the bombardier's keen eye and stead hand. But
  Johnnie's job is to see that they are accurate, and to do it, he checks and re-checks,
  adjusts and replaces, performs miracles of maintenance to keep those instruments right.
Incidental music
  2nd Lt. Donald P. Briggs: Yes, Johnnie, it's a job you can be proud to do. A mighty
    important job! Just as surely as if you were piloting a plane, dropping the bombs, or
    manning a waist gun, you're helping to blaze a trail of destruction to Berlin and
    Tokyo! Day after day, and night after night, as the bombers roar over on their way to
    the target, and the bombs rain down. You're playing a vital part in one of the
    biggest jobs that ever faced mankind. And you'll go on playing it, and playing it
    well, 'til the last enemy resistance has been blasted from our path, and victory is
    ours!]
Captain Glenn Miller: Your papa's off to the Seven Seas, that mean's "Shoo-Shoo Baby" and
  "Shoo-Shoo Baby" means the Crew Chiefs. Gentlemen, you're on.
SHOO-SHOO BABY
  Vocal refrain by the Crew Chiefs
Captain Glenn Miller: Now here's a dedication to all those gallant lads of Uncle Sam's
  Armed Forces who are spending a red, white and blue Christmas overseas. P.F.C. Johnny
  Desmond sings "White Christmas."
WHITE CHRISTMAS
  Vocal refrain by Private First Class Johnny Desmond

Corporal Paul A. Dubov: Tomorrow, Sunday, December twelfth, has been set aside as an official day of tribute to members of the Women's Army Corps serving in the Army Air Forces. Parades, dinners, and other appropriate ceremonies will be held throughout the country in honor of these women who are doing so much to help "Keep 'Em Flying." Make arrangements to visit your nearest airfield and see these Air WACs in action. They're handling all sorts of essential jobs, operating control towers, working in aerial photog[raphy units, and doing many other jobs that call for the special skill of trained women. They're adding strength to America's air arm, performing a wonderful, war-winning service, and finding real pleasure in doing it! Because they know the work is indispensable, the life interesting and rewarding. The cause, the cause of America itself! To all WACs now serving in the A.A.F., we of the A.A.F. Training Command offer our sincerest tribute and thanks. To every woman who may be eligible to become an Air WAC, we say, "Join! Join now!" Now here's Captain Miller.]
Captain Glenn Miller: (Thank you, Corporal. We're all rooting for this next song to need new words by Christmas 1944. We hope by then we'll be singing about the past instead of the future to the tune of) the "Vict'ry Polka."
VICT'RY POLKA
Vocal refrain by the Glee Club
I SUSTAIN THE WINGS (closing theme)
Captain Glenn Miller: That all for now. Speaking for the Band of the Training Command, thanks to all you folks for your swell letters. Keep 'em comin'. And you guys and gals in the service, let us know your favorite tunes because this program is dedicated to you.
2nd Lt. Donald P. Briggs: "I Sustain the Wings" has presented the Band of the Training Command of the A.A.F.; [Captain Glenn Miller; Corporal Ray McKinley; Corporal Mel Powell; P.F.C. Johnny Desmond; Johnnie, the kid next door; and many of your old friends. Next week you'll learn more about Johnnie at Pratt Whitney Engine School in Hartford, Connecticut. Be with us again next Saturday, same time, same station.
2nd Lt. Donald P. Briggs: This program is produced and written entirely by soldiers of the A.A.F., and came to you from New York City.]

The parts of Pilot Bill, Navigator Ed, Bombardier, Radio, and Tail gunner were played by Cpl. Paul A. Dubov, Pfc. Joseph Shulman and other members of the band.

11Dec43 (Sat) 11:30PM-Midnight EWT WEAF, NBC Vanderbilt Theatre, New York, New York
  I SUSTAIN THE WINGS broadcast   Audience

THE ARMY AIR CORPS (opening fanfare)
2nd Lt. Donald P. Briggs: "I Sustain the Wings."
I SUSTAIN THE WINGS (opening theme)
  2nd Lt. Donald P. Briggs: "I Sustain the Wings." The Army Air Forces Training Command
    presents the Band of the Training Command; Captain Glenn Miller; Corporal Ray
    McKinley; Corporal Mel Powell; P.F.C. Johnny Desmond; Johnnie, the kid next door; and
    many of your old friends. And now Captain Glenn Miller.
Captain Glenn Miller: Thank you, Lieutenant Don Briggs, and good evening, everybody.
  Tonight's program, one of a series dedicated to the men of the A.A.F. Training Command,
  salutes the A.A.F. instrument maintenance men at Randolph Field, Texas, Colonel Walter
  C. White, commanding officer. Now the boys in the band are all set to go with "Snafu
  Jump."
SNAFU JUMP
Captain Glenn Miller: Now it's medley time, a serenade for the mothers, wives and
  sweethearts of the officers and enlisted men at Randolph Field. Here's something old,
  something new, something borrowed and something blue. The old song, "Flow Gently, Sweet
  Afton."
FLOW GENTLY, SWEET AFTON (Old tune)
  Captain Glenn Miller: For something new, the Crew Chiefs sing "Later Tonight." Johnny
    Desmond starts it out.
LATER TONIGHT (New tune)
  Vocal refrain by Private First Class Johnny Desmond and the Crew Chiefs
  Captain Glenn Miller: We borrow one of Benny Goodman's old timers, "Don't Be That Way."
DON'T BE THAT WAY (Borrowed tune)
  Captain Glenn Miller: Last in our medley, something blue, "Blue Champagne."
BLUE CHAMPAGNE (Blue tune)
2nd Lt. Donald P. Briggs: Bombs away. [An American bomber unloads its "eggs" on an enemy
  target, then turns and roars homeward. As the giant bomber heads for home the pilot
  puts the plane into a steep dive to pick up speed, then takes a quick glance at his
  panel, checking the instruments to make sure everything is set for the trip back. Each
  one has a message for him. The altimeter tells him ...
Cpl. Paul A. Dubov: Altitude is ten thousand feet.
2nd Lt. Donald P. Briggs: Air speed.
Cpl. Paul A. Dubov: Air speed is one sixty-five.
2nd Lt. Donald P. Briggs: Engine speed.
Cpl. Paul A. Dubov: Engine speed is two thousand revolutions per minute.
2nd Lt. Donald P. Briggs: Manifold pressure.
Cpl. Paul A. Dubov: Manifold pressure is twenty-nine inches.
2nd Lt. Donald P. Briggs: To the pilot each instrument tells some vital fact, reports to
  him on the position of the plane, its speed and the condition of its engines. It's just
  as though Johnnie himself were there at the pilot's elbow, an unseen member of the crew
  speaking to him through those instruments. For Johnnie is the man behind these
  instruments, the instrument maintenance man in the plane's ground crew, the fellow who
  services the instruments and makes them accurate. You remember Johnnie, I'm sure.
  Johnnie, the kid next door. He's the same kid who made you laugh when he wrecked the
  family phonograph trying to see what made it work. And today he's still seeing what
  make things work, and seeing that they work right, as an instrument specialist in Uncle
  Sam's fighting A.A.F. He learned his job in the A.A.F. Training Command and, believe
  me, he learned it well. Learned all about altimeters, rate-of-climb indicators, fuel
  gauges, and all the complex tubes, wires and electrical gadgets that make them tick.
  His knowledge is vital to every mission. The bombardier, as he unloaded his bombs on
  that enemy base, counted on the altimeter to do his job. The slightest flaw in this
  delicate instrument would have sent his bombs wide of the target. The navigator counted
  on instruments to set the course for home. And now, as the pilot glances at the
  instruments in front of him, he too counts on them for an accurate report.
Cpl. Paul A. Dubov: Danger! Your oil pressure on engines one and four is only 45 and 50
  pounds. Your cylinder head temperatures are 2-50 and 2-63 centigrade.

Pilot Bill: Pilot to navigator. Engines one and four overheating. Oil lines acting up. Cutting two engines.

Navigator Ed: Navigator to pilot. Mountain range ahead. Map says ninety-five hundred feet. Can we clear on two engines?

Pilot Bill: Pilot to navigator. Can't say, Ed. Still over enemy territory. Losing altitude. Shall we try to clear mountains? Come in, everybody.

Navigator Ed: Navigator. Don't think we'll make it, Bill, but I'm game.

Bombardier: Bombardier. O.K. by me, Bill.

Radio: Radio. Let's go.

Tail gunner: Tail gunner. Shoot the works, but keep her tail up.

Pilot Bill: Pilot to crew. Thanks, gang. It's one chance in a million. Still losing altitude.

Cpl. Paul A. Dubov: Your altitude is ninety-seven hundred feet. Your altitude is ninety-six hundred and fifty feet. Your altitude is ninety-six hundred feet.

Pilot Bill: Pilot to navigator. Altimeter reads ninety-six hundred feet. Running into heavy clouds. Can't see mountains. Have to go over them blind. Can have hundred feet clearance if altimeter correct.

2nd Lt. Donald P. Briggs: And if it isn't correct, Johnnie? If you made the slightest error in checking it before the flight, a bomber and its crew will never get home. In just about a minute they'll be a tangle of smoking wreckage on a mountain peak. They're betting their lives that you were right, Johnnie. If that altimeter of yours is wrong even by so much as a quiver ...

Cpl. Paul A. Dubov: Your altitude is ninety-five hundred and fifty feet.

Pilot Bill: Pilot to crew. Only fifty feet clearance left. Throw out everything to lighten plane. Pilot to crew. Take crash stations. Take crash stations. It's now or never, fellows. Here we go.

Navigator Ed: How about it, Bill? Bill, come in, Bill.

Pilot Bill: O.K., Ed. That's it. We're over!

2nd Lt. Donald P. Briggs: And another plane comes home safe, another crew comes back alive, because Johnnie was on the job! Because Johnnie knew his job! Johnnie, the instrument maintenance man, upon whose skill and knowledge hang the lives of men, the fate of every mission! For without instruments, no plane could get off the ground, or get back to Earth safely. Navigation instruments alone are essential to ninety per cent of all missions flown by the A.A.F. And these instruments must be correct, accurate to the last degree. If they're not, everything else counts for nothing, the pilot's skill, the navigator's precise calculations, the bombardier's keen eye and stead hand. But Johnnie's job is to see that they are accurate, and to do it, he checks and re-checks, adjusts and replaces, performs miracles of maintenance to keep those instruments right.

Incidental music

2nd Lt. Donald P. Briggs: Yes, Johnnie, it's a job you can be proud to do. A mighty important job! Just as surely as if you were piloting a plane, dropping the bombs, or manning a waist gun, you're helping to blaze a trail of destruction to Berlin and Tokyo! Day after day, and night after night, as the bombers roar over on their way to the target, and the bombs rain down. You're playing a vital part in one of the biggest jobs that ever faced mankind. And you'll go on playing it, and playing it well, 'til the last enemy resistance has been blasted from our path, and victory is ours!]

Captain Glenn Miller: Your papa's off to the Seven Seas, that mean's "Shoo-Shoo Baby" and "Shoo-Shoo Baby" means the Crew Chiefs. Gentlemen, you're on.

SHOO-SHOO BABY

Vocal refrain by the Crew Chiefs

Captain Glenn Miller: Now here's a dedication to all those gallant lads of Uncle Sam's Armed Forces who are spending a red, white and blue Christmas overseas. P.F.C. Johnny Desmond sings "White Christmas."

WHITE CHRISTMAS

Vocal refrain by Private First Class Johnny Desmond

Corporal Paul A. Dubov: Tomorrow, Sunday, December twelfth, has been set aside as an
    official day of tribute to members of the Women's Army Corps serving in the Army Air
    Forces. Parades, dinners, and other appropriate ceremonies will be held throughout the
    country in honor of these women who are doing so much to help "Keep 'Em Flying." Make
    arrangements to visit your nearest airfield and see these Air WACs in action. They're
    handling all sorts of essential jobs, operating control towers, working in aerial
    photography units, and doing many other jobs that call for the special skill of trained
    women. They're adding strength to America's [air arm, performing a wonderful, war-
    winning service, and finding real pleasure in doing it! Because they know the work is
    indispensable, the life interesting and rewarding. The cause, the cause of America
    itself! To all WACs now serving in the A.A.F., we of the A.A.F. Training Command offer
    our sincerest tribute and thanks. To every woman who may be eligible to become an Air
    WAC, we say, "Join! Join now!" Now here's Captain Miller.]
Captain Glenn Miller: Thank you, Corporal. We're all rooting for this next song to need
    new words by Christmas 1944. We hope by then we'll be singing about the past instead of
    the future to the tune of the "Vict'ry Polka."
VICT'RY POLKA
    Vocal refrain by the Glee Club
I SUSTAIN THE WINGS (closing theme)
    Captain Glenn Miller: That all for now. Speaking for the Band of the Training Command,
        thanks to all you folks for your swell letters. Keep 'em comin'. And you guys and
        gals in the service, let us know your favorite tunes because this program is dedicated
        to you.
    2nd Lt. Donald P. Briggs: "I Sustain the Wings" has presented the Band of the Training
        Command of the A.A.F. Next week you'll learn more about Johnnie, the kid next door,
        at the A.A.F. Engine Training School at the Pratt and Whitney factory in East
        Hartford, Connecticut. Be with us again next Saturday, same time, same station.
    2nd Lt. Donald P. Briggs: This program is produced and written entirely by soldiers of
        the A.A.F., and came to you from New York City.

The parts of Pilot Bill, Navigator Ed, Bombardier, Radio, and Tail gunner were played by
Cpl. Paul A. Dubov, Pfc. Joseph Shulman and other members of the band.

18Dec43 (Sat) NBC Vanderbilt Theatre, New York, New York
HELLO LATIN-AMERICA recordings

Captain Glenn Miller: Today we add another big wish to our hope for quick and complete
    victory, that's our wish that you're enjoying a happy Christmas. We know it could be
    happier amid the spirit of peace this day represents, but until V-Day we'll go right on
    makin' the most of the good things like this All-American song which carries our
    Yule-tide greetings to you. The band plays and P.F.C. Johnny Desmond sings "White
    Christmas."

Captain Glenn Miller: That's it, friends. And now this is Captain Glenn Miller wishing
    you a Merry Christmas and a victorious New Year from the Band of the Training Command of
    the Army Air Forces. Now we turn you back to the West coast of the U.S.A.

18Dec43 (Sat) 6:00-6:30PM EWT WEAF, NBC Vanderbilt Theatre, New York, New York
  I SUSTAIN THE WINGS broadcast   Audience

THE ARMY AIR CORPS (opening fanfare)
2nd Lt. Donald P. Briggs: "I Sustain the Wings."
I SUSTAIN THE WINGS (opening theme)
  2nd Lt. Donald P. Briggs: ["I Sustain the Wings."] The Army Air Forces Training
    Command presents [the Band of the Training Command,] under the direction of Captain
    Glenn Miller, with Corporal Ray McKinley at the drums, and the story of Johnnie, the
    kid next door. [And now Captain] Glenn Miller.
Captain Glenn Miller: Thank you, Lieutenant Don Briggs, and good evening, everybody.
  Tonight the words and music pay tribute to the Army Air Forces Training Command boys
  stationed up at Pratt and Whitney Engine School, Hartford, Connecticut. So, here's to
  ya fellows and we're off with a tune that should be plenty rugged, "I Hear You
  Screamin'."
I HEAR YOU SCREAMIN'
Captain Glenn Miller: And now it's medley time. A serenade for the mothers, wives and
  sweethearts of the officers and enlisted men of the Pratt and Whitney Engine Training
  School. Here's something old, something new, something borrowed, something blue. The
  old tune, "In the Gloaming."
IN THE GLOAMING (Old tune)
  Captain Glenn Miller: For something new, P.F.C. Johnny Desmond sings.
FOR THE FIRST TIME (I've Fallen in Love) (New tune)
  Vocal refrain by Private First Class Johnny Desmond
  Captain Glenn Miller: From our good friend Benny Goodman we borrow "Stompin' at the
    Savoy."
STOMPIN' AT THE SAVOY (Borrowed tune)
  Captain Glenn Miller: Last in our medley something bluer than blue, "Deep Purple."
DEEP PURPLE (Blue tune)
2nd Lt. Donald P. Briggs (as Johnnie): ... fifteen, sixteen, seventeen, eighteen,
  nineteen, twenty! That's all of 'em!
Narrator: Yeah, that's all of 'em. The last of a squadron of twenty Martin Marauders off
  on a mission over occupied France, powered to their destination by plenty of horsepower.
  Horsepower packed into the precision smooth walls of a modern aircraft engine! Those
  engines are kept running by those men you see standing around the field and hangars.
  Yeah, yeah, those men over there, those soldiers in coveralls with the grease stained
  faces and weary eyes, watching anxiously after the planes, their planes, as they
  disappear toward the coast of France. Those men of the ground crew like the one in the
  leather jacket coming this way. That, that one right there. He's probably on his way
  to grab a little shut-eye.
2nd Lt. Donald P. Briggs: I heard that, mister, but you've got me wrong. I'm not goin'
  to hit the hay, 'cause my job is never done. It goes on 24 hours 'round the clock, and
  the hardest part of it is right now, when the planes are on their way, just waiting,
  waiting for 'em to come back. Sure, I could lie down and try to get a little rest, but
  I couldn't sleep. I'd be thinking about those planes and the trouble they might run
  into. I'd still be wondering if those engines we've been checking and adjusting and
  nursing are perking the way they should. No, uh, uh, I'm not sentimental, mister, but
  the engines I checked have got to take those guys over and bring 'em back. Maybe I'm
  just a worrier, but with a responsibility like that on your mind, there's not much use
  of a squadron engineering officer trying to sleep.
Sergeant Mechanic: Ah, 'scuse me, Lieutenant, ...
2nd Lt. Donald P. Briggs: Yeah?
Sergeant Mechanic: ... but the ignition on the R-20-2800 is snafued. Mind taking a look
  at it?
2nd Lt. Donald P. Briggs: No, I'll be right with you, Sergeant.
Sergeant Mechanic: O.K., sir.
2nd Lt. Donald P. Briggs: Ah, see what I mean, Mister? Ah, stick around, I'll be back in
  a minute. These jobs can't wait.

Narrator: There he goes, "Johnnie-Engine-Specialist," the guy that's got to know all the
   answers. He's engineering officer for one of the many squadrons of the Eighth Air Force
   stationed in England. He keeps the engines running. He got his Know-how at the A.A.F.
   Engine Training School at the Pratt and Whitney plant in East Hartford, Connecticut.
   They really taught him the answers. You know, you've met Johnnie before; he's Johnnie,
   the kid next door, that solemn-faced youngster that always took life so seriously.
   Well, he still takes things seriously, like those twenty Martin Marauders that took off
   at nine o'clock. It's ten o'clock now, and Johnnie's been thinking about them every
   minute.
2nd Lt. Donald P. Briggs: They should be at the rendezvous point now. Yeah, twelve might
   be a little behind the others. Her right engine was overheating the other day. Ah, no,
   no, we, we checked through and found that trouble. It's all taken care of.
Narrator: Eleven o'clock!
2nd Lt. Donald P. Briggs: If they're on schedule, they, they're at the target, ready for
   that ride over the hot spot. Number nine's carburetors weren't flowin' just right. If
   they should choke up on the bombing run it'd be, aw, what's - what's eating me? We had
   those carburetors on the flow bench and they were one hundred per cent O.K. when we got
   through.
Narrator: Twelve o'clock.
2nd Lt. Donald P. Briggs: Well, they should be on the way back now. Huh, bet they got a
   flock of ME-1-0-9s on their tail. Yeah, but there's nothin' to worry about. Our boys
   can fly circles around those Jerries. Unless maybe the number four's engines are out of
   time. They weren't quite right yesterday. I went all over the ignition and timing and
   had those engines running smooth as silk.
Narrator: One o'clock.
2nd Lt. Donald P. Briggs: Hey, ah, hey, mister, you seen anything of those B-26s yet?
Narrator: No, no. Ah, are they due?
2nd Lt. Donald P. Briggs: Huh, they're overdue. And believe me, mister, it's plenty
   tough waiting, always waiting, for those planes to get back. Why I babied those engines
   along, I've taken 'em apart and put 'em back together again. I know every one of their
   ten thousand odd parts and I can tell you if there's anything wrong with 'em. Ah, I've
   learned to love those engines like they were human. Why they're almost part of me, I
   know they're O.K., but kind of gets you just - just standing here waitin', wondering if
   those planes and their crews are gonna make it back here to the field and knowin' all
   the time there's nothin' I can do to hurry them up. Sorta like bein' on a ... Hey,
   hey, here comes somethin'. Ah, huh, those are P-38s. Hey, wait a minute, wait a
   minute, our babies are right behind them. There's number one. Hey, look at 'em come.
   Number two, there's three, four, ...
Incidental music
   2nd Lt. Donald P. Briggs: ... five, six.
2nd Lt. Donald P. Briggs: Fifteen, sixteen, seventeen, eight ... seventeen. Yeah, but
   twenty planes took off on that mission and only seventeen came back. Three of our
   aircraft are missing. Yeah. Three of our planes are missing. Wonder what happened?
   The engines you'd, ah, no, no, no, those - those engines were O.K. I checked every one
   of 'em myself. I gotta stop worryin'. I can't wish 'em home, I - I, hey look, look,
   look, they're comin' in, mister. They're comin' in. There's number eighteen, ...
The Army Air Corps Incidental music
   2nd Lt. Donald P. Briggs: ... nineteen, twenty.
2nd Lt. Donald P. Briggs: Eighteen, nineteen and twenty. The three missing planes.
   They're flyin' low, limping a little, but their engines are bringing them safely home
   again. Yeah, safely home again. It, it, it, it's a prayer answered by the safe return
   of our planes and their crews. And the reward? Well, I - I get my ...
I Sustain the Wings Incidental music
   2nd Lt. Donald P. Briggs: ... payoff just in knowin' that I'm doin' my job down here,
      backin' up those guys who are doin' their job up there. And as long as there's a need
      for planes to fly, to blast the Nazis and the Japs from the face of the Earth, I
      promise, I promise you we'll be on the job making sure those engines are operating
      because we know they'll furnish the power to speed us on the flight to victory.
Captain Glenn Miller: Special orders read, "Go West, young man," so P.F.C. Johnny Desmond
   hitches a ride with the band and sings "Santa Fe Trail."

ALONG THE SANTA FE TRAIL
  Vocal refrain by Private First Class Johnny Desmond
Cpl. Paul A. Dubov: You know, no one has to tell any of us to help win this war. We all
  want to help, every one of us. But I can tell you how you can help. I'm speaking now
  especially to you women who may be listening. You can help and help a lot by serving
  your country in the Women's Army Corps. Today in the A.A.F. thousands of Air WACs are
  working as clerks, stenographers, control tower operators, photographic technicians,
  Link trainer instructors, why, that's to mention only a few of their vital services.
  They're doing a tremendous job these Air WACs, but they need your help, the help of
  every woman eligible to join them. So how about lending them a hand? Over a hundred
  trained, specialized jobs await your choice in either the Air, Ground or Service Forces.
  Visit the nearest WAC encampment and get a personal picture of the interesting life they
  lead and the useful work they do. Then call at any WAC Recruiting Station and talk to
  the WAC officer there. If you're not engaged in essential war work, enlist now as an
  Air WAC and help "Keep 'Em Flying." Now here's Captain Miller.
Captain Glenn Miller: Thank you, Corporal. Folks, there isn't much left to say or play
  about the music from "Oklahoma." However Private Jerry Gray has a few new ideas on the
  subject and he sort of gets them off his chest in an all-out arrangement of "Oh, What a
  Beautiful Mornin'."
OH, WHAT A BEAUTIFUL MORNIN'
  Vocal refrain by Private First Class Johnny Desmond, the Crew Chiefs and the Glee Club
I SUSTAIN THE WINGS (closing theme)
  Captain Glenn Miller: That's all for now. Speaking for the Band of the Training
    Command, thanks to all you folks listening for your swell letters. You guys and gals
    in the service, let us know your favorite tunes, 'cause this program is dedicated to
    you.
  2nd Lt. Donald P. Briggs: "I Sustain the Wings" has presented the Band of the A.A.F.
    Training Command. Next Saturday, on Christmas, "I Sustain the Wings" will be heard
    from Halloran Army Hospital, Staten Island, New York, where we'll be playing for some
    of the boys who are sitting this one out away from home. So tune in same time, same
    station.
2nd Lt. Donald P. Briggs: This program is produced and written entirely by soldiers of
  the Army Air Forces and came to you from New York City.
NBC announcer: This is the National Broadcasting Company.

The parts of Narrator and Sergeant Mechanic were played by Cpl. Paul A. Dubov and Pfc.
Joseph Shulman.

18Dec43 (Sat) 11:30PM-Midnight EWT WEAF, NBC Vanderbilt Theatre, New York, New York
  I SUSTAIN THE WINGS broadcast   Audience

THE ARMY AIR CORPS (opening fanfare)
2nd Lt. Donald P. Briggs: "I Sustain the Wings."
I SUSTAIN THE WINGS (opening theme)
  2nd Lt. Donald P. Briggs: "I Sustain the Wings." The Army Air Forces Training Command
    presents the Band of the Training Command, under the direction of Captain Glenn
    Miller, with Corporal Ray McKinley at the drums, and the story of Johnnie, the kid
    next door. And now Captain Glenn Miller.
Captain Glenn Miller: Thank you, Lieutenant Don Briggs, and good evening, everybody.
  Tonight the words and music pay tribute to the Army Air Forces Training Command boys
  stationed up at Pratt and Whitney Engine School, Hartford, Connecticut. So, here's to
  ya fellows and we're off with a tune that should be plenty really rugged, "I Hear You
  Screamin'."
I HEAR YOU SCREAMIN'
Captain Glenn Miller: Nice going, Red. And now it's medley time, folks. A serenade for
  the mothers, wives and sweethearts of the officers and enlisted men of the Pratt and
  Whitney Engine Training School. Here's something old, something new, something
  borrowed, something blue. The old tune, "In the Gloaming."
IN THE GLOAMING (Old tune)
  Captain Glenn Miller: For something new, P.F.C. Johnny Desmond sings.
FOR THE FIRST TIME (I've Fallen in Love) (New tune)
  Vocal refrain by Private First Class Johnny Desmond
  Captain Glenn Miller: From our good friend Benny Goodman we borrow "Stompin' at the
    Savoy."
STOMPIN' AT THE SAVOY (Borrowed tune)
  Captain Glenn Miller: Last in our medley something bluer than blue, "Deep Purple."
DEEP PURPLE (Blue tune)
2nd Lt. Donald P. Briggs (as Johnnie): ... fifteen, sixteen, seventeen, eighteen,
  nineteen, twenty! That's all of 'em!
Narrator: Yeah, that's all of 'em. The last of a squadron of twenty Martin Marauders off
  on a mission over occupied France, powered to their destination by plenty of horsepower.
  Horsepower packed into the precision smooth walls of the modern aircraft engine! Those
  engines are kept running by those men you see standing around the field and hangars.
  Yeah, yeah, those - those men over there, those soldiers in coveralls with the grease
  stained faces and weary eyes, watching anxiously after the planes, their planes, as they
  disappear toward the coast of France. Those men of the ground crew like the one in the
  leather jacket coming this way. That - that one right there. He's probably on his way
  to grab a little shut-eye.
2nd Lt. Donald P. Briggs: I heard that, mister, yeah, but you've got me wrong. Huh, I'm
  not gonna to hit the hay, 'cause my job's never done, goes on 24 hours 'round the clock,
  and the hardest part of it's right now, when the planes are on their way, waiting, just
  waiting for 'em to come back. Huh, sure, I could lie down and try to get a little rest,
  but I couldn't sleep. Yeah, yeah, I'd be thinking about those planes and the trouble
  they might run into. I'd still be wondering if those engines we've been checking and
  adjusting and nursing, are perking the way they should. Huh, no, I - I'm not
  sentimental, mister, but the engines I checked have got to take those guys over and
  bring 'em back. Maybe I'm just a worry-wart, but with a responsibility like that on
  your mind, there's not much use of a squadron engineering officer trying to sleep.
Sergeant Mechanic: Ah, 'scuse me, Lieutenant, but the ignition on the
  R-twenty-eight-hundred is snafued. Mind taking a look at it?
2nd Lt. Donald P. Briggs: Yeah, be right with you, Sergeant.
Sergeant Mechanic: O.K., sir.
2nd Lt. Donald P. Briggs: Huh, see what I mean, Mister? Stick around, I'll be back in a
  minute. These jobs can't wait.

Narrator: There he goes, "Johnnie-Engine-Specialist," the guy that's got to know all the answers. He's engineering officer for one of the many squadrons of the Eighth Air Force stationed in England. He keep the engines running. He got his Know-how at the A.A.F. Engine Training School at the Pratt and Whitney plant in East Hartford, Connecticut. They really taught him the answers. You know, ah you've met Johnnie before; he's Johnnie, the kid next door, that solemn-faced youngster that always took life so seriously. Well, he still takes things seriously, like those twenty Martin Marauders that took off at nine o'clock. It's ten o'clock now, and Johnnie's been thinking about them every minute.

2nd Lt. Donald P. Briggs: They should be at the rendezvous point now. Ah, twelve might be a little behind the others. Her right engine was overheating the other day. Aw, no, no, no, we checked through and found that trouble. It's all taken care of.

Narrator: Eleven o'clock!

2nd Lt. Donald P. Briggs: If they're on schedule, they're at the target, ready for that ride over the hot spot. Yeah, number nine's carburetors weren't flowin' just right. If they should choke up on the bombing run it'd be, aw, what's eating me? We had those carburetors on the flow bench and they were one hundred per cent O.K. when we got through.

Narrator: Twelve o'clock.

2nd Lt. Donald P. Briggs: Yeah, they should be on the way back now. Yeah, bet they got a flock of ME-1-0-9s on their tail. Yeah, but there's nothin' to worry about. Our boys can fly circles around those Jerries. Unless maybe the number four's engines are out of time. They weren't quite right yesterday, but I went all over the ignition and timing and had those engines running smooth as silk.

Narrator: One o'clock.

2nd Lt. Donald P. Briggs: Hey, hey, mister, mister, you seen anything of those B-26s yet?

Narrator: No, no. Ah, are they due?

2nd Lt. Donald P. Briggs: They're overdue. Believe me, mister, it's plenty tough waitin' for those planes to get back. Why I - I - I babied those engines along, I've taken 'em apart and put 'em back together again. I know every one of their ten thousand odd parts and can tell you if there's anything wrong with 'em. Why, I've learned to love those engines like they were human. Why they're almost part of me, I know they're O.K., but it kind of gets you just standing here waitin', wondering if those planes and their crews are gonna make it back here to the field and knowin' all the time there's nothin' I can do to hurry them up. Sorta like bein' on a ... Hey, here comes somethin'. Ah, yeah, those are P-38s. Hey, wait a minute, wait a minute, our babies are right behind them. Yeah, there's number one. Hey, look at 'em come. Number two, there's three, four, ...

Incidental music

2nd Lt. Donald P. Briggs: ... five, six.

2nd Lt. Donald P. Briggs: Fifteen, sixteen, seventeen, eight ... seventeen. Yeah, but twenty planes took off on that mission and only seventeen came back. Three of our aircraft are missing. Yeah. Three of our planes are missing. Wonder what happened? The engines you'd, ah, no, no, no, tho - those engines were O.K. I checked every one of 'em myself. I gotta stop worryin'. I can't wish 'em home, I - I, hey look, look, they're comin' in, mister. They're comin' in. There's number eighteen, ...

The Army Air Corps Incidental music

2nd Lt. Donald P. Briggs: ... nineteen, twenty.

2nd Lt. Donald P. Briggs: Eighteen, nineteen and twenty. The three missing planes. They're flyin' low, limping a little, but their engines are bringing them safely home again. Yeah, safely home again. It, it, it's a prayer answered by the safe return of our planes and their crews. And the reward? Well, I - I get my payoff just in ...

I Sustain the Wings Incidental music

2nd Lt. Donald P. Briggs: ... knowin' that I'm doin' my job down here, backin' up those guys who are doin' their job up there. And as long as there's a need for planes to fly, to blast the Nazis and the Japs from the face of the Earth, I - I promise, I promise you we'll be on the job making sure those engines are operating because we know they'll furnish the power to speed us on the flight to victory.

Captain Glenn Miller: The special orders read, "Go West, young man," so P.F.C. Johnny Desmond hitches a ride with the band and sings "Santa Fe Trail."

ALONG THE SANTA FE TRAIL
Vocal refrain by Private First Class Johnny Desmond
Cpl. Paul A. Dubov: You know, no one has to tell any of us to help win this war. We all
    want to help, every one of us. But I can tell you how you can help. I'm speaking now
    especially to you women who may be listening. You can help and help a lot by serving
    your country in the Women's Army Corps. Today in the A.A.F. thousands of Air WACs are
    working as clerks, stenographers, control tower operators, photographic technicians,
    Link trainer instructors, well, that's to mention only a few of their vital services.
    They're doing a tremendous job these Air WACs, but they need your help, the help of
    every woman eligible to join them. So how about lending them a hand? Over a hundred
    trained, specialized jobs await your choice in either the Air, Ground or Service Forces.
    Visit the nearest WAC encampment and get a personal picture of the interesting life they
    lead and the u - useful work they do. Then call at any WAC Recruiting Station and talk
    to the WAC officer there. If you're not engaged in essential war work, enlist now as an
    Air WAC and help "Keep 'Em Flying." and now here's Captain Miller.
Captain Glenn Miller: Thank you, Corporal. There isn't much left to say or play about
    the music from "Oklahoma." However Private Jerry Gray has a few new ideas on the
    subject and he gets 'em off his chest in an all-out arrangement of "Oh, What a Beautiful
    Mornin'."
OH, WHAT A BEAUTIFUL MORNIN'
Vocal refrain by Private First Class Johnny Desmond, the Crew Chiefs and the Glee Club
I SUSTAIN THE WINGS (closing theme)
    Captain Glenn Miller: And that's all for now, folks. Speaking for the Band of the
        Training Command, thanks to all you for listening and for your swell letters. You
        guys and gals in the service, let us know your favorite tunes, because this program is
        dedicated to you.
    2nd Lt. Donald P. Briggs: "I Sustain the Wings" has presented the Band of the A.A.F.
        Training Command. Next Saturday, on Christmas, "I Sustain the Wings" will be heard
        from Halloran Army Hospital, Staten Island, New York, where we'll be playing for some
        of the boys who are sitting this one out away from home. So tune in same time, same
        station.
2nd Lt. Donald P. Briggs: This program is produced and written entirely by soldiers of
    the Army Air Forces and came to you from New York City.
NBC announcer: This is the National Broadcasting Company.
NBC chimes

The parts of Narrator and Sergeant Mechanic were played by Cpl. Paul A. Dubov and Pfc.
Joseph Shulman.

25Dec43 (Sat) 6:00-6:30PM EWT WEAF, NBC
  Auditorium, Halloran General Hospital, Staten Island, New York
  I SUSTAIN THE WINGS broadcast   Audience

THE ARMY AIR CORPS (opening fanfare)
Cpl. Paul A. Dubov: "I Sustain the Wings."
I SUSTAIN THE WINGS (opening theme)
  Cpl. Paul A. Dubov: "I Sustain the Wings." The Army Air Forces Training Command
  presents the Band of the Training Command, with Corporal Mel Powell, Corporal Ray
  McKinley, and songs by P.F.C. Johnny Desmond. And now Lieutenant Donald Briggs.
  2nd Lt. Donald P. Briggs: Thank you, Corporal, and hello, everybody. Tonight I'm
  pinch-hitting in the words department for Captain Glenn Miller, who's fighting it out
  with the flu, while Private Jerry Gray does the leading in the music department.
  There's no doubt about it, at Christmas time there's no place like home. But this
  Christmas there's one place we'd rather be and that's where we are, right here with
  the Army boys who are sitting this one out at Halloran Army Hospital in Staten Island,
  New York. It'll be a happier Christmas for us making this a merrier Christmas for
  them. First thing to do is light up the place and there's nothing much brighter than
  "Caribbean Clipper."
CARIBBEAN CLIPPER
2nd Lt. Donald P. Briggs: Plenty of boys in uniform who'll be romancing the - the only
  girl during their Christmas furlough home. And if they're sitting out there waiting for
  some romantic music ...
STAR EYES
  2nd Lt. Donald P. Briggs: ... here it is. P.F.C. Johnny Desmond sings "Star Eyes."
  Vocal refrain by Private First Class Johnny Desmond
  2nd Lt. Donald P. Briggs: Right after the program, Corporal Ray McKinley and Corporal Mel
  Powell and all the rest of the gang will scatter and take their stations out in the
  wards and rooms here at Halloran General Hospital to play for the boys who couldn't make
  it here to the auditorium. And one of the things there's sure to be a call for is the
  musical good cheer of "Tuxedo Junction."
TUXEDO JUNCTION
Cpl. Paul A. Dubov: Christmas 1943. The Christmas spirit needs no setting other than a
  holy heart. And no matter where they may be, in a foxhole of hot hostile islands, or
  chilled in the icy grip of screaming Arctic gales, American boys in uniform everywhere
  feel deeply the comforting glow of this holy day. And here star bound to greet the dawn
  of Christmas an American pilot flying his island in the sky.
Incidental music
  2nd Lt. Donald P. Briggs: Here beneath the Earth and moon, between this war, and the
  peace that is in my heart, I seek the warmth of the Christmas star. I make my prayer
  to Thee o Lord within this small, strange chapel where the organ sound is the engine
  roar, where no choir sings but the freezing wings, where no candles burn but the
  dim-lit dials as they guide me on my mission toward victory and peace. The memory of
  far off home fires burns within my heart as I pray. Dear, Lord, protect all those for
  whom I fight as defender of their faith. And on this holy Christmas I pray for all
  the strength which I may need to do my share for freedom's cause against depression of
  this Earth. I give full thanks for Thy blessings of which I am armed to show the
  might of right. And I go forth on my mission upon my poor wings to search the skies
  for the dove of peace. And the Yuletide gift I bear is but the message that we shall
  win back Christmas for all mankind in this Thy world.
Cpl. Paul A. Dubov: Now medley time, delivering our greetings to the mothers, wives and
  sweethearts of the men here at Halloran Hospital, something old, something new,
  something borrowed and something blue. In the old department, "Silent Night."
SILENT NIGHT (Old tune)
  2nd Lt. Donald P. Briggs: Now something new, P.F.C. Johnny Desmond sings "I'll Be Home
  for Christmas." Maybe next Christmas, Johnny.
I'LL BE HOME FOR CHRISTMAS (New tune)
  Vocal refrain by Private First Class Johnny Desmond
  2nd Lt. Donald P. Briggs: We put the touch on old Santa himself for our borrowed tune,
  here's "Jingle Bells."

JINGLE BELLS (Borrowed tune)
  Vocal refrain by the Crew Chiefs
  2nd Lt. Donald P. Briggs: Something blue, the blue lights on the Halloran Christmas
    tree spell out "White Christmas."
WHITE CHRISTMAS (Blue tune)
2nd Lt. Donald P. Briggs: Chances are you'll find Christmas quartets harmonizing this
  next tune all over the country. Well, the band and the Crew Chiefs are coming up with a
  few fancy curves of their own on "I'll Be Around."
I'LL BE AROUND
  Vocal refrain by Private First Class Johnny Desmond and the Crew Chiefs
2nd Lt. Donald P. Briggs: The boys here at Halloran General Hospital know all about what
  it takes to make victory. One of the things is plenty of that good old American spirit,
  and here it is all wrapped up in a song ...
WITH MY HEAD IN THE CLOUDS
  2nd Lt. Donald P. Briggs: ... dedicated to General H. H. Arnold, "With My Head in the
    Clouds."
  Vocal refrain by Private First Class Johnny Desmond and the Glee Club
I SUSTAIN THE WINGS (closing theme)
  2nd Lt. Donald P. Briggs: Well, that's all for now. Speaking for Captain Miller and
    the Band of the Training Command, thanks to all you folks listening for your swell
    letters. You guys and gals in the service, let us know your favorite tunes because
    this program is dedicated to you.
  Cpl. Paul A. Dubov: "I Sustain the Wings" has presented the Band of the Training
    Command of the A.A.F., Lieutenant Donald Briggs, Corporal Ray McKinley, Corporal Mel
    Powell, P.F.C. Johnny Desmond, and many of your old friends. Be with us again next
    Saturday, same time, same station.
Cpl. Paul A. Dubov: This program is produced and written entirely by soldiers of the
  A.A.F. and came to you from Halloran General Hospital, Staten Island, New York.
NBC announcer: This is the National Broadcasting Company.

25Dec43 (Sat) 11:30PM-Midnight EWT WEAF, NBC Vanderbilt Theatre, New York, New York
 I SUSTAIN THE WINGS broadcast   Audience

   ...

2nd Lt. Donald P. Briggs: ... "Caribbean Clipper."
CARIBBEAN CLIPPER
STAR EYES
   2nd Lt. Donald P. Briggs: Plenty of boys in uniform will be romancing the only girl
     during their Christmas furloughs at home. If they're sitting out there waiting for
     some romantic music, here it is, P.F.C. Johnny Desmond sings.
   Vocal refrain by Private First Class Johnny Desmond
2nd Lt. Donald P. Briggs: Following our, ah, first broadcast out at Halloran Hospital
   this afternoon, Corporal Ray McKinley, Corporal Mel Powell, and all the rest of the
   gang, scattered through the rooms and ...

   ...

TUXEDO JUNCTION
   Cpl. Paul A. Dubov: Christmas 1943. The Christmas spirit needs no setting other than a
   holy heart. No matter where ...

   ...

SILENT NIGHT (Old tune)
   2nd Lt. Donald P. Briggs: Something new, P.F.C. Johnny Desmond sings "I'll Be Home for
     Christmas." Maybe next Christmas, Johnny.
I'LL BE HOME FOR CHRISTMAS (New tune)
   Vocal refrain by Private First Class Johnny Desmond
   2nd Lt. Donald P. Briggs: We put the touch on old Santa himself for our borrowed tune,
     here's "Jingle Bells."
JINGLE BELLS (Borrowed tune)
   Vocal refrain by the Crew Chiefs
   2nd Lt. Donald P. Briggs: Something blue, the blue lights on the Christmas tree spell
     out "White Christmas."
WHITE CHRISTMAS (Blue tune)
   2nd Lt. Donald P. Briggs: Chances are you'll find Christmas quartets harmonizing this
     next tune all over the country. The band and the Crew Chiefs are coming up with a few
     fancy curves of their own on "I'll Be Around."
I'LL BE AROUND
   Vocal refrain by Private First Class Johnny Desmond and the Crew Chiefs

   ...

I SUSTAIN THE WINGS (closing theme)
   2nd Lt. Donald P. Briggs: Well, that's all for now. Speaking for Captain Miller and
     the Training Command Band, thanks to all you folks listening for your swell letters.
     You guys and gals in the service, let us know your favorite tunes because this program
     is dedicated to you.
   Cpl. Paul A. Dubov: "I Sustain the Wings" has presented the Band of the Training
     Command of the A.A.F., Corporal Ray McKinley, Corporal Mel Powell, P.F.C. Johnny
     Desmond, and many of your old friends. Be with us again next Saturday, same time,
     same station.
   Cpl. Paul A. Dubov: This program is produced and written entirely by soldiers of the
     A.A.F. and came to you from New York City.

01Jan44 (Sat) 11:30PM-Midnight EWT WEAF, NBC Vanderbilt Theatre, New York, New York
  I SUSTAIN THE WINGS broadcast   Audience

THE ARMY AIR CORPS (opening fanfare)
2nd Lt. Donald P. Briggs: "I Sustain the Wings."
I SUSTAIN THE WINGS (opening theme)
  2nd Lt. Donald P. Briggs: "I Sustain the Wings." The Army Air Forces Training Command
    presents the Band of the Training Command, under the direction of Captain Glenn
    Miller, with Corporal Ray McKinley at the drums. And now Captain Glenn Miller.
Captain Glenn Miller: Thank you, Lieutenant Don Briggs, and good evening, everybody. Old
  Pop Time has given us the nod to start a new year and this year we've got plenty to do
  to make it a victorious 1944. Tonight we're startin' things off with Private Jerry
  Gray's own idea of what a New Year's noise maker should be, "Here We Go Again."
HERE WE GO AGAIN
Captain Glenn Miller: And now it's medley time and we salute the mothers, wives,
  sweethearts and sisters of every man in the Armed Forces of the United States. For the
  gals they left behind, something old, something new, something borrowed and something
  blue. The old song, "Londonderry Air."
LONDONDERRY AIR (Old tune)
  Captain Glenn Miller: Off with the old, on with the new. P.F.C. Johnny Desmond sings.
ABSENT MINDED (New tune)
  Vocal refrain by Private First Class Johnny Desmond
  Captain Glenn Miller: Our loan department recommends for a borrowed tune Charlie
    Barnet's theme, "Cherokee."
CHEROKEE (Indian Love Song) (Borrowed tune)
  Captain Glenn Miller: In the blue department, the "Blue Danube" waltz.
BEAUTIFUL BLUE DANUBE (Blue tune)
Incidental music

  . . .

Captain Glenn Miller: ... Pfc. Johnny Desmond sings you a pin-up song, "How Sweet You
  Are."
HOW SWEET YOU ARE
  Vocal refrain by Private First Class Johnny Desmond
Captain Glenn Miller: Looking back through the American years up until this 1944, every
  American heart is filled with pride. Those who have marched before us through our
  nation's history did a big job and a good one. They fought to establish the greatest
  symbol of freedom in all the world and we're fightin' for it now. Here's our musical
  salute to "Old Glory."
OLD GLORY
  Vocal refrain by 2nd Lieutenant Donald P. Briggs, Corporal Ray McKinley, Private First
    Class Johnny Desmond and the Ensemble

  . . .

O8Jan44 (Sat) NBC, New York, New York
  UNCLE SAM PRESENTS recording

I SUSTAIN THE WINGS (opening theme)
  2nd Lt. Donald P. Briggs: From the United States of America, to the other united
    nations of the world, "Uncle Sam Presents" the Band of the A.A.F. Training Command,
    under the direction of Captain Glenn Miller, with Sergeant Ray McKinley, Sergeant Mel
    Powell, and many of your old friends.
2nd Lt. Donald P. Briggs: And here is Captain Glenn Miller.
Captain Glenn Miller: Thank you, Lieutenant Don Briggs, and howdy to you folks out there.
  We're off on another mission salutin' the boys and gals of the Army Air Forces. We're
  on runway number one and ready to take to the air with a special that should be a real
  cloud-buster, "Must Be Jelly 'cause Jam Don't Shake Like That."
IT MUST BE JELLY ('Cause Jam Don't Shake Like That)
Captain Glenn Miller: Yeah. And now, for the gals who keep the letters a flyin' to the
  boys in the Armed Forces, here's a love song and Sergeant Johnny Desmond to sing it.
SPEAK LOW (When You Speak Love)
  Vocal refrain by Sergeant Johnny Desmond
Captain Glenn Miller: Sergeant McKinley and the Crew Chiefs give you a yardbird's
  reaction to all this "G.I. Jive."
G.I. JIVE
  Vocal refrain by Sergeant Ray McKinley and the Crew Chiefs
Captain Glenn Miller: 1944 finds a battle scarred tune of two wars still in there
  pitchin' with our boys. A star-spangled veteran for the lads with the fightin' hearts,
  "Over There!"
OVER THERE!
  Vocal refrain by the Crew Chiefs
I SUSTAIN THE WINGS (closing theme)
  Captain Glenn Miller: Time now to take our leave until next week's meeting. You keep
    the letters a comin' and we'll keep the music a goin'. Speaking for Lieutenant Don
    Briggs, Sergeant Ray McKinley, Sergeant Mel Powell, Sergeant Johnny Desmond, the whole
    gang, thanks for listenin' and so long.
  2nd Lt. Donald P. Briggs: The Band of the A.A.F. Training Command, under the direction
    of Captain Glenn Miller, has come to you from New York City. Don't forget tomorrow,
    same time, same station, "Uncle Sam Presents" another famous service band with music
    from us to you.
JEEP JOCKEY JUMP (fade-out tune)
  2nd Lt. Donald P. Briggs: This is the United States of America, one of the united
  nations.

08Jan44 (Sat) 6:00-6:30PM EWT WEAF, NBC Vanderbilt Theatre, New York, New York
  I SUSTAIN THE WINGS broadcast   Audience

THE ARMY AIR CORPS (opening fanfare)
2nd Lt. Donald P. Briggs: "I Sustain the Wings."
I SUSTAIN THE WINGS (opening theme)
  2nd Lt. Donald P. Briggs: "I Sustain the Wings." The Army Air Forces Training Command
    presents the Band of the Training Command, under the direction of Captain Glenn
    Miller, with Sergeant Ray McKinley at the drums. And now Captain Glenn Miller.
Captain Glenn Miller: Thank you, Lieutenant Don Briggs, and good evening, everybody.
  We're off on another Saturday night mission salutin' the boys and the gals of the Army
  Air Force. We're on runway number one and ready to take to the air with a tune that
  should be a real cloud-buster, "It Must Be Jelly 'cause Jam Don't Shake Like That."
IT MUST BE JELLY ('Cause Jam Don't Shake Like That)
Captain Glenn Miller: For you gals who keep the letters a flyin' to the boys in the Armed
  Forces, here's a love song. The band playin' and Sergeant Johnny Desmond singin'.
SPEAK LOW (When You Speak Love)
  Vocal refrain by Sergeant Johnny Desmond
Cpl. Paul A. Dubov: Would any woman listening to this program like to make a new
  resolution today that would really help win this war? Well, let me tell you how you can
  do it. By just resolving now that you're going to join the Women's Army Corps. Now you
  can choose your branch of the service with the Air Forces, Ground Forces, or Service
  Forces. If you choose the Air Forces you'll find that Air WACs today are very
  important. They're serving with the A.A.F. in many capacities. Some of them are
  driving jeeps at busy air fields. Some are handling key assignments as clerks and
  stenographers. Others are doing skilled technical work, perhaps just the kind of work
  that you can do yourself. And all of them are really doing something to help bring the
  day of victory closer and closer. Visit the nearest Air WAC encampment and get a
  personal picture of the useful work they do and the interesting life they lead. Then
  talk with a WAC officer at any WAC Recruiting Station and let her explain how you can
  become an Air WAC and help "Keep 'Em Flying." Now, Captain.
Captain Glenn Miller: Thank you, Corporal. Sergeant McKinley and the Crew Chiefs give
  you a yardbird's reaction to all this "G.I. Jive."
G.I. JIVE
  Vocal refrain by Sergeant Ray McKinley and the Crew Chiefs
Captain Glenn Miller: Now it's medley time, saluting the mothers, wives, sweethearts and
  sisters of the boys in the A.A.F. Something old, something new, something borrowed,
  something blue. The old song, "Long, Long Ago."
LONG, LONG AGO (Old tune)
  Captain Glenn Miller: Something new from the romance department, Sergeant Johnny
    Desmond sings "The Music Stopped."
THE MUSIC STOPPED (New tune)
  Vocal refrain by Sergeant Johnny Desmond
  Captain Glenn Miller: We borrow our friend Larry Clinton's famous theme, "Dipsy
    Doodle."
THE DIPSY DOODLE (Borrowed tune)
  Captain Glenn Miller: Last, our blue tune, "Blues in My Heart."
BLUES IN MY HEART (Blue tune)

  . . .

08Jan44 (Sat) 11:30PM-Midnight EWT   WEAF, NBC Vanderbilt Theatre, New York, New York
  I SUSTAIN THE WINGS broadcast   Audience

THE ARMY AIR CORPS (opening fanfare)
2nd Lt. Donald P. Briggs: "I Sustain the Wings."
I SUSTAIN THE WINGS (opening theme)
  2nd Lt. Donald P. Briggs: "I Sustain the Wings." The Army Air Forces Training Command
    presents the Band of the Training Command, under the direction of Captain Glenn
    Miller, with Sergeant Ray McKinley at the drums. And now Captain Glenn Miller.
Captain Glenn Miller: Thank you, Lieutenant Don Briggs, and good evening, everybody.
  We're off on another Saturday night mission saluting the boys and the girls of the Army
  Air Forces. We're on runway number one and ready to take to the air with a special tune
  that should be a real cloud-buster, "It Must Be Jelly 'cause Jam Don't Shake Like That."
IT MUST BE JELLY ('Cause Jam Don't Shake Like That)
Captain Glenn Miller: Yes, sir. That's what I'm talking about. Now for you gals who
  keep the letters a flyin' to the boys in the Armed Forces, here's a love song. The band
  playin' and Sergeant Johnny Desmond singin'.
SPEAK LOW (When You Speak Love)
  Vocal refrain by Sergeant Johnny Desmond
Cpl. Paul A. Dubov: Would any woman listening to this program like to make a new
  resolution today that would really help win this war? Well, let me tell you how you can
  do it. By just resolving now that ...

  ...

Captain Glenn Miller: ... McKinley and the Crew Chiefs gives you, ah, ah, you've got me
  doing it, Corporal, a yardbird's reaction to all this "G.I. Jive."
G.I. JIVE
  Vocal refrain by Sergeant Ray McKinley and the Crew Chiefs
Captain Glenn Miller: Now it's medley time, saluting the mothers, wives, sweethearts and
  sisters of the boys in the A.A.F. Something old, something new, something borrowed and
  something blue. Our old song, "Long, Long Ago."
LONG, LONG AGO (Old tune)
  Captain Glenn Miller: Something new from the romance department, Sergeant Johnny
    Desmond sings "The Music Stopped."
THE MUSIC STOPPED (New tune)
  Vocal refrain by Sergeant Johnny Desmond
  Captain Glenn Miller: We borrow our old friend Larry Clinton's famous theme, "The Dipsy
    Doodle."
THE DIPSY DOODLE (Borrowed tune)
  Captain Glenn Miller: Last, our blue tune, "Blues in My Heart."
BLUES IN MY HEART (Blue tune)
Incidental music
  Captain Glenn Miller: Germany took, Germany took ten years to create her Air Force; we
    built ours in one and fought with it in four corners of the Earth at the same time.
    This week the story of this amazing achievement is told by the Commanding General of
    the Army Air Forces, General H. H. Arnold, in his report to the Secretary of War and
    to the nation. In this report, one of the most important documents of the war, the
    growth of our A.A.F. from blueprint to reality is dramatically summarized.
  Captain Glenn Miller: But most stirring of all is the tribute paid by General Arnold to
    the men behind the machines and planes, America's dauntless air crews, who fly our
    planes to victory, and the hard-working, highly-trained men of the ground crews, who
    "Keep 'Em Flyin'." Because these men are your sons, brothers, husbands, sweethearts, we
    know you will enjoy hearing this closing section of General Arnold's report.

  ...

Captain Glenn Miller: ... (194)4 finds a battled-scarred tune of two wars still in there
 pitchin'. A star-spangled veteran for the lads with the fightin' hearts, "Over There!"
OVER THERE!
 Vocal refrain by the Crew Chiefs
I SUSTAIN THE WINGS (closing theme)
 Captain Glenn Miller: That's all for now. Speaking for the Band of the Training
 Command, thanks to all you folks listening for your swell letters. You guys and gals
 in the service, let us know your favorite tunes, because this program is dedicated to
 you.
 2nd Lt. Donald P. Briggs: "I Sustain the Wings" has presented the Band of the Training
 Command of the A.A.F., Captain Glenn Miller, Sergeants Ray McKinley, Mel Powell, and
 Johnny Desmond, and many of your old friends. Be with us again next Saturday, same
 time, same station.
 2nd Lt. Donald P. Briggs: This program is produced by the Second A.A.F. Training Command
 Radio Unit and came to you from New York City.

15Jan44 (Sat) NBC, New York, New York
UNCLE SAM PRESENTS recording

I SUSTAIN THE WINGS (opening theme)
 2nd Lt. Donald P. Briggs: From the United States of America, to the other united
 nations of the world, "Uncle Sam Presents" the Band of the A.A.F. Training Command
 under the direction of Captain Glenn Miller with Sergeant Ray McKinley, Sergeant Mel
 Powell and many of your old friends.
 2nd Lt. Donald P. Briggs: Here's Captain Glenn Miller.
 Captain Glenn Miller: Ah, thank you, Lieutenant Don Briggs. Howdy to all you guys and
 gals out there. We're all set for a musical good will tour saluting the Army Air
 Forces, and our instrumental crew with composer Sergeant Mel Powell navigatin' at the
 piano, Sergeant Mike Hucko pilotin' the clarinet, takes off on a "Mission to Moscow."
MISSION TO MOSCOW
Captain Glenn Miller: Next we deliver a V-Mail special from the boys on the flyin' front
 to their one and onlys back here in the States. Sergeant Johnny Desmond sings "My Heart
 Tells Me."
MY HEART TELLS ME (Should I Believe My Heart?)
 Vocal refrain by Sergeant Johnny Desmond
Captain Glenn Miller: Quite some time now the strings have had things pretty much their
 own way when it came to playin' this next tune. But Sergeant Jerry Gray has other
 ideas. Listen to "Holiday for Strings."
HOLIDAY FOR STRINGS
I SUSTAIN THE WINGS (closing theme)
 Captain Glenn Miller: Time now to take our leave until next week's meeting. You keep
 the letters comin', we'll keep the music a goin'. Speakin' for Lieutenant Don Briggs,
 Sergeants Ray McKinley, Mel Powell, Johnny Desmond, the whole gang, thanks for
 listenin' and so long for now.
 2nd Lt. Donald P. Briggs: The Band of the A.A.F. Training Command under the direction
 of Captain Glenn Miller has come to you from New York City. Don't forget tomorrow,
 same time, same station, "Uncle Sam Presents" another famous service band with music
 from us to you.
A STRING OF PEARLS (fade-out tune)
 2nd Lt. Donald P. Briggs: This is the United States of America, one of the united
 nations.

15Jan44 (Sat) 6:00-6:30PM EWT WEAF, NBC Vanderbilt Theatre, New York, New York
 I SUSTAIN THE WINGS broadcast   Audience

   ...

Captain Glenn Miller: Now for medley time, delivering a bouquet of tunes to mothers,
  wives, sisters and sweethearts and their boys in uniform. Here's something old,
  something new, something borrowed, something blue. The oldie, "Old Black Joe."
OLD BLACK JOE (Old tune)
  Captain Glenn Miller: Now for our new tune, Sergeant Johnny Desmond sings "Someone to
  Love."
SOMEONE TO LOVE (New tune)
  Vocal refrain by Sergeant Johnny Desmond
  Captain Glenn Miller: A bit of reverse Lend-Lease gets us our borrowed tune. A
  marching song from England sung now by Corporal Malvin and the gang.
I'VE GOT SIXPENCE (As We Go Rolling Home) (Borrowed tune)
  Vocal refrain by Corporal Artie Malvin and the Crew Chiefs
  Captain Glenn Miller: Something blue from the pen of an outstanding contributor to the
  musical quality of the red, white and blue, George Gershwin, "Rhapsody in Blue."
RHAPSODY IN BLUE (Blue tune)
Cpl. Paul A. Dubov: Today women can join the WACs and elect to serve in either the Air
  Forces, Ground Forces, or Service Forces. If any of you women listening in have been
  wondering what kind of job the WACs are doing in this war, here's a suggestion. Don't
  depend on second or third hand information. Just visit the nearest air field where Air
  WACs are stationed and see for yourself. You'll find Air WACs working in control
  towers, doing technical work in photographic units, handling specialized jobs of all
  kinds. Chances are you'll decide that this is a job you'd be proud to do too, for it
  offers you a chance to get training that will prove valuable in post-war years and an
  unequaled opportunity to do a job that's vital to victory. So, follow our suggestion,
  visit any WAC encampment, then have a talk with the WAC officer at your nearest WAC
  Recruiting Station. Remember, your opportunities as a WAC are many. The need for your
  services is urgent. Join now. Captain Miller.
Captain Glenn Miller: Thank you, Corporal. For quite some time now the strings have had
  things pretty much their own way when it came to playing this next tune. But Sergeant
  Jerry Gray had other ideas. So he took his pen and manuscript in hand and listen to
  what happened to "Holiday for Strings."
HOLIDAY FOR STRINGS
I SUSTAIN THE WINGS (closing theme)
  Captain Glenn Miller: That's all for now. Speaking for the Band of the Training
  Command, thanks to all you folks listening for your swell letters. You guys and gals
  in the service, let us know your favorite tunes, because this program is dedicated to
  you.
  2nd Lt. Donald P. Briggs: "I Sustain the Wings" has presented the Band of the Training
  Command of the A.A.F., Captain Glenn Miller, Sergeants Ray McKinley, Mel Powell, and
  Johnny Desmond, and many of your old friends. Be with us again next Saturday, same
  time, same station.
2nd Lt. Donald P. Briggs: This program is produced by the Second A.A.F. Training Command
  Radio Unit and came to you from New York City.

15Jan44 (Sat) 11:30PM-Midnight EWT WEAF, NBC Vanderbilt Theatre, New York, New York
 I SUSTAIN THE WINGS broadcast   Audience

NBC announcer: 11:30PM, Eastern War Time, WEAF, New York.
THE ARMY AIR CORPS (opening fanfare)
2nd Lt. Donald P. Briggs: "I Sustain the Wings."
I SUSTAIN THE WINGS (opening theme)
  2nd Lt. Donald P. Briggs: "I Sustain the Wings." The Army Air Forces Training Command
    presents the Band of the Training Command, under the direction of Captain Glenn
    Miller, with Sergeant Ray McKinley at the drums. And now Captain Glenn Miller.
Captain Glenn Miller: Thank you, Lieutenant Don Briggs, and good evening, everybody.
  Takes a mighty big salute to pay the nation's respects to the fightin' guys and gals on
  Uncle Sam's All-American team. The best way to do it is by backing them up with every
  ounce of home front support you can give them. You keep pluggin' at your job, they'll
  keep sluggin' at their's. We're here tonight to play 'em the music they asked to hear.
  And one hot tip, based from a training camp feedbag, asks us to give a friendly nod to
  our gallant Russian allies. We're playin' Sergeant Mel Powell's "Mission to Moscow."
MISSION TO MOSCOW
MY HEART TELLS ME (Should I Believe My Heart?)
  Captain Glenn Miller: To be a good soldier a fellow must have something to fight for.
    First comes his country and then a lot of other things, usually including the gal he
    left behind. So here, for the boys and their gals, Sergeant Johnny Desmond sings
    something on the romantic side.
  Vocal refrain by Sergeant Johnny Desmond
The Army Air Corps (Incidental music)
  Captain Glenn Miller: Tonight we bring you a story. One of the many stories born in
    battle and brought back by the men of the A.A.F. Training Command, radio operators,
    mechanics, flight engineers, and gunners, who have returned from combat. Many of the
    tales they tell are epics of quiet courage. Others, like this one, have their moments
    of grim humor. But all reflect glory upon these men to whom danger is day long.
    Heroism habitual...

  ...

Captain Glenn Miller: Now for medley time, delivering a bouquet of tunes to mothers,
  wives, sisters and sweethearts and their boys in uniform. Here's something old,
  something new, something borrowed and something blue. The oldie, "Old Black Joe."
OLD BLACK JOE (Old tune)
  Captain Glenn Miller: Now for our new tune, Sergeant Johnny Desmond sings "Someone to
    Love."
SOMEONE TO LOVE (New tune)
  Vocal refrain by Sergeant Johnny Desmond
  Captain Glenn Miller: A bit of reverse Lend-Lease gets us our borrowed tune. A
    marching song from England sung by Corporal Malvin and the gang.
I'VE GOT SIXPENCE (As We Go Rolling Home) (Borrowed tune)
  Vocal refrain by Corporal Artie Malvin and the Crew Chiefs
  Captain Glenn Miller: Something blue from the pen of an outstanding contributor to the
    musical quality of the red, white and blue, George Gershwin, and it's his "Rhapsody in
    Blue."
RHAPSODY IN BLUE (Blue tune)
Cpl. Paul A. Dubov: Today women can join the WACs and elect to serve in either the Air
  Forces, Ground Forces, or Service Forces. If any of you women listening in have been
  wondering what kind of job the WACs are doing in this war, here's a suggestion. Don't
  depend on second or third hand information. Just visit the nearest air field where Air
  WACs are stationed and see for yourself. You'll find Air WACs working in control
  towers, doing technical work in photographic units, and handling specialized jobs of all
  kinds. Chances are you'll decide that this is a job you'd be proud to do too, for it
  offers you a chance to get training that will prove valuable in post-war years and an
  unequaled opportunity to do a job that's vital to victory. So, follow our suggestion,
  visit any WAC encampment, and have a talk with the WAC officer at your nearest WAC

Recruiting Station.   Remember, your opportunities as a WAC are many.   The need for your
services is urgent.   Join now.   Captain Miller.
Captain Glenn Miller: Thank you, Corporal.   For quite some time now the strings have had
things pretty much their own way when it came to playing this next tune.   But Sergeant
Jerry Gray had other ideas.   So he took his pen and manuscript in hand and listen to
what happened to "Holiday for Strings."
HOLIDAY FOR STRINGS
I SUSTAIN THE WINGS (closing theme)
Captain Glenn Miller: That's all for now.   Speaking for the Band of the Training
Command, thanks to all you folks listening for your swell letters.   You guys and gals
in the service, let us know your favorite tunes, because this program is dedicated to
you.
2nd Lt. Donald P. Briggs: "I Sustain the Wings" has presented the Band of the Training
Command of the A.A.F., Captain Glenn Miller, Sergeants Ray McKinley, Mel Powell, and
Johnny Desmond, and many of your old friends.   Be with us again next Saturday, same
time, same station.

17Jan44 (Mon) 9:00-10:00PM   NBC, New York, New York
  LET'S BACK THE ATTACK broadcast   CBS, NBC, Mutual, Blue Network, Shortwave
  Official opening of the Fourth War Loan Drive   Audience

  ...

Captain Glenn Miller: Mr. Secretary, this is Captain Glenn Miller reporting, sir.   And if
there's going to be an American parade, Private Jones, let's start it off right with
"Old Glory."
OLD GLORY
  Vocals, talks, etc. by members of the band and the cast

  ...

22Jan44 (Sat) 2:15-2:30PM EWT NBC, New York, New York
UNCLE SAM PRESENTS recording

I SUSTAIN THE WINGS (opening theme)
    2nd Lt. Donald P. Briggs: From the United States of America, to the other united
      nations of the world, "Uncle Sam Presents" the Band of the A.A.F. Training Command,
      under the direction of Captain Glenn Miller, with Sergeant Ray McKinley, Sergeant Mel
      Powell and many of your old friends.
    2nd Lt. Donald P. Briggs: Here's Captain Glenn Miller.
    Captain Glenn Miller: Thank you, Lieutenant Don Briggs, and howdy to all you sons and
      daughters of Uncle Sam scattered all over the world. We have some music comin' up we
      think that you'll like and Sergeant Jerry Gray's responsible for the opener-upper,
      "Enlisted Men's Mess."
ENLISTED MEN'S MESS
Captain Glenn Miller: Now here's the band playin' and Sergeant Johnny Desmond, the Crew
    Chiefs singin' a swell new tune, "Moon Dreams."
MOON DREAMS
    Vocal refrain by Sergeant Johnny Desmond and the Crew Chiefs
Captain Glenn Miller: Very pretty, boys. Ever since it opened last spring, Broadway's
    hit show "Oklahoma" has been packin' 'em in. One of the main reasons is the swell
    music. Our boys and gals in uniform seem to like it a lot, especially this next tune,
    "Oh, What a Beautiful Mornin'."
OH, WHAT A BEAUTIFUL MORNIN'
    Vocal refrain by Sergeant Johnny Desmond and the Crew Chiefs
I SUSTAIN THE WINGS (closing theme)
    Captain Glenn Miller: Time now to take our leave until next week's meeting. You keep
      the letters a comin', we'll keep the music a goin'. Speaking for Lieutenant Don
      Briggs, Sergeants Ray McKinley, Mel Powell and Johnny Desmond, the whole gang, thanks
      for listenin' and so long.
    2nd Lt. Donald P. Briggs: The Band of the A.A.F. Training Command, under the direction
      of Captain Glenn Miller, has come to you from New York City. Don't forget tomorrow,
      same time, same station, "Uncle Sam Presents" another famous service band with music
      from us to you.
BUBBLE BATH (fade-out tune)
    2nd Lt. Donald P. Briggs: This is the United States of America, one of the united
      nations.

22Jan44 (Sat) 6:00-6:30PM EWT WEAF, NBC Vanderbilt Theatre, New York, New York
  I SUSTAIN THE WINGS broadcast   Audience

THE ARMY AIR CORPS (opening fanfare)
2nd Lt. Donald P. Briggs: "I Sustain the Wings."
I SUSTAIN THE WINGS (opening theme)
  2nd Lt. Donald P. Briggs: "I Sustain the Wings." The Army Air Forces Training Command
    presents the Band of the Training Command, under the direction of Captain Glenn
    Miller, with Sergeant Ray McKinley at the drums. And now Captain Glenn Miller.
Captain Glenn Miller: Thank you, Lieutenant Don Briggs, and good evening, everybody.
  This week America is firing a 21-gun salute to Uncle Sam's fighting guys and gals by
  opening the Fourth War Loan Drive to back the attack. One way for you on the home front
  to show your appreciation and support for the swell job they're doing on the fighting
  front is to buy that "extry" War Bond today. In the music department Sergeant Jerry
  Gray has a new type of G.I. dinner music, "Enlisted Men's Mess."
ENLISTED MEN'S MESS
Captain Glenn Miller: Now Sergeant Johnny Desmond and the Crew Chiefs sing a swell new
  tune, "Moon Dreams."
MOON DREAMS
  Vocal refrain by Sergeant Johnny Desmond and the Crew Chiefs
The Army Air Corps (Incidental music)
  Captain Glenn Miller: It takes 59 different men, all of them specialists in their
    individual jobs, to maintain a Fortress in combat and to keep it there. Only ten of
    these men actually fly in the plane, the rest work on the ground. They're the
    mechanics, armorers, ignition experts, guys who do a million and one terrifically
    important jobs to keep those planes flying the way they should. Each one of these 59
    specialists learned his job in the A.A.F. Training Command. They're plenty good,
    these men. Able to fix up a plane with almost nothing at all. But there comes a time
    when they've got to have tools and spare parts for replacements, ...
Captain Glenn Miller: ... supplies flown to them by guys just like themselves. Here's an
  interesting story and according to the way one of these unsung heroes tells it.
2nd Lt. Donald P. Briggs: My job's just a job. Dull, unexciting, routine stuff. Nothing
  much ever happens. Sure, I've done a lot of flying since I was sent to India, just
  shuttling back and forth, delivering men and supplies from one base to another. Picking
  up wounded, taking them to the hospital. Things like that. Like I said before, just
  routine stuff. The Training Command made a mechanic out of me, only they tagged it with
  a fancy name, aerial engineer. Huh, like working in a garage, just fixing the engines
  and keeping them running on the ground and in the air. We fly all day and spend most of
  the night getting the plane in shape for the next day. Like the time I worked all night
  fixing up a carburetor with some spare parts I got from a wrecked plane. It was four
  o'clock in the morning by the time I had those engines perking. I was just getting set
  to knock off for a little shut-eye when bang, all of a sudden we got orders to be ready
  to take off at six o'clock. It was after we lost Burma and the Japs had closed the
  Burma Road. Flyin' Tigers were operating a base in China and they needed some tools and
  spare parts fast. Well, we loaded up the plane, took off on the dot, headed for the
  Chinese base, Lo Sang they called it, just a routine trip, nothin' to write home about.
  That C-47 just kept eatin' up the miles over jungles and mountains. And it seemed like
  no time at all until we were over the field at Lo Sang, ready to come in.
We'd hardly stopped movin' before those ground crew boys were swarming around the plane,
  ready to help us unload. They looked pretty tired with their red-rimmed eyes and
  unshaven faces, but all they could think about was gettin' the tools and stuff 'cause,
  as they put it, they just about run out of things that they could do to a plane with
  balin' wire and a prayer.
We just started to unload when a bunch of Chinese came runnin' toward the plane,
  pointin' up at the sky and shoutin', "Ling bo, ling bo!" Huh, it didn't take us long to
  figure out there was an air raid comin', and soon. Sure enough, we could hear the Jap
  bombers and see 'em in the distance. We didn't even have time to unload the rest of our
  cargo. We had to get out of there fast. We waited long enough to get some wounded
  pilots on board and then we started to take off.

Those Japs were gettin' closer and closer and we were havin' trouble gettin' off the field because the runways were so short. There was a ditch at one end of it and as we kept gettin' closer and closer to it that ditch looked bigger than the Grand Canyon. But we cleared it O.K. and got out of there just ahead of the Japs. We could see 'em dropping their bombs on the field that we just left, made us plenty mad, but if we'd stayed a couple of minutes longer it'd have been the finish for us 'cause the Japs messed up Lo Sang plenty that day. We couldn't stick around and get in on the excitement, swap punches with those Japs, 'cause, you see, we don't have guns or ammunition on a cargo plane. And, besides, we had to fly our stuff to a safer base, further into the interior of China, and unload there. Well, we picked up a fast tail wind and then it started cloudin' up.

Incidental music

2nd Lt. Donald P. Briggs: Clouds got thicker and thicker and we couldn't get above or below 'em. It was as black as the ace of spades. We were really flying blind. We kept goin' right through that soup, there was nothin' else to do and Bingo!

2nd Lt. Donald P. Briggs: We were right smack in the middle of a monsoon. And, brother, that's not my idea of fun. The storm kept slappin' at the plane. The pilot figured it was time to set down at our base and he tried for a beam on the field, but that tail wind had carried us a couple of hundred miles beyond the base and we didn't know where we were. Things didn't look any too good. Finally, after foolin' around for a while the pilot managed to get a fix and set a course for the base. We all relaxed, but only for a minute, 'cause when we reached the field we might as well have been a thousand miles away. It was ceiling zero. The storm had that field blacked out like a curtain. So we just kept circling, ...

Incidental music

2nd Lt. Donald P. Briggs: ... circling, circling. Gas got lower and lower. Finally the pilot made a pass at the field but he overshot his mark and had to pull up again. Down below they were doin' what they could to help us, linin' the runway with lights, sendin' up rocket flares, but it was like tryin' to light up Madison Square Garden with a match. That one bad try made us all a little jittery but the pilot got set for another try. He circled again, then pointed the nose down, down, down.

2nd Lt. Donald P. Briggs: Sure, we made it O.K., and without damaging the plane too much, thanks to the pilot. He's a good man. Course, it took us most of the night to get the plane in flyin' shape again for the next day, but that's how it goes. Our job's delivering parts and stuff where they're needed the most. Just routine flights, that's us, the pack mules of the A.A.F. Excitement? Huh, that's for the other guys. They have all the fun. Nothin' ever happens to us.

Incidental music

Captain Glenn Miller: Now it's medley time. And the boys of the Ground Crew have asked us to send a special delivery package of tunes to all their mothers, wives, sisters and sweethearts. Something old, something new, something borrowed, something blue. The old tune, "Jeanie with the Light Brown Hair."

JEANIE WITH THE LIGHT BROWN HAIR (Old tune)

Captain Glenn Miller: For our new tune Sergeant Johnny Desmond and the Crew Chiefs sing "I Couldn't Sleep a Wink Last Night."

I COULDN'T SLEEP A WINK LAST NIGHT (New tune)

Vocal refrain by Sergeant Johnny Desmond and the Crew Chiefs

Captain Glenn Miller: We borrow the next tune from friend Artie Shaw, "Begin the Beguine."

BEGIN THE BEGUINE (Borrowed tune)

Captain Glenn Miller: Last in our medley, something blue, "Blue Rain."

BLUE RAIN (Blue tune)

Cpl. Paul A. Dubov: Today any woman joining the Women's Army Corps may pick her branch of the service, either Air, Ground or Service Forces. If the Air Force is your choice, you'll be trained for a specialized assignment in one of more than a hundred skilled jobs, all of them are interesting, all of them are essential to victory. And as an Air WAC you'll have the proud satisfaction of helping win this war in as direct a way as any woman can. The knowledge that your service really counts. Visit any Army Recruiting Station and discover for yourself the many opportunities that can be yours in the

Women's Army Corps. Join now and help "Keep 'Em Flying" as an Air WAC in the A.A.F.
Captain Miller.
Captain Glenn Miller: Thank you, Corporal. Next an all-ow, all, wait a minute, an
all-out arrangement of "Oh, What a Beautiful Mornin'."
OH, WHAT A BEAUTIFUL MORNIN'
Vocal refrain by Sergeant Johnny Desmond and the Crew Chiefs
I SUSTAIN THE WINGS (closing theme)
Captain Glenn Miller: "I Sustain the Wings" has presented the Band of the Training
Command of the A.A.F., Lieutenant Don Briggs, Sergeants Ray McKinley, Mel Powell,
Johnny Desmond, and many of your old friends. Be with us again next Saturday, same
time, same station.
2nd Lt. Donald P. Briggs: This program is produced by the Second A.A.F. Training
Command Radio Unit and came to you from New York City.
NBC announcer: This is the National Broadcasting Company.
NBC chimes

22Jan44 (Sat) 11:30PM-Midnight EWT WEAF, NBC Vanderbilt Theatre, New York, New York
  I SUSTAIN THE WINGS broadcast   Audience

THE ARMY AIR CORPS (opening fanfare)
2nd Lt. Donald P. Briggs: "I Sustain the Wings."
I SUSTAIN THE WINGS (opening theme)
  2nd Lt. Donald P. Briggs: "I Sustain the Wings." The Army Air Forces Training Command
    presents the Band of the Training Command, under the direction of Captain Glenn
    Miller, with Sergeant Ray McKinley at the drums. And now Captain Glenn Miller.
Captain Glenn Miller: Thank you, Lieutenant Don Briggs, and good evening, everybody.
  This week America's firing a 21-gun salute to Uncle Sam's fighting guys and gals by
  opening the Fourth War Loan Drive to back the attack. One way for you on the home front
  to show your appreciation and support for the swell job they're doing on the fighting
  front is to buy, at least, that extra hundred dollar War Bond today. Now in the music
  department Sergeant Jerry Gray has a new type of G.I. dinner music, "Enlisted Men's
  Mess."
ENLISTED MEN'S MESS
Captain Glenn Miller: Now Sergeant Johnny Desmond and the Crew Chiefs sing a swell new
  tune, "Moon Dreams."
MOON DREAMS
  Vocal refrain by Sergeant Johnny Desmond and the Crew Chiefs
The Army Air Corps (Incidental music)
  Captain Glenn Miller: Takes 59 different men, all of them specialists in their
    individual jobs, to maintain a Fortress in combat and to keep it there. Only ten of
    those men actually fly in the plane, the rest work on the ground. They're the
    mechanics, armorers, hydraulic experts, guys who do a million and one terrifically
    important jobs to keep those planes flying the way they should. Each one of these 59
    specialists learned his job in the A.A.F. Training Command. They're pretty good,
    these men. Able to fix up a plane with almost nothing at all. But there comes a time
    when they've got to have ...
Captain Glenn Miller: ... tools and spare parts for replacements, supplies flown to them
  by guys just like themselves. Here's an interesting story and according to the way one
  of these unsung heroes tells it.
2nd Lt. Donald P. Briggs: Well, our job's just a job. Dull, unexciting, routine stuff.
  Nothing much ever happens. Oh sure, I've done a lot of flying since I was sent to
  India, just shuttling back and forth, delivering men and supplies from one base to
  another. Picking up wounded, taking them to the hospital. Things like that. Like I
  said before, just routine stuff. Training Command made a mechanic out of me, only they
  tagged it with a fancy name, aerial engineer. Huh, like working in a garage, just
  fixing the engines and keeping them running on the ground and in the air. We fly all
  day and spend most of the night getting the plane in shape for the next day. Heh, like
  the time I worked all night fixing up a carburetor with some spare parts I got from a
  wrecked plane. It was four o'clock in the morning by the time I had those engines
  perking. I was just getting set to knock off for a little shut-eye when bang, ... all
  ready to take off ... appears to be ...

  ...

Captain Glenn Miller: ... Something old, something new, something borrowed, something
  blue. The old tune, "Jeanie with the Light Brown Hair."
JEANIE WITH THE LIGHT BROWN HAIR (Old tune)
  Captain Glenn Miller: For our new tune Sergeant Johnny Desmond and the Crew Chiefs sing
    "I Couldn't Sleep a Wink Last Night."
I COULDN'T SLEEP A WINK LAST NIGHT (New tune)
  Vocal refrain by Sergeant Johnny Desmond and the Crew Chiefs
  Captain Glenn Miller: We borrow the next tune from friend Artie Shaw, "Begin the
    Beguine."
BEGIN THE BEGUINE (Borrowed tune)

  ...

BLUE RAIN (Blue tune)

Cpl. Paul A. Dubov: Today any woman joining the Women's Army Corps may pick her branch of the service, either Air, Ground or Service Forces. If the Air Force is your choice, you'll be trained for a specialized assignment in one of more than a hundred skilled jobs, all of them are interesting, all of them are essential to victory. And as an Air WAC you'll have the proud satisfaction of helping win this war in as direct a way as any woman can. The knowledge that your service really counts. Visit any Army Recruiting Station and discover for yourself the many opportunities that can be yours in the Women's Army Corps. Join now and help "Keep 'Em Flying" as an Air WAC in the A.A.F. Captain Miller.

Captain Glenn Miller: Thank you, Corporal. Next an all-out arrangement of "Oh, What a Beautiful Mornin'."

OH, WHAT A BEAUTIFUL MORNIN'

Vocal refrain by Sergeant Johnny Desmond and the Crew Chiefs

I SUSTAIN THE WINGS (closing theme)

Captain Glenn Miller: "I Sustain the Wings" has presented the Band of the Training Command of the A.A.F., Lieutenant Don Briggs, Sergeants Ray McKinley, Mel Powell, Johnny Desmond, and many of your old friends. Be with us again next Saturday, same time, same station.

2nd Lt. Donald P. Briggs: This program is produced by the Second A.A.F. Training Command Radio Unit and came to you from New York City.

29Jan44 (Sat) NBC, New York, New York
UNCLE SAM PRESENTS recording

...

2nd Lt. Donald P. Briggs: Here's Captain Glenn Miller.

Captain Glenn Miller: Thank you, Lieutenant Don Briggs, and hello, everybody. The boys in the band are ready and waitin' and Sergeant Jerry Gray is responsible for the opener, "Jeep Jockey Jump."

JEEP JOCKEY JUMP

Captain Glenn Miller: Song writers still can't find a better way to say it, but we'll take a chance on Sergeant Johnny Desmond findin' a better way to sing the tune "I Love You."

I LOVE YOU

Vocal refrain by Sergeant Johnny Desmond

...

Captain Glenn Miller: ... One three-striper has turned these talents toward a popular tune and put it through some mighty fancy paces. Here's Sergeant Jerry Gray's fancy dress parade arrangement of the "Vict'ry Polka."

VICT'RY POLKA

Vocal refrain by Sergeant Johnny Desmond, the Crew Chiefs and the Glee Club

I SUSTAIN THE WINGS (closing theme)

...

29Jan44 (Sat) 6:00-6:30PM EWT WEAF, NBC Vanderbilt Theatre, New York, New York
I SUSTAIN THE WINGS broadcast   Audience

THE ARMY AIR CORPS (opening fanfare)
2nd Lt. Donald P. Briggs: "I Sustain the Wings."
I SUSTAIN THE WINGS (opening theme)
    2nd Lt. Donald P. Briggs: "I Sustain the Wings." The Army Air Forces Training Command
        presents the Band of the Training Command, under the direction of Captain Glenn
        Miller, with Sergeant Ray McKinley at the drums. And now Captain Glenn Miller.
Captain Glenn Miller: Thank you, Lieutenant Don Briggs, and good evening, everybody. Our
    musical takeoff tonight is a quiet little ear-splitter called "Stealin' Apples."
STEALIN' APPLES
Captain Glenn Miller: The song writers still can't find a better way to say it, but we'll
    take a chance on Sergeant Johnny Desmond finding a better way to sing it. The tune, "I
    Love You."
I LOVE YOU
    Vocal refrain by Sergeant Johnny Desmond
Incidental music
    2nd Lt. Donald P. Briggs: If you're Mister Bombardier, you and the rest of the team ...

    ...

2nd Lt. Donald P. Briggs: Your big Liberator's coming in fast now. Pouring head-on
    through black bursts of flak that rock you like a canoe. From your grandstand seat in
    the greenhouse you can see fires down below. That's where the first wave of planes laid
    its bombs. You're next.
    Sometimes back at preflight school it didn't quite add up, logarithms, formulas, classes
    all day. You couldn't see how you could ever use the stuff that the Training Command
    crammed into your head but you stuck it out. You wanted those bombardier's wings.
    The top turret guns begin to spit as you hunch down over your bomb-sight. Check for
    altitude. Check for airspeed. The guns are going faster now but you won't let yourself
    look up. Check for wind drift. Suddenly you realize you're doing things automatically,
    all the things that came so hard in training, and you're doing them right. In advance
    school you got pretty cocky. Pilots, navigators, huh, O.K. for some guys maybe, but
    you're the man that they build bombers around. You pack the knockout punch.
    The Liberator heels and straightens out on her target. Then Pete comes in over the
    interphone.
Cpl. Paul A. Dubov (as Pilot Pete): O.K., slugger, she's yours. Make it good.
2nd Lt. Donald P. Briggs: All right, you're the boss now. This is what you've been
    waiting for. You glue your eye into the sights, you talk into your throat microphone.
    "Level, Pete. Hold it level. Bomb bay doors open. Left a little. Level now. Level.
    Perfect." All right, there's your target, caught on the cross hairs like a fly in a
    spider's web. You jab the release. Bombs away. Now you've done it. The seconds drag
    out and then B.Z., back at the tail gun, yells out "Hit! Hit!" Well, you - you just
    start to swell and then all at once you see that it wasn't just you who smeared that
    Nazi base. No, no, it - it was Pete up in the pilot's seat, Flip with his navigation
    charts, and the gunners Jim, Tony, B.Z., and Lou. It was you and the rest of the crew
    flying as a team, a part of the same team that paved the way for the landings in the
    Gilberts, that flattened Bremen and Williamsshaumen, that's carrying the war to Japan,
    the A.A.F., the greatest team in the world. And it makes you pretty proud to be a part
    of that team. Now, I know 'cause I'm playing on the same team, me, myself, yeah, and I
    helped deliver those bombs to the target just now. Though I wasn't actually in the
    plane, I was flying with you all the time. I'm the Air Force technician. I make it
    possible for flyers to be heroes and heroes to be fliers. I drill and work and fight.
    I work that others may fly and fight. I fight that I may work to "Keep 'Em Flying."
    I'm the mechanic, the machinist, the armorer, the weather observer, the instrument man,
    the radio man. I'm a technician, but I fight like a commando. I'm one of an unbeatable
    trio, the plane, the air crew, and the ground crew, each indispensable to the other two.
    Without me the plane would be a motionless machine, the pilot a helpless gladiator.

When I trained I - I beefed at the constant stream or repetition of routine, but now I realize I was learning to act on instinct. I griped at scrubbing and shining and cleaning but now I realize neatness means a clean job at every task. An unbuttoned pocket seemed trivial but now I know a forgotten button might be a forgotten cotter key and that key might mean a plane destroyed and a crew lost. Because of strict training, I'm good and I know I'm good. The folks at home may never know how important I am, the public may never see my name in print. I'm the plodding lineman of modern football. I make long runs possible for All-Americans. I'm the blocker that never carries the ball.

Incidental music

2nd Lt. Donald P. Briggs: That pilot there knows me. He knows that when he climbs on board, that plane's ready. He knows those engines are perfect. The radio, his ears; the instruments, his eyes. That bombardier knows his hits are going to be perfect. And when they come back there's something in their handshake no newspaper could describe, no medal could equal. It's the grip of men whose lives depend on me. I Sustain the Wings.

Captain Glenn Miller: Sergeant Mel Powell has written and arranged a wonderful piece of music, wonderful to these tired ears, at any rate. To make it an all-out job on the Sergeant's part, he is featured as piano soloist. The title, "Pearls on Velvet." Sergeant Powell.

PEARLS ON VELVET

Captain Glenn Miller: Now for medley time. The music from the boys in uniform to their mothers, wives, sweethearts and sisters. To the gals they left behind. Something old, something new, something borrowed and something blue. The old song, "Annie Laurie."

ANNIE LAURIE (Old tune)

Captain Glenn Miller: Something new, Sergeant Johnny Desmond sings "My Ideal."

MY IDEAL (New tune)

Vocal refrain by Sergeant Johnny Desmond

Captain Glenn Miller: We'll put the bite on Irving Berlin for our borrowed tune and come up smilin' with "Alexander's Ragtime Band."

ALEXANDER'S RAGTIME BAND (Borrowed tune)

Captain Glenn Miller: One now for the blue department, "Blue Is the Night" above me.

BLUE IS THE NIGHT (Blue tune)

Cpl. Paul A. Dubov: One of the biggest opportunities open to women who join the Women's Army Corps is the chance to get valuable training. Training that'll be useful to you in the years after the war. Why, right now in the Air Forces alone are thousands of Air WACs learning new skills or improving abilities they already possess, and their jobs are important war-winning jobs, interesting specialized work that's vital to victory. In joining the Women's Army Corps you may pick any branch of the service, Air, Ground, or Service Forces. So, if you're not in essential war work, visit the nearest WAC Recruiting Station and volunteer as an Air WAC to help "Keep 'Em Flying." Captain Miller.

Captain Glenn Miller: Thank you, Corporal. Here's Sergeant Jerry Gray's fancy dress parade arrangement of the "Vict'ry Polka."

VICT'RY POLKA

Vocal refrain by Sergeant Johnny Desmond, the Crew Chiefs and the Glee Club

2nd Lt. Donald P. Briggs: Yesterday an important statement was made by the commanding general of the A.A.F. Training Command. Statistics that were confidential for years were released to the public so that you, Mr. and Mrs. America, may know about your Air Forces. Here are the facts.

Voice 1: There are more than two million, three hundred thousand officers and enlisted men in the Army Air Forces.

Voice 2: Since January first, 1939 the A.A.F. Training Command has turned out over one hundred thousand pilots, ...

Voice 3: ... twenty thousand bombardiers, ...

Voice 4: ... one hundred and ten thousand aerial gunners, ...

Voice 5: ... half a million highly specialized technicians.

2nd Lt. Donald P. Briggs: And, Mr. and Mrs. America, there are thousands and thousands more to come. The A.A.F. is in high gear smashing the enemy whenever and wherever he may be found.

I SUSTAIN THE WINGS (closing theme)
    Captain Glenn Miller: "I Sustain the Wings" has presented the Band of the Training
      Command of the A.A.F., Lieutenant Don Briggs, Sergeants Ray McKinley, Mel Powell,
      Johnny Desmond, and many of your old friends. So be with us again next Saturday, same
      time, same station.
    2nd Lt. Donald P. Briggs: This program is a presentation of the Army Air Forces
      Training Command and came to you from New York City.
NBC announcer: This is the National Broadcasting Company.
NBC chimes

The parts of Voice 1, Voice 2, Voice 3, Voice 4 and Voice 5 were played by Cpl. Paul A.
Dubov and other members of the band.

05Feb44 (Sat) 2:15-3:00PM EWT   NBC, New York, New York
    UNCLE SAM PRESENTS recording

I SUSTAIN THE WINGS (opening theme)
    2nd Lt. Donald P. Briggs: From the United States of America, to the other united
      nations of the world, "Uncle Sam Presents" the Band of the A.A.F. Training Command,
      under the direction of Captain Glenn Miller, with Sergeant Ray McKinley, Sergeant Mel
      Powell and many of your old friends.
    2nd Lt. Donald P. Briggs: Here's Captain Glenn Miller.
    Captain Glenn Miller: Thank you, Lieutenant Don Briggs, and hello, everybody. Startin'
      off we salute those rugged lads who have that dangerous rear guard spot in every fighter
      formation, the "Tail End Charlies."
TAIL END CHARLIE
Captain Glenn Miller: Now a new tune that looks like it's headed for a long run in the
    top brackets of popularity. Sergeant Johnny Desmond sings "Now I Know."
NOW I KNOW
    Vocal refrain by Sergeant Johnny Desmond
Captain Glenn Miller: A fine tune gives a fine arranger plenty of inspiration. And
    there's no better example of that than what happened when Staff Sergeant Jerry Gray
    bumped into "Holiday for Strings."
HOLIDAY FOR STRINGS
I SUSTAIN THE WINGS
    Captain Glenn Miller: Time now to take our leave until next week's meeting. You keep
      the letters a comin', we'll keep the music a goin'. And speaking for Lieutenant Don
      Briggs, Sergeants Ray McKinley, Mel Powell, Johnny Desmond, the whole gang, thanks for
      listenin' and so long for now.
    2nd Lt. Donald P. Briggs: The Band of the A.A.F. Training Command, under the direction
      of Captain Glenn Miller, has come to you from New York City. Don't forget tomorrow,
      same time, same station, "Uncle Sam Presents" another famous service band with music
      from us to you.
7-0-5 (fade-out tune)
    2nd Lt. Donald P. Briggs: This is the United States of America, one of the united
    nations.

05Feb44 (Sat) 6:00-6:30PM EWT WEAF, NBC Vanderbilt Theatre, New York, New York
I SUSTAIN THE WINGS broadcast   Audience

THE ARMY AIR CORPS (opening fanfare)
2nd Lt. Donald P. Briggs: "I Sustain the Wings."
I SUSTAIN THE WINGS (opening theme)
  Cpl. Broderick Crawford: "I Sustain the Wings." The Army Air Forces Training Command
    presents the Band of the Training Command, under the direction of Captain Glenn
    Miller, with Lieutenant Donald Briggs, and Sergeant Ray McKinley at the drums. And
    now Captain Glenn Miller.
Captain Glenn Miller: Thank you, Corporal Broderick Crawford, and good evening,
  everybody. One of the greatest supplies of ammunition with which our nation is fighting
  this war is a plentiful supply of good old-fashioned faith. Faith in our purpose and
  faith in the kind of guy who climbs into the tiny caboose of a high flying Fortress to
  shoot it out with the Jap and German flyers. Those are the boys we salute, the "Tail
  End Charlies."
TAIL END CHARLIE
Captain Glenn Miller: A new tune that looks like its headed for a long run in the top
  brackets of popularity, Sergeant Johnny Desmond sings "Now I Know."
NOW I KNOW
  Vocal refrain by Sergeant Johnny Desmond
Incidental music
  2nd Lt. Donald P. Briggs: This is our home. It's not a cozy cottage in the country.
    It's not a little white bungalow on a quiet side street, with roses in the door yard.
    It's not a farm house on the prairie, set in the windbreak of pines. But it's our
    home. Fifty-one feet long, about six feet wide, high enough to stand up in, here and
    there, that's our home. There's no street number above the door because we move
    around quite a bit. In the past two months our address has been a lot places. North
    Africa, Sicily, Italy, wherever our business takes us. Our job? We deliver things
    for Uncle Sam. Mostly bombs.
  2nd Lt. Donald P. Briggs: I guess you might say this old B-25 bomber, this home of ours,
    is sort of a trailer, a sky trailer with wings. It takes us anywhere we want to go, in
    a hurry, too, and brings us back. But like a trailer, it's just a bit crowded for
    space. Especially with five of us living in it. Then, of course, the machine guns take
    up space, too. Strange furniture for a home, you say? Yeah, but very comforting at
    times. Traveling around the way we do, you never know who you might run into. Course,
    it is a bit noisy, this home of ours. The two engines make quite a racket sometimes and
    the ventilation isn't perfect either. Sometimes there's not enough air and we have to
    wear oxygen masks to keep going, and then other times it's too drafty. Especially when
    certain rowdy neighborhood characters knock holes in the house with cannon shells. Oh,
    yeah, yeah, I almost forgot to warn you, if you step out the door watch that first step.
    You're liable to fall and hurt yourself badly. But, all in all, it's not a bad home.
Incidental music
  2nd Lt. Donald P. Briggs: Each of us has his own room. The bombardier lives up in
    front on the sun porch. His room's all nicely glassed-in with a wonderful view of the
    country. And right behind him's the office of the pilot and the co-pilot, who also
    serves as navigator. Not very big, their room, but with all their dials and switches
    real handy. And just behind the bomb bay that's where I stay, snug as a bug in a rug
    in my little radio room. And in the top turret, just above me, sits the top turret
    gunner in his small, cozy den with a skylight roof and a brace of machine guns, just
    in case burglars might try to climb down the chimney.
  2nd Lt. Donald P. Briggs: Heh, yeah, like I said, there's five in our family. Eh, eh,
    look. Here - here - here's a snapshot I took of them just after we returned from a
    little business trip to Sicily last year. That lanky fellow in front, that's our pilot,
    Captain Hank Beaton, lean-jawed guy from down Texas way. Yeah, he's made out of cast
    iron and gunpowder. Never guess he was once a certified public accountant, would you?
    Looking over his shoulder in the picture is Lieutenant Joe Sims, the co-pilot and
    navigator, from Louisiana. Yeah, he's as dangerous in a fight as a loaded revolver.
    Always joking, though. That big guy beside him's Lieutenant Moose Krozinsky, the
    bombardier. You can see why we call him Moose. Always happy, Moose is. And sing?

Heh, heh. You should hear him singing over the interphone, sometimes in Polish, that's really gruesome. The - the top turret gunner is that short kid beside the Captain, Sergeant Johnny Burk. Yeah, his hair always looks like that. Won't stay combed. Teeth far apart in front when he grins, which is often. Always threatening to quit and take a safer job. But he never will. He's got six burglars to his credit already. Then there's the rest of the family, our brothers in battle, the guys of the ground crew who look after the place when we're not using it. Did I say, "look after it?" Hey, mister, they love it. They take care of this house of ours like a mother watching over her children. When we leave on a trip, they're there to see us off, to wish us luck and to smother us with last minute advice, and then gaze after us 'til we're swallowed up in the sky. While we're gone they wait and worry out the long hours that we're away. When we finally get back, there they are again, the first to greet us, watching us come in, with big, happy grins on their faces, but stealing anxious glances at the house to see that nothing happened to it. Almost before the engines stopped they're there swarming all over the place, cleaning out the empty shell cases, spending hours of loving care on the engines, filling the fuel tanks, making all the necessary household repairs. Never satisfied, always fixing, checking or something, working day and night, each one a specialist trained to do his job and do it perfectly, each one devoted to this house of ours as we are. Swell bunch, all of them. Without them we couldn't do our job and this house of ours couldn't exist.

Incidental music
  2nd Lt. Donald P. Briggs: Well, that's it, I guess. Just a handful of guys living in one home for the duration. A strange home, I'll admit that, but it's the only one we've got. Here we live and here we work, always together in this house of ours in the sky. We came from all over, we've got different ideas on lots of things, but none of that counts now. It's us against the world. All for one and one for all. Before we go on each trip we kneel down with the chaplin and say a prayer. And I always manage to sneak in a word for our home. "God bless our happy home," I say. And I know the others do, too. Some day when the last bomb is delivered, when the last trip is over, we'll leave our house in the sky and go back to other homes where folks are waiting for us. But in the meantime, this is our home.
Captain Glenn Miller: Now it's medley time. Serenade for the mothers, wives and sweethearts of those gallant guys who are fighting Uncle Sam's battle all over the world. Here's something old, something new, something borrowed and something blue. The old tune, "Flow Gently, Sweet Afton."
FLOW GENTLY, SWEET AFTON (Old tune)
  Captain Glenn Miller: Something new now, Sergeant Johnny Desmond sings.
MY HEART TELLS ME (Should I Believe My Heart?) (New tune)
  Vocal refrain by Sergeant Johnny Desmond
  Captain Glenn Miller: We borrow from our good friend Benny Goodman "Don't Be That Way."
DON'T BE THAT WAY (Borrowed tune)
  Captain Glenn Miller: Last in our medley, something blue, "Blue Champagne."
BLUE CHAMPAGNE (Blue tune)
Cpl. Broderick Crawford: Folks, the next time you see an Army Air Forces plane roaring through the sky, just remember that part of the credit for keeping that plane in the air belongs to women, members of the Women's Army Corps serving in the A.A.F. and known as Air WACs. As an Air WAC you have a chance to fill more than one hundred specialized jobs now available, each one of them interesting and vitally important to victory. So, join now. You can pick the branch of the service you prefer, either the Air, Ground, or Service Forces. Talk to the WAC officer at any WAC Recruiting Station and let her explain how you, as an Air WAC, can help "Keep 'Em Flying." Now, Captain.
Captain Glenn Miller: Thank you, Corporal. A fine tune gives a fine arranger plenty of inspiration, and there's no better example of that than what happened when Staff Sergeant Jerry Gray bumped into "Holiday for Strings."
HOLIDAY FOR STRINGS
2nd Lt. Donald P. Briggs: A university so big that it totals over a million men. Its schools cover every State in the Union. Its graduates number in the hundreds of thousands. That's the A.A.F. Training Command. Its purpose? To train each man to serve his country most efficiently. Through its schools have already passed every man now flying in the A.A.F., as well as more than a half a million ground crew technicians.

No wonder they call it the biggest university in the world. No wonder its motto is "I Sustain the Wings."
I SUSTAIN THE WINGS (closing theme)
    Captain Glenn Miller: "I Sustain the Wings" has presented the Band of the Training Command of the A.A.F., Lieutenant Don Briggs, Sergeant Ray McKinley, Mel Powell, Johnny Desmond, and Corporal Brod Crawford. Be with us again next Saturday, same time, same station.
    Cpl. Broderick Crawford: This program is a presentation of the Army Air Forces Training Command and came to you from New York City.
NBC announcer: This is the National Broadcasting Company.
NBC chimes

05Feb44 (Sat) 11:30PM-Midnight EWT WEAF, NBC Vanderbilt Theatre, New York, New York
  I SUSTAIN THE WINGS broadcast
                                                                                       Audience

  ...

FLOW GENTLY, SWEET AFTON (Old tune)
    Captain Glenn Miller: Something new, Sergeant Johnny Desmond sings.
MY HEART TELLS ME (Should I Believe My Heart?) (New tune)
    Vocal refrain by Sergeant Johnny Desmond
    Captain Glenn Miller: We borrow from our good friend Benny Goodman "Don't Be That Way."
DON'T BE THAT WAY (Borrowed tune)
    Captain Glenn Miller: Last in our medley, something blue, "Blue Champagne."
BLUE CHAMPAGNE (Blue tune)

  ...

HOLIDAY FOR STRINGS
    2nd Lt. Donald P. Briggs: A university so big that it totals over a million men. Its schools cover every State of the Union. Its graduates number in the hundreds ...

  ...

11Feb44 (Fri) 1:45-4:00PM NBC, New York, New York
TREASURY STAR PARADE recording (First show)

I SUSTAIN THE WINGS (opening theme)
  2nd Lt. Donald P. Briggs: Now here's Captain Glenn Miller.
Captain Glenn Miller: Thank you, Lieutenant Briggs, and hello, everybody. In the music
  department here's one of Sergeant Jerry Gray's latest and best, "Caribbean Clipper."
CARIBBEAN CLIPPER
Captain Glenn Miller: Switching over now to the romance department, Sergeant Johnny
  Desmond sings "Speak Low."
SPEAK LOW (When You Speak Love)
  Vocal refrain by Sergeant Johnny Desmond
Captain Glenn Miller: Sergeant Ray McKinley and the Crew Chiefs give you a yardbird's
  slant on "G.I. Jive."
G.I. JIVE
  Vocal refrain by Staff Sergeant Ray McKinley and the Crew Chiefs
Captain Glenn Miller: One of the greatest stories to come out of this war is the history
  that has been made in the sky by the A.A.F. So, in tribute to the Air Forces, the Crew
  Chiefs and the orchestra bring you "The Squadron Song."
THE SQUADRON SONG
  Vocal refrain by Sergeant Johnny Desmond, the Crew Chiefs and the Glee Club
I SUSTAIN THE WINGS (closing theme)

11Feb44 (Fri) 1:45-4:00PM NBC, New York, New York
TREASURY STAR PARADE recording (Second show)

I SUSTAIN THE WINGS (opening theme)
  2nd Lt. Donald P. Briggs: Now here's Captain Glenn Miller.
Captain Glenn Miller: Thank you, Lieutenant Briggs, and hello, everybody. To start our
  "Treasury Star Parade," we play a tune dedicated to those gallant guys who man the tail
  guns in the last bomber in formation, the "Tail End Charlies."
TAIL END CHARLIE
Captain Glenn Miller: Now Sergeant Johnny Desmond and the top tune from Cole Porter's new
  show, "Mexican Hayride." The title, "I Love You."
I LOVE YOU
  Vocal refrain by Sergeant Johnny Desmond
Captain Glenn Miller: Here's Sergeant Jerry Gray's arrangement of "Holiday for Strings."
HOLIDAY FOR STRINGS

12Feb44 (Sat) NBC, New York, New York
  UNCLE SAM PRESENTS recording

I SUSTAIN THE WINGS (opening theme)
  2nd Lt. Donald P. Briggs: From the United States of America, to the other united
    nations of the world, "Uncle Sam Presents" the Band of the A.A.F. Training Command,
    under the direction of Captain Glenn Miller, with Sergeant Ray McKinley, Sergeant Mel
    Powell and many of your old friends.
  2nd Lt. Donald P. Briggs: Here's Captain Glenn Miller.
  Captain Glenn Miller: Thank you, Lieutenant Don Briggs, and hello, everybody. Comin' up
    first is the band playin' Sergeant Jerry Gray's tribute to the lads who pilot one of
    America's newest institutions, "Jeep Jockey Jump."
JEEP JOCKEY JUMP
  Captain Glenn Miller: According to the cash customers on the receiving end of this
    program, they like Sergeant Johnny Desmond singin' "Speak Low." So, "Speak Low" again,
    Sergeant.
SPEAK LOW (When You Speak Love)
  Vocal refrain by Sergeant Johnny Desmond
  Captain Glenn Miller: The Crew Chiefs and Sergeant Bobby Nichols give you a nickel's
    worth of some of your musical favorites, "Juke Box Saturday Night."
JUKE BOX SATURDAY NIGHT
  Vocal refrain by the Crew Chiefs
WITH MY HEAD IN THE CLOUDS
  Captain Glenn Miller: Now a song written by Irving Berlin and dedicated to the
    commanding general of the A.A.F., General H. H. Arnold, "With My Head in the Clouds."
  Vocal refrain by the Crew Chiefs and the Glee Club
I SUSTAIN THE WINGS (closing theme)
  Captain Glenn Miller: Time now to take our leave until next week's meeting. You keep
    the letters a comin', we'll keep the music a goin'. And speakin' for Lieutenant Don
    Briggs, Sergeants Ray McKinley, Mel Powell, Johnny Desmond, the Crew Chiefs, and the
    whole gang, thanks for listenin' and so long for now.
  2nd Lt. Donald P. Briggs: The Band of the A.A.F. Training Command, under the direction
    of Captain Glenn Miller, has come to you from New York City. Don't forget tomorrow,
    same time, same station, "Uncle Sam Presents" another famous service band with music
    from us to you.
OH, LADY BE GOOD! (fade-out tune)
  2nd Lt. Donald P. Briggs: This is the United States of America, one of the united
    nations.

12Feb44 (Sat) 6:00-6:30PM EWT WEAF, NBC Vanderbilt Theatre, New York, New York
I SUSTAIN THE WINGS broadcast   Audience

THE ARMY AIR CORPS (opening fanfare)
2nd Lt. Donald P. Briggs: "I Sustain the Wings."
I SUSTAIN THE WINGS (opening theme)
  Cpl. Broderick Crawford: "I Sustain the Wings." The Army Air Forces Training Command
    presents the Band of the Training Command, under the direction of Captain Glenn
    Miller. And now Captain Glenn Miller.
Captain Glenn Miller: Good evening, everybody. Speaking for Corporal Brod Crawford,
    Sergeants Mel Powell, Ray McKinley, Johnny Desmond, the Crew Chiefs, and Lieutenant Don
    Briggs, and the whole gang, in fact, welcome to the thirty-first program of "I Sustain
    the Wings." We're in the home stretch of the Fourth War Loan Drive and that's where the
    final burst of speed really counts. So you take it from there and buy that "extry" one
    hundred dollar bond, you know, the one you can't afford. Musically, here's Sergeant
    Jerry Gray's tribute to the lads who pilot one of America's newest institutions, "Jeep
    Jockey Jump."
JEEP JOCKEY JUMP
Captain Glenn Miller: According to the cash customers on the receiving end of this
    program, they like "Speak Low" by the band and Sergeant Johnny Desmond. Well, the
    customer's always right, so, "Speak Low" again.
SPEAK LOW (When You Speak Love)
  Vocal refrain by Sergeant Johnny Desmond
Cpl. Broderick Crawford: Are airplanes people? Well, to men of the A.A.F. ground crews
    the world over, they are. You know it's pretty hard not to feel that way about a plane
    when you live with it, share danger with it and take care of it for 24 hours a day. It
    comes to be more than a complicated collection of metal. It gets to be more like an old
    friend. You give it a name, you learn its peculiarities that set it apart from other
    planes. You work with it, polish it, repair it and sometimes you do even more than that
    for it, like the ground crew of the Bouncing Bess in our story today. But that story
    really belongs to Sergeant Mat Johnson, the crew chief. So let's let him tell it.
2nd Lt. Donald P. Briggs (as Sgt. Mat Johnson): Yeah, yeah.
Incidental music
  2nd Lt. Donald P. Briggs: I - I remember like it was yesterday the day old Bouncing
    Bess came back from the raid that ended her career. She'd gone out that morning with
    a flock of other Forts to drop some "cabbages" on Frankfurt and while she was gone us
    guys on the ground crew just sat around smokin' and talkin' and waitin' for her to
    come back. At about noon the other Forts started comin' in, Desperate Desmond, Good
    Time Charlie, Birmingham Blitz, and all the rest. But no Bouncing Bess. And then,
    then when we'd about given her up for lost, there she came, like a wounded bird,
    tilted over on one wing, engines smokin', shootin' red flares to warn of wounded
    aboard. Well, she bounced into the field, then rolled to a shuttering stop and we
    raced out to look at her. A wreck, that's all, big scramble of twisted metal, two
    engines shot, a hole in the waist big enough to throw a gunner through, a wreck.
    Well, we pulled her over to one side, Hank, Dave, Morty, Ed and the rest of us on the
    ground crew. And, as we stood there looking at her, our hearts were way down in our
    shoes. We didn't talk much, just waited while the squadron engineers went out in a
    jeep to look her over, waited like a sick person's family waiting for the doctor's
    verdict. Then it came. No more flying for Bouncing Bess, Colonel's orders. From now
    on she's be used as a hangar queen, just left standin' around to supply parts to fix
    other planes. Yeah, that hit us hard, all of us. Bouncing Bess had been our plane
    for almost a year, mission after mission we, we got up before dawn to send her off,
    we'd, we'd sweated out her return, we'd worked on her, taking care of her like she was
    a human being or somethin', and now she was gone, a hangar queen.
  2nd Lt. Donald P. Briggs: Aw, it was a tough moment, I tell you. Well, we pulled a
    canvas over her two good engines and pushed her over to one side of the field and then
    we transferred over to another plane, feeling heartless and hatin' ourselves. But it
    was nothing else to do. Meanwhile the other guys started taking parts off Bouncing Bess
    to fix their planes. Well, a Fort came in with its hydraulic system shot away, so they
    took the spare parts out of Bess. Another plane came in with its tail assembly chewed

up, so Bouncing Bess gave up hers. Yeah, that's the way it went. Aw, let's see, the next thing to go was her props. Yeah, I remember now, they stripped them off for G.I. Joe that had crash landed. Then out came one engine, a wing for V for Vengeance that ground-looped in a tough breeze. Huh, fact is, it seemed like every morning when you looked out there at Bouncing Bess, she got smaller, another part or two missing. Ah, I was afraid to think of the day when I'd look out there and see nothing left of her except just two chocks sitting there alone in the runway where the wheels used to be. Well, then one day, one day we got a big shipment of wings in and other spare parts. Suddenly there was plenty for everything, and I got a great idea. Why not rebuild Bouncing Bess? Sure, I - I know it sounds crazy, that's what the other guys said at first. At first they couldn't see it at all, felt too gloomy, I guess, too discouraged. But I - I - I kept right on talkin'. Finally they began to get stirred up about it, too. Well, we - we - we put on a new wing that same day. Yeah, Bouncing Bess looked better already. A few days later we - we got our hands on a new tail assembly. We put it on, workin' at it after our other jobs were done. Ho, ho, aw, that was better. Even Bouncing Bess began to notice it. There was a sort of a - a - a gleam in her plexiglass windows that wasn't there before. Ah, before she's been, well, sort of sad lookin', cast down like any lady'd be who couldn't present her best face to the world but now, now, now she spruced up a little. Well, we - we picked up some odds and ends of hydraulic equipment and patched it in. Well, the fellows were really gettin' excited now. The officers just shook their heads and smiled sadly. Maybe they thought we were mad. Huh, maybe we were. Well, here and there we found other parts, installed them every time we got a chance. Heh, we were like vultures when new parts arrived and we could smell a spare part a mile. If it wasn't tied down it disappeared and a few hours later it'd show up bright and shiny in Bouncing Bess. And then, then came the day when we installed the last part. Boy, I'll never forget it. The Colonel came out to look her over. They tested her, hardly believing their eyes, checked her in every way. She was O.K. We'd worked hard on her. Yeah, she looked like a ship right off the assembly line, except for a tell-tale dent here and a bit of scratched paint there.

Incidental music
> 2nd Lt. Donald P. Briggs: And at last the morning came when she went up with her old squadron. Ed and Morty and I put the guns back in her and she - she straightened up with pride. Hank and Dave gave her a taste of gas and oil and she looked positively giddy with joy. Nobody said anything, just - just watched her, feelin' all - all funny inside. Then the crew climbed in and the pilot, Lieutenant Nelson, waved at us from the pilot's window and taxied her out to the runway. When, when her turn came to take off we, we stood there in the half light of dawn just, just lookin' our hearts out. We felt good. We were just a bunch of ground crew guys but we'd done somethin' good. Yeah, and I, I know old Bouncin' Bess thanked us. When she roared down the runway and then lifted airborne into the morning mist, her nose pointed again toward the Channel, I swear she winked at us. Yes, she winked as if to say, "Thanks, boys. This one's for you."

> Captain Glenn Miller: And now for mom, the missis, sis and the only gal in the world here's something old, something new, something borrowed and something blue. The old tune, "Londonderry Air."

LONDONDERRY AIR (Danny Boy) (Old tune)
> Captain Glenn Miller: For something new, Sergeant Johnny Desmond sings "Absent Minded."

ABSENT MINDED (New tune)
> Vocal refrain by Sergeant Johnny Desmond
> Captain Glenn Miller: Friend Charlie Barnet's theme is our borrowed tune, "Cherokee."

CHEROKEE (Indian Love Song) (Borrowed tune)
> Captain Glenn Miller: Last, the blue tune, "Blue Danube" waltz.

BEAUTIFUL BLUE DANUBE (Blue tune)
> 2nd Lt. Donald P. Briggs: Today women who join the Women's Army Corps can choose any branch of the service they prefer, the Air, Ground, or Service Forces. You can choose your job, too. Request an assignment that uses your skill, or get training in some new specialty. And you can choose your station. Make a request when you join the WAC to be stationed at any Army post near your home. Visit the nearest Army Recruiting Station and find out all about these new opportunities. With our Air Forces growing bigger

every day, Air WACs are especially needed. Join now as an Air WAC in the A.A.F. and
help "Keep 'Em Flying."

WITH MY HEAD IN THE CLOUDS
  Captain Glenn Miller: Now a song written by Irving Berlin and dedicated to the
  commanding general of the A.A.F., General H. H. Arnold. The tune, "With My Head in
  the Clouds."
  Vocal refrain by Sergeant Johnny Desmond, the Crew Chiefs and the Glee Club
Cpl. Broderick Crawford: It fires over six hundred shots per minute. It contains over
  two hundred complex parts. That's Uncle Sam's fifty-caliber aircraft machine-gun. Yet
  the A.A.F. Training Command can teach a man the care and construction of this gun in one
  week. Using the most modern training methods, the Training Command gives every A.A.F.
  armorer thorough instruction in every phase of guns, bombs and ammunition, and turns him
  out in only ten weeks, a specialist in aircraft armament. In this and it's many other
  teaching jobs, the Training Command lives up to its proud motto, "I Sustain the Wings."

I SUSTAIN THE WINGS (closing theme)
  Captain Glenn Miller: Captain Miller saying so long for the band of the Training
  Command, Corporal Brod Crawford, Sergeants Mel Powell, Ray McKinley, Johnny Desmond,
  the Crew Chiefs and Lieutenant Don Briggs. See you again next Saturday, same time,
  same station. In the meantime, don't forget those lads that are sluggin' it out
  overseas. They go for those V-Mail letters, don't let 'em down.
  Cpl. Broderick Crawford: "I Sustain the Wings" is a presentation of the Army Air Forces
  and came to you from New York City.
NBC announcer: This is the National Broadcasting Company.
NBC chimes

12Feb44 (Sat) 11:30PM-Midnight EWT WEAF, NBC Vanderbilt Theatre, New York, New York
  I SUSTAIN THE WINGS broadcast   Audience

  ...

Captain Glenn Miller: ... "Jeep Jockey Jump."
JEEP JOCKEY JUMP
Captain Glenn Miller: According to the cash customers on the receiving end of this
  program, they like "Speak Low" by the band and Sergeant Johnny Desmond. Well, the
  customer's always right, so, "Speak Low" again.
SPEAK LOW (When You Speak Love)
  Vocal refrain by Sergeant Johnny Desmond
Cpl. Broderick Crawford: Are airplanes people? Well, to men of the A.A.F. ground crews
  the world over, they are. You know it's pretty hard not to feel that way about a plane
  ...

  ...

DANNY BOY (Old tune)
  Captain Glenn Miller: For something new, Sergeant Johnny Desmond sings "Absent Minded."
ABSENT MINDED (New tune)
  Vocal refrain by Sergeant Johnny Desmond
  Captain Glenn Miller: Friend Charlie Barnet's theme is our borrowed tune, "Cherokee."
CHEROKEE (Indian Love Song) (Borrowed tune)
  Captain Glenn Miller: Last, the blue tune, the "Blue Danube" waltz.
BEAUTIFUL BLUE DANUBE (Blue tune)

  ...

WITH MY HEAD IN THE CLOUDS
  Captain Glenn Miller: ... Berlin and dedicated to the commanding general of the A.A.F.,
       ...
  Vocal refrain by Sergeant Johnny Desmond, the Crew Chiefs and the Glee Club
Cpl. Broderick Crawford: It fires over six hundred shots per minute. It contains over
  two hundred complex parts. That's Uncle Sam's fifty-caliber aircraft machine-gun. Yet
  the A.A.F. Training Command can teach a man the care and construction of this gun in one
  week. Using the most modern training methods, the Training Command gives every A.A.F.
  armorer thorough instruction in every phase of guns, bombs and ammunition, and turns him
  out in only ten weeks, a specialist in aircraft arma(ment.) ...

  ...

19Feb44 (Sat) NBC, New York, New York
  UNCLE SAM PRESENTS recording

  ...

Captain Glenn Miller: ... big guns of the brass section are trained on all you guys and
  gals, with a right fancy musical salute. It's "Sun Valley Jump."
SUN VALLEY JUMP
Captain Glenn Miller: Now a little wishful singing on the part of Sergeant Johnny
  Desmond, "Suddenly It's Spring."
SUDDENLY IT'S SPRING
  Vocal refrain by Sergeant Johnny Desmond
Captain Glenn Miller: Now the Crew Chiefs and "Shoo-Shoo Baby."
SHOO-SHOO BABY
  Vocal refrain by the Crew Chiefs
Captain Glenn Miller: Here's Sergeant Jerry Gray's arrangement of a new tune that should
  hit the jackpot with the men in our Armed Forces. The band plays, the Crew Chiefs and
  Sergeant McKinley sing "There Are Yanks."
THERE ARE YANKS (From the Banks of the Wabash)
  Vocal refrain by Staff Sergeant Ray McKinley and the Crew Chiefs
I SUSTAIN THE WINGS (closing theme)
  Captain Glenn Miller: Time now to take our leave until next week's meeting. You keep
    the letters a comin', we'll keep the music a goin'. Speakin' for Lieutenant Don
    Briggs, Sergeants Ray McKinley, Mel Powell, Johnny Desmond, the gang, thanks for
    listening and so long for now.
  2nd Lt. Donald P. Briggs: The Band of the A.A.F. Training Command, under the direction
    of Captain Glenn Miller, has come to you from New York City. Don't forget tomorrow,
    same time, same station, "Uncle Sam Presents" another famous service band with music
    from us to you.
MISSION TO MOSCOW (fade-out tune)
  2nd Lt. Donald P. Briggs: This is the United States of America, one of the united
    nations.

19Feb44 (Sat) 6:00-6:30PM EWT WEAF, NBC Vanderbilt Theatre, New York, New York
I SUSTAIN THE WINGS broadcast   Audience

THE ARMY AIR CORPS (opening fanfare)
2nd Lt. Donald P. Briggs: "I Sustain the Wings."
I SUSTAIN THE WINGS (opening theme)
  2nd Lt. Donald P. Briggs: "I Sustain the Wings." The Army Air Forces presents the Band
    of the Training Command, under the direction of Captain Glenn Miller. And now Captain
    Glenn Miller.
Captain Glenn Miller: Good evening, everybody. Speaking for Corporal Broderick Crawford,
  Sergeants Mel Powell, Ray McKinley, John Desmond, the Crew Chiefs, Lieutenant Don
  Briggs, and the whole gang, welcome to "I Sustain the Wings." The big guns of the brass
  section are trained on all you guys and gals, with a right fancy musical salute, "Sun
  Valley Jump."
SUN VALLEY JUMP
Captain Glenn Miller: A little wishful singing on the part of Sergeant John Desmond,
  "Suddenly It's Spring."
SUDDENLY IT'S SPRING
  Vocal refrain by Sergeant Johnny Desmond
Captain Glenn Miller: Today the Army Air Forces is making an immediate appeal to
  thousands of new Air WACs. There's an urgent need for volunteers to join the Women's
  Army Corps and serve with the A.A.F., so in place of our Training Command dramatization,
  usually presented at this time, Lieutenant Briggs has a message for you. Listen to it
  carefully. It's important. Lieutenant.
2nd Lt. Donald P. Briggs: Every one of us knows that this hour is a crucial hour.
  America's gathering its total strength for the greatest military blow in history. And
  we're calling on every resource to make this a final victorious effort. Many thousands
  of Air WACs are at their posts this very minute, lending their indispensable help.
  They're working side by side with our fighting men of the A.A.F. They're driving jeeps
  on busy air fields. They're operating control towers, working as weather observers,
  photographers and secretaries, a vital, absolutely necessary part of our mighty Air
  Force. Their work's interesting and exciting. It's never humdrum or unimportant.
  They're learning new jobs, traveling all over the world, receiving training that will be
  invaluable to them in post-war life and they're proud of the job that they're doing.
  They're proud to be part of our army. They're glad to be able to do something really
  essential toward winning this war and bringing our boys back sooner. They know the
  urgency of their work. They know that not one of them can be spared. They know the job
  is so big that many more Air WACs are needed. And they call on every woman qualified
  for Air WAC service to join them and join them now, when the need is the greatest. So,
  if you're not in essential war work, answer their call. Join either the Air, Ground of
  Service Forces, you can take your pick, but do it now. Don't say, "It doesn't concern
  me," because it does. This call for Air WACs concerns every qualified woman in this
  country. The need is immediate and tremendous. The cause is the cause of every
  American. Thousands of Air WACs are already doing their share to help win this war.
  How about you?
Captain Glenn Miller: Thank you, Lieutenant. Medley time now, delivering love and kisses
  from the boys over there to their gals over here, for their mothers, wives, sweethearts
  and sisters. Something old, something new, something borrowed and something blue. The
  old song, "All through the Night."
ALL THROUGH THE NIGHT (Old tune)
  Captain Glenn Miller: Sergeant Johnny Desmond sings.
I LOVE YOU (New tune)
  Vocal refrain by Sergeant Johnny Desmond
  Captain Glenn Miller: Guy Lombardo made it popular, we borrow it, "Take It Easy."
TAKE IT EASY (Borrowed tune)
  Vocal refrain by the Crew Chiefs and the Glee Club
  Captain Glenn Miller: Something blue now, "Blue Hawaii."
BLUE HAWAII (Blue tune)
Captain Glenn Miller: The Crew Chiefs and Sergeant Bobby Nichols with a nickel's worth of
  some of your favorite music, "Juke Box Saturday Night."

JUKE BOX SATURDAY NIGHT
  Vocal refrain by the Crew Chiefs
Captain Glenn Miller: A piano solo composed, arranged and played by Sergeant Mel Powell,
  repeated at the request of those of you who liked the way Mel played it on one of our
  earlier programs, "Pearls on Velvet."
PEARLS ON VELVET
Cpl. Broderick Crawford: Nothing means more to our soldiers overseas than mail from home.
  They look forward to it, wait for it anxiously, depend on it for encouragement and
  comfort. So, see that they get it. Use V-Mail when you write because it's quickest.
  It travels on priorities, usually by plane, and it takes up less shipping space than
  ordinary letters and it's safer. Not a single V-Mail has been reported lost since the
  war began. V-Mail stationery is available for the asking at any post office. Use it
  and write often. Don't forget how much a letter means to that soldier boy or girl of
  yours. Write tonight. Captain.
Captain Glenn Miller: Thank you, Corporal. Here's Sergeant Jerry Gray's arrangement of a
  new tune that should hit the jackpot with the men in our Armed Forces. The band plays,
  the Crew Chiefs and Sergeant McKinley sing "There Are Yanks."
THERE ARE YANKS (From the Banks of the Wabash)
  Vocal refrain by Staff Sergeant Ray McKinley and the Crew Chiefs
I SUSTAIN THE WINGS (closing theme)
  Captain Glenn Miller: This is Captain Miller saying so long for the Band of the
    Training Command, Corporal Brod Crawford, Sergeants Mel Powell, Ray McKinley, Johnny
    Desmond, the Crew Chiefs, and Lieutenant Don Briggs. Hope to see you again next
    Saturday, same time, same station.
  2nd Lt. Donald P. Briggs: "I Sustain the Wings" is a presentation of the Army Air
    Forces Training Command and came to you from New York City.
NBC announcer: This is the National Broadcasting Company.

19Feb44 (Sat) 11:30PM-Midnight EWT WEAF, NBC Vanderbilt Theatre, New York, New York
  I SUSTAIN THE WINGS broadcast   Audience

  ...

SUN VALLEY JUMP
Captain Glenn Miller: A little wishful singing on the part of Sergeant Johnny Desmond,
  "Suddenly It's Spring."
SUDDENLY IT'S SPRING
  Vocal refrain by Sergeant Johnny Desmond

  ...

Captain Glenn Miller: ... The old song tonight, "All through the Night."
ALL THROUGH THE NIGHT (Old tune)
  Captain Glenn Miller: Sergeant Johnny Desmond sings.
I LOVE YOU (New tune)
  Vocal refrain by Sergeant Johnny Desmond
  Captain Glenn Miller: Guy Lombardo made it popular, we borrow it, "Take It Easy."
TAKE IT EASY (Borrowed tune)
  Vocal refrain by the Crew Chiefs and the Glee Club
  Captain Glenn Miller: Something blue now, "Blue Hawaii."
BLUE HAWAII (Blue tune)

  ...

Captain Glenn Miller: ... Chiefs and Sergeant Bobby Nichols ...

  ...

26Feb44 (Sat) 2:15-3:00PM EWT NBC, New York, New York
   UNCLE SAM PRESENTS recording

I SUSTAIN THE WINGS (opening theme)
   2nd Lt. Donald P. Briggs: From the United States of America, to the other united
   nations of the world, "Uncle Sam Presents" the Band of the A.A.F. Training Command,
   under the direction of Captain Glenn Miller, with Sergeants Ray McKinley, Johnny
   Desmond, and many of your old friends.
2nd Lt. Donald P. Briggs: Here's Captain Glenn Miller.
Captain Glenn Miller: Thank you, Lieutenant Don Briggs, and hello, everybody. Here's
   some special G.I. music for all you G.I. guys and gals listening to this program, "Snafu
   Jump."
SNAFU JUMP
Captain Glenn Miller: Beautiful new melody with a fancy set of lyrics is the contribution
   of Sergeant Johnny Desmond and the Crew Chiefs to the romance department, "Moon Dreams."
MOON DREAMS
   Vocal refrain by Sergeant Johnny Desmond and the Crew Chiefs
Captain Glenn Miller: This one comin' up is bad medicine for the master race according to
   all reports we've been hearing lately, "Volga Boatmen."
SONG OF THE VOLGA BOATMEN
Captain Glenn Miller: The Crew Chiefs and the band and "What Do You Do in the Infantry."
   You ready, Red?
WHAT DO YOU DO IN THE INFANTRY
   Vocal refrain by the Crew Chiefs and the Glee Club
I SUSTAIN THE WINGS (closing theme)
   Captain Glenn Miller: Time now to take our leave until next week's meeting. You keep
   the letters comin', we'll keep the music a goin'. Speaking for Lieutenant Don Briggs,
   Sergeants Ray McKinley, Johnny Desmond, the Crew Chiefs, and the whole gang, thanks
   for listenin' and so long until next time.
   2nd Lt. Donald P. Briggs: The Band of the A.A.F. Training Command, under the direction
   of Captain Glenn Miller, has come to you from New York City. Don't forget tomorrow,
   same time, same station, "Uncle Sam Presents" another famous service band with music
   from us to you.
NINE TWENTY SPECIAL (fade-out tune)
   2nd Lt. Donald P. Briggs: This is the United States of America, one of the united
   nations.

26Feb44 (Sat) 6:00-6:30PM EWT WEAF, NBC Vanderbilt Theatre, New York, New York
I SUSTAIN THE WINGS broadcast   Audience

THE ARMY AIR CORPS (opening fanfare)
2nd Lt. Donald P. Briggs: "I Sustain the Wings."
I SUSTAIN THE WINGS (opening theme)
   2nd Lt. Donald P. Briggs: "I Sustain the Wings." The Army Air Forces presents the Band
      of the Training Command, under the direction of Captain Glenn Miller. And now Captain
      Glenn Miller.
Captain Glenn Miller: Thank you, Lieutenant Briggs, good evening, everybody. Speaking
   for Corporal Brod Crawford, Sergeants Ray McKinley, John Desmond, the Crew Chiefs, and
   the whole gang, welcome to another program of "I Sustain the Wings." First off, the big
   guns in the brass section bust out in a G.I. serenade to an old army tradition, "Snafu
   Jump."
SNAFU JUMP
Captain Glenn Miller: A beautiful new melody with a fancy set of lyrics is the
   contribution of Sergeant Johnny Desmond and the Crew Chiefs to the romance department
   tonight, "Moon Dreams."
MOON DREAMS
   Vocal refrain by Sergeant Johnny Desmond and the Crew Chiefs
The Army Air Corps (Incidental music)
2nd Lt. Donald P. Briggs (as Sgt. "Holly" Hollis): Aw, brother, would you look at that
   pile of junk? Perfume, silk stockings, shawls, jewelry. Huh, boy, you must have been a
   sucker for every merchant in Paris.
Cpl. Broderick Crawford (as Sgt. Joe Carson): Sucker, your maiden aunt. This stuff's
   hard to get back to the States.
2nd Lt. Donald P. Briggs: Hum, you've got enough of it to open a store. I suppose it's
   all for your wife.
Cpl. Broderick Crawford: Yeah, and what if it is?
2nd Lt. Donald P. Briggs: Oh, nothing, except you'll have to get rid of a lot of it.
Cpl. Broderick Crawford: Says who?
2nd Lt. Donald P. Briggs: Says the C.O. They're sending our plane home for a bond tour
   and we're flying her there as soon as she's fixed up.
Cpl. Broderick Crawford: Yeah, Holly was right. We were flying our plane back to the
   States. The Air Forces felt we needed a rest and it was O.K. with me. Well, we loaded
   up and we took off for home, the good old U.S.A. When we landed another crew took over
   the ship and Holly and I reported to the liaison officer at the nearest port of
   debarkation.
2nd Lt. Donald P. Briggs: Sergeants Hollis and Carson reporting to the liaison officer.
Liaison officer: At ease. Welcome home, gentlemen.
Cpl. Broderick Crawford: You can say that again, sir.
Liaison officer: I, ah, I know how you feel. You have your records?
2nd Lt. Donald P. Briggs: Here, sir.
Liaison officer: I'll take these and forward them to the A.A.F. Redistribution Station at
   Atlantic City. Oh, ah, before you report there, you both have a 21-day furlough.
Cpl. Broderick Crawford: 21 days. 21 wonderful days at home with Babe. That was too
   good to be true. I nearly went nuts the next 24 hours, questioning my intelligence,
   arranging transportation, that kind of stuff. But they got it over with as soon as they
   could and before I knew it I was on a train headin' home. My wife met me at the station
   and the way Babe greeted me, well, that's kind of our own business. 21 days went by so
   fast it seemed like next day Holly and I were on our way to Atlantic City. We were both
   pretty down because our furloughs were over, but we figured we couldn't complain, we'd
   had our fun and we were in the Army. We got to Atlantic City and they met us at the
   station with a bus and drove us to a fancy hotel on the Boardwalk. We piled out and
   walked into the lobby. There was a dance goin' on, the music ...
All the Things You Are (Incidental music)
   2nd Lt. Donald P. Briggs: Hey, hey, they must have brought us to the wrong place.
   Cpl. Broderick Crawford: Yeah, this place is too rich for my blood.
   2nd Lt. Donald P. Briggs: Hey, you're tellin' me. I stayed here once in the good old
      days, twenty bucks a day it cost me.

Cpl. Broderick Crawford: Twenty bucks?

2nd Lt. Donald P. Briggs: Yeah.

Cpl. Broderick Crawford: Let's get out o' here before they charge us five for just standin' here.

2nd Lt. Donald P. Briggs: Check. This ain't the right place.

Cpl. Broderick Crawford: And it ain't the Army.

2nd Lt. Donald P. Briggs: Yeah, but it was the right place and it was the Army. Aw, it was really somethin'. Comfortable? And how. Real beds, not G.I. bunks, in the room Joe and I had. It was just like when I paid twenty bucks for one just like it. Ocean view, swell furniture, everything just like a regular hotel.

Cpl. Broderick Crawford: Say, you know somethin', Holly?

2nd Lt. Donald P. Briggs: Huh?

Cpl. Broderick Crawford: I could stay in this for the duration.

2nd Lt. Donald P. Briggs: Aw, this is for me. Hey, did you hear what the guy said downstairs?

Cpl. Broderick Crawford: Naw.

2nd Lt. Donald P. Briggs: No roll call 'til one o'clock. Yeah, that means we can sleep 'til noon. We don't have to make our own beds. The maid'll do it for us.

Cpl. Broderick Crawford: Aw, this joint's lousy. No breakfast in bed.

2nd Lt. Donald P. Briggs: Huh, you would, you lug. If it was raining five dollar bills you'd want a raincoat before you'd ... Hey, chum.

Cpl. Broderick Crawford: Huh?

2nd Lt. Donald P. Briggs: Get a load o' this.

Cpl. Broderick Crawford: What's that?

2nd Lt. Donald P. Briggs: Aw, it's a pamphlet, ah, Flight Sergeant gave it to me.

Cpl. Broderick Crawford: How do you like that, they even give us books.

2nd Lt. Donald P. Briggs: Hey, Joe, Joe, listen to this. Welcome to Atlantic City and the Army Air Forces Redistribution Station. This is to tell you briefly of the purposes of the Redistribution Center. Headquarters of the Center's here in Atlantic City.

Cpl. Broderick Crawford: Yeah, and it ain't bad.

2nd Lt. Donald P. Briggs: Huh. It's a working part of the Air Staff who was set up by General Arnold so that all the Air Forces men coming back from overseas would have certain things accomplished for 'em.

Cpl. Broderick Crawford: Yeah. And they're sure doin' plenty for us, Holly.

2nd Lt. Donald P. Briggs: We know that you've undergone tremendous nervous and physical fatigue, that you're tired and in need of rest.

Cpl. Broderick Crawford: You can say that again, brother.

2nd Lt. Donald P. Briggs: Heh, heh. So it's very important that you men be properly placed in domestic commands. The experience that you've had overseas must be passed on to men now undergoing training in this country. The benefit of your experience overseas will be very valuable to them.

Cpl. Broderick Crawford: Yeah. We could really tell them a thing or two.

2nd Lt. Donald P. Briggs: I'll say. It's likewise very important that you receive every possible attention. Many of you have been under great strain and we want to be assured that you're in excellent physical condition. The government owes that to each of you and it's our responsibility to see that it's fulfilled. Signed Colonel A. W. Snyder, Commanding Officer.

Cpl. Broderick Crawford: They sure took that responsibility seriously. They did everything for us. They even arranged for us married men to have our wives down there with us. And you can bet I didn't lose any time in sending for Babe. She got down there on the double and we had a swell time. You might call is a second honeymoon. Of course, during the day we had appointments for physical and medical examinations, reclassification tests, just to make sure we'd be put in the right spot when we returned to duty. But most of the time we were on our own and there was plenty to do, parties, free movies, concerts given by Broadway stars, and the best dance bands in the country. We had golf, skeet shooting, horseback riding and a million other things we'd been dreaming about overseas. And the chow, well, maybe I shouldn't mention it, the chow, but I put on 35 pounds. All in all it was a real vacation. It was plenty easy to take after seventeen months of combat flying. Well, the honeymoon was over when I was placed

on shipping alert. I sent Babe home so she wouldn't be stuck down there alone, and was
    feeling pretty lousy when Holly busted into the room.
2nd Lt. Donald P. Briggs: Hey, Joe, Joe. I got my assignment. I'm goin' back with the
    skipper.
Cpl. Broderick Crawford: Lieutenant Stokey? On the level?
2nd Lt. Donald P. Briggs: On the level. He's organizing a combat crew for duty in the
    South Pacific in about three months and he asked for me to be in his crew. They told me
    I could stick around in this country as an instructor if I wanted to.
Cpl. Broderick Crawford: Aw, who wants to? Boy, would I like to fly with Lieutenant
    again.
2nd Lt. Donald P. Briggs: Well, you can if you want to. He asked for you, too.
Cpl. Broderick Crawford: He did? No foolin'?
2nd Lt. Donald P. Briggs: No foolin'.
Cpl. Broderick Crawford: Boy, that was somethin'. A chance to be with the Lieutenant and
    Holly and the old crew again, and the Lieutenant asking for me. There's no pilot I'd
    rather fly with, he's the world's best. But, well, I'd sorta been lookin' forward to an
    instructor's job in this country where I could have Babe with me and maybe I could get a
    family started. Of course, it's up to me to make up my own mind. I don't have to
    return to combat duty, not for some months at any rate, unless I say it's O.K. Boy, I'd
    sure like to take a crack at the Japs, though, before this thing's over. Be kinda hard
    to leave Babe again so soon after ... well, so soon after just gettin' to know her real
    well. What am I gonna do? Babe'll be waitin' when I come home!
I Sustain the Wings (Incidental music)
Captain Glenn Miller: This one comin' up is bad medicine for the master race according to
    all reports we've been hearin' lately, "Volga Boatmen."
SONG OF THE VOLGA BOATMEN
Captain Glenn Miller: It's medley time and that means old, new, borrowed and blue tunes
    played for servicemen's ladies be they mom, sis or Mrs. to be. The old tune, "Jeanie
    with the Light Brown Hair."
JEANIE WITH THE LIGHT BROWN HAIR (Old tune)
    Captain Glenn Miller: Sergeant Desmond and the Crew Chiefs sing the new tune.
I COULDN'T SLEEP A WINK LAST NIGHT (New tune)
    Vocal refrain by Sergeant Johnny Desmond and the Crew Chiefs
    Captain Glenn Miller: Little Lend-Lease from the Navy now as we borrow Chief Petty
        Officer Artie Shaw's "Begin the Beguine."
BEGIN THE BEGUINE (Borrowed tune)
    Captain Glenn Miller: Last, the blue tune, "Blue Rain."
BLUE RAIN (Blue tune)
2nd Lt. Donald P. Briggs: One of the biggest opportunities open to women who join the
    Women's Army Corps is the chance to get valuable training, training that'll be useful to
    you in the years after the war. Why, right now in the Air Forces alone are thousands of
    Air-WACs learning new skills or improving abilities they already possess. Their jobs
    are important war-winning jobs, interesting specialized work that's vital to victory.
    In joining the Women's Army Corps you may choose any branch of the service, Air, Ground,
    or Service Forces. So, if you're not in essential war work, visit the nearest WAC
    Recruiting Station and volunteer as an Air WAC to help "Keep 'Em Flying."
WHAT DO YOU DO IN THE INFANTRY
    Vocal refrain by the Crew Chiefs and the Glee Club
I SUSTAIN THE WINGS (closing theme)
    Captain Glenn Miller: This is Captain Glenn Miller saying so long for the Band of the
        Training Command, Corporal Brod Crawford, Sergeants Mel Powell, Ray McKinley, Johnny
        Desmond, the Crew Chiefs, and Lieutenant Don Briggs. Hope to see you again next
        Saturday, same time, same station. In the meantime, don't forget those lads that are
        slugging it out overseas, they go for those V-Mail letters, don't let 'em down.
    2nd Lt. Donald P. Briggs: "I Sustain the Wings" is a presentation of the Army Air
        Forces Training Command, came to you from New York City.
NBC announcer: This is the National Broadcasting Company.

The part of Liaison officer was played by either Cpl. Paul A. Dubov or Cpl. Joseph
Shulman.

26Feb44 (Sat) 11:30PM-Midnight EWT WEAF, NBC Vanderbilt Theatre, New York, New York
   I SUSTAIN THE WINGS broadcast
                                                                    Audience

   . . .

JEANIE WITH THE LIGHT BROWN HAIR (Old tune)
   Captain Glenn Miller: Sergeant Johnny Desmond and the Crew Chiefs sing the new tune.
I COULDN'T SLEEP A WINK LAST NIGHT (New tune)
   Vocal refrain by Sergeant Johnny Desmond and the Crew Chiefs
   Captain Glenn Miller: Little Lend-Lease from the Navy now as we borrow Chief Petty
      Officer Artie Shaw's "Begin the Beguine."
BEGIN THE BEGUINE (Borrowed tune)
   Captain Glenn Miller: Last, the blue tune, "Blue Rain."
BLUE RAIN (Blue tune)

   . . .

WHAT DO YOU DO IN THE INFANTRY
   Vocal refrain by the Crew Chiefs and the Glee Club
I SUSTAIN THE WINGS (closing theme)
   Captain Glenn Miller: This is Captain Glenn Miller saying so long for the Band of the
      Training Command, Corporal Brod Crawford, Sergeants Ray McKinley, John Desmond, the
      Crew Chiefs, and Lieutenant Don Briggs. Hope to see you again next Saturday, same
      time, same station. In the meantime, don't forget those lads that are slugging it out
      overseas, they go for those V-Mail letters, don't let 'em down.
   2nd Lt. Donald P. Briggs: "I Sustain the Wings" is a presentation of the Army Air
      Forces Training Command and came to you from New York City.

04Mar44 (Sat) 2:15PM NBC, New York, New York
  UNCLE SAM PRESENTS recording

I SUSTAIN THE WINGS (opening theme)
  2nd Lt. Donald P. Briggs: From the United States of America, to the other united
    nations of the world, "Uncle Sam Presents" the Band of the A.A.F. Training Command,
    under the direction of Captain Glenn Miller, with Sergeants Ray McKinley, Johnny
    Desmond, and many of your old friends.
2nd Lt. Donald P. Briggs: Here's Captain Glenn Miller.
Captain Glenn Miller: Thank you, Lieutenant Don Briggs, and hello, everybody. For your
  listenin' pleasure here's one of the top tunes on our request list, "In the Mood."
IN THE MOOD
Captain Glenn Miller: Sergeant Johnny Desmond's coming up now with the lyrics to one of
  the better new tunes, "Now I Know."
NOW I KNOW
  Vocal refrain by Sergeant Johnny Desmond
THE DIPSY DOODLE
  Captain Glenn Miller: From the pen of ex-bandleader, now Air Force Lieutenant Larry
    Clinton, the old Dipsy-Doodler, the tune that earned him the title.
Captain Glenn Miller: A musical tribute to those rugged gentlemen who man the stingers in
  our fightin' planes, "Guns in the Sky."
GUNS IN THE SKY
  Vocal refrain by Sergeant Johnny Desmond, the Crew Chiefs and the Ensemble
I SUSTAIN THE WINGS (closing theme)
  Captain Glenn Miller: Time now to take our leave until next week's meeting. Keep the
    letters a comin', we'll keep the music a goin'. I'm speaking for Lieutenant Don
    Briggs, Sergeants Ray McKinley, Johnny Desmond, Mel Powell, and the gang, thanks for
    listening and so long.
  2nd Lt. Donald P. Briggs: The Band of the A.A.F. Training Command, under the direction
    of Captain Glenn Miller, has come to you from New York City. Don't forget tomorrow,
    same time, same station, "Uncle Sam Presents" another famous service band with music
    from us to you.
SWING LOW, SWEET CHARIOT (fade-out tune)
  2nd Lt. Donald P. Briggs: This is the United States of America, one of the united
    nations.

04Mar44 (Sat) 6:00-6:30PM EWT WEAF, NBC Vanderbilt Theatre, New York, New York
  I SUSTAIN THE WINGS broadcast   Audience

THE ARMY AIR CORPS (opening fanfare)
2nd Lt. Donald P. Briggs: "I Sustain the Wings."
I SUSTAIN THE WINGS (opening theme)
  2nd Lt. Donald P. Briggs: "I Sustain the Wings." The Army Air Forces present the Band
    of the Training Command, under the direction of Captain Glenn Miller. And now Captain
    Glenn Miller.
Captain Glenn Miller: Good evening, everybody. Speaking for Sergeant Brod Crawford, Mel
  Powell, Ray McKinley, Johnny Desmond, the Crew Chiefs, Lieutenant Don Briggs, and the
  whole gang, welcome to another program of "I Sustain the Wings." Now for your listening
  pleasure one of the top tunes on our request list, "In the Mood."
IN THE MOOD
Captain Glenn Miller: Sergeant Johnny Desmond's comin' up now with the lyrics of one of
  the better new tunes, "Now I Know."
NOW I KNOW
  Vocal refrain by Sergeant Johnny Desmond
Incidental music
  2nd Lt. Donald P. Briggs (as Jerry): Dear, Mom. The rest of the crew just took off on
    another mission over Italy. So, while I'm sittin' here, sweatin' it out, waitin' for
    'em to come back, I thought I'd better grab the chance to answer some of the swell
    letters I've been gettin' from you. Maybe you're wondering why I'm not flyin' with
    Dick and the others today. Well, I'm grounded on account of a cold and I'm puttin' in
    the time with the ground crew, helpin' out as a mechanic. You know, the Training
    Command made a gunner-mechanic out of me. Cold's nothing to worry about, though.
    I'll be O.K. in a day or two. You sure write wonderful letters, Mom, tellin' about
    every little thing at home. Sort of like I was there myself, seeing it all happen.
    Yeah, and you're smart to use V-Mail, too. The Army gets it to us awful fast. Your
    last letter took less than a week. Yeah, they know how much it means to us. A guy
    doesn't get nearly so lonesome when there's a lot of mail from home to read.
2nd Lt. Donald P. Briggs: Eh, speaking about mail, there's one thing I wish you'd do for
  me. Make a point of asking Doris Bailey to write to Dick more often. I know she's
  awful busy with the baby and everything, but it's Dick's baby too and he'd like to know
  every little thing about the kid and Doris. I know she's probably been writing but I'll
  give you odds she doesn't use V-Mail and she should 'cause you can't tell about regular
  mail. It's been an awful long time since Dick got his last letter from home and he's
  really down about it. He doesn't seem to care about anything. He just sits around and
  mopes. All the fun's gone out ...
  Ah, Dick. Hey, Dick. C-47 just came in with mail aboard. Let's see what goes.
Sgt. Broderick Crawford (as Dick Bailey): Aw, what's the use? There won't be anything
  for me. There never is.
2nd Lt. Donald P. Briggs: Aw, you can't be sure. Maybe this is the day.
Sgt. Broderick Crawford: Yeah, and maybe it isn't. You don't know how I feel, Jerry.
  There's always somethin' for you. But me, I stand there while the Sergeant calls out
  the names. Allison, Alford, Babcock. And it seems like I wait a thousand years for the
  next name but it's never Bailey. He goes on to Brantano, then Cassidy, Collins, but
  never Bailey. Every time that happens it takes something out of me, Jerry, makes me
  feel like I'm a forgotten man. Maybe Doris has found ...
2nd Lt. Donald P. Briggs: Aw, don't - don't say it, Dick. You know Doris is nuts about
  you.
Sgt. Broderick Crawford: Yeah, I know it deep down inside of me but why doesn't she
  write, Jerry? It's been weeks since I've heard from her. There's a million and one
  things could happen to her and the little guy.
2nd Lt. Donald P. Briggs: You shouldn't think about things like that.
Sgt. Broderick Crawford: Well, a man can't stop thinkin'. That's all there is to do in
  this God forsaken place when we're not flyin'.
2nd Lt. Donald P. Briggs: Aw, don't let it get you, Dick. I'm sure everything's all
  right.

Sgt. Broderick Crawford: I wish I were sure. If I think they're all O.K., that's fine.
  If they're not, well, I could take that too. It's not knowin' that's gettin' me down.
  I just gotta know somethin', Jerry. I tell you I gotta know.
2nd Lt. Donald P. Briggs: Telling me over and over again, "I gotta know, I gotta know."
  Well, Mom, that was just before we went over to the briefing room and got our
  instructions for the day's mission. I didn't get a chance to see Dick again until we
  climbed into the plane and settled down for the long ride. There's nothing much to do
  until we get near the target, so we laugh and kid and swap yarns. Wasn't long 'til I
  noticed Dick wasn't having any part of the fun. He was just sittin' by himself, away
  from the rest of us, staring off into space. I could see he was thinkin' about home and
  Doris so I tried talking to him but he'd give me a short answer and then climb back out
  of this world. He was still daydreamin' when we hit the danger zone and we all had to
  take our stations. Dick climbed into the turret and I grabbed my waist gun, Cookie was
  handling the other. When we got near the target we were right in the middle of trouble
  and havin' a busy time of it when the pilot called on the intercom.
Pilot: Pilot to radio. See what happened to Bailey. He doesn't answer.
2nd Lt. Donald P. Briggs: Ah, roger. Can you handle both guns, Cookie?
Cookie: I got two hands, ain't I?
2nd Lt. Donald P. Briggs: And so, Mom, I crawled over to the turret. I could see Dick
  was sort of slumped over. When I got to him he was out like a light. He wasn't
  bleeding or anything, just - just out. Then I saw his face. It was kind of bluish and
  I knew right away he wasn't getting any oxygen. His oxygen valve wasn't turned on.
  Well, I got him out of there in a hurry and started working on him to bring him to. Ah,
  Cookie climbed in the turret and took over, and the bombardier, who'd already done his
  main job, came back to handle the waist guns. And, boy, they didn't get those guns back
  in action any too soon 'cause the MEs had a spigot for a lame duck and were diving in
  for the kill. I kept working on Dick, giving him oxygen, artificial respiration.
  Wasn't long before he started coming to again.
  Hey, Dick. Hey, you lug, this ain't no place to be passin' out.
Sgt. Broderick Crawford: Passin' out?
2nd Lt. Donald P. Briggs: Yeah, that's what you did. You should do your sleeping at
  nights.
Sgt. Broderick Crawford: What happened, Jerry?
2nd Lt. Donald P. Briggs: All I know is you forgot to turn on your oxygen.
Sgt. Broderick Crawford: Oh, yeah, yeah. Now - now I remember. I was up in the turret
  gettin' things ready, thinkin' o' Doris, all of a sudden I started feelin' awful funny.
  I just didn't care about anything, Jerry. I knew I wasn't gettin' any oxygen and I
  started reaching over to turn it on. It's about the last thing I remember.
2nd Lt. Donald P. Briggs: Why'd ya wait so long, Dick? You must have been out of your
  mind.
Sgt. Broderick Crawford: I wasn't thinking, Jerry. I've been so worried about not
  hearin' from Doris. Why doesn't she write, Jerry? Why doesn't she write?
2nd Lt. Donald P. Briggs: So, that's the way it was, Mom. Dick didn't know it but he put
  himself and the rest of us in a spot because he was so worried about not gettin' any
  mail. Heh, sure, we got back to the base all right. I wouldn't be writin' you this
  letter if we didn't.
I Sustain the Wings (Incidental music)
  2nd Lt. Donald P. Briggs: But you see, Mom, this thing they call morale isn't just a
    word. It - it's sorta hard to explain but it's awful important to us fellows over
    here doin' the fightin'. We gotta have it if we're gonna win this war. We don't mind
    takin' our chances if we know you folks back home are thinkin' about us, standin'
    behind us a hundred per cent. So tell Doris to write Dick, and soon. And tell her to
    use V-Mail 'cause, like I said, it gets over here a lot quicker and her letters can't
    get here any too fast to suit him. You've been swell about writin', Mom, and I know I
    don't have to remind you that a letter a day chases the gloom away. Give my love to
    Dad, the rest of the family and a special lot of it to Mary. Tell 'em all to keep the
    V-Mail comin'. It means an awful lot to us guys over here. Well, so long, Mom. I'll
    be seein' you. Your lovin' son, Jerry.
Captain Glenn Miller: Sergeant Johnny Desmond, the Crew Chiefs sing one of today's top
  tunes, "I'll Be Around."

I'LL BE AROUND
  Vocal refrain by Sergeant Johnny Desmond and the Crew Chiefs
Captain Glenn Miller: Now it's medley time, saluting the mothers, wives, sweethearts and
  sisters of the boys in the A.A.F. Something old, something new, something borrowed,
  something blue. The old song, "Long, Long Ago."
LONG, LONG AGO (Old tune)
  Captain Glenn Miller: Something new, Sergeant Johnny Desmond sings "The Music Stopped."
THE MUSIC STOPPED (New tune)
  Vocal refrain by Sergeant Johnny Desmond
  Captain Glenn Miller: We borrow Lieutenant Larry Clinton's theme, "Dipsy Doodle."
THE DIPSY DOODLE (Borrowed tune)
  Captain Glenn Miller: Last, the blue tune, "Blues in My Heart."
BLUES IN MY HEART (Blue tune)
Cpl. Paul A. Dubov: Partners in victory. That's just what you women can become by
  joining the Women's Army Corps and helping to win this war along with the men of the
  Armed Forces. And you can pick your branch of the service, either Air, Ground, or
  Service Forces. If you choose the Air Forces, there are unlimited opportunities in one
  of more than a hundred skilled jobs and you'll receive training in these specialized
  assignments that'll be invaluable to you after the war is won. Visit any WAC Recruiting
  Station and discover for yourself the interesting work that awaits you in the Women's
  Army Corps. Join now and as an Air WAC in the A.A.F. become a partner in victory. Now,
  Captain Miller.
Captain Glenn Miller: Nice going, Corporal. Now a musical tribute to those rugged
  gentlemen who man the stingers in our fightin' planes, "Guns in the Sky."
GUNS IN THE SKY
  Vocal refrain by Sergeant Johnny Desmond and the Glee Club
Sgt. Broderick Crawford: It's a pretty fancy job to take a man who's only been a Mister
  Fix-It around the house and teach him to repair airplane engines in only a few short
  months. The Army Air Forces Training Command performs this miracle every day in its
  training of A.A.F. mechanics. To date the Training Command has turned out over a half
  million mechanics and other ground crew specialists, a job that has won it the name of
  the biggest university in the world, a job that makes every man in the Training Command
  proud to say, "I Sustain the Wings."
I SUSTAIN THE WINGS (closing theme)
  Captain Glenn Miller: This is Captain Glenn Miller saying so long for the Band of the
    Training Command, Sergeants Brod Crawford, Mel Powell, Ray McKinley, Johnny Desmond,
    the Crew Chiefs, Lieutenant Don Briggs, and the whole gang. Hope to see you again
    next Saturday, same time, same station. In the meantime, don't forget those lads that
    are slugging it out overseas. They're dependent on the Red Cross and the Red Cross is
    depending on you. Don't let 'em down.
  2nd Lt. Donald P. Briggs: "I Sustain the Wings" is a presentation of the Army Air
    Forces Training Command and came to you from New York City.
NBC announcer: This is the National Broadcasting Company.

The parts of Pilot and Cookie were played by Cpl. Paul A. Dubov and Cpl. Joseph Shulman.

04Mar44 (Sat) 11:30PM-Midnight EWT WEAF, NBC Vanderbilt Theatre, New York, New York
  I SUSTAIN THE WINGS broadcast   Audience

THE ARMY AIR CORPS (opening fanfare)
2nd Lt. Donald P. Briggs: "I Sustain the Wings."
I SUSTAIN THE WINGS (opening theme)
  2nd Lt. Donald P. Briggs: "I Sustain the Wings." The Army Air Forces present the Band
    of the Training Command, under the direction of Captain Glenn Miller. And now Captain
    Glenn Miller.
Captain Glenn Miller: Good evening, everybody. Speaking for Sergeants Brod Crawford, Mel
  Powell, Ray McKinley, Johnny Desmond, the Crew Chiefs, Lieutenant Don Briggs, the whole
  gang, welcome to another program of "I Sustain the Wings." Now for your listening
  pleasure one of the top tunes on our request list, "In the Mood."
IN THE MOOD (Beginning)
NBC announcer 1 (interrupting "In the Mood"): Ladies and gentlemen, we interrupt this
  program to bring you a special bulletin.
NBC announcer 2: News has just been flashed from Sing Sing Prison that Lewis Lepke
  Buckhalter has been electrocuted. Dying in the electric chair also were Emmanuel Weiss
  and Louis Capone, associates of Lepke. The trio was put to death on a charge they
  murdered Joseph Rosen, Brooklyn candy store proprietor in 1936. Thus is written the
  final chapter in the unparalleled saga of crime enacted by a gang which came to be known
  as Murder Incorporated. This bulletin has come to you from the N.B.C. news room in New
  York.
IN THE MOOD (Conclusion)
Captain Glenn Miller: Sergeant Johnny Desmond comin' up now with the lyrics to one of the
  better new tunes, "Now I Know."
NOW I KNOW
  Vocal refrain by Sergeant Johnny Desmond
Incidental music
  2nd Lt. Donald P. Briggs (as Jerry): Dear, Mom. The rest of the crew just took off on
    another mission over Italy. While I'm sittin' here, sweatin' it out, waitin' for 'em
    to come back, I thought I'd better grab the chance to answer some of the swell letters
    I've been gettin' from you. Maybe you're wondering why I'm not flyin' with Dick and
    the others today. Well, I'm grounded on account of a cold and I'm puttin' in the time
    with the ground crew, helpin' out as a mechanic. You know, the Training Command made
    a gunner-mechanic out of me. Cold's nothing to worry about, though. I'll be O.K. in
    a day or two. You sure write wonderful letters, Mom, tellin' about every little thing
    at home. Sort of like I was there myself, seeing it all happen. Yeah, and you're
    smart to use V-Mail, too. The Army gets it to us awful fast. Your last letter took
    less than a week. They know how much it means to us. A guy doesn't get nearly so
    lonesome when there's a lot of mail from home to read.
  2nd Lt. Donald P. Briggs: Eh, speaking about mail, there's one thing I wish you'd do for
    me. Make a point of asking Doris Bailey to write to Dick more often. I know she's
    awful busy with the baby and everything, but it's Dick's baby too and ...

    ...

Captain Glenn Miller: ... "I'll Be Around."
I'LL BE AROUND
  Vocal refrain by Sergeant Johnny Desmond and the Crew Chiefs
Captain Glenn Miller: Now it's medley time, a salute the mothers, wives, sweethearts and
  sisters of the boys in the A.A.F. Something old, something new, something borrowed,
  something blue. The old song, "Long, Long Ago."
LONG, LONG AGO (Old tune)
  Captain Glenn Miller: Something new, Sergeant Johnny Desmond sings "The Music Stopped."
THE MUSIC STOPPED (New tune)
  Vocal refrain by Sergeant Johnny Desmond
  Captain Glenn Miller: We borrow Lieutenant Larry Clinton's old theme, "Dipsy Doodle."
THE DIPSY DOODLE (Borrowed tune)
  Captain Glenn Miller: Last, the blue tune, "Blues in My Heart."

BLUES IN MY HEART (Blue tune)
Cpl. Paul A. Dubov: Partners in victory. That's just what you women can become by
  joining the Women's Army Corps ...
  ...

Captain Glenn Miller: ... Now a musical tribute to those rugged gentlemen who man the
  stingers in our fighting planes, "Guns in the Sky."
GUNS IN THE SKY
  Vocal refrain by Sergeant Johnny Desmond and the Glee Club
Sgt. Broderick Crawford: It's a pretty fancy job to take a man who's only had been a
  Mister Fix-It around the house and teach him to repair airplane engines in only a few
  short months. The Army Air Forces Training Command performs this miracle every day in
  its training of A.A.F. mechanics. To date the Training Command has turned out over a
  half million mechanics and other ground crew specialists, a job that has won it the name
  of the biggest university in the world, a job that makes every man in the Training
  Command proud to say, "I Sustain the Wings."
I SUSTAIN THE WINGS (closing theme)
  Captain Glenn Miller: This is Captain Glenn Miller saying so long for the Band of the
    Training Command, Sergeants Brod Crawford, Mel Powell, Ray McKinley, Johnny Desmond,
    the Crew Chiefs, Lieutenant Don Briggs, and the whole gang. Hope to see you again
    next Saturday, same time, same station. Meantime, don't forget those lads that are
    slugging it out overseas. They're dependent on the Red Cross, the Red Cross is
    depending on you. Don't let 'em down.

  ...

11Mar44 (Sat)   NBC, New York, New York
UNCLE SAM PRESENTS recording

  ...

LONG AGO (And Far Away)
  Vocal refrain by Sergeant Johnny Desmond
Captain Glenn Miller: Beautiful melody that's been bangin' around for a long time and
  lately the customers are askin' for it, and it looks like it's on the way to becoming
  one of today's top tunes, "Poinciana."
POINCIANA (Song of the Tree)
  Vocal refrain by Sergeant Johnny Desmond and the Crew Chiefs

  ...

11Mar44 (Sat) 6:00-6:30PM EWT WEAF, NBC Vanderbilt Theatre, New York, New York
  I SUSTAIN THE WINGS broadcast   Audience

THE ARMY AIR CORPS (opening fanfare)
2nd Lt. Donald P. Briggs: "I Sustain the Wings."
I SUSTAIN THE WINGS (opening theme)
  2nd Lt. Donald P. Briggs: "I Sustain the Wings." The Army Air Forces present the Band
    of the Training Command, under the direction of Captain Glenn Miller. And now Captain
    Glenn Miller.
Captain Glenn Miller: Thank you, Lieutenant Don Briggs, and good evening, everybody.
  Speaking for Sergeants Brod Crawford, Mel Powell, Ray McKinley, Johnny Desmond, the Crew
  Chiefs, and the gang, welcome to another program of "I Sustain the Wings." First, a
  right fancy dish on the musical menu, "Must Be Jelly 'cause Jam Don't Shake Like That."
IT MUST BE JELLY ('Cause Jam Don't Shake Like That)
Captain Glenn Miller: Sergeant Johnny Desmond sings the new tune you'll be hearing more
  of come spring and summer. Johnny, you're on and the tune, "Long Ago and Far Away."
LONG AGO (And Far Away)
  Vocal refrain by Sergeant Johnny Desmond
The Army Air Corps (Incidental music)
  Captain Glenn Miller: It couldn't be done, so we did it. That might well be the motto
    of the men of the A.A.F. Training Command, the men of the ground crews and the men of
    our air crews who fly the planes. The history of the Air Force is full of stories of
    impossible deeds that were, never the less, done. Stories like that of Benny, tail
    gunner on a Flying Fortress in England.
Captain Glenn Miller: Here's the way we heard it from the bombardier in Benny's crew as
  he says ...
Sgt. Broderick Crawford: If you know gunners you know they're a pretty rough and tumble
  bunch of kids, full of fun and always clowning. Phil, the tail gunner we used to have,
  was that way. When he stopped a piece of flak and had to be shipped home we hated to
  see him go. He was the life of every mission. And we weren't too happy when this quiet
  kid Benny showed up to take his place. We found out he was a ground crew mechanic who
  wanted to get off the ground. He was as different from Phil as a Liberator and Piper
  Cub. A silent kid who sort of stayed apart from the others, just stood around with a
  serious frown on his face, like he was thinking about something. After he arrived we
  went up for a few practice missions over England. He hardly said one word the whole
  time. Most crews talk back and forth on long trips, kidding each other over the
  interphone. But when you called instructions to Benny during a flight, all he'd answer
  was just the usual "roger." That's all, just "roger." The fellows even started
  nicknaming him "Roger." And I had a hunch they might ask Big Sid, our pilot, to trade
  Benny for another gunner because guys on a bomber have to click together to do a good
  job. But they kept it to themselves even though they didn't know what to make of him.
  Then about a week after he joined us he made his first combat mission with us to
  Frankfurt. We climbed into the plane at 0-5-5-0 that morning. I went up to my place in
  the bombardier's greenhouse in the nose of the plane and the rest of the crew took their
  stations and we were off. Everything went fine 'til we reached the target. As we came
  in over Frankfurt, flak started whistling up and Focke-Wulfs started diving back and
  forth through the formation, the gun turrets of our planes whirling around to follow
  'em. Then suddenly I heard Benny in the tail open fire. His first tracers caught a
  Focke-Wulf square in the one wing. Down he went, gushing flame. And I yelled into the
  interphone, "Nice shootin', kid, keep it up." I waited for his answer, knowing what it
  would be. Sure enough, you guessed it.
Benny: Roger.
Sgt. Broderick Crawford: "Roger," always "roger." But I had to admit, the kid could
  shoot. I wiped the frost off the window of my compartment with a piece of waste, and
  dead ahead I could see the factories at Frankfurt, our target. I ordered the bomb bay
  doors open and checked the row of red lights above the rack switches on the bomb
  indicator. Everything was O.K. A quick adjustment in the sight, then another, the
  automatic pilot was holding her steady, the cross-hairs were on the factory, I gave her
  the trigger and the ship jumped as the bombs left, and I hollered out, "Bombs away!
  Come on, let's get out of here." Big Sid banked her around to head back and just as he

did, bang, we got it. The flak had knocked out our number two and four engines. Right away we started to lose altitude. I heard Big Sid on the interphone telling us to lighten the ship by throwing out everything we could. Out went the guns, next the heavy flak suits we wear, the armor plating, everything we could get loose. We were down to twelve thousand feet already. Nothing we did seemed to keep us from losing altitude. Then suddenly I heard a voice on the interphone.

Benny: How about dropping the ball turret, sir?

Sgt. Broderick Crawford: It was Benny. For a minute I was too surprised to realize what he'd said. Then I called back, "What's the matter, kid, are you flak-happy? You can't drop a ball turret."

Benny: Why not, sir?

Sgt. Broderick Crawford: It's too hard to get loose. Even if you could do it, it'd take you three or four hours. We haven't got time, now forget it.

Benny: Roger.

Sgt. Broderick Crawford: There was that 'roger" again. Drop the ball turret. It's a great idea. It had never been done and couldn't be done. Meanwhile we were losing altitude and dodging from cloud to cloud to hide away from any Jerries that might be following us. I was busy hunting clouds for Big Sid when Benny cut in again.

Benny: I still think we could do it, sir. It would lighten ship over half a ton if we could.

Sgt. Broderick Crawford: Well, by this time I was so busy looking for clouds that I didn't care what he did. So I called back, "Go ahead. Don't let me stop you. Only, I think you're crazy."

Benny: Can I have the radio man, the ball turret man and the waist gunner to help me, sir?

Sgt. Broderick Crawford: Sure, take everybody. But keep your 'chutes handy. We'll be jumpin' before you get the first bolt loose. I didn't hear anything more from him. And back I went to hunting clouds. We were dropping like a lead balloon, carrying too much weight for our two engines. It wouldn't be long now. I called the top turret gunner. "Those guys making any headway with the ball turret?" He said they were working at it but it seemed to be a tough job. I had to smile at that. A tough job. That kid Benny must have blown his top. I crawled back through the ship to see for myself. There they were, clustered around the ball turret, four of them, sweat pouring down their face. First, one would take a few minutes, then another would take over. All they had was a crescent wrench and a pair of pliers. I went back up front and waited for the word to jump. Out the window I could see the ground moving up to meet us. And I was just figuring how many minutes we had left when the ship gave a mighty lurch and I heard somebody yell on the interphone, "Bombs away!" Back I went in a hurry. Where that ball turret was there was just a big hole in the floor now. Benny, wrench in hand, was starring down at it, frowning that funny, serious way of his. The rest of the guys were grinning. Not at me, at Benny. I could feel the ship climbing under me. We're gonna be all right now, I thought. Then I looked at my watch. It had taken them just fifteen minutes. The other guys were still looking at Benny and still grinning. And one look at their sweaty, grease-stained faces was all you needed. From now on there wasn't going to be any more talk about Benny leaving us. He was in. He was one of us. Well, we got back O.K. and when we told the Colonel the story he said ...

Colonel: Gentlemen, it was a splendid job. The entire crew deserves the highest commendation.

Sgt. Broderick Crawford: The crew itself said ...

Crew man: That Benny boy is tops, a swell guy.

Sgt. Broderick Crawford: And Benny? Well, he just said ...

Benny: Roger.

I Sustain the Wings (Incidental music)

Captain Glenn Miller: Now it's medley time, saluting the mothers, wives, sweethearts and sisters of the boys in the A.A.F. Something old, something new, something borrowed and something blue. The old tune, "Songs My Mother Taught Me."

SONGS MY MOTHER TAUGHT ME (Old tune)

Captain Glenn Miller: For something new, the Crew Chiefs singin' "It's Love, Love, Love!"

IT'S LOVE, LOVE, LOVE! (New tune)

Captain Glenn Miller: Raymond Scott collaborated with Mr. Mozart for our borrowed tune, "Eighteenth Century Drawing Room."
IN AN EIGHTEENTH CENTURY DRAWING ROOM (Borrowed tune)
Captain Glenn Miller: The blue tune, Sergeant Johnny Desmond sings "Blue Orchids."
BLUE ORCHIDS (Blue tune)
Vocal refrain by Sergeant Johnny Desmond
2nd Lt. Donald P. Briggs: Women of America, you can become a partner with the men of the Armed Forces in the world's biggest job, the business of winning this war, merely by enlisting in the Women's Army Corps, and you can choose your branch of the service, either Air, Ground, or Service Forces. If it's your choice to join the Air Force and become an Air WAC, you'll be given a specialized assignment in one of more than a hundred interesting, specialized and skilled jobs. You'll be thoroughly trained and the training you receive will be invaluable to you after the war is won. Go to the nearest WAC Recruiting Station, talk to the officer in charge. She'll help you select the job for which you are best suited and the one that you'll like. Do it now. And, as an Air WAC in the A.A.F., help to win this war and become a partner in victory. Captain Miller.
Captain Glenn Miller: Thank you, Lieutenant Briggs. Now a beautiful melody that's been bangin' around for a long time. Lately the customers are asking for it and it looks like it's on the way to becoming one of today's top tunes, "Poinciana."
POINCIANA (Song of the Tree)
Vocal refrain by Sergeant Johnny Desmond and the Crew Chiefs
2nd Lt. Donald P. Briggs: Write that letter soon, tonight, and write often. Use V-Mail. It gets there faster because it's the only kind of mail that's always sent by air. And V-Mail is safer. The Army retains the original until the photographic reproduction is actually delivered. Go to your nearest post office and obtain special V-Mail stationery. It's yours for the asking. Start writing that letter right now. And remember, V-Mail gets there first.
I SUSTAIN THE WINGS (closing theme)
Captain Glenn Miller: This is Captain Miller saying so long for the Band of the Training Command, Sergeants Brod Crawford, Mel Powell, Ray McKinley, Johnny Desmond, the Crew Chiefs, and Lieutenant Don Briggs. Hope to see you again next Saturday, same time, same station. In the meantime, don't forget those lads that are slugging it out overseas. They go for those V-Mail letters, don't let 'em down.
NBC announcer: This is the National Broadcasting Company.
NBC chimes

The parts of Benny, Colonel and Crewmen were played by Cpl. Paul A. Dubov, Cpl. Joseph Shulman and other members of the band.

11Mar44 (Sat) 11:30PM-Midnight EWT WEAF, NBC Vanderbilt Theatre, New York, New York
  I SUSTAIN THE WINGS broadcast   Audience

THE ARMY AIR CORPS (opening fanfare)
2nd Lt. Donald P. Briggs: "I Sustain the Wings."
I SUSTAIN THE WINGS (opening theme)
  2nd Lt. Donald P. Briggs: "I Sustain the Wings." The Army Air Forces present the Band
    of the Training Command, under the direction of Captain Glenn Miller. And now Captain
    Glenn Miller.
Captain Glenn Miller: Thank you, Lieutenant Don Briggs, and good evening, everybody.
  Speaking for Sergeants Brod Crawford, Mel Powell, Ray McKinley, Johnny Desmond, the Crew
  Chiefs, and the gang, welcome to another program of "I Sustain the Wings." First, a
  right fancy dish on the musical menu, "Must Be Jelly 'cause Jam Don't Shake Like That."
IT MUST BE JELLY ('Cause Jam Don't Shake Like That)
Captain Glenn Miller: Sergeant Johnny Desmond sings the new tune you'll be hearing more
  of come spring and summer. Johnny, you're on and the tune, "Long Ago and Far Away."
LONG AGO (And Far Away)
  Vocal refrain by Sergeant Johnny Desmond
The Army Air Corps (Incidental music)
  Captain Glenn Miller: It couldn't be done, so we did it. That might well be the motto
    of the men of the A.A.F. Training Command, the men of the ground crews and ...

    ...

Captain Glenn Miller: ... for the sweethearts and sisters of the boys in the A.A.F.
  Something old, something new, something borrowed, something blue. The old tune, "Songs
  My Mother Taught Me."
SONGS MY MOTHER TAUGHT ME (Old tune)
  Captain Glenn Miller: For something new, the Crew Chiefs singin' "It's Love, Love,
    Love!"
IT'S LOVE, LOVE, LOVE! (New tune)
  Captain Glenn Miller: Raymond Scott collaborated with Moz - Mr. Mozart for our borrowed
    tune, "Eighteenth Century Drawing Room."
IN AN EIGHTEENTH CENTURY DRAWING ROOM (Borrowed tune)
  Captain Glenn Miller: The blue tune, Sergeant Johnny Desmond sings "Blue Orchids."
BLUE ORCHIDS (Blue tune)
  Vocal refrain by Sergeant Johnny Desmond

    ...

Captain Glenn Miller: ... for it and it looks like it's on the way to becoming one of
  today's top tunes, Sergeant Jerry Gray's arrangement of "Poinciana."
POINCIANA (Song of the Tree)
  Vocal refrain by Sergeant Johnny Desmond and the Crew Chiefs
2nd Lt. Donald P. Briggs: A letter from home. Those few words are a magic prescription
  to give a lift to a lonely soldier stationed overseas. He wants to know what's going on
  at home, how his loved ones are doing, the hundreds of little details of their familiar
  daily life. And the sooner he knows these things the better. So write that letter
  soon, tonight, and write often. Use V-Mail. It gets there faster because it's the only
  kind of mail that's always sent by air. And V-Mail is safer. The Army retains the
  original until the photographic reproduction is actually delivered. Go to your nearest
  post office and obtain special V-Mail stationery. It's yours for the asking. Start
  writing that letter right now. And remember, V-Mail gets there first.

I SUSTAIN THE WINGS (closing theme)
  Captain Glenn Miller: This is Captain Miller saying so long for the Band of the
    Training Command, Sergeants Brod Crawford, Mel Powell, Ray McKinley, Johnny Desmond,
    the Crew Chiefs, and Lieutenant Don Briggs. Hope to see you again next Saturday, same
    time, same station. In the meantime, don't forget those lads that are slugging it out
    overseas. They go for those V-Mail letters.
  2nd Lt. Donald P. Briggs: "I ...

  ...

18Mar44 (Sat) NBC, New York, New York
  UNCLE SAM PRESENTS recording

I SUSTAIN THE WINGS (opening theme)
  2nd Lt. Donald P. Briggs: From the United States of America, to the other united
    nations of the world, "Uncle Sam Presents" the Band of the A.A.F. Training Command,
    under the direction of Captain Glenn Miller, with Sergeants Ray McKinley, Mel Powell
    and Johnny Desmond, and many of your old friends.
  2nd Lt. Donald P. Briggs: Here's Captain Glenn Miller.
  Captain Glenn Miller: Thank you, Lieutenant Don Briggs, and howdy to all you guys and
    gals out there. Sergeant Ray McKinley's ready to roll off the band with the big
    hammers. The tune, "Anvil Chorus."
ANVIL CHORUS
  Captain Glenn Miller: Nice goin', Sergeant McKinley. Here's the Crew Chiefs and Sergeant
    Johnny Desmond now singin' about "A Lovely Way to Spend an Evening."
A LOVELY WAY TO SPEND AN EVENING
  Vocal refrain by Sergeant Johnny Desmond and the Crew Chiefs
  Captain Glenn Miller: For those of you who like your music on the pretty side, a chorus
    of "Annie Laurie."
ANNIE LAURIE
  Captain Glenn Miller: Just in case things aren't warm enough in what's left of a certain
    German capitol, here's the whole gang playin' and singin' the rest of the story,
    "There'll Be a Hot Time In the Town of Berlin."
(There'll Be a) HOT TIME IN THE TOWN OF BERLIN (When the Yanks Go Marching In)
  Vocal refrain by Technical Sergeant Ray McKinley, the Crew Chiefs and the Glee Club
I SUSTAIN THE WINGS (closing theme)
  Captain Glenn Miller: Time now to take our leave until next week's meeting. You keep
    the letters a comin', we'll keep the music a goin'. Speaking for Lieutenant Don
    Briggs, Sergeants Ray McKinley, Mel Powell, Johnny Desmond, the Crew Chiefs and the
    gang, thanks for listening and so long.
  2nd Lt. Donald P. Briggs: The Band of the A.A.F. Training Command, under the direction
    of Captain Glenn Miller, has come to you from New York City. Don't forget tomorrow,
    same time, same station, "Uncle Sam Presents" another famous service band with music
    from us to you.
OH! SO GOOD! (fade-out tune)
  2nd Lt. Donald P. Briggs: This is the United States of America, one of the united
    nations.

18Mar44 (Sat) 6:00-6:30PM EWT WEAF, NBC Vanderbilt Theatre, New York, New York
  I SUSTAIN THE WINGS broadcast   Audience

  . . .

Captain Glenn Miller: ... the "Anvil Chorus."
ANVIL CHORUS
Captain Glenn Miller: Here's the Crew Chiefs and Sergeant Johnny Desmond singin' about "A
  Lovely Way to Spend an Evening."
A LOVELY WAY TO SPEND AN EVENING
  Vocal refrain by Sergeant Johnny Desmond and the Crew Chiefs

  . . .

I SUSTAIN THE WINGS (closing theme)
  Captain Glenn Miller: This is Captain Miller saying so long for the Band of the
    Training Command, Sergeants Brod Crawford, Mel Powell, Ray McKinley, Johnny Desmond,
    the Crew Chiefs, and Lieutenant Don Briggs, and the gang. Hope to see you again next
    Saturday, same time, same station. In the meantime, don't forget those lads that are
    doin' the dirty work ...

  . . .

18Mar44 (Sat) 11:30PM-Midnight EWT WEAF, NBC Vanderbilt Theatre, New York, New York
  I SUSTAIN THE WINGS broadcast   Audience

  . . .

ANNIE LAURIE (Old tune)
  Captain Glenn Miller: Something new, Corporal Bob Carroll sings.
STAR EYES (New tune)
  Vocal refrain by Corporal Bob Carroll

  . . .

ALEXANDER'S RAGTIME BAND (Borrowed tune)
  Captain Glenn Miller: Last, something blue, "Blue Is the Night."
BLUE IS THE NIGHT (Blue tune)

  . . .

25Mar44 (Sat) 2:15PM NBC, New York, New York
  UNCLE SAM PRESENTS recording

I SUSTAIN THE WINGS (opening theme)
  2nd Lt. Donald P. Briggs: ... the Band of the A.A.F. Training Command, under the
    direction of Captain Glenn Miller, with Sergeants Ray McKinley, Mel Powell, Johnny
    Desmond, and many of your old friends.
  2nd Lt. Donald P. Briggs: Here's Captain Glenn Miller.
  Captain Glenn Miller: Thank you, Lieutenant Don Briggs, and hello to all you guys and
    gals, wherever you are. Time for some music again, so here's the gang with "I Hear You
    Screamin'."
I HEAR YOU SCREAMIN'
  Captain Glenn Miller: Here's Sergeant Johnny Desmond singin' what we predict will be one
    of the year's top tunes, "Long Ago and Far Away."
LONG AGO (And Far Away)
  Vocal refrain by Sergeant Johnny Desmond
  Captain Glenn Miller: We turn to a page from Charlie Barnet's musical book and it's the
    war paint and fancy feathers of "Cherokee."
CHEROKEE (Indian Love Song)
  Captain Glenn Miller: Sergeant Ray McKinley and the Crew Chiefs with a musical salute to
    one of G.I. Joe's favorite characters, "Peggy the Pin-up Girl."
PEGGY THE PIN-UP GIRL
  Vocal refrain by Technical Sergeant Ray McKinley and the Crew Chiefs
I SUSTAIN THE WINGS (closing theme)
  Captain Glenn Miller: Time now to take our leave until next week's meeting. Speaking
    for Lieutenant Don Briggs, Sergeants Ray McKinley, Mel Powell, Johnny Desmond, the
    Crew Chiefs, and the gang, thanks for listening and so long.
  2nd Lt. Donald P. Briggs: The Band of the A.A.F. Training Command, under the direction
    of Captain Glenn Miller, has come to you from New York City. Don't forget tomorrow,
    same time, same station, "Uncle Sam Presents" another famous service band with music
    from us to you.
FLYING HOME (fade-out tune)
  2nd Lt. Donald P. Briggs: This is the United States of America, one of the united
    nations.

25Mar44 (Sat) 6:00-6:30PM EWT WEAF, NBC Vanderbilt Theatre, New York, New York
  I SUSTAIN THE WINGS broadcast   Audience

THE ARMY AIR CORPS (opening fanfare)
2nd Lt. Donald P. Briggs: "I Sustain the Wings."
I SUSTAIN THE WINGS (opening theme)
  2nd Lt. Donald P. Briggs: "I Sustain the Wings." The Army Air Forces present the Band
    of the Training Command, under the direction of Captain Glenn Miller. And now Captain
    Glenn Miller.
Captain Glenn Miller: Thank you, Lieutenant Don Briggs. Good evening, everybody, and
  hello again from Sergeants Ray McKinley, Brod Crawford, Mel Powell, Johnny Desmond, the
  Crew Chiefs, and the whole gang. Tonight "I Sustain the Wings" salutes the men of the
  Army Air Forces Troop Carrier Command. The boys of the band join in on the chorus with
  "I Hear You Screamin'."
I HEAR YOU SCREAMIN'
Captain Glenn Miller: Here's Sergeant Johnny Desmond singing Sergeant Norm Leyden's
  arrangement of what we predict will be one of the year's top tunes, "Long Ago."
LONG AGO (And Far Away)
  Vocal refrain by Sergeant Johnny Desmond
The Army Air Corps (Incidental music)
  Captain Glenn Miller: Many of the men trained by the A.A.F. Training Command are today
    serving in the Troop Carrier Command of the Army Air Forces. Their job is to
    transport troops, freight and the wounded to and from America's fighting front. It's
    a mighty important job and many are the tales of courage and heroism that come out of
    it. Such is the story of Captain Cecil Petty, pilot of a C-47 ...
Captain Glenn Miller: ... transport in the 13th Troop Carrier Squadron, operating in the
  South Pacific. It all began on October 20th, 1942 when Captain Petty took off from
  Guadalcanal with 19 sick and wounded soldiers aboard, bound for New Caledonia. They
  were still a hundred miles from their destination when the first trouble came. Captain
  Petty threw a quick glance at the instrument panel in front of him, called to his
  co-pilot.
2nd Lt. Donald P. Briggs (as Captain Cecil Petty): Hey, Bill, Bill. Take a look at that
  voltage regulator.
Sgt. Broderick Crawford (as Co-pilot Bill): I am looking. Brother, it's dead as a
  doornail. What happens now?
2nd Lt. Donald P. Briggs: We gotta set her down.
Sgt. Broderick Crawford: What are we, sea gulls? It's all open water. Try to push her
  in. We've got 19 wounded boys aboard.
2nd Lt. Donald P. Briggs: The old needle's kicking zero. We gotta let down.
Sgt. Broderick Crawford: Davy Jones, here we come.
2nd Lt. Donald P. Briggs: Now hold it. Bill, over there. Coral reef down there to the
  right.
Sgt. Broderick Crawford: It's too small and half under water. You'll never make it.
2nd Lt. Donald P. Briggs: We've gotta. Go back and tell the medical Sergeant to watch
  for those wounded guys. Tell them to hold tight. Hurry.
Sgt. Broderick Crawford: O.K.
2nd Lt. Donald P. Briggs: How about it, Bill? They all right?
Sgt. Broderick Crawford: They'll be O.K. But look, stand on those brakes. We're gonna
  overrun. Watch it, we're going into the water.
2nd Lt. Donald P. Briggs: Can't help it. We've used up the island. Hold on.
Sgt. Broderick Crawford: Let's get out those life rafts. Quick!
2nd Lt. Donald P. Briggs: No, it's no use. Not enough, not enough of them for everybody.
  Let's tie the plane so it won't sink.
Sgt. Broderick Crawford: With what, our shoestrings?
2nd Lt. Donald P. Briggs: Yeah, that's right. Oh, wait. I've got an idea. Control
  cables. We'll tear out the control cables, loop them around the wings and tail and
  anchor the plane to the reef. Then we'll radio the squadron for help. Let's go.
Incidental music
2nd Lt. Donald P. Briggs: Hello, Palm Tree. Hello, Palm Tree. This is Shamrock 2-7-1
  calling Palm Tree. Come in, Palm Tree. Come in, anybody.

Sgt. Broderick Crawford: How about it, you gettin' through?
2nd Lt. Donald P. Briggs: Naw, I've been sitting here for five days yelling hello into this thing. Not a word. Let's go back and take a look-see at the men. How are they today?
Sgt. Broderick Crawford: Not so good. Mac over there is getting worse all the time. His leg's in a bad way.
Mac: One more chance.
2nd Lt. Donald P. Briggs: What did you say, Mac?
Sgt. Broderick Crawford: He's kinda out of his head at times. He keeps saying, "One more chance," over and over.
Mac: One more chance.
2nd Lt. Donald P. Briggs: What's he talking about?
Sgt. Broderick Crawford: I don't know. Sergeant says he's a fighter pilot and aced six Zeros to his credit. I think he was up one day and they got him. Guess that hurt him worse than the leg. Kind of on his mind.
Mac: One more chance.
2nd Lt. Donald P. Briggs: All right now, easy, kid, easy. You guys will all get another chance if we can get it for you. That's our job, giving you guys a second chance, seeing that you get to a hospital and then back to try again. Don't worry, we'll pull through. I don't know how but we'll do it. O.K., Bill, get back to that radio. We've got to get help some way, but quick.
Incidental music
2nd Lt. Donald P. Briggs: Hello, hello. Shamrock 2-7-1 calling. Shamrock 2-7-1 calling.
Sgt. Broderick Crawford: Why don't you let it go? You've been at that radio for nine days and nine nights. You've got a cold. You're all in. Come in, let me take over for a while.
2nd Lt. Donald P. Briggs: Listen, Bill, those guys are counting on us to get them out of this. We've got to do it.
Sgt. Broderick Crawford: But you're just about half dead yourself.
2nd Lt. Donald P. Briggs: I'll be O.K. If we can just get an answer. Hello. Hello. Shamrock 2-7-1 calling. Hello. Hello. Ah, I guess It's no use. Even the Japs won't cut in on us.
Benson: Hello. Hello, 2-7-1.
2nd Lt. Donald P. Briggs: Bill, do you hear that?
Sgt. Broderick Crawford: Yes.
Benson: I hear your call. This is Shamrock 8-4-6. Where are you? We've been looking for you.
2nd Lt. Donald P. Briggs: Bill, it's a plane from our squadron.
Sgt. Broderick Crawford: Sure it's not a Jap?
2nd Lt. Donald P. Briggs: No, no, no, it's Benson. I know his voice. Hello, hello, Benson. This is Petty 2-7-1. We're down on a coral reef. Location C for Charlie, K for Kane, Z for Zebra, S for Sugar, 2-3-1-5. Plane in water, wounded aboard, can't stay afloat much longer. Can you help? Can you help?
Benson: Hello, Petty. Hang on. I'm heading your way. I'll drop food and water. I must be near you. I see a lot of reefs but no plane. Keep in touch with me.
2nd Lt. Donald P. Briggs: Hey, hey, listen.
Sgt. Broderick Crawford: Huh? Listen, there he is now. Come on. Let's get outside.
2nd Lt. Donald P. Briggs: Hello, 8-4-6. We hear your engines. Watch for us.
Benson: Roger. I see you now. I'm gonna drop supplies. Ready?
2nd Lt. Donald P. Briggs: We'll get 'em. Drop ahead. Come on, open that hatch. Let's get outside on the wing. There he is, look, circling low. Boy, food at last. My stomach feels like my throat's been cut. He's throwing stuff out on a parachute. Ah, here it comes. No, no. The wind's carrying it away. It's going into the water.
Sgt. Broderick Crawford: It'll sink. We'll never get it.
2nd Lt. Donald P. Briggs: By God, I'm going in after it.
Sgt. Broderick Crawford: Now, don't be crazy. You're all keyed up now. Let me go. I can't swim very good but maybe I can make it.
2nd Lt. Donald P. Briggs: Don't argue. I'm all right. The guys down there got to have food and I'm going to get it. Look out.
Incidental music

2nd Lt. Donald P. Briggs: Hey, Bill. Bring up the binoculars when you come. I'm in the cabin.

Sgt. Broderick Crawford: I'll be right with you. Boy, after a week I can hardly get out of this hatch anymore. Why don't you go down in the cabin and get yourself some sleep. We'll have you in a litter before long.

2nd Lt. Donald P. Briggs: Forget it. The medical Sergeant's got your hands full with those guys below. I got to stay up here on the wing and watch. Benson said he'd send help. That was two days ago.

Sgt. Broderick Crawford: Yeah, it's blowing up a storm, too. When it gets here those cables won't hold for a minute.

2nd Lt. Donald P. Briggs: Yeah. Funny, I don't care about myself so much. It's Mac and those other guys. They trusted us to get them another chance, all of them. That's our job, helping guys to get back and fight again, but I guess this time we failed.

Sgt. Broderick Crawford: Hey, look, what's that?

2nd Lt. Donald P. Briggs: Where?

Sgt. Broderick Crawford: Over there. Looks like smoke or something. It - it's a destroyer.

2nd Lt. Donald P. Briggs: Give me those glasses, quick. It - it's one of ours. They're putting down a boat. You stay here and keep wavin'. I'm goin' down and tell the boys. Hey, Sergeant. On the double. Destroyer comin' up. Start gettin' everything ready to take off. I'll give you a lift with the litters when they get here.

Mac: One more chance.

2nd Lt. Donald P. Briggs: It's O.K., Mac. You'll get your chance. You'll get your chance.

I Sustain the Wings (Incidental music)

Captain Glenn Miller: Now it's medley time, saluting the mothers, wives, sweethearts and sisters of the men of the Troop Carrier Command. Something old, something new, something borrowed and something blue. The old tune, "Schubert's Serenade."

SHUBERT'S SERENADE (Old tune)

    Captain Glenn Miller: Something new, Corporal Bob Carroll and the Crew Chiefs singin' "Irresistible You."

IRRESISTIBLE YOU (New tune)

    Vocal refrain by Corporal Bob Carroll and the Crew Chiefs

    Captain Glenn Miller: We reached way back in the books for our borrowed tune, it's "Little Brown Jug."

LITTLE BROWN JUG (Borrowed tune)

    Captain Glenn Miller: The blue tune, "Rhapsody in Blue."

RHAPSODY IN BLUE (Blue tune)

Captain Glenn Miller: Sergeant Jerry Gray's arrangement and Sergeant Ray McKinley and the Crew Chiefs singing a musical salute to one of G.I. Joe's favorite characters, "Peggy the Pin-Up Girl."

PEGGY THE PIN-UP GIRL

    Vocal refrain by Technical Sergeant Ray McKinley and the Crew Chiefs

2nd Lt. Donald P. Briggs: Eighteen thousand passengers transported, six thousand wounded evacuated, four and one-half billion pounds of freight hauled. All in less than a year. That's the tremendous record of only one squadron of the Troop Carrier Command, an important branch of the fighting A.A.F. And like all men of the A.A.F., the personnel of this highly efficient delivery service is trained by the A.A.F. Training Command, the world's biggest university, whose job it is to furnish the men to fly our planes and to "Keep 'Em Flying." Because of the knowledge obtained from the Training Command, every one of the men of the Troop Carrier Command can proudly boast, "I Sustain the Wings."

I SUSTAIN THE WINGS (closing theme)

    Captain Glenn Miller: This is Captain Glenn Miller saying so long for the Band of the Training Command, Sergeants Brod Crawford, Mel Powell, Ray McKinley, Johnny Desmond, the Crew Chiefs and "Lietanent" - Lieutenant Don Briggs, and the whole gang. Hope to see you again next Saturday, same time, same station. In the meantime, don't forget those lads that are slugging it out overseas. Write 'em a letter. Use V-Mail.

    2nd Lt. Donald P. Briggs: "I Sustain the Wings" is a presentation of the Army Air Forces Training Command and came to you from New York City.

NBC announcer: This is the National Broadcasting Company.

NBC chimes

The parts of Mac and Benson were played by Cpl. Paul A. Dubov and another member of the band.

25Mar44 (Sat) 11:30PM-Midnight EWT   WEAF, NBC Vanderbilt Theatre, New York, New York
  I SUSTAIN THE WINGS broadcast
                                                                          Audience

THE ARMY AIR CORPS (opening fanfare)
2nd Lt. Donald P. Briggs: "I Sustain the Wings."
I SUSTAIN THE WINGS (opening theme)
   2nd Lt. Donald P. Briggs: "I Sustain the Wings." The Army Air Forces present the Band
     of the Training Command, under the direction of Captain Glenn Miller. And now Captain
     Glenn Miller.
Captain Glenn Miller: Thank you, Lieutenant Briggs. Good evening, everybody, and hello
  again from Sergeants Ray McKinley, Brod Crawford, Mel Powell, Johnny Desmond, the Crew
  Chiefs, and the whole gang. Tonight "I Sustain the Wings" salutes the men of the Army
  Air Forces Troop Carrier Command. The boys of the band join in on the chorus with "I
  Hear You Screamin'."
I HEAR YOU SCREAMIN'
Captain Glenn Miller: Now here's Sergeant Johnny Desmond singing Sergeant Norm Leyden's
  arrangement and one that we predict will be top tunes this year, "Long Ago and Far Away"
LONG AGO (And Far Away)
   Vocal refrain by Sergeant Johnny Desmond
The Army Air Corps (Incidental music)
   Captain Glenn Miller: Many of the men trained by the A.A.F. Training Command are today
     serving in the Troop Carrier Command of the Army Air Forces. Their job is to
     transport troops, freight and the wounded to and from America's fighting front. It's
     a mighty important job and many are the tales of courage and heroism that have come
     out of it. Such is the story of Captain Cecil Petty, pilot of a C-47 transport in the
     13th Troop Carrier Squadron, operating in the South Pacific.
Captain Glenn Miller: It all began on October 20th, 1942 when Captain Petty took off from
  Guadalcanal with 19 sick and wounded soldiers aboard, bound for New Caledonia. They
  were still a hundred miles from their destination when the first trouble came. Captain
  Petty threw a quick glance at the instrument panel in front of him, called to his
  co-pilot.
2nd Lt. Donald P. Briggs (as Captain Cecil Petty): Hey, Bill. Take a look at that
  voltage regulator.
Sgt. Broderick Crawford (as Co-pilot Bill): I am looking. Brother, it's dead as a
  doornail. What happens now?
2nd Lt. Donald P. Briggs: We gotta set her down.
Sgt. Broderick Crawford: What are we, sea gulls? It's all open water. Try to push her
  in. We've got 19 wounded boys aboard.
2nd Lt. Donald P. Briggs: The old needle's kicking zero. We gotta let down.
Sgt. Broderick Crawford: Davy Jones, here we come.
2nd Lt. Donald P. Briggs: Now hold it. Bill, over there. Coral reef down there to the
  right.
Sgt. Broderick Crawford: Too small and half under water. You'll never make it.
2nd Lt. Donald P. Briggs: We've gotta. Go back and tell the medical Sergeant to watch
  for those wounded guys. Tell them to hold tight. Hurry.
Sgt. Broderick Crawford: O.K.
2nd Lt. Donald P. Briggs: How about it, Bill? They all right?
Sgt. Broderick Crawford: They'll be O.K. But look, stand on those brakes. We're gonna
  overrun. Watch it, we're going into the water.
2nd Lt. Donald P. Briggs: Can't help it. We've used up the island.
Sgt. Broderick Crawford: All right. Come on, get out the life rafts. Quick!
2nd Lt. Donald P. Briggs: Oh, it's no use. Not enough for for everybody. Got to tie the
  plane so it won't sink.
Sgt. Broderick Crawford: With what, our shoestrings?
2nd Lt. Donald P. Briggs: Yeah, that's right. Oh, wait. I've got an idea. Control
  cables. We'll tear out the control cables, loop them around the wings and tail and
  anchor the plane to the reef. Then we'll radio the squadron for help. Let's go.
Incidental music
2nd Lt. Donald P. Briggs: Hello, Palm Tree. Hello, Palm Tree. This is Shamrock 2-7-1
  calling Palm Tree. Come in, Palm Tree. Come in, anybody.

Sgt. Broderick Crawford: How about it, getting through?

2nd Lt. Donald P. Briggs: Ah, I've been sitting here for five days yelling hello into this thing. Not a word. Ah, let's go back and take a look-see at the men. How are they today?

Sgt. Broderick Crawford: Not so good. Mac over there is getting worse all the time. His leg's in a bad way.

Mac: One more chance.

2nd Lt. Donald P. Briggs: What did you say, Mac?

Sgt. Broderick Crawford: He's out of his head at times. He keeps saying, "One more chance," over and over.

Mac: One more chance.

2nd Lt. Donald P. Briggs: What's he talking about?

Sgt. Broderick Crawford: I don't know. Sergeant says he's a fighter pilot and aced six Zeros to his credit. One day he goes up and, well, they got him. Guess that hurt him worse than the leg. Kind of on his mind.

Mac: One more chance.

2nd Lt. Donald P. Briggs: All right now, easy, kid, easy. You guys will all get another chance if we can get it for you. That's our job, giving you guys a second chance, seeing that you get to a hospital and then back to try again. Don't worry, we'll pull through. I don't know how but we'll do it. O.K., Bill, let's get back to that radio. We've got to get help some way, but quick.

Incidental music

2nd Lt. Donald P. Briggs: Hello, hello. Shamrock 2-7-1 calling. Shamrock 2-7-1 calling.

Sgt. Broderick Crawford: Oh, why don't you let it go? You've been at that radio nine days and nine nights. You've got a cold. You're all in. Come on, let me take over for a while.

2nd Lt. Donald P. Briggs: Listen, Bill, those guys are counting on us to get them out of this. We've got to do it.

Sgt. Broderick Crawford: But you're just about half dead yourself.

2nd Lt. Donald P. Briggs: I'll be O.K. If we can just get an answer. Hello. Hello. Shamrock 2-7-1 calling. Hello. Hello. Ah, I guess It's no use. Even the Japs won't cut in on us.

Benson: Hello. Hello, 2-7-1.

2nd Lt. Donald P. Briggs: Bill, do you hear that?

Sgt. Broderick Crawford: Yes.

Benson: I hear your call. This is Shamrock 8-4-6. Where are you? We've been looking for you.

2nd Lt. Donald P. Briggs: It's a plane from our squadron.

Sgt. Broderick Crawford: Sure it's not a Jap?

2nd Lt. Donald P. Briggs: No, no, it's Benson. I know his voice. Hello, hello, Benson. This is Petty 2-7-1. We're down on a coral reef. Location C for Charlie, K for Kane, Z for Zebra, S for Sugar, 2-3-1-5. Plane in water, wounded aboard, can't stay afloat much longer. Can you help? Can you help?

Benson: Hello, Petty. Hang on. I'm heading your way. I'll drop food and water. I must be near you. I see a lot of reefs but no plane. Keep in touch with me.

2nd Lt. Donald P. Briggs: Hey, listen.

Sgt. Broderick Crawford: Huh? Listen, there he is now. Come on. Let's get outside.

2nd Lt. Donald P. Briggs: Hello, 8-4-6. We hear your engines. Watch for us.

Benson: Roger. I see you now. I'm gonna drop supplies. Ready?

2nd Lt. Donald P. Briggs: We'll get 'em. Drop ahead. Come on, open that hatch. Let's get outside on the wing. There he is, look, circling low. Boy, food at last. My stomach feels like my throat's been cut. Throwing stuff out on a parachute. Here, here comes. No, no. The wind's carrying it away. It's going into the water.

Sgt. Broderick Crawford: It'll sink. We'll never get it.

2nd Lt. Donald P. Briggs: God, I'm going in after it.

Sgt. Broderick Crawford: Now, don't be crazy. You're all keyed up. Let me go. I can't swim very good but maybe I can make it.

2nd Lt. Donald P. Briggs: Don't argue. I'm all right. The guys down there got to have food and I'm going to get it. Look out.

Incidental music

2nd Lt. Donald P. Briggs: Hey, Bill. Bring up the binoculars when you come. I'm in the cabin.

Sgt. Broderick Crawford: Be right with you. Boy, after a week I can hardly get out of this hatch anymore. Why don't you go down in the cabin and get some sleep before we have you in a litter, too.

2nd Lt. Donald P. Briggs: Aw, forget it. The medical Sergeant's got your hands full with those guys below. I got to stay up here on the wing and watch. Benson said he'd send help. That was two days ago.

Sgt. Broderick Crawford: Yeah, and it's blowing up a storm. When it gets here those cables won't hold for a minute.

2nd Lt. Donald P. Briggs: Yeah. Funny, I don't care about myself so much. It's Mac and those other guys. They trusted us to get them another chance, all of them. That's our job, helping guys to get back and fight again, but I guess this time we failed.

Sgt. Broderick Crawford: Hey, what's that?

2nd Lt. Donald P. Briggs: Where?

Sgt. Broderick Crawford: Over there. Looks like smoke or something. It - it's a destroyer.

2nd Lt. Donald P. Briggs: Give me those glasses, quick. One of ours. They're putting down a boat. You stay here and keep ...

  ...

SHUBERT'S SERENADE (Old tune)
  Captain Glenn Miller: Something new, Corporal Bob Carroll and the Crew Chiefs singin' "Irresistible You."
IRRESISTIBLE YOU (New tune)
  Vocal refrain by Corporal Bob Carroll and the Crew Chiefs
  Captain Glenn Miller: We reach way back in the books for our borrowed tune tonight, "Little Brown Jug."
LITTLE BROWN JUG (Borrowed tune)
  Captain Glenn Miller: L - last in the medley is the blue tune, "Rhapsody in Blue."
RHAPSODY IN BLUE (Blue tune)
Sgt. Broderick Crawford: Women of America, we all want to help win this war. If you have any doubt about the part you're playing in this business of victory, then enlist in the Women's Army Corps. You can select your own branch of the service, either Air, Ground, or Service Forces. If you choose the Army Air Forces and become an Air WAC, you will be given excellent training in one of more than a hundred specialized jobs. And with the thousands of men in the fighting A.A.F., become a partner in victory.
Captain Glenn Miller: Now Sergeant Jerry Gray's arrangement, Sergeant Ray McKinley and the Crew Chiefs singing a musical salute to one of G.I. Joe's favorite characters, "Peggy the Pin-Up Girl."
PEGGY THE PIN-UP GIRL
  Vocal refrain by Technical Sergeant Ray McKinley and the Crew Chiefs
2nd Lt. Donald P. Briggs: Eighteen thousand passengers transported, six thousand wounded evacuated, four and one-half billion pounds of freight hauled. All in less than a year. That's the tremendous record of only one squadron of the Troop Carrier Command, an important branch of the fighting A.A.F. And like all men of the A.A.F., the personnel of this highly efficient delivery service is trained by the A.A.F. Training Command, the world's biggest university, whose job it is to furnish the men to fly our planes and to "Keep 'Em Flying." Because of the knowledge obtained from the Training Command, every one of the men of the Troop Carrier Command can proudly boast, "I Sustain the Wings."
I SUSTAIN THE WINGS (closing theme)
  Captain Glenn Miller: This is Captain Glenn Miller saying so long for the Band of the Training Command, Sergeants Brod Crawford, Mel Powell, Ray McKinley, Johnny Desmond, the Crew Chiefs and Lieutenant Don Briggs. Hope to see you again next Saturday, same time, same station. And in the meantime, don't forget those lads that are slugging it out overseas. They go for those V-Mail letters. Don't let 'em down.
  2nd Lt. Donald P. Briggs: "I Sustain the Wings" is a presentation of the Army Air Forces Training Command and came to you from New York City.

The parts of Mac and Benson were played by Cpl. Paul A. Dubov and another member of the band.

01Apr44 (Sat) 2:15-3:00PM EWT   NBC, New York, New York
  UNCLE SAM PRESENTS recording

I SUSTAIN THE WINGS (opening theme)
  2nd Lt. Donald P. Briggs: From the United States of America, to the other united
    nations of the world, "Uncle Sam Presents" the Band of the A.A.F. Training Command,
    under the direction of Captain Glenn Miller.
  2nd Lt. Donald P. Briggs: Here's Captain Glenn Miller.
  Captain Glenn Miller: Thank you, Lieutenant Don Briggs. Speaking for Corporal Bob
    Carroll, Sergeants Mel Powell, Ray McKinley, and all the boys, welcome to another go
    around with the Band of the Training Command. Sergeant Ray McKinley rolls off, the band
    plays "American Patrol."
AMERICAN PATROL
Captain Glenn Miller: Corporal Bob Carroll and the Crew Chiefs sing one of the more
  promising of the new tunes, "Good Night, wherever You Are."
GOOD NIGHT, WHEREVER YOU ARE
  Vocal refrain by Corporal Bob Carroll and the Crew Chiefs
Captain Glenn Miller: According to the mailman, all the cash customers want a return bout
  with Sergeant Jerry Gray's arrangement of "Holiday for Strings." Here it 'tis.
HOLIDAY FOR STRINGS
I SUSTAIN THE WINGS (closing theme)
  Captain Glenn Miller: Time now to take our leave until next week's meeting. Speaking
    for Lieutenant Don Briggs, Corporal Bob Carroll, Sergeants Ray McKinley, Mel Powell,
    and the gang, thanks for listening and so long 'til next time.
  2nd Lt. Donald P. Briggs: The Band of the A.A.F. Training Command, under the direction
    of Captain Glenn Miller, has come to you from New York City. Don't forget tomorrow,
    same time, same station, "Uncle Sam Presents" another famous service band with music
    from us to you.
SUN VALLEY JUMP (fade-out tune)
  2nd Lt. Donald P. Briggs: This is the United States of America, one of the united
    nations.

01Apr44 (Sat) 6:00-6:30PM EWT WEAF, NBC Vanderbilt Theatre, New York, New York
  I SUSTAIN THE WINGS broadcast   Audience

THE ARMY AIR CORPS (opening fanfare)
2nd Lt. Donald P. Briggs: "I Sustain the Wings."
I SUSTAIN THE WINGS (opening theme)
  2nd Lt. Donald P. Briggs: "I Sustain the Wings." The Army Air Forces present the Band
    of the Training Command, under the direction of Captain Glenn Miller. And now Captain
    Glenn Miller.
Captain Glenn Miller: Good evening, everybody. Speaking for Sergeants Brod Crawford, Mel
  Powell, Ray McKinley, Johnny Desmond, the Crew Chiefs, Lieutenant Don Briggs, the whole
  gang, welcome to another program of "I Sustain the Wings." Now Sergeant Ray McKinley
  rolls off, the band plays "American Patrol."
AMERICAN PATROL
Captain Glenn Miller: Corporal Bob Carroll and the Crew Chiefs singin' one of the more
  promising new tunes, "Good Night, wherever You Are."
GOOD NIGHT, WHEREVER YOU ARE
  Vocal refrain by Corporal Bob Carroll and the Crew Chiefs
Incidental music
  Captain Glenn Miller: A good example of the skilled technicians turned out by the
    A.A.F. Training Command is the aerial engineer, the boss of the bomber, they call him.
    He's the guy who keeps the engines purring like tiger cubs. He nurses the last flying
    minutes out of a crippled ship. He makes all repairs in flight. He mans a pair of
    guns in the top turret. And if he has to, he can bring the ship home almost
    single-handed, like Steve, the engineer in tonight's story. Steve and his pilot,
    Dave, had both been in the auto racing game before the war. Dave as a driver, Steve
    riding with him as a mechanic. And after they joined the Air Forces they wound up
    together again, Dave pilot, and Steve engineer, on the big Liberator, "Bad Medicine,"
    raiding Jap airfields in Burma.
2nd Lt. Donald P. Briggs (as Pilot Dave): Pilot to top turret. How's it going up there,
  Steve? Everything all right?
Sgt. Broderick Crawford (as Aerial Engineer Steve): Top turret. It's O.K. here, Dave.
  Just takin' it easy, like old times.
2nd Lt. Donald P. Briggs: What do you mean, "like old times?"
Sgt. Broderick Crawford: Yeah, you remember the old days. You did the drivin'. All I
  did after the race started was ride along as mechanic and watch the scenery. The same
  thing now.
2nd Lt. Donald P. Briggs: You won't watch much scenery on this track, brother. This
  track is tough.
Sgt. Broderick Crawford: Maybe for you, you have to do the drivin'. Us mechanics just go
  along for the drive. Not a worry in the world.
2nd Lt. Donald P. Briggs: Wait'll those Zeros come pouring in on the back stretch.
  You'll do some worrying then.
Sgt. Broderick Crawford: Not me. All I have to do is hemstitch a few of those babies
  with my twin fifties and my job's done. You're the guy that's got to get us home. I'm
  just goin' along for the ride, remember?
2nd Lt. Donald P. Briggs: Heh, heh, O.K., wise guy. But you better get those fifties
  ready right now. We'll be over the target in a minute. Heads up, gang. We're goin'
  in. Let's make it a good one this time.
Incidental music
2nd Lt. Donald P. Briggs: Nice shooting, gang. We dug 'em a hole that time. O.K.,
  Steve, we're heading back for the home stretch. If anybody tries to pass us on the
  curves, heave a wrench at them.
Sgt. Broderick Crawford: Top turret to pilot. A couple of Jap drivers pulling up on our
  tail, Dave. Here goes the first wrench, Dave. One of them out of the races. Here
  comes the other one.
2nd Lt. Donald P. Briggs: Bail out. B - bail out, we're falling. Bail out before it's
  ...
Sgt. Broderick Crawford: Dave. Hello, Dave. Are you all right, Dave? Engineer to
  radio. Take over here. I got to see what's wrong.

Incidental music
Cpl. Paul A. Dubov (as Navigator Bill): Navigator to pilot.
Sgt. Broderick Crawford: Engineer here.
Cpl. Paul A. Dubov: We're calling Dave. Get off the wire, Steve. Hello, Dave.
Sgt. Broderick Crawford: Dave's been hit, Bill. I'm taking over for him at the controls.
Cpl. Paul A. Dubov: How about co-pilot? Better let him do it.
Sgt. Broderick Crawford: Joe's gone. Same shell got him.
Cpl. Paul A. Dubov: Hold it level, if you can. I'll get the first aid kit and bring it
  in.
Sgt. Broderick Crawford: Roger. How you feeling, Dave?
2nd Lt. Donald P. Briggs: Pretty rocky, Steve. I'll be all right. Just watch those
  rudders. It's - it's a rough track.
Sgt. Broderick Crawford: You're telling me. Say, what am I doing driving this thing?
  I'm a mechanic. I'm just along for the ride.
2nd Lt. Donald P. Briggs: Huh, you're in the driver's seat now, kid. You're the guy
  that's got to bring us home, if we get home.
Sgt. Broderick Crawford: We'll get there. Don't worry, Dave, we'll make it.
Cpl. Paul A. Dubov: Ah, Steve, how's it going? It's the first air kit. See if you can
  bandage Dave up and then you better get back to the guns.
Sgt. Broderick Crawford: But the ship. Somebody's got to ...
Cpl. Paul A. Dubov: All right. I'll try to hold her level until you get back. We need
  you at those guns, we're still over enemy territory and may have visitors any minute.
Incidental music
Sgt. Broderick Crawford: Top turret to navigator. Three Tojos coming in at nine o'clock.
  Evasive action if you can, Bill. They're coming in for the kill. Two of 'em are
  turning back. I think I got the other one, he's heading down, out of control. It's all
  clear again.
Cpl. Paul A. Dubov: Got a minute, Steve? Come back and see what's wrong with the tail
  gunner. He doesn't answer.
Sgt. Broderick Crawford: I'll go back right now.
Incidental music
  Cpl. Paul A. Dubov: Navigator to engineer. Manifold pressure on number three down.
    Check turbo controls. See if you can fix it, Steve.
  Sgt. Broderick Crawford: I'll take care of it.
  Cpl. Paul A. Dubov: Navigator to engineer. Waist gunner reports hydraulic lines
    broken. Think you can patch them up?
  Sgt. Broderick Crawford: I'll do what I can.
  Cpl. Paul A. Dubov: Navigator. Steve, prop governor on number four engine frozen.
    What are we going to do about it?
  Sgt. Broderick Crawford: I'll see about it just as soon as I get this hydraulic line.
  Cpl. Paul A. Dubov: Hello, Steve. Zeros coming up on our tail. I need you back in the
    turret. Hurry.
  Sgt. Broderick Crawford: I'm going right away.
  Cpl. Paul A. Dubov: Navigator to engineer. Can you come up to the flight deck, take
    the controls again? I want to plot us a course home.
  Sgt. Broderick Crawford: I'll be right there.
Cpl. Paul A. Dubov: According to this course I've plotted, Steve, we're near Emergency
  Field Y. Better land there. How's tail gunner? Check on him?
Sgt. Broderick Crawford: Well, he's coming along O.K. He had a fifty in the shoulder,
  but I bandaged him up.
Cpl. Paul A. Dubov: Did you get the hydraulic line fixed?
Sgt. Broderick Crawford: I patched it up but the pressure won't hold.
Cpl. Paul A. Dubov: How about that prop on number four?
Sgt. Broderick Crawford: Frozen solid. But it won't hurt anything at cruising speed.
Cpl. Paul A. Dubov: You better check the gas supply, Steve. I want to see if we can make
  it.
Sgt. Broderick Crawford: I checked it on the way forward, it's all right.
Cpl. Paul A. Dubov: Well, we're almost there now. Put the wheels down for me, will you?
Sgt. Broderick Crawford: Roger.

Cpl. Paul A. Dubov: Huh, what's the matter with them, Steve? They don't lock. What's wrong?

Sgt. Broderick Crawford: The hydraulic system's shot. I ...

Cpl. Paul A. Dubov: Can you crank it down, Steve? We're almost ready to go down for the landing.

Sgt. Broderick Crawford: Roger. And I thought I was just supposed to watch the scenery.

Cpl. Paul A. Dubov: What'd you say, Steve?

Sgt. Broderick Crawford: Oh, nothin', nothin'. I'll crank those wheels down right away. Take over.

Cpl. Paul A. Dubov: Did you get them down, Steve?

Sgt. Broderick Crawford: All O.K., Bill. They ought be ...

Cpl. Paul A. Dubov: And you'd better land this thing, Steve. You know more about it than I do. Dave says you can do it.

Sgt. Broderick Crawford: I don't know how to land the planes, Dave. I never flew one before in my life.

2nd Lt. Donald P. Briggs: You gotta try, Steve, if we're gonna get down. Go ahead, I'll tell you what to do. You can do it.

Sgt. Broderick Crawford: Well, I'll try it, but I ain't sure.

2nd Lt. Donald P. Briggs: Now, forward on the controls a bit. That's right. Now hold them there. Looks good. Now hold back, back harder, hold back. We - we're touchin' the runway. Keep those rudders straight. That's it. Now the brakes. Take it easy. Not too heavy. You did it, Steve. We're in.

Cpl. Paul A. Dubov: All right, come on, Dave. We're gonna get you out of here.

Sgt. Broderick Crawford: Easy, unbuckle his safety belt.

Cpl. Paul A. Dubov: All right, Steve.

Sgt. Broderick Crawford: Open the hatch, I'll lift him up.

Cpl. Paul A. Dubov: Hmm.

Sgt. Broderick Crawford: Now don't worry, Dave. You're gonna be O.K.

Cpl. Paul A. Dubov: I'm sure he'll be O.K. Steve, if it hadn't been for you workin' the guns, fixin' the plane, and keepin' us goin', I don't know what we'd o' done. You did a great job.

2nd Lt. Donald P. Briggs: Yeah, you don't mean Steve, Bill. Why, all he did was watch the scenery.

Sgt. Broderick Crawford: Yeah, sure, that's right, Bill. I just went along for the ride.

I Sustain the Wings (Incidental music)

Captain Glenn Miller: Now it's medley time, saluting the mothers, wives, sweethearts and sisters of the boys in the A.A.F. Something old, something new, something borrowed, something blue. Our old song, "All through the Night."

ALL THROUGH THE NIGHT (Old tune)

Captain Glenn Miller: Something new, Sergeant Johnny Desmond sings.

I LOVE YOU (New tune)

Vocal refrain by Sergeant Johnny Desmond

Captain Glenn Miller: Friend Guy Lombardo furnishes the Crew Chiefs with the borrowed tune, "Take It Easy."

TAKE IT EASY (Borrowed tune)

Vocal refrain by the Crew Chiefs

Captain Glenn Miller: Last, something blue, "Blue Hawaii."

BLUE HAWAII (Blue tune)

Captain Glenn Miller: According to the mailman, all the cash customers want a return bout with Sergeant Jerry Gray's arrangement of "Holiday for Strings." Here it is.

HOLIDAY FOR STRINGS

2nd Lt. Donald P. Briggs: The aerial engineer is more than just a mechanic, he's the watchdog of a plane when it's flying. It's his job to keep a plane functioning smoothly in flight, to know if all the engines are perking as they should, to watch the fuel supply and transfer it to the proper tank at the proper time, plus hundreds of other details necessary to the most efficient plane operation. The pilot knows the aerial engineer's opinion of a plane is reliable because of the knowledge and training he's received from the Army Air Forces Training Command, the world's biggest university. And with the thousands of other graduates of the Training Command, the aerial engineer can proudly say, "I Sustain the Wings."

I SUSTAIN THE WINGS (closing theme)
  Captain Glenn Miller: This is Captain Glenn Miller saying so long for the Band of the
    Training Command, Sergeants Brod Crawford, Mel Powell, Ray McKinley, Johnny Desmond,
    Bob Carroll, the Crew Chiefs, and Lieutenant Don Briggs. Hope to see you again next
    Saturday, same time, same station. In the meantime, don't forget those lads that are
    doin' the dirty work overseas. They're doin' the fightin', you do the writin'.
  2nd Lt. Donald P. Briggs: "I Sustain the Wings" is a presentation of the Army Air
    Forces Training Command and came to you from New York City.
NBC announcer: This is the National Broadcasting Company.
NBC chimes

01Apr44 (Sat) 11:30PM-Midnight EWT WEAF, NBC Vanderbilt Theatre, New York, New York
  I SUSTAIN THE WINGS broadcast   Audience

THE ARMY AIR CORPS (opening fanfare)
2nd Lt. Donald P. Briggs: "I Sustain the Wings."
I SUSTAIN THE WINGS (opening theme)
  2nd Lt. Donald P. Briggs: "I Sustain the Wings." The Army Air Forces present the Band
    of the Training Command, under the direction of Captain Glenn Miller. And now Captain
    Glenn Miller.
Captain Glenn Miller: Good evening, everybody. Speaking for Sergeants Brod Crawford, Mel
  Powell, Ray McKinley, Johnny Desmond, the Crew Chiefs, Lieutenant Don Briggs, the whole
  gang, welcome to another program of "I Sustain the Wings." Now Sergeant Ray McKinley
  rolls off, the band plays "American Patrol."
AMERICAN PATROL
Captain Glenn Miller: Corporal Bob Carroll and the Crew Chiefs sing one of the more
  promising new tunes, "Good Night, wherever You Are."
GOOD NIGHT, WHEREVER YOU ARE
  Vocal refrain by Corporal Bob Carroll and the Crew Chiefs
Incidental music
  Captain Glenn Miller: A good example of the skilled technicians turned out by the
    A.A.F. Training Command is the aerial engineer, the boss of the bomber, they call him.
    He's the guy who keeps the engines purring like tiger cubs. He nurses the last flying
    minutes out of a crippled ship. He makes all repairs in flight. He mans a pair of
    guns in the top turret. And if he has to, he can bring the ship home almost
    single-handed, like Steve, the engineer in tonight's story. Steve and his pilot,
    Dave, had both been in the auto racing game before the war. Dave as a driver, Steve
    riding with him as a mechanic. And after they joined the Air Forces they wound up
    together again, Dave pilot, and Steve engineer, on the big Liberator, "Bad Medicine,"
    raiding Jap airfields in Burma.
2nd Lt. Donald P. Briggs (as Pilot Dave): Pilot to top turret. How's it going up there,
  Steve? Everything all right?
Sgt. Broderick Crawford (as Aerial Engineer Steve): Top turret. O.K. here, Dave. Just
  taking it easy, like old times.
2nd Lt. Donald P. Briggs: What do you mean, "like old times?"
Sgt. Broderick Crawford: Yeah, you remember the old days. You did the driving. All I
  did after the race started was ride along as mechanic and watch the scenery. The same
  thing now.
2nd Lt. Donald P. Briggs: You won't watch much scenery on this track, brother. This
  track is tough.
Sgt. Broderick Crawford: It is for you, you have to do the driving. Us mechanics just go
  along for the drive. Not a worry in the world.
2nd Lt. Donald P. Briggs: Wait'll those Zeros come pouring in on the back stretch.
  You'll do some worrying then.
Sgt. Broderick Crawford: Huh, huh, not me. All I have to do is hemstitch a few of those
  babies with my twin fifties and my job's done. You're the guy that has to get us home.
  I'm just along for the ride, remember?
2nd Lt. Donald P. Briggs: Heh, heh, O.K., wise guy. But you better get those fifties
  ready right now. We'll be over the target in a minute. Heads up, gang. We're going
  in. Let's make it a good one this time.
Incidental music
2nd Lt. Donald P. Briggs: Nice shooting, gang. We dug them a hole that time. O.K.,
  Steve, we're heading back for the home stretch. If anybody tries to pass us on the
  curves, heave a wrench at them.
Sgt. Broderick Crawford: Top turret to pilot. A couple of Jap drivers pulling up on our
  tail, Dave. Here goes the first wrench. One of them out of the race. Here comes the
  other one.
2nd Lt. Donald P. Briggs: We - we're falling. We're falling.
Sgt. Broderick Crawford: Dave. Dave. Hello, Dave. Are you all right, Dave? Engineer
  to radio. Take over. I got to see what's wrong.
Incidental music

Cpl. Paul A. Dubov (as Navigator Bill): Navigator to pilot.
Sgt. Broderick Crawford: Engineer here.
Cpl. Paul A. Dubov: I'm calling Dave. Get off the wire, Steve. Hello, Dave.
Sgt. Broderick Crawford: Dave's been hit, Bill. I'm taking over for him at the controls.
Cpl. Paul A. Dubov: How about co-pilot? Better let him do it.
Sgt. Broderick Crawford: Joe's gone. The same shell got him.
Cpl. Paul A. Dubov: Hold it level, if you can. I'll get the first aid kit and bring it in.
Sgt. Broderick Crawford: Roger. How you feeling, Dave?
2nd Lt. Donald P. Briggs: Pretty rotten, Steve. I'll be all right. Just watch those rudders. It's a rough track.
Sgt. Broderick Crawford: You're telling me. What am I doing driving this thing? I'm a mechanic. I just came along for the ride.
2nd Lt. Donald P. Briggs: Huh, you're in the driver's seat now, kid. You're the guy that's got to bring us home, if we get home.
Sgt. Broderick Crawford: You'll get there. Don't worry, Dave, we'll make it.
Cpl. Paul A. Dubov: Ah, Steve, how's it going? First air kit. See if you can get Dave bandaged up and then you better get back to the guns.
Sgt. Broderick Crawford: But the ship. Somebody's got to ...
Cpl. Paul A. Dubov: All right. I'll try to hold her level until you get back. We need you at those guns, we're still over enemy territory and may have visitors any minute.
Incidental music
Sgt. Broderick Crawford: Top turret to navigator. Three Tojos coming in at nine o'clock. Evasive action if you can, Bill. They're coming in for the kill. Two of them turning back. I think I got the other one, he's heading down, out of control. It's all clear again.
Cpl. Paul A. Dubov: Got a minute, Steve? Come back and see what's wrong with the tail gunner. He doesn't answer.
Sgt. Broderick Crawford: I'll go back now.
Incidental music
Cpl. Paul A. Dubov: Navigator to engineer. Manifold pressure on number three down. Check turbo controls. See if you can fix it, Steve.
Sgt. Broderick Crawford: I'll take care of it.
Cpl. Paul A. Dubov: Navigator to engineer. Waist gunner reports hydraulic lines broken. Think you can patch them up?
Sgt. Broderick Crawford: I'll do what I can.
Cpl. Paul A. Dubov: Navigator. Steve, prop governor on number four engine frozen. What are we going to do about it?
Sgt. Broderick Crawford: I'll see about it just as soon as I get this hydraulic line.
Cpl. Paul A. Dubov: Hello, Steve. Zeros coming up on our tail. I need you back in the turret. Hurry.
Sgt. Broderick Crawford: I'm going right away.
Cpl. Paul A. Dubov: Navigator to engineer. Can you come up to the flight deck, take the controls again? Want to try to plot us a course home.
Sgt. Broderick Crawford: I'll be right there.
Cpl. Paul A. Dubov: According to this course I've plotted, Steve, we're near Emergency Field Y. Better land there. How's the tail gunner? Did you check on him?
Sgt. Broderick Crawford: Oh, he's coming along O.K. He had a fifty in the shoulder, but I band...
Cpl. Paul A. Dubov: Did you get the hydraulic line fixed?
Sgt. Broderick Crawford: Well, I patched it up but the pressure won't hold.
Cpl. Paul A. Dubov: How about that prop on number four?
Sgt. Broderick Crawford: Frozen solid. But it won't hurt anything at cruising speed.
Cpl. Paul A. Dubov: You better check the gas supply, Steve. I want to see if we can make it.
Sgt. Broderick Crawford: I checked it on the way forward, ...

...

Captain Glenn Miller: And now it's medley time, saluting the mothers, wives, sweethearts
    and sisters of the boys in the A.A.F. Something old, something new, something borrowed
    and something blue. Our old song, "All through the Night."
ALL THROUGH THE NIGHT (Old tune)
    Captain Glenn Miller: Something new, Sergeant Johnny Desmond sings.
I LOVE YOU (New tune)
    Vocal refrain by Sergeant Johnny Desmond
    Captain Glenn Miller: Friend Guy Lombardo furnishes the Crew Chiefs with the borrowed
        tune and it's "Take It Easy."
TAKE IT EASY (Borrowed tune)
    Vocal refrain by the Crew Chiefs
    Captain Glenn Miller: Last, something blue, "Blue Hawaii."
BLUE HAWAII (Blue tune)
Captain Glenn Miller: According to the mailman, all the cash customers want a return bout
    with Sergeant Jerry Gray's arrangement of "Holiday for Strings." Here it is.
HOLIDAY FOR STRINGS
2nd Lt. Donald P. Briggs: The aerial engineer is more than just a mechanic, he's the
    watchdog of a plane when it's flying. It's his job to keep a plane functioning smoothly
    in flight, to know if all the engines are perking as they should, to watch the fuel
    supply and transfer it to the proper tank at the proper time, plus hundreds of other
    details necessary to the most efficient plane operation. The pilot knows the aerial
    engineer's opinion of a plane is reliable because of the knowledge and training he's
    received from the Army Air Forces Training Command, the world's biggest university. And
    with the thousands of other graduates of the Training Command, the aerial engineer can
    proudly say, "I Sustain the Wings."
I SUSTAIN THE WINGS (closing theme)
    Captain Glenn Miller: This is Captain Glenn Miller saying so long for the Band of the
        Training Command, Sergeants Brod Crawford, Mel Powell, Ray McKinley, Johnny Desmond,
        Bob Carroll, the Crew Chiefs, and Lieutenant Don Briggs. Hope to see you again next
        Saturday, same time, same station. In the meantime, don't forget those lads that are
        doing the dirty work overseas. They're doing the fightin', you do the writin'.
    2nd Lt. Donald P. Briggs: "I Sustain the Wings" is a presentation of the Army Air
        Forces Training Command and came to you from New York City.
NBC announcer: This is the National Broadcasting Company.

06Apr44 (Thu) NBC, New York, New York
  HOME BASE recording for the US Treasury Department   For broadcast 01Jun44

2nd Lt. Donald P. Briggs: Here's "Home Base," presented by the United States Treasury in
  cooperation with the Armed Forces Radio Service, a home front report to the Armed Forces
  overseas.
I SUSTAIN THE WINGS (opening theme)
  2nd Lt. Donald P. Briggs: A hop across the Atlantic, a skip over the Pacific and a jump
    to every Allied listening post overseas, "Home Base" tells you what's new in the old
    hometown, sends you music by the Army Air Forces Band of the Training Command, under
    the direction of Captain Glenn Miller.
2nd Lt. Donald P. Briggs: Captain Miller.
Captain Glenn Miller: Thank you, Lieutenant Don Briggs, and hello to you guys and gals
  who are givin' American history something to brag about. The kids of tomorrow will get
  plenty of thrills reading about the things you are accomplishing today. Later in the
  show you'll be hearin' from an old gal friend who'll sing you a song, then there'll be
  news from your home town war front correspondent, but first here's a high jumpin' tune
  dedicated to the kind of action we want to see you enjoyin' mighty soon, "Flyin' Home."
FLYING HOME
Captain Glenn Miller: There's no two things get along any better than a soldier and a
  song. Here's Sergeant Johnny Desmond to sing "Long Ago, Far Away."
LONG AGO (And Far Away)
  Vocal refrain by Sergeant Johnny Desmond
2nd Lt. Donald P. Briggs: Lieutenant Don Briggs reporting.
Sgt. Broderick Crawford: Sergeant Brod Crawford reporting.
2nd Lt. Donald P. Briggs: Subject, backing the attack.
Sgt. Broderick Crawford: Coming right up, the Fifth War Loan.
2nd Lt. Donald P. Briggs: Starting date, June 12th.
Sgt. Broderick Crawford: Goal, 16 billion dollars.
2nd Lt. Donald P. Briggs: Six billion of that to come out of the earnings and savings of
  the little fellow, John Q. Public himself.
Sgt. Broderick Crawford: Will the people of America make that 16 billion dollar goal?
2nd Lt. Donald P. Briggs: The people of America have never failed to beat a War Loan goal
  yet.
Sgt. Broderick Crawford: Slogan for the Fifth War Loan, "Buy more than before. Back the
  attack."
2nd Lt. Donald P. Briggs: 16 billion American dollars. Stand by for action.
Captain Glenn Miller: And that's the story in a bombshell. And now we drop a nickel in
  the Crew Chiefs to hear "Juke Box Saturday Night."
JUKE BOX SATURDAY NIGHT
  Vocal refrain by the Crew Chiefs
2nd Lt. Donald P. Briggs: This is your "Home Base" Orientation Officer. This is a brief
  report on the doings along the domestic war front. If you're an American, this report
  should make you feel better. If you're a Nazi doing some eavesdropping on this
  broadcast, this report should make you feel worse. Here are some simple facts. The
  thing you Americans seem to be most interested in is the state of mind and health of
  your families and the gals you left behind. Well, sir, as far as keeping them healthy
  both physically and spiritually goes, you're the doctor. The job you're doing over
  there is doing a job of its own over here. You've given the folks at home one great
  thing and that's confidence. It's good for a mother or a father whose boy is away from
  home to know that her son marches and fights side by side with men like those whose
  exploits and heroisms are recounted here in the daily press. All thoughts these days
  are upon invasion, all hopes are upon its speedy success. All this has had a
  tremendously positive effect on war production. Good results are no longer good enough.
  Labor disputes are few and of minor nature. In brief, our nation's sense of wartime
  responsibility is strengthening, as contrasted with the weakening morale evident along
  the home fronts of the enemy. In just a few days now the Treasury Department will call
  upon Americans to once again pledge their faith in their nation and to evidence their
  whole-hearted desire to back your attack. This will be the Fifth War Loan Drive. The
  goal is high --- over 16 billion dollars. The slogan is, "Buy more than before. Back

the attack." And more than ever before the man in the street is being called upon to do the buying. Yeah, the little guy'll have to be the big guy this time. And the spirit of one for all will never be more in evidence. The Treasury Department is confident of that. The people here at home by and large are conscientiously investing in War Bonds and in the American future, in your future as well as their own. What they're doing today will make the tomorrow that you're making possible a better tomorrow for all Americans. The War Bonds of today shall be the wealth of tomorrow, a wealth in the hands of the people. No matter how much a man is doing here at home, he feels deeply and sincerely that it is as nothing compared to what you're doing over there. This nation of ours has the greatest sense of appreciation the nation ever had. Sometimes we may not give ourselves that much credit but there's always the proof, the kind of proof you guys and gals over there are exemplifying every day of this war. It all adds up to this, when the chips are down the spirit is up.

Incidental music
Captain Glenn Miller: Sergeant Jerry Gray hasn't left a note unturned to bring you an all out arrangement of a tune that's doin' pretty well around "Home Base," "Poinciana."

POINCIANA (Song of the Tree)
Vocal refrain by Sergeant Johnny Desmond and the Crew Chiefs

I SUSTAIN THE WINGS (closing theme)
2nd Lt. Donald P. Briggs: The United States Treasury in cooperation with the Armed Forces Radio Service has presented "Home Base," an overseas report from the home front. You'll soon be hearing another edition of "Home Base" with your favorite singing stars, your home front war correspondent and music by the Army Air Forces Band of the Training Command under the direction of Captain Glenn Miller.

08Apr44 (Sat) 6:00-6:30PM EWT WEAF, NBC Vanderbilt Theatre, New York, New York
  I SUSTAIN THE WINGS broadcast   Audience

    ...

Captain Glenn Miller: Now it's medley time, saluting the mothers, wives, sweethearts and
    sisters of the men who teach our boys of the A.A.F. how to fly those planes. Something
    old, something new, something borrowed and something blue. Our old song, "Killarney."
KILLARNEY (Old tune)
    Captain Glenn Miller: For something new, Corporal Carroll and the Crew Chiefs with
    "I've Got a Heart Filled with Love."
I'VE GOT A HEART FILLED WITH LOVE (For You Dear) (New tune)
    Vocal refrain by Corporal Bob Carroll and the Crew Chiefs
    Captain Glenn Miller: For something borrowed, one of my favorite tunes.
MOONLIGHT SERENADE (Borrowed tune)
    Captain Glenn Miller: Last, something blue, "Wabash Blues."
WABASH BLUES (Blue tune)
JOIN THE WAC
    2nd Lt. Donald P. Briggs: Women of America, march with Uncle Sam's Army. Join the WAC.
    Vocal refrain by the Crew Chiefs
    2nd Lt. Donald P. Briggs: As an Air WAC you can be a member of the world's greatest
       team, the A.A.F., and serve in one of more than a hundred important jobs here and
       overseas.
    Vocal refrain by the Crew Chiefs
Captain Glenn Miller: In answer to a lot of requests, here's a repeat performance on
    Sergeant Jerry Gray's arrangement of "Poinciana."
POINCIANA (Song of the Tree)
    Vocal refrain by Sergeant Johnny Desmond and the Crew Chiefs
Sgt. Broderick Crawford: Folks, you've heard and read all about the famous Flying
    Fortress "Memphis Belle." Now you can actually see the heroic actions of the plane and
    her crew. Documentary films shot by the Army Air Forces combat camera crews of the
    Eighth Air Force are soon to be released in theaters all over the country. Consult your
    local newspaper for the time and place it'll be shown in your neighborhood. Don't miss
    this remarkable picture. It's an epic story of the bravery and courage of the men who
    fly the planes and of the men of the ground crew whose motto is "I Sustain the Wings."
I SUSTAIN THE WINGS (closing theme)
    Captain Glenn Miller: This is Captain Glenn Miller saying so long for the Band of the
       Training Command, Sergeants Brod Crawford, Mel Powell, Ray McKinley, Johnny Desmond,
       Corporal Bob Carroll, the Crew Chiefs, and Lieutenant Don Briggs. Hope to see you
       again next Saturday, same time, same station.
2nd Lt. Donald P. Briggs: "I Sustain the Wings" is a presentation of the Army Air Forces
    Training Command and came to you from New York City.
NBC announcer: This is the National Broadcasting Company.

08Apr44 (Sat) 11:30PM-Midnight EWT WEAF, NBC Vanderbilt Theatre, New York, New York
 I SUSTAIN THE WINGS broadcast   Audience

THE ARMY AIR CORPS (opening fanfare)
2nd Lt. Donald P. Briggs: "I Sustain the Wings."
I SUSTAIN THE WINGS (opening theme)
  2nd Lt. Donald P. Briggs: "I Sustain the Wings." The Army Air Forces present the Band
    of the Training Command, under the direction of Captain Glenn Miller. And now Captain
    Glenn Miller.
Captain Glenn Miller: Thank you, Lieutenant Don Briggs, and good evening, everybody.
  Tonight we toss a salute to some guys who rate a lot of credit for America's success in
  the air, the instructors of the A.A.F. They're the men who give our ground crews the
  know-how they need to keep our planes in fightin' trim. They're the men behind the men
  of America's great Air Forces. And they're doing a big job in a big way. Musically
  now, fasten your safety belts and get ready for the takeoff, 'cause we're "Flying Home."
FLYING HOME
Captain Glenn Miller: Shine those shoes, polish up those buckles, and set a sharp crease
  in those G.I. slacks 'cause here comes the band, with Sergeant Johnny Desmond and the
  Crew Chiefs leading the "Easter Parade."
EASTER PARADE
  Vocal refrain by Sergeant Johnny Desmond and the Crew Chiefs
Cpl. Paul A. Dubov (as Newsboy): Extra! Extra! Read all about the big air battle.
  American planes raid Germany again. Extra! Read all about it. Extra!
2nd Lt. Donald P. Briggs: You know, just about every day now you read stories like this
  one in the papers. All about how American flyers have dropped another load of bombs on
  Hitler's Europe. Every now and then you see a name in one of those stories that sounds
  familiar. Yeah, like the other day when I read the name Lieutenant Bob Nelson. Yeah,
  there it was, right in the middle of the story. Lieutenant Bob Nelson, it said, piloted
  one of the escort fighters. Flying a new P-51, he moved into the ranks of American aces
  by bagging three German rocket planes and bringing his score to seven. Lieutenant
  Nelson is being considered for the Distinguished Flying Cross. Heh, Lieutenant Nelson.
  It's funny reading your name like that in the papers, Bob. Sort of hard to imagine that
  clear over there, this minute, chopping down Germans. A fighter pilot in the big league
  at last. Huh, it's just like you and I always wanted to be. Way back when we were
  kids, together we read every airplane magazine we could get our hands on. We built
  model planes in your basement. We saved our nickels and dimes to buy rides at the local
  airport. All we could think about was planes and flying 'em and being fighter pilots.
  And when the war came it seemed like our big chance. Morning after Pearl Harbor we
  signed up as aviation cadets, started our training a few months later. You remember the
  day we arrived at primary flight school together, Bob? As we came in on the train we -
  we could see the school in the distance. Planes in the air everywhere. We were both so
  excited we could hardly talk.
Sgt. Broderick Crawford (as Lieutenant Bob Nelson): Hey, hey, look. There it is over
  there.
2nd Lt. Donald P. Briggs: Yeah, that's it, all right. Ah, wow, what a place. Look at
  those fighters.
Sgt. Broderick Crawford: Yeah, PT-19s. Boy, I can hardly wait to get my hands on one of
  those grasshoppers.
2nd Lt. Donald P. Briggs: Yeah, just wait, we'll show those guys how to really fly them.
Sgt. Broderick Crawford: Yeah, you said it. This time next year we'll be flying the big
  stuff, P-47s and '51s and the rest of 'em. Maybe overseas, shooting down Germans and
  Japs.
2nd Lt. Donald P. Briggs: Yeah, that whistle of the train, it still sends shivers down my
  spine. But before we got through with our preflight training we heard plenty of
  whistles.
Cpl. Paul A. Dubov (as Drill Sergeant): Come, you misters, fall out. On the double.
  Squadron, attention. O.K. If you want to buy the place you can look it over later.
  Wipe that smile off your face, Mister.

2nd Lt. Donald P. Briggs: Well, at preflight we got a careful physical checkup for any defects that might disqualify us as flyers. We drilled and studied and we went through hours of psychological tests to help them decide if we ought to be pilots, navigators, or bombardiers. Ah, it was a shaky moment while we waited for the verdict. What if we got separated right this moment? What if neither one of us gets to be a pilot? Pilots it was for both of us. We were still together. Heh, we celebrated with three straight Cokes at the P.K. Primary and actual flying followed free flights ... schools. Studied aircraft engines ...

   ...

Incidental music
2nd Lt. Donald P. Briggs: We're on the same team. Fighting the same fight. When you're up there, Bob, with the flak bursting and the Messerschmitts come screaming in, get one for me.
Captain Glenn Miller: Now it's medley time, saluting the mothers, wives, sweethearts and sisters of the men who teach our boys of the A.A.F. how to fly those planes. Something old, something new, something borrowed something blue. The old song, "Killarney."
KILLARNEY (Old tune)
Captain Glenn Miller: Something new, Corporal Carroll and the Crew Chiefs, "I've Got a Heart Filled with Love."
I'VE GOT A HEART FILLED WITH LOVE (For You Dear) (New tune)
Vocal refrain by Corporal Bob Carroll and the Crew Chiefs
Captain Glenn Miller: Something borrowed, one of my favorite tunes.
MOONLIGHT SERENADE (Borrowed tune)
Captain Glenn Miller: Last, something blue, the "Wabash Blues."
WABASH BLUES (Blue tune)
JOIN THE WAC
2nd Lt. Donald P. Briggs: Women of America, march with Uncle Sam's Army. Join the WAC.
Vocal refrain by the Crew Chiefs
2nd Lt. Donald P. Briggs: As an Air WAC you can be a member of the world's greatest team, the A.A.F., and serve in one of more than a hundred important jobs here and overseas.
Vocal refrain by the Crew Chiefs
Captain Glenn Miller: In answer to a lot of requests, here's Sergeant Jerry Gray's arrangement of "Poinciana."
POINCIANA (Song of the Tree)
Vocal refrain by Sergeant Johnny Desmond and the Crew Chiefs
Sgt. Broderick Crawford: You've heard and read all about the famous Flying Fortress the "Memphis Belle." Now you can actually see the heroic actions of the plane and her crew. Documentary films shot by the Army Air Forces combat camera crews of the Eighth Air Force are soon to be released in theaters all over the country. Consult your local newspaper for the time and place it'll be shown in your neighborhood. Don't miss this remarkable picture. It's an epic story of the bravery and courage of the men who fly the planes and of the men of the ground crew whose motto is "I Sustain the Wings."
I SUSTAIN THE WINGS (closing theme)
Captain Glenn Miller: This is Captain Glenn Miller saying so long for the Band of the Training Command, Sergeants Brod Crawford, Mel Powell, Ray McKinley, Johnny Desmond, Corporal Bob Carroll, the Crew Chiefs, and Lieutenant Don Briggs, and all the gang. Hope to see you again next Saturday, same time, same station.
2nd Lt. Donald P. Briggs: "I Sustain the Wings" is a presentation of the Army Air Forces Training Command and came to you from New York City.
NBC announcer: This is the National Broadcasting Company.

15Apr44 (Sat) 6:00-6:30PM EWT WEAF, NBC Vanderbilt Theatre, New York, New York
  I SUSTAIN THE WINGS broadcast   Audience

THE ARMY AIR CORPS (opening fanfare)
2nd Lt. Donald P. Briggs: "I Sustain the Wings."
I SUSTAIN THE WINGS (opening theme)
  2nd Lt. Donald P. Briggs: "I Sustain the Wings." The Army Air Forces present the Band
    of the Training Command, under the direction of Captain Glenn Miller. And now Captain
    Glenn Miller.
Captain Glenn Miller: Good evening, everybody. Speaking for the Crew Chiefs, Corporal
  Bob Carroll, Sergeants Brod Crawford, Mel Powell, Ray McKinley, Johnny Desmond,
  Lieutenant Don Briggs, the whole gang, welcome to another program of "I Sustain the
  Wings." We're coming up with some music for your listenin' pleasure now and the takeoff
  is aboard the "Caribbean Clipper."
CARIBBEAN CLIPPER
Captain Glenn Miller: Nice going, men. Now Sergeant Johnny Desmond singin' one of
  today's top tunes, "Now I Know."
NOW I KNOW
  Vocal refrain by Sergeant Johnny Desmond
The Army Air Corps (Incidental music)
  Captain Glenn Miller: Among all the men on Uncle Sam's great Air Force team, there's
    none more important than the aerial photographer. The eyes of the A.A.F. they call
    him, and that's just what they are. Before an air attack, these flying shutter bugs
    take off on reconnaissance flights to spy out the target. After the smoke of bombing
    settles, they go back with their cameras to record the damage. The A.A.F. Training
    Command gives them the finest training in the world, but they've got something else
    too, plenty of courage and resourcefulness. And it's this training and courage that
    carries them through experiences like those in our story tonight. It was told to us
    by a Sergeant whom we'll call Bill, an aerial photographer just back from the
    Aleutians.
Sgt. Broderick Crawford (as Sergeant Bill): Well, now that I think back on those days, I
  don't see how we did it. We had to work under the worst conditions in the world, bad
  weather, fog, lack of repair parts, and freezing cold. We flew missions, developed our
  film in tents, and thought nothing of turning out six hundred to a thousand prints a
  night. Camera parts froze up and our fingers ached with cold. The dampness loosened
  the joints of our ground cameras. Somehow we managed, don't ask me how. All I know is
  that when the lives of a thousand men and the success of the mission depend on your
  work, you do it and you do it good. Every day seemed to bring a new problem. I
  remember one morning my buddy Joe and I were working in a tent we used for a lab when a
  guy came in and said the Captain of our photographic unit wanted to see me. When I got
  to his tent he was busy looking at some photos. Finally he looked up.
2nd Lt. Donald P. Briggs (as Captain): Ah, sit down, Sergeant. Got a job for you.
Sgt. Broderick Crawford: Yes, sir.
2nd Lt. Donald P. Briggs: Yesterday, as you know, our boys made their first raid on a
  target on Attu.
Sgt. Broderick Crawford: Yes, sir. They blew it right off the map.
2nd Lt. Donald P. Briggs: So we thought. But these recon photographs made after the raid
  show they didn't.
Sgt. Broderick Crawford: But they said every bomb was right on the target. I don't
  understand.
2nd Lt. Donald P. Briggs: Well, I don't understand either. They're Dead-Eye-Dicks, those
  bombardiers. They dropped the bombs, the bombs exploded, but there's the pictures.
  They show the target largely undamaged.
Sgt. Broderick Crawford: Well, what happened?
2nd Lt. Donald P. Briggs: Well, I don't know, Sergeant. That's what I want you to find
  out. Want you to go along on this morning's mission. Shoot pictures of the bombing
  from the time the bombs leave the plane until they hit. There's another mission
  scheduled for this afternoon, but unless you come through on this, we'll have to call it
  off. I know it's a tough assignment, you'll meet plenty of Zeros, usual ground haze and
  fog, but remember this, we've got to have those pictures.

Incidental music

Sgt. Broderick Crawford: I couldn't figure it out. How could you drop bombs on a target and not damage it? It didn't seem possible, but there was no time to think about it. I hurried back to the lab and told Joe the story. Told him to stand by with everything ready when I got back so we could start running off the prints the minute I arrived. Then I got out my favorite K-17 camera. Old Eagle-Eye I called it. It had seen plenty of action. It'd been shot up and repaired a dozen times. Materials were short up there in those days, but ships could get in through bad weather, carried food, medicine, and plane parts. And we had to make camera repairs with whatever we could find handy. Well, we used bed springs, adhesive tape, gum, string, everything we could get our hands on. Old Eagle-Eye itself had a shutter leaf made out of the lid of an old tomato can. Wasn't exactly the camera you'd pick for an important job like this, but there was no other choice. Well, I took Old Eagle-Eye and I mounted her in the plane I'd been assigned to. And around 0-8-3-5 we took off. Things began popping when we came in over the target area. Zeros, a whole swarm of them, came whining up to meet us.

Tail Gunner: Tail gunner to pilot. Zeros at 5 o'clock, two thousand yards.

Sgt. Broderick Crawford: I hunched over the camera and gave Old Eagle-Eye a tender pat or two. Everything depended on these pictures. Unless I could get them and get them back, we'd have to call the whole thing off. I sat there thinking about how much it meant and wondering if everything was all right. I checked the shutter speed again to make sure, and waited for the pilot's voice to announce the bomb run. Finally it came.

Pilot: Pilot to crew. Going in for the run. Bomb bay doors open. Start the camera.

Sgt. Broderick Crawford: I pushed the button and the camera hummed into action. As the bombardier called "Bombs away" I looked down through the view finder and saw the bombs falling. I could have sworn they were heading right for the target, but there was so much smoke down there you couldn't tell for sure. Unless Old Eagle-Eye came through for us, we were whipped. We swung over the island and headed for home. The Zeros followed us snipping at us for a long ways. Then they turned back. Well, we came in O.K. with one engine sputtering and a fuselage full of holes. The minute we stopped rolling I tore the film magazine out and raced to the lab tent. Joe was waiting for me.

Joe: Hurry it up, Bill. I've got everything ready.

Sgt. Broderick Crawford: What a ride. I thought we'd never get back. How much time have we got?

Joe: Not much. The next mission's coming up in about an hour. We've got to work fast now.

Sgt. Broderick Crawford: If we don't work fast we'll freeze to death. It's like an ice-box in here.

Joe: I better put some more coal in the stove. I'll be right with you.

Sgt. Broderick Crawford: O.K. That water ready?

Joe: If you call melted snow water. You can't even dig for water with the ground frozen like this.

Sgt. Broderick Crawford: How about the developer?

Joe: All set, but it's a pretty weak solution. You think it'll work on this?

Sgt. Broderick Crawford: It's all we got, it's got to work.

Joe: Huh, melted snow for water, weak developing fluid, temperatures all wrong, cameras made out of tomato cans. Well, there's one thing you can say.

Sgt. Broderick Crawford: What's that?

Joe: We're making suckers out of the rule books.

Sgt. Broderick Crawford: Yeah, we were at that. We heated the hypo solution with a blow-torch. When it came to drying the prints, we held them in front of the stove, hoping they wouldn't wrinkle too much. But there was no time to worry about things like that, we had to work fast, and we did. We had seven of the twelve prints finished when the Captain hurried in to see how we were doing.

2nd Lt. Donald P. Briggs: Ah, how's it going, Sergeant? Got any prints yet?

Sgt. Broderick Crawford: Well, we finished seven, sir. The others will be ready in a minute.

2nd Lt. Donald P. Briggs: Well, let me see the ones you got. If they show what's wrong we've got just enough time to get those ships off for the next mission. Haven't got a minute to lose.

Sgt. Broderick Crawford: Here's the first one.

2nd Lt. Donald P. Briggs: Here, let's see. Ah, there go the bombs. Huh, nothing new in this next one. Hand me that third one. Heh, well, they seem to be heading right for the target. Well, these next ones are just smoke. Well, it looks like the target ought to be wiped out completely.

Joe: Here's the last one, sir.

2nd Lt. Donald P. Briggs: Here, let me see. No, no, look. In - in this one the smoke's cleared away. You can see the target wasn't damaged at all.

Sgt. Broderick Crawford: My heart sank right down to my shoes. We'd failed after all. Old Eagle-Eye had let us down. The whole thing had been for nothing. I started to gather up the prints and put them away. The Captain stopped me.

2nd Lt. Donald P. Briggs: Sergeant, wait a minute. Let me look at that sixth one again. I think I see it. And look down there in the left hand corner. It's a bomb and it's bouncing. Bouncing and then exploding. As much as two hundred feet from the target. Well, there's just one thing that can cause it, the fuses must be too delayed for the low altitude we're forced to bomb at. Let me take those prints with me. Thanks for getting us the answers, Sergeant. Swell job. We'll shorten those fuses on this mission and blow that target right off the map.

Sgt. Broderick Crawford: So we hadn't failed after all.

The Army Air Corps (Incidental music)

  Sgt. Broderick Crawford: It was bitter cold as I stood there in the tent, listening to the bombers take off. But I had a warm feeling in spite of the cold and fog, Zeros and bullets, and cameras made of tin cans, we'd made it. Oh, it had been a tough job, but it had been worth it just to know that the whole thing had depended on you and you'd come through. And you weren't a bombardier and you couldn't push the button that sent the bombs tumbling down, but you could push the button on a camera and because of you the tiny flick of its shutter would be magnified into the roar of a thousand bombs blasting a pathway to victory.

Captain Glenn Miller: Now it's medley time, saluting the mothers, wives, sweethearts and sisters of the men of the Photographic School at Lowry Field out in Colorado. Something old, something new, something borrowed, something blue. The old tune, "Songs My Mother Taught Me."

SONGS MY MOTHER TAUGHT ME (Old tune)

  Captain Glenn Miller: Something new, the Crew Chiefs and "It's Love, Love, Love!"

IT'S LOVE, LOVE, LOVE! (New tune)

  Vocal refrain by the Crew Chiefs

  Captain Glenn Miller: Our borrowed tune is a hit by Mozart with an assist by Sergeant Mel Powell and Raymond Scott, "Eighteenth Century Drawing Room."

IN AN EIGHTEENTH CENTURY DRAWING ROOM (Borrowed tune)

  Captain Glenn Miller: Last, something blue, Corporal Bob Carroll sings "Blue Orchids."

BLUE ORCHIDS (Blue tune)

  Vocal refrain by Corporal Bob Carroll

JOIN THE WAC

  2nd Lt. Donald P. Briggs: Women of America, march with Uncle Sam's Army. Join the WAC.

  Vocal refrain by the Crew Chiefs

  2nd Lt. Donald P. Briggs: Aerial photographs must be developed and printed before their full value can be realized. As an Air WAC you can become a laboratory technician and do this highly skilled work.

  Vocal refrain by the Crew Chiefs

2nd Lt. Donald P. Briggs: And now Sergeant Ray McKinley and the Crew Chiefs vocalizin' and the band playin' "There Are Yanks."

THERE ARE YANKS (From the Banks of the Wabash)

  Vocal refrain by Technical Sergeant Ray McKinley and the Crew Chiefs

2nd Lt. Donald P. Briggs: The eyes of the A.A.F., that's the aerial photographer, a special kind of soldier who does his fighting with a camera instead of a gun. His reconnaissance flights produce pictures that help our tactical officers plan their campaigns, show weaknesses in the enemy's defenses, lead our bombers straight to the target. Like thousands of other specialized technicians, the aerial photographer is a graduate of the A.A.F. Training Command, the world's biggest university. And because of the know-how received from the Training Command, he and over a million ground crew specialists can proudly boast "I Sustain the Wings."

I SUSTAIN THE WINGS (closing theme)
  Captain Glenn Miller: This is Captain Glenn Miller saying so long for the Band of the
    Training Command, the Crew Chiefs, Corporal Bob Carroll, Sergeants Brod Crawford, Mel
    Powell, Ray McKinley, Johnny Desmond, and Lieutenant Don Briggs. Hope to see you
    again next Saturday, same time, same station.
  2nd Lt. Donald P. Briggs: Keep those V-Mail letters flyin' to the boys overseas. Mail
    from home is number one on their Hit Parade. They're doin' the fightin', you do the
    writin'.
Sgt. Broderick Crawford: The "Memphis Belle," fighting queen of the skies. You've heard
  and read all about this famous plane. Well, now you can actually see her splendid
  exploits in all the brilliance of Technicolor. The War Department is releasing
  documentary films of the Memphis Belle in action to theaters all over the country.
  Consult your local newspaper for the time and place this remarkable picture, taken by
  the A.A.F. combat crews of the Eighth Air Force, is to be shown in your neighborhood.
  Put it on your must list. It's a chance to see one of the many reasons why the A.A.F.
  is the greatest team in the world.
2nd Lt. Donald P. Briggs: "I Sustain the Wings" is a presentation of the Army Air Forces
  Training Command and came to you from New York City.
NBC announcer: This is the National Broadcasting Company.
NBC chimes

The parts of Tail Gunner, Pilot and Joe were played by Cpl. Paul A. Dubov and other
members of the band.

15Apr44 (Sat) 11:30PM-Midnight EWT WEAF, NBC Vanderbilt Theatre, New York, New York
  I SUSTAIN THE WINGS broadcast   Audience

THE ARMY AIR CORPS (opening fanfare)
2nd Lt. Donald P. Briggs: "I Sustain the Wings."
I SUSTAIN THE WINGS (opening theme)
  2nd Lt. Donald P. Briggs: "I Sustain the Wings." The Army Air Forces present the Band
    of the Training Command, under the direction of Captain Glenn Miller. And now Captain
    Glenn Miller.
Captain Glenn Miller: Good evening, everybody. Speaking for the Crew Chiefs, Corporal
  Bob Carroll, Sergeants Brod Crawford, Mel Powell, Ray McKinley, Johnny Desmond,
  Lieutenant Don Briggs, the whole gang, welcome to another program of "I Sustain the
  Wings." We're coming up with some music for your listenin' pleasure now and the takeoff
  is aboard the "Caribbean Clipper."
CARIBBEAN CLIPPER
Captain Glenn Miller: Now Sergeant Johnny Desmond singin' one of today's top tunes, "Now
  I Know."
NOW I KNOW
  Vocal refrain by Sergeant Johnny Desmond
The Army Air Corps (Incidental music)
  Captain Glenn Miller: Among all the men on Uncle Sam's great Air Force team, there's
    none more important than the aerial photographer. The eyes of the A.A.F. they call
    him, and that's just what they are. Before an air attack, these flying shutter bugs
    take off on reconnaissance flights to spy out the target. And after the smoke of
    bombing settles, they go back with their cameras to record the damage. The A.A.F.
    Training Command gives them the finest training in the world, but they've got
    something else too, plenty of courage and resourcefulness. And it's this training and
    courage that carries them through experiences like those in our story tonight. It was
    told to us by a Sergeant whom we'll call Bill, an aerial photographer just back from
    the Aleutians.
Sgt. Broderick Crawford (as Sergeant Bill): Well, now that I think back on those days, I
  don't see how we did it. We had to work under the worst conditions in the world, bad
  weather, fog, lack of repair parts, and freezing cold. We flew missions and developed
  our film in tents, and thought nothing of turning out six hundred to a thousand prints a
  night. Camera parts froze up and our fingers ached with cold. The dampness loosened
  the joints of our ground cameras. But somehow we managed, don't ask me how. All I know
  is that when the lives of a thousand men and the success of the mission depend on your
  work, you do it and you do it good. Every day brought us a new problem. I remember one
  morning my buddy Joe and I were working in the tent we used for a lab when a guy came in
  and said the Captain of our photographic unit wanted to see me. And when I got to his
  tent he was busy looking at some photos. Finally he looked up.
2nd Lt. Donald P. Briggs (as Captain): Ah, sit down, Sergeant. Got a job for you.
Sgt. Broderick Crawford: Yes, sir.
2nd Lt. Donald P. Briggs: Yesterday, as you know, our boys made their first raid on a
  target on Attu.
Sgt. Broderick Crawford: Yes, sir. They blew it right off the map.
2nd Lt. Donald P. Briggs: So we thought. These recon photographs made after the raid
  show they didn't.
Sgt. Broderick Crawford: But they said every bomb was right on the target. I don't
  understand it.
2nd Lt. Donald P. Briggs: Well, I don't understand either. They're Dead-Eye-Dicks, those
  bombardiers. They dropped the bombs, the bombs exploded, but there's the pictures.
  They show the target largely undamaged.
Sgt. Broderick Crawford: What happened?
2nd Lt. Donald P. Briggs: I don't know, Sergeant. That's what I want you to find out.
  Want you to go along on this morning's mission and shoot pictures of the bombing from
  the time the bombs leave the plane until they hit. There's another mission scheduled
  for this afternoon, but unless you come through on this, we'll have to call it off. I
  know it's a tough assignment, you'll meet plenty of Zeros, usual ground haze and fog,
  but remember this, we've got to have those pictures.

Incidental music
Sgt. Broderick Crawford: I couldn't figure it out. How could you drop bombs on a target
    and not damage it? It didn't seem to make any sense but there was no time to think
    about it. I went back to the lab tent and told Joe the story and told him to stand by
    with everything ready when I got back so we could start running off the prints the
    minute I arrived. Then I got out my favorite K-17 camera. Old Eagle-Eye I called it.
    It had seen plenty of action. It'd been shot up and repaired a dozen times. Materials
    were short up here in those days, but ships could get through bad weather and what not,
    carried food, medicine, and plane parts. And we had to make camera repairs with
    whatever we could find handy. Well, we used bed springs, adhesive tape, gum, string,
    everything we could g - get our hands on. Old Eagle-Eye itself had a shutter leaf made
    out of the lid of an old tomato can. Well, it wasn't exactly the camera you'd pick for
    an important job like this, but there was no other choice. Well, I took Old Eagle-Eye
    and I mounted her in the plane I'd been assigned to. And around 0-8-3-5 we took off.
    Things began popping when we came in over the target area. Zeros, a whole swarm of
    them, came whining up to meet us.
Tail Gunner: Tail gunner to pilot. Zeros at 5 o'clock, two thousand yards.

    ...

Captain Glenn Miller: Now it's medley time, saluting the mothers, wives, sweethearts and
    sisters of the men of the Photographic School at Lowry Field out in Colorado. Something
    old, something new, something borrowed and something blue. The old tune, "Songs My
    Mother Taught Me."
SONGS MY MOTHER TAUGHT ME (Old tune)
    Captain Glenn Miller: Something new, the Crew Chiefs singing "It's Love, Love, Love!"
IT'S LOVE, LOVE, LOVE! (New tune)
    Vocal refrain by the Crew Chiefs
    Captain Glenn Miller: Our borrowed tune is a hit by Mozart with an assist by Sergeant
    Mel Powell and Raymond Scott, "Eighteenth Century Drawing Room."
IN AN EIGHTEENTH CENTURY DRAWING ROOM (Borrowed tune)
    Captain Glenn Miller: Last, something blue, Corporal Bob Carroll sings "Blue Orchids."
BLUE ORCHIDS (Blue tune)
    Vocal refrain by Corporal Bob Carroll
JOIN THE WAC
    2nd Lt. Donald P. Briggs: Women of America, march with Uncle Sam's Army. Join the WAC.
    Vocal refrain by the Crew Chiefs
    2nd Lt. Donald P. Briggs: Aerial photographs must be developed and printed before their
    full value can be realized. As an Air WAC you can become a laboratory technician and
    do this highly skilled work.
    Vocal refrain by the Crew Chiefs
2nd Lt. Donald P. Briggs: And now Sergeant Ray McKinley and the Crew Chiefs vocalizing
and the band playing "There Are Yanks."
THERE ARE YANKS (From the Banks of the Wabash)
    Vocal refrain by Technical Sergeant Ray McKinley and the Crew Chiefs
2nd Lt. Donald P. Briggs: The eyes of the A.A.F., that's the aerial photographer, a
    special kind of soldier who does his fighting with a camera instead of a gun. His
    reconnaissance flights produce pictures that help our tactical officers plan their
    campaigns, show weaknesses in the enemy's defenses, lead our bombers straight to the
    target. Like thousands of other specialized technicians, the aerial photographer is a
    graduate of the A.A.F. Training Command, the world's biggest university. And because of
    the know-how received from the Training Command, he and over a million ground crew
    specialists can proudly boast "I Sustain the Wings."
I SUSTAIN THE WINGS (closing theme)
    Captain Glenn Miller: This is Captain Glenn Miller saying so long for the Band of the
    Training Command, the Crew Chiefs, Corporal Bob Carroll, Sergeants Brod Crawford and
    Mel Powell, Ray McKinley, Johnny Desmond, Lieutenant Briggs, the whole gang. Hope to
    see you again next Saturday, same time, same station.

2nd Lt. Donald P. Briggs: Keep those V-Mail letters flying to the boys overseas. Mail from home is number one on their Hit Parade. They're doin' the fightin', you do the writin'.

Sgt. Broderick Crawford: The "Memphis Belle," fighting queen of the skies. You've heard and read all about this famous plane. Well, now you can actually see her splendid exploits in all the brilliance of Technicolor. The War Department is releasing documentary films of the Memphis Belle in action to theaters all over the country. Consult your local newspaper for the time and place this remarkable picture, taken by the A.A.F. combat camera crews of the Eighth Air Force, is to be shown in your neighborhood. Put it on your must list. It's a chance to see one of the many reasons why the A.A.F. is the greatest team in the world.

2nd Lt. Donald P. Briggs: "I Sustain the Wings" is a presentation of the Army Air Forces Training Command and came to you from New York City.

NBC announcer: This is the National Broadcasting Company.

The parts of Tail Gunner, Pilot and Joe were played by Cpl. Paul A. Dubov and other members of the band.

22Apr44 (Sat) NBC, New York, New York
  UNCLE SAM PRESENTS recording

  ...

2nd Lt. Donald P. Briggs: Here's Captain Glenn Miller.

Captain Glenn Miller: Thank you, Lieutenant Don Briggs. Speaking for Sergeants Mel Powell, Ray McKinley, Corporal Bob Carroll, the Crew Chiefs, and all the gang, welcome to another program of "Uncle Sam Presents." Musically now, our good-will ambassadors are waitin' to take off on "Mission to Moscow."

MISSION TO MOSCOW

Captain Glenn Miller: Here's Corporal Bob Carroll singin' the new tune that should hit the popularity jackpot any day now. It's "Time Alone Will Tell."

TIME ALONE WILL TELL
  Vocal refrain by Corporal Bob Carroll

Captain Glenn Miller: From the hits of a few years back, here's a swell old tune with a fancy new dress, "Wabash Blues."

WABASH BLUES

Captain Glenn Miller: Sergeant Ray McKinley, the Crew Chiefs, and band playin' and singin' "There'll Be a Hot Time in the Town of Berlin."

(There'll Be a) HOT TIME IN THE TOWN OF BERLIN (When the Yanks Go Marching In)
  Vocal refrain by Technical Sergeant Ray McKinley, the Crew Chiefs and the Glee Club

I SUSTAIN THE WINGS (closing theme)

  ...

22Apr44 (Sat) 6:00-6:30PM EWT WEAF, NBC Vanderbilt Theatre, New York, New York
  I SUSTAIN THE WINGS broadcast   Audience

THE ARMY AIR CORPS (opening fanfare)
2nd Lt. Donald P. Briggs: "I Sustain the Wings"
I SUSTAIN THE WINGS (opening theme)
  2nd Lt. Donald P. Briggs: "I Sustain the Wings." The Army Air Forces present the Band
    of the Training Command, under the direction of Captain Glenn Miller. And now Captain
    Glenn Miller.
Captain Glenn Miller: Good evening, everybody. Speaking for the Crew Chiefs, Corporal
  Bob Carroll, Sergeants Brod Crawford, Mel Powell, Ray McKinley, Johnny Desmond,
  Lieutenant Don Briggs, and the gang, welcome to another program of "I Sustain the
  Wings." Musically, our good-will ambassadors are waitin' to take off on a "Mission to
  Moscow."
MISSION TO MOSCOW
Captain Glenn Miller: Now Corporal Bob Carroll singing the new tune that should hit the
  popularity jackpot any day now. It's "Time Alone Will Tell."
TIME ALONE WILL TELL
  Vocal refrain by Corporal Bob Carroll
Incidental music
  Captain Glenn Miller: Wind and fog can drive the biggest bomber off its course. And
    snow and ice can flip the wings of the fastest fighter, but the fact that they seldom
    do is a tribute to the skilled weather observers and forecasters trained by the A.A.F.
    Training Command. Before each flight these weather-wise experts furnish air crews
    with a full report of flying conditions. They guard our fliers against weather
    hazards of all kinds, help plan every mission.
Captain Glenn Miller: And much of our success in the air is due directly to their
  vigilance and courage. This might be the typical story of any one of these men. It was
  told to us by a Sergeant we'll call Joe Blake, who served with the mobile weather unit
  in the Battle of Salerno.
2nd Lt. Donald P. Briggs (as Sgt. Joe Blake): Yeah, there were ten in our unit when we
  took off for Salerno back in September 1943. One Captain; Master Sergeant; Tech
  Sergeant; four Staffs; a buddy, Red, a Sergeant like myself; that's nine of us and
  Mickey. Mickey, huh, huh, there was a real soldier for you, a guy you could count on to
  pull you through anything. The rougher the going got the better he seemed to like it.
  And what a pal. And he never argued or complained, never bummed cigarettes, in fact, he
  didn't smoke, except when his valves needed regrinding, and he never drank except a
  little gasoline now and then for his carburetor's sake. Yeah, but before you start
  thinking that this job of mine has me weather-wacky, maybe I better explain that Mickey
  was a jeep. Yeah, he'd been with our mobile weather unit ever since we landed in Africa
  and I guess without him we'd have never got along at all. When we first got him we
  stripped him down 'til there wasn't much left on him but the squeal of his brakes. Then
  we built him up again, installed a small radio unit, aneroid barometer for gauging air
  pressure, compass, thermometers, a dozen other things and an old auto horn that Red and
  I picked up cheap from a native in Algiers. Well, the day we left Sicily for the
  invasion of Italy, we loaded Mickey and all this equipment on an LST boat. Mickey
  seemed to be in fine fettle except for a nervous muttering in his gearbox. I was
  driving and Red was on the seat beside me, keeping an eye on the equipment.
Sgt. Broderick Crawford (as Sgt. Red): Well, this is it, Joe.
2nd Lt. Donald P. Briggs: Yeah, looks like they got us in front row seat for this one all
  right.
Sgt. Broderick Crawford: Mickey's the guy I pity with all this stuff to carry. Bet he
  thought he was getting something easy when he picked weather, poor guy.
2nd Lt. Donald P. Briggs: Yeah, don't worry about him. He's seen plenty tough days
  already.
Sgt. Broderick Crawford: Yeah, but if my guess is any good, this is gonna be tougher than
  any of them. Huh, Mickey?

2nd Lt. Donald P. Briggs: Well, we laughed a little then but we weren't laughing when we hit Salerno. No, sir. Shore batteries and dive bombers rolled out a welcome mat right away. And we had a pretty rough time even gettin' to shore. When we did we left Mickey in the protection of a clump of trees and started digging foxholes with our helmets. Every time the Junkers-88s came over, we dug deeper until we had a regular trench. And when we finally got back to Mickey, even he was up to his hub caps in sand. I swear he was trying to dig in too. We set up shop alongside a landing strip the bulldozers had made and got to work. We sent out weather reports to bases back in Africa and Sicily. We supplied data for artillery, information on wind velocity and upper air conditions useful to 'em in firing their long range shells. And we even made weather forecasts for the infantry to help them in moving their motorized equipment. For seven days the battle for Salerno beachhead raged back and forth. At one point we had all our classified material piled up ready to set fire to it, and all our stuff was loaded onto Mickey in case we had to evacuate. But reinforcements came up and drove the Jerries back and we unloaded again. Then on the eighth day, the day the tide finally turned in our favor, the Jerries came over for a last big try. Their special target, our outfit's landing strip. A couple of fields to the south of us our anti-aircraft battery went into action and Red and I headed for shelter. But just as we did the field telephone rang. Hello, weather unit.

Cpl. Paul A. Dubov (as Sergeant): Anti-aircraft battery number 6 calling. We need some information, quick.

2nd Lt. Donald P. Briggs: What's wrong?

Cpl. Paul A. Dubov: Our range finders are knocked out. But they're coming over us at cloud level. Give us the height of the clouds and we'll set our range at that. How about it?

2nd Lt. Donald P. Briggs: Just a second. I got it right here. The cloud height today ... Hello. Hello, ack-ack. Hey, Red, phone's out. That last one must have got it. I'll have to take Mickey and go over there myself.

Sgt. Broderick Crawford: Don't be crazy, Joe. They'll get you for sure.

2nd Lt. Donald P. Briggs: I can't help it. Come on, Mickey, it's you and me for it. Let's go. Out across those fields we went like a rabbit with a hot foot. There was so much dust and smoke that I couldn't see where we were going, but Mickey seemed to know. All I could do was grab the steering wheel and hold on. We dodged bomb craters, turning, twisting, bouncing our way across the fields. We tore through bushes, into ditches, in and out of shell holes, leaving a zigzag trail of dust behind us all the way. As we raced up to the ack-ack battery I tooted the horn and out ran a Sergeant to meet me, waving his arms. Weather reporting. Those clouds at ten thousand five hundred feet. Anything else we can do?

Cpl. Paul A. Dubov: Ten thousand five hundred, thanks, pal. Hit the cover, they're coming over again.

2nd Lt. Donald P. Briggs: I drove Mickey down into a sandy gully nearby and lay down beside him. Heard the ack-ack go into action again. This time they were right on the button. One Jerry rode high into a flak burst and came smoking to Earth. Then another and another until five of them had spun down and the rest of them turned back. Our landing strip was safe. They hadn't hit it once. Well, when the dust had settled the Sergeant came running back.

Cpl. Paul A. Dubov: Hey, hey, did you see that? We got five of them.

2nd Lt. Donald P. Briggs: Yeah, man, we sure poured it on.

Cpl. Paul A. Dubov: Thanks to you guys. Paint five swastikas on that jeep of yours, brother. You really earned them.

2nd Lt. Donald P. Briggs: Well, we painted them on all right. I wish you could have seen Mickey after that. He was so proud he wouldn't look at another jeep for days. Yeah, but we didn't need swastikas to make us proud. It was enough just to be doing the job. Because of us the bombers could bomb and the fighters could fight. Yeah, weather's our work like flying's theirs, and we're still over here, keeping our eye on the sky, giving theme all the help we can. Of course, Mickey's getting a little old now. He hasn't got the old bounce he used to have but I've cleaned him up, painted him again, got him a new transmission, put new points in his distributor, and he looks as good as ever. We've been a lot of places together already, Africa, Sicily, now Italy. And before this thing's over we'll ... say, Mickey, I wonder how the weather is in Berlin.

Incidental music
Captain Glenn Miller: Here's Sergeant Jerry Gray's hit tune of a few season's back,
  "String of Pearls."
A STRING OF PEARLS
Captain Glenn Miller: Now medley time, saluting the mothers, wives, sweethearts and
  sisters of the men of the Weather Observer School at Chanute Field, Illinois. Our old
  song, "Flow Gently, Sweet Afton."
FLOW GENTLY, SWEET AFTON (Old tune)
  Captain Glenn Miller: Something new, Sergeant Johnny Desmond, the Crew Chiefs singin'
    "Moon Dreams."
MOON DREAMS (New tune)
  Vocal refrain by Sergeant Johnny Desmond and the Crew Chiefs
  Captain Glenn Miller: From friend Benny Goodman we borrow "Don't Be That Way."
DON'T BE THAT WAY (Borrowed tune)
  Captain Glenn Miller: Last, something blue, "Blue Champagne."
BLUE CHAMPAGNE (Blue tune)
JOIN THE WAC
  2nd Lt. Donald P. Briggs: Women of America, march with Uncle Sam's Army. Join the WAC.
  Vocal refrain by the Crew Chiefs
  2nd Lt. Donald P. Briggs: Air WACs as weather observers are using weather as a weapon
    of war and making the skyways safe ways for our planes and the men who fly them.
  Vocal refrain by the Crew Chiefs
Captain Glenn Miller: Sergeant Ray McKinley, the Crew Chiefs and the band playing and
  singing "There'll Be a Hot Time in the Town of Berlin."
(There'll Be a) HOT TIME IN THE TOWN OF BERLIN (When the Yanks Go Marching In)
  Vocal refrain by Technical Sergeant Ray McKinley, the Crew Chiefs and the Glee Club
Sgt. Broderick Crawford: The weather observer furnishes information so that our fighting
  flyers can make use of weather as a weapon of war. Like over a million other ground
  crew specialists, each weather observer has been thoroughly trained for his job by the
  A.A.F. Training Command, the world's biggest university. This training has given him
  the privilege of adopting as his motto "I Sustain the Wings."
I SUSTAIN THE WINGS (closing theme)
  Captain Glenn Miller: This is Captain Miller saying so long for the Band of the
    Training Command, the Crew Chiefs, Corporal Bob Carroll, Sergeants Brod Crawford, Mel
    Powell, Ray McKinley, Johnny Desmond, and Lieutenant Don Briggs. See you again next
    Saturday, same time, same station.
2nd Lt. Donald P. Briggs: "I Sustain the Wings" is a presentation of the Army Air Forces
  Training Command and came to you from New York City.
NBC announcer: This is the National Broadcasting Company.
NBC chimes

22Apr44 (Sat) 11:30PM-Midnight EWT WEAF, NBC Vanderbilt Theatre, New York, New York
  I SUSTAIN THE WINGS broadcast   Audience

THE ARMY AIR CORPS (opening fanfare)
2nd Lt. Donald P. Briggs: "I Sustain the Wings"
I SUSTAIN THE WINGS (opening theme)
  2nd Lt. Donald P. Briggs: "I Sustain the Wings." The Army Air Forces present the Band
    of the Training Command, under the direction of Captain Glenn Miller. And now Captain
    Glenn Miller.
Captain Glenn Miller: Good evening, everybody. Speaking for the Crew Chiefs, Corporal
  Bob Carroll, Sergeants Brod Crawford, Mel Powell, Ray McKinley, Johnny Desmond,
  Lieutenant Don Briggs, and the whole gang, welcome to another program of "I Sustain the
  Wings." Musically, our good-will ambassadors are waitin' to take off on a "Mission to
  Moscow."
MISSION TO MOSCOW
Captain Glenn Miller: Now Corporal Bob Carroll singing the new tune that should hit the
  popularity jackpot any day now. It's "Time Alone Will Tell."
TIME ALONE WILL TELL
  Vocal refrain by Corporal Bob Carroll
Incidental music
  Captain Glenn Miller: Wind and fog can drive the biggest bomber off its course. And
    snow and ice can flip the wings of the fastest fighter, but the fact that they seldom
    do is a tribute to the skilled weather observers and forecasters trained by the A.A.F.
    Training Command. Before each flight these weather-wise experts furnish air crews
    with a full report of flying conditions. They guard our fliers against weather
    hazards of all kinds, help plan every mission. And much of our success in the air is
    due directly to their vigilance and courage. This might be the ...
Captain Glenn Miller: ... typical story of any one of these men. It was told to us by a
  Sergeant we'll call Joe Blake, who served with the mobile weather unit in the Battle of
  Salerno.
2nd Lt. Donald P. Briggs (as Sgt. Joe Blake): Yeah, there were ten in our unit when we
  took off for Salerno back in September 1943. One Captain; Master Sergeant; Tech
  Sergeant; four Staffs; a buddy, Red, a Sergeant like myself; that's nine of us and
  Mickey. Huh, huh, Mickey, ah, there was a real soldier for you, a guy you could count
  on to pull you through anything. The rougher the going got the better he seemed to like
  it. And what a pal. Never argued or complained, never bummed cigarettes, in fact, he
  didn't smoke, except when his valves needed regrinding, and he never drank except a
  little gasoline now and then for his carburetor's sake. Ah, but before you start
  thinking this job of mine has me weather-wacky, maybe I'd better explain that Mickey was
  a jeep. Yes, sir, he'd been with our mobile weather unit ever since we landed in Africa
  and I guess without him we'd have never got along at all. When we first got him we
  stripped him down 'til there wasn't much left of him but the squeal of his brakes. Then
  we built him up again, installed a small radio unit, aneroid barometer for gauging air
  pressure, compass, thermometers, a dozen other things and an old auto horn that Red and
  I picked up cheap from a native in Algiers. The day we left Sicily for the invasion of
  Italy, we loaded Mickey and all this equipment on an LST boat. Ah, Mickey seemed to be
  in fine fettle except for a nervous muttering in his gearbox. I was driving, Red was on
  the seat beside me, keeping an eye on the equipment.
Sgt. Broderick Crawford (as Sgt. Red): Well, this is it, Joe.
2nd Lt. Donald P. Briggs: Yeah, looks like they got us a front row seat for this one all
  right.
Sgt. Broderick Crawford: Well, Mickey's the guy I pity with all this stuff to carry. I
  bet he thought he was getting something easy when he picked weather, poor guy.
2nd Lt. Donald P. Briggs: Ah, don't worry about him. He's seen plenty tough days
  already.
Sgt. Broderick Crawford: Yeah, but if my guess is any good, this is gonna be tougher than
  any of them. Huh, Mickey?

2nd Lt. Donald P. Briggs: Well, we laughed a little then but we weren't laughing when we hit Salerno. Shore batteries and dive bombers rolled out a welcome mat right away. And we had a pretty rough time even getting to shore. When we did we left Mickey in the protection of a clump of trees and started digging foxholes with our helmets. Every time the Junkers-88s came over, we dug deeper until we had a regular trench. And when we finally got back to Mickey, even he was up to his hub caps in sand. I swear he was trying to dig in too. We set up shop alongside a landing strip the bulldozers had made and got to work. We sent out weather reports to bases back in Africa and Sicily. We supplied data for artillery, information on wind velocity and upper air conditions useful to 'em in firing their long range shells. And we even made weather core - forecasts for the infantry to help them in moving their motorized equipment. Well, for seven days the battle for Salerno beachhead raged back and forth. At one point we had all our classified material piled up ready to set fire to it, and all our stuff was loaded onto Mickey in case we had to evacuate. But reinforcements came up and drove the Jerries back and we unloaded again. Then on the eighth day, the day the tide finally turned in our favor, the Jerries came over for a last big try. Their special target, our outfit's landing strip. A couple of fields to the south of us our anti-aircraft battery went into action and Red and I headed for shelter. But just as we did the field telephone rang. Hello, weather unit.
Cpl. Paul A. Dubov (as Sergeant Tony): Anti-aircraft out on 6, Tony. We need some information, quick.
2nd Lt. Donald P. Briggs: Yeah, what's wrong?
Cpl. Paul A. Dubov: Our range finders are knocked out. But they're coming over us at the cloud level. Give us the height of the clouds and we'll set our range at that. How about it?
2nd Lt. Donald P. Briggs: Just a second. I got it right here. The cloud height is ... Hello. Hello, ack-ack. Hey, Red, phone's out. Last one must have got it. I'll have to take Mickey and go over there myself.
Sgt. Broderick Crawford: What are you, crazy, Joe? They'll get you for sure.
2nd Lt. Donald P. Briggs: I can't help it. Come on, Mickey, it's you and me for it. Let's go. Out across those fields we went like a rabbit with a hot foot. There was so much dust and smoke that I couldn't see where we were going, but Mickey seemed to know. All I could do was grab the steering wheel and hold on. We dodged bomb craters, turning, twisting, bouncing our way across the fields. We tore through bushes, into ditches, in and out of shell holes, leaving a zigzag trail of dust behind us all the way. As we raced up to the ack-ack battery I tooted the horn and out ran a Sergeant to meet me, waving his arms. Ah, weather reporting. Those clouds, ten thousand five hundred feet. Anything else we can do?
Cpl. Paul A. Dubov: Ten thousand five hundred, thanks, pal. Hey, hit the cover, they're coming over again.
2nd Lt. Donald P. Briggs: I drove Mickey down into a sandy gully nearby and lay down beside him. Heard the ack-ack go into action again. And this time they were right on the button. One Jerry rode right into a flak burst and came smoking to Earth. Then another and another until five of them had spun down and the rest of them turned back. Our landing strip was safe.

...

Captain Glenn Miller: Here's Sergeant Jerry Gray's hit tune of a few season's back, "String of Pearls."
A STRING OF PEARLS
Captain Glenn Miller: Medley time now, saluting the mothers, wives, sweethearts and sisters of the men of the Weather Observer School at Chanute Field, Illinois. Our old song, "Flow Gently, Sweet Afton."
FLOW GENTLY, SWEET AFTON (Old tune)
Captain Glenn Miller: Something new, Sergeant Johnny Desmond, the Crew Chiefs singin' "Moon Dreams."
MOON DREAMS (New tune)
Vocal refrain by Sergeant Johnny Desmond and the Crew Chiefs
Captain Glenn Miller: From friend Benny Goodman we borrow "Don't Be That Way."

DON'T BE THAT WAY (Borrowed tune)
  Captain Glenn Miller: Last, something blue, "Blue Champagne."
BLUE CHAMPAGNE (Blue tune)
JOIN THE WAC
  2nd Lt. Donald P. Briggs: Women of America, march with Uncle Sam's Army. Join the WAC.
  Vocal refrain by the Crew Chiefs
  2nd Lt. Donald P. Briggs: Air WACs as weather observers are using weather as a weapon
    of war and making the skyways safe ways for our planes and the men who fly them.
  Vocal refrain by the Crew Chiefs
Captain Glenn Miller: Now Sergeant Ray McKinley, the Crew Chiefs and the band playing and
  singing "There'll Be a Hot Time In the Town of Berlin."
(There'll Be a) HOT TIME IN THE TOWN OF BERLIN (When the Yanks Go Marching In)
  Vocal refrain by Technical Sergeant Ray McKinley, the Crew Chiefs and the Glee Club
Sgt. Broderick Crawford: The weather observer furnishes information so that our fighting
  flyers can make use of weather as a weapon of war. Like over a million other ground
  crew specialists, each weather observer has been thoroughly trained for his job by the
  A.A.F. Training Command, the world's biggest university. This training has given him
  the privilege of adopting as his motto "I Sustain the Wings."
I SUSTAIN THE WINGS (closing theme)
  Captain Glenn Miller: This is Captain Miller saying so long for the Band of the
    Training Command, the Crew Chiefs, Corporal Bob Carroll, Sergeants Brod Crawford, Mel
    Powell, Ray McKinley, Johnny Desmond, and Lieutenant Don Briggs. See you again next
    Saturday, same time, same station.
2nd Lt. Donald P. Briggs: "I Sustain the Wings" is a presentation of the Army Air Forces
  Training Command and came to you from New York City.
NBC announcer: This is the National Broadcasting Company.

29Apr44 (Sat) NBC, New York, New York
  UNCLE SAM PRESENTS recordings

I SUSTAIN THE WINGS (opening theme)
  2nd Lt. Donald P. Briggs: From the United States of America, to the other united
    nations of the world, "Uncle Sam Presents" the Band of the A.A.F. Training Command,
    under the direction of Captain Glenn Miller.
  2nd Lt. Donald P. Briggs: And here is Captain Glenn Miller.

I SUSTAIN THE WINGS (closing theme)
  Captain Glenn Miller: Time now to take our leave until next week's meetin'. Speakin'
    for Lieutenants Don Briggs, Sergeants Ray McKinley, Mel Powell, Johnny Desmond, the
    Crew Chiefs, and all the gang, thanks for listenin' and so long for now.
    2nd Lt. Donald P. Briggs: The Band of the A.A.F. Training Command, under the direction
    of Captain Glenn Miller, has come to you from New York City. Don't forget tomorrow,
    same time, same station, "Uncle Sam Presents" another famous service band with music
    from us to you.
  2nd Lt. Donald P. Briggs: This is the United States of America, one of the united
  nations.

Captain Glenn Miller: Thank you, Lieutenant Don Briggs. Speakin' for Sergeants Mel
  Powell, Ray McKinley, Johnny Desmond, the Crew Chiefs --- Stop!

Captain Glenn Miller: Thank you, Lieutenant Don Briggs. Speaking for Sergeants Mel
  Powell, Ray McKinley, Johnny Desmond, the Crew Chiefs, welcome to another program of
  "Uncle Sam Presents." First off in the music department, "Tuxedo Junction."

Captain Glenn Miller: Thank you, Lieutenant Don Briggs. Speaking for Sergeants Mel
  Powell, Ray McKinley, Johnny Desmond, the Crew Chiefs, welcome to another program of
  "Uncle Sam Presents." We're comin' up with some music for your listenin' pleasure now
  and the takeoff is aboard the "Caribbean Clipper."

Captain Glenn Miller: Here's an old girl friend with a brand new permanent, "Jeanie with
  the Light Brown Hair."

Captain Glenn Miller: Sergeant Mel Powell at the piano now and he turns triple-threat man
  this next number. He wrote it, arranged it, and now plays "Pearls on Velvet."

Captain Glenn Miller: Now a song written by Irving Berlin and dedicated to the commanding
  general of the A.A.F., General H. H. Arnold, "With My Head in the Clouds."

Captain Glenn Miller: Thank you, Lieutenant Don Briggs. Speaking for Sergeants Mel
  Powell, Ray McKinley, Johnny Desmond, the Crew Chiefs, welcome to another program of
  "Uncle Sam Presents." Musically now, our good-will ambassadors are waitin' to take off
  on "Mission to Moscow."

Captain Glenn Miller: Sergeant Mel Powell is the head man on this next arrangement. It's
  "Honeysuckle Rose."

Captain Glenn Miller: One of the most popular tunes of any season. I'm sure you'll say it's one of your favorites, "Star Dust."

Captain Glenn Miller: Sergeant Ray McKinley picks up the big hammers and we go into "Anvil Chorus."

Captain Glenn Miller: Thank you, Lieutenant Don Briggs. Speaking for Sergeants Mel Powell, Ray McKinley, Johnny Desmond, and the Crew Chiefs, welcome to another program of "Uncle Sam Presents." For your listenin' pleasure here's one of the top tunes on our request list, "In the Mood."

Captain Glenn Miller: Now a new arrangement of an old favorite, "In the Gloaming."

Captain Glenn Miller: Here's the Band of the Training Command playing "Stormy Weather."

Captain Glenn Miller: 1944 finds a battle-scarred tune of two wars still in there pitchin' with our boys in training. A star-spangled veteran for the fighting heart and it's "Over There."

Captain Glenn Miller: 1944 finds a battle-scarred tune of two wars still in there pitchin' with our boys in service. A star-spangled veteran for the fighting heart, it's "Over There."

29Apr44 (Sat) 6:00-6:30PM EWT WEAF, NBC Vanderbilt Theatre, New York, New York
I SUSTAIN THE WINGS broadcast
Audience

THE ARMY AIR CORPS (opening fanfare)
2nd Lt. Donald P. Briggs: "I Sustain the Wings"
I SUSTAIN THE WINGS (opening theme)
  2nd Lt. Donald P. Briggs: "I Sustain the Wings." The Army Air Forces present the Band
    of the Training Command, under the direction of Captain Glenn Miller. And now Captain
    Glenn Miller.
Captain Glenn Miller: Good evening, everybody. Speaking for the Crew Chiefs, Sergeants
  Brod Crawford, Mel Powell, Ray McKinley, Johnny Desmond, Lieutenant Don Briggs, and the
  whole gang, welcome to another program of "I Sustain the Wings." In the music
  department tonight's curtain lifter-upper is "Here We Go Again."
HERE WE GO AGAIN
Captain Glenn Miller: Sergeant Norm Leyden's arrangement of a swell new tune, "Going My
  Way." Sergeant Johnny Desmond sings the lyric.
GOING MY WAY
  Vocal refrain by Sergeant Johnny Desmond
Incidental music
  Captain Glenn Miller: Many are the stories brought back from overseas by men who have
    graduated from the A.A.F. Training Command. Some are stories of heroism, stories of
    men who achieve the impossible, epics of quiet courage and resourcefulness. But
    there's humor too in their everyday life of fighting and hardship. Stories like the
    one told to us by a mechanic just returned from England. One of his friends over
    there was a waist gunner on a Flying Fort at the same field. One day word came that
    his friend had been hurt on the morning mission. So this mechanic hurried over to the
    hospital to offer his sympathy. The doctor in charge let him into the ward.
Cpl. Paul A. Dubov (as Doctor): You'll find your friend down the line there, Sergeant.
  It's the third bed on the left. Oh, don't stay too long.
2nd Lt. Donald P. Briggs (as Sgt. Mike): Thank you, sir. I'll just stay a few minutes.
  Hello, Jim. Gosh, fellow, I'm sure sorry to hear about this. How're you feelin'?
Sgt. Broderick Crawford (as Jim): Oh, hello, Mike. There's nothing wrong with me. My
  bag of luck just ran out, I guess. Sit down. Have a chair.
2nd Lt. Donald P. Briggs: Oh, thanks. Where'd you get it, Jim? In the leg? I see
  you've got it all bandaged up there.
Sgt. Broderick Crawford: Yeah, yeah, it's my leg. It doesn't hurt much now but sure was
  an awful way to get it, wasn't it?
2nd Lt. Donald P. Briggs: Well, I didn't hear yet how it happened. That's what I wanted
  to ask you.
Sgt. Broderick Crawford: Well, I'd rather not talk about it, Mike, if you don't mind.
2nd Lt. Donald P. Briggs: Well, that's O.K., kid, I know how you feel. Anything you say.
Sgt. Broderick Crawford: Well, I suppose there's no use being persistent about it. It's
  probably all over the field by now anyway.
2nd Lt. Donald P. Briggs: Anything you say, kid.
Sgt. Broderick Crawford: Well, well, Mike, it happened like this. We took off this
  morning, everything O.K. Just routine, you know. We climbed to about fifteen thousand
  feet and picked up our fighter escort right on schedule. As we neared the target we
  could see Messerschmitts coming up. They're coming from all directions. We go on
  automatic pilot and level off for the bomb run, the Jerries firing faster than ever.
  Oh, it's terrible, Mike. Fighters everywhere you look. Then one of them comes droning
  head on at me, like he had his sights on me alone. Bloey he comes. I fire like mad,
  the gun jumps in my hand, but he keeps comin'. Three thousand yards, two thousand
  yards. My tracers seem to go right through him, but he comes right on, not firing
  himself, holding his own fire. When all of a sudden at five hundred yards, point blank
  range, he let's go. Bang! I feel something hit me. Boy, I just stood there for a
  minute. All of a sudden I began to feel cold, like an icy hand on the pit of my
  stomach.
2nd Lt. Donald P. Briggs: Boy, no wonder.
Sgt. Broderick Crawford: I'll say no wonder. It's thirty degrees below up there and that
  coat blowing open in the wind.

2nd Lt. Donald P. Briggs: Your coat?
Sgt. Broderick Crawford: Sure, sure, the bullet ripped the zipper right off. It didn't touch me at all, just ripped the zipper off.
2nd Lt. Donald P. Briggs: And didn't touch you?
Sgt. Broderick Crawford: No, it didn't touch me. We got that fighter, too, Mike, believe me. He rolled away under us, folded up like a Roman candle. That was his finish.
2nd Lt. Donald P. Briggs: Oh, that's what I call a narrow escape. Took the zipper right off and never touched you. Wh - what about the leg, Jim?
Sgt. Broderick Crawford: Huh, oh, oh that. Well, that came later. You see, we headed for home after dropping the bomb load and fighters came right after us, the flak heavy all the time. We tossed around in the explosion like a feather in a cyclone. The flak made big holes in our wings, one engine smoking, we're dodging every which way to escape the flak, when all of a sudden a big jagged chunk of it smashes right up through the roof.
2nd Lt. Donald P. Briggs: Holy smoke, it must have almost tore your leg off.
Sgt. Broderick Crawford: My leg? How could it?
2nd Lt. Donald P. Briggs: Well, I mean, if it came up and hit you like that, you ...
Sgt. Broderick Crawford: Hey, who's telling you I was hit by flak? These guys around here, what are they being funny or something?
2nd Lt. Donald P. Briggs: Nobody told me, Jim. I just figured ...
Sgt. Broderick Crawford: Well, it didn't touch me, the flak didn't. You see, just a split second before it came through the floor I stepped over to get another box of ammunition and it missed me completely.
2nd Lt. Donald P. Briggs: Oh, what a lucky break. That's the narrowest escape I ever heard of. Well, how did it happen then?
Sgt. Broderick Crawford: Well, you see, we went on, practically limping along with that one bad engine finally giving out all together. We headed for the channel as fast as we could go and suddenly another batch of fighters circled up from some hidden field near the French coast. They were laying for us cripples, that's what they was doing. It looks like about eighteen million of them. They're everywhere. They dive at us from out of the sun and fill us with lead through the fuselage. We're trapped in a circle of fire, Mike. They get the plane just ahead of us and down she goes without parachutes. Then they head for us. It's whooping from every direction. I can see two of them high at nine o'clock coming at top speed, spitting flames from their wing guns. All of a sudden bang! Everything goes black for a minute.
2nd Lt. Donald P. Briggs: Holy smoke, they got you.
Sgt. Broderick Crawford: Well, all at once I ... What did you say?
2nd Lt. Donald P. Briggs: I said, "They got you."
Sgt. Broderick Crawford: Who got who?
2nd Lt. Donald P. Briggs: The Jerries, they hit you.
Sgt. Broderick Crawford: When?
2nd Lt. Donald P. Briggs: When everything went black.
Sgt. Broderick Crawford: Oh, no, no. That wasn't when I got it. You see, as I reeled back I put my hand up to my head and there was a slug of that Jerry's gun embedded right in my flight helmet.
2nd Lt. Donald P. Briggs: Yeah?
Sgt. Broderick Crawford: Yeah, yeah, it hit something else first, spent its force, then bounced off and hit me. Didn't even scratch me, just gave me a good wallop in the head, that's all.
Sgt. Broderick Crawford: But how did you get it in the leg? That's what I want to know.
Sgt. Broderick Crawford: Well, take it easy, I'm coming to that. You see ...
Cpl. Paul A. Dubov: Sergeant.
2nd Lt. Donald P. Briggs: Yeah.
Cpl. Paul A. Dubov: Sergeant, I see you're still here.
2nd Lt. Donald P. Briggs: Yes, sir. I was just going.
Cpl. Paul A. Dubov: I think maybe you'd better. This really isn't visiting hours, you know, and your friend here has had a pretty bad shock.
2nd Lt. Donald P. Briggs: Yes, sir, ah ... so long, Jim. I better go now, I guess. I'll come back tomorrow and then you can tell me how.
Cpl. Paul A. Dubov: Coming, Sergeant?

2nd Lt. Donald P. Briggs: Ah, yes, sir. See you later, Jim.
Sgt. Broderick Crawford: O.K., Mike. Thanks for coming over.
Cpl. Paul A. Dubov: Your friend had quite a rough trip, didn't he?
2nd Lt. Donald P. Briggs: Yes, sir. He sure did.
Cpl. Paul A. Dubov: Well, he's going to be all right. So don't worry.
2nd Lt. Donald P. Briggs: I guess he's lucky to be alive after a trip like that. Boy, he had more narrow escapes than anybody I've ever heard of. A bullet rips a zipper off his flying suit, doesn't scratch him. Flak tears up the floor right where he was standing but he isn't touched. Another bullet hits him smack in the head but doesn't even go through his helmet. Yes, sir, that guy's really lucky. Ah, how did he finally set it, sir?
Cpl. Paul A. Dubov: Oh, didn't he tell you? Well, after the plane landed he started to climb out through the hatch and slipped and broke his leg.
Incidental music
Captain Glenn Miller: Now it's medley time, saluting the mothers, wives, sweethearts and sisters of the men of the A.A.F. Something old, something new, something borrowed and something blue. Our old song, "My Buddy."
MY BUDDY (Old tune)
  Captain Glenn Miller: Something new, Sergeant Johnny Desmond and the Crew Chiefs with "Good Night, wherever You Are."
GOOD NIGHT, WHEREVER YOU ARE (New tune)
  Vocal refrain by Sergeant Johnny Desmond and the Crew Chiefs
  Captain Glenn Miller: Something borrowed from friend Harry James, "Music Makers."
MUSIC MAKERS (Borrowed tune)
  Captain Glenn Miller: Last, something blue, "Farewell Blues."
FAREWELL BLUES (Blue tune)
JOIN THE WAC
  2nd Lt. Donald P. Briggs: Women of America, march with Uncle Sam's Army. Join the WAC.
  Vocal refrain by the Crew Chiefs
  2nd Lt. Donald P. Briggs: As an Air WAC you can become a Link trainer instructor and teach future pilots the use of instruments for blind flying.
  Vocal refrain by the Crew Chiefs
Captain Glenn Miller: Sergeant Ray McKinley and the Crew Chiefs singin' Sergeant Jerry Gray's arrangement of "Peggy the Pin-Up Girl."
PEGGY THE PIN-UP GIRL
  Vocal refrain by Technical Sergeant Ray McKinley and the Crew Chiefs
2nd Lt. Donald P. Briggs: Precision instruments play an important part in all missions flown by the A.A.F. These instruments, upon which the lives of a plane and her crew often depend, must be maintained at the peak of operational efficiency. That's the job of the instrument maintenance man who, like thousands of other specialized technicians, is a graduate of the A.A.F. Training Command, the world's biggest university. Because of the knowledge and skill obtained in the Training Command, the instrument specialist and over a million fellow members of the A.A.F. ground crews translate by action the Latin words of their proud motto "Sustineo Alas," "I Sustain the Wings."
I SUSTAIN THE WINGS (closing theme)
  Captain Glenn Miller: This is Captain Glenn Miller saying so long for the Band of the Training Command, Sergeants Brod Crawford, Mel Powell, Ray McKinley, Johnny Desmond, the Crew Chiefs, and Lieutenant Don Briggs. Hope to see you again next Saturday, same time, same station.
  2nd Lt. Donald P. Briggs: Keep those V-Mail letters flying to the boys overseas. Mail from home is number one on their Hit Parade. You can make your boy's day bright by writing that letter tonight.
2nd Lt. Donald P. Briggs: "I Sustain the Wings" is a presentation of the Army Air Forces Training Command and came to you from New York City.
NBC announcer: This is the National Broadcasting Company.
NBC chimes

29Apr44 (Sat) 11:30PM-Midnight EWT   WEAF, NBC Vanderbilt Theatre, New York, New York
I SUSTAIN THE WINGS broadcast   Audience

THE ARMY AIR CORPS (opening fanfare)
2nd Lt. Donald P. Briggs: "I Sustain the Wings"
I SUSTAIN THE WINGS (opening theme)
   2nd Lt. Donald P. Briggs: "I Sustain the Wings." The Army Air Forces present the Band
     of the Training Command, under the direction of Captain Glenn Miller. And now Captain
     Glenn Miller.
Captain Glenn Miller: Good evening, everybody. Speaking for the Crew Chiefs, Sergeants
   Brod Crawford, Mel Powell, Ray McKinley, Johnny Desmond, Lieutenant Don Briggs, and the
   gang, welcome to another program of "I Sustain the Wings." In the music department
   tonight's curtain lifter-upper is "Here We Go Again."
HERE WE GO AGAIN
Captain Glenn Miller: Sergeant Norm Leyden's arrangement of a swell new tune, "Going My
   Way." Sergeant Johnny Desmond sings the lyric.
GOING MY WAY
   Vocal refrain by Sergeant Johnny Desmond
Incidental music
   Captain Glenn Miller: Many are the stories brought back from overseas by men who have
     graduated from the A.A.F. Training Command. Some are stories of heroism, stories of
     men who achieve the impossible, epics of quiet courage and resourcefulness. But
     there's humor too in their everyday life of fighting and hardship. Stories like the
     one told to us by a mechanic just returned from England. One of his friends over
     there was a waist gunner on a Flying Fort at the same field. And one day word came
     that his friend had been hurt on the morning mission. So this mechanic hurried over
     to the hospital to offer his sympathy. The doctor in charge let him into the ward.

   ...

Captain Glenn Miller: Now it's medley time, saluting the mothers, wives, sweethearts and
   sisters of the men of the A.A.F. Something old, something new, something borrowed and
   something blue. Our old song, "My Buddy."
MY BUDDY (Old tune)
   Captain Glenn Miller: Something new, Sergeant Johnny Desmond and the Crew Chiefs, "Good
     Night, wherever You Are."
GOOD NIGHT, WHEREVER YOU ARE (New tune)
   Vocal refrain by Sergeant Johnny Desmond and the Crew Chiefs
   Captain Glenn Miller: Something borrowed from friend Harry James, "Music Makers."
MUSIC MAKERS (Borrowed tune)
   Captain Glenn Miller: Last, something blue, "Farewell Blues."
FAREWELL BLUES (Blue tune)
JOIN THE WAC
   2nd Lt. Donald P. Briggs: Women of America, march with Uncle Sam's Army. Join the WAC.
   Vocal refrain by the Crew Chiefs
   2nd Lt. Donald P. Briggs: As an Air WAC you can become a ...

   ...

Captain Glenn Miller: ... Sergeant Jerry Gray's arrangement of "Peggy the Pin-Up Girl."
PEGGY THE PIN-UP GIRL
   Vocal refrain by Technical Sergeant Ray McKinley and the Crew Chiefs
2nd Lt. Donald P. Briggs: Precision instruments play an important part in all missions
   flown by the A.A.F. These instruments, upon which the lives of a plane and her crew
   often depend, must be maintained at the peak of operational efficiency. That's the job
   of the instrument maintenance man who, like thousands of other specialized technicians,
   is a graduate of the A.A.F. Training Command, the world's biggest university. Because
   of the knowledge and skill obtained in the Training Command, the instrument specialist
   and over a million fellow members of the A.A.F. ground crews translate by action the
   Latin words of their proud motto "Sustineo Alas," "I Sustain the Wings."

I SUSTAIN THE WINGS (closing theme)
  Captain Glenn Miller: This is Captain Glenn Miller saying so long for the Band of the
    Training Command, Sergeants Brod Crawford, Mel Powell, Ray McKinley, Johnny Desmond,
    the Crew Chiefs, and Lieutenant Don Briggs. Hope to see you again next Saturday, same
    time, same station.
  2nd Lt. Donald P. Briggs: Keep those V-Mail letters flying to the boys overseas. Mail
    from home is number one on their Hit Parade. You can make your boy's day bright by
    writing that letter tonight.
  2nd Lt. Donald P. Briggs: "I Sustain the Wings" is a presentation of the Army Air Forces
  Training Command and came to you from New York City.

06May44 (Sat) 6:00-6:30PM EWT WEAF, NBC Vanderbilt Theatre, New York, New York
I SUSTAIN THE WINGS broadcast   Audience

...

1st Lt. Donald P. Briggs (as Lt. Ed Barker): ... and then I was in the plane once again
   with the machine guns chattering, the roar of the engines in my ears, the whine of Zeros
   as they came diving at us from all directions. And through it all I could hear a voice.
Sgt. Broderick Crawford (as Jim Wilson): This is your chance, Ed. Yours and mine. It's
   a chance I never had. Make it a good one, kid, for me.
1st Lt. Donald P. Briggs: I reached out, touched the bomb release, the destroyer was
   square in the cross-hairs of the sight, and, as I watched the bombs curving silently
   down toward the target, somehow I knew they wouldn't miss. It was our turn now and from
   now on it would always be our turn. We were hitting back and we'd keep on hittin' 'em
   harder and harder on land and sea, and by night, never stopping, never resting, until
   the last trace of their treachery vanished from the Earth. Bombs away, Jim.
Incidental music
Captain Glenn Miller: And now it's medley time, saluting the mothers, wives, sweethearts
   and sisters of the men of the Bombardier School at Saint Angelo, Texas. Here's
   something old, something new, something borrowed and something blue. Our old song,
   "Songs My Mother Taught Me."
SONGS MY MOTHER TAUGHT ME (Old tune)
   Captain Glenn Miller: Something new, the Crew Chiefs and "It's Love, Love, Love!"
IT'S LOVE, LOVE, LOVE! (New tune)
   Vocal refrain by the Crew Chiefs
   Captain Glenn Miller: For our borrowed tune, "Eighteen Century Drawing Room."
IN AN EIGHTEENTH CENTURY DRAWING ROOM (Borrowed tune)
   Captain Glenn Miller: "Blue Orchids" with Sergeant Johnny Desmond doin' the singin'.
BLUE ORCHIDS (Blue tune)
   Vocal refrain by Sergeant Johnny Desmond
JOIN THE WAC
   1st Lt. Donald P. Briggs: Women of America, march with Uncle Sam's Army. Join the WAC.
   Vocal refrain by the Crew Chiefs
   1st Lt. Donald P. Briggs: Air WACs work to keep our planes in fighting trim and help to
      pack the punch that wallops the Axis.
   Vocal refrain by the Crew Chiefs
WITH MY HEAD IN THE CLOUDS
   1st Lt. Donald P. Briggs: And now a song written by Irving Berlin for the all-soldier
      hit picture "This Is the Army." Written for and dedicated to the commanding general
      of the A.A.F., General H. H. Arnold, "With My Head in the Clouds."
   Vocal refrain by Sergeant Johnny Desmond and the Glee Club
Sgt. Broderick Crawford: Bombardiers of the A.A.F. have a habit of dropping their bombs
   where they'll do the most good, right on the target. No little part of this accuracy is
   due to a piece of mechanical magic, the bombsight. The bombsight is a precision
   instrument wh - which must be checked, adjusted and accurately maintained. That's the
   job of the bombsight maintenance man, another graduate of the world's largest
   university, the A.A.F. Training Command. The Training Command has given him skill and
   the know-how to keep these bombsights at the peak of operating efficiency. Though the
   bombsight maintenance man stays on the ground, he's riding with the bombardier every
   second of that dangerous bombing run. And he, like the millions of other graduates of
   the A.A.F. Training Command, can proudly say, "I Sustain the Wings."
I SUSTAIN THE WINGS (closing theme)
   Captain Glenn Miller: This is Captain Glenn Miller saying so long for the Band of the
      Training Command, the Crew Chiefs, Sergeants Brod Crawford, Mel Powell, Ray McKinley,
      Johnny Desmond and Lieutenant Don Briggs. Hope to see you again next Saturday, same
      time, same station.
   1st Lt. Donald P. Briggs: Keep those V-Mail letters flying to the boys overseas. Mail
      from home's number one on their Hit Parade." They're doing the fightin', you do the
      writin'.

1st Lt. Donald P. Briggs: "I Sustain the Wings" is a presentation of the Army Air Forces
  Training Command and came to you from New York City.
NBC announcer: This is the National Broadcasting Company.
NBC chimes

06May44 (Sat) 11:30PM-Midnight EWT WEAF, NBC Vanderbilt Theatre, New York, New York
  I SUSTAIN THE WINGS broadcast   Audience

THE ARMY AIR CORPS (opening fanfare)
1st Lt. Donald P. Briggs: "I Sustain the Wings"
I SUSTAIN THE WINGS (opening theme)
  1st Lt. Donald P. Briggs: "I Sustain the Wings." The Army Air Forces present the Band
    of the Training Command, under the direction of Captain Glenn Miller. And now Captain
    Glenn Miller.
Captain Glenn Miller: Good evening, everybody. Speaking for the Crew Chiefs, Sergeants
  Brod Crawford, Mel Powell, Ray McKinley, Johnny Desmond, Lieutenant Don Briggs, and the
  gang, welcome to another program of "I Sustain the Wings." Now a little petty larceny
  in the music department, "Stealin Apples."
STEALIN' APPLES
Captain Glenn Miller: Now here's Sergeant Johnny Desmond singing one of this season's top
  show tunes, "Speak Low."
SPEAK LOW (When You Speak Love)
  Vocal refrain by Sergeant Johnny Desmond
Incidental music
  Captain Glenn Miller: When a Flying Fortress wings her way to the target, it takes ten
    men in the crew to get her there and at least forty others on the ground. But in
    those last twenty seconds over the target it's all one man, the lord of the bombsight,
    the bombardier. He's trained for his job by the A.A.F. Training Command and it's on
    that training that everything depends in those final precious seconds when the whole
    success of the mission hangs on his skill and courage.
Captain Glenn Miller: Take our story tonight. It's the story of a bombardier we'll call
  Lieutenant Ed Barker, and as Lieutenant Barker tells it, it all began one morning two
  and a half years ago in Hawaii.
1st Lt. Donald P. Briggs (as Lt. Ed Barker): It was Sunday morning. The kind of Sunday
  morning that used to make you think of picnics and walks in the woods when you were back
  home. The sun had just come up a few minutes before and everything was peaceful and
  quiet. Some of the boys were still asleep in the barracks at Hickham Field, but I got
  up early that morning and was sitting on a bunk talking to my buddy, Jim Wilson, another
  bombardier. It was a day of rest for us. We were busy making plans for a trip into
  Honolulu that afternoon to see the sights. Suddenly Jim stopped talking.
Sgt. Broderick Crawford (as Jim Wilson): Hey. Hey, listen.

  ...

Captain Glenn Miller: ... saluting the mothers, wives, sweethearts and sisters of the men
  of the Bombardier School at Saint Angelo, Texas. Here's something old, something new,
  something borrowed and something blue. The old song, "Songs My Mother Taught Me."
SONGS MY MOTHER TAUGHT ME (Old tune)
  Captain Glenn Miller: Something new, the Crew Chiefs singing "It's Love, Love, Love!"
IT'S LOVE, LOVE, LOVE! (New tune)
  Vocal refrain by the Crew Chiefs
  Captain Glenn Miller: For our borrowed tune, "Eighteen Century Drawing Room."
IN AN EIGHTEENTH CENTURY DRAWING ROOM (Borrowed tune)
  Captain Glenn Miller: For the blue tune, "Blue Orchids" with Sergeant Johnny Desmond
    singing.
BLUE ORCHIDS (Blue tune)
  Vocal refrain by Sergeant Johnny Desmond
JOIN THE WAC
  1st Lt. Donald P. Briggs: Women of America, march with Uncle Sam's Army. Join the WAC.
  Vocal refrain by the Crew Chiefs
  1st Lt. Donald P. Briggs: Air WACs work to keep our planes in fighting trim and help to
    pack the punch that wallops the Axis.
  Vocal refrain by the Crew Chiefs

WITH MY HEAD IN THE CLOUDS

1st Lt. Donald P. Briggs: And now a song written by Irving Berlin for the all-soldier hit picture "This Is the Army." Written for and dedicated to the commanding general of the A.A.F., General H. H. Arnold, "With My Head in the Clouds."

Vocal refrain by Sergeant Johnny Desmond and the Glee Club

Sgt. Broderick Crawford: Bombardiers of the Army Air Forces have a habit of dropping their bombs where they'll do the most good, right on the target. No little part of this accuracy is due to a piece of mechanical magic, the bombsight. The bombsight is a precision instrument which must be checked, adjusted and maintained. That's the job of the bombsight maintenance man, another graduate of the world's biggest university, the Army Air Forces Training Command. The Training Command has given him skill and the know-how to keep these bombsights at the peak of operating efficiency. Though the bombsight maintenance man stays on the ground, he's riding with the bombardier every second of that dangerous bombing run. And he, like the millions of other graduates of the Army Air Forces Training Command, can proudly say, "I Sustain the Wings."

I SUSTAIN THE WINGS (closing theme)

Captain Glenn Miller: This is Captain Glenn Miller saying so long for the Band of the Training Command, the Crew Chiefs, Sergeants Brod Crawford, Mel Powell, Ray McKinley, Johnny Desmond and Lieutenant Don Briggs. Hope to see you again next Saturday, same time, same station.

1st Lt. Donald P. Briggs: Keep those V-Mail letters flying to the boys overseas. Mail from home is number one on their Hit Parade." They're doing the fightin', you do the writin'.

1st Lt. Donald P. Briggs: "I Sustain the Wings" is a presentation of the Army Air Forces Training Command and came to you from New York City.

NBC announcer: This is the National Broadcasting Company.

13May44 (Sat) 6:00-6:30PM EWT WEAF, NBC Vanderbilt Theatre, New York, New York
  I SUSTAIN THE WINGS broadcast   Audience

  ...

1st Lt. Donald P. Briggs: ... "It Must Be Jelly 'cause Jam Don't Shake Like That."
IT MUST BE JELLY ('Cause Jam Don't Shake Like That)
  Chant by the Ensemble

  ...

1st Lt. Donald P. Briggs: ... "Mother Machree."
MOTHER MACHREE (Old tune)
  1st Lt. Donald P. Briggs: Something new, Sergeant Johnny Desmond and the Crew Chiefs
    sing.
I COULDN'T SLEEP A WINK LAST NIGHT (New tune)
  Vocal refrain by Sergeant Johnny Desmond and the Crew Chiefs
  1st Lt. Donald P. Briggs: And now Sergeants Hucko and Privin singin' and playin' our
    tune borrowed from King Louie Armstrong.
I CAN'T GIVE YOU ANYTHING BUT LOVE (Baby) (Borrowed tune)
  Vocal refrain by Sergeant Michael A. Hucko
  1st Lt. Donald P. Briggs: Something blue song, you can't find them much bluer than the
    "Wang-Wang Blues."
WANG-WANG BLUES (Blue tune)
1st Lt. Donald P. Briggs: And here's where Sergeant Jerry Gray covers all the bases, and
  pitches all the curves in a new nine-inning arrangement of "I've Got a Heart Filled with
  Love."
I'VE GOT A HEART FILLED WITH LOVE (For You Dear)
  Vocal refrain by Sergeant Johnny Desmond, the Crew Chiefs and the Glee Club
1st Lt. Donald P. Briggs: Tomorrow marks the second anniversary of the Women's Army
  Corps. Originally the WACs were organized as an auxiliary of the Armed Forces, but
  their important and invaluable work for the three branches of the service, the Air, the
  Ground, and the Service Forces, entitle them to be recognized and accepted as an
  integral part of the Army and today they're serving on many fronts with America's
  fighting soldiers. We salute these partners in victory, and the men of the A.A.F. give
  a special vote of thanks to the Air WACs who, because of their technical skill and
  training, can truthfully say "I Sustain the Wings."
I SUSTAIN THE WINGS (closing theme)
  1st Lt. Donald P. Briggs: This is Lieutenant Don Briggs saying so long for the Band of
    the Training Command, the Crew Chiefs, Sergeants Jerry Gray, Brod Crawford, Mel
    Powell, Ray McKinley and Johnny Desmond. Hope to see you again next Saturday, same
    time, same station.

  ...

13May44 (Sat) 11:30PM-Midnight EWT WEAF, NBC Vanderbilt Theatre, New York, New York
  I SUSTAIN THE WINGS broadcast   Audience

THE ARMY AIR CORPS (opening fanfare)
1st Lt. Donald P. Briggs: "I Sustain the Wings"
I SUSTAIN THE WINGS (opening theme)
  1st Lt. Donald P. Briggs: "I Sustain the Wings." The Army Air Forces present the Band
    of the Training Command, with music from us to you. 1st Lt. Donald P. Briggs: Good
    evening, everybody. This is Lieutenant Don Briggs speaking for the Band of the
    Training Command and saying welcome to another program of "I Sustain the Wings."
    Tonight I'm pinch-hitting in the words department for Captain Glenn Miller, while
    Sergeant Jerry Gray does the leadin' in the music department. First off, a nice thick
    slice of music covered with something better than butter, "It Must Be Jelly 'cause Jam
    Don't Shake Like That."
IT MUST BE JELLY ('Cause Jam Don't Shake Like That)
  Chant by the Ensemble
1st Lt. Donald P. Briggs: Now the band with something on the sweet side, "Star Dust."
STAR DUST
Sgt. Broderick Crawford: When guys go overseas to fly one of Uncle Sam's bombers, they
  stop being separate persons and become a team. They taught me that while I was still in
  this country at Army Air Forces Training Command School learning to be an aerial gunner.
  Over there in the Pacific I found it was true. The fellows in a bomber crew live
  together, fly together, and fight together. But here's the tough thing, when we come
  back from overseas there's one member of the team we have to leave behind, the plane
  itself. You never expect to see her again and you feel kind of bad because it's like
  leaving an old friend. But sometimes the unexpected happens, as it did a few weeks ago,
  like right right here at this Nevada air field where I'm stationed now as a mechanic.

  ...

Incidental music
  Sgt. Broderick Crawford: ... up there where there's nothing but stars, but God. And
    there's always a tailwind to help you home and the takeoffs are never bumpy, and the
    landings always smooth. But until then, so long, Lucy. Take care of yourself.
1st Lt. Donald P. Briggs: And now it's medley time with something old, something new,
  something borrowed and something blue. Our old song, just as sweet as the gals that we
  officially honor tomorrow. So for the mothers of the boys in the Armed Forces, "Mother
  Machree."
MOTHER MACHREE (Old tune)
  1st Lt. Donald P. Briggs: Something new, Sergeant Johnny Desmond and the Crew Chiefs
    sing.
I COULDN'T SLEEP A WINK LAST NIGHT (New tune)
  Vocal refrain by Sergeant Johnny Desmond and the Crew Chiefs
  1st Lt. Donald P. Briggs: And now Sergeants Hucko and Privin singin' and playin' our
    tune borrowed from King Louie Armstrong.
I CAN'T GIVE YOU ANYTHING BUT LOVE (Baby) (Borrowed tune)
  Vocal refrain by Sergeant Michael A. Hucko
  1st Lt. Donald P. Briggs: Something blue song, you can't find 'em much bluer than the
    "Wang-Wang Blues."
WANG-WANG BLUES (Blue tune)
1st Lt. Donald P. Briggs: And here's where Sergeant Jerry Gray covers all the bases, and
  pitches all the curves in a new nine-inning arrangement of "I've Got a Heart Filled with
  Love."
I'VE GOT A HEART FILLED WITH LOVE (For You Dear)
  Vocal refrain by Sergeant Johnny Desmond, the Crew Chiefs and the Glee Club

1st Lt. Donald P. Briggs: Tomorrow marks the second anniversary of the Women's Army
  Corps. Originally the WACs were organized as an auxiliary of the Armed Forces, but
  their important and invaluable work for the three branches of the service, the Air, the
  Ground, and the Service Forces, entitle them to be recognized and accepted as an
  integral part of the Army and today they're serving on many fronts with America's
  fighting soldiers. We salute these partners in victory, and the men of the A.A.F. give
  a special vote of thanks to the Air WACs who, because of their technical skill and
  training, can truthfully say "I Sustain the Wings."
I SUSTAIN THE WINGS (closing theme)
  1st Lt. Donald P. Briggs: This is Lieutenant Don Briggs saying so long for the Band of
    the Training Command, the Crew Chiefs, Sergeants Jerry Gray, Brod Crawford, Mel
    Powell, Ray McKinley and Johnny Desmond. Hope to see you again next Saturday, same
    time, same station.
  Sgt. Broderick Crawford: Keep those V-Mail letters flyin' to the boys overseas. Mail
    from home is number one on their Hit Parade. They're doin' the fightin', you do the
    writin'.
1st Lt. Donald P. Briggs: "I Sustain the Wings" is a presentation of the Army Air Forces
  Training Command and came to you from New York City.
NBC announcer: This is the National Broadcasting Company.

20May44 (Sat) 6:00-6:30PM EWT WEAF, NBC Vanderbilt Theatre, New York, New York
  I SUSTAIN THE WINGS broadcast   Audience

THE ARMY AIR CORPS (opening fanfare)
1st Lt. Donald P. Briggs: "I Sustain the Wings"
I SUSTAIN THE WINGS (opening theme)
  1st Lt. Donald P. Briggs: "I Sustain the Wings." The Army Air Forces present the Band
  of the Training Command, with music from us to you.
Sgt. Broderick Crawford: This is Sergeant Broderick Crawford pinch-hitting for Captain
  Glenn Miller and saying hello for the Band of the Training Command, with Lieutenant Don
  Briggs, Sergeants Jerry Gray, Mel Powell, Johnny Desmond and Ray McKinley. For the take
  off tune tonight, an oldie with bright new clothes. Sergeant Jerry Gray leads the band
  in "Everybody Loves My Baby."
EVERYBODY LOVES MY BABY (But My Baby Don't Love Nobody but Me)
Sgt. Broderick Crawford: And here's some mighty easy listening, Sergeant Johnny Desmond
  and the Crew Chiefs do the vocalizing as the band plays "Poinciana."
POINCIANA (Song of the Tree)
  Vocal refrain by Sergeant Johnny Desmond and the Crew Chiefs
Sgt. Broderick Crawford: There are times that can only be described as a hush in history.
  Such a moment is this one. The world stands waiting on the eve of great events.
  Fascism has spoken its piece. Its hours are rushing out. The hands of the clock move
  relentlessly on, minute by minute, bringing nearer and nearer the day of decision. It
  is a moment that calls for a searching of hearts, a review of our reasons for fighting.
  That is why we believe you'll be interested in the thoughts that follow. They're the
  thoughts of a soldier now stationed overseas, written as he waits on the eve of that
  action that should see these same thoughts and hopes fulfilled. They are the thoughts
  of all of us, every American, our solemn answer in this hushed moment of history to the
  question "Why Do I Fight?"
Incidental music
  1st Lt. Donald P. Briggs: This is why I fight.
    I fight because it's my fight.
    I fight because my eyes are unafraid to look into other eyes. Because they've seen
    happiness and because they've seen suffering. Because they're curious and searching,
    because they're free.
    I fight because my ears can listen to both sides of a question. Because they can hear
    the groanings of a tormented people as well as the laughter of a free people. Because
    they're a channel for information, not a route for repetition. Because if I hear and
    do not think, I am deaf.
    I fight because my mouth does not fear to utter my opinions. Because though I am only
    one, my voice helps forge my destiny. Because I can speak from a soapbox or from a
    letter to the newspapers or from a question that I may ask my representatives in
    Congress. Because when my mouth speaks and can only say what everyone's forced to
    say, it is gagged.
    I fight because my knees kneel only to God.
    I fight because my feet can go where they please. Because they need no passport to go
    from New York to New Jersey and back again. Because if I want to leave my country I
    can go without being forced, without bribing, and without the lose of my savings.
    Because I can plant my feet in farm soil or city concrete without anybody's
    by-your-leave. Because when my feet walk only the way they're forced to walk, they're
    hobbled.
    I fight because of all of these and because I have a mind, a mind which is being
    trained in a free school to accept or to reject, to ponder and to weigh, a mind which
    knows the flowing stream of thought, not the stagnant swamp of blind obedience. A
    mind schooled to think for itself, to be curious, skeptical, to analyze, to formulate
    and to express its opinions. A mind capable of digesting the intellectual food it
    receives from a free press, because if a mind does not think, it is the brain of a
    slave.
    I fight because I think I'm as good as anybody else. Because of what other people
    have said better than ever I could; certain inalienable rights, right to life, liberty

and the pursuit of happiness; the government of the people, by the people and for the
people; give me liberty or give me death.
I fight because of my memory, the laughter and play of my childhood, the ball games I
was in and the better ones I watched, my mother telling me why my father and she came
to America at the turn of the century, my sisters marrying, my high school graduation,
the first time I saw a cow, the first year we could afford a vacation, there's the
crib at Camp Surprise Lake after the crowds had polluted Coney Island waters, the
hikes in the fall with the many-colored leaves falling, the weenie and marshmallow
roasts over a hot fire, the first time I voted, my first date and the slap in the face
I got instead of the kiss I attempted, the way the nostrum quack would alternate with
political orators on our street corner, yes, and seeing the changes for the better in
my neighborhood, the el going down and the streets being widened to let the sun in,
the new tenements replacing the old slums, the crowd applauding the time I came
through with a hit that won us the Borough Championship, the memories, which if people
like me do not fight, our children will never have.
I fight because I have something to fight for.
I fight because of the life I hope to live when the fighting's finished. Because that
life offers opportunity and security and the freedom to read and write and listen and
think and talk. Because, as before, my home will be my castle with the drawbridge
down only to those I invite. Because if I do not fight, life itself will be dead.
I fight because I believe in progress, not merely action. Because despite our faults,
there is hope in our manner of life. Because if we lose, there is no hope.
I fight because some day I'll want to get married, I want my children to be born into
a free world. Because my forefathers left me a heritage of freedom which is my duty
to pass on. Because if we lost, it would be a crime to have children.
I fight because it's an obligation. Because free people must fight to remain free.
Because when the freedom to one nation or one person is taken away, the lives of all
nations and all people are threatened. And because through our elected
representatives (I have the choice to fight or not to fight.
I fight not so much because of Pearl Harbor but because of what Pearl Harbor meant.
Because, finally, after skirmishes with the Ethiopians, the Manchurians, the Chinese,
the Austrians,) the Czechoslovakians, the Danes, the Spaniards and the Norwegians,
fascism is menacing us as we've never before been menaced. And because only the
craven will not defend themselves.
I fight because it's better to die than to live on one's knees.
I fight because only by fighting today will there be peace tomorrow.
I fight because I'm thankful that I'm not on the other side. Because, but for the
grace of God, or an accident of nature, the brutalized Nazi could have been me, and
but for my fighting, will be my child.
I fight in the fervent hope that those who follow me will not have to fight again, but
in the knowledge that if they have to, they will not be found wanting in the crisis.
I fight to remain free.
Sgt. Broderick Crawford: And now it's medley time, with something old, something new,
  something borrowed and something blue. The old tune, "In the Gloaming."
IN THE GLOAMING (Old tune)
  Sgt. Broderick Crawford: Something new, Sergeant Johnny Desmond sings "Fellow on a
  Furlough."
A FELLOW ON A FURLOUGH (New tune)
  Vocal refrain by Sergeant Johnny Desmond
  Sgt. Broderick Crawford: From friend Benny Goodman we borrow "Stompin' at the Savoy."
STOMPIN' AT THE SAVOY (Borrowed tune)
  Sgt. Broderick Crawford: That bluer than blue tune, "Deep Purple."
DEEP PURPLE (Blue tune)
JOIN THE WAC
  1st Lt. Donald P. Briggs: Women of America, march with Uncle Sam's army. Join the WAC.
  Vocal refrain by the Crew Chiefs
  1st Lt. Donald P. Briggs: Be an Air WAC, share in the fight, you'll share in the
  victory. The spirit that makes you join is the spirit that'll make the victory.
  Vocal refrain by the Crew Chiefs

Sgt. Broderick Crawford: Now a 21-gun salute to those gallant guys who keep 'em firing in Uncle Sam's giant bombers. Here's the Crew Chiefs and the whole gang with "Guns in the Sky."

GUNS IN THE SKY
Vocal refrain by Sergeant Johnny Desmond, the Crew Chiefs and the Glee Club

Sgt. Broderick Crawford: The world's biggest university, that's the Army Air Forces Training Command, whose job it is to train the men to fly our planes and to "Keep 'Em Flying." The graduates of the Training Command include not only pilots, navigators, bombardiers and gunners and men of the flying crews, but also the more than a million men of the ground crew. Each man on the ground is a specialist in his particular job, whether it be mechanic, weather observer, instrument man, armorer or radio man. He knows that his work is vital to the smooth and efficient operation of the A.A.F. Because he has an important job to do and does it well, it is no idle boast when each man of the ground crew says "I Sustain the Wings."

I SUSTAIN THE WINGS (closing theme)
Sgt. Broderick Crawford: This is Sergeant Brod Crawford saying so long for the Band of the Training Command, Lieutenant Don Briggs, the Crew Chiefs, Sergeants Jerry Gray, Mel Powell, Ray McKinley and Johnny Desmond. Hope to see you again next Saturday, same time, same station.
1st Lt. Donald P. Briggs: Write those V-Mail letters and "Keep 'Em Flying" to the boys overseas. Letters are a sure cure for the blues. They're doing the fightin', you do the writin'.

Sgt. Broderick Crawford: "I Sustain the Wings" is a presentation of the Army Air Forces Training Command and came to you from New York City.

NBC announcer: And this is the National Broadcasting Company.

20May44 (Sat) 11:30PM-Midnight EWT WEAF, NBC Vanderbilt Theatre, New York, New York
 I SUSTAIN THE WINGS broadcast   Audience

THE ARMY AIR CORPS (opening fanfare)
1st Lt. Donald P. Briggs: "I Sustain the Wings"
I SUSTAIN THE WINGS (opening theme)
  1st Lt. Donald P. Briggs: "I Sustain the Wings." The Army Air Forces present the Band
    of the Training Command, with music from us to you.
Sgt. Broderick Crawford: This is Sergeant Broderick Crawford pinch-hitting for Captain
  Glenn Miller and saying hello for the Band of the Training Command, Lieutenant Don
  Briggs, Sergeants Jerry Gray, Mel Powell, Johnny Desmond and Ray McKinley. For the take
  off tune tonight, an oldie with bright new clothes. Sergeant Jerry Gray leads the band
  in "Everybody Loves My Baby."
EVERYBODY LOVES MY BABY (But My Baby Don't Love Nobody but Me)
Sgt. Broderick Crawford: And here's some easy listening, Sergeant Johnny Desmond and the
  Crew Chiefs do the vocalizing as the band plays "Poinciana."
POINCIANA (Song of the Tree)
  Vocal refrain by Sergeant Johnny Desmond and the Crew Chiefs
Sgt. Broderick Crawford: There are times that can only be described as a hush in history.
  Such a moment is this one. The world stands waiting on the eve of great events.
  Fascism has spoken its piece. Its hours are rushing out. The hands of the clock move
  relentlessly on, minute by minute, bringing nearer and nearer the day of decision. It
  is a moment that calls for a searching of hearts, a review of our reasons for fighting.
  That is why we believe you'll be interested in the thoughts that follow. They're the
  thoughts of a soldier now stationed overseas, written as he waits on the eve of that
  action that should see these same thoughts and hopes fulfilled. They are the thoughts
  of all of us, every American, our solemn answer in this hushed moment of history to the
  question "Why Do I Fight?"
Incidental music
  1st Lt. Donald P. Briggs: This is why I fight.
    I fight because it's my fight.
    I fight because my eyes are unafraid to look into other eyes. Because they've seen
  happiness and because ...

    ...

  1st Lt. Donald P. Briggs: ... representatives I have the choice to fight or not to
    fight.
    I fight not so much because of Pearl Harbor but because of what Pearl Harbor meant.
  Because, finally, after skirmishes with the Ethiopians, the Manchurians, the Chinese,
  the Austrians, the Czechoslovakians, the Danes, the Spaniards and the Norwegians,
  fascism is menacing us as we've never before been menaced. Because only the craven
  will not defend themselves.
    I fight because it's better to die than to live on one's knees.
    I fight because only by fighting today will there be peace tomorrow.
    I fight because I'm thankful that I'm not on the other side. Because, for the grace
  of God, or an accident of nature, the brutalized Nazi could have been me, and but for
  my fighting, will be my child.
    I fight in the fervent hope that those who follow me will not have to fight again, but
  in the knowledge that if they have to, they will not be found wanting in the crisis.
    I fight to remain free.
Sgt. Broderick Crawford: And now it's medley time, with something old, something new,
  something borrowed and something blue. The old tune, "In the Gloaming."
IN THE GLOAMING (Old tune)
  Sgt. Broderick Crawford: Something new, Sergeant Johnny Desmond sings "Fellow on a
    Furlough."
A FELLOW ON A FURLOUGH (New tune)
  Vocal refrain by Sergeant Johnny Desmond
  Sgt. Broderick Crawford: From friend Benny Goodman we borrow "Stompin' at the Savoy."
STOMPIN' AT THE SAVOY (Borrowed tune)

Sgt. Broderick Crawford: That bluer than blue tune, "Deep Purple."
DEEP PURPLE (Blue tune)
JOIN THE WAC
  1st Lt. Donald P. Briggs: Women of America, march with Uncle Sam's army. Join the WAC.
  Vocal refrain by the Crew Chiefs
  1st Lt. Donald P. Briggs: Be an Air WAC, share in the fight and you'll share in the
    victory. The spirit that makes you join is the spirit that'll make the victory.
  Vocal refrain by the Crew Chiefs
Sgt. Broderick Crawford: Now a 21-gun salute to those gallant guys who keep 'em firing in
  Uncle Sam's giant bombers. Here's the Crew Chiefs and the whole gang with "Guns in the
  Sky."
GUNS IN THE SKY
  Vocal refrain by Sergeant Johnny Desmond, the Crew Chiefs and the Glee Club
Sgt. Broderick Crawford: The world's biggest university, that's the Army Air Forces
  Training Command, whose job it is to train the men to fly our planes and to "Keep 'Em
  Flying." The graduates of the Training Command include not only pilots, navigators,
  bombardiers and gunners and men of the flying crews, but also the more than a million
  men of the ground crew. Each man of the ground crew is a specialist in his particular
  job, whether it be mechanic, weather observer, instrument man, armorer or radio man.
  And he knows that his work is vital to the smooth and efficient operation of the A.A.F.
  Because he has an important job to do and does it well, it is no idle boast when each
  man of the ground crew says "I Sustain the Wings."
I SUSTAIN THE WINGS (closing theme)
  Sgt. Broderick Crawford: This is Sergeant Brod Crawford saying so long for the Band of
    the Training Command, Lieutenant Don Briggs, the Crew Chiefs, Sergeants Jerry Gray,
    Mel Powell, Ray McKinley and Johnny Desmond. Hope to see you again next Saturday,
    same time, same station.
  1st Lt. Donald P. Briggs: Write those V-Mail letters and "Keep 'Em Flying" to the boys
    overseas. Letters are a sure cure for the blues. They're doing the fightin', you do
    the writin'.
Sgt. Broderick Crawford: "I Sustain the Wings" is a presentation of the Army Air Forces
  Training Command and came to you from New York City.
NBC announcer: And this is the National Broadcasting Company.

27May44 (Sat) 6:00-6:30PM EWT WEAF, NBC Vanderbilt Theatre, New York, New York
  I SUSTAIN THE WINGS broadcast   Audience

  ...

IRRESISTIBLE YOU (New tune)
  Vocal refrain by Sergeant Johnny Desmond and the Crew Chiefs
  1st Lt. Donald P. Briggs: From the boss himself, Captain Glenn Miller, the Band of the
    Training Command borrows "Little Brown Jug."
LITTLE BROWN JUG (Borrowed tune)
  1st Lt. Donald P. Briggs: Something blue, "Rhapsody in Blue."
RHAPSODY IN BLUE (Blue tune)
JOIN THE WAC
  1st Lt. Donald P. Briggs: Women of America, march with Uncle Sam's army. Join the WAC.
  Vocal refrain by the Crew Chiefs
  1st Lt. Donald P. Briggs: Are you doing all you can? Be an Air WAC and be in on the
    fight. Join up, join in on the victory.
  Vocal refrain by the Crew Chiefs
1st Lt. Donald P. Briggs: Music makes the miles fly faster and here's a song that's
  flying a lot of them, the alma mater tune for the lads doing the training and the
  fighting the Air Force way.
THE ARMY AIR CORPS
  Vocal refrain by Sergeant Johnny Desmond, the Crew Chiefs and the Glee Club
1st Lt. Donald P. Briggs: Parachute rigging is the kind of insurance that pays off any
  time it's needed. The lives of the most precious cargoes ever carried in the air, Uncle
  Sam's pilots and crewmen, depend upon the job done by the parachute rigger, who, like
  thousands of other specialized technicians, is a graduate of the A.A.F. Training
  Command, the world's biggest university. Because of the knowledge and skill obtained in
  the Training Command, the parachute rigger and over a million fellow members of the
  A.A.F. ground crews translate by action the Latin words of their proud motto, "Sustineo
  Alas," "I Sustain the Wings."
I SUSTAIN THE WINGS (closing theme)
  1st Lt. Donald P. Briggs: This is Lieutenant Don Briggs saying so long for the Band of
    the Training Command, the Crew Chiefs, Sergeants Jerry Gray, Brod Crawford, Mel
    Powell, Ray McKinley and Johnny Desmond. Hope to see you again next Saturday, same
    time, same station.

  ...

27May44 (Sat) 11:30PM-Midnight EWT WEAF, NBC Vanderbilt Theatre, New York, New York
I SUSTAIN THE WINGS broadcast   Audience

THE ARMY AIR CORPS (opening fanfare)
1st Lt. Donald P. Briggs: "I Sustain the Wings"
I SUSTAIN THE WINGS (opening theme)
  1st Lt. Donald P. Briggs: "I Sustain the Wings." The Army Air Forces present the Band
    of the Training Command, with music from us to you
  1st Lt. Donald P. Briggs: Good evening, everybody. This is Lieutenant Don Briggs
    standing in for Captain Glenn Miller and saying hello for the Band of the Training
    Command, with Sergeants Jerry Gray, Brod Crawford, Ray McKinley, Johnny Desmond, and the
    Crew Chiefs. And here's Sergeant Jerry Gray leading the boys off in "I Hear You
    Screamin'."
I HEAR YOU SCREAMIN'
1st Lt. Donald P. Briggs: Playing for all the fellows and gals in uniform you can't go
  wrong with a love song. So, here's Sergeant Johnny Desmond to sing "Time Alone Will
  Tell."
TIME ALONE WILL TELL
  Vocal refrain by Sergeant Johnny Desmond
Incidental music
  Sgt. Broderick Crawford (as Charlie): If you folks were to say to me, "Charlie, tell us
    about some of the experiences you had as a gunner on a B-17 in the Pacific," I'd have
    to tell you that most of our trips were just routine.
  Sgt. Broderick Crawford: Nothing unusual happened because there'd been ...

  ...

1st Lt. Donald P. Briggs: And now it's medley time, saluting the mothers, wives, sisters
  and sweethearts of the men in the Armed Forces. Something old, something new, something
  borrowed and something blue. The old song, "Schubert's Serenade."
SCHUBERT'S SERENADE (Old tune)
  1st Lt. Donald P. Briggs: A song that's mighty new and mighty nice, Sergeant Johnny
    Desmond sings.
IRRESISTIBLE YOU (New tune)
  Vocal refrain by Sergeant Johnny Desmond and the Crew Chiefs
  1st Lt. Donald P. Briggs: From the boss himself, Captain Glenn Miller, the Band of the
    Training Command borrows "Little Brown Jug."
LITTLE BROWN JUG (Borrowed tune)
  1st Lt. Donald P. Briggs: Something blue, "Rhapsody in Blue."
RHAPSODY IN BLUE (Blue tune)
JOIN THE WAC
  1st Lt. Donald P. Briggs: Women of America, march with Uncle Sam's army. Join the WAC.
  Vocal refrain by the Crew Chiefs
  1st Lt. Donald P. Briggs: Are you doing all you can? Be an Air WAC and be in on the
    fight. Join up, join in on the victory.
  Vocal refrain by the Crew Chiefs
1st Lt. Donald P. Briggs: Music makes the miles fly faster and here's a song that's
  flying a lot of them, the alma mater tune for the lads doing the training and the
  fighting the Air Force way.
THE ARMY AIR CORPS
  Vocal refrain by Sergeant Johnny Desmond, the Crew Chiefs and the Glee Club
1st Lt. Donald P. Briggs: Parachute rigging is the kind of insurance that pays off any
  time it's needed. The lives of the most precious cargoes ever carried in the air, Uncle
  Sam's pilots and crewmen, depend upon the job done by the parachute rigger, who, like
  thousands of other specialized technicians, is a graduate of the A.A.F. Training
  Command, the world's biggest university. Because of the knowledge and skill obtained in
  the Training Command, the parachute rigger and over a million fellow members of the
  A.A.F. ground crews can proudly say "I Sustain the Wings."

I SUSTAIN THE WINGS (closing theme)

    1st Lt. Donald P. Briggs: This is Lieutenant Don Briggs saying so long for the Band of the Training Command with the Crew Chiefs, Sergeants Jerry Gray, Brod Crawford, Mel Powell, Ray McKinley and Johnny Desmond. Hope to see you again next Saturday, same time, same station.

    Sgt. Broderick Crawford: Keep those V-Mail letters flying to the boys overseas. Mail from home is number one on their Hit Parade. They're doing the fightin', you do the writin'.

1st Lt. Donald P. Briggs: "I Sustain the Wings" is a presentation of the Army Air Forces Training Command and came to you from New York City.

NBC Announcer: This is the National Broadcasting Company.

03Jun44 (Sat) 6:00-6:30PM EWT WEAF, NBC Vanderbilt Theatre, New York, New York
  I SUSTAIN THE WINGS broadcast   Audience

THE ARMY AIR CORPS (opening fanfare)
1st Lt. Donald P. Briggs: "I Sustain the Wings"
I SUSTAIN THE WINGS (opening theme)
  1st Lt. Donald P. Briggs: "I Sustain the Wings." The Army Air Forces present the Band
    of the Training Command, under the direction of Captain Glenn Miller. And now Captain
    Glenn Miller.
Captain Glenn Miller: Thank you, Lieutenant Don Briggs, and good evening, everybody.
  Speaking for the Crew Chiefs, Sergeants Jerry Gray, Brod Crawford, Mel Powell, Ray
  McKinley, Johnny Desmond, the gang, welcome to another program of "I Sustain the Wings."
  For your listening pleasure in the music department now, here's "Sun Valley Jump."
SUN VALLEY JUMP
Captain Glenn Miller: A soldier and a song, Sergeant Johnny Desmond singin' "Going My
  Way."
GOING MY WAY
  Vocal refrain by Sergeant Johnny Desmond
Incidental music
  1st Lt. Donald P. Briggs: Of all the men trained by the A.A.F. Training Command none is
    more important than the crew chief, the guiding genius of the bomber's crew. When the
    ships go out, his is the final O.K. When they come limping home from battle, the job
    of supervising the repair is his. He knows his plane like the face of an old friend.
    He knows how to fix it and, if need be, how to fight for it. And many are the stories
    of his skill and initiative in the face of emergency, such as our story tonight. It's
    told by one of the men in a bomber ground crew now stationed in England.
Sgt. Broderick Crawford (as Phil): Well, I guess the whole thing started that morning the
  Colonel posted a notice on the bulletin board listing the ships on the field that had
  the most missions without aborting. "Aborting," as you may know, means turning back
  from a mission because of engine failure or failing to take off with the others. There
  was quite a crowd of guys around the board when I happened to be there that day with
  Lefty, our crew chief on the Lazy Susan. Lefty noticed the bulletin first.
Lefty: Hey, Phil. Look at that.
Sgt. Broderick Crawford: What?
Lefty: That memo up there. Take a gander at it.
Sgt. Broderick Crawford: 864th Bomb Squadron, Lazy Susan, 46 missions, no abort. Hey,
  we're leading the whole bunch.
Lefty: Sure, what'd you think? We've got the best ground crew in the business. We'll
  hit the fifty mark before any of 'em.
Eddie: Ah, a hundred bucks say you won't.
Lefty: Well, look who's here, Phil, our old friend Eddie from the good ship Storm King.
Eddie: That's right. And I'm still saying you won't hit fifty before we do.
Phil: No. That crate of yours has only had 45 without an abort. We've had 46. Now, how
  are you going to beat us if we both fly every day?
Eddie: You guys'll mess up. You're bound to.
Phil: Not us, brother. We never miss.
Eddie: That hundred smackers still does my talking. Put up or shut up.
Lefty: Sure, we'll put up. Come around this afternoon. I'll collect our share, you have
  yours. We'll leave the stakes with Captain Mercer here at engineering.
Eddie: It's a bet?
Lefty: It's a bet.
Sgt. Broderick Crawford: Well, to tell the truth, I wasn't too sure about the whole
  thing. We'd been lucky, I knew that, and don't let on I told you, but those guys who
  tooled the Storm King with Eddie were plenty good. They had a first class bunch of boys
  on that bomber, inside and out. There wasn't much that ground crew of Eddie's didn't
  know. But then we had Lefty. Lefty, I guess must be the best crew chief in the Air
  Force and, brother, there's plenty of 'em. There wasn't nothing he didn't know about a
  plane. He was an engine mechanic, prop man, instrument expert and a half a dozen other
  specialists all rolled into one. Ingenuity was his middle name. Yeah, he was tops, our
  ace in the hole, so I didn't worry so much about that hundred, not at first. Then the

trouble started. That same day our ship came back with a busted rudder and we worked half the night getting it ready for the next morning's mission. The Storm King, not a scratch. And sure enough, when we started to work that evening, who shows up for a laugh but Eddie.

Eddie: Hello, boys. Having a little trouble, I see. Nothing trivial, I hope.

Lefty: I figured you'd be around. How'd you guys come out?

Eddie: Hardly worth mentioning, old man. Bit of paint chipped off here and there. I fixed it up myself while the pilot was unbuckling his safety belt.

Lefty: Yeah. Well, how about getting out of here and letting us work? If we need any help we'll send up flares.

Eddie: O.K. Sorry to rush off with you boys still working, but I've got a date in town with that little dark doll you've been seeing so much of, Phil. Can't let that gal get lonesome, you know.

Sgt. Broderick Crawford: If you don't get out of here I'll ...

Eddie: My, my. What a temper. Well, I'll see you. You can sign a statement and charge us for that wrench tomorrow.

Sgt. Broderick Crawford: Well, with Lefty pushing us and doing most of the work himself, we finished about three A.M. In the next two days our luck returned, the Lazy Susan came back untouched. Eddie's ship drew a bent bomb bay door and a broken hydraulic line. We felt too good to kid him. We had 49 missions now and the next day would make it fifty. We looked a cinch to win. I woke up nervous the next morning and went out early to look over the ship. Lefty warmed it up and we checked it inch by inch. Not a thing wrong, everything perfect. It looked like we couldn't lose. Take off time came and the ships started taxiing out to the runway. I saw Eddie watching our plane and looking pretty glum. Suddenly his face broke into a look of wild glee. He started jumping up and down and pointing to the Lazy Susan. I looked, too, and my heart did a flip-flop. The tail wheel on the ship was flatter than a stove lid. The other fellows in our crew saw it, too, and you could see 'em kissing that hundred bucks good bye. But not Lefty. He hesitated for a minute and then ...

Lefty: Mike, quick, bring the jack over here. We're gonna put a new wheel on it.

Sgt. Broderick Crawford: Aw, we can't do it, Lefty. The other ships are out on the runway. We're licked.

Lefty: We'll make it. Sam, bring up those tools. Wally, you hop in the tug, go down to supply and get a new tail wheel. Jump!

Sgt. Broderick Crawford: As the first plane took off, we went into action. Up went the tail of the Lazy Susan on a jack and hands reached for tools. Off came the fairing plate, hub cap, and retaining washer. Wrenches clattered on metal. Sweat was running into our eyes. Out on the runway we could hear the planes taking off one after the other. Only five of 'em left out there. The Storm King was next and then it was gone. As it roared away, the tail wheel wobbled and came loose. We jammed with the new one, fumbling in our haste. Back went the fairing, the wheel was on. But would there be time? The pilot began to clear the props and the engines started to roar. Out on the runway only three planes were left. One raced forward, that left two. Another one took off. Then, as the last one moved away, the Lazy Susan taxied out to her place at the head of the runway. She wasn't a second too soon. A signal from the tower and she was away after the others, climbing swiftly into the haze of the horizon. We'd made it, fifty missions. Thanks to Lefty, we made it. I looked at him. He was smiling as his eyes followed the Lazy Susan out of sight. Good old Lefty. I could read him like a book. Just looking at him I could see he'd forgotten all about the bet. Money didn't count. What counted for him was gettin' that plane in the air every day. Any minute I knew he was going to turn to me and say, "Phil, let's forget the bet. It doesn't matter. Just the pleasure of doing your job is enough. That's all that matters." Suddenly he noticed me watching him, smiled and looked back in the sky.

Lefty: Phil.

Sgt. Broderick Crawford: Yeah, Lefty?

Lefty: I was just thinking. Could we talk Eddie into betting we wouldn't reach 75 before he does? Suppose we could?

Incidental music

Captain Glenn Miller: Now it's medley time, saluting the mothers, wives, sisters and
   sweethearts of the men in the Armed Forces. Something old, something new, something
   borrowed and something blue. And the old song, "Mighty Lak' a Rose."
MIGHTY LAK' A ROSE (Old tune)
   Captain Glenn Miller: Something new, Sergeant Johnny Desmond sings.
AMOR (New tune)
   Vocal refrain by Sergeant Johnny Desmond
   Captain Glenn Miller: From the whole state of Tennessee we borrow "Chattanooga Choo
      Choo."
CHATTANOOGA CHOO CHOO (Borrowed tune)
   Vocal refrain by Technical Sergeant Ray McKinley and the Crew Chiefs
   Captain Glenn Miller: Last in the medley something blue, "Bye Bye Blues."
BYE BYE BLUES
Captain Glenn Miller: Now, just before we send it to the back of the book for a hard
   earned holiday, "Holiday for Strings."
HOLIDAY FOR STRINGS
1st Lt. Donald P. Briggs: Upon the shoulders of the crew chief rests the burden of
   mechanical efficiency of a plane. It's the business of the crew chief to check the work
   done on a ship, and on his final O.K. the plane takes to the air. The lives of the
   pilots and the crew, the success of the missions, the condition of the plane, these are
   responsibilities of the crew chief, who, like thousands of others, is a graduate of the
   A.A.F. Training Command, the world's biggest university. Through his knowledge and
   skill, obtained in the Training Command, the crew chief, like a million fellow members
   of the A.A.F., can proudly say "I Sustain the Wings."
I SUSTAIN THE WINGS (closing theme)
   Captain Glenn Miller: This is Captain Glenn Miller saying so long for the Band of the
      Training Command, the Crew Chiefs, Sergeants Jerry Gray, Brod Crawford, Mel Powell,
      Ray McKinley, Johnny Desmond. Hope to see you again next Saturday, same time, same
      station.
   1st Lt. Donald P. Briggs: Next Saturday night we'll bring the show in for a landing in
      Chicago, Illinois as we swing around the nation for the Fifth War Loan Drive.
1st Lt. Donald P. Briggs: "I Sustain the Wings" is a presentation of the Army Air Forces
   Training Command and came to you from New York City.
I SUSTAIN THE WINGS (closing theme)
NBC announcer: This is the National Broadcasting Company.
NBC chimes

The parts of Lefty and Eddie were played by Cpl. Paul A. Dubov and another member of the
band.

03Jun44 (Sat) 11:30PM-Midnight EWT WEAF, NBC Vanderbilt Theatre, New York, New York
  I SUSTAIN THE WINGS broadcast   Audience

THE ARMY AIR CORPS (opening fanfare)
1st Lt. Donald P. Briggs: "I Sustain the Wings"
I SUSTAIN THE WINGS (opening theme)
  1st Lt. Donald P. Briggs: "I Sustain the Wings." The Army Air Forces present the Band
    of the Training Command, under the direction of Captain Glenn Miller. And now Captain
    Glenn Miller.
Captain Glenn Miller: Thank you, Lieutenant Don Briggs, and good evening, everybody.
  Speaking for the Crew Chiefs, Sergeants Jerry Gray, Brod Crawford, Mel Powell, Ray
  McKinley, Johnny Desmond, the whole gang, welcome to another program of "I Sustain the
  Wings." For your listening pleasure in the music department here's "Sun Valley Jump."
SUN VALLEY JUMP
Captain Glenn Miller: A soldier and a song, Sergeant Johnny Desmond singing "Going My
  Way."
GOING MY WAY
  Vocal refrain by Sergeant Johnny Desmond
Incidental music
  1st Lt. Donald P. Briggs: Of all the men trained by the A.A.F. Training Command none is
    more important than the crew chief, the guiding genius of the bomber's crew. When the
    ships go out, his is the final O.K. When they come limping home from battle, the job
    of supervising the repair is his. He knows his plane like the face of an old friend.
    He knows how to fix it and, if need be, how to fight for it. Many are the stories of
    his skill and initiative in the face of emergency, such as our story tonight. It's
    told by one of the men in a bomber ground crew now stationed in England.
Sgt. Broderick Crawford (as Phil): Well, I guess the whole thing started that morning the
  Colonel posted a notice on the bulletin board listing the ships on the field that had
  the most missions without aborting. "Aborting," as you may know, means turning back
  from a mission because of engine failure or failing to take off with the others. There
  was quite a crowd of guys around the board when I happened to be there with Lefty, our
  crew chief on the Lazy Susan. Lefty noticed the bulletin first.
Lefty: Hey, Phil. Look at that.
Sgt. Broderick Crawford: What?
Lefty: That memo up there. Take a gander at it.
Sgt. Broderick Crawford: 864th Bomb Squadron, Lazy Susan, 46 missions, no abort. Hey,
  we're leading the whole bunch.
Lefty: Sure, what'd you think? We've got the best ground crew in the business. We'll
  hit the fifty mark before any of 'em.
Eddie: Hundred bucks say you won't.
Lefty: Well, look who's here, Phil, our old friend Eddie from the good ship Storm King.
Eddie: That's right. And I'm still saying you won't hit fifty before we do.
Phil: No. That crate of yours has had only had 45 without an abort. Now, we've had 46.
  How are you going to beat us if we both fly every day?
Eddie: You guys'll mess up. You're bound to.
Phil: Not us, brother. We never miss.
Eddie: That hundred smackers still does my talking. Put up or shut up.
Lefty: Sure, we'll put up. Come around this afternoon. I'll collect our share, you have
  yours. We'll leave the stakes with Captain Mercer here at engineering.
Eddie: It's a bet?
Lefty: It's a bet.
Sgt. Broderick Crawford: Well, to tell the truth, I wasn't too sure about the whole
  thing. We'd been lucky, I knew that, and don't let on I told you, but those guys who
  tooled the Storm King with Eddie were plenty good. They had a first class bunch of boys
  on that bomber, inside and out. There wasn't much that ground crew of Eddie's didn't
  know. But then we had Lefty. Lefty, I guess must be the best crew chief in the Air
  Force and, brother, there's plenty of 'em. There wasn't nothing he didn't know about a
  plane. He was an engine mechanic, prop man, instrument expert and a half a dozen other
  specialists all rolled into one. Ingenuity was his middle name. Yeah, he was tops, our
  ace in the hole, so I didn't worry so much about that hundred, not at first. Then the

trouble started. That same day our ship came back with a busted rudder and we worked half the night getting it ready for the next morning's mission. The Storm King, uh, uh, not a scratch. Sure enough, when we started to work that evening, who shows up for a laugh but Eddie.

Eddie: Hello, boys. Having a little trouble, I see. Nothing trivial, I hope.

Lefty: I figured you'd be around. How'd you guys come out?

Eddie: Well, hardly worth mentioning, old man. Bit of paint chipped off here and here. I fixed it up myself while the pilot was unbuckling his safety belt.

Lefty: Yeah. Well, how about getting out of here and lettin' us work? If we need any help we'll, ah, send up flares.

Eddie: O.K. Sorry to rush off with you boys still working, but I've got a date in town with that little dark doll you've been seeing so much of, Phil. Can't let that gal get lonesome, you know.

Sgt. Broderick Crawford: Look, if you don't get out of here I'll ...

Eddie: My, my. What a temper. Well, I'll see you. You can sign a statement and charge us for that wrench tomorrow.

Sgt. Broderick Crawford: With Lefty pushing us and doing most of the work himself, we finished about three A.M. In the next two days our luck returned, the Lazy Susan came back untouched. Eddie's ship drew a bent bomb bay door and a broken hydraulic line. We felt too good to kid him. We had 49 missions now and the next day would make it fifty. We looked a cinch to win. I woke up nervous that next morning and went out early to look the ship over. Lefty warmed it up and we checked it inch by inch. Not a thing wrong, everything perfect. It looked like we couldn't lose. Take off time came and the ships started taxiing out to the runway. I saw Eddie watching our plane and looking pretty glum. Suddenly his face broke into a look of wild glee. He started jumping up and down and pointing to the Lazy Susan. I looked, too, and my heart did a flip-flop. The tail wheel on our ship was flatter than a stove lid. The other fellows in our crew saw it, too, and you could see 'em kissing that hundred bucks good bye. But not Lefty. He hesitated for a minute and then ...

Lefty: Mike, quick, bring a jack over here. We're gonna put a new wheel on.

Sgt. Broderick Crawford: Aw, we can't do it, Lefty. The other ships are out on the runway already. We're licked.

Lefty: We'll make it. Sam, bring up those tools. Wally, you hop in the tug, go down to supply and get a new tail wheel. Jump!

Sgt. Broderick Crawford: As the first plane took off, we went into action. Up went the tail of the Lazy Susan on a jack and hands reached for tools. Off came the fairing plate, hub cap, and retaining washer. Wrenches clattered on metal. Sweat was runnin' down in our eyes. Out on the runway we could hear the planes taking off one after the other. Only five left out there. The Storm King was next and then it was gone. As it roared away, the tail wheel wobbled and came loose. We jammed on the new one, fumbling in our haste. Back went the fairing and the wheel was on. But would there be time? The pilot began to clear the props and the engines started to roar. Out on the runway only three planes were left. One raced forward, that left two. Another one took off. Then, as the last one moved away, the Lazy Susan taxied out to her place at the head of the runway. Not a second too soon. A signal from the tower and she was away after the others, climbing swiftly into the haze of the horizon. Yeah, We'd made it, fifty missions. Thanks to Lefty, we'd made it. I looked at him. He was smiling a bit as his eyes followed the Lazy Susan out of sight. Good old Lefty. I could read him like a book. Just looking at him I could see he'd forgotten all about the bet. Money didn't count. What counted for him was gettin' that plane in the air every day. Any minute I knew he was going to turn to me and say, "Phil, let's forget the bet. It doesn't matter. Just the pleasure of doing our job is enough. That's all that matters." Suddenly he noticed me watching him, smiled and looked up at the sky.

Lefty: Phil.

Sgt. Broderick Crawford: Yeah, Lefty?

Lefty: I was just thinking. Could we talk Eddie into betting we wouldn't reach 75 before he does? Suppose we could?

Incidental music

Captain Glenn Miller: Something old, something new, something borrowed and something blue means medley time. The old song tonight, "Mighty Lak' a Rose."
MIGHTY LAK' A ROSE (Old tune)
    Captain Glenn Miller: Something new, Sergeant Johnny Desmond sings.
AMOR (New tune)
    Vocal refrain by Sergeant Johnny Desmond
    Captain Glenn Miller: From the whole state of Tennessee we borrow "Chattanooga Choo Choo."
CHATTANOOGA CHOO CHOO (Borrowed tune)
    Vocal refrain by Technical Sergeant Ray McKinley and the Crew Chiefs
    Captain Glenn Miller: Something blue, "Bye Bye Blues."
BYE BYE BLUES
Captain Glenn Miller: Now, just before we send it back of the book for a hard earned holiday, here's "Holiday for Strings."
HOLIDAY FOR STRINGS
1st Lt. Donald P. Briggs: Upon the shoulders of the crew chief rests the burden of mechanical efficiency of a plane. It's the business of the crew chief to check the work done on a ship, and on his final O.K. the plane takes to the air. The lives of the pilots and the crew, the success of the missions, the condition of the plane, these are responsibilities of the crew chief, who, like thousands of others, is a graduate of the A.A.F. Training Command, the world's biggest university. Through his knowledge and skill, obtained in the Training Command, the crew chief, like a million fellow members of the A.A.F., can proudly say "I Sustain the Wings."
I SUSTAIN THE WINGS (closing theme)
    Captain Glenn Miller: This is Captain Glenn Miller saying so long for the Band of the Training Command, the Crew Chiefs, Sergeants Jerry Gray, Brod Crawford, Mel Powell, Ray McKinley, Johnny Desmond and Lieutenant Briggs. Hope to see you again next Saturday, same time, same station.
    1st Lt. Donald P. Briggs: Next Saturday night we'll bring the show in for a landing in Chicago, Illinois as we swing around the nation for the Fifth War Loan Drive.
1st Lt. Donald P. Briggs: "I Sustain the Wings" is a presentation of the Army Air Forces Training Command and came to you from New York City.
NBC announcer: This is the National Broadcasting Company.

The parts of Lefty and Eddie were played by Cpl. Paul A. Dubov and another member of the band.

10Jun44 (Sat) 5:00-5:30PM CWT NBC, Service Men's Center No. 2, Chicago, Illinois
  I SUSTAIN THE WINGS broadcast   Audience

THE ARMY AIR CORPS (opening fanfare)
  1st Lt. Donald P. Briggs: "I Sustain the Wings."
I SUSTAIN THE WINGS (opening theme)
  1st Lt. Donald P. Briggs: "I Sustain the Wings." The Army Air Forces present the Band
    of the Training Command under the direction of Captain Glenn Miller. And now Captain
    Glenn Miller.
Captain Glenn Miller: Thank you, Lieutenant Don Briggs, and good evening, everybody.
  It's been a big week for our side. Over on the beaches of Normandy our boys have fired
  the opening guns of the long awaited drive to liberate the world. And over here the
  folks who are backing up those boys are staging another big push of their own, the Fifth
  War Loan Drive. To lend a hand with the band we're swinging around the countryside
  ourselves to do what we can to keep those invasion dollars moving over to the fighting
  front where they're needed in the shape of guns, tanks and planes. And tonight we're at
  the Service Men's Center here in Chicago where already over twelve million service men
  and women have been guests of the city of Chicago. Now to get to a little music here
  are the boys with their rocket gun version of "Flying Home."
FLYING HOME
Captain Glenn Miller: Now here's Sergeant Johnny Desmond.
LONG AGO (And Far Away)
  Vocal refrain by Sergeant Johnny Desmond
Incidental music
  1st Lt. Donald P. Briggs: As the quitting whistle blows at a large war plant in Denver,
    Colorado, the men of the day shift leave their benches and machines and file over to
    the office entrance. It's payday and the pay line is forming.
Corporal Paul Dubov (as Joe): Next man.
Sergeant Broderick Crawford (as Mike McGuire): Mike McGuire.
Corporal Paul Dubov: Mike McGuire, let --- let's see. Here's your envelope. Say, it
  looks kind of fat, doesn't it?
Sergeant Broderick Crawford: Yeah, yeah --- I had a pretty good week I guess.
Corporal Paul Dubov: I suppose you'll be buying some new tires for that jalopy of yours,
  huh?
Sergeant Broderick Crawford: Wrong number, Joe. I ain't buyin' nothin' I don't have to.
  Any extra dough I get is goin' right into War Bonds. Now that I think about it, how
  about putting me down for another bond on that payroll plan of yours?
Corporal Paul Dubov: Here, let me look at your card. Mavic, McGerritt, McGerritt,
  McGuire. Here it is. It says here you're buying two bonds a month, Mike.
Sergeant Broderick Crawford: Yeah, well make it three. It's gonna take a lot of 'em,
  bonds to win this thing, Joe. A lot of 'em. You know what it costs just to get one of
  them big bombers off the ground?
Corporal Paul Dubov: Probably plenty.
Sergeant Broderick Crawford: Plenty, he says. It takes about one and one-half million
  dollars counting the costs of the plane and training the crew.
Corporal Paul Dubov: I never thought it was that much.
Sergeant Broderick Crawford: Well, it is. Go ahead, put me down for that other bond.

1st Lt. Donald P. Briggs: It's H-Hour, D-Day. The breeze of approaching dawn stirs the
  mist over the English countryside. The hour, long awaited, gropes for fulfillment. The
  hand is clinched, the blow prepares. On the airfield the propeller blades of the giant
  bomber shimmer and twinkle, revolving slowly in the first rays of light from the East.
  In the shadows the ground crews stand silent in little groups as the bombers move out to
  the runway. The sparrows nesting under the eaves of the barracks watch in wonder as
  these strange birds of the night waddle slowly across the field. The waist gunners wave
  from their windows. The signal is given. With a spurt of dark smoke from its engines
  the lead bomber gathers itself together and leaps down the runway. Then slowly, gently
  it lifts, it rises from the runway, its nose glimmering in the dawn, pointed toward the
  invasion coast of France.

1st Lt. Donald P. Briggs: It's eight o'clock in Milwaukee, Wisconsin. Two men are just coming out of a newsreel theater, talking as they pass through the lobby to the street.
T/Sgt. Ray McKinley: Yeah, and what about those last shots, the pictures of the pre-invasion raid on the French coast? Boy, did they plaster that place.
Corporal Paul Dubov (as Ed): Boy, I'll say. Say, I wonder how much it costs for a raid like that? A thousand planes.
T/Sgt. Ray McKinley: I don't know. Seems like I read it takes better than a thousand bucks just for one plane for gas alone.
Corporal Paul Dubov: Huh, not to mention a million dollars worth of nerve. How those guys in the bombers keep it up day after day is more than I know.
T/Sgt. Ray McKinley: Yeah, it's rough, all right. Funny thing, Ed, all the time I was watching those kids in the picture I kept wanting to reach out and help them, push them along or something, you know what I mean.
Corporal Paul Dubov: Yeah, well, what's stopping us?
T/Sgt. Ray McKinley: Huh?
Corporal Paul Dubov: See that booth over there in the lobby?
T/Sgt. Ray McKinley: Yeah.
Corporal Paul Dubov: They sell War Bonds there. If you want to help those kids along --- well, what are we waiting for?
T/Sgt. Ray McKinley: Well, who's waiting. I'm way ahead of you. Come on, we'll give those guys in the bombers a boost.

1st Lt. Donald P. Briggs: Over the quiet sleeping English hills the bomber soars. Flocks of sheep in the fields far below look up as its sudden shadow races over the long meadow grass and over the smoke of early morning chimneys, the trees and shadowy country lanes. Then the glittering wind-whipped channel below, crawling with barges, transports, destroyers, stretching endlessly toward the chalky cliffs of Normandy in the distance where patches of smoke and flame mark the first hard won beachheads. The pilot, white-lipped, watches the battle below, the navigator bends over his charts plotting the course of the bomber straight at the railroad yards of Rouen. The enemy is frantically rushing up troops to meet our knock-out blow. The gunners swing their guns idly back and forth, squinting at the clouds on the horizon for enemy fighters and flak. As the bomber gains height the invasion coast below flows into a pattern of green and blue, the chessboard of war over which the bombers move. And leaving long vapor trails behind it, the formation roars through the freezing air pointed like a spear toward Rouen.

1st Lt. Donald P. Briggs: In Dayton, Ohio in a downtown auditorium a crowd is gathered for a big bond rally. The speaker is auctioning off bonds.
Sergeant Broderick Crawford: All right, thank you, thank you, folks, that was wonderful. A thousand dollars for this German field helmet brought back from Italy. How much for this deck of playing cards? It was the personal property of a bomber gunner over in England. A boy from right here in Dayton. Let me hear the first bid.
Voice from audience: Five hundred dollars.
Sergeant Broderick Crawford: Five hundred, five hundred. Will anybody raise that? I'm not going to let this go for less than two thousand, just about what it costs to buy the ammunition that gunner and his pals'll need on one mission. Two thousand, who'll buy these bullets?
Voice from audience: Seven fifty.
Sergeant Broderick Crawford: I hear seven fifty. Who'll make it a thousand? Who'll pass the ammunition to these kids?
Voices from audience: One thousand. One thousand five hundred. Two thousand.

1st Lt. Donald P. Briggs: As the huge bomber groans nearer and nearer the target the fighters swarm up desperately, wings glinting in the early sun, dancing in the gunners' sights like dragon flies darting over a blue pond in summer. Bursts of orange flame wink on their wings as they feel for the bomber with their cannon. Then suddenly the bomber's guns shutter in reply. Threads of flame crisscross the blue air between bombers and fighters as the glowing tracers race from the turrets. The guns burn hot beneath the hands of the sweating gunners. Empty shells cascade and dance on the floor of the bomber. Small fighters dive in, guns spurting fire, get through this hurricane

of lead and death, the bomber flies on, shaken with flak, riddled with bullets, yet tied
to its purpose, fighting its way to the target just ahead, Rouen, with its sprawling
maze of railroad tracks and shops spread out below in the smoky sunlight. In the
glassed-in nose of the bomber the bombardier hunches over his instruments. He sees the
target, trapped like a frightened fly on the cross hairs of his bombsight. His hand
creeps out to the bomb release and then silently the bombs stream out of the plane
tumbling down, growing smaller and smaller until they flower in fire on the earth below.
The bombers fly on. On the wings of America's patriotism they fly on. The roar of
their engines is the voice of America. The thunder of their bombs the pledge of a
united people at war, working, sacrificing, buying the bombs that are making the
invasion possible. What Americans have done and are doing is known to our enemies.
They know that their only hope is that we're too soft to carry this fight to the finish.
But that hope is hopeless. Each plume of smoke from a ruined German rail center or
blasted Jap island is another milestone on the road to Berlin and Tokyo. The fight is
on. The bombers are flying and they'll keep on flying until those who took up the sword
in hate shall lay it down in death and defeat and victory is ours.

Incidental music

Captain Glenn Miller: And now it's medley time. That means something old, something new,
  something borrowed and something blue. The old song, "My Buddy."

MY BUDDY (Old tune)

  Captain Glenn Miller: Something new, Sergeant Desmond sings ...

NOW I KNOW (New tune)

  Vocal refrain by Sergeant Johnny Desmond
  Captain Glenn Miller: From friend Harry James we borrow "Music Makers."

MUSIC MAKERS (Borrowed tune)

  Captain Glenn Miller: For something blue, "Farewell Blues."

FAREWELL BLUES (Blue tune)

Captain Glenn Miller: And now the band playing, Sergeant Desmond, the Crew Chiefs singing
  "Poinciana."

POINCIANA (Song of the Tree)

  Vocal refrain by Sergeant Johnny Desmond and the Crew Chiefs

Sergeant Broderick Crawford: To keep those planes firing and fighting it takes hard work,
  courage, and skill. But that's not all, it takes money as well, the dollars you've been
  putting into War Bonds. The Fifth War Loan Drive is your chance to share in the
  invasion, to keep the sky over those Normandy beaches ours and ours alone. So buy bonds
  and hold on to 'em. That way you can join in the proud boast of every man of the Army
  Air Forces Training Command and say I too Sustain the Wings.

I SUSTAIN THE WINGS (closing theme)

  Captain Glenn Miller: This is Captain Glenn Miller saying so long for all our gang.
    Next week "I Sustain the Wings" will be brought to you by another band of the Training
    Command of the Army Air Forces with Captain Bob Jennings the C.O. and the music under
    the direction of Sergeant Harry Bluestone. We've enjoyed playing for you and we hope
    you've enjoyed listening to us.

  1st Lt. Donald P. Briggs: Don't forget to listen again to "I Sustain the Wings"
    nex-next Saturday, same time, same station and remember, keep those V-Mails flying to
    the boys overseas. They're doin' the fighting, you do the writin'.

1st Lt. Donald P. Briggs: "I Sustain the Wings" is a presentation of the Army Air Forces
  Training Command and came to you from Chicago, Illinois.

NBC announcer: This is the National Broadcasting Company.

NBC chimes

10Jun44 (Sat) 10:30-11:00PM CWT   NBC, Service Men's Center No. 2, Chicago, Illinois
I SUSTAIN THE WINGS broadcast
                                                                                    Audience

THE ARMY AIR CORPS (opening fanfare)
  1st Lt. Donald P. Briggs: "I Sustain the Wings."
I SUSTAIN THE WINGS (opening theme)
  1st Lt. Donald P. Briggs: "I Sustain the Wings." The Army Air Forces present the Band
    of the Training Command under the direction of Captain Glenn Miller. And now Captain
    Glenn Miller.
Captain Glenn Miller: Thank you, Lieutenant Don Briggs, and good evening, everybody.
    It's been a big week for our side. Over on the beaches of Normandy our boys have fired
    the opening guns of the long awaited drive to liberate the world. Over here the folks
    who are backing up those boys are staging another big push of their own, the Fifth War
    Loan Drive. And that's to lend a hand with the band, as far as we're concerned, for
    swinging around the --- we're swinging around the countryside ourselves to do all we can
    to keep those invasion dollars moving over to the fighting front where they're needed in
    the shape of guns, tanks and planes. Tonight we're broadcasting from the Service Men's
    Center here in Chicago where already over twelve million service men and women have been
    guests of the city of Chicago. Getting to the music department now here are the boys
    with their rocket gun version of "Flying Home."
FLYING HOME
Captain Glenn Miller: Nice going, Lieutenant, that's great. Atta boy ---. Now here's
    Sergeant Johnny Desmond.
LONG AGO (And Far Away)
  Vocal refrain by Sergeant Johnny Desmond
Incidental music
  1st Lt. Donald P. Briggs: As the quitting whistle blows at a large war plant in Denver,
    Colorado, the men of the day shift leave their benches and machines and file over to
    the office entrance. It's payday and the pay line is forming.
Corporal Paul Dubov (as Joe): Next man.
Sergeant Broderick Crawford (as Mike McGuire): Mike McGuire.
Corporal Paul Dubov: Mike McGuire, let's see, ah. Oh, here's your envelope. Say, it
    looks kind of fat, doesn't it?
Sergeant Broderick Crawford: Yeah, a little. Had a pretty good week I guess.
Corporal Paul Dubov: I suppose you'll be buying some new tires for that jalopy of yours,
    huh?
Sergeant Broderick Crawford: You got the wrong number, Joe. I ain't buyin' nothin' I
    don't have to. Any extra dough I get's goin' right into War Bonds. Say, now that I
    think about it, how about putting me down for another bond on that payroll plan of
    yours?
Corporal Paul Dubov: Well, let me look at your card. Mavic, McGerritt, McGuire. Here it
    is. It says here you're buying two bonds a month, Mike.
Sergeant Broderick Crawford: Well, make it three. It's gonna take a lot of bonds to win
    this thing, Joe. A lot of 'em. You know what it costs just to get one of them big
    bombers off the ground?
Corporal Paul Dubov: Probably plenty.
Sergeant Broderick Crawford: Plenty, he says. It takes about one and one-half million
    dollars counting the costs of the plane and training the crew.
Corporal Paul Dubov: Huh, I never thought it was that much.
Sergeant Broderick Crawford: Well, it is. Go on, put me down for that other bond, will
    you?
Corporal Paul Dubov: Sure.

1st Lt. Donald P. Briggs: It's H-Hour, D-Day. The breeze of approaching dawn stirs the
    mist over the English countryside. The hour, long awaited, gropes for fulfillment. The
    hand is clinched, the blow prepares. On the airfield the propeller blades of the giant
    bomber shimmer and twinkle, revolving slowly in the first rays of light from the East.
    In the shadows the ground crews stand silent in little groups as the bombers move out to
    the runway. The sparrows nesting under the eaves of the barracks watch in wonder as
    these strange birds of the night waddle slowly across the field. The waist gunners wave

from their windows. The signal is given. With a spurt of dark smoke from its engines
the lead bomber gathers itself together and leaps down the runway. Then slowly, gently
it lifts, it rises from the runway, its nose glimmering in the dawn, pointed toward the
invasion coast of France.

1st Lt. Donald P. Briggs: It's eight o'clock in Milwaukee, Wisconsin. Two men are just
coming out of a newsreel theater, talking as they pass through the lobby to the street.
T/Sgt. Ray McKinley: Hey, how 'bout those last shots, the pictures of the pre-invasion
raid on the French coast? Boy, did they plaster that place.
Corporal Paul Dubov (as Ed): Wonder how much it costs for a raid like that? A thousand
planes.
T/Sgt. Ray McKinley: I don't know. Seems like I read it takes better than a thousand
bucks just for one plane for gas alone.
Corporal Paul Dubov: Say, and not to mention a million dollars worth of nerve. How those
guys in the bombers keep it up day after day is more than I know.
T/Sgt. Ray McKinley: Yeah, it's rough, all right. Funny thing, Ed, you know all the time
I was watching those kids in the picture I kept wanting to reach out and help 'em, push
'em along or something, you know what I mean.
Corporal Paul Dubov: Well, what's stopping us?
T/Sgt. Ray McKinley: What's that?
Corporal Paul Dubov: See that booth over there in the lobby?
T/Sgt. Ray McKinley: Yeah.
Corporal Paul Dubov: They sell War Bonds there and if you want to help those kids along,
what are you waitin' for?
T/Sgt. Ray McKinley: Well, who's waiting. I'm way ahead of you. Come on, we'll give
those guys in the bombers a boost.

1st Lt. Donald P. Briggs: Over the quiet sleeping English hills the bomber soars. Flocks
of sheep in the fields far below look up as its sudden shadow races over the long meadow
grass, over the smoke of early morning chimneys, the trees and shadowy country lanes.
Then the glittering wind-whipped channel below, crawling with barges, transports,
destroyers, stretching endlessly toward the chalky cliffs of Normandy in the distance
where patches of smoke and flame mark the first hard won beachheads. The pilot,
white-lipped, watches the battle below, the navigator bends over his charts plotting the
course of the bomber straight at the railroad yards of Rouen where the enemy is
frantically rushing up troops to meet our knock-out blow. The gunners swing their guns
idly back and forth, squinting at the clouds on the horizon for enemy fighters and flak.
As the bomber gains height the invasion coast below flows into a pattern of green and
blue, the chessboard of war over which the bombers move. And leaving long vapor trails
behind it, the formation roars through the freezing air pointed like a spear toward
Rouen.
1st Lt. Donald P. Briggs: In Dayton, Ohio in a downtown auditorium a crowd is gathered
for a big bond rally. The speaker is auctioning off bonds.
Sergeant Broderick Crawford: All right, thank you, thank you, folks, that's wonderful. A
thousand dollars for this German field helmet brought back from Italy. How much for
this deck of playing cards? It was the personal property of a bomber gunner over
England. A boy right from Dayton. Let me hear the first bid.
Voice from audience: Five hundred dollars.
Sergeant Broderick Crawford: Five hundred dollars, come on now, let's go. Will anybody
raise that? I'm not going to take less than two thousand, folks, just about what it
costs to buy ammunition that gunner and his pals need on a mission. Two thousand,
who'll buy these bullets?
Voice from audience: Seven hundred and fifty.
Sergeant Broderick Crawford: I hear seven hundred and fifty. Who'll make it a thousand?
Who'll pass the ammunition to these kids?
Voices from audience: One thousand. One thousand five hundred. Two thousand.
1st Lt. Donald P. Briggs: As the huge bomber groans nearer and nearer the target the
fighters swarm up desperately, wings glinting in the early sun, dancing in the gunners'
sights like dragon flies darting over a blue pond in summer. Bursts of orange flame
wink on their wings as they feel for the bomber with their cannon. Then suddenly the

bomber's guns shutter in reply. Threads of flame crisscross the blue air between bombers and fighters as the glowing tracers race from the turrets. The guns burn hot beneath the hands of the sweating gunners. Empty shells cascade and dance on the floor of the bomber. More fighters dive in, guns spurting fire, get through this hurricane of lead and death, the bomber flies on, shaken with flak, riddled with bullets, yet tied to its purpose, fighting its way to the target just ahead, Rouen, with its sprawling maze of railroad tracks and shops spread out below in the smoky sunlight. In the glassed-in nose of the bomber the bombardier hunches over his instruments. He sees the target, trapped like a frightened fly in the cross hairs of his bombsight. His hand creeps out to the bomb release and then silently the bombs stream out of the plane tumbling down, growing smaller and smaller until they flower in fire on the earth below. The bombers fly on. On the wings of America's patriotism they fly on. The roar of their engines is the voice of America. The thunder of their bombs the pledge of a united people at war, working, sacrificing, buying the bombs that are making the invasion possible. What Americans have done and are doing is known to our enemies. They know that their only hope is that we're too soft to carry this fight to the finish. But that hope is hopeless. Each plume of smoke from a ruined German rail center or blasted Jap island is another milestone on the road to Berlin and Tokyo. The fight is on. The bombers are flying and they'll keep on flying until those who took up the sword in hate shall lay it down in death and defeat and victory is ours.

Incidental music

Captain Glenn Miller: And now it's medley time, something old, something new, something borrowed and something blue. The old song, "My Buddy."

MY BUDDY (Old tune)

Captain Glenn Miller: Something new, Sergeant Desmond sings ...

NOW I KNOW (New tune)

Vocal refrain by Sergeant Johnny Desmond

Captain Glenn Miller: From friend Harry James we borrow "Music Makers."

MUSIC MAKERS (Borrowed tune)

Captain Glenn Miller: Something blue, "Farewell Blues."

FAREWELL BLUES (Blue tune)

Captain Glenn Miller: Now the band playing, Sergeant Johnny Desmond, the Crew Chiefs singing "Poinciana."

POINCIANA (Song of the Tree)

Vocal refrain by Sergeant Johnny Desmond and the Crew Chiefs

Sergeant Broderick Crawford: To keep those planes firing and fighting takes hard work, courage, and skill. But that's not all, it takes money as well, the dollars you've been putting into War Bonds. The Fifth War Loan Drive is your chance to share in the invasion, to keep the sky over those Normandy beaches ours and ours alone. So buy bonds and hold on to 'em. In that way you can join in the proud boast of every man of the Army Air Forces Training Command and say I too Sustain the Wings.

I SUSTAIN THE WINGS (closing theme)

Captain Glenn Miller: This is Captain Glenn Miller saying so long for all our gang. Next week "I Sustain the Wings" will be brought to you by another band of the Training Command of the Army Air Forces with Captain Bob Jennings the C.O. and the music under the direction of Sergeant Harry Bluestone. We've enjoyed playing for you and we hope you've enjoyed listening to us.

1st Lt. Donald P. Briggs: Don't forget to listen again to "I Sustain the Wings" next Saturday, same time, same station and keep those V-Mails flying to the boys overseas. They're doing the fighting, you do the writing.

1st Lt. Donald P. Briggs: "I Sustain the Wings" is a presentation of the Army Air Forces Training Command and came to you from Chicago, Illinois.

NBC announcer: This is the National Broadcasting Company.

09Jul44 (Sun) 7:15-8:00PM Corn Exchange, Bedford, England   SWN-18891
  WELCOME TO AMERICAN BAND broadcast   Script   Attendance: 1000

Corporal Paul Dubov: This is the Allied Expeditionary Forces Program of the BBC. And
  here is your compere, Leslie Mitchell.
Leslie Mitchell: Good evening. This is about the time of a Sunday evening when our good
  sense of hospitality would be hoping for a visitor to our home. If it happens to be an
  old friend, we might even recognize his knock on the door. (Rhythm knock from band)
  Then we'd say, "Cecil, old boy, come right in. Make yourself at home." And that's the
  idea. Now tonight here we are sitting at home, in our radio home, hoping for a visitor.
  I believe I hear his footsteps on the walk outside. Let's see if we recognize the knock
  on the door.
MOONLIGHT SERENADE (opening theme)
  Leslie Mitchell: That's right. Tonight's visitor is Glenn Miller. Captain Glenn
    Miller of the U.S. Army Air Forces, playing the song by which he identified himself to
    radio audiences all over the world, "Moonlight Serenade," played by the Moonlight
    Serenader himself.
Leslie Mitchell: A happy surprise indeed. But we have more surprises. We find that
  Captain Glenn Miller has come to stay for a while. Yes, he's come to this country to
  bring his music direct to you boys and girls of the Allied Forces. And from now on
  he'll be knocking at your radio door with a new theme, "The Flaming Sword of
  Liberation," by which you'll always be able to recognize The American Band of the
  Supreme Allied Command.
WINGS ON PARADE (The Flaming Sword of Liberation) (opening theme)
  Corporal Paul Dubov: The American Band of the Supreme Allied Command with Captain Glenn
    Miller. A special program saying hello to the Moonlight Serenader, with Dorothy
    Carless, Bruce Trent and Leslie Mitchell.
Leslie Mitchell: Welcome, Captain Miller.
Captain Glenn Miller: Thank you, Leslie Mitchell, and good evening, everybody. The
  reason we're here is simple. You folks seem to like plenty of music, and we've got
  plenty of it to play for you. You'll be hearing the band on the Allied Expeditionary
  Forces Network, and you'll be seeing us again at the bases and up front where the
  fireworks are a-poppin'. We've brought along a lot of your old friends, like Sergeant
  Mel Powell, Ray McKinley, Johnny Desmond and the Crew Chiefs, and a lot of your old
  musical friends like tonight's first tune, "In the Mood."
IN THE MOOD
Leslie Mitchell: This is Leslie Mitchell again. As compere of this welcome to Captain
  Glenn Miller program, it's my duty to be, let's see, I believe our producer said I was
  to be charming, warm, unbelievable and friendly. All of which becomes most difficult in
  the face of the competition offered by this next typical Miller arrangement of a typical
  American tune. I believe you'll find it more charming, warm, believable and friendly
  than any man can be expected to be. Here is "Star Dust."
STAR DUST
Leslie Mitchell: Ah, that was beautiful, Captain. Now let's see. Back to my duties as
  compere. As I recall, I was not only supposed to be charming, warm, believable and
  friendly, but I believe the producer chap said something about keeping what I said - er
  - gracious, lovely and lyrical. And once again I find myself forced to bow and make way
  this time for something unsurpassably gracious, lovely and lyrical. One of England's
  favorite singing sweethearts. Just as you Yanks are proud of your Captain Glenn Miller,
  so we are proud of our own Dorothy Carless. So with double pride and being musically
  allied, here we have this remarkable combination, England's Dorothy Carless, America's
  Band of the Supreme Allied Command, singing and playing "Begin the Beguine."
BEGIN THE BEGUINE
  Vocal refrain by Dorothy Carless
Leslie Mitchell: Splendid, Dorothy Carless. Captain Miller, absolutely splendid. Now
  let's see. Here's another item to tick off my list of duties as compere. Em - yes -
  here it is. A compere must be resourceful. Now let's see, how would one go about that?
Captain Glenn Miller: Well, one of lads went about it this way, Leslie. Years ago when
  we were searching for an original idea for a musical comedy, this bright lad came up
  with the thought of building a medley around an old American saying, the one that refers

to the different things a bride wears to bring her good luck, something old, something new, something borrowed, something blue. Tonight's old song, "My Buddy."

MY BUDDY (Old tune)
   Captain Glenn Miller: A soldier and a song. For something new, Sergeant Johnny Desmond sings "Now I Know."

NOW I KNOW (New tune)
   Vocal refrain by Sergeant Johnny Desmond
   Captain Glenn Miller: For our borrowed tune we've put the bite on friend Harry James for his "Music Makers."

MUSIC MAKERS (Borrowed tune)
   Captain Glenn Miller: The blue tune, soft and sweet, "Farewell Blues."

FAREWELL BLUES (Blue tune)
Leslie Mitchell: Ah, me. Some men work from sun 'til sun. But a compere's work is never done. Here it says I must put in something gay and witty. Well, the something gay and witty I'm going to put in is Sergeant Ray McKinley, who joins the Crew Chiefs and the band in "G. I. Jive."

G.I. JIVE
   Vocal refrain by Technical Sergeant Ray McKinley and the Crew Chiefs
Leslie Mitchell: Ah, here it is. Here's a page in the advanced "Complete Little Dandy Guide and Handbook for Radio Comperes." Here's the one that says, "A compere must be virile, dashing, romantic." This is where I can cut myself a few touches.
Captain Glenn Miller: Leslie.
Leslie Mitchell: Yes, Captain Miller?
Captain Glenn Miller: You want our audience to have nothing but the best?
Leslie Mitchell: Right.
Captain Glenn Miller: You want them to hear the most virile?
Leslie Mitchell: Rather.
Captain Glenn Miller: The most dashing?
Leslie Mitchell: Absolutely.
Captain Glenn Miller: The most romantic?
Leslie Mitchell: Oh, Captain. Now, really.
Captain Glenn Miller: Then I suggest you listen along as we have a song from England's popular singing star, Bruce Trent. And Bruce Trent is going to sing "I Couldn't Sleep a Wink Last Night."
Leslie Mitchell: Oh, dash it all.

I COULDN'T SLEEP A WINK LAST NIGHT
   Vocal refrain by Bruce Trent
Leslie Mitchell: Now the American Band of the Supreme Allied Command with Sergeant Jerry Gray's distinguished arrangement of "Poinciana."

POINCIANA (Song of the Tree)
   Vocal refrain by Sergeant Johnny Desmond and the Crew Chiefs
Leslie Mitchell: Out comes the rule book again. This is Leslie still-in-there-pitching Mitchell speaking. And here I see that one of my great responsibilities as compere of this program is to strike just the proper note. Personally, I can't distinguish tar from fire. So I'll once again leave everything up to the gentlemen who seem to possess a veritable bundle of proper notes. And this time the American Band of the Supreme Allied Command offers "What Do You Do in the Infantry."

WHAT DO YOU DO IN THE INFANTRY
   Vocal refrain by Corporal Artie Malvin and the Crew Chiefs
Leslie Mitchell: Now for all of us, Dorothy Carless, Bruce Trent and everybody listening, thanks to you, Captain Glenn Miller, and to the American Band of the Supreme Allied Command who are most welcome to the European Theatre of Operations, and we want to wish you God speed and success in your radio and in-person journeys to the boys and girls of the Allied Forces. And now this is your compere, Leslie Mitchell, who has managed not to be charming, warm, believable, friendly, resourceful, gay, witty, virile, dashing, romantic, etc., but who has managed to be royally entertained.
Captain Glenn Miller: Thank you, Leslie. And, by the way, I've just found out something.
Leslie Mitchell: Yes, old chap, what's that?
Captain Glenn Miller: I've just found out that compere business you've been talking about all evening is just old-fashioned Master of Ceremonies.

Leslie Mitchell: Oh, really?
WINGS ON PARADE (The Flaming Sword of Liberation) (closing theme)
    Corporal Paul Dubov: Watch your papers and listen to your radio for announcements of
      radio programs and personal appearances of the American Band of the Supreme Command
      under the direction of Glenn Miller.

20Jul44 (Thu) 8:30-9:00PM Corn Exchange, Bedford, England   SWN-18901
AMERICAN BAND OF THE SUPREME ALLIED COMMAND broadcast   Attendance: 1000

[Captain Franklin Engelmann: This is the Allied Expeditionary Forces Program of the BBC.
Corporal Paul Dubov: This is a feature of the American Band] of the Supreme Allied
  Command.
MOONLIGHT SERENADE (opening theme)
  Captain Franklin Engelmann: The American Band of the Supreme Allied Command under the
    direction of Captain Glenn Miller, a program featuring the voices of Britain's Vera
    Lynn and Royal Air Force Sergeant Jimmy Miller. And here is Captain Glenn Miller.
  Captain Glenn Miller: Thank you, Captain Franklin Engelmann, and good evening, everybody.
    We've been over here a few weeks now and before we go any further I want to pass along a
    word of thanks to all the fine folks in the British Isles. The way you've made us feel
    welcome is a real thrill. You've made us feel that you've not only taken us into your
    home but into your hearts as well. And to you Yanks over here, well all I can say is
    we're mighty glad to be here with you. But our job is making music, not conversation,
    so here goes with a Jerry Gray arrangement of the Sergeant's own tune, "Caribbean
    Clipper."
CARIBBEAN CLIPPER
[Captain Franklin Engelmann: Er, Captain Miller, may I pop in here for a moment?
Captain Glenn Miller: You certainly may, Captain Engelmann, any time.
Captain Franklin Engelmann: Well, I want to introduce you to a young man who no only
    bears a similar responsibility, but also your name. Captain Glenn Miller, may I present
    Sergeant Jimmy Miller, leader of the RAF's famous "Squadronaires?"
Captain Glenn Miller: How d'you do, Sergeant Miller?
Sergeant Jimmy Miller: Very well indeed, Captain Miller. I've looked forward to this
    moment.
Captain Glenn Miller: No more than we have, Sarge. Sharin' the same mission with a band
    like yours is nice work, and we've got it.
Sergeant Jimmy Miller: Well, Captain, I do a bit of singin' y'know, and I've been hopin'
    to share the same song with a band like yours.
Captain Glenn Miller: All right, Jimmy, you name it, we'll play it.
Sergeant Jimmy Miller: This is "A Lovely Way to Spend an Evening."
A LOVELY WAY TO SPEND AN EVENING
  Vocal refrain by Royal Air Force Sergeant Jimmy Miller
Captain Glenn Miller: Thank you, Sergeant Jimmy Miller, I hope we fly together again
    soon. Besides fighting a common enemy, the English Tommy and the American Yank share
    the same language and a mutual admiration for a beautiful gal. So, we're taking the
    responsibility of dedicating this next tune from you fighting partners to your lovely
    ladies.
PUT YOUR ARMS AROUND ME, HONEY
  Captain Glenn Miller: The Crew Chiefs and the whole gang join voices in "Put Your Arms
    Around Me, Honey."
  Vocal refrain by Sergeant Johnny Desmond and the Crew Chiefs
Captain Glenn Miller: And now it's medley time with somethin' old, somethin' new,
    somethin' borrowed and somethin' blue. Our old song, "Mighty Lak' a Rose."
MIGHTY LAK' A ROSE (Old tune)
  Captain Glenn Miller: For somethin' new, Sergeant Johnny Desmond sings "Amor."
AMOR (New tune)
  Vocal refrain by Sergeant Johnny Desmond
  Captain Glenn Miller: For our borrowed song we put the touch on our pre-war stock of
    arrangements. Here's "Chattanooga Choo Choo."
CHATTANOOGA CHOO CHOO (Borrowed tune)
  Vocal refrain by Technical Sergeant Ray McKinley and the Crew Chiefs
  Captain Glenn Miller: For somethin' blue, here's a whisperin' arrangement of "Bye Bye
    Blues."
BYE BYE BLUES (Blue tune)
Captain Glenn Miller: Now, here's a special bit of introducin' to do, so I suggest we
    call on an expert in that department to do it, Captain Franklin Engelmann.

Captain Franklin Engelmann: Well, Captain Miller, I believe most of our listening friends
    already know the lady I am about to introduce. When she hasn't been singing for them on
    the radio, she has been out on the various fronts singing for our soldiers in person.
    She is known as "the sweetheart of the forces" and her name is Vera Lynn.
Vera Lynn: Thank you. Captain Miller, this is indeed a pleasure.
Captain Glenn Miller: The pleasure's all ours, Miss Lynn, and the microphone's all yours.
Vera Lynn: Well, tonight I'd like to sing "Besame Mucho."
Captain Glenn Miller: That's all we needed to know. "Besame Mucho" comin' right up!
BESAME MUCHO (Kiss Me Much)
    Vocal refrain by Vera Lynn
Captain Glenn Miller: Thank you] Vera Lynn for some mighty fancy singing and now Sergeant
    Ray McKinley is up there with the big hammers ready to make the welcome ring with the
    "Anvil Chorus."
ANVIL CHORUS
[Captain Glenn Miller: This is Captain Glenn Miller sayin' thanks for the band to Vera
    Lynn, Sergeant Jimmy Miller and Captain Franklin Engelmann for bein' here. To you
    listeners, thanks for the visit and we'll be lookin' forward to seeing you again next
    week same time. In the meantime, we'll be out playin' at the bases for you of the
    Allied Forces. For now, good luck and good night.
MOONLIGHT SERENADE (closing theme)
    Corporal Paul Dubov: You have been listening to the regular Thursday night broadcast of
        the American Band of the Supreme Allied Command under the direction of Captain Glenn
        Miller. Tonight's half hour featured the voices of Britain's Vera Lynn and Sergeant
        Jimmy Miller.]

22Jul44 (Sat) 10:30-11:00AM Co-Partners Hall, Bedford, England   SWN-18971
  THE SWING SHIFT recording   Aired 01Aug44

Miss Jean Metcalf: This is the Allied Expeditionary Forces Program of the B.B.C.
Corporal Paul Dubov: This is a feature of the American Band of the Supreme Allied
  Command.
Miss Jean Metcalf: Presenting "The Swing Shift" with Sergeant Ray McKinley and his music.
SONG AND DANCE (opening theme)
  Vocal refrain by Technical Sergeant Ray McKinley:
    This is Sergeant Ray McKinley sayin', "All Aboard."
    We're gonna take a trip we can all afford.
    Well, we gotta fly fast, it's a cross country hop.
    Now here are some of the places where we're liable to stop.
    First we cut a carpet out in Russia way.
    Then even though we'd all kinda like to stay,
    We hop down to Dixie where they talk so slow,
    Where the peaches and the melons and the "you alls" grow.
    Then by train and rather hurriedly,
    We take the old L and N up to Tennessee.
    Then northward to Harlem where they sing a song,
    About a tailor named Sam who's done 'em wrong.
    Such are some of the stops and there are even more.
    I just meant to sketch the itinerary in store.
    For the details we have a guy to give with the gab.
    Meet the lady in charge, Jean Metcalf.
Miss Jean Metcalf: Thank you, Sergeant Mac. And, to borrow one of your American
  expressions, what's buzzin', Cousin?
T/Sgt. Ray McKinley: Oh, conversation Lend Lease, aye? Well, we're gonna tee off with a
  tune that we think is not only smashing and jolly but absolutely ripping, actually.
Miss Jean Metcalf: Then let's have at it.
T/Sgt. Ray McKinley: O.K., men, have at Mel Powell's "Mission to Moscow."
MISSION TO MOSCOW
Miss Jean Metcalf: And here "The Swing Shift" swings into a lazier cadence, offering a
  tune that makes might easy listening. It also gives the boys from Georgia a chance to
  go collecting memories all along the line. Here's "Georgia on My Mind."
GEORGIA ON MY MIND
Miss Jean Metcalf: This is "The Swing Shift" of the American Band of the Supreme Allied
  Command with Sergeant Ray McKinley at the throttle. Now it's all aboard for
  "Chattanooga Choo Choo."
CHATTANOOGA CHOO CHOO
  Vocal refrain by Technical Sergeant Ray McKinley and the Crew Chiefs

  ...

GOING MY WAY
  Vocal refrain by Sergeant Johnny Desmond

  ...

CAN'T GET STUFF IN YOUR CUFF
  Vocal refrain by Technical Sergeant Ray McKinley

  ...

IT'S LOVE, LOVE, LOVE!
  Vocal refrain by the Crew Chiefs

  ...

HERE WE GO AGAIN
Miss Jean Metcalf: There'll be more of this sort of doing Saturday morning when you'll
  again hear "The Swing Shift" of the American Band of the Supreme Allied Command with
  Sergeant Ray McKinley and his music.
SONG AND DANCE (closing theme)
  Vocal refrain by Technical Sergeant Ray McKinley:
    Well, so long, everybody, glad you tuned us in.
    If you liked us, please notify your next of kin.
    It was indeed quite a pleasure to play for you all.
    Here are a few of the boys to take a curtain call.
  Vocal refrain by Sergeant Johnny Desmond:
    This is Sergeant Johnny Desmond. It was lots of fun.
  Vocal refrain by the Crew Chiefs:
    This is the Crew Chiefs saying thanks indeed.
  Vocal refrain by Technical Sergeant Ray McKinley:
    Well, upon that point I guess we're all agreed.
    And all the guys in the band would like to wish you well.
    This includes little Jeannie who was nonpareil.
    We're all very happy to be over here.
    So once or twice each week please lend an ear.
    And whether you like it sweet, whether you like it jive,
    Tune your radio to medium two-eight-five.
    We'll be back swingin' for Tommy and Joe.
    So until next Saturday, toodle-oo.
  Whistling by Technical Sergeant Ray McKinley

23Jul44 (Sun) 8:30-9:00PM Co-Partners Hall, Bedford, England   SWN-18908
AMERICAN BAND OF THE SUPREME ALLIED COMMAND recording   Aired 27Jul44

Corporal Paul Dubov: ... the Allied Expeditionary Forces Program of the B.B.C.
T/Sgt. Paul Dudley: This is a feature of the American Band of the Supreme Allied Command.
MOONLIGHT SERENADE (opening theme)
  T/Sgt. Paul Dudley: The American Band of the Supreme Allied Command under the direction
    of Captain Glenn Miller. Your Thursday night thirty minutes with the Moonlight
    Serenader and tonight's guest, Britain's own Anne Shelton. And here is Captain Glenn
    Miller.
Captain Glenn Miller: Thank you and good evening, everybody. Tonight's marching orders
  tell us that this show is headed first to you members of the forces and then to you
  folks who are listening to the Home Service of the B.B.C. And whether you happen to be
  listening by the home fire or by the battle fire, we're sure you partners in victory are
  all hoping for that big day when the Tommies and Yanks come "Flyin' Home."
FLYING HOME
Captain Glenn Miller: Nice goin', m'lads. And now whether you happen to take one sugar
  or two in your tea or coffee, you fightin' guys seem to like your lovin' and your music
  on the sweet side. So Tommy and Joe, with that in mind, you furnish the gal, we'll
  furnish the music. "Smoke Gets in Your Eyes."
(When Your Heart's on Fire) SMOKE GETS IN YOUR EYES
Captain Glenn Miller: Besides the same ideals, the same language, and a common enemy,
  Britain and America share the same colors in flags. So up with the red, the white and
  the blue lights as the Crew Chiefs and the whole gang join voices singin' the "Vict'ry
  Polka."
VICT'RY POLKA
  Vocal refrain by Sergeant Johnny Desmond, the Crew Chiefs and the Ensemble
Captain Glenn Miller: Since coming over here it's been our good fortune to play for some
  of the finest singing stars in the British Isles. Tonight our luck holds good for
  here's a young lady, lovely to look at, delightful to hear, Miss Anne Shelton.
Anne Shelton: Thank you, Captain Miller, that was a charming welcome to your program.
  And now that I feel right at home would you care to join me in a spot of song?
Captain Glenn Miller: Well, the idea sounds right delightful. What'll it be?
Anne Shelton: Ah, how about "I'll Get By?"
Captain Glenn Miller: O.K., Anne m'gal, come out singin'
I'LL GET BY (As Long As I Have You)
  Vocal refrain by Anne Shelton
Captain Glenn Miller: Thank you, Anne Shelton. That was lovely. And now it's medley
  time calling for something old, something new, something borrowed and something blue.
  Our old song, "In the Gloaming."
IN THE GLOAMING (Old tune)
  Captain Glenn Miller: For something new, Sergeant Johnny Desmond sings "A Fellow on a
    Furlough."
A FELLOW ON A FURLOUGH (New tune)
  Vocal refrain by Sergeant Johnny Desmond
  Captain Glenn Miller: We make a slight touch on friend Benny Goodman for our borrowed
    tune and he let us have "Stompin' at the Savoy."
STOMPIN' AT THE SAVOY (Borrowed tune)
  Captain Glenn Miller: The bluer than blue tune, "Deep Purple."
DEEP PURPLE (Blue tune)
Captain Glenn Miller: Popular tunes from home seem to have a tough time catching up with
  you boys at the front, so by way of a tip to you Yanks, here's a song that's just what
  the well-dressed voice is wearing this season. Sergeant Johnny Desmond sings it for you
  and it's called "Time Alone Will Tell."
TIME ALONE WILL TELL
  Vocal refrain by Sergeant Johnny Desmond
Captain Glenn Miller: Nice goin', Johnny. Tonight's anchor tune is dedicated to those
  Allies who gave Jerry a big surprise by taking a quick trip Eastward. A rip-roarin'
  arrangement dedicated to the gallant fighters of the Red Army. Sergeant Ray McKinley
  pulls stoke oar for "The Volga Boatmen."

SONG OF THE VOLGA BOATMEN

Captain Glenn Miller: That's what I'm talking about. This is Captain Glenn Miller saying thanks to Anne Shelton for the nice visit. Reminding you folks out there that we'll be holding down this same spot at this same time next Thursday. Now from the American Band of the Supreme Allied Command, it's good luck and good night.

MOONLIGHT SERENADE (closing theme)

T/Sgt. Paul Dudley: The American Band of the Supreme Allied Command under the direction of Captain Glenn Miller has been heard on the Allied Expeditionary Forces Program of the B.B.C. and on the Home Service.

27Jul44 (Thu) 3:30-4:00PM Dunkers Den, Piccadilly, London, England   DOX-36114
American Red Cross Rainbow Corner Club (run by Adele Astaire)   Aired 29Jul44
AMERICAN EAGLE IN BRITAIN recording   190th Program   Attendance: 1000

Announcer: This is London calling. The "American Eagle in Britain," a weekly program
  from Rainbow Corner in London. The duration is approximately 30 minutes. Standby now
  for the "American Eagle." This is London calling. The British Broadcasting Corporation
  presents its weekly "American Eagle in Britain" program. Your host today is Cecil
  Madden.
Cecil Madden: This is London calling from American Red Cross Rainbow Corner.
Let's Sing a Happy Song (opening theme --- recording, not Miller band)
Cecil Madden: For the 190th time it's hello to all of you in America. Flying bombs or
  no, London always carries on and so this is Cecil Madden of the British Broadcasting
  Corporation saying pull up a chair, join us on our "American Eagle in Britain" program
  sent to you, as usual, with good wishes from the B.B.C. in London, England. This
  opening spot is always given to six of the smaller towns of the United States.
First Sergeant Kastelanetz: First Sergeant Kastelanetz calling Palatka,   Florida.
David McNeil: David McNeil calling Georgetown, Louisiana.
Private Rausch: Private Rausch calling Green Bay, Wisconsin.
Sergeant Gregory: Sergeant Gregory calling Barnsdall, Oklahoma.
Sergeant Ralph Crandall: Sergeant Ralph Crandall calling New Castle, Indiana.
Sergeant Klein Smith: Sergeant Klein Smith calling Avon Lake, Ohio.
Cecil Madden: And those six, which I've picked out at random in this room under the
  pavement in Dunkers Den in the famous American Red Cross Rainbow Corner Club in
  Piccadilly, London. Now I step out, I introduce our musical guests, they're G.I.s,
  they're a unit of the American Band of the Supreme Allied Command, they're headed by
  Sergeant Ray McKinley of Fort Worth, Texas, and this American band is over here with us,
  working on the new Allied Expeditionary Forces Programs, and are personally directed by
  Captain Glenn Miller who's right here. Captain Miller, what's it like to be in London?
Captain Glenn Miller: Well, Cecil, I'm speaking for the whole gang when I say that this
  is the kind of a place that makes music in our ears. Being here with these boys from
  home is a big thrill, and this place makes all of us feel right at home.
Cecil Madden: Thank you, Captain, and like all American soldiers, you're more than
  welcome any time.
Captain Glenn Miller: Thank you, Cecil. I'd like to add a word about how this show of
  your's goes back home. American mothers and fathers and wives, sweethearts of boys over
  here tie up the radio whenever you're on.
Cecil Madden: Well, Captain, we've had nearly four years of being on, and perhaps you
  have a mother and a wife over there listening?
Captain Glenn Miller: Well, if they aren't, I'll be mighty disappointed in Denver,
  Colorado and Tenafly, New Jersey, and that goes for every town where there's a mother or
  a wife or family of any man in the band.
Cecil Madden: Well, I add my greetings to all those places. So, with the help of
  Sergeant Mel Powell at the piano of New York City, the band and the usual help of our
  song master Sergeant Cecil Elmore of Cadillac, Michigan, we've been talking over a song
  your men would like to sing you, and today their choice at rehearsal has gone to "Me and
  My Gal."
FOR ME AND MY GAL (S/Sgt. Mel Powell, piano)
  Vocal refrain by Sergeant Cecil Elmore, the audience and the band members
Cecil Madden: This is where I introduce our interviewer, the man who makes New Rochelle
  famous, member of the 8th Air Force, so once again we give our London welcome to our
  good friend Major Ken Tredwell.
Major Ken Tredwell: Thank you, Cecil, and one thing we'd like to emphasize today is that
  this is not just another banner Thursday in Dunkers Den. The light spirits and the
  glowing faces are lighter and more glowing than ever. The reason is obvious. Ah, with
  us here today we have no less than Captain Glenn Miller who's bringing United States the
  best popular mosac - music it has ever had, no laughter please, and the best music we've
  ever heard right here to our very eyes and believe me, our eyes are popping out on our
  checks. This is a day we can remember and cherish for a long while to come. The first
  man we're going to talk to today is T/5 Jerome Huff. Is that right, Jerry?

T/5 Jerome Huff: That's right, sir.
Major Ken Tredwell: Where's your home?
T/5 Jerome Huff: Ah, New York City, sir, Bronx.
Major Ken Tredwell: The Bronx, the Bronx. The first thing I see about Jerry is that he's
    wearing a Presidential Citation, the Combat Infantryman's Badge and the ETO Ribbon with
    two clusters, all of which means he's a top flight fighting man. Let's give him a hand.
    And what --- I see that you're a paratrooper, Jerry. How many jumps have you had?
T/5 Jerome Huff: I have 25, sir.
Major Ken Tredwell: 25 jumps!
T/5 Jerome Huff: Yes, sir.
Major Ken Tredwell: And how many of those have been combat jumps?
T/5 Jerome Huff: Three, sir.
Major Ken Tredwell: Three combat jumps! That's very unusual. One paratrooper, three
    combat jumps and looking pretty healthy, too. Too healthy. I imagine your last jump
    was in Normandy. Is that right, Jerry?
T/5 Jerome Huff: That's right, sir.
Major Ken Tredwell: Tell me, about how big a load were you carrying?
T/5 Jerome Huff: Well, sir, everybody carries at least a hundred pounds.
Major Ken Tredwell: A hundred pounds on your back!
T/5 Jerome Huff: Yes, sir.
Major Ken Tredwell: And what was the objective of your organization?
T/5 Jerome Huff: Well, sir, our objective was to - ah - take and to hold a town.
Major Ken Tredwell: And did you take and hold that town?
T/5 Jerome Huff: Yes, sir. The boys in the battalions did a swell job. For a regiment
    and myself but I'd like to give them every credit that we possibly can because they did
    a job.
Major Ken Tredwell: Jerry, did your organization, your unit, your outfit - ah - win the
    Presidential Citation for holding that town?
T/5 Jerome Huff: Yes, sir. They did.
Major Ken Tredwell: And for how long did you hold it?
T/5 Jerome Huff: Well, sir, we held it for about 36 hours.
Major Ken Tredwell: That's mighty fine. Against superior forces?
T/5 Jerome Huff: Ah, yes, sir.
Major Ken Tredwell: Jerome Huff, T/5, there's a name to remember, America, and when he
    and his boys get back home let's give them a royal welcome. Thanks a lot to Jerry Huff.
    And we're goin' from the Army to the Navy. This is Leroy Swan. Leroy, you've got one
    inverted red stripe - ah - a white globe and a white eagle. That means you're what rank
    in the Navy?
Leroy Swan: Electrician Mate Third, sir.
Major Ken Tredwell: A Electrician's Mate Third Class?
Leroy Swan: That's right.
Major Ken Tredwell: And where's your home, Leroy?
Leroy Swan: Aberdeen, South Dakota.
Major Ken Tredwell: What is your job in the Navy, Leroy?
Leroy Swan: I'm a electrician, sir.
Major Ken Tredwell: On what sort of a ship?
Leroy Swan: LST, 3-35.
Major Ken Tredwell: I hear a lot of applause. What do you think of LSTs?
Leroy Swan: Think the LSTs are the best. And we've got the best one that there is.
Major Ken Tredwell: You've got a good crew, too?
Leroy Swan: We've got the best crew that ever sailed on any LST.
Major Ken Tredwell: Boy, that's, ha, ha, that's, that's, that's sure the kinda talk the
    Navy likes to hear. Tell me, where has your LST taken you?
Leroy Swan: Spent nine months in the Mediterranean, sir, making two invasions, one at
    Gela, Sicily and Salerno of Italy.
Major Ken Tredwell: And you're in on the Normandy show too?
Leroy Swan: That's right, sir.
Major Ken Tredwell: Three invasions in one LST. How many times have you been over to
    Normandy?
Leroy Swan: Eleven trips, sir.

Major Ken Tredwell: Eleven trips, oh, that's a-plenty. Leroy, you're back here now, I
  imagine your ship's in dry dock, is that correct?
Leroy Swan: That's right, sir.
Major Ken Tredwell: And when do you re-report back to it?
Leroy Swan: I have to at eight o'clock tomorrow morning.
Major Ken Tredwell: Oh, my. That's a shame. That's a shame. Well, we want to wish you
  good luck tomorrow morning and on every morning from now on until you hit Aberdeen
  again. Thank you, Leroy.
Leroy Swan: And thank you, sir.
Cecil Madden: Thank you, Ken. Now we call in Captain Glenn Miller and musical guests Ray
  McKinley and his merry men to play you "Flying Home."
FLYING HOME
Cecil Madden: It, it's the roving microphone now. A regular feature in our B.B.C.
  "American Eagle in Britain" program. So listen out for home towns first and then the
  names of someone you know. So, take over, Ken, with the roving microphone.
Major Ken Tredwell: Thank you Cecil, and we'll get going right away. How I'm ever gonna
  get through this jam-packed crowd I don't know, but let's start right out with the Navy.
Frank E. O'Brian: Philadelphia, Pennsylvania, Frank E. O'Brian.
Major Ken Tredwell: Boy, he sounds belligerent. He doesn't really mean that.
A. J. Rousoff: Waterbury, Connecticut, A. J. Rousoff.
Major Ken Tredwell: And two soldiers.
Morris Klingerman: San Marcos, Texas, Morris Klingerman.
Corporal Coleman Davis: Suffolk, Virginia, Corporal Coleman Davis.
Major Ken Tredwell: From Texas to Virginia, and here's a very lovely WAC right on the end
  seat, a big smile, we've all got big smiles for her.
Jeannette Baum: Hollis, New York, Jeannette Baum.
Major Ken Tredwell: Jeannette Baum. Here we go.
James Jackson: Kincaid, Illinois, James Jackson.
Corporal Mayhew: Chicago, Illinois, Corporal Mayhew.
Major Ken Tredwell: And here's the 9th Air Force.
Edward Dow: Edw - ah - Kansas City, Missouri, Edward Dow.
Major Ken Tredwell: Come on you wild haired man, let's hear about it.
Chester Rosenfeld: Newark, New Jersey, Chester Rosenfeld.
Major Ken Tredwell: And on Chester's right.
Buddy Strucker: Philadelphia, Pennsylvania, Buddy Strucker.
Major Ken Tredwell: Another Philadelphia man heard from. Let's get back to the Army on
  the other side of the aisle.
Reuben Fauch: Ah - Twin Lakes, Wisconsin, Reuben Fauch.
Major Ken Tredwell: Very calm voice, he's not excited. Doin' O.K.
Rodney Stuart: Aurora, Illinois, Rodney Stuart.
Major Ken Tredwell: And from Illinois where are we goin'?
Boyd Bergren: Martinsburg, West Virginia, Boyd Bergren.
Major Ken Tredwell: Quite a hop. Here comes the Army again.
Bob Slack: Shreveport, Louisiana, Bob Slack.
Major Ken Tredwell: You, you, you, you, him.
Cristie Savone: Clarendon, New York, Cristie Savone.
Major Ken Tredwell: And a good town. Here are three more.
Gus Cocus: Dearborn, Michigan, Gus Cocus.
George Canuel: South Norwalk, Connecticut, George Canuel.
John Thusy: San Jose, California, John Thusy.
Private Doma J. DeLafanta: Jersey City, New Jersey, Private Doma J. DeLafanta.
Major Ken Tredwell: Well, what'dja think I was throwing in your face there, soldier? How
  about it, Sergeant?
Julius Greenwald: Brooklyn, New York, Julius Greenwald.
Major Ken Tredwell: And the 8th Air Force heard from.
Dick Helpful: Fishkill, New York, Dick Helpful.
Major Ken Tredwell: And she's a brunette and in a WAC uniform and very pretty.
Vicky Washiac: Cleveland, Ohio, Vicky Washiac.
Major Ken Tredwell: Hello, Vicky. Hello, Vicky. Here's the Navy.
William J. Coleman: William J. --- Charleston, West Virginia, William J. Coleman.

Major Ken Tredwell: Once again, Bill.
William J. Coleman: Charleston, West Virginia, William J. Coleman.
Major Ken Tredwell: I bet they couldn't hear that all the way back to Charleston, no
  kidding.
Covy Cornival: New York City, Covy Cornival.
Al Michaels: Thomson, New York, Al Michaels.
James Madison: "Metatocheese," James Madison.
Major Ken Tredwell: That's a fine haircut you've got there, too, Jim.
Don T. King: Humboldt, Tennessee, Don T. King.
Major Ken Tredwell: From Humboldt where are we going?
Bill Dollun: To Rothsville, Pennsylvania, Bill Dollun.
Major Ken Tredwell: And another, a very trim little creature in WAC uniform.
Lila Graham: New Orleans, Louisiana, Lila Graham.
Major Ken Tredwell: This is no fun.
Arild Warmill: Arild Warmill, Syracuse, New York.
Charles Dewey: East Hartford, Connecticut, Charles Dewey.
Major Ken Tredwell: Young ladies like this upset the whole program, don't they? By gosh.
John Austin: "Firestan," New York, John Austin.
Major Ken Tredwell: Right behind Johnny, leaning up against the door.
Charles Rulof: Boston, Massachusetts, Charles Rulof.
Major Ken Tredwell: And a big man too. Here we are.
Joseph Dopheld: New York City, Joseph Dopheld.
Major Ken Tredwell: Great place, New York City. Let's move on over.
Corporal Roland Short: Port Chester, New York, Corporal Roland Short.
Major Ken Tredwell: He's been here every week for six weeks. Get's on every week, too.
  Here we go.
Merrideth Watts: Decatur, Illinois, Merrideth Watts.
Rayfield Smith: Opelousas, Louisiana, Rayfield Smith.
Major Ken Tredwell: And the Navy again.
Ted Hauskins: "Warrenwood," Illinois, Ted Hauskins.
Major Ken Tredwell: And two in the Army with the brand new, the newest in hat styles
  here.
Michael Pravus: "Brave," Massachusetts, Michael Pravus.
Private Vigerio: Lawrence, Massachusetts, Vigerio, Private Vigerio.
Major Ken Tredwell: Hello, Major. You look like a Midwesterner. How about it?
Major Harry Becroft: Topeka, Kansas, Harry Becroft.
Major Ken Tredwell: Yeah, man. Ha, ha. And here's the American Red Cross.
Georgia Lightfoot: Detroit, Michigan, Georgia Lightfoot.
Major Ken Tredwell: Write that down, men. Here's a light haired boy.
Peter Volcalbule: Hartford, Connecticut, Peter Volcalbule.
Major Ken Tredwell: How about you, Sergeant?
Sergeant Glenn Schweitzer: LaPorte, Indiana, Glenn Schweitzer.
Major Ken Tredwell: Let's end up with seven men right in a row, all fast. I'll run right
  down and getcha all.
William Cardona: Brooklyn, New York, William Cardona.
Major Ken Tredwell: Let's have no more Brooklyn today.
Clayton Doe: Chicago, Illinois, Clayton Doe.
Richard Burman: Brooklyn, New York, Richard Burman.
Ernest Myer: Brooklyn, New York, Ernest Myer.
Robert Bell: "Glenboe," West Virginia, Robert Bell.
Major Ken Tredwell: Cecil, it's time to turn the microphone and Brooklyn all the way back
  to you. Take it over.
Cecil Madden: Thank you, Ken, for that tour around the room. The other nine hundred and
  eighty of you make a point to come back next week. Today we spotlight station WIP,
  Philadelphia, Pennsylvania, the famous, the famous Philadelphia pioneer voice serving on
  the air day or night. Many thanks to you, Mr. Wallace, for your charming message about
  the program. We were very glad to get it. There's a fellow here from Philadelphia,
  maybe you'd like to meet him.
Private Battlesinski: Private Battlesinski from Newportville. I want to say hello to my
  mom and dad and all the friends and I'm starting my fourth year in the E.T.O. today.

Cecil Madden: Graham, many thanks. So now it's back to Glenn Miller, to Ray McKinley and the American Dance Orchestra, the Supreme Allied Command to you "Stealing Apples."

STEALIN' APPLES

Cecil Madden: This is where we introduce our special feature in our "American Eagle in Britain" program. We take you out now into the countryside of Britain where in a hospital some of your men have been brought back wounded from the fighting in France with our invasion forces. Once again that talented and great-hearted lady Bebe Daniels, famous on stage, screen and radio, is at a hospital now waiting to talk to some of your men. I received a letter from one of you in the United States saying when Bebe Daniels went through that hospital last week just about everybody in the United States went in with her. So over now to somewhere in Britain, so come in will you, Bebe Daniels.

Bebe Daniels: Thank you, Cecil Madden, and a special hello to you mothers, fathers, wives and sweethearts in America. This hospital is built entirely of Nissen huts, you know, those tunnel-shaped, corrugated, iron structures which are being used all over the world in this war. Well, let's go in and have a look inside. Like all the wards in this hospital, this one has plenty of windows set in and the walls are decorated with cream-colored compo board and brown stripping. Ha, ha. By the way, the cur-curved walls here are an ideal place for pin-up girls. The boys don't even have to turn around to look at them. And now, who's in this bed?

William Sheely: Ah, do you want to know my name?

Bebe Daniels: Yes, and where you from?

William Sheely: I'm from Binghamton, New York. I'm Chief Quartermaster of the U.S. Navy and my name is William Sheely.

Bebe Daniels: Do your folks call you William?

William Sheely: No, they call me Bill.

Bebe Daniels: Bill Sheely. That sounds like an Irish name to me.

William Sheely: It is.

Bebe Daniels: Isn't there a saying that wherever there's a good fight you'll always find an Irishman?

William Sheely: Yes. I guess so. But I prove the exception to the rule.

Bebe Daniels: What do you mean?

William Sheely: Well, I'm not a combat man. I'm a mine sweeper.

Bebe Daniels: One of the most dangerous jobs in the war.

William Sheely: Oh, I don't know about that.

Bebe Daniels: Well, I do. Now in this bed we have Corporal Earl Davis of the 29th Infantry Division. Where you from, Earl?

Earl Davis: "Paudhill," North Carolina.

Bebe Daniels: And what were you before the war started?

Earl Davis: A carpenter.

Bebe Daniels: And since then you've been building up trouble for the Germans, eh?

Earl Davis: That's right.

Bebe Daniels: When did you first see action, Earl?

Earl Davis: I went in on D-Day on an LCVP. I was about 20 feet from shore when there was a terrible explosion. The next thing I remember I was in the water. I rolled over on my back, reached down and then phased my life belt. Then I got my knife out to cut my assault jacket off, but I couldn't use my left hand. That's when I found I was hurt. The tide was coming in very fast and nearly got me. I tried to crawl to shore, but I couldn't and it looked like I was trapped. Then a Caterpillar came along and the boys pulled me in to shallow water where I finally cut my jacket off and crawled up on the beach.

Bebe Daniels: Then what?

Earl Davis: I got on a bank and tried to dig in. I could dig a bit with my right hand but 88s kept hitting and a few mortar shells landed about 40 feet from me.

Bebe Daniels: Wasn't there a first aid man about?

Earl Davis: Yes, but he got hit by one of the mortar shells.

Bebe Daniels: Oh, that was too bad. Wasn't there any other first aid men around?

Earl Davis: Yes, but there was so many wounded it was some time before they could get to me.

Bebe Daniels: And you stayed there until ...

Earl Davis: Until a medical Captain came along. I asked him to help me. He got some of
  my clothes off to see the wound and then he gave me morphine. Later that evening I was
  carried out to the beach by a group of German prisoners who put me on a boat. I was a
  little afraid of them at first. I thought they might drop me accidentally on purpose,
  but they didn't. They did a good job.
Bebe Daniels: And the doctors and nurses are doin' a good job for you here, aren't they,
  Earl?
Earl Davis: They sure are. The medical attention here is first class.
Bebe Daniels: And now over here, writing a letter and occasionally glancing up at a
  picture of his wife and son is one of our chaplains. It's Chaplain Jerry Dean of ...
Chaplain Jerry Dean: Little Rock, Arkansas, Bebe.
Bebe Daniels: Thank you. You know, you're the first chaplain I've seen who's been
  wounded over here. How did it happen?
Chaplain Jerry Dean: Well, those bullets don't seem to care much whether you're a
  chaplain or not.
Bebe Daniels: Oh, oh, I didn't mean that. I meant - ah - what were you doin' when you
  got it?
Chaplain Jerry Dean: Well, I went in with the boys on D-Day.
Bebe Daniels: Yes, and then what?
Chaplain Jerry Dean: Well, when we got down on the beach I dug a foxhole. I got in it, I
  prayed and shook and dodged bullets.
Bebe Daniels: Ha, I've heard a different story.
Chaplain Jerry Dean: What's that?
Bebe Daniels: Aw, about a certain chaplain who went into the front lines and got wounded
  while he was giving medical aid to two of our soldiers.
Chaplain Jerry Dean: You don't say?
Bebe Daniels: Yes. Tell me, Chaplain Dean, what happened to those two fellows you helped
  to fix up?
Chaplain Jerry Dean: Well, one had a broken leg and the other had a bad scalp injury.
Bebe Daniels: Did you send them back to the Red Cross station?
Chaplain Jerry Dean: Yes, and me too.
Bebe Daniels: What happened to you?
Chaplain Jerry Dean: Well, we came under artillery fire and I got a piece of shrapnel in
  my left hip. You want to see it?
Bebe Daniels: What?
Chaplain Jerry Dean: Here it is. Ah.
Bebe Daniels: The hip?
Chaplain Jerry Dean: Not the hip, I - shrapnel, I mean.
Bebe Daniels: Oh, I see. I'm sorry. Say, that's a mighty rugged piece of shrapnel.
  What are you gonna do with it?
Chaplain Jerry Dean: I'm going to take it home to my wife.
Bebe Daniels: Well, I'm sure she'll treasure it. Now, getting back to the front lines
  over in France, how long did it take after you were wounded before you were safe in this
  hospital?
Chaplain Jerry Dean: I was hit at nine o'clock in the morning, was on the beach in France
  at five o'clock the same evening, and was landed over here the next day.
Bebe Daniels: Uh huh.
Chaplain Jerry Dean: I'd say that was a pretty good schedule, won't you, Bebe?
Bebe Daniels: I'd certainly would. Well, Chaplain Dean, I, I won't keep you any longer
  because I see you want to get back and finish your letter.
Chaplain Jerry Dean: That's all right, Bebe.
Bebe Daniels: Well, thank you very much for your story.
Chaplain Jerry Dean: And thank you for your visit.
Bebe Daniels: Well, folks, ... and next week at the same time on Purple Heart Corner. So
  until then, good bye for now and back to Cecil Madden in London.
Cecil Madden: Thank you, Bebe Daniels, and we're now back in the club. We call on our
  famous G.I. musical guests to play you "I Hear You Screamin'."
I HEAR YOU SCREAMIN'
Cecil Madden: Thank you, Glenn Miller, Ray McKinley and all of you. Next here's Ken
  Tredwell with his second lot of good stories for you.

Major Ken Tredwell: Thank you, Cecil, and without further ado we're gonna introduce Captain John West and Staff Sergeant Harold Zoller, standing up here together. Captain Johnny West, how about your home town first?
Captain John West: Ah, Sardis, Mississippi.
Major Ken Tredwell: How do you spell that Sardis?
Captain John West: Capital S-A-R-D-I-S.
Major Ken Tredwell: With a capital. And Sergeant Harold Zoller, your home town.
Sergeant Harold Zoller: Dorchester, Massachusetts.
Major Ken Tredwell: Tell me - ah -, Captain, why are you two here together?
Captain John West: It just happens that I was the pilot on a crew that landed in - ah - Normandy. Sergeant Zoller was a member of my crew.
Major Ken Tredwell: Ah, you're both on the same plane.
Captain John West: That is correct.
Major Ken Tredwell: And what kind of a plane is that?
Captain John West: That's a B-26, the best ship in the E.T.O.
Major Ken Tredwell: I'll buy that.

Announcer: That was the "American Eagle in Britain" program presented from London by the British Broadcasting Corporation.

28Jul44 (Fri) 11:00-11:15AM Co-Partners Hall, Bedford, England   SLO-59930
THE UPTOWN HALL recording   Aired 29Jul44

MY GUY'S COME BACK (opening theme)
   Corporal Paul Dubov: Hear that theme, folks? It tells you you're in "The Uptown Hall," meeting place of those who like their music soft but solid. And it also says we're ready to go with Sergeant Mel Powell's first tune of the evening, "Liza."
LIZA
Corporal Paul Dubov: Here to answer present when her name's called tonight is a little lady who's done a lot to make these meetings really enjoyable. Fellow members I give you "Sweet Lorraine."
SWEET LORRAINE
Corporal Paul Dubov: As chairman of the meeting I just received a rather curious note from one of the members. The idea seems to be that if we don't hurry up and play his favorite tune said member will personally take the old Hall apart stone by stone. Well, naturally we don't frighten easily but just to keep harmony in the Hall here it is, "Blue Room."
THE BLUE ROOM
Corporal Paul Dubov: Next those old insomniacs, the Crew Chiefs, and "I Couldn't Sleep a Wink Last Night."
I COULDN'T SLEEP A WINK LAST NIGHT
   Vocal refrain by the Crew Chiefs
Corporal Paul Dubov: Mel wrote it, Mel arranged it and Mel plays it. It's the boys and a little number dedicated to swing pianist Earl Hines. Mel calls it "The Earl."
THE EARL
Corporal Paul Dubov: And that's all from "The Uptown Hall."

Jul-Dec44 Co-Partners Hall, Bedford England
CORPORAL PAUL DUBOV DIALOGUE recordings

1. O.K. Well, let's go do a one take. If we don't make out we'll do it again. Oh, good. Corporal Jack Rusin. ... he plays a boogie piece called ... O.K.
(Test)

2. For his first number this Saturday mornin' Corporal Jack Rusin plays a boogie piece called "Left Swings Right." (Piano Parade)

3. Presenting "A Soldier and a Song," the voice of Sergeant Johnny Desmond and songs for you, you and you. (A Soldier and a Song)

4. To start this Sunday afternoon program Sergeant Johnny Desmond sings "Speak Low". (A Soldier and a Song)

5. To start this Sunday afternoon program Sergeant Johnny Desmond sings "Star Eyes." (A Soldier and a Song)

6. For his second song Johnny Desmond sings one of his own favorites, "I'll Walk Alone." (A Soldier and a Song)

7. For his second song Sergeant Johnny Desmond sings one of his own particular favorites, "Homesick." (A Soldier and a Song)

8. Now the good Sergeant takes a short rest while the orchestra plays one from the past, "Tuxedo Junction." (A Soldier and a Song)

9. Now the good Sergeant takes a short rest while the orchestra plays one of Jerry Gray's originals, "Jeep Jockey Jump." (A Soldier and a Song)

10. For the last song on this week's program we close with "The Music Stopped." Kind of apropos. (A Soldier and a Song)

11. For the last song on this week's program we close with "Now I Know." (A Soldier and a Song)

12. "A Soldier and a Song" has presented the voice of Sergeant Johnny Desmond, vocalist with the American Band of the A.E.F. Until next Sunday it's good bye and good luck. This is the American Forces Network. (A Soldier and a Song)

13. Wha-what I think is wrong, obviously I'm not modulating my voice. So, I tell you what, for the hell of it I'm going to try it one more time. And this time we'll try and give it some modulation. I think you'll understand what I mean after I get through this second take. So here goes.

14. For his first number this Saturday mornin' Corporal Jack Rusin plays a boogie piece called "Left Swings Right." (Piano Parade)

15. Presenting "A Soldier and a Song," the voice of Sergeant Johnny Desmond and songs for you, you and you. (A Soldier and a Song)

16. To start this Sunday afternoon program Sergeant Johnny Desmond sings "Speak Low". (A Soldier and a Song)

17. Just a minute, that didn't sound right.

18. To start this Sunday afternoon program Sergeant Johnny Desmond sings "Star Eyes." (A Soldier and a Song)

19. For his second song Johnny Desmond sings one of his own favorites, "I'll Walk Alone." (A Soldier and a Song)

20. For his second song Sergeant Johnny Desmond sings one of his own particular favorites, "Homesick." (A Soldier and a Song)

21. Now the good Sergeant takes a short rest while the orchestra plays one from the original pen of Jerry Gray, "Tuxedo Junction." (A Soldier and a Song)

22. And now we let the good Sergeant take a short rest while the orchestra plays one of Jerry Gray's originals, "Jeep Jockey Jump."
(Hums tune) Yeah, I know that one. (A Soldier and a Song)

23. For the last song on this week's program we close with "The Music Stopped." Kind of apropos. (A Soldier and a Song)

24. For the last song on this week's program we close with "Now I Know." (A Soldier and a Song)

25. "A Soldier and a Song" has presented the voice of Sergeant Johnny Desmond, vocalist with the American Band of the A.E.F. Until next Sunday it's good bye and good luck from all of us. This is the American Forces Network. (A Soldier and a Song)

26. Luncheon.

29Jul44 (Sat) late afternoon Wycombe Abbey (Pinetree), High Wycombe, England
V-8 BOND RALLY opening   Attendance: 4000

General Jimmy Doolittle: The war is going well. Substantial advances are being made on
  all three of the ground fronts, in Russia, in Italy, and in Norway. The air battle is
  going well, too. We're able to go any place we want in Germany. The Hun air force is
  being gradually crushed. The Hun manufacturing capacity for munitions is being
  destroyed. Our loses are substantially a quarter of what they were a few months ago.
  But in the prize ring when the battle's going well, when a fighter has his opponent on
  the ropes, he doesn't slow down, he gives him everything he has, he knocks him out.
  We've got the Hun groggy, we don't want to slow down now, we want to knock him out. One
  way to knock him out is to buy bonds.

WAC: Good, good afternoon, General. We would like to have you purchase the first
  Intrasquadron War Bond.
General Jimmy Doolittle: I'd be very pleased to.
WAC: Ah, would you prefer to make the allotment, sir, or by cash?
General Jimmy Doolittle: In cash.
WAC: Thank you, sir. And will Mrs. Doolittle be the co-owner?
General Jimmy Doolittle: That's right.
WAC: And here, sir, is your membership card. And we would like you to be the first to
  sign in our book which will go to General Arnold.
General Jimmy Doolittle: I shall be glad to.
Announcer (Lt.): Now General Doolittle ... the first pledge in this War Bond Drive.
General Jimmy Doolittle: Now I shall like to --- now I shall like to sell a bond.
WAC: All right, sir.
T/Sgt. Lutz: Tech. Sergeant Lutz buying, sir.
General Jimmy Doolittle: How would you like to buy a bond?
T/Sgt. Lutz: Well, sir, I'd like to take out one on a G.I. allotment.
General Jimmy Doolittle: All right. If you'd just sign the book, the Corporal will make
  out the papers.
T/Sgt. Lutz: Yes, sir. Sergeant.
General Jimmy Doolittle: Don't forget to drop your tickets in the box.
T/Sgt. Lutz: I won't, sir. Thank you very much, sir.
Announcer (Lt.): Hello, American Forces Network. You have just seen General Doolittle
  buy the first bond for the kickoff ...

    ...

IN THE MOOD

    ...

STAR DUST

    ...

Captain Glenn Miller: ... action which is composed of gentlemen from the various high
  grade orchestras throughout the United States, the New York Philharmonic, the Boston
  Symphony, Cleveland Orchestra, and Stokowski's little group down in Philadelphia and the
  head man in that outfit is Sergeant George Ockner. George, will you rise with your boys
  there, please?
  The saxophone section is presided over by that rather portly gentleman in the - near the
  center there and he used to occupy that same position with Artie Shaw before Artie went
  in the Navy. His name is Sergeant Hank Freeman. He's in charge of the boys.
  Gentlemen.
  That, ah, original gum-chum kid there leaning on the bass is a lad that had the dubious
  pleasure of working for me at one time. His name's Sergeant Trigger Alpert.
  Over in the trombone sections here there ...

...

Ah, the lad seated next to him is the Master Sergeant, the head man in the band, worked for all the famed leaders that Sergeant Privin did and some old country band by the name of Miller, Sergeant Zarchy.

...

WHAT DO YOU DO IN THE INFANTRY
Vocal refrain by Sergeant Johnny Desmond and the Crew Chiefs

...

I'LL GET BY (As Long As I Have You)
Vocal refrain by Sergeant Johnny Desmond

03Aug44 (Thu) 8:30-9:00PM Co-Partners Hall, Bedford, England   SWN-18951
AMERICAN BAND OF THE AEF broadcast   Attendance: 100

Corporal Paul Dubov: This program is heard over the Allied Expeditionary Forces Program of the B.B.C. and on the Home Service. This is a feature of the American Band of the A.E.F.

MOONLIGHT SERENADE (opening theme)

  Corporal Paul Dubov: The American Band of the A.E.F. under the direction of Captain Glenn Miller, your Thursday night thirty minutes with the Moonlight Serenader with tonight's special guests Britain's Sam Browne and a recent arrival to the A.E.F., America's famous singing star Dinah Shore. And here is Captain Glenn Miller.

Captain Glenn Miller: Thank you and good evening, everybody. It's a big night in our lives seeing a gal from back home. Dinah Shore has made the big hop across the ocean to do some singin' for you Tommies and Yanks and she'll be seein' a lot of you in person right soon. Tonight we're happy that Dinah's sayin' hello to the E.T.O. on our show and first thing we want to do is to make her feel right at home over here. So here's a tune that was born and brought up back in the States all wrapped up in a Sergeant Jerry Gray arrangement, "Sun Valley Jump."

SUN VALLEY JUMP

Captain Glenn Miller: Music speaks the universal language and just so long as it's good music it doesn't make much difference who sings it. Just as fightin' Tommy likes America's Dinah Shore, well good old fightin' Yank likes Britain's Sam Browne. Sam's in the big league no matter who he's singin' for and tonight he's singin' for every Allied fighter within listenin' distance. Here's a British voice feeling right at home in an American song, "Time on My Hands."

TIME ON MY HANDS (You in My Arms)

  Vocal refrain by Sam Browne

Captain Glenn Miller: Seein' as how this is a sort of a house warming for Dinah Shore, let's light up the front parlor and the --- give the gal a warm reception with a jumper from home.

IT MUST BE JELLY ('Cause Jam Don't Shake Like That)

Captain Glenn Miller: Thanks to the fact that England and America share a common language, common interests and a common enemy, we know and like a lot of things about each other, whether it's cricket or baseball, or there's hot dogs or fish and chips, we share many a taste. That's one reason Tommy, as well as G.I. Joe, will be mighty happy to know that Dinah Shore is on this side of the ocean to sing for them right up at the fightin' front. And here she is, Dinah Shore.

Dinah Shore: Thank you, Captain Miller.

Captain Glenn Miller: The pleasure's all ours, Captain Dinah.

Dinah Shore: Oh, I'm just a simulated Captain.

Captain Glenn Miller: Well, that's all right, Dinah. There's one thing we know, you aren't here to do simulated singin'. You've brought along the real thing.

Dinah Shore: Well, I'm here to sing my head off, I know that. And to you boys listening, I'm fresh from the States and I've brought you a love letter song. As a matter of fact I brought two, they're straight from the gal you left behind.

Captain Glenn Miller: Well, tonight the postman sings twice, and what's your first choice, Dinah?

Dinah Shore: Well, here's a song that's bound to be humming around in the heart of any gal who's longing for her man, "Long Ago and Far Away."

LONG AGO (And Far Away)

  Vocal refrain by Dinah Shore

Captain Glenn Miller: Nice goin', Dinah Shore, and just as we read 'em slow when mail call brings us two letters, we're gonna save a song for later. Right now it's medley time callin' for something old, something new, something borrowed and something blue. The old song, "Flow Gently, Sweet Afton."

FLOW GENTLY, SWEET AFTON (Old tune)

  Captain Glenn Miller: Here's a soldier and a song, Sergeant Johnny Desmond sings the new tune.

MOON DREAMS (New tune)

  Vocal refrain by Sergeant Johnny Desmond and the Crew Chiefs

Captain Glenn Miller: The vice-president in charge of our loan department puts the bite
   on Benny Goodman for our borrowed tune, "Don't Be That Way."
DON'T BE THAT WAY (Borrowed tune)
   Captain Glenn Miller: Last, the blue tune, "Blue Champagne."
BLUE CHAMPAGNE (Blue tune)
Captain Glenn Miller: And here once again is the gal who U.S.O. camp shows delivered over
   here to you guys on the fightin' front, Dinah Shore.
Dinah Shore: Thank you, Captain Glenn Miller, and here's that other love letter song I
   brought along for all you Tommies and Yanks. Straight from the gal you left behind,
   "I'll Be Seeing You."
I'LL BE SEEING YOU
   Vocal refrain by Dinah Shore
Captain Glenn Miller: That's wrappin' it up, Dinah Shore, and speakin' for every man in
   the A.E.F. it's mighty nice havin' you over here with us. Now for the last go around a
   salute to you boys we've had the pleasure of meeting this last few weeks out at the
   fighter and bomber bases.
WITH MY HEAD IN THE CLOUDS
   Captain Glenn Miller: The Crew Chiefs sing and the whole gang join in to sing "With My
   Head in the Clouds."
   Vocal refrain by Sergeant Johnny Desmond, the Crew Chiefs and the Ensemble
Captain Glenn Miller: This is Captain Glenn Miller sayin' thanks to Britain's Sam Browne
   for being here and thanks and a great big welcome to Dinah Shore, bringin' a great big
   hunk o' home to every American in the A.E.F. and to you folks out there listenin', if
   you like this kind of listenin' there's plenty more to be had same time every Thursday.
   For now it's good luck and good night.
MOONLIGHT SERENADE (closing theme)
   Corporal Paul Dubov: You have been listening to the American Band of the A.E.F. under
   the direction of Captain Glenn Miller. Tonight's special guest stars were America's
   Dinah Shore and Britain's Sam Browne. This program reached you through the Allied
   Expeditionary Forces Program of the B.B.C. and on the Home Service.

03Aug44 (Thu) 9:00PM Co-Partners Hall, Bedford, England
  THE UPTOWN HALL recording session with Dinah Shore

31214 (17214)   S/Sgt. Mel Powell: Hi, fellows. This is Sergeant Mel Powell sort of
Aired 11Aug44   sideling in here sidewise to see if I can get a word in edgewise. And
                  the word, you folks will be glad to know, is Dinah. Seems like people
                  hereabouts have been talking about nothing but Dinah Shore since the last
                  few visits to the program. So in response to a mailbag full of requests,
                  here she is again. And, Dinah, the boys say your tune tonight has got to
                  be "Night and Day."
                NIGHT AND DAY
                  Vocal refrain by Dinah Shore

31217 (17217)   S/Sgt. Mel Powell: Hello, fellows. This is Sergeant Mel Powell and I'm
Aired 16Aug44   supposed to be proprietor of this here "Uptown Hall." So taking my job
                  seriously it's a right proud moment when comes the time, as it does now,
                  to announce that Miss Dinah Shore is winding up to make a pitch. That's
                  baseball talk, for you Tommies. To put it correctly, she's going to sing
                  you a song. Dinah, you do the sayin', we'll do the playin'.
                Dinah Shore: Right you are, Mel Powell. And this one is about as American
                  as that baseball you were talking about or apple pie or the Hudson River
                  night boat. Not only that, it's been getting a lot of humming around the
                  places where the Tommies get their fun. So that makes it just cut out
                  for the job it's here to do. Tommy and Yank cut yourself a slice of
                  "Honeysuckle Rose."
                HONEYSUCKLE ROSE
                  Vocal refrain by Dinah Shore

07Aug44 or 06Sep44 7:45-8:00PM Co-Partners Hall, Bedford, England
  STRINGS WITH WINGS broadcast   Script

I SUSTAIN THE WINGS (opening theme)
Corporal Paul Dubov: Hello there. Welcome to another program of "Strings with Wings."
  Here we are back again with more of your favorite tunes, played as only violins can
  play them. So take time out, if you can, to lean back and listen to some of the old
  tunes you remember and enjoy. The first one tonight, "With a Song in My Heart."
WITH A SONG IN MY HEART

09Aug44 (Wed) 11:00-11:15AM Co-Partners Hall, Bedford, England   SOX-36628
  THE UPTOWN HALL recording   Aired 09Aug44

MY GUY'S COME BACK (opening theme)

  ...

Corporal Paul Dubov: Our business here is to bring you folks some of that soft but solid
  music we know you like and that's what we're going to do right now as Mel and the boys
  take off on their first tune of the evening, "Makin' Whoopee!"
MAKIN' WHOOPEE!
Corporal Paul Dubov: Sergeant Mel gets the green light for a second tune tonight and here
  it is, a little something on the sweet side, "Confessin'."
(I'm) CONFESSIN' (That I Love You)
Corporal Paul Dubov: Our good friend the censor tells us we can't mention any weather
  information in our V-Mail but he puts his personal O.K. on this next one and I think you
  will too. It's "Blue Skies."
BLUE SKIES

  ...

I SURRENDER, DEAR
  Vocal refrain by Sergeant Johnny Desmond

  ...

Corporal Paul Dubov: We just can't adjourn without letting you hear this next one. It's
  Mel and the boys in a fancy arrangement of "I'll Remember April."
I'LL REMEMBER APRIL
BBC female announcer: There'll be another program by the Swing Sextet next Friday evening
  at 7:15.

  ...

MY GUY'S COME BACK (closing theme)

10Aug44 (Thu) 3:30-4:00PM Dunkers Den, Piccadilly, London, England   DOX-36727
  American Red Cross Rainbow Corner Club (run by Adele Astaire)   Aired 12Aug44
  AMERICAN EAGLE IN BRITAIN recording   192nd Program   Attendance: 500
  Material within [ ] was deleted from the recording before it was broadcast.

Announcer: This is London calling. The British Broadcasting Company presents its weekly
  program "American Eagle in Britain." Your host today is Cecil Madden.
[Cecil Madden: This is London Calling from American Red Cross Rainbow Corner.]
Let's Sing a Happy Song (opening theme --- recording, not Miller band)
Cecil Madden: Once again and for the 192nd time it's hello to all of you in America.
  Flying bombs or no, London will always carry on and this is Cecil Madden of the British
  Broadcasting Corporation saying call in the family, join us on our "American Eagle in
  Britain" program sent to you with our usual good wishes from the B.B.C. in London,
  England. And this opening spot is always given to six of the smaller towns of the
  United States.
Corporal Vincent Begin: This is Corporal Vincent Begin calling Wayne, Michigan.
Corporal Peter Anastos: This is Corporal Peter Anastos calling Newport, New Hampshire.
Sergeant Gordon Westwood: This is Sergeant Gordon Westwood calling Moab, Utah.
Sergeant Ben Moja: This is Sergeant Ben Moja calling Hayward, California.
Sergeant Steinberg: This is Sergeant Steinberg calling Potsdam, New York.
Corporal Richard Adams: This is Corporal Richard Adams calling Hartford, Connecticut.
Cecil Madden: And here we are, under the pavement in Dunkers Den in the famous American
  Red Cross Rainbow Corner Club in Piccadilly, London. Our musical guests today are G.I.s
  They are "The Swing Shift," the unit of the American Band of the Allied Expeditionary
  Force, who are over here broadcasting with us. They're headed by Sergeant Ray McKinley
  and they're under the personal direction of Captain Glenn Miller. Let's give 'em both a
  cheer. The Captain's looking as suave as ever but I guess he's waiting to hear about
  this program from Denver, Colorado and Monrovia, California. So with the help of
  Sergeant Mel Powell at the piano and the usual help of our song master Sergeant Cecil
  Elmore of Cadillac, Michigan, we've been talking over a song your men would like to sing
  you. And today their choice at rehearsal has gone to "I've Been Working on the
  Railroad."
I'VE BEEN WORKING ON THE RAILROAD (S/Sgt. Mel Powell, piano)
  Vocal refrain by Sergeant Cecil Elmore, the audience and the band members
Cecil Madden: Stand by, New Rochelle, here's your favorite son, a member of the 8th Air
  Force, our good friend and interviewer in our program, Major Ken Tredwell.
Major Ken Tredwell: Thank you, Cecil Madden, and before we go any further we want to
  acknowledge - ah - the great part that Colonel Ed Kirby of Nashville, Tennessee has done
  to get Glenn Miller for us today and to get Glenn Miller for us over here in the E.T.O.
  with Ray McKinley and all the boys. So to Colonel Ed Kirby and his folks back home we
  want to say thanks. And now standing in front of our microphone is P.F.C. Paul
  Stafsholt. Is that right, Paul?
Pfc. Paul Stafsholt: That's right, sir.
Major Ken Tredwell: Where's your home?
Pfc. Paul Stafsholt: Mason, Wisconsin, sir.
Major Ken Tredwell: Mason, Wisconsin. Look at him sweat. How about that? Whereabouts
  in Mason, Wisconsin do you live?
Pfc. Paul Stafsholt: I - just south of it, sir. At a - a little tavern of Biden, right
  south of it.
Major Ken Tredwell: A little tavern of - he lives in a tavern, that's what I like.
Pfc. Paul Stafsholt: Right next to it, sir.
Major Ken Tredwell: It's a good life if you can get it. [What's the population back
  there, Paul?
Pfc. Paul Stafsholt: It's a very small town, sir, only 400 people.
Major Ken Tredwell: 400. Are your dad and mother back there?
Pfc. Paul Stafsholt: Yes, sir.
Major Ken Tredwell: Any brothers or sisters?
Pfc. Paul Stafsholt: I have one brother.
Major Ken Tredwell: And any sisters?
Pfc. Paul Stafsholt: I have sisters but they're not there.

Major Ken Tredwell: How many sisters have you?
Pfc. Paul Stafsholt: I have three sisters. One's in Seattle, one in Los Angeles,
  California and the other in Superior, Wisconsin.
Major Ken Tredwell: Here in Paul's home town there are four - seven - Stafsholts. Well
  that's about 2% of the population. I wonder how many other men could say they represent
  2% of the population of a town. Have you got a girl, Paul?
Pfc. Paul Stafsholt: Yes, sir.
Major Ken Tredwell: What's her name, or would you rather not talk about her?
Pfc. Paul Stafsholt: Oh, there might be a lot of them there, sir!]
Major Ken Tredwell: I see you're a paratrooper. I see you're wearing the Purple Heart,
  the E.T.O. with one - ah - Combat Star and the Presidential Citation. Let's give him a
  hand. Tell me, Paul, have you been in Norway?
Pfc. Paul Stafsholt: Yes, sir.
Major Ken Tredwell: When did you go there?
Pfc. Paul Stafsholt: About six hours before H-Hour on D-Day.
Major Ken Tredwell: Six hours before D-Day?
Pfc. Paul Stafsholt: Yes, sir.
Major Ken Tredwell: And what was your unit's objective?
Pfc. Paul Stafsholt: Ah, we were supposed to blow up a few bridges, sir.
Major Ken Tredwell: Did you blow them up?
Pfc. Paul Stafsholt: Ah, you're not lyin'.
Major Ken Tredwell: Good, good. Were you with them at the time, Paul?
Pfc. Paul Stafsholt: No, sir.
Major Ken Tredwell: Where were you?
Pfc. Paul Stafsholt: I was about four and a half miles south of Carentan, nine miles
  below the line.
Major Ken Tredwell: Behind the enemy line. What did you exist on? What did you eat
  while you were back there?
Pfc. Paul Stafsholt: Well, we had a K-ration apiece when we went in there and for the
  next five days we lived - lived on milk and butter.
Major Ken Tredwell: Milk and butter. How about that? Tell me, did you contact any
  French at all?
Pfc. Paul Stafsholt: Yes, sir. We did.
Major Ken Tredwell: Were they good to you?
Pfc. Paul Stafsholt: What we contacted were very good.
Major Ken Tredwell: Mighty fine. And when did you get back to your outfit finally? How
  long did it take?
Pfc. Paul Stafsholt: Nine days later, sir.
Major Ken Tredwell: Nine days on milk and butter. What a life. Wow! When were you
  wounded, Paul?
Pfc. Paul Stafsholt: I was wounded on the eleventh day, sir.
Major Ken Tredwell: Whereabout?
Pfc. Paul Stafsholt: I was - ah -
Major Ken Tredwell: That is, where - whereabouts on your body?
Pfc. Paul Stafsholt: In the arm, sir.
Major Ken Tredwell: In the arm.
Pfc. Paul Stafsholt: Right forearm.
Major Ken Tredwell: And then you came back to England?
Pfc. Paul Stafsholt: Yes, sir.
Major Ken Tredwell: How did England look to you when you got back here?
Pfc. Paul Stafsholt: Well, she looked better than it ever looked before.
Major Ken Tredwell: Paul. I'd like to say to P.F.C. Paul Stafsholt that he and all the
  boys like him that are really doing the job look mighty good to us. Thank you a lot,
  Paul. And here's a sailor man. It's Joseph H. Gross. Joe, what rank are you? I see
  an insignia on your left arm.
Joseph H. Gross: That's - ah - Aviation Machinist's Mate, 3rd Class.
Major Ken Tredwell: And the shoulder wings you're - you're wearing indicate that you're a
  ...
Joseph H. Gross: Air - Air Crew Man.
Major Ken Tredwell: I see. What's your home town, Joe?

Joseph H. Gross: It's Towson, Maryland.
[Major Ken Tredwell: Close to what other town?
Joseph H. Gross: Oh, it's eight miles north of Baltimore.
Major Ken Tredwell: When did you last see Baltimore?
Joseph H. Gross: Well, it was Thanksgiving morning.
Major Ken Tredwell: You had a Thanksgiving dinner at home, did you?
Joseph H. Gross: Yes.
Major Ken Tredwell: Tell us what you had.
Joseph H. Gross: When I got home, it was my last time home, I was just bringing my car
   there to leave it, I didn't know it was Thanksgiving 'til I saw my mother dressing the
   turkey. Then we had pumpkin pie and salads and sweet potatoes and candied, sweet ...
Major Ken Tredwell: That's all, that's all, brother. He's had it.] Joe, how long have
   you been in the Navy?
Joseph H. Gross: I've been here 23 months.
Major Ken Tredwell: And you've been in - ah - E.T.O. how long?
Joseph H. Gross: Oh, let's see, eight months.
Major Ken Tredwell: Eight months. Have you made any flights? I see you're with the Air
   Corps, that is, Air Corps Navy.
Joseph H. Gross: Well, yes, I've had nine missions. Right now I'm not flying.
Major Ken Tredwell: You're not flying. Have you been in many - ah - different types of
   craft since you've been in the Navy?
Joseph H. Gross: Well, I trained in CBYs at Jacksonville.
Major Ken Tredwell: How about on the sea itself? Any ocean going craft?
Joseph H. Gross: No. I - I had eleven days on the way over here. That's all the sea
   duty I've had and I got sick as a dog. I couldn't eat. Couldn't eat for three days.
Major Ken Tredwell: A sailor - huh, huh - a sailor in the Navy for 23 months, he's been
   eleven days on the water and that was getting over here. How about that? That's like a
   barber without any hair, a dentist without any teeth, like a mess without any Spam. How
   about that? Joe, you're a dry land sailor. How do you do that?
Joseph H. Gross: I like it that way.
Major Ken Tredwell: That's - that's mighty swell. Thanks a lot, Joe Gross, and good luck
   to the sailor on land.
Joseph H. Gross: Thank you.
Cecil Madden: Thank you, Ken. Now we call in our musical guests, Ray McKinley and the
   Crew Chiefs to play you "G.I. Jive."
G.I. JIVE
   Vocal refrain by Technical Sergeant Ray McKinley and the Crew Chiefs
Cecil Madden: Thank you, Ray McKinley, for that fine bit of yardbird yodeling. I hope
   they heard it in New Haven.
Sergeant Ray McKinley: Thank you, Cecil. We sort of enjoyed it ourselves.
Cecil Madden: Well, you've done something for us. Is there anything in return we can do
   for you?
Sergeant Ray McKinley: Yes, there is. You see, we know all about your roving microphone
   coming on - ah - now and how about letting it roam over our way, over towards the band?
Cecil Madden: Certainly, and as it's the roving microphone next, take over, Ken, will
   you, with our roving microphone.
Major Ken Tredwell: Thank you, Cecil, and Ray, we'll get all those boys that we can.
   Let's dig right back here by the band. The first man we're gonna hit is Tech. Sergeant
   who has plenty to do with their routings, their bookings and all the arrangements they
   have to make.
T/Sgt. Paul Dudley: New York City, Paul Dudley.
Major Ken Tredwell: Good old New York City. And right next to him with one of these good
   singing men.
Corporal Murray Kane: New York City, Murray Kane.
Major Ken Tredwell: Three more of them right in a row.
Pfc. Gene Steck: Gene Steck, Olyphant, P.A.
Pfc. Lynn Allison: Chicago, Illinois, Lynn Allison.
Major Ken Tredwell: You're not the bass, are you?
Corporal Artie Malvin: New York City, Corporal Artie Malvin.
Major Ken Tredwell: And one more right in the corner here. Sergeant, how about it?

Sergeant James B. Jackson: New York City, Sergeant James B. Jackson.
Major Ken Tredwell: My, my. And here are four sax men right in front that have been
    dishing out some of this terrific music to us. Let's start right with you, Sergeant.
Sergeant Vincent Carbone: Tyrone, New York, Vince Carbone.
S/Sgt. Hank Freeman: New Haven, Connecticut, Sergeant Hank Freeman.
Major Ken Tredwell: How can they talk so softly and play so loud? How about that?
Sergeant Michael Hucko: Syracuse, New York, Michael Hucko.
Corporal Jack Ferrier: Springfield, Mass., Jack Ferrier.
Major Ken Tredwell: Now we'll get this man with the big "geetar." Looks like an
    overgrown "geetar." How about it, Sergeant?
Sergeant Carmen Mastren: New York City, Carmen Mastren.
Major Ken Tredwell: And a big bass man. I think they call him Trigger.
S/Sgt. Trigger Alpert: Trigger Alpert, Indianapolis, Indiana.
Major Ken Tredwell: And here's a piano man and one of the best. Wait 'til you hear his
    name. Here we go.
S/Sgt. Mel Powell: New York City, Mel Powell.
Major Ken Tredwell: I wish I could get back there to the back row and get some of you
    swell trumpet men. I see "Red" Nichols and the big Z.Z. back there with Master Sergeant
    stripes on him. Here we go. Here's one man I missed, by gosh. Come on back here.
Private Mannie Thaler: Brooklyn, New York, Mannie Thaler.
Major Ken Tredwell: We had to get Brooklyn in there somewhere. And here are two very
    attractive WACs, get out your pens and pencils, boys, we'll get all the information.
Mellor Wizner: Souder, Missouri, Mellor Wizner.
Major Ken Tredwell: Missouri. Here we go. Here's another.
Esther Figlas: Cleveland, Ohio, Esther Figlas.
Major Ken Tredwell: And three very comfortable soldiers, coats off across their laps,
    very comfortable, not perspiring, very happy.
Dan Oakley: Augusta, Georgia, Dan Oakley.
Bob Monsen: Saint Johns, Pennsylvania, Bob Monsen.
Paul Tranford: Chelsea, Massachusetts, Paul Tranford.
Major Ken Tredwell: Let's move over across the aisle. Here's another soldier.
Vince Murgolski: Pittsburgh, Pennsylvania, Vince Murgolski.
Major Ken Tredwell: And here sits a G.I. with brown and green suspenders. How about
    that?
Ben Olman: Brooklyn, New York, Ben Olman.
Major Ken Tredwell: We should have known it. We should have known it. Here we go.
Jerome Budd: Chicago, Illinois, Jerome Budd.
Major Ken Tredwell: And a Tech. Sergeant in the Air Corps.
T/Sgt. Robert Bale: Glenville, West Virginia, Sergeant Robert Bale.
Major Ken Tredwell: Here's a 9th Air Force boy.
John R. Shaydon: Stevensville, Pennsylvania, John R. Shaydon.
Major Ken Tredwell: And two sailors right next to a pillar here.
Charles Raves: Memphis, Tennessee, Charles Raves.
Walter Brank: Munford, Tennessee, Walter Brank.
Major Ken Tredwell: And to show that we've got complete spirit of cooperation, a soldier
    sitting right next to that sailor.
Andrew Stephans: Seattle, Washington, Andrew Stephans.
Major Ken Tredwell: And a stack of boys standing up in the back. Let's get five or six
    of you right in a row. Sergeant.
Sergeant Eugene Litt: Mahoning, Pennsylvania, Eugene Litt.
Major Ken Tredwell: And a man with a very - ah - where do you part your hair, soldier?
Daniel Olenberg: Madison, Nebraska, Daniel Olenberg.
Cliff Dodds: Akron, Ohio, Cliff Dodds.
Jim Foley: Milwaukee, Wisconsin, Jim Foley.
Major Ken Tredwell: He can't think of it. He can't think of it, by gosh. Sergeant,
    gonna try you once more.
Sergeant Edward Vale, Jr.: Omaha, Nebraska, Sergeant Ed - Edward Vale, Junior.
Major Ken Tredwell: Got him that time. Thank you, Sergeant. Now [let's run down this
    middle aisle and get right to the center of the floor again. I see a lot of bright eyes
    and eager lads. We'll get just as many as we can. Here's an Air Corps man.

S/Sgt. Franklin Orr: Staff Sergeant Franklin Orr, Corpus Christi, Texas.
Major Ken Tredwell: And here's an old-timer, he's really been in the Army.
Benjamin Agen: Brooklyn, New York, Benjamin Agen.
Major Ken Tredwell: Hello, Brooklyn. Here's the Air Corps again.
Harold Egood: Lowell, Massachusetts, Harold Egood.
Ed Gregory: Lawrenceville, Oklahoma, Ed Gregory.
Major Ken Tredwell: From Oklahoma to Massachusetts. Sergeant, how about you?
Raddy Sturtz: Rantoul, Illinois, Raddy Sturtz.
Major Ken Tredwell: Say, you have got buttons on those cuffs. You don't have to button
    them up but you have got buttons, haven't you? What's your name and home town?
Reuben Barks: Clear Lake, Wisconsin, Reuben Barks.]
Frank Mackintosh: Portland, Oregon, Frank Mackintosh.
Phil Hamley: Columbus, Kansas, Phil Hamley.
Major Ken Tredwell: How about the other side? Hello, sailor.
Jack Bord: Jack Bord, Gaffney, South Carolina.
Major Ken Tredwell: You look as if you want to eat that microphone. Do you? How about
    it, Sergeant?
Sergeant Elton Shuggers: Jackson, Michigan, Elton Shuggers.
Major Ken Tredwell: And here's a slim - ah - wisp of a fellow, just - just about able to
    sit on a seat here. How about it, soldier?
Jake Culpepper: Athens, Georgia, Jake Culpepper.
Charles S. Nova: Jamesville, North Carolina, Charles S. Nova.
Major Ken Tredwell: Can't help wondering what they feed Culpepper at home. How about
    that? Here we go.
Artie Mann: Chicago, Illinois, Artie Mann.
William Jordan: Evansville, Indiana, William Jordan.
James Allan: Flint, Michigan, James Allan.
Major Ken Tredwell: And here's that Lieutenant the band was singing about.
Lieutenant Thomas Lee: Rockingham, North Carolina, Lieutenant Thomas Lee.
Major Ken Tredwell: And right next to Lieutenant Lee.
Lieutenant Cons: Pekin, Illinois, Lieutenant Cons.
Major Ken Tredwell: Look like good men, soldiers. And this hasn't done any good,
    Lieutenant, in this Army, by god. Let's get down - ah - back to this other aisle. I
    see plenty of sailors here. We're going to hit four in the front row. Get them one -
    one right after the other.
John Hodd: Akron, Ohio, John Hodd.
George Block: Tyler, Alabama, George Block.
Allen Lloyd: Grand Rapids, Minnesota, Allen Lloyd.
Major Ken Tredwell: I hope Minnesota could hear that.
Robert Croft: Orangeville, Pennsylvania, Robert Croft.
Major Ken Tredwell: We're really getting around the country. Curly, how about you?
Leonard Ross: Prescott, Arizona, Leonard Ross.
Major Ken Tredwell: Don't laugh. He can't help it if he's got curly hair. Leave the,
    leave the man alone. How about it, sailor?
Robin Ramos: Bronx, New York, Robin Ramos.
Major Ken Tredwell: The Bronx. Right, right. Sailor, how about it?
Jim Shakley: State College, Pennsylvania, Jim Shakley.
Major Ken Tredwell: The 9th Air Force.
Andrew Kesacki: Allport, Pennsylvania, Andrew Kesacki.
Major Ken Tredwell: And the dark haired boy.
Dick Nihestle: Boulder, Colorado, Dick Nihestle.
Major Ken Tredwell: The 9th Air Force again.
Allan Trayvord: Boston, Massachusetts, Allan Trayvord.
Major Ken Tredwell: And again.
Bob Stocker: Evansville, Indiana, Bob Stocker.
Major Ken Tredwell: Sailor, have I gotten you yet? You want to be gotten? Here we go.
Bill Hall: Indianapolis, Indiana, Bill Hall.
Major Ken Tredwell: And next to Bill another sailor.
Eddie Sampolski: Eddie Sampolski, Rahway, New Jersey.

Major Ken Tredwell: And I see a Purple Heart, and E.T.O. and two Combat Stars on this sailor.
Al Marlow: Brooklyn, New York, Al Marlow.
Peter Shedler: Phillipsburg, New Jersey, Peter Shedler.
Major Ken Tredwell: Let's get some soldiers back here. Here's an 8th Air Force man.
Joe Mersey: Cleveland, Ohio, Joe Mersey.
Nick Carter: Portland, Maine, Nick Carter.
Albert Minns: North Brookfield, Massachusetts, Albert Minns.
Major Ken Tredwell: I love those accents from up there. Park your car in the car yard. Yeah. Good stuff. How about it, Sergeant?
Art Tampson: Detroit, Michigan, Art Tampson.
Major Ken Tredwell: Say, here are some suspenders again. How do you guys get away with it?
Dick Merle: Pocomoke City, Maryland, Dick Merle.
Major Ken Tredwell: And a man, we can see his identification tags right here, he's blood type "O." How about it, Sergeant?
Sergeant Nat Ruse: St. Louis, Missouri, Nat Ruse.
John Trunow: Cleveland, Ohio, John Trunow.
Charles Martin: Leesville, Louisiana, Charles Martin.
Major Ken Tredwell: Boys, I'll get as many as I can back there. Here we go. How about it, blondy?
Private Mullen: Warren, Indiana, Private Mullen.
Major Ken Tredwell: A D.F.C., an Air Medal and three Clo - Clusters, a Presidential Citation, a Staff Sergeant.
S/Sgt. Don Crutcher: Kiowa, Kansas, Don Crutcher.
Freddy Moser: Burney, Indiana, Freddy Moser.
Major Ken Tredwell: And here is the eagerest beaver in the whole room. Let's get him.
Chuck Capualo: Prov - Providence, Rhode Island, Chuck Capualo.
Major Ken Tredwell: He doesn't need a mike. Ha, ha, ha. They can hear that from Providence without a mike. Cecil, I guess it's about time to take it back. Take over, will you please?
Cecil Madden: Thank you, Ken, for that tour around the room. Now standby, Connecticut. Today we spotlight station WICC, Bridgeport, that great capital of industry where you do so much to back up the men in uniform. And just as I came in here I was handed a letter from William Street, Bridgeport. We also spotlight station WNLC, New London, the friendly voice of the Thames. That's pretty difficult for me to say because we have a little river around here which we call the Thames. And so, greetings to you of the Electric Boat Company and the Coast Guard Academy, not forgetting the Connecticut College for Women. The very best of luck to all of you in Bridgeport, New London, and those orchestra wives in New Haven from all of us in London. There are two fellows from Connecticut in the room, I'm just going to bring them up to say hello to you.
Corporal Andy Terence: Hello, Connecticut. This is Corporal Andy Terence calling Stafford Springs to say hello to the folks and all the boys back there. Are you boys still having those matches at the bowling alleys? I hope so, because I'll be joining you in them soon.
Cecil Madden: Now here's the other one.
S/Sgt. Joseph J. Wojnar: Calling Thompsonville, Connecticut. Hello, friends and folks. Staff Ser - Staff Sergeant Joseph J. Wojnar speaking. Bigelow, how's those G.I. blankets comin'? We'll be seeing you soon.
Cecil Madden: Grand. And especially for you, Connecticut, Ray McKinley and the band play "King Porter Stomp."
KING PORTER STOMP
Cecil Madden: For the second time we take you now to Normandy, where in a casualty collecting station, the second link in the chain, that talented and great-hearted lady, Bebe Daniels, famous on stage and radio, is waiting to talk to some of your doctors and some of your men. Over now to somewhere in France, so come in, will you, Bebe Daniels.

Bebe Daniels: Thank you, Cecil Madden, and hello to all of you folks back home in America. Last week Purple Heart Corner took you to a battalion first aid station 600 yards behind the front lines in Normandy with a promise that this week we'd take you to the second link in the chain of the evacuation of our wounded, the collecting station. So here we are. This time we're 2000 yards behind the front line. And now I'll try and give you a brief description of this particular collecting station. It's set up in a large field. There's no camouflage here, only a large red cross on the ground. The doctors and aid men are all very busy right now, going about taking care of the wounded who are lying on the grass on litters, covered with blankets. Ambulances and jeeps continue to arrive and depart. The more seriously wounded are being treated in the tents while the slightly wounded are being treated here on the, in the open. Colonel Unger, I don't think the doctors here would mind if I talk to the boys out here, do you?

Colonel Unger: No, go ahead, Bebe.

Bebe Daniels: Well, fellow, what's your name?

Pfc. Edward Baylan: Ah, P.F.C. Edward Baylan from Manteca, California.

Bebe Daniels: What happened to you?

Pfc. Edward Baylan: Well, I was just in a little cave-in, is all.

Bebe Daniels: Is that all? You're looking fine now.

Pfc. Edward Baylan: Yeah. Feeling good, too.

Bebe Daniels: I guess your folk'll be glad to hear that. By the way, who have you got back home?

Pfc. Edward Baylan: Oh, my mother, my father, and little sister.

Bebe Daniels: What about a girl friend?

Pfc. Edward Baylan: Yes, a girl friend I hope to get back to and make her mine just as soon as I can.

Bebe Daniels: I'm sure you will. I hope the wedding bells'll ring out for you very soon.

Pfc. Edward Baylan: Yeah.

Bebe Daniels: And who's this sitting next to you?

Private Diginene Mare: Private Diginene Mare.

Bebe Daniels: Have you a girl friend back home, too?

Private Diginene Mare: Not yet.

Bebe Daniels: Not yet? Who have you, your ma?

Private Diginene Mare: My mother and my sister and I have two brothers in - one brother in the Navy.

Bebe Daniels: What are you going to do the first thing when you get home?

Private Diginene Mare: Well. Call my mother and sister.

Bebe Daniels: That's fine.

Private Diginene Mare: See 'em.

Bebe Daniels: I hope that'll be very soon. ... I betcha aren't. What's your name?

Private Raymond Anthonely: Private Raymond Anthonely.

Bebe Daniels: And where are you from?

Private Raymond Anthonely: Chicago, Illinois.

Bebe Daniels: Chicago, Illinois. And who's back home listening to you today?

Private Raymond Anthonely: My wife.

Bebe Daniels: Your wife?

Private Raymond Anthonely: That's right.

Bebe Daniels: Would you like to say something to her?

Private Raymond Anthonely: I don't know what to say.

Bebe Daniels: Aw, you know what to say.

Private Raymond Anthonely: All I can say is just keep writin' them letters, that's all.

Bebe Daniels: Aw. That's fine. And I know she will. I see you're walking, soldier, so I guess you're feeling all right.

Rocco Ballenino: Yes, ma'am, but I'm a bit tired.

Bebe Daniels: You are? I bet it's pretty tough up at the front, isn't it?

Rocco Ballenino: Hotter than hell.

Bebe Daniels: Tell me something, how'd you get that scratch over your eye?

Rocco Ballenino: We were all around the beach trying to evacuate some casualties when a shell hit, a shell hit in the road and shrapnel flew all over the place and just whizzed by me.

Bebe Daniels: That's tough. Well, what's your name?

Rocco Ballenino: Rocco Ballenino.
Bebe Daniels: From where?
Rocco Ballenino: Brooklyn, New York.
Bebe Daniels: Colonel Unger, how about your doing your usual job and introducing us to
  the Commanding Officer?
Colonel Unger: Bebe, I sure know what I'm going to do after this war. I'm going to be a
  receptionist. Well, anyhow, I want you to meet Captain Stanley.
Bebe Daniels: Very glad to know you, Captain Stanley. You have a very, very comfortable
  looking station here.
Captain Stanley: Thank you, Bebe. We try hard to make our boys comfortable as soon as we
  can. You see, we have three tents here with an emergency dressing station where our
  wounded are cared for before we take them on to the clearing station.
Bebe Daniels: Yes, I could see that.
Captain Stanley: We have brought them here mostly by jeeps that are fixed up to carry
  litters and they really ride comfortably.
Bebe Daniels: Tell me, do you use ambulances?
Captain Stanley: Yes, when it's possible to get through with them.
Bebe Daniels: How about your staff?
Captain Stanley: We have three doctors and two medical administration officers who take
  care of all our records. It assures us of the fact that our wounded are checked.
Bebe Daniels: Tell me, what other setups have you, doctor?
Captain Stanley: We have our kitchen, which is mobile, and our men live in foxholes. But
  this all goes to make up a more mobile outfit. By the way, there are some patients
  coming in now.
Bebe Daniels: Well, is it all right if I go up and talk to some of them?
Captain Stanley: Why sure, of course it is.
Bebe Daniels: Hello, fellow. What's your name?
Private Edward T. McNaley: Private Edward T. McNaley.
Bebe Daniels: You feelin' all right?
Private Edward T. McNaley: Pretty good.
Bebe Daniels: Would you like to say something back home?
Private Edward T. McNaley: I'd like to say hello to my wife, Mary.
Bebe Daniels: Mary. Where's Mary?
Private Edward T. McNaley: Chicago, Illinois.
Bebe Daniels: And I know she'll be glad to know you're feeling all right.
Sergeant Walren Mullins: Sergeant Walren Mullins of Avondale, West Virginia.
Bebe Daniels: And what happened to you?
Sergeant Walren Mullins: Well, I was in the wrong place at the right time, I guess.
Bebe Daniels: Where were you hit?
Sergeant Walren Mullins: I got a piece of shrapnel in my left hand.
Bebe Daniels: Does it hurt you much now?
Sergeant Walren Mullins: No, it feels O.K. now.
Bebe Daniels: What were you doing up there?
Sergeant Walren Mullins: To clean up a German mine field.
Bebe Daniels: Hey, speaking of Germans, are we getting many prisoners at the front?
Sergeant Walren Mullins: Yeah, we're getting quite a few. I saw 84 in one group.
Bebe Daniels: What they look like?
Sergeant Walren Mullins: Yeah, they all - all seemed to be pretty young, they wasn't 14
  to 20 years old.
Bebe Daniels: Huh, are they sullen?
Sergeant Walren Mullins: Oh, yes, scared to death, and they're gonna be scareder a lot
  more before this thing's over with.
Bebe Daniels: That's right, soldier. Tell me, is anyone back home that you'd like to
  send a message to?
Sergeant Walren Mullins: Yes, I would. I'd like to tell my sis, Mrs. Florence Shufbach
  of West Virginia, I'm getting along O.K. now and I hope I continue being as lucky as I
  have been up until yesterday.
Bebe Daniels: I'm sure you will, soldier. Good luck to you. Captain, after you get this
  boy in shape he'll be taken to a clearing station, won't he?

Captain Stanley: That's right, Bebe. One of these boys will take him over by ambulance. Here's an ambulance driver now. Hey, Jack, tell Miss Daniels about your work.
Jack Davidson: You bet, but we all call her Babesette.
Bebe Daniels: That's right. What's your name, fellow, and where are you from?
Jack Davidson: Jack Davidson from Kentucky.
Bebe Daniels: Well, Jack, tell us something about your work, will you?
Jack Davidson: Yes, we place the patients as carefully as possible in an ambulance and drive as slow as we can over these rough roads to - in order not to injure 'em any more and take 'em back to the clearing.
Bebe Daniels: That's fine. Tell me, Jack, is there somebody back home that you want to talk to, give a message to?
Jack Davidson: Yes, ah, my wife's in Florida. I hope she's listening.
Bebe Daniels: I hope she is, too, and I hope she hears it nice and clearly. Well, good luck to you, fellow.
Jack Davidson: Thanks.
Colonel Unger: Bebe, the old watchman is here again. I think we better start back to headquarters.
Bebe Daniels: O.K., Colonel Unger. Is that an order? Well, there seems to be a lull now and anyway it's time to say good bye again from the front lines of Normandy. Believe me, it isn't very pretty up here, but I won't trade the privilege of being with our soldiers and medical men for anything in the world. They're really fine men, America. Fine because they believe in the things that are right. Fine because every day unselfishly and uncomplainingly they risk their lives so we may live in the way we desire. And now, America, I return you to London with the promise that next week Purple Heart Corner will come to you from a clearing station hospital where again you'll hear the voices and the stories of more of your men. And now, Cecil Madden in London, it's all yours.
Cecil Madden: Thank you, Bebe Daniels, for your fine enterprise on our behalf and we're now back in the club. [Thank you, Ken. Thank you all of you.] Again, our short half-hour is nearing its close. But even if these flying bombs without pilots still attack us in London, everyone is still cheerful and carrying on, still able to sing. Here are your men singing you a song chosen by them at rehearsal, their own choice to end, and today it's "Roll Out the Barrel."
BEER BARREL POLKA (Roll Out the Barrel) (S/Sgt. Mel Powell, piano;   , trumpet) Vocal refrain by the audience
Cecil Madden: Well, this is my spot and I'm using it just to say goodbye for another wartime week. I'd just like to say one thing before we part, 'cause we over here seem it a pleasure and a privilege to be able to do and send you this program every week for nearly four years now as a very small gesture to the families wherever you are in United States. I think that you like it from your wonderful letters. We're always ready to try to improve it. Thank you for writing last week from Norwalk and Bridgeport, Connecticut and it's all your's, Connecticut, today; Baltimore, Maryland; Philadelphia, Pennsylvania; Arlington and Montague City, Massachusetts; Seattle, Washington; Buffalo, Cohoes, North Rose and Brooklyn, New York; Barberton and East Cleveland, Ohio; Miami, Florida; Woodbury Heights, New Jersey; San Francisco and Los Angeles and all our good friends in California. So it's au revoir from me and thanks from me today to Bebe Daniels, Major Ken Tredwell, Captain Glenn Miller, Sergeant Cecil Elmore, Sergeant Ray McKinley, the Crew Chiefs and the band, the American Red Cross and all of you, hoping you'll be tuned in to us next week wherever you live, when you join us over here 3, 4, 5, or 6000 miles away in London, England.
Let's Sing a Happy Song (closing theme --- recording, not Miller band)
Announcer: That was the "American Eagle in Britain" program presented from London.

10Aug44 (Thu) 8:30-9:00PM Paris Cinema, London, England   SWN-18986
    AMERICAN BAND OF THE AEF broadcast   Attendance: 200

    ...

Captain Glenn Miller: Whenever the band gets a chance they do a lot of listening to the
    radio. Last week they sort of listened to "Variety Bandbox" and along with it a
    charmin' gal who sings a charmin' song. We asked her to sing this one out with us
    tonight. So here she is, an English gal whose singin' has brought a lot of pleasure to
    a lot of listenin' Americans, Miss Paula Green.
Paula Green: Thank you, Captain Glenn Miller, and you've made this English girl feel
    right at home.
Captain Glenn Miller: Well, England's your front parlor, Paula. You're the one who's
    helped to make us feel right at home.
Paula Green: Well, since we're all feeling right at home, how about a spot of tea?
Captain Glenn Miller: Well, it's a right nice offer but I'm sure there's somethin'
    everybody would enjoy more than a spot of tea and that's a spot of song. So we'll do
    the pourin', you do the singin'. Here's "Tess's Torch Song."
TESS'S TORCH SONG
    Vocal refrain by Paula Green

    ...

Captain Glenn Miller: And here's time to play our ace in the hole, a Sergeant Jerry Gray
    arrangement we broadcast when we first reached this side of the Atlantic. Since then
    we've had quite a few requests to repeat it. So, just by way of provin' that one way of
    gettin' somethin' is askin' for it, here's "Holiday for Strings."
HOLIDAY FOR STRINGS
MOONLIGHT SERENADE (closing theme)
    Captain Glenn Miller: This is Captain ...
    ...

12Aug44 (Sat) 2:35-2:55PM Co-Partners Hall, Bedford, England
THE UPTOWN HALL recording

SLO-60537/A
Aired 16Aug44

MY GUY'S COME BACK (opening theme)
Corporal Paul Dubov: Good evening, all, it's "The Uptown Hall," music for you of the
    Allied Liberation Forces presented by members of the American Band of the A.E.F.,
    featuring Sergeant Mel Powell at the piano.
Corporal Paul Dubov: Welcome to "The Uptown Hall," fellow members. Tonight the Hall
    plays host again to Dinah Shore. And in just a few minutes she's gonna bring us another
    one of those songs that sends you guys and gals crowding right up to the radio when you
    hear it's Dinah. But before we get around to that big moment, Mel and the boys have
    racked up a little music you might like to give a little listen to and right on top is
    "Liza."
LIZA (All the Clouds'll Roll Away)
Corporal Paul Dubov: Now here's Mel and the boys tying a few bright ribbons on an old
    favorite that I know you'll remember, "The Very Thought of You."
THE VERY THOUGHT OF YOU
Corporal Paul Dubov: Comin' up next a little resolution offered by Mel and his committee
    of seven which I know will be warmly seconded by all members present. Be it resolved
    that "Love Is the Sweetest Thing."
LOVE IS THE SWEETEST THING

    ...

    At this point in the recording, the 03Aug44 recording of Dinah Shore singing
    "Honeysuckle Rose" with "The Uptown Hall," 31217 (17217), was inserted.

    ...

Corporal Paul Dubov: Thank you, Dinah Shore. It was mighty nice of you to drop in on our
    last four meetings and bring us some of those songs that nobody can sing like Dinah.
    And any time you're not singing for the guys and gals over there in Normandy, why you
    can call this place home. Thanks again, Dinah, and don't forget that latchstring's
    always out at the Hall. Now it's back to Mel and the boys and "Flying Home."
FLYING HOME

    ...

MY GUY'S COME BACK (closing theme)

12Aug44 (Sat) 2:55-3:15PM Co-Partners Hall, Bedford, England   SLO-60537/B
  THE UPTOWN HALL recording   Aired 18Aug44

Corporal Paul Dubov: This is a feature of the American Band of the A.E.F.
MY GUY'S COME BACK (opening theme)
  Corporal Paul Dubov: Good evening, all, it's "The Uptown Hall," music for you of the
    Allied Liberation Forces, presented by members of the American Band of the A.E.F.,
    featuring Sergeant Mel Powell at the piano.
Corporal Paul Dubov: Welcome to "The Uptown Hall," fellow members. Well, the minutes of
  the last meeting have been read and approved and the secretary's got his pen all ready
  to start another page in the book of proceedings. Glancing over his shoulders I see him
  writing down that the first order of business for today is Sergeant Mel and the boys
  playing, ah, what's those next two words? I - I can't make them out very clearly but
  they look like, ah, "Blow Top."
BLOW TOP
Corporal Paul Dubov: Now the boys climb down from "Blow Top" and take this next one in a
  slower tempo. It's "Where or When."
WHERE OR WHEN
Corporal Paul Dubov: Now Mel and the boys come before the meeting to read a short paper
  entitled "romance in relation to certain celestial magnitudes." And since it looks like
  it might be a little tough going for some of us, I've asked Mel to give it to us in
  words of one syllable and here it is, "How High the Moon."
HOW HIGH THE MOON

   ...

    At this point in the recording, the 03Aug44 recording of Dinah Shore singing "Night
    and Day" with "The Uptown Hall," 31214 (17214), was inserted.

   ...

Corporal Paul Dubov: Always welcome in the Hall is one of these oldies that everybody
  remembers and everybody likes. Fellow members, I give you "Rosetta."
ROSETTA
Corporal Paul Dubov: Well, it's time to lock up the doors and pull down the shades in
  "The Uptown Hall." But we'll be swinging and singing here tomorrow night, so come one,
  come all. Until then this is Corporal Paul Dubov saying so long and good luck to you.
MY GUY'S COME BACK (closing theme)

18Aug44 (Fri) 9:30-10:00AM Co-Partners Hall, Bedford, England   SLO-60496
  THE SWING SHIFT recording   Aired 19Aug44

...

THE MUSIC STOPPED
  Vocal refrain by Sergeant Johnny Desmond
Corporal Paul Dubov: "The Swing Shift's" little chamber music ... of Sergeants Hucko,
  Powell and McKinley. Very often these gentlemen perform feats of musical legerdemain
  upon simple original themes. Today we bring you one that is marked "allegro monon
  fumoso" or, if you prefer, positively a Lulu. The title is again something to defeat
  the imagination, "Tinicongle Tinkle."
TINICONGLE TINKLE (trio: Hucko, Powell, McKinley)
Corporal Paul Dubov: And that, my friends, was "Tinicongle Tinkle" as tinkled by
  Sergeants Hucko, Powell and McKinley. So from the sublime we turn to the sublimer,
  Sergeant Johnny Desmond soothes an aching heart with "Time Alone Will Tell."
TIME ALONE WILL TELL
  Vocal refrain by Sergeant Johnny Desmond
Corporal Paul Dubov: The Swing Shifters and Sergeant Ray McKinley close up shop with
  "Flying Home."
FLYING HOME
Corporal Paul Dubov: And that wraps it up for today. "The Swing Shift" of the American
  Band of the A.E.F., with music by Sergeant Ray McKinley and company, will be back doing
  business again next Saturday at the same time. This is Corporal Paul Dubov.
SONG AND DANCE (closing theme)
  Vocal refrain by Technical Sergeant Ray McKinley:
    Well, so long, everybody, hope you got your fill.
    Never mind the tip, just step up and pay the bill.
    It was indeed quite a pleasure to serve you all.
    Now here are a few of the boys to take a curtain call.
  Vocal refrain by Sergeant Johnny Desmond:
    This is Sergeant Johnny Desmond saying, "Hey, thanks to you!"
  Vocal refrain by Technical Sergeant Ray McKinley:
    My, my goodness, scramble two.
  Vocal refrain by the Crew Chiefs:
    This is the Crew Chiefs saying, "Drink more stout."
  Vocal refrain by Technical Sergeant Ray McKinley:
    Or, as the late Allie Aulwurm would say, spread out.
    Well, all of the boys in the kitchen wish you well.
    This includes Paul Muny Dubov, who is nonpareil.
    We're all happy to be over here.
    So once or twice each week please to lend an ear.
    Maybe you like it sweet or maybe you like it jive.
    In either case keep tuned to 2, 8, 5.
    We'll be back again with a bit of jump.
    So until next Tuesday, carry on.

22Aug44 (Tue) 11:15-11:30AM Co-Partners Hall, Bedford, England   SLO-61066
   THE UPTOWN HALL recording   Aired 23Aug44

...

Corporal Paul Dubov: ... with another favorite of folks here in the Hall and this time
   it's "Don't Blame Me."
DON'T BLAME ME
Corporal Paul Dubov: You charter members here in the Hall know that the password is
   always "happy listenin'," and just to make sure you know what that means, here's another
   sample. It's Sergeant Mel and company playin' "On the Sunny Side of the Street."
ON THE SUNNY SIDE OF THE STREET

...

Corporal Paul Dubov: ... these little sermons real short. Tonight it's just three words
   long, "Lady Be Good!"
OH, LADY BE GOOD!

...

24Aug44 (Thu) 8:30-9:00PM Co-Partners Hall, Bedford, England   SWN-19041
   AMERICAN BAND OF THE AEF broadcast

...

Major Glenn Miller: Mighty nice, Doreen. And now it's medley time, saluting the mothers,
   wives, sweethearts and sisters of the men of the Allied Forces. Something old,
   something new, something borrowed, something blue. Our old song, "Long, Long Ago."
LONG, LONG AGO (Old tune)
   Major Glenn Miller: Fresh as a daisy and just as sweet, that's our new song sung now by
      Sergeant Johnny Desmond.
THE MUSIC STOPPED (New tune)
   Vocal refrain by Sergeant Johnny Desmond
   Major Glenn Miller: They put the tap on Air Corps Lieutenant Larry Clinton for the
      borrowed tune and up comes "The Dipsy Doodle."
THE DIPSY DOODLE (Borrowed tune)
   Major Glenn Miller: The blue spotlight now for the anchor tune in medley time, "Blues
      in My Heart."
BLUES IN MY HEART (Blue tune)
Major Glenn Miller: On that ever lovin' map of the U.S.A. there's a place where you can
   stand and watch the sun take its evening dip into the Pacific. That's the tall, thin,
   good looking state called California. That's also where a lot of Yanks'll be heading
   when the war curtain rings down. And for those of us who feel the urge to sing about
   that happy day a'coming, Corporal Art Malvin has fitted just the right words to some
   music that came straight out of my heart right into my own little music pen. Here for
   the first time out is Ray McKinley backed up by the Crew Chiefs singing "I'm Heading for
   California."
I'M HEADIN' FOR CALIFORNIA
   Vocal refrain by Technical Sergeant Ray McKinley and the Crew Chiefs

...

27Aug44 (Sun) 6:00-7:00PM Queensbury All-Services Club, London, England   DLO-69978
VARIETY BANDBOX recording   Aired 29Aug44

...

Tommy Handley: Now, folks. You know what's coming, mate. And now it's my great pleasure
  to introduce one of the grandest fellows in the world, that great artist we are very,
  very glad to welcome in London. There's only one of him so let's give him a great big
  hand. Here he is, Bing Crosby. Have you got any gum, chum?
Bing Crosby: I have some. Here, Tom, here.
Tommy Handley: Thank you very much. Well, we got ... Well, I'm delighted to meet you,
  Bing. Welcome to London. My name's Tommy, so - ah - you won't call me Bob, I hope.
Bing Crosby: Certainly not, Bob.
Tommy Handley: Well, thank you for being so frank, Sinatra.
Bing Crosby: Yike.
Tommy Handley: And to show my appreciation I've brought this for you, sir.
Bing Crosby: Oh, isn't that nice. What ever is it?
Tommy Handley: Well, it's a pipe. What did you think it was, a cigar with a   knob on?
Bing Crosby: Well, just a minute here, Tommy. There's a piece of paper stuck inside it.
  Let's see what this says here.
Tommy Handley: Oh, is there?
Bing Crosby: Somebody stopped me on a horse, I guess. Oh, I read it. "A present from
  Tommy to Bing. You were grand in 'The Road to Morocco,' you open your glasses and sing,
  and I'll buy you an ounce of tobacco." Well, forever more.
Tommy Handley: That's right. Well, what do you think, chum?
Bing Crosby: Well, Tommy, let me tell you, I get a great big boot out of arriving on this
  side of the big water jump and finding the warm water of friendship waitin' for me. I
  don't know what I'm doing here unless it's tryin' to bring a little hunk o' home to a
  couple of million Yanks and Tommies. But believe me, I'll be eternally grateful that I
  was accorded a chance to come. Imagine what a routine I'm going to give my
  grandchildren about it. Ah, yes, sittin' around a can of canned heat, sittin' 'n'
  sippin' 'n' sippin' 'n' sippin', old grandpappy Bing will be able to say that he was
  invited over to do some singin' for the Tommies and the Yanks while they were winding up
  a little production called "The Road to Victory." I know exactly how big-leaguer Major
  Glenn Miller and the Dixie Diva, lovely Dinah Shore, must have felt when they arrived
  here, proud, happy and anxious to get to work. Well, Private First Class Jack Rusin, if
  you'll join me in a bit of buskin' we'll have at it, aye?
SAN FERNANDO VALLEY (I'm Packin' My Grip) (Pfc. Jack Rusin, piano)
  Vocal refrain by Bing Crosby

...

LONG AGO (And Far Away) (Pfc. Jack Rusin, piano)
  Vocal refrain by Bing Crosby
Bing Crosby: Go ahead, Jack. This is the song I had a request to do. I don't know if I
  remember all of it but we'll struggle along. Let's carry on.
MOONLIGHT BECOMES YOU (Pfc. Jack Rusin, piano)
  Vocal refrain by Bing Crosby
Pat Kirkwood: Thank you very much, Bing Crosby.
Bing Crosby: Aye.
Pat Kirkwood: So there you are, everybody. That's "Variety Bandbox" for today. I hope
  it was O.K. Huh! This is where I say good bye until another time. Here's Bing to say
  so long.
Bing Crosby: Good luck to all of you boys in France, India, the Middle East, Italy,
  Africa and the Pacific. It was swell being with you and I'll see you again soon. So
  long.
BBC announcer: Thank you, Pat Kirkwood, and thank you, Bing Crosby.

...

27Aug44 (Sun) after 7:00PM Queensbury All-Services Club, London, England
  SPECIAL SHOW for audience at the preceding "Variety Bandbox" recording

  . . .

Bing Crosby: Anne, now 'bout - ah - how 'bout you and I takin' a whack at a duet? Think
  we could handle it? I'll try it. I may want to louse you up but, think. All right?
Anne Shelton: For years I've been dreaming of this moment.
Bing Crosby: Aw, get out. Go ahead, Jack. Lay it on us.
EASTER PARADE (Pfc. Jack Rusin, piano)
  Bing Crosby: In your --- what's the key, Jack?
  Vocal refrain by Bing Crosby and Anne Shelton

  . . .

31Aug44 (Thu) 3:30-4:00PM Dunkers Den, Piccadilly, London, England   DOX-37918
  American Red Cross Rainbow Corner Club (run by Adele Astaire)   Aired 02Sep44
  AMERICAN EAGLE IN BRITAIN recording   195th Program   Attendance: 1000
  Material within [ ] was deleted from the recording before it was broadcast.

Announcer: This is London calling. The British Broadcasting Corporation presents its
  weekly program the "American Eagle in Britain." Your host is Cecil Madden.
[Cecil Madden: This is London calling from American Red Cross Rainbow Corner.]
Let's Sing a Happy Song (opening theme --- recording, not Miller band)
Cecil Madden: Once again and for the 195th time it's hello to all of you in America.
  Flying bombs or no, London always carries on and this is Cecil Madden of the British
  Broadcasting Corporation saying call in the family, it's time for the "American Eagle in
  Britain" program sent to you with the usual good wishes from the B.B.C. in London,
  England. And this opening spot is always given to six of the smaller towns in the
  United States.
Pfc. John H. Terry: This is Pfc. John H. Terry calling Onondaga, New York.
Pfc. Dan Strampo: This is Pfc. Dan Strampo calling Reedsburg, Wisconsin.
Private Danny Walsh: This is Private Danny Walsh calling Coon Rapids, Iowa.
Pfc. Arthur Sbrille: This is Pfc. Arthur Sbrille calling Highland Park, New Jersey.
Pfc. Donald Strong: This is Pfc. Donald Strong calling Shiocton, Wisconsin.
Pfc. Larry Bird: This is Pfc. Larry Bird calling Fayetteville, Arkansas.
Cecil Madden: And those six were just picked out at random in this room under the
  pavement in Dunkers Den in the famous American Red Cross Rainbow Corner Club in London.
  Now I step out, I introduce our musical guests, they're G.I.s, they're extremely popular
  on this program, they're the famous "Swing Shift" led by Sergeant Ray McKinley, a unit
  of the American Band of the Allied Expeditionary Force under the personal direction of
  Major Glenn Miller. With their help and pianist Mel Powell, who's made a great name for
  himself too over with his "Swing Sextet" unit, we've been talking over a song your men
  would like to sing to you. And today for no reason except the composer is down here
  with us, you'll see why in a moment, we're in London so we're singing about Mexico, and
  this song is "South of the Border."
SOUTH OF THE BORDER (Down Mexico Way) (S/Sgt. Mel Powell, piano)
  Vocal refrain by the audience
Cecil Madden: And this is where I'll introduce our interviewer, member of the 8th Air
  Force, so once again we give our London welcome to our good friend Major Ken Tredwell.
Major Ken Tredwell: And as they say in England, ta, Cecil, ta. We're here with a
  terrific crowd here in Dunkers Den Rainbow Corner today and one reason for the crowd is
  Ray McKinley from Glenn Miller's bunch and we'll hear a little bit about the other
  reason in a few minutes. But for the moment here's Private Charles Noonan from
  Birmingham, Alabama. Is that right, Charlie?
Private Charles Noonan: That's right.
Major Ken Tredwell: Look at that big, personable smile on that man. And, Charlie, what
  do they call you? Chuck?
Private Charles Noonan: Chuck.
Major Ken Tredwell: I see that you're a paratrooper, you're wearing the Purple Heart and
  also the Presidential Citation. [That means he's put his life on the block for Uncle
  Sam already at least once. Let's welcome him, boys. Chuck, what did you do back in
  civilian life?
Private Charles Noonan: Chemical engineer.
Major Ken Tredwell: Doing what in chemical engineering?
Private Charles Noonan: Research in explosives.
Major Ken Tredwell: With what organization was that?
Private Charles Noonan: DuPont Powder Company.
Major Ken Tredwell: Explosives with DuPont. Are you a single man?
Private Charles Noonan: Single.
Major Ken Tredwell: Any plans?
Private Charles Noonan: Definitely.
Major Ken Tredwell: Ah! Tell me, will you reveal the name of that plan?
Private Charles Noonan: Marjorie Woodley.
Major Ken Tredwell: And where is Marjorie?

Private Charles Noonan: Birmingham, Alabama.
Major Ken Tredwell: Are the letters coming through?
Private Charles Noonan: Not too well, sir, right now.
Major Ken Tredwell: I hope Margie takes careful note. How long have you been in the
    Army, Chuck?
Private Charles Noonan: About four and a half years.
Major Ken Tredwell: And you're a volunteer in the paratroopers?]
Private Charles Noonan: Yes.
Major Ken Tredwell: Have you had any combat jumps?
Private Charles Noonan: Two.
Major Ken Tredwell: Whereabouts?
Private Charles Noonan: Sicily and France, Normandy.
Major Ken Tredwell: Oh, my, rough all the way through. You sure look healthy now though,
    Chuck.
Private Charles Noonan: Recuperating fast.
Major Ken Tredwell: Tell me - ah - what was - what was your job or your organization's
    job in Normandy?
Private Charles Noonan: We had a bridge mission there and also a supply line we had to
    cut off. We occupied some higher ground overlooking the supply lines and the bridge
    head. The mission was accomplished successfully.
Major Ken Tredwell: Your job was to either blow up the bridge or grab it?
Private Charles Noonan: To capture it.
Major Ken Tredwell: And you get to "throw" on it?
Private Charles Noonan: Yes.
Major Ken Tredwell: When were you wounded?
Private Charles Noonan: The fourth day after D-Day, sir.
Major Ken Tredwell: Well, were you hurt badly?
Private Charles Noonan: Ah, I was twice in the hip, ah, three times in the hip and twice
    in the side.
Major Ken Tredwell: How long were you in the hospital?
Private Charles Noonan: Since - ah - the tenth day of June. Just getting out.
Major Ken Tredwell: Aw, buddy, that's rough, that's rough. How are you feeling now,
    Chuck?
Private Charles Noonan: Ah, I feel all right. I miss the American nurses, though.
Major Ken Tredwell: Don't we all. Don't we all. After Berlin and Tokyo are you going
    back to that explosives job? Demolition?
Private Charles Noonan: Ah - with Marjorie Woodley.
Major Ken Tredwell: Ah, that's explosive in a way, too. That's a good start. Thanks
    very much to Charles Noonan and good luck to you. And now it's from the paratroops to
    the 8th Air Force, it's Staff Sergeant Dave Ellis. I - I understand, Dave, that they
    call you Lloyd. Is that right?
S/Sgt. Dave Ellis: Yes, sir. Pleasure.
[Major Ken Tredwell: Where's your home town, Lloyd?
S/Sgt. Dave Ellis: Collingdale, Pennsylvania.
Major Ken Tredwell: Right outside of Philadelphia?
S/Sgt. Dave Ellis: That's right.
Major Ken Tredwell: Are your folks there?
S/Sgt. Dave Ellis: Yes, sir.
Major Ken Tredwell: Any brothers or sisters?
S/Sgt. Dave Ellis: I have three brothers in the service and one sister.
Major Ken Tredwell: Three brothers in the service, that means you've got a very proud
    four-star service flag in your window back home, is that right?
S/Sgt. Dave Ellis: That's right, sir.
Major Ken Tredwell: Single or married? I was going to say double there for a moment.
S/Sgt. Dave Ellis: Single.
Major Ken Tredwell: Have you any plans as Chuck Noonan had?
S/Sgt. Dave Ellis: Yes, sir.
Major Ken Tredwell: What are they?
S/Sgt. Dave Ellis: Lorraine Taves.
Major Ken Tredwell: Lorraine Taves. You're a goner is that it?

S/Sgt. Dave Ellis: Just about.]
Major Ken Tredwell: I see, Lloyd, that you're wearing those Silver Wings, the D.F.C., the Air Medal and three Clusters and the E.T.O. Ribbon with two Combat Stars. He's got it coming, boy. Have you finished your missions, Lloyd?
S/Sgt. Dave Ellis: Yes, sir.
Major Ken Tredwell: And in what sort of a ship did you make them?
S/Sgt. Dave Ellis: In a Fort.
Major Ken Tredwell: What was the name of the Fort?
S/Sgt. Dave Ellis: The Fickle Finger.
Major Ken Tredwell: Yeah, man. Quiet please. Heh, heh. What was your job in the Fickle Finger?
S/Sgt. Dave Ellis: I'm a ball turret gunner.
Major Ken Tredwell: That's in the lead spitting belly of a B-17, right?
S/Sgt. Dave Ellis: That's right.
Major Ken Tredwell: What have some of your targets been, Lloyd?
S/Sgt. Dave Ellis: I've been to Berlin twice, Kiel, Paris, Petermunday, Stattin, ah -
Major Ken Tredwell: Hit just about all the big, tough jobs.
S/Sgt. Dave Ellis: - Hamburg and
Major Ken Tredwell: Which one stands out in your memory as being the toughest of all?
S/Sgt. Dave Ellis: Saarbrücken definitely.
Major Ken Tredwell: And why Saarbrücken?
S/Sgt. Dave Ellis: Come back on one engine, I
Major Ken Tredwell: Holy Moses. A - a four-engine ship, did you come all the way back on one engine?
S/Sgt. Dave Ellis: All the way back on two engines and we landed on one.
Major Ken Tredwell: That is really tough, and you got back O.K., huh?
S/Sgt. Dave Ellis: Yes, sir.
[Major Ken Tredwell: Are you with a squadron that is known by any particular name or nickname?
S/Sgt. Dave Ellis: The famous Fightin' Bitin'.
Major Ken Tredwell: And Fightin' Bitin', famous they are. Any Fightin' Bitin' men here? Hot dog, I hear one back there. The squadron is still going strong. Have you any chance of going back now that you've finished your missions?
S/Sgt. Dave Ellis: I expect to go back soon.
Major Ken Tredwell: Perhaps we'd better deliver an advance message to the U.S.A., both to the U.S.A. and to Lorraine, that they'd better both open their arms, here comes a curly-haired, smiling, fighting son. Thanks a lot.]
Cecil Madden: We call in more of our musical guests now, the Glenn Miller Crew Chiefs to sing you a new British song which is sweeping this country. It was written by an ace British song writer, Michael Carr, who also wrote "South of the Border," which we all sang just now. If you in the room can get it, join in, we see how we go, he's in the room with us, so let's hear the Crew Chiefs sing "All's Well Mademoiselle."

ALL'S WELL MADEMOISELLE
Vocal refrain by the Crew Chiefs

Cecil Madden: Thank you, Crew Chiefs, and that was "All's Well Mademoiselle." It's the roving microphone now, a regular feature in our B.B.C. "American Eagle in Britain" program. Standby for the home towns first and then the names of someone you know in this room with us in London. And, by the way, I notice, sort of promised, Ken, that you'd start off over by the band 'cause some of them didn't get their names in last time. So take over, Ken, with the roving microphone.
Major Ken Tredwell: Thank you, Cecil. That's the least we can do to get that band first. And I think the first man we ought to get is Ray McKinley, their leader. We understand, by the way, that September 6th is a mighty important day to him because he's got a wife back home with a bit of a birthday then. What is she gonna get for a birthday present? The voice of her husband. She couldn't ask for more.
T/Sgt. Ray McKinley: Well, hello there, Sugar. Take it easy now.
Major Ken Tredwell: But - but you didn't give your home town, Ray. Let's have it.
T/Sgt. Ray McKinley: Fort Worth, Texas.
Major Ken Tredwell: And here are some of the other boys in the band. Come on up, boys. Let's have your heads.

Corporal Fred Guerra: Boston, Mass., Fred Guerra.
Major Ken Tredwell: A little louder, gents. Want to hear it all the way back there in
    Boston.
Pfc. Nat Peck: Brooklyn, New York, Nat Peck.
Major Ken Tredwell: You can keep that Brooklyn down low. Here we are, Sergeant.
S/Sgt. Jimmy Priddy: Huntington, West Virginia, Jimmy Priddy.
Sergeant Johnny Halliburton: Des Moines, Iowa, Johnny Halliburton.
Major Ken Tredwell: And right on Johnny's right with a big trombone in his hand.
Pfc. Larry Hall: Yonkers, New York, Larry Hall.
Major Ken Tredwell: Here's a man that also plays some drums.
Pfc. Frank Ippolito: Bronx, New York, Frank Ippolito.
Major Ken Tredwell: We're coming up behind Frank - ah - a little bit - ah - low on the
    hairline. Get that hair out of your eyes, Sergeant. We'll get to you.
Sergeant Bernie Privin: New York, Bernie Privin.
Sergeant William E. Thomas: Rocky Mount, North Carolina, Sergeant William E. Thomas.
Major Ken Tredwell: Some really fine musical names here. Hello, Sergeant, seen you
    before.
M/Sgt. Zeke Zarchy: Brooklyn, New York, Zeke Zarchy.
Major Ken Tredwell: Thank you, Zeke. And here's the red-headed boy.
Sergeant Bob Nichols: Boston, Massachusetts, Bob Nichols.
Major Ken Tredwell: Right behind Bob Nichols, the last one with the trumpet in his hands.
Pfc. Jack Steele: Connersville, Indiana, Jack Steele.
[Major Ken Tredwell: Thank you, Jack. And now let's get around this room a bit and get
    as many of these G.I.s as we can. Here we go.
John Wallis: John Wallis, Steubenville, Ohio.
Major Ken Tredwell: Oh, Johnny, let's have that home town first, let's have that again,
    re-run.
John Wallis: Steubenville, Ohio, John Wallis.
Major Ken Tredwell: Much better, sounded better from here, didn't it? Here we go.
Private Sherman Oider: Wellington, Kansas, Private Sherman Oider.
Major Ken Tredwell: Right next to Sherman.
Warren Heyne: Grand Forks, North Dakota, Warren Heyne.
Major Ken Tredwell: And two soldiers and a sailor in rapid succession.
Johnny Sims: Staten Island, New York, Johnny Sims.
Donny Dyall: Pullman, Washington, Donny Dyall.
Chester Gidonski: New Bedford, Mass., Chester Gidonski
Major Ken Tredwell: And that's a good-looking cigar you've got there, Chester. And
    here's a Corporal in the WACs.
Virginia Roy: Carleton, Michigan, Virginia Roy.
Major Ken Tredwell: And another WAC, and look at that smile.
Corporal Tokowski: Trenton, New Jersey, Corporal Tokowski.
Major Ken Tredwell: You boys on the other side of the room who didn't hear that, I've got
    it. I'll give it to you for a price. Here we go.
Ray Vines: Avril, Mass., Ray Vines.
Major Ken Tredwell: And another sailor.
Willard Sallers: Nashville City, North Carolina, Willard Sallers.
Major Ken Tredwell: A WAC and a soldier, both look quite happy.
Sylvia Powell: Jackson Heights, New York, Sylvia Powell.
Sergeant Cleveland: Nashua, Iowa, Sergeant Cleveland.
Major Ken Tredwell: Nashua and Jackson Heights, they've got together. Here we go.
Bob Furgeson: Los Angeles, California, Bob Furgeson.
Major Ken Tredwell: He's not going to say a word. If he thinks of his name, write it
    down and we'll come back to him.
Thomas Cooway: Dublin, Georgia, Thomas Cooway.
Ern Budday: Detroit, Michigan, Ern Budday.
Major Ken Tredwell: And a big stack of men standing up at the back of the room, we'll get
    all we can. Put your heads over here, boys.
Hines Noel: New York, New York, Hines Noel.
Jack Walden: Chicago, Illinois, Jack Walden.
Eddie Muchwertz: Long Beach, California, Eddie Muchwertz.

Major Ken Tredwell: Hello, curly.
Paul Erdvil: Hamilton, Ohio, Paul Erdvil.
Major Ken Tredwell: It's the first man I've ever called curly who wasn't bald-headed. He
  really is curly. Here we go.
Manuel Hauser: Quincy, Mass., Manuel Hauser.]
Robert Pull: Manawa, Wisconsin, Robert Pull.
Major Ken Tredwell: How about it, Sergeant?
Sergeant Carl Eyre: Allentown, Pennsylvania, Carl Eyre.
Major Ken Tredwell: And six feet, three of man here.
Frank Alexander: Owatonna, Minnesota, Frank Alexander.
Major Ken Tredwell: Now let's see if I can get down that middle aisle, if I can get this
  wire all the way back there. Here are two men, oh, oh. Here's some band boys I missed.
  Let's get 'em.
T/Sgt. Jerry Gray: Sommerville, Massachusetts, Jerry Gray.
Major Ken Tredwell: Thank you, Jerry. Here's another. Corporal, how about it?
Corporal Julius Zifferblatt: Ah, New York City, Julie Zifferblatt.
Major Ken Tredwell: Thank you, Julie. And two men sitting on the end.
John N. Sterns: Albany, Kentucky, John Nobue Sterns.
Doug Benson: Jamestown, New York, Doug Benson.
Major Ken Tredwell: We're really getting around the country today. Let's get down this
  middle aisle. Ah, she's not in uniform but she'd sure be nice to get on this program.
Dawn Mills: Akron, Ohio, Dawn Mills.
Abe Esrick: Philadelphia, Pennsylvania, Abe Esrick.
Major Ken Tredwell: And three sailors, blond, darker and darkest.
James Criftsver: Pittsburgh, Pennsylvania, James Criftsver.
Mike Donoghue: East Orange, New Jersey, Mike Donoghue.
Charles Simpson: Denver, Colorado, Charles Simpson.
Frank Keyes: Portland, Maine, Frank Keyes.
Major Ken Tredwell: Frank is the next Army man and here are three more sailors. Boy,
  they're really with us today.
John Rondy: Kingston, Pennsylvania, John Rondy.
Albert Marje: Norwich, Connecticut, Albert Marje.
Gene Munhills: Armagh, Pennsylvania, Gene Munhills.
Major Ken Tredwell: Thank you, boys. And three sailors sitting right in front of them.
  One with Yank magazine. Good old Yank magazine in his hands.
Sergeant Bert Halbert: Lexington, Kentucky, Bert Halbert.
Major Ken Tredwell: Do you like Yank, Sergeant?
Sergeant Bert Halbert: Ah, roger.
Ivor Minney: Highland Park, Illinois, Ivor Minney.
Major Ken Tredwell: Wilco, and right next to him.
Dick Hodgens: Milwaukee, Wisconsin, Dick Hodgens.
Major Ken Tredwell: How about it, blondy?
Dan Mills: Ah - Pueblo, New Mexico, Dan Mills.
[Major Ken Tredwell: I want to get some of you one-stripers over here. Believe me,
  they're the backbone of the Army. Two Pfcs. right here. Let's go.
Sidney Drew: Greenfield, Mass., Sidney Drew.
Jack Craver: Bronx, New York, Jack Craver.
Major Ken Tredwell: Thank you Sid and Jack, good stuff. And here we come back. Here's a
  Yank, here's an eager beaver.
Joseph Grummols: Cudahy, Wisconsin, Joseph Grummols.
Major Ken Tredwell: Next to Joe?
Sergeant Hayne: Coffeyville, Kansas, Sergeant Hayne.
Major Ken Tredwell: Where are we going from Kansas?
Millard Fuller: Auburn, Alabama, Millard Fuller.
Major Ken Tredwell: I almost knocked a man out with that mike. I'm sorry. Here we go.
Lawrence Kesebowski: Detroit, Michigan, Lawrence Kesebowski.
Major Ken Tredwell: Lawrence who?
Lawrence Kesebowski: Lawrence Kesebowski.
Major Ken Tredwell: Thank you, Detroit.
Sergeant Siprielli: Camden, New Jersey, Sergeant Siprielli.

Charles Pearson: Burlingame, California, Charles Pearson.
Major Ken Tredwell: Let's say this so they can hear it without the mike all the way back
   in the States, make it loud.
Hal Jacobs: Hal Jacobs, Brooklyn, New York.
Major Ken Tredwell: And let's get three more. A WAC and two soldiers.
Mary Novecheck: Eau Claire, Wisconsin, Mary Novecheck.
Thomas E. Sissil: Revere, Massachusetts, Thomas E. Sissil.
Calvin R. Black: Tuscaloosa, Alabama, Calvin R. Black.
Major Ken Tredwell: Tuscaloosa, Alabama. He's really from down under. Now if I can get
   this wire untangled we'll try the next row down. Here's a soldier right here.
Pfc. Don Strampo: Reedsburg, Wisconsin, Pfc. Don Strampo.
Major Ken Tredwell: Don, we got you once already, that's a repeat. No extra charge, it's
   all on the house.
Zal Kowski: Detroit, Michigan, Zal Kowski.
Rel Ovey: Okatowa, Idaho, Rel Ovey.
Harry Noble: Houston, Texas, Harry Noble.
Major Ken Tredwell: What's the paper you're reading, Harry? Evening Standard, published
   right here in London. Here we go, Corporal.
Corporal Harry Crussle: St. Louis, Missouri, Corporal Harry Crussle.
Major Ken Tredwell: And three sailors.
Lucien J. Palakeer: Albion, Rhode Island, Lucien J. Palakeer.
Victor House: Chicago, Illinois, Victor House.
Frank Ainsworth: Akron, Ohio, Frank Ainsworth.
Major Ken Tredwell: Chicago and Ohio. And a soldier, he's shaking his head, I think he
   can be talked into it. How about it, Sergeant?
Chester Green: Longview, Texas, Chester Green.
Major Ken Tredwell: And here is a nurse, a Lieutenant. Hello, Lieutenant, name and home
   town.
Dorothy C. Longeniger: Lancaster, Pennsylvania, Dorothy C. Longeniger.
Major Ken Tredwell: I bet that sounded good in Lancaster, very good. Sergeant, how about
   it?
Don McDougall: Providence, Rhode Island, Don McDougall.
Major Ken Tredwell: And a Staff Sergeant wearing those Silver Wings.
S/Sgt. Dick Jackson: Hinckley, Ohio, Dick Jackson.
Major Ken Tredwell: Another Staff Sergeant with the Silver Wings.
S/Sgt. Howard Haley: Austin, Minnesota, Howard Haley.
Major Ken Tredwell: And straight from the Infantry.
R. C. Smith: Terre Haute, Indiana, R. C. Smith.
Major Ken Tredwell: How about it, sailor?
Bill Rekowski: Garfield, New Jersey, Bill Rekowski.
Major Ken Tredwell: What was that last name, Bill?
Bill Rekowski: Bill Rekowski.
Major Ken Tredwell: Good enough, and next to Bill?
Thomas Pridner: Long Branch, New Jersey, Thomas Pridner.]
Major Ken Tredwell: And wearing the patch of SHAEF.
Noyse Scott: Ah - Burbank, California, Noyse Scott.
Major Ken Tredwell: Now we get about five more, Cecil, then we're gonna run right back to
   you. Here's number one.
Russ Bowen: Pasadena, California, Russ Bowen.
Harry Levine: Kalamazoo, Michigan, Harry Levine.
Major Ken Tredwell: I see you sailors waving back there but how am I gonna get to you?
   Come on over here.
Bill Malone: St. Louis, Missouri, Bill Malone.
Major Ken Tredwell: If the sailors can get to me we'll grab 'em. Here's a soldier.
Raymond Anderson: Minneapolis, Minnesota, Raymond Anderson.
Major Ken Tredwell: Sailor one.
Pat Rodgers: Brooklyn, New York, Pat Rodgers.
Major Ken Tredwell: Sailor two.
Wally Yusemina: Ah - Wally Yusemina, Hyde Park, Massachusetts.
Major Ken Tredwell: Let's have that home town first. Sailor three.

Paul Knapp: Syracuse, New York, Paul Knapp.

Major Ken Tredwell: Look at 'em line up. It's like a chow line here.

Gerry Lester: Newburgh, New York, Gerry Lester.

Major Ken Tredwell: And three soldiers sitting on two tables apiece.

Bill Berrick: Philadelphia, Pennsylvania, Bill Berrick.

Don T. Mustang: Quakersville, Virginia, Don T. Mustang.

Bob Trolton: Berkeley, California, Bob Trolton.

Major Ken Tredwell: And the swan song by a Tech. Sergeant. Let's go, Sergeant.

T/Sgt. Leroy Barnett: Independence, Missouri, Leroy Barnett.

Major Ken Tredwell: Cecil Maddem from Casablanca, take it back.

Cecil Madden: Thank you, Ken, and today we spotlight station KVNU located at Logan and Cash Valley, Utah. You who also give our program to the people of Southern Idaho and Western Wyoming, good luck to all of you of the Utah Agricultural College. And I guess we dedicate our coming surprise to you. Greetings and the very best wishes to all of you at Lit - ah - Logan from all of us in London. As I've often told you before, this room, Dunkers Den, though it's technically part of the American Red Cross, very technically, really belongs to a member of the Astaire family, to wit, Adele, who works here. In fact I'm standing by her own desk where she helps G.I.s to write letters home. We're able today to unite the Astaire family on this side of the Atlantic, where they're so well known, because a charming, long-legged fellow has breezed in looking as debonair as we've always known him in London in his great stage triumphs at the London Strand and Empire theatres in the great picture "Holiday Inn." So let's give a grand welcome to our great surprise, Fred Astaire. Fred, we're thrilled to have you here and your sister, too, she's a very good friend of this program. And one of the things we do on this program are these G.I. interviews. So we're going to subject you to a G.I. interview, if that's O.K., by Major Ken Tredwell. O.K.?

Fred Astaire: Yeah. Yeah.

Cecil Madden: Come on, Ken.

Major Ken Tredwell: Here we go and it's really a thrill to have Fred and Adele Astaire with us in person and together today. Ah, Fred, I'd like to ask you a couple of questions if I may. Ah, are you married?

Fred Astaire: Yeah. Yes, I am.

Major Ken Tredwell: Yes. Yeah. Any gum, chum?

Fred Astaire: Wait a minute, wait until I get this gum out of my mouth.

Major Ken Tredwell: Ah, have you any family, Fred?

Fred Astaire: You bet I have.

Major Ken Tredwell: That's mighty fine. How many have you?

Fred Astaire: Three.

Major Ken Tredwell: Three. That sounds fine.

Fred Astaire: Three children.

Major Ken Tredwell: Three children?

Fred Astaire: Isn't that what you asked me?

Major Ken Tredwell: I sure did. I sure did. Tell me, Fred, ah, what ...

Fred Astaire: Lovely wife, too.

Major Ken Tredwell: ... ah, before the war what did you do for a living?

Fred Astaire: Oh, ah.

Major Ken Tredwell: That was - that was nasty and I certainly take it back. When were you last here in London, Fred?

Fred Astaire: About - ha - five years ago.

Major Ken Tredwell: Five years ago. Does it look very much different to you now?

Fred Astaire: Somewhat.

Major Ken Tredwell: I'll bet it does. We can't see London in her real electrical brilliance these days, can we?

Fred Astaire: No, hardly.

Major Ken Tredwell: I bet, I bet what he heard about was the Spam lines and he wanted to get in on one. I've never seen - ah - Dally Astaire, whom we all know very well, I've never seen her looking so happy. Ah - it's been five years since, since she and Fred were together.

Fred Astaire: Right.

Major Ken Tredwell: Very sincerely and without horseplay - ah - although Fred is not in uniform he's probably the best G.I. of us all and it's a great thrill, a great thrill to have him with us.

Adele Astaire: I'm a G.I., too.

Major Ken Tredwell: All right. That, that was Dally and she means it. God bless you to both of you.

Fred Astaire: Thanks a lot.

Major Ken Tredwell: We're not going to let Fred Astaire leave this stage without a dance, are we?

Audience: No!

Fred Astaire: Well.

Major Ken Tredwell: Back goes the gum in his mouth, here goes the piano, make it anything, Mel. Here we go.

Unidentified trio tune (S/Sgt. Mel Powell, piano; Sgt. Michael Hucko, clarinet; T/Sgt. Ray McKinley, drums)

   Fred Astaire: This is strictly from fright, I tell you. Don't make it too long, boys. I can't dance to that too long.

Cecil Madden: Thank you, Fred Astaire, and thank you, Ken. Now we introduce our feature from France. A few weeks ago Bebe Daniels, that talented and great-hearted lady, famous on stage and radio, visited some of your wounded and some of your doctors on our behalf. We're able to give you now her second visit to the evacuation hospital, so come in will you, Bebe Daniels.

Bebe Daniels: Thank you, Cecil Madden, and a very cheerful hello to you, America, from all your daughters and sons in liberated France. Last week Purple Heart Corner came to you from one of our evacuation hospitals nine miles from the front lines in Normandy, with the promise that this week we would pay that same hospital another visit. Well, here we are and Colonel Adams from Abilene, Texas is still showing us around.

Colonel Adams: Now, Bebe, sitting on this cart is Captain James Mayhorn of "Shiktashill," Oklahoma.

Bebe Daniels: What happened to you up there, Captain?

Captain James Mayhorn: I was flying an artillery observation plane. I located two target tanks, dropped too close, and one of them bit back at me.

Bebe Daniels: How are you feeling now?

Captain James Mayhorn: Fine.

Bebe Daniels: You must be to be sitting up the way you are.

Captain James Mayhorn: Yes, they only got me in the shoulder. You know, I've written home telling them I was going to keep my skin all in one piece. Well, I've kept my promise with the exception of a couple of little holes.

Bebe Daniels: Hmm, good. How'd you land the aircraft, Captain?

Captain James Mayhorn: Well, I wasn't - ah - hurt badly so I went in and finished my mission.

Bebe Daniels: Meaning?

Captain James Mayhorn: I directed the fire of the artillery so that the tanks were knocked out.

Bebe Daniels: Good work, Captain. Tell me, who have you got back home in Oklahoma who'll be proud to hear that?

Captain James Mayhorn: My wife and my mother.

Bebe Daniels: Have you been getting mail from them lately?

Captain James Mayhorn: Yes, it comes in quite regularly.

Bebe Daniels: It helps a lot with these fellows over here, doesn't it?

Captain James Mayhorn: You bet it does.

Bebe Daniels: Well, here's hoping the mail keeps coming in regularly. And remember, Captain, keep 'em flying.

Captain James Mayhorn: Right.

Colonel Adams: Bebe, on this next cart we have Private First Class Alfred W. Beard of "Credonia," Kansas.

Bebe Daniels: Well, Al, what happened to you?

Pfc. Alfred W. Beard: I got a piece of 88 shrapnel in my leg, but it ain't bad.

Bebe Daniels: Any pain now?

Pfc. Alfred W. Beard: No, there's no pain.

Bebe Daniels: Tell me, how does it feel to be up there at the front facing those Jerry bullets?
Pfc. Alfred W. Beard: Well, there's enough excitement, you don't have time to be scared.
Bebe Daniels: You don't, huh?
Pfc. Alfred W. Beard: As a matter of fact, I miss my pals and I think I'll get right up and get right back and join 'em.
Bebe Daniels: Good luck to you, soldier. Colonel, who's this in the cot over here?
Colonel Adams: Ah, Bebe, this is Robert Tyler of Los Angeles, California, First Lieutenant.
Bebe Daniels: Where do you live back there in Los Angeles, Robert?
1st Lt. Robert Tyler: On South Normandy Avenue.
Bebe Daniels: And who's living there now?
1st Lt. Robert Tyler: Ah, my wife and mother-in-law.
Bebe Daniels: Oh. Sounds like you get along very well with your mother-in-law.
1st Lt. Robert Tyler: Yes, we get along O.K. She's a bit unusual.
Bebe Daniels: I think they'd like to know how you're feeling now.
1st Lt. Robert Tyler: I'm feeling fine. I just got a few shell fragments in my leg and they're healing up.
Bebe Daniels: No pain?
1st Lt. Robert Tyler: None at all.
Bebe Daniels: By the way, what's your wife's name?
1st Lt. Robert Tyler: Frances.
Bebe Daniels: Well, I'll bet Frances and your mother-in-law will be mighty happy to know that you're feeling so well.
1st Lt. Robert Tyler: Yes, and under the circumstances I think it's a bit unusual I'm feeling well.
Bebe Daniels: Well, what do you mean, Lieutenant?
1st Lt. Robert Tyler: Well, you see, I'm going to be a father in a couple of weeks.
Bebe Daniels: Ha, ha, ha. Well, don't worry. The doctors here tell me that they lose very few fathers.

Colonel Adams: Say, Bebe, here comes Colonel Hair with Colonel Rodgers.
Colonel Hair: And, Bebe, I want you to meet Colonel John Rodgers of Washington, D.C., who is Chief Surgeon of all the American medical services of the 1st Army in France.
Bebe Daniels: Well, it's a great honor to meet you, Colonel Rodgers. I've seen a lot of your stations and hospitals and you're doing a mighty wonderful job for our boys over here.
Colonel John Rodgers: Thank you, and that is because I have such a wonderful staff, particularly Colonel Jim Snyder of Washington, D.C. and Colonel Bill Ampspecial of Oklahoma, they are my right and left arms. Together we spent months before D-Day planning this entire operation. And I would like to pay tribute to the wonderful work of the officers, nurses and men who are operating our medical units.
Bebe Daniels: You're right.

Colonel Adams: Here it is, Bebe.
Bebe Daniels: Ah, then I guess we'll have to say good bye, folks, until next week when Purple Heart Corner will come to you from the fifth link in the chain of evacuation of our wounded, the landing strip. So now I return you to Cecil Madden in London.

[Cecil Madden: Thank you, Bebe Daniels, and we're now back in the club. We call on our musical guests, Ray McKinley and his G.I.s, to play you "Sun Valley Jump."
SUN VALLEY JUMP]
Cecil Madden: You may know that Bing Crosby is over here in London. Bing has made an instantaneous hit with the London public by his good nature and his good humor. You've probably heard the story of his singing to a crowd of 2000 people out of the window of a small restaurant in Soho in the dark with the only lighting their torches turned on his face. The story is perfectly true because I was right there with him where he was dining. We liked everything about Bing, and in appearing in my own radio program, "Variety Bandbox" at the Queensbury All-Services Club, he made a great hit by comedy dialogue with Britain's leading radio comedian Tommy Handley. Not only were there

nearly 5000 men and girls of all the services of all the united nations assembled in that club while he was singing, but it's estimated that the radio audience here, through the Allied Expeditionary Forces Program and the other B.B.C. network was approximately 30,000,000s at one time. I thought you might like to hear his opening in our show, so here's a flash of Bing Crosby in London.

...

At this point in the recording, the 27Aug44 recording of Bing Crosby and Tommy Handley, and Bing Crosby singing ""San Fernando Valley (I'm Packin' My Grip)" accompanied by Pfc. Jack Rusin on piano, was inserted.

...

[Cecil Madden: Once again our short half hour is nearing its close. We're going to make a change today and instead of all of us singing a community song, here's Ray McKinley, we're going to ask him to do something.
T/Sgt. Ray McKinley: Thank you, Cecil. I think the folks on both sides of the puddle would get a big kick out of an old favorite which the boys made a record of back there and it takes a nice little hunk of Americana and brings it right over here. It's called "Chattanooga Choo Choo."]
CHATTANOOGA CHOO CHOO
  Vocal refrain by Technical Sergeant Ray McKinley and the Crew Chiefs
Cecil Madden: Well it's, well it's time to say good bye for another wartime week. I'd just like to say one thing before we part, it's a great privilege to be able to do and send you this program each week for nearly four years now as a very small gesture to the families wherever you are in United States. Thank you for your really marvelous letters received last week from Denver and Colorado Springs, Colorado; Dedham and Cambridge, Massachusetts; Macon, Georgia; Buffalo; New York City; from Palmyra, New Jersey; St. Petersburg and Tallahassee, Florida; good luck WTAL and welcome; Philadelphia and Sharon Hill, Pennsylvania; Bountiful, Utah; Portsmouth and Oakton, Virginia; Emporia, Kansas; Lewiston, Auburn, Maine; and Taft, Eureka, San Marino and Los Angeles, California. So it's au revoir from me and thanks to Adele Astaire, Fred Astaire, Bebe Daniels, Major Ken Tredwell; Sergeant Ray McKinley, the American Red Cross, U.S.O. camp shows, to the band and all of you. This is Cecil Madden of the British Broadcasting Corporation saying so long for now, hoping you'll be tuned in to us next week, wherever you live, when you join us over here, 3, 4, 5 or 6000 miles away from London, England.
Let's Sing a Happy Song (closing theme --- recording, not Miller band)

31Aug44 (Thu) 8:30-8:59PM Paris Cinema, London, England   SWN-19136
  AMERICAN BAND OF THE AEF broadcast

Corporal Paul Dubov: This is a feature of the American Band of the A.E.F.
MOONLIGHT SERENADE (opening theme)
  Corporal Paul Dubov: The American Band of the A.E.F. under the direction of Major Glenn
    Miller. This is your Thursday night thirty minutes with the Moonlight Serenader,
    presenting tonight's starring guest Bing Crosby. And here is Major Glenn Miller.
Major Glenn Miller: Thank you and good evening, everybody. Tommies and Yanks, this is
    another of your very own shows being broadcast over your very own radio network. Over
    in the corner tonight there's a tin hat, a gas mask, a bed roll, and a B-4 bag ready to
    go. Which all means that Bing Crosby is on his way out there to the fighting lines to
    pay you a personal visit. However, we managed to snag him for this half hour just
    before take off time. So during the next thirty minutes you'll hear him singin' some of
    the new home town tunes. Now, just by way of gettin' the curtain up in a hurry, here's
    a Sergeant Jerry Gray high jumper, "Here We Go Again."
HERE WE GO AGAIN
Major Glenn Miller: Tonight we're forgetting the idea of saving the best for the last by
    moving the main attraction up to the two spot. Nothing I could say could top the
    feeling you Tommies and Yanks have already expressed toward this guy, so I'm just gonna
    lay it on the line short and sweet. Here's Bing Crosby.
Bing Crosby: Well, it's certainly high honor, Major Glenn Miller, sharing this all Allied
    audience and the music of your All-American band. You know, if I were making tanks or
    airplanes or something like that, I'd - I'd be a lot closer to understanding why you
    guys out there might be wanting anything that I have to offer. I'm just hoping that
    your demand lasts as long as my supply. So whatever I got to sell ain't gonna get any
    closer to a deal if I don't chase the conversation here and swing into a slight sonata.
    Shall we say something that would be doing big business around the rumble seat circuit
    if you Yanks were back there to take up with your summer night spy service? Major.
LONG AGO (And Far Away)
  Vocal refrain by Bing Crosby
Major Glenn Miller: Mighty fancy, Mr. Crosby, as usual. Your voice is what the well
    dressed song should be wearing and I mean any season. Now it's medley time saluting the
    mothers, wives, sweethearts and sisters of the men of the Allied Forces, to the gals you
    left behind here's something old, something new, something borrowed and something blue.
    Our old song, "My Buddy."
MY BUDDY (Old tune)
  Major Glenn Miller: Tonight's new song is entrusted to the loving care of the voice of
    Bing.
AMOR (New tune)
  Vocal refrain by Bing Crosby
  Major Glenn Miller: We put the bite on friend Harry James for tonight's borrowed tune,
    and up jumps "Music Maker."
MUSIC MAKERS (Borrowed tune)
  Major Glenn Miller: Tonight the blue department offers a song shaded in whispering blue,
    "Farewell Blues."
FAREWELL BLUES (Blue tune)
Major Glenn Miller: Now just by way of makin' the most of a good thing, we've scheduled
    brother Bing Crosby to take another cut at the ball right here and right now. Bing.
Bing Crosby: Major, I'm all rosinned up, I got a good toe hold and I aim to meet the ball
    where it's gonna do the most good.
Major Glenn Miller: Well, make yourself right at home, Mr. C., and get to it.
Bing Crosby: You know ...
MY GUY'S COME BACK (The Uptown Hall)
  Bing Crosby: ... what I'd like to do, I'd like to pay a little visit to the Miller
    family ice box and avail myself of what I consider one of the choice cuts of your
    organization. I'm referring to the tenderloin of tempo or the sirloin of swing as it
    were. The boys from "Uptown Hall," Mel Powell and his little group.
  S/Sgt. Mel Powell: Whatcha got, Bing?
  Bing Crosby: Just bust me a beat, Sergeant Powell ...

SWINGING ON A STAR (The Uptown Hall)
    Bing Crosby: ... and I'll join you at the water hole.
    Vocal refrain by Bing Crosby and the Crew Chiefs
Major Glenn Miller: Nice work, Mr. C and company. Now a word to you Tommies and Yanks
    out there on the listenin' end of this program. We know just how you feel about this
    guy Crosby, so in your name we're invitin' him to join the Crew Chiefs and the gang in
    the last go around, Sergeant Jerry Gray's league leadin' arrangement of "Poinciana."
POINCIANA (Song of the Tree)
    Vocal refrain by Bing Crosby and the Crew Chiefs
Major Glenn Miller: Do you have a few last words, Bing?
Bing Crosby: Well, I got a few to you, Major Glenn, words of thanks for letting me hitch
    a ride on your high flyin' half hour. And another few to you Tommies and Yanks out
    there. In just a - just a few minutes here I should be getting plenty of laughs tryin'
    to carry that tin hat and bed roll and gas mask and B-4 bag that the Major mentioned
    earlier. And if I don't lose traction entirely, I'll get to you. So long for now.
    I'll be gettin' around.
Major Glenn Miller: Thank you, Bing Crosby, and now this is Major Glenn Miller checkin'
    along until next Thursday night. So in the next six days and nights we'll be meetin'
    and playin' for a lot of you fightin' guys. For now, good luck, good night.
MOONLIGHT SERENADE (closing theme)
    Corporal Paul Dubov: This has been your regular Thursday night thirty minutes with the
        Moonlight Serenader, presenting the American Band of the A.E.F. under the direction of
        Major Glenn Miller with tonight's starring guest Bing Crosby.

02Sep44 (Sat) 6:30-7:00PM London time/12:30-1:00PM New York time BBC Studio
London, England   FWN-19139, O.P.647
ATLANTIC SPOTLIGHT broadcast   London attendance: 200

Announcer: This is "Atlantic Spotlight."
Theme [Atlantic Spotlight Orchestra (NBC Orchestra)]
Announcer: Again the British Broadcasting Corporation and the National Broadcasting
  Company of America join wave bands across the sea to bring you high spots of
  entertainment from both countries. Today's masters of ceremonies are Ronnie Waldman in
  London and Herb Sheldon in New York.
Herb Sheldon: Good morning, Ronnie.
Ronnie Waldman: Good evening, Herb.
Herb Sheldon: Say, ah, Ben Grauer's a bit under the weather today so I'm sitting in.
Ronnie Waldman: Glad to hear that. We're delighted to have you.
Herb Sheldon: Ha, ha. Thanks very much. By the way, the "Spotlight" is going
  Anglo-American in a big way today, isn't it, Ronnie?
Ronnie Waldman: It certainly is, what with Major Glenn Miller and that superb orchestra
  of his, the American Band of the A.E.F., who are giving immense pleasure to listeners in
  Britain and France these days.
Herb Sheldon: And that very popular leader of a British band, Roy Fox, who happens to be
  in New York at the moment, as guest conductor of our American Spotlight Orchestra.
Ronnie Waldman: Well, it looks as though we're in for two highly appetizing musical
  courses at today's picnic.
Herb Sheldon: Ha.
Ronnie Waldman: Have you anything to add as an extra dish?
Herb Sheldon: Well, Ronnie, if you were up to date with your American slang you won't
  call it a dish.
Ronnie Waldman: Sorry.
Herb Sheldon: Ha, ha. Let's say several dishes and also a glass of good wine with
  luncheon.
Ronnie Waldman: Dinner.
Herb Sheldon: Now don't blame me if you got up six, ah, hours too early.
Ronnie Waldman: All right. Let's settle the time question about this meal and call it
  dunch.
Herb Sheldon: Dunch? O.K., dunch it is.
Ronnie Waldman: Right. Well, what's the good wine?
Herb Sheldon: The Modernaires with Paula Kelly from here and Marion Hutton from Atlantic
  City.
Ronnie Waldman: Well, that sounds good to us, Herb. And now to prove that old world
  courtesy still lives, we'll say, "After you in New York."
Herb Sheldon: Thanks, Ronnie. And now, Ronnie, and for that matter, England, Australia
  and the British Dominions, stand by for a familiar greeting.
Ronnie Waldman: That sounds very interesting. Who is it?
Herb Sheldon: Ah, listen.
Whispering (Atlantic Spotlight Orchestra)
  Roy Fox: Hello, ladies and gentlemen, this is ...
  Ronnie Waldman: Roy Fox.
  Herb Sheldon: Right, Ronnie. I didn't think you could miss that greeting.
  Ronnie Waldman: Well, hardly, Herb.
Ronnie Waldman: Roy Fox happens to be one of the most popular and famous of our pre-war
  bandleaders.
Herb Sheldon: We know that, Ronnie. That's why we thought it'd be a pleasant surprise
  for you.
Ronnie Waldman: It certainly is. I say, Roy, do you ever get homesick for London?
Roy Fox: Of course I do. Most Americans who work over there for any length of time
  develop a real affection for it. I hope to be back there soon and conduct a British
  band again. The one I had before the war broke us up made work a pleasure.
Ronnie Waldman: To say nothing of listening. Ah, some of your discoveries have done
  extremely well, haven't they, Roy?
Herb Sheldon: Ah, what discoveries, Roy?

Roy Fox: Now don't try to lure me into the ranks of the people who claim to have discovered stars, Herb.

Ronnie Waldman: Ah, yes, but you will admit that you helped a good many of them up the ladder. For instance, one of Ella Logan's first important jobs was with you, and also Denny Dennis, Mary Lee and a few more, wasn't it?

Roy Fox: Yes, that's quite true. I was lucky to be among the first to find them.

Herb Sheldon: Well, Roy, ah, now's your chance to discover a new baritone. While in my bath this morning I sang "Long Ago And Far Away" in a way that would make Bing Crosby feel ashamed.

Roy Fox: Of whom?

Herb Sheldon: Me.

Roy Fox: Then promise me you won't try to sing anything while we play.

Herb Sheldon: All right, Roy, I promise. Incidentally, you might tell them what you're going to play.

Roy Fox: Gladly. It's a medley of "Amor" and "Tico-Tico."

Amor (American Spotlight Orchestra)

Tico-Tico (American Spotlight Orchestra)

Herb Sheldon: Now then, Ronnie. I say, Ronnie.

Ronnie Waldman: Hello there, Herb.

Herb Sheldon: Ah, Ronnie.

Ronnie Waldman: Yes.

Herb Sheldon: Ah, standby now for some transatlantic yelling.

Ronnie Waldman: Why, what's going on, Herb?

Herb Sheldon: Well, when old American friends get together there's usually a lot of back slapping and yelling and right now we're gonna bring some old friends together. Is Major Glenn Miller standing by over there?

Ronnie Waldman: Yes, he's standing by on this side of the Atlantic just as he was standing by on your side of the Atlantic on the first "Atlantic Spotlight" back on January the first this year.

Major Glenn Miller: You can bet we're standing by, Herb.

Herb Sheldon: Well, then meet some old employees of yours, the Modernaires.

The Modernaires: Hi ya, boss.

Major Glenn Miller: Hi, gang, the Modernaires. How about Paula? She there too?

Herb Sheldon: Ah.

Herb Sheldon and Paula Kelly: Here, Glenn.

Major Glenn Miller: In the flesh.

Herb Sheldon: Yes, she's right in the flesh, Glenn.

Major Glenn Miller: Well, that's a good deal. How they sounding these days, Herb?

Herb Sheldon: Well, solid as ever. As a matter of fact just as solid as when the Modernaires and Paula Kelly were an integral part of Glenn Miller's Moonlight Serenaders way back there in peacetime.

Major Glenn Miller: Well, we thought they were a pretty good outfit then. Too bad we can't arrange a transatlantic duet.

Herb Sheldon: Ah, we thought of that, Glenn, but we couldn't rush the Modernaires' arrangements to you fast enough and besides we didn't want to clutter up the mails going overseas. Incidentally, Glenn, we know that you'll be happy to learn that the Modernaires are currently knockin' 'em dead at the Adams Theater in Newark, New Jersey.

Major Glenn Miller: Well, that's great. I'm sorry that we can't hear them over there. The best we can do is to put them on the wireless over here. So let's get goin'. Go ahead, children.

I've Got a Heart Filled with Love (American Spotlight Orchestra)
   Vocal refrain by Paul Kelly and the Modernaires

Herb Sheldon: Well, well. What do you say to that, Glenn? What do you say to that, Glenn?

Major Glenn Miller: Only one thing, Herb. That's terrific.

Herb Sheldon: Ha, ha. How about you, Ronnie?

Ronnie Waldman: Only two things, solid and encore.

Herb Sheldon: Well, then encore it is. The Modernaires and Paula Kelly, get this, Glenn, with a new tune knocked out by Hal Dickinson, one of the boys, "Tabby Cat."
Tabby the Cat (American Spotlight Orchestra)
   Vocal refrain by Paula Kelly and the Modernaires
Herb Sheldon: Yes, solid, solid, Ronnie.
Ronnie Waldman: That was fine. That was fine, Herb. I wish you could have seen the faces of the boys in the band here. They loved it.
Herb Sheldon: Loved it, huh. That's great, Ronnie.
Ronnie Waldman: Yep.
Herb Sheldon: What now, Ronnie?
Ronnie Waldman: Well, now, Herb, we come to Major Glenn Miller and the kind of orchestra that composers dream about. World newspapers have told you of their great success here but we've been impressed not only by their artistry but their tireless energy. They give innumerable concerts for the Forces, they broadcast regularly to the Forces overseas, and they somehow still find time to eat, sleep and rehearse, although it looks like now the implied word "sleep" was a typographical error.
Herb Sheldon: Say, we're lucky to get them for a few minutes now at that rate.
Ronnie Waldman: I agree and so as not to lose another few seconds of it let me now introduce Major Glenn Miller, as if he needed an introduction.
Herb Sheldon: Well, not to the folks at home anyway. Hello, Major Glenn Miller and all your famous orchestra.
Major Glenn Miller: Hello, Herb. Here we go. It isn't often we pick a tune for its title but today that's the main reason we're shooting one particular melody back to the big 48. In the name of all the boys over here, whether they're from 79th Street in New York or from Monrovia, California or Washington, D.C., this is the cue song for a happy day a comin' when we all go "Flying Home."
FLYING HOME
Major Glenn Miller: Everybody's playin' real loud then so his best gal would hear him. Here we go again with another tune. Ever since we've been over here flying around the A.E.F. we've had the pleasure of seeing a lot of new faces and a lot of new places. Our old friends the Yanks, our new friends the Tommies, all seem to get a big boot out of the same kind of music. And here's Sergeant Johnny Desmond to sing one of the songs that's hittin' the big time on both sides of the Atlantic, "I'll Be Seeing You."
I'LL BE SEEING YOU
   Vocal refrain by Sergeant Johnny Desmond
Herb Sheldon: Well, you said it, fellow. Thanks very much, we'll be seeing you. Hope soon, too.
Ronnie Waldman: Herb, you can warn the United States for me that it's going to take a lot of force to get the orchestra away from their host of fans over here.
Herb Sheldon: Well, we're waiting for them patiently and impatiently I should say.
Ronnie Waldman: I'll bet.
Herb Sheldon: Ah, Ronnie, if ...
Ronnie Waldman: Yes?
Herb Sheldon: ... I may, I'd like to interrupt this little shindig for some history making.
Ronnie Waldman: History, Herb? Not another transatlantic bridge game?
Herb Sheldon: Oh, well, practically the same thing. A transaclan-atlantic duet. Is Glenn Miller still standing by over there?
Major Glenn Miller: Right here, Herb.
Herb Sheldon: Well, good, because it's time for you to meet another one of your peacetime hirelings. Now, if the Atlantic City, New Jersey end of this party line is working we should hear from somebody else you know. How about it, Marion Hutton?
Marion Hutton: This is Marion Hutton in Atlantic City.
Major Glenn Miller: What do you say, Marion? What are you doin' so far from New York?
Marion Hutton: You should talk! I'm down here selling an engagement at the Steel Pier.
Major Glenn Miller: Well, fine. We're over here with a couple o' million lads who are fillin' a sort of a cute engagement over here, too.
Marion Hutton: Yes, we've heard that they've been a smash hit of late.
Herb Sheldon: Well, this is really like old home week. Now if - if everything works out all right our history should be made with a melodious bang.

Ronnie Waldman: Oh? I get it. Glenn Miller's band in London accompanies Marion Hutton singing in Atlantic City in a number announced by Herb Sheldon in New York. That's simple.
Herb Sheldon: Oh, yeah? Very simple. I - I like to have you working the switches in this hook-up, bub. Well, enough of that anyway. On with our duet.
Ronnie Waldman: Right. Major Glenn Miller raises his baton in London.
Herb Sheldon: And Marion Hutton raises her voice in Atlantic City and the two neatly join to form an old favorite done now in transatlantic style.
JUKE BOX SATURDAY NIGHT
  Vocal refrain by Marion Hutton and the Crew Chiefs
Herb Sheldon: Oh say, say that was great, Marion, and good luck to you in Atlantic City. Now I think we have time for more of that Major Glenn Miller music. What say, Glenn?
Major Glenn Miller: Well, I'll tell you what, it's, ah, got a little tune cooked up here that's, ah, makes every Yank over here feel right at home because its', ah, brings back a little touch in of old times, if you know what I mean.
Herb Sheldon: Right.
Major Glenn Miller: Makes, makes him think of his gal friend, his Polly, or Kay, or Joy, Helen, Marge, Nancy, or Connie, some gal like that, you know?
Herb Sheldon: Right.
Major Glenn Miller: And I'm happy to say it's just about as popular here as it is over there, it's "In the Mood."
Herb Sheldon: Fine.
IN THE MOOD
  Ronnie Waldman: Everything's over, Major Glenn Miller.
  Herb Sheldon: Well, the clock says we must sign off. So this is Herb Sheldon in ...
Herb Sheldon: ... New York signing off and saying good bye 'til next week. Our thanks to the Modernaires and everybody. So long, gang.
Theme (American Spotlight Orchestra)
Female BBC announcer: The program you've just heard was "Atlantic ...
NBC announcer: "Atlantic Spotlight" is presented jointly each Saturday by the British Broadcasting Corporation and the National Broadcasting Company. Script in London is by Jim Dyrenfort, in New York by Peter Harkins. Next week "Atlantic Spotlight" presents a special broadcast from Hollywood. "Atlantic Spotlight" is produced by Tom Ronald in London and in New York by Ross Filion. This is the National Broadcasting Company.
NBC chimes.

06Sep44 (Wed) c. 3:00-3:15PM Co-Partners Hall, Bedford, England   SWN-19244
  THE UPTOWN HALL recording   Aired 19Sep44

  ...

Corporal Paul Dubov: ... Miss Beryl Davis, one of England's favorite singers, back to bring us another song. And while we're looking forward to that, here's Mel and the boys to pass the time with a tune, "China Boy."
CHINA BOY
Corporal Paul Dubov: Back with us again tonight is none other than our good old friend old Sergeant Bernie Privin, he of the toy trumpet. He's taking a five-minute furlough from the American Band of the A.E.F. to sit in with Mel and the boys on another number. It's a tune he played a few meetings ago here in the Hall and one that you folks said you just had to hear again, "You Go to My Head."
YOU GO TO MY HEAD

  ...

06Sep44 (Wed) c. 3:30-3:45PM Co-Partners Hall, Bedford, England   SWN-19245
THE UPTOWN HALL recording   Aired 20Sep44

...

Corporal Paul Dubov: You charter members here in the Hall know that the password is
   always "Happy Listenin'" and just to make sure you know what that means, here's another
   sample with Sergeant Mel and the company playin'. It's "I Want to Be Happy."
I WANT TO BE HAPPY
Corporal Paul Dubov: The boys hark back now to a hit tune from the pen of composer Johnny
   Green. It's that unforgettable, unforgotten "Body and Soul."
BODY AND SOUL
Corporal Paul Dubov: For this next number we go a little down our little aggregation to
   just four men. It's "Uptown Hall's" band within a band, Sergeant Mel at the piano, Ray
   McKinley at the drums, Trigger Alpert at the string bass and Michael Hucko supplying the
   hot licks on the clarinet. Their tune tonight is "What Is This Thing Called Love?"
WHAT IS THIS THING CALLED LOVE? (quartet: Hucko, Powell, Alpert, McKinley)
Corporal Paul Dubov: Miss Beryl Davis is back with us tonight with another one of those
   songs you've been hollering for. Beryl, from where I stand it looks to me like the
   folks are ready.
Beryl Davis: Well, if they've got the time I've got the tune. So, if the boys will back
   me up with a few bars I'll swing right in on the chorus of "Sweet Lorraine."
SWEET LORRAINE
   Vocal refrain by Beryl Davis
Corporal Paul Dubov: Beryl, that was really great. And here's a standing note of thanks
   from all the members for sharing these meetings with us. And, by the way, don't forget,
   if you're ever in the neighborhood again you'll find the key to the Hall right under the
   doormat. And now it's time for another tune and here's Mel and the boys ridin' a happy
   ending for our little meeting with "Rosette."
ROSETTE

...

07Sep44 (Thu) 8:30-8:59PM Co-Partners Hall, Bedford, England   SWN-19167
  AMERICAN BAND OF THE AEF broadcast   Attendance: 100

...

Major Glenn Miller: ... U.S.A. way. We think maybe it'll do when it comes to stirring up
  a few pleasant memories. So step right up and help yourself to "Body and Soul."
BODY AND SOUL

...

Cpl. Paul A. Dubov: ... later Glenn Miller takes us all down to "Tuxedo Junction."
TUXEDO JUNCTION

...

Major Glenn Miller: And now it's medley time, salutin' the mothers, wives, sweethearts
  and sisters of you Tommies and Yanks with something old, something new, something
  borrowed, something blue. The old song, "Songs My Mother Taught Me."
SONGS MY MOTHER TAUGHT ME (Old tune)
  Major Glenn Miller: For our new tune here comes the Crew Chiefs singin' "It's Love,
    Love, Love!"
IT'S LOVE, LOVE, LOVE! (New tune)
  Vocal refrain by the Crew Chiefs
  Major Glenn Miller: For the borrowed tune we pay a visit to our musical antique dealer,
    pickin' up a fine old piece designed by Mozart, refinished by Raymond Scott and
    polished by Sergeant Mel Powell, "Eighteenth Century Drawing Room."
IN AN EIGHTEENTH CENTURY DRAWING ROOM (Borrowed tune)
  Major Glenn Miller: Sergeant Johnny Desmond turns the heat on our blue tune singin'
    "Blue Orchids."
BLUE ORCHIDS (Blue tune)
  Vocal refrain by Sergeant Johnny Desmond
Major Glenn Miller: Whoever does the pickin' of the guest artist for this program not
  only has a fine ear for music but also exhibits a fine eye for beauty. Tonight they've
  sent us a gal just returned from singin' her way around the camps and bases in the U.K.
  Here's Britain's Gloria Brent singin' "Time Alone Will Tell."
TIME ALONE WILL TELL
  Vocal refrain by Gloria Brent
Major Glenn Miller: Nice goin', Gloria. Your kind o' singin' makes our kind o'
  listenin'. Now you boys, Tommies and Yanks, Johnny Canucks, who are flyin' an' drivin'
  an' marchin' the road to victory, made this happy new song possible. It not only
  inspired the boys who wrote it, it also popped a lot o' new ideas into the head of the
  soldier who arranged it. Here's Sergeant Jerry Gray's most recent piece of writin',
  markin' the first time out of our startin' gate for "All's Well Mademoiselle."
ALL'S WELL MADEMOISELLE
  Vocal refrain by Sergeant Johnny Desmond and the Crew Chiefs
Major Glenn Miller: That's the rundown for tonight and now this is Major Glenn Miller
  thankin' Gloria Brent for stoppin' by, reminding you all that one week from now we'll be
  back to deliver another half hour cut along these same lines. This is your kind of
  music, well, your kind o' band will be right here to play it for you. So it's good
  luck, good night.
MOONLIGHT SERENADE (closing theme)
  Corporal Paul Dubov: You have heard your regular weekly half hour with the Moonlight
    Serenader, presenting the American Band of the A.E.F., under the direction of Major
    Glenn Miller, with tonight's starring guest, Britain's own Gloria Brent.

08Sep44 (Fri) 7:30-8:00PM Co-Partners Hall, Bedford, England
THE UPTOWN HALL recording   Script   Aired 16Nov44

Announcer: This is a feature of the American Band of the A.E.F.
MY GUY'S COME BACK (opening theme)
   Corporal Paul Dubov: Good evening, all, it's "The Uptown Hall," music for you of the
    Allied Liberation Forces, presented by members of the American Band of the A.E.F.,
    featuring Sergeant Mel Powell at the piano.
Corporal Paul Dubov: Welcome to "The Uptown Hall," fellow members. If you're lookin' for
  a few cheerful little earfuls tonight, well, let me say right off, you've come to the
  right place. Yes, sir, here in the old Hall we've lined up another session of happy
  listening for the members. And you're all invited to stick around and join in the fun,
  which begins right now with Mel and the boys playin' "I Remember April."
I'LL REMEMBER APRIL
Corporal Paul Dubov: One down and four to go. And here's brother Mel sparkin' the boys
  in a sparklin' arrangement of "These Foolish Things."
THESE FOOLISH THINGS
Corporal Paul Dubov: Now it's recess time for some of the boys while we turn the next
  tune over to our little "Band within a Band." It's Sergeant Mel Powell, piano; Sergeant
  Ray McKinley, drums; Sergeant Michael Hucko, clarinet; and Corporal Joe Shulman, string
  bass givin' the special treatment to "Exactly Like You."
EXACTLY LIKE YOU (quartet: Hucko, Powell, Shulman, McKinley)
Corporal Paul Dubov: Time now for our "Soldier and a Song." The soldier, Sergeant Johnny
  Desmond, the song, "I'll Be Seeing You."
I'LL BE SEEING YOU
   Vocal refrain by Sergeant Johnny Desmond
Corporal Paul Dubov: We always like to wind up our meetings here in the Hall on a
  pleasant note. And believe me, there's plenty of pleasant notes in this It's "Caravan."
CARAVAN
Corporal Paul Dubov: Well, while we've been playin', the clock has been tickin' away just
  as if nothin' else mattered. And now it's time for us to turn the lights out and light
  out ourselves. But remember, we're right here doin' business every Tuesday, Wednesday,
  Friday and Saturday. So be sure to catch us the next time around. Until then, this is
  Corporal Paul Dubov saying, "So long, and good luck to you."
MY GUY'S COME BACK (closing theme)
   Corporal Paul Dubov: You've been listening to music by members of the American Band of
    the A.E.F. Don't forget to join us again for our next musical meeting in "The Uptown
    Hall."

09Sep44 (Sat) 5:00-5:15PM Co-Partners Hall, Bedford, England   SLO-61673
  STRINGS WITH WINGS recording   Aired 11Sep44

Corporal Paul Dubov: This is a feature of the American Band of the A.E.F.
I SUSTAIN THE WINGS (opening theme)
    Corporal Paul Dubov: "Strings with Wings." "Strings with Wings," a program of music
      for you of the Allied Liberation Forces, presented by the string section of the
      American Band of the A.E.F., featuring Sergeant George Ockner and his violin.
Corporal Paul Dubov: Hello there. Those violins you've just heard in the background have
    probably already told you steady customers that it's Sergeant George Ockner and the boys
    back with another rack full of tunes for you folks. So borrow a cigarette from the chap
    next to you and lean back and listen as the boys bring you our first tune this evening,
    "I'll Get By."
I'LL GET BY (As Long As I Have You)
Corporal Paul Dubov: Here's one of those numbers that explain just what we mean when we
    talk about tunes played as only violins can play them. You heard it many times before
    played many ways. Now listen to our all violin version of "Sweet and Low."
SWEET AND LOW
Corporal Paul Dubov: Take some blue skies, add a dash of bright sunshine, some ripening
    apples, and a pleasant fragrance of burning leaves and you've got a pretty good tip-off
    on the title of our next tune, "Indian Summer."
INDIAN SUMMER
Corporal Paul Dubov: You've heard this next one before, too. But like the river it's
    written about it just seems to keep on rolling along. The string orchestra and their
    new arrangement of "Old Man River."
OL' MAN RIVER
Corporal Paul Dubov: Which brings us right down to the bottom of tonight's program,
    folks. Sorry we can't stay and play, but don't forget, we'll be back Wednesday with
    more music, so be sure to be listening. Until then, this is Corporal Paul Dubov saying,
    "Good night and good luck to you."
I SUSTAIN THE WINGS (closing theme)
    Corporal Paul Dubov: You've been listening to music by the string section of the
      American Band of the A.E.F., featuring Sergeant George Ockner and his violin.
      Remember to join us this coming Wednesday, same time, when we again present "Strings
      with Wings."

13Sep44 (Wed) 8:15-8:45PM Co-Partners Hall, Bedford, England   SLO-61750
  STRINGS WITH WINGS recording   Script   Aired 18Dec44

Announcer: This is a feature of the American Band of the A.E.F.
I SUSTAIN THE WINGS (opening theme)
  Corporal Paul Dubov: "Strings with Wings." "Strings with Wings," a program of music
    for you of the Allied Liberation Forces, presented by the string section of the
    American Band of the A.E.F., featuring Sergeant George Ockner and his violin.
Corporal Paul Dubov: Well, last week we had a long talk with the chap in the next bunk
  who handles our horoscopes for us. And he assured us that today would be one of our
  lucky days. He said the stars showed that today would be ideal for doing just as we
  pleased. And since the thing that pleases us most is playing for you folks, here we
  are. We've brought along Sergeant Ockner and the boys and they've brought along their
  music. So it looks like we're ready to go with the first tune, "All the Things You
  Are."
ALL THE THINGS YOU ARE
Corporal Paul Dubov: Sergeant Mel Powell, who plays a right fancy bit of piano for the
  American Band of the A.E.F., can also turn out a right fancy tune himself. A few months
  ago he tore himself away from the piano long enough to compose a little string number
  for the boys in the violin section, and we've brought it along to play tonight.
  Sergeant Mel's "Waltz for Strings."
WALTZ FOR STRINGS
Corporal Paul Dubov: If this next one doesn't bring back memories to you guys and gals,
  well, I guess nothin' will. It's Sergeant Ockner and the boys reminiscin' about that
  sunny season of ripening apples, harvest moons and walks in the woods, "Indian Summer."
INDIAN SUMMER
Corporal Paul Dubov: Sergeant Ockner must have done a mind-reading when he picked this
  next one. It's the thing that a lot of us are doin' a lot of thinking about these days.
  And here's hopin' the day won't be too far off when the job'll be done and we'll be
  "Goin' Home."
GOIN' HOME
I SUSTAIN THE WINGS (closing theme)
  Corporal Paul Dubov: You've been listening to music by the string section of the
    American Band of the A.E.F., featuring Sergeant George Ockner and his violin. Don't
    forget to join us again for our next program of "Strings with Wings."

14Sep44 (Thu) BBC studio, London, England
  HERE'S WISHING YOU WELL recording   Aired 21Sep44
  MAJOR GLENN MILLER INTERVIEW BY VERNON HARRIS   "The Wishing Well" segment

Vernon Harris: As many of you know, Glenn Miller, now Major Glenn Miller, is here just
  now as conductor of the American Band of the Allied Expeditionary Force and that's a bit
  of luck for "The Wishing Well" and for you, Jeff, Rodney and Rocky in East Africa,
  because Glenn has some along especially today to meet you.
Major Glenn Miller: Thank you, Vernon, and hello to all you guys and gals on the all
  Allied fighting team. Like to put that hello into capital letters to the three
  gentlemen who invited me here, Jeff, Rodney and Rocky.
Vernon Harris: I'm sure that many of the Forces who are listening, as well as Jeff and
  Rodney and Rocky, will paste this moment well into their memory books, Major Miller.
Major Glenn Miller: Take it easy now, Vernon.
Vernon Harris: And now how about bouncing a few answers back at the questions that have
  been bowling in about you and your American Band of the A.E.F.?
Major Glenn Miller: Well, you start asking, we'll do our best.
Vernon Harris: Well, I think first we should start right from the beginning of your visit
  to this country. Now how long have you been over here?
Major Glenn Miller: Ah, just about three months, but in those ninety odd days it seems
  like we've lived a lifetime of really wonderful experiences.
Vernon Harris: Sounds as if you've been kept busy every moment.
Major Glenn Miller: Well, the flak has been a little heavy at times and this might give
  you a rough idea of what it's been like. In the month of August, for instance, we
  played 89 separate jobs. That includes 35 concerts at the bases and camps, as well as
  maintaining our regular broadcasting schedule.
Vernon Harris: Shouldn't think there was much time left for eating and sleeping.
Major Glenn Miller: Well, sometimes there isn't.
Vernon Harris: Ah, rumor has it, Glenn, that you and your boys will soon be going
  overseas.
Major Glenn Miller: Ah, the sooner we have it, Vernon, the better we like it.
Vernon Harris: Have you enjoyed being here, I mean in the few moments you've found
  outside work?
Major Glenn Miller: The real enjoyment comes from the moments inside our work. Once we
  heard the happy sound of a music-hungry bunch of servicemen yelling for more of whatever
  we had to offer, we knew that we could never enjoy a more satisfying payoff in our
  lives.
Vernon Harris: Ah, I can understand that.
Major Glenn Miller: It's really been a great kick. Not only that but we've had the
  pleasure of playing with such fine British artists and new friends like Vera Lynn, Anne
  Shelton, Paula Green and many others, a couple of old friends of ours like Dinah Shore
  and Bing Crosby.
Vernon Harris: And how do you feel about the British reaction to your American Band of
  the A.E.F.?
Major Glenn Miller: Ah, from a personal standpoint it's really been wonderful. The
  Tommies we have played for have made us feel right at home. Ah, we were surprised to
  find that the British youngsters in the service are well educated to our American style
  of music.
Vernon Harris: Well, don't forget your records got here before you did.
Major Glenn Miller: Well, I hadn't thought of that. Anyway I hope we can send some of
  our bands over here and bring some of your bands over to the States after the war so
  we'll get to know each other a little better musically.
Vernon Harris: Well, that's a grand idea and thank you, Major Glenn Miller, for your
  visit to our program.
Major Glenn Miller: Pleasure's been all ours, Vernon. It's always a treat to talk to the
  men and women of the Forces. So to you out there, thanks again for the invitation to
  come here and for now, good luck, good bye.

23Sep44 (Sat) 10:45-11:00AM Co-Partners Hall, Bedford, England   SAL-16667
THE UPTOWN HALL recording   Script   Aired 23Nov44

Announcer: This is a feature of the American Band of the A.E.F.
MY GUY'S COME BACK (opening theme)
  Corporal Paul Dubov: Good evening, all, it's "The Uptown Hall," music for you of the
    Allied Liberation Forces, presented by members of the American Band of the A.E.F.,
    featuring Sergeant Mel Powell at the piano.
Corporal Paul Dubov: Welcome to "The Uptown Hall," fellow members. "The Uptown Hall"
  society for the improvising, harmonizing and popularizing of tantalizing
  instrumentalizing is now in session! The members have all filed in, the Sergeant at
  Arms has closed the door, and the band's on the stand ready to go. So let's have it
  quiet please while Mel and the boys lift the roof off the Hall to give you a glimpse of
  "Blue Skies."
BLUE SKIES
Corporal Paul Dubov: Comes now Sergeant Bernie Privin up the steps to the platform and
  totin' his trumpet along to sit in with Mel and the boys on "You Go to My Head."
YOU GO TO MY HEAD
Corporal Paul Dubov: First vice-president in charge of vocalizing here in the Hall is
  Sergeant Johnny Desmond. And tonight he steps up in front of the assembled members to
  deliver a few trillable syllables on the subject of "Long Ago and Far Away."
LONG AGO (And Far Away)
  Vocal refrain by Sergeant Johnny Desmond
Corporal Paul Dubov: Nice goin', Johnny, you did it again! But now as we get along
  toward the end of the meetin', here's Mel and the boys to top off tonight's tally of
  tunes with Sergeant Ralph Wilkinson's rapturous arrangement of "Perdido."
PERDIDO
Corporal Paul Dubov: Well, they say the show must go on. But if it did, we'd be right
  smack-dab in the middle of our next meetin'. So I guess that's gotta be all for now.
  But don't forget, we're holdin' open house here in the Hall every Tuesday, Wednesday,
  Friday and Saturday. And you've all got a big welcome waitin' for you, any time you can
  drop in. Until then, this is Corporal Paul Dubov saying, "So long, and good luck to
  you."
MY GUY'S COME BACK (closing theme)
  Corporal Paul Dubov: You've been listening to music by members of the American Band of
    the A.E.F. Don't forget to join us for our next musical meeting here in "The Uptown
    Hall."

26Sep44 (Tue) 8:45-9:15PM Co-Partners Hall, Bedford, England   SLO-62523
THE UPTOWN HALL recording   Aired 16Dec44

[Announcer: This is a feature of the American Band of the A.E.F.
MY GUY'S COME BACK (opening theme)
    Corporal Paul Dubov: Good evening, all, it's "The Uptown Hall," music for you of the
      Allied Liberation Forces, presented by members of the American Band of the A.E.F.,
      featuring Sergeant Mel Powell at the piano.
Corporal Paul Dubov: Welcome to "The Uptown Hall," fellow members. "The Uptown Hall"
    society for the modernizing and multiplication of mellifluous melodies and memorable
    masterpieces is now in session. We've locked the doors to keep out all those folks who
    don't know a good thing when they hear it. And sittin' up there on the platform are Mel
    and the boys fixin' to play. Here comes the wind-up, the pitch, and it's "Rosetta."
ROSETTA
Corporal Paul Dubov: Now maestro Mel's foot reaches over toward the soft pedal on the
    piano as the boys ease over into the easy groove. And if you listen carefully in this
    next one, you'll dig the dulcet French Horn of our own Corporal Addison S. Collins,
    horning in on a solo or two. O.K., "Love Is the Sweetest Thing."
LOVE IS THE SWEETEST THING
Corporal Paul Dubov: Time now for a bit of streamlined swing as three of the boys peel
    off and we carry on with our little "Band within a Band." It's Sergeant Mel at the
    piano, Sergeant Ray McKinley at the] drums, Sergeant Trigger Alpert, string bass and
    Sergeant Michael Hucko, doubling up on clarinet and tenor sax. They're coming at you
    now with a little dissertation called "As Long As I Live."
AS LONG AS I LOVE (quartet: Hucko, Powell, Alpert, McKinley)
Corporal Paul Dubov: Boy meets song, [boy likes song, boy sings song. All of which leads
    up to the fact that Sergeant Johnny Desmond is about to add the vocal trimmings to an
    old favorite of yours. "What a Diff'rence a Day Made."
WHAT A DIFF'RENCE A DAY MADE
    Vocal refrain by Sergeant Johnny Desmond
Corporal Paul Dubov: Now before we adjourn our madcap musicale for tonight,] there's just
    time to squeeze in one more tune and we bring the whole thing to a happy, snappy ending
    with "The Sheik (of Araby)."
THE SHEIK (of Araby)
Corporal Paul Dubov: Which nails the lid down on another meeting here in "The Uptown
    Hall." Yes, good friends, it's time to go. But on your way out be sure to pick up your
    invitation to join us for our next go-around of rhythm. [We're doin' business right
    here every Tuesday, Wednesday, Friday and Saturday. So don't forget to drop around.
    Until then, this is Corporal Paul Dubov saying, "So long, and good luck to you."
MY GUY'S COME BACK (closing theme)
    Corporal Paul Dubov: You've been listening to music by members of the American Band of
      the A.E.F. And remember to join us again for our next musical meeting in "The Uptown
      Hall."]

BBC announcer: There'll be another program by the Swing Sextet next Friday evening.

28Sep44 (Thu) 3:30-4:00PM Dunkers Den, Piccadilly, London, England
DOX-39135/DLO-62311/DLO-62354A
American Red Cross Rainbow Corner Club (run by Adele Astaire)   Aired 30Sep44
AMERICAN EAGLE IN BRITAIN recording   199th Program   Attendance: 1000

Let's Sing a Happy Song (opening theme --- recording, not Miller band)
Cecil Madden: Once again, and for the 199th time, it's hello to all of you in America.
   This is Cecil Madden of the British Broadcasting Corporation saying call in the family,
   it's time for the "American Eagle in Britain" program sent to you with the usual good
   wishes of the B.B.C. in London. And this opening spot is always given to six of the
   smaller towns of the United States.
Sergeant Jack C. Feet: This is Sergeant Jack C. Feet calling Plymouth, Michigan.
Motorman Second Class Weldon Whitsel: This is Weldon Whitsel, Motorman Sen-Second Class,
   calling Maramec, Oklahoma.
Private James A. Griner: This is Private James A. Griner calling Bedford, Ohio.
Carpenter's Mate Second Class Henry Timpson, Jr.: This is Henry Timpson, Jr., Carpenter's
   Mate Second Class, calling Tulare, California.
Sergeant Willard R. Hill: This is Sergeant Willard R. Hill calling Littlefield, Texas.
Machinist's Mate Third Class Ronald Talmason: This is Ronald Talmason, Machinist's Mate
   Third Class, calling Great Falls, South Carolina.
Cecil Madden: And those three soldiers and those three sailors were picked at random in
   this room under the pavement in Dunkers Den in this famous American Red Cross Rainbow
   Corner Club in London. Now I step out, I introduce our musical guests, they're G.I.s,
   they're very popular on this program. It's Ray McKinley and his "Swing Shift," a unit
   of the American Band of the A.E.F., under the personal direction of Major Glenn Miller.
   With their help and the help of Murray Kane of the Crew Chiefs, we've been talking over
   a song your men would like to sing you, and their choice is "Tipperary."
IT'S A LONG, LONG WAY TO TIPPERARY (S/Sgt. Mel Powell, piano)
   Vocal refrain by Corporal Murray Kane and the audience
Cecil Madden: This is where I introduce our interviewer, a member of the 8th Air Force.
   Once again we give our London welcome to our good friend Major Ken Tredwell.

29Sep44 (Sat) 2:45-3:30PM Co-Partners Hall, Bedford, England   SLO-62604
  THE SWING SHIFT recording   Script   Aired 16Dec44

Announcer: This is a feature of the American Band of the A.E.F.
Corporal Paul Dubov: Presenting "The Swing Shift," featuring Sergeant Ray McKinley and
  his music.
SONG AND DANCE (opening theme)
  Vocal refrain by Technical Sergeant Ray McKinley
Corporal Paul Dubov: And that was Sergeant Ray McKinley laying out the welcome mat for
  all you khaki-clad and blue-bedecked members of the Allied Expeditionary Forces.
T/Sgt. Ray McKinley: O.K., Paul. Sergeant Zeke Zarchy called the role just a few minutes
  ago and "The Swing Shift" is present in full force, with Sergeant Johnny Desmond, the
  Crew Chiefs and the orchestra anxious to go into production. Music is our business and
  rhythm is the keynote, and to illustrate our claims here's item number one, "Get Happy."
GET HAPPY
Corporal Paul Dubov: Do I hear cries for more? Frankly, you don't have to work too hard
  at coaxing us along because that's precisely why we are here. Slowing down the tempo a
  bit and schmaltzing the melody like a lot, "The Swing Shift" eases into a sentimental
  sortie that you should recognize easily, "In a Sentimental Mood."
IN A SENTIMENTAL MOOD
Corporal Paul Dubov: As I glance around me, I suddenly find that somebody let a crowd
  into the place. However, being a nonchalant sort of gent, I don't even flicker a vowel
  because I recognize the crowd as the Crew Chiefs, who carol with us from time to time.
  And if that isn't enough, here's Sergeant Mac on the opposite side of the mike to join
  the boys and take the lead in the operetta titled "I'm Headin' for California." Hear,
  hear!
I'M HEADIN' FOR CALIFORNIA
  Vocal refrain by Technical Sergeant Ray McKinley and the Crew Chiefs
Corporal Paul Dubov: At this point we are stumped as to what to say about our "Soldier
  and a Song," Sergeant Johnny Desmond. So, taking the bull by the horns, I think I'll
  reveal a few facts concerning his talents. Johnny dances like Fred Astaire, plays piano
  like Vladimir Horowitz, looks like Johnny Desmond and sings like, well he sings like,
  show 'em, will ya, Johnny?
HOW BLUE THE NIGHT
  Vocal refrain by Sergeant Johnny Desmond
Corporal Paul Dubov: Thank you, Johnny, thank you. High time we were hearing from "The
  Swing Shift's" Boogie Woogie Trio, also sometimes known as the "Chamber Music Society of
  the Upper Thames River - Drainage Canal Division." The trio contains Sergeant Mel
  Powell, piano; Michael Hucko, tenor sax; and Ray McKinley, drums. Looking at the music
  that isn't there we find it is titled "Shine."
SHINE (trio: Hucko, Powell, McKinley)
Corporal Paul Dubov: A low bow to you gentlemen, a low bow. That was refreshing. Now
  for more ambitious doings, the boys get together on a nefarious musical excursion called
  "Stealin' Apples."
STEALIN' APPLES
Corporal Paul Dubov: The routine calls for another appearance of Sergeant Johnny Desmond.
  And here he is with "The Music Stopped."
THE MUSIC STOPPED
  Vocal refrain by Sergeant Johnny Desmond
Corporal Paul Dubov: A short while back, at one of the American Band's numerous
  appearances, a charming elderly lady walked up to Sergeant McKinley and said, "My, I
  never knew anyone could make such beautiful noise." And that's what happens now.
  Sergeant Ray McKinley featured in "Anvil Chorus."
ANVIL CHORUS
Corporal Paul Dubov: That puts a brilliant finish on today's session of "Swing Shift."
  We'll be expectin' you when we hit the ether on 5-1-4 again. This is Corporal Paul
  Dubov saying, "So long" and turning over to Sergeant Mac.

SONG AND DANCE (closing theme)
   Vocal refrain by Technical Sergeant Ray McKinley
Corporal Paul Dubov: The American Band of the A.E.F. has presented "The Swing Shift,"
   with Sergeant Ray McKinley and his music.

30Sep44 (Sun) 11:00-11:30AM Co-Partners Hall, Bedford, England   SAL-16706
THE UPTOWN HALL recording   Script   Aired 21Dec44

Announcer: This is a feature of the American Band of the A.E.F.
MY GUY'S COME BACK (opening theme)
   Corporal Paul Dubov: Good evening, all, it's "The Uptown Hall," music for you of the
      Allied Liberation Forces, presented by members of the American Band of the A.E.F.,
      featuring Sergeant Mel Powell at the piano.
Corporal Paul Dubov: Welcome to "The Uptown Hall," fellow members. "The Uptown Hall"
   society for paying timely tribute to all the old toe-tingling tunes and teasing,
   tempestuous tempos, is now in session! We're back again with some more of that music
   that's soft but solid. And out in front of the Hall, swing movers from everywhere are
   queuing up to get in. So while they're bucking the line out there, what d'ya say we
   give 'em a little preview of what we're up to inside. We're "Makin' Whoopee!"
MAKIN' WHOOPEE!
Corporal Paul Dubov: Now that even the tallest members have entered and claimed their
   seats, we'll ask the Crew Chiefs to stand up and address the meeting. Here they are
   extolling the verbal felicities of "I Don't Know Why."
I DON'T KNOW WHY (I Just Do)
   Vocal refrain by the Crew Chiefs
Corporal Paul Dubov: Like the Major says, sometimes ya gotta take the bitter with the
   sweet. And just to prove it can be done, here's Sergeant Johnny Desmond puttin' 'em
   both together in a bittersweet ballad called "When Your Lover Has Gone."
WHEN YOUR LOVER HAS GONE
   Vocal refrain by Sergeant Johnny Desmond
Corporal Paul Dubov: If I were you, folks, down in front, I wouldn't get too close to
   that piano now, because in this next number it really throws off sparks. There's the
   boys gettin' all set to hot up the Hall with "You're Driving Me Crazy!"
YOU'RE DRIVING ME CRAZY! (What Did I Do?)
MY GUY'S COME BACK (closing theme)
   Corporal Paul Dubov: You've been listening to music by members of the American Band of
      the A.E.F. Don't forget to join us for our next swing session in "The Uptown Hall."

05Oct44 (Thu) 8:30-9:00PM Queensbury All-Services Club, London, England   SWN-19353
  AMERICAN BAND OF THE AEF broadcast   Attendance: 2500

Corporal Paul Dubov: This is a feature of the American Band of the A.E.F.
MOONLIGHT SERENADE (opening theme)
  Corporal Paul Dubov: This is your regular weekly half hour with the Moonlight
    Serenader, presenting the American Band of the A.E.F., under the direction of Major
    Glenn Miller, with tonight's starring guest Britain's own Regimental Sergeant Major
    George Melachrino. And here is Major Glenn Miller.
Major Glenn Miller: Thank you, Corporal Paul Dubov, and good evening, everybody. All
  through the week Sergeant Ray McKinley's "Swing Shift" band, Sergeant Mel Powell's
  "Uptown Hall" boys, and Sergeant George Ockner's "Strings with Wings" section have been
  on the musical firing line and here tonight again they've all gathered together for the
  weekly big push through the air lane. First we'll light up the runway with an
  arrangement that was once just a gleam in arranger Sergeant Jerry Gray's eye. Now it's
  a reality. "Great Day."
GREAT DAY
Major Glenn Miller: Tonight we tap the supply line of British talent not for a gal, as is
  the usual custom, but for the man who leads the British Band of the A.E.F., Regimental
  Sergeant Major George Melachrino. George.
Regimental Sergeant Major George Melachrino: Thank you up there. Thank you, Major Glenn
  Miller. As you know, I've looked forward to appearing with your band.
Major Glenn Miller: Well, we've looked forward to having you, George. You're a mighty
  handy guy to have around. I - I understand that you not only can direct an orchestra
  but I know that you play violin, viola, saxophone, clarinet, oboe and trumpet.
Regimental Sergeant Major George Melachrino: That's right.
Major Glenn Miller: Well, how about it? Do you play anything else?
Regimental Sergeant Major George Melachrino: Oh, a bit of cricket and a fair game of
  darts.
Major Glenn Miller: Oh, that's great. That darts is for me. Well, what are you going to
  play tonight?
Regimental Sergeant Major George Melachrino: Oh, nothing at all, I'm just going to sing.
Major Glenn Miller: Well, you're a really a dangerous man to have around, George.
  What'll it be?
Regimental Sergeant Major George Melachrino: Well, I'm going to sing "Good Night Good
  Neighbor."
Major Glenn Miller: Good choice, George. Come out singing.
GOOD NIGHT GOOD NEIGHBOR
  Vocal refrain by Regimental Sergeant Major George Melachrino
Major Glenn Miller: Mighty fancy piece of singing there Regimental Sergeant Major George
  Melachrino. And now to answer some of the mail that's coming in from the boys fighting
  on the all Allied team, they ask for, they're gonna get it, "String of Pearls."
A STRING OF PEARLS

  ...

08Oct44 (Sun) 4:15-5:00PM Co-Partners Hall, Bedford, England   SLO-63029A
  THE SWING SHIFT recording   Script   Aired 21Dec44

Announcer: This is a feature of the American Band of the A.E.F.
Corporal Paul Dubov: Presenting "The Swing Shift," featuring Sergeant Ray McKinley and
  his music.
SONG AND DANCE (opening theme)
  Vocal refrain by Technical Sergeant Ray McKinley
Corporal Paul Dubov: Howdy, Sergeant Mac. I see you and the boys have punched the
  time-clock for another "Swing Shift" soiree.
T/Sgt. Ray McKinley: Yes, sir, and we're gonna belt that music clear out to the Allied
  Expeditionary Forces here in the E.T.O.
Corporal Paul Dubov: Good, but talk about belting things around, you sound as though a
  few cold germs have been shoving you all over the place.
T/Sgt. Ray McKinley: Brother, they've been shoving, mauling, kicking and making a general
  playground outta me. But us Texas boys is made of sterner stuff, so I'm giving those
  microscopic meanies a run for their money. I'm pouring anything that can cure a cold
  right into me, and letting my front-line defenses wage a bitter battle against the foe.
Corporal Paul Dubov: That just about makes you a walking laboratory, Sergeant Mac.
  Evidently you don't care what happens to you.
T/Sgt. Ray McKinley: Maybe not, but we do care about starting a program right about now.
  So lemme motion to you outfielders to get way out, 'cause this first baby stands a
  chance of being belted clear outta this theater. Ready, boys, a-one, a-two.
EVERYBODY LOVES MY BABY (But My Baby Don't Love Nobody but Me)
Corporal Paul Dubov: "Everybody Loves My Baby," a musical house-warming by Sergeant
  McKinley and the boys. Now the good Sarge and his good music change tempo, tone and
  tactics to bring us a real old friend, "In a Sentimental Mood."
IN A SENTIMENTAL MOOD
Corporal Paul Dubov: No program would be complete without a vocal contribution from
  Sergeant Mac. So, taking the boogie-woogie form, he puts on it four sturdy legs, a
  swishing tail, gives it a familiar face and a few necessary accouterments and we have
  "Cow-Cow Boogie."
COW-COW BOOGIE
  Vocal refrain by Technical Sergeant Ray McKinley
Corporal Paul Dubov: Back to our high-powered "Swing Shift" 18 cylinder job now, as
  Sergeant Mac takes the wheel, and pulls the throttle for an increase in tempo. The road
  map points to "Somebody's Wrong."
SOMEBODY'S WRONG
Corporal Paul Dubov: On these cool harvest evenings as the wind rustles through the
  leaves and the bright moon lights up the landscape, romance and moon dreams fill the
  heart. I know if I could sing, my choice would be something like "I Dream of You."
  Inasmuch as I can't and Sergeant Johnny Desmond can, here he is to complete the picture.
  Johnny.
I DREAM OF YOU (More Than You Dream I Do)
  Vocal refrain by Sergeant Johnny Desmond
Corporal Paul Dubov: Let's leave moon dreams behind and come back to earth with another
  toe-tapping, ear-pleasing number by the "Swing Shift's" trio. Answering to the role
  call are Sergeants Mel Powell, piano; Michael Hucko, clarinet; and Ray McKinley, drums.
  The object of their musical mission is a mellifluous madrigal yclept, "If Dreams Come
  True."
IF DREAMS COME TRUE (trio: Hucko, Powell, McKinley)
Corporal Paul Dubov: Mission completed. Results - excellent. And so we turn to our
  "Soldier and a Song" Sergeant Johnny Desmond to waft us away on wings of song. Upon our
  ears fall the familiar and satisfying strains of "My Ideal."
MY IDEAL
  Vocal refrain by Sergeant Johnny Desmond
Corporal Paul Dubov: Sergeant Mac and the boys have it all over Jules Verne when it comes
  to gallivanting around ways and byways, and if given the chance they could circle this
  tired world by air in nothing flat. To illustrate the point here's a single lap to our
  neighbors across the sea via the "Caribbean Clipper."

CARIBBEAN CLIPPER
Corporal Paul Dubov: And as the "Caribbean Clipper" comes to a stop, we decide to call it a day for the time being. But "The Swing Shift" with all its regular members will resume it's musical missions soon again. So be around, won't you? This is Corporal Paul Dubov saying so long and turning over to Sergeant Ray McKinley.
SONG AND DANCE (closing theme)
   Vocal refrain by Technical Sergeant Ray McKinley
Corporal Paul Dubov: "The Swing Shift" is a presentation of the American Band of the A.E.F.

12Oct44 (Thu) 8:30-9:00PM Queensbury All-Services Club, London, England
AMERICAN BAND OF THE AEF broadcast   Attendance: 2500   SLO-63391

   . . .

MY BLUE HEAVEN (Blue tune)
Major Glenn Miller: Tonight our British guest star is a man who is as famous back home in the big 48 as he is over here. He used to be the leader of an orchestra, a mighty swell one too. A few years ago he decided to sort of go straight. At that time he embarked on a career that made him what he is today, ah, London, and I dare say Britain's greatest theatrical producer and impresario. Ladies and gentlemen, Hylton's back. Here's Jack Hylton.
Jack Hylton: Thank you, Glenn, for those kind words and even more for the invitation to join you on this program.
Major Glenn Miller: Well, there's no thanks necessary, Jack. As a matter of fact, ah, we invited you here to sort of put you to work.
Jack Hylton: Sounds bad.
Major Glenn Miller: Sounds good. There's not a guy in the band or a Yank in our audience who doesn't remember and admire the records you've made and sent to our nation.
Jack Hylton: Well, what's that got to do with putting me to work?
Major Glenn Miller: Well, just this, Jack. We dug up an arrangement that sold a heap of records over on our side of the Atlantic and tonight we want you to conduct the American Band of the A.E.F. playing that same arrangement.
Jack Hylton: You might find me a bit rusty or a bit dusty, you know.
Major Glenn Miller: Well, we'll take that chance. The band's all yours, the pleasure's all ours, and the tune, "She Shall Have Music."
SHE SHALL HAVE MUSIC
   Vocal refrain by Sergeant Johnny Desmond

   . . .

17Oct44 (Tue) 6:30-7:00PM Co-Partners Hall, Bedford, England
   THE SWING SHIFT broadcast

   ...

Corporal Paul Dubov: Now the moment you've all been waiting for, a number from "The Swing
   Shift's" trio, sometimes known as the "Champion Music Society of the Lower Thames
   Estuary - Dry Dock Division." These music faring gentlemen pose before the microphone
   and upon closer observation we find them to be Sergeant Mel Powell, piano; Michael
   Hucko, tenor sax; and Ray McKinley, drums. Rubbing his drum sticks with a glee,
   Sergeant Mac gives the nod and we hear an intermezzo titled "Sensation."
SENSATION RAG [trio: Hucko (tenor saxophone), Powell, McKinley]
Corporal Paul Dubov: That was "Sensation" and a sparkling performance by our trio. Well,
   as we've said before, we aim to please and please we will. So many of you have ...

   ...

30Oct44 (Mon) EMI studio, St. John's Wood, Abbey Road, London, England
OWI RECORDING SESSION for ABSIE Network   Aired 08Nov44

CTPX-12753-1 **MOONLIGHT SERENADE** (opening theme)   Program 1, Record 1

Ilse Weinberger: Deutsche Soldaten, hier spricht Ilse. Für die nächste halbe Stunde
  habe ich für Euch etwas ganz besonderes arrangiert, ein Rendezvous mit dem
  Kapellmeister eines der bekanntesten Orchester. Heute ist er der Dirigent des
  Amerikanischen Orchesters der Allierten Expeditionsstreitkräfte, Major Glenn Miller.
  Major Miller begrüsst Sie zunächst mit seiner Sendezeichen Musik.
MOONLIGHT SERENADE (opening theme)
  Ilse Weinberger: Mit dieser allen Amerikanern bekannten Melodie beginnt und endet
    Glenn Miller stets seine musikalischen Darbietungen. Es ist seine eigene
    Komposition, die er Mondscheinserenade nennt.
  Ilse Weinberger: Ehe ich Major Miller selbst ans Mikrofon bitte, möchte ich Sie näher
    mit seiner Persönlichkeit bekanntmachen. Glenn Miller ist ein Zauberer beschwingter
    Tanzmusik. Ein Musiker, der im Ballsaal, auf Schallplatten und im Rundfunk schon seit
    vielen Jahren ganz Amerika begeistert hat. Denn der Rhythmus seiner Musik geht in die
    Beine, aber er geht auch ins Herz. Als der krieg ausbrach hat Glenn Miller all seine
    Erfolge im Stich gelassen und sich zum Militär gemeldet, um die Allierten Truppen mit
    seiner Kunst zu erfreuen. Soldaten, hier ist Major Glenn Miller persönlich.
  Major Glenn Miller: Thank you, Ilse. You speak German very well. Ich kann nur sehr
    wenig Deutsch spechen.
  Ilse Weinberger: Nur mutig drauf los, ich werde Ihnen schon helfen.
  Major Glenn Miller: Good evening, I mean Guten Abend, Deutsche Soldaten, im Sprechen
    bin ich immer sehr kurz, denn ich folge immer dem Sprichwort, "Lasst Blumen sprechen."
    Have I said that right?
  Ilse Weinberger: Ich glaube, sie wollten sagen, "Lasst Musik sprechen."
  Major Glenn Miller: Oh, yes. Ich lasse immer gern Musik für mich sprechen. Ilse, you
    better announce our first number in German, it's "In the Mood."
  Ilse Weinberger: Glenn Miller und sein Orchester spielt den amerikanischen Schlager "In
    the Mood," "In Stimmung."

Translation:
  Ilse Weinberger: German soldiers, this is Ilse speaking. For the next half hour I have
    arranged something special for you, a rendezvous with the bandleader of one of the
    best known orchestras. Today he is the leader of the American Band of the Allied
    Expeditionary Forces, Major Glenn Miller. Major Miller greets you first with his
    theme song.
MOONLIGHT SERENADE (opening theme)
  Ilse Weinberger: With this melody, which is well known to all Americans, Glenn Miller
    starts and ends all his programs. It is his own composition which he calls
    "Moonlight Serenade."
  Ilse Weinberger: Before I call Major Miller to the microphone I want to say something
    about his personality. Glenn Miller is a magician of swing dance music. A musician
    who has enchanted for years all of America on the dance floor, on records, and on the
    radio. The rhythm of his music goes into your legs, but it also goes into your heart.
    When the war started Glenn Miller left all his success behind and enlisted in order to
    let the Allied troops enjoy his music. Soldiers, here is Glenn Miller in person.
  Major Glenn Miller: Thank you, Ilse. You speak German very well. I can only speak
    very little German.
  Ilse Weinberger: Go ahead, I will help you.
  Major Glenn Miller: Good evening, I mean good evening, German soldiers. When speaking
    I always make it very short, because I always follow the saying, "let flowers speak."
    Have I said that right?
  Ilse Weinberger: I think you meant to say, "let music speak."
  Major Glenn Miller: Oh, yes. I always prefer to let music do the talking for me.
    Ilse, you better announce our first number in German, it's "In the Mood."
  Ilse Weinberger: Glenn Miller and his orchestra will play the American hit "In the
    Mood," "In the Mood."

CTPX-12755-1 STAR DUST   Program 1, Record 3

Ilse Weinberger: Major Miller, das war wirklich ausgezeichnet. Dieser erste Schlager
  "In the Mood" brachte uns gleich in die richtige Stimmung. Dar fich vielleicht jetzt
  "Sternschnuppen" vorschlagen?
Major Glenn Miller: "Sternschnuppen?" Wer hat Schnupfen?
Ilse Weinberger: Nein, Herr Major, niemand hat Schnupfen, ich meine das Lied
  "Sternschnuppen," "Star Dust."
Major Glenn Miller: Oh, "Star Dust" ist "Sternschnuppen."
Ilse Weinberger: Jawohl, und "Sternschnuppen" ist "Star Dust" und zwar gespielt vom
  Amerikanischen Orchester der Allierten Expeditionsstreitkräfte Glenn Miller.
Major Glenn Miller: Sehr gut.
STAR DUST
Ilse Weinberger: Wir gönnen unseren fleissigen Musikern eine kleine Rastpause und ich
  übergebe das Mikrofon unserem Berichter.

Translation:

Ilse Weinberger: Major Miller, that was excellent, this first hit, "In the Mood,"
  really put us in the right mood. May I suggest that you now play "Star Dust?"
Major Glenn Miller: "Star Dust?" Who has a cold?
Ilse Weinberger: No, Major, nobody has a cold, I mean the song "Star Dust," "Star
  Dust."
Major Glenn Miller: Oh, "Star Dust" is "Star Dust."
Ilse Weinberger: Yes, and "Star Dust" is "Star Dust" and played by the American Band of
  the Allied Expeditionary Forces of Glenn Miller.
Major Glenn Miller: Very good.
STAR DUST
Ilse Weinberger: We allow our busy musicians a little break and I hand over the
  microphone to our reporter.

CTPX-12756-1 **SONG OF THE VOLGA BOATMEN**   Program 1, Record 4

Ilse Weinberger: Nun, Herr Major Miller, was darf ich jetzt ankündigen?
Major Glenn Miller: "The Volga Boatmen," that well known Russian song in our own
   version, and we play it as a tribute to our fightin' Russian Allies.
Ilse Weinberger: "Volga Boatmen," das sind "Die Wolgaschiffer," und Glenn Miller sagte
   er spielt diese bekannte Melodie im modernen Tanzrhythmus, gewidmet unseren heroisch
   kämpfenden russischen Verbündeten.
SONG OF THE VOLGA BOATMEN
Ilse Weinberger: Oh, Herr Major Miller, es ist doch wirklich wunderbar, dass es für
   einen amerikanischen Musiker kein verbot und keine Einschränkungen gibt. Er spielt
   die Musik, die er will, die Musik die seinen Hörern gefällt, gleichgültig, ob es
   amerikanische, deutsche, russische, chinesische oder juedische Musik ist.
Major Glenn Miller: Ich versteh Sie. America means freedom and there's no expression
   of freedom quite so sincere as music.
Ilse Weinberger: Sehr richtig, Herr Major. Hoffentlich haben das, was Sie soeben
   sagten, auch alle verstanden. Wenn nicht, Major Miller sagte, "Amerika bedeutet
   Freiheit und es gibt keinen besseren Ausdruck für Freiheit als die Musik." Und Musik
   werden Sie gleich wieder hören. Doch vorerst bittet unser Berichterstatter um Ihr
   gehör.

Translation:

Ilse Weinberger: Now, Major Miller, what may I now announce?
Major Glenn Miller: "The Volga Boatmen," that well known Russian song in our own
   version and we play it as a tribute to our fightin' Russian Allies.
Ilse Weinberger: "Volga Boatmen," that is "The Volga Boatmen," and Glenn Miller said he
   plays this familiar melody in modern dance rhythms for our heroic, fighting Russian
   Allies.
SONG OF THE VOLGA BOATMEN
Ilse Weinberger: Oh, Major Miller, it is really wonderful that for an American musician
   there are no restrictions and no barriers, he plays the music he likes, the music his
   audiences like, whether the music is American, German, Russian, Chinese or Jewish.
Major Glenn Miller: I understand you. America means freedom and there's no expression
   of freedom quite so sincere as music.
Ilse Weinberger: Quite right, Major. I hope that everybody here understood what you
   just said. If not, Major Miller said, "America means freedom and there is no
   expression of freedom quite so sincere as music." And music you will hear again
   shortly. But first please listen to our reporter.

CTPX-12757-1 **LONG AGO (And Far Away)** (JD-German)   Program 1, Record 5

Major Glenn Miller: Ilse, this is Sergeant Johnny Desmond. I wish you'd tell the
   audience that he will sing in German our tune "Long Ago and Far Away."
Ilse Weinberger: With pleasure. Major Miller stellte mir soeben Feldwebel Desmond vor,
   ...
   LONG AGO (And Far Away)
   Ilse Weinberger: ... der den nächsten amerikanischen Schlager mit deutschem Text
      singen wird, und Sie hören "Long Ago and Far Away," "Lang Ist Es Her Und Weit
      Zurück."
   Vocal refrain by Sergeant Johnny Desmond (in German)

Translation:

   Major Glenn Miller: Ilse, this is Sergeant Johnny Desmond. I wish you'd tell the
      audience that he will sing in German our tune "Long Ago and Far Away."
   Ilse Weinberger: With pleasure. Major Miller introduces me to Sergeant Desmond, ...
   LONG AGO (And Far Away)
   Ilse Weinberger: ... who will sing the next American hit with German lyrics, and you
      will hear "Long Ago and Far Away," "It's been some time ago and far in the past."
   Vocal refrain by Sergeant Johnny Desmond (in German)

CTPX-12758-1 **IS YOU IS OR IS YOU AIN'T MY BABY?** (RM)   Program 1, Record 6

Ilse Weinberger: Das war schön. Vielen Dank, Feldwebel Desmond.
Sergeant Johnny Desmond: Bitte schön.
Ilse Weinberger: "Lang Ist Es Her Und Weit Zurück," ein schöner Titel und ein grosser
  Schlager. Übrigens, was hören Sie von zu Hause, Herr Major Miller?
Major Glenn Miller: Meine Frau hat mir soeben telegraphiert. Wait a moment, here's the
  telegram. Sie telegraphiert, "Vergiss nicht, dass Du verheiratet bist."
Ilse Weinberger: Und was haben Sie ihr daraufhin geantwortet?
Major Glenn Miller: Telegramm zu spät erhalten.
(Laughter from the band)
Ilse Weinberger: Hoffentlich wird sie Sie nicht falsch verstehen.
Major Glenn Miller: Don't worry, Ilse. Now we want you to meet another member of our
  orchestra, Sergeant Ray McKinley.
Ilse Weinberger: Es freut mich, Sie kennenzulernen, Herr Feldwebel McKinley. Was darf
  ich für Sie ankündigen?
T/Sgt. Ray McKinley: "Is You Is or Is You Ain't My Baby?"
Ilse Weinberger: Feldwebel McKinley singt "Bist Du Oder Bist Du Nicht Mein Baby?"
IS YOU IS OR IS YOU AIN'T MY BABY?
  Vocal refrain by Technical Sergeant Ray McKinley
Ilse Weinberger: Vielen Dank, Feldwebel McKinley, das war ausgezeichnet. Während Major
  Miller das nächste musikalische Stück wählt, hören Sie was unser Berichterstatter
  jetzt zu sagen hat.

Translation:

  Ilse Weinberger: That was beautiful. Thank you very much, Sergeant Desmond.
  Sergeant Johnny Desmond: You're welcome.
  Ilse Weinberger: "Long Ago and Far Away," a beautiful title and a great hit. By the
  way, what do you hear from home, Major Miller?
  Major Glenn Miller: My wife just now has sent me a telegram. Wait a moment, here's the
  telegram. She wired, "Don't forget that you are married."
  Ilse Weinberger: And what did you reply to that?
  Major Glenn Miller: Telegram was received too late.
  (Laughter from the band)
  Ilse Weinberger: I hope she won't misinterpret that.
  Major Glenn Miller: Don't worry, Ilse. Now we want you to meet another member of our
  orchestra, Sergeant Ray McKinley.
  Ilse Weinberger: I am very pleased to meet you, Sergeant McKinley. What may I announce
  for you?
  T/Sgt. Ray McKinley: "Is You Is or Is You Ain't My Baby?"
  Ilse Weinberger: Sergeant McKinley sings "Is You or Is You Not My Baby?"
  IS YOU IS OR IS YOU AIN'T MY BABY?
  Vocal refrain by Technical Sergeant Ray McKinley
  Ilse Weinberger: Thank you very much, Sergeant McKinley, that was excellent. While
  Major Miller selects the next musical piece, listen to what our reporter now has to
  say.

CTPX-12759-1 **GREAT DAY**   Program 1, Record 7

Ilse Weinberger: Hier ist nun Major Millers nächste musikalische Darbietung. Es ist der grosse amerikanische Schlager "Great Day," auf deutsch "Der Grosse Tag." Es ist ein Musikstück, das bestimmt dem Tage des Sieges und des Friedens gewidmet ist, "Great Day."
GREAT DAY
Ilse Weinberger: Bei Ihrer Musik vergeht die Zeit wie im Fluge, Herr Major.
Major Glenn Miller: Sagt man "im Fluche?"
Ilse Weinberger: Nein, Herr Major, das heisst ganz etwas anderes.
Major Glenn Miller: Na ja, ich weiss schon, deutsche Sprache, schwere Sprache.
Ilse Weinberger: Nur keine Sorge. Unsere Zuhörer werden Sie bestimmt gut verstanden haben. Doch leider sehe ich, unsere Zeit ist um. Unser musikalisches Rendezvous muss jetzt leider ein Ende nehmen. Aber nächste Woche sehen wir uns wieder zur selben Zeit. Nicht wahr, Herr Major?
Major Glenn Miller: Jawohl.
Ilse Weinberger: Und was sagen Sie uns zum Abschied, Herr Major? Auf deutsch, meine ich.
Major Glenn Miller: I know, I know, Auf Wiedersehen.
Ilse Weinberger: Ausgezeichnet, und ich sage, Auf Wiederhören.

Translation:

Ilse Weinberger: Now here is Glenn Miller's next musical number. It is the big American hit "Great Day," in German "Der Grosse Tag." It is a piece of music which is dedicated surely to the day of victory and peace, "Great Day."
GREAT DAY
Ilse Weinberger: By listening to your music time flies, Major.
Major Glenn Miller: One says "in swearing?"
Ilse Weinberger: No, Major, that means something quite different.
Major Glenn Miller: Oh, well, I know by this time, German language, difficult language.
Ilse Weinberger: Don't worry. Our listeners will surely understand you well. But to my regret, I see our time is up. Unfortunately your musical rendezvous must now come to an end. But next week we will see each other again at the same time. Isn't that true, Major.
Major Glenn Miller: Yes indeed.
Ilse Weinberger: And what do you say to us in parting, Major? In German, I mean.
Major Glenn Miller: I know, I know, see you again.
Ilse Weinberger: Excellent, and I say, hear you again.

01Nov44 (Wed) 6:15-6:30PM Co-Partners Hall, Bedford, England
  THE UPTOWN HALL broadcast   Script

Announcer: This is a feature of the American Band of the A.E.F.
MY GUY'S COME BACK (opening theme)
  Corporal Paul Dubov: Good evening, all, it's "The Uptown Hall." Music for you of the
    Allied Liberation Forces, presented by members of the American Band of the A.E.F.,
    featuring Sergeant Mel Powell at the piano.
Corporal Paul Dubov: Welcome to "The Uptown Hall," fellow members. Well, we're back here
    in the Hall at harmony headquarters, all ready to run over another set of tunes for you.
    Whether you like 'em sweet or like 'em hot, we got. And now that Mel's got the kinks
    out of the keys, and the boys are ready to go, I move that we get the music movin'. And
    for the first go-round, we're gonna build a fire under one of your old favorites,
    "Makin' Whoopee!"
MAKIN' WHOOPEE!
Corporal Paul Dubov: Now if you folks down there in front will remain nice and quiet, I
    believe prexy Powell has a few things to say to you. Here he is heel-and-toeing it up
    to the microphone to make with the vowels and consonants. Mel.
S/Sgt. Mel Powell:

    ...

YOU GO TO MY HEAD
Corporal Paul Dubov: Thanks for coming again, Sergeant Bernie Privin. The door's open
    anytime for you. Now Sergeant Johnny Desmond takes star billing on this next one.
    Here's Mel and the boys riding top cover for him as he sings "She's Funny That Way."
(I Got a Woman Crazy for Me) SHE'S FUNNY THAT WAY
  Vocal refrain by Sergeant Johnny Desmond
Corporal Paul Dubov: Every once in a while, here in the Hall, we like to close the
    meeting with a word of wisdom for the folks. But tonight we promise to keep it short
    and sweet. It's Mel and the boys in a bit of musical moralizing called "Lady Be Good!"
OH, LADY BE GOOD!
Corporal Paul Dubov: And this is yours truly fightin' his way out of that last blizzard
    of eighth notes to say, "Sorry, we gotta go." But the latch'll be hangin' out at the
    Hall Friday night, so drop around and latch on to some more of that soft but oh so solid
    music that features Sergeant Mel Powell at the piano. Until then this is Corporal Paul
    Dubov locking up the Hall and saying "So long, and good luck to you."
MY GUY'S COME BACK (closing theme)
  Corporal Paul Dubov: You've been listening to music by members of the American Band of
    the A.E.F. Don't forget to join us Friday night for another big helping of harmony in
    "The Uptown Hall."

01Nov44 (Wed) 7:45-8:00PM Co-Partners Hall, Bedford, England
STRINGS WITH WINGS broadcast   Script

Announcer: This is a feature of the American Band of the A.E.F.
I SUSTAIN THE WINGS (opening theme)
  Corporal Paul Dubov: "Strings with Wings," a program of music for you of the Allied
    Liberation Forces, presented by the string section of the American Band of the A.E.F.,
    featuring Sergeant George Ockner and his violin.
Corporal Paul Dubov: Hello there, folks. Welcome to "Strings with Wings." You've tuned
  yourself right in at the beginning of another sack-time serenade, a little program of
  the songs you like best, played as only violins can play 'em. Sergeant Ockner and the
  boys are all ready to go, and now that you're here there's nothing to stop us. So light
  up and lean back while we dream a few favorite tunes your way. The first one, "Lover,
  Come Back to Me!"
LOVER, COME BACK TO ME!
Corporal Paul Dubov: The boys flip over a page in their music books, tuck their violins
  back under their chins, and we're ready to go with tune number two. See if you remember
  "Someday I'll Find You."
SOMEDAY I'LL FIND YOU
Corporal Paul Dubov: Now the boys dream another one your way. This time they're
  brightening up the barracks with something mighty charming in the line of musical
  bouquets, "Orchids in the Moonlight."
ORCHIDS IN THE MOONLIGHT
Corporal Paul Dubov: Well, it's time for the boys to pick up the music and pack away the
  fiddles for tonight. But if you've enjoyed these few minutes of music, how about all of
  us getting together again? Next Monday evening ought to make especially good listening
  because Sir Adrian Boult, distinguished conductor of the B.B.C. Symphony Orchestra, will
  be here as our guest to direct the program. So don't forget to tune in. Meanwhile,
  this is Corporal Paul Dubov saying, "So long, and good luck to you."
I SUSTAIN THE WINGS
  Corporal Paul Dubov: You've been listening to music by the string section of the
    American Band of the A.E.F., featuring Sergeant George Ockner and his violin. Don't
    forget to join us next Monday night when we again present "Strings with Wings."

02Nov44 (Thu) 8:30-9:00PM Queensbury All-Services Club, London, England   SWN-19498
  AMERICAN BAND OF THE AEF broadcast   Script   Attendance: 2500

Corporal Paul Dubov: This is a feature of the American Band of the A.E.F., originating at
  the Queensbury All-Services Club in London.
MOONLIGHT SERENADE (opening theme)
  Corporal Paul Dubov: This is your regular weekly half hour with the Moonlight
    Serenader, presenting music by the American Band of the A.E.F., under the direction
    Major Glenn Miller. And here is Major Glenn Miller.
Major Glenn Miller: Thank you, Corporal Paul Dubov, and hello, everybody. We're here
  again to see what we can do about making the next thirty minutes a listening pleasure
  for you, Tommy and Yank and Johnny Canuck. And our first shot at that target is a
  smile-a-minute arrangement hot off the mind of Sergeant Jerry Gray. "Get Happy."
GET HAPPY
Major Glenn Miller: The big heart-throb man around the American Band of the A.E.F. is a
  lad named Sergeant Johnny Desmond. And right now John is on singin' "I'll Be Seeing
  You."
I'LL BE SEEING YOU
  Vocal refrain by Sergeant Johnny Desmond
Major Glenn Miller: Carrying the ball in this week's musical salute to our American
  football teams is the hard-hitting eleven that represents the U.S. Navy. Sergeant Ray
  McKinley up in the tailback position calls the signals for "Anchors Aweigh."
ANCHORS AWEIGH
Major Glenn Miller: And now we turn to medley time, saluting the mothers, wives,
  sweethearts and sisters of the Allied Forces with somethin' old, somethin' new,
  somethin' borrowed and somethin' blue. Our old, old song, "Long, Long Ago."
LONG, LONG AGO (Old tune)
  Major Glenn Miller: Squirin' our new song is Sergeant Johnny Desmond singin' "The Music
    Stopped."
THE MUSIC STOPPED (New tune)
  Vocal refrain by Sergeant Johnny Desmond
  Major Glenn Miller: From friend and Army teammate Sergeant Larry Clinton we borrow "The
    Dipsy Doodle."
THE DIPSY DOODLE (Borrowed tune)
  Major Glenn Miller: And holdin' down the blue spot, good old "Blues In My Heart."
BLUES IN MY HEART (Blue tune)
Major Glenn Miller: On this particular program we're about to unveil a tune written by
  one of our vocal group, the Crew Chiefs, and that same combination now steps up to chew
  over the lyrics of Corporal Murray Kane's composition "Have Ya Got Any Gum, Chum?"
HAVE YA GOT ANY GUM, CHUM?
  Vocal refrain by Sergeant Johnny Desmond and the Crew Chiefs

  ...

JERRY'S AACHEN BACK (trio: Hucko, Powell, McKinley)
Major Glenn Miller: Now for the anchor tune of our show, an all out salute to the
  magnificent Red Army that has the Eastern front Jerries singin' the blues. To our
  fightin' Russian Allies we pay tribute with the "Song of the Volga Boatmen."
SONG OF THE VOLGA BOATMEN
Major Glenn Miller: Now, this is Major Glenn Miller hangin' out the latchstring to
  welcome you back to next week's show by the American Band of the A.E.F. During the next
  six days we'll be sprinkled around the air lanes with programs by Sergeants Ray
  McKinley, Mel Powell and George Ockner. Then next week, same time, same station, we'll
  be back with more music by the big band. If you'd care for another basin-full of the
  same, help yourself. For now it's good luck and goodnight.
MOONLIGHT SERENADE (closing theme)
  Corporal Paul Dubov: You have been listening to your regular weekly half hour with the
    Moonlight Serenader, presenting music by the American Band of the A.E.F., under the
    direction of Major Glenn Miller.

04Nov44 (Sat) 11:45AM-Noon Co-Partners Hall, Bedford, England
PIANO PARADE broadcast   Script

Announcer: This is a feature of the American Band of the A.E.F.
CHOPSTICKS (opening theme)
    Corporal Paul Dubov: "Piano Parade," a daily quarter hour of piano music that today
        brings you Private First Class Jack Rusin in a medley of memory melodies.
Corporal Paul Dubov: Glancing over the list of tunes that Jack just handed me, I see he's
    put his finger right on a few of your special favorites. On the program today there's
    "Darn That Dream," "Easy to Love," "I'll Walk Alone," the "Merry Widow Waltz," "Oh! Look
    at Me Now" and "Lady Be Good!" That's the line-up, so O.K., Jack, take it from there.
DARN THAT DREAM
EASY TO LOVE
I'LL WALK ALONE
MERRY WIDOW WALTZ
OH! LOOK AT ME NOW
OH, LADY BE GOOD!
CHOPSTICKS (closing theme)
    Corporal Paul Dubov: You've been listening to "Piano Parade," fifteen minutes of your
        favorite tunes, with Private First Class Jack Rusin at the keyboard. Heard today were
        "Darn That Dream," "Easy to Love," "I'll Walk Alone," the "Merry Widow Waltz," "Oh!
        Look at Me Now" and "Lady Be Good!" That's all for now, but don't forget to be around
        listening when we come marching this way again with another "Piano Parade."

04Nov44 (Sat) 3:01-3:30PM Co-Partners Hall, Bedford, England
THE SWING SHIFT broadcast   Script

Announcer: This is a feature of the American Band of the A.E.F.

Corporal Paul Dubov: Presenting "The Swing Shift," featuring Sergeant Ray McKinley and his music.

SONG AND DANCE (opening theme)
    Vocal refrain by Technical Sergeant Ray McKinley

Corporal Paul Dubov: Good afternoon to all you guys and gals of the Allied Expeditionary Forces, and welcome to "The Swing Shift." This is a new time for our program and from now on we'll be holding forth every Saturday afternoon at 1501 to 1530 hours. Now here's Sergeant Ray McKinley to tell you more.

T/Sgt. Ray McKinley: Thank you, Corporal Paul Dubov, and howdy, gang. Just like Paul said, our time will be your time from 1501 to 1530 hours every Saturday afternoon. Answering the roll call will be Sergeant Johnny Desmond, the Crew Chiefs, the boys in the band, and yours truly. So, actions speaking louder that words, let's stir up the ether around you with a sample of what I'm talking about. First to ride the waves is "Flying Home." Ready, boys, one, two.

FLYING HOME

Corporal Paul Dubov: Sergeant Mac faces the microphone now and is about to be cross examined. Looking him straight in the eyes, the band demands "Whatcha Know Joe."

WHATCHA KNOW JOE
    Vocal refrain by Technical Sergeant Ray McKinley

Corporal Paul Dubov: Now Sergeant Johnny Desmond and the Crew Chiefs have been polishing up a new arrangement for you. It's a thumbnail description of your number one heart-throb, "Sweet and Lovely."

SWEET AND LOVELY
    Vocal refrain by Sergeant Johnny Desmond and the Crew Chiefs

Corporal Paul Dubov: Nice heart throbbing, Johnny and Crew Chiefs. Swing rears its ugly head, Sergeant Ray McKinley and "The Swing Shift" band open the throttle and really get goin' on the "Nine Twenty Special."

NINE TWENTY SPECIAL

Corporal Paul Dubov: Thumbing over some of your old favorites, Sergeant Mac decided on a sub-Dixie line favorite of some years back. So for the G.I. crackers down Georgia way here's "Georgia on My Mind."

GEORGIA ON MY MIND

Corporal Paul Dubov: The band takes five as the hard working "Boogie Woogie Trio" of "The Swing Shift" belt the mercury about fifty degrees with one of their rhythmic blockbusters. Sergeant McKinley at the drums gives the nod to Sergeants Powell at the piano and Hucko on the clarinet and harmony prevails as the boys ease into "Uptown Flavor."

UPTOWN FLAVOR (trio: Hucko, Powell, McKinley)

Corporal Paul Dubov: That was "The Swing Shift's" "Boogie Woogie Trio" laying the rhythm on "Uptown Flavor". Sergeant Johnny Desmond is on again. Johnny's all set with your current favorite, "I'll Walk Alone."

I'LL WALK ALONE
    Vocal refrain by Sergeant Johnny Desmond

Corporal Paul Dubov: "The Swing Shift" orchestra consists of nineteen khaki-clad music makers. Fifteen of these lads play "horns," horn being the general word for trumpet, saxophone or trombone. Of these fifteen, five play trumpet, and it's these raucous gentlemen who will now blow off the studio roof in our winder upper titled "I Hear You Screamin'."

I HEAR YOU SCREAMIN'

Corporal Paul Dubov: Our five Gabriels having blown off the studio roof, "The Swing Shift" will now retire 'til next Tuesday evening at 1830 hours. Repairs will be made in the meantime so that we may bring you another program of music you like to hear. This is Corporal Paul Dubov saying so long and turning you over to Sergeant Ray McKinley.

SONG AND DANCE (closing theme)
  Vocal refrain by Technical Sergeant Ray McKinley
Corporal Paul Dubov: "The Swing Shift" is a presentation of the American Band of the
  A.E.F.

04Nov44 (Sat) 6:15-6:30PM Co-Partners Hall, Bedford, England
THE UPTOWN HALL broadcast   Script

Announcer: This is a feature of the American Band of the A.E.F.
MY GUY'S COME BACK (opening theme)
  Corporal Paul Dubov: Good evening, all, it's "The Uptown Hall," music for you of the
    Allied Liberation Forces, presented by members of the American Band of the A.E.F.,
    featuring Sergeant Mel Powell at the piano.
Corporal Paul Dubov: And here's brother Mel himself comin' up with the big scissors to
  cut the lid off tonight's program. Mel, you can cut right in here.
S/Sgt. Mel Powell: Thank you, Paul, and welcome to "Uptown Hall," fellow members. The
  by-laws of the Hall plainly read that it's our job to drop around here three times each
  week and swank up the swing for you. And we're back tonight to do the same. This
  evening we've set an extra plate on the table for an old and valued guest of ours. He's
  a guy that never wears out his welcome because he always brings along that high-note
  trumpet of his to play for his supper. But more about our guest later on. Right now
  it's time to open the doors of the Hall. Paul, here's the key.
Corporal Paul Dubov: The key Mel's given me tonight is the key of F minor. And we're
  using it to open up with "Caravan."
CARAVAN
Corporal Paul Dubov: Now just to get real cozy, we cut the band down from seven men to
  three, and lo and behold, it's the "Band within a Band." Sergeant Mel at the piano,
  Sergeant Ray McKinley at the drums, Sergeant Trigger Alpert, string bass; and Sergeant
  Michael Hucko, clarinet. The subject of their little musical mumbo-jumbo tonight seems
  to be "Dream a Little Dream of Me."
DREAM A LITTLE DREAM OF ME (quartet: Hucko, Powell, Alpert, McKinley)
Corporal Paul Dubov: Next up, Sergeant Johnny Desmond to carry on with a song. And with
  Mel and the boys hitch-hiking along in the background, here's Johnny to give out with
  the lovelorn lyrics of "I'll Be Seeing You."
I'LL BE SEEING YOU
  Vocal refrain by Sergeant Johnny Desmond
Corporal Paul Dubov: As I told you a few minutes ago, our guest tonight has been bucking
  the guest register here for quite some time. He's Sergeant Bernie Privin, who plays a
  lot of trumpet for the band of the A.E.F. Tonight he's signed his talents over to us.
  And we're gonna hear him now as he rides along with the band on "Struttin' with Some
  Barbecue."
STRUTTIN' WITH SOME BARBECUE
Corporal Paul Dubov: Well, the roof's rockin' and the neighbors are knockin'. So it's
  time for us to get out. But don't forget, we'll be back next Wednesday night with more
  of that soft but oh so solid music that features Sergeant Mel Powell at the piano.
  Until then this is Corporal Paul Dubov saying, "So long, and good luck to you."
MY GUY'S COME BACK (closing theme)
  Corporal Paul Dubov: You've been listening to music by members of the American Band of
    the A.E.F. Don't forget to join us next Wednesday evening when we again open the
    doors on another musical meeting in "The Uptown Hall."

05Nov44 (Sun) 12:45-1:00PM Co-Partners Hall, Bedford, England
   SONGS BY SGT. JOHNNY DESMOND broadcast   Script

Announcer: This is a feature of the American Band of the A.E.F.
TIME ON MY HANDS (opening theme)
   Corporal Paul Dubov: Presenting "Songs by Sergeant Johnny Desmond."
   Vocal refrain by Sergeant Johnny Desmond
   Corporal Paul Dubov: Sunday songs, as a background for letter-writing to the gal you
      left behind. Old songs, new songs, just-for-you songs.
Sergeant Johnny Desmond: Good afternoon, everyone. This is Sergeant Johnny Desmond
   falling in for our weekly song session. I've got a handy song bag overflowing with the
   kinda music you like to hear 'long about this time. So here's hoping that what comes
   out will be to your liking. First off the top this afternoon is an old Jerome Kern
   favorite, "All the Things You Are."
ALL THE THINGS YOU ARE
   Vocal refrain by Sergeant Johnny Desmond
Sergeant Johnny Desmond: Now reaching way down into the song bag we come up with two of
   your all-time all timers. So with a thought to those pretty gals who are waiting for us
   on the other side of the Atlantic, here's "My Heart Stood Still" and "I Only Have Eyes
   for You."
MY HEART STOOD STILL
   Vocal refrain by Sergeant Johnny Desmond
Corporal Paul Dubov: And now Sergeant Desmond sings "I Only Have Eyes for You."
I ONLY HAVE EYES FOR YOU
   Vocal refrain by Sergeant Johnny Desmond
Sergeant Johnny Desmond: Now before doin' the final tune, I'd like to point out that this
   is our last Sunday program. Next time we come through on the A.E.F. wave-length it will
   be on Monday night, November the 13th at 1901 hours, that will be our new time, and I'm
   looking forward to continuing our get-togethering then. Meantime, here are a few
   pleasant memories of home, all wrapped up in Norm Leyden's arrangement of a brand new
   tune, "Deep Summer Music."
DEEP SUMMER MUSIC
   Vocal refrain by Sergeant Johnny Desmond
TIME ON MY HANDS (closing theme)
   Corporal Paul Dubov: You've been listening to "Songs by Sergeant Johnny Desmond," old
      songs, new songs, just-for-you songs. Don't forget to join Sergeant Johnny Desmond
      again when he continues this series on Monday nights at 1901 hours starting November
      the 13th. That's Monday night at 1901 hours, November the 13th. See you then.
   Vocal refrain by Sergeant Johnny Desmond
Corporal Paul Dubov: "Songs by Sergeant Johnny Desmond" is a feature of the American Band
   of the A.E.F.

06Nov44 (Mon) EMI studio, St. John's Wood, Abbey Road, London, England
  OWI RECORDING SESSION for ABSIE Network
  Program 2 aired 15Nov44; Program 3 aired 22Nov44

CTPX-12762-1 **MOONLIGHT SERENADE (opening theme)/AMERICAN PATROL**   Program 2, Record 1

Ilse Weinberger: Deutsche Soldaten, hier spricht Ilse. Ich lade Euch alle ein zu einem
  Rendezvous mit dem Zauberer amerikanischer Tanzmusik, mit einem Meister des Rhythmus,
  mit Major Glenn Miller und seinem famosen Amerikanischen Orchester der Allierten
  Expeditionsstreitkräfte.
MOONLIGHT SERENADE (opening theme)
  Ilse Weinberger: Erkennen Sie seine romantische Sendezeichen Musik? Es ist seine
    eigene Komposition "Moonlight Serenade," "Mondscheinserenade." Im Frieden hat Glenn
    Miller sämtliche Tanzbeine Amerikas rebellisch gemacht. Und heute bringt er mit der
    Wunderwaffe, seiner schwungvollen Musik Unterhaltung für die Soldaten. Hier ist er
    selbst, Major Glenn Miller.
Major Glenn Miller: Thanks, Ilse, and Grüss Gott to everybody. What do you say to our
  progress in die deutsche Sprache?
Ilse Weinberger: Die Forschritte sind gross, aber die Tonart war noch ein bisschen
  falsch, Herr Kapellmeister. Man sagt, "in der deutschen Sprache."
Major Glenn Miller: Oh, in der deutschen Sprache. Ob Englisch oder Chinesisch, es
  bleibt sich einerlei, Musik wird von jedem verstanden. Especially when we play the
  "American Patrol" with Sergeant Ray McKinley at the drums.
Ilse Weinberger: Sehr richtig, Herr Major. Glenn Millers Orchester spielt den
  bekannten Militärmarsch "Amerikanische Patrouille" und Feldwebel Ray McKinley schlägt
  die Trommel.
AMERICAN PATROL

Translation:

  Ilse Weinberger: German soldiers, this is Ilse speaking. I invite all of you to a
    rendezvous with the magician of American dance music, with a master of rhythm, with
    Major Glenn Miller and his famous American Band of the Allied Expeditionary Forces.
MOONLIGHT SERENADE (opening theme)
  Ilse Weinberger: Do you recognize his romantic theme song? It is his own composition
    "Moonlight Serenade," "Moonlight Serenade." In peacetime Glenn Miller made quite a
    splash with American dancers. And today he brings, with the magic weapon of his
    lively music, entertainment for the soldiers. Here he is himself, Major Glenn
    Miller.
Major Glenn Miller: Thanks, Ilse, and greetings to everybody. What do you say to our
  progress in the German language?
Ilse Weinberger: The progress is great but the intonation was a little wrong, Mr.
  Bandleader. One says, "in the German language."
Major Glenn Miller: Oh, in the German language. Whether English or Chinese, it remains
  the same, music is understood by everybody. Especially when we play the "American
  Patrol" with Sergeant Ray McKinley at the drums.
Ilse Weinberger: So right, Major. Glenn Miller's orchestra plays the well known
  military march "American Patrol" and Sergeant Ray McKinley beats the drums.
AMERICAN PATROL

CTPX-12763-1 **SUMMERTIME**   Program 2, Record 2

   Ilse Weinberger: Und jetzt Herr Major hätte ich eine grosse Bitte.
   Major Glenn Miller: Granted, I mean bewilligt.
   Ilse Weinberger: Spielen Sie Sommerzeit.
   Major Glenn Miller: Sommerzeit? What's that?
   Ilse Weinberger: Aber Herr Major, ich meine "Summertime," den grossen Musikschlager.
   Major Glenn Miller: Warum reden Sie nicht gleich Deutsch mit mir? Boys,
     let's play "Summertime."
SUMMERTIME
   Ilse Weinberger: Das war der bekannte Schlager "Sommerzeit." Herr Major, vor ein paar
    Wochen noch hätten Sie Sommerzeit zwimal spielen müssen.
   Major Glenn Miller: Warum?
   Ilse Weinberger: Haben Sie vergessen, da hatten wir hier in England noch doppelte
    Sommerzeit.
   Major Glenn Miller: You're very bright, Ilse. You think of everything, don'tcha?
   Ilse Weinberger: Ja, und ich denke gerade daran, dass es Zeit ist unserem
    Berichterstatter das Mikrofon zu überlassen. Hier ist er.

Translation:

   Ilse Weinberger: And now, Major, I have a big request.
   Major Glenn Miller: Granted, I mean granted.
   Ilse Weinberger: Please play "Summertime."
   Major Glenn Miller: "Summertime?" What's that?
   Ilse Weinberger: But Major, I mean "Summertime," the big hit.
   Major Glenn Miller: Why don't you speak in German to me right away? Boys, let's play
    "Summertime."
SUMMERTIME
   Ilse Weinberger: That was the well-known hit "Summertime." Major, only a few weeks ago
    you would have had to play "Summertime" twice.
   Major Glenn Miller: Why?
   Ilse Weinberger: Have you forgotten, we still had double summertime here in England.
   Major Glenn Miller: You're very bright, Ilse. You think of everything, don't 'cha?
   Ilse Weinberger: Yes, and I just remembered that it is time to hand over the microphone
    to our reporter. Here he is.

CTPX-12764-1 **TUXEDO JUNCTION**   Program 2, Record 3

   Ilse Weinberger: Und nun ist Major Miller bereit mit seinem Orchester Ihnen sein
    eigenes Arrangement eines typisch amerikanischen Jazzbandschlagers zu bringen.
   Major Glenn Miller: Don't forget the title, Ilse. It's "Tuxedo Junction."
TUXEDO JUNCTION

Translation:

   Ilse Weinberger: And now Major Miller is ready with his orchestra to play for you his
    own arrangement of a typical American jazz band hit.
   Major Glenn Miller: Don't forget the title, Ilse. It's "Tuxedo Junction."
TUXEDO JUNCTION

CTPX-12765-1 **NOW I KNOW** (JD-German)   Program 2, Record 4

    Ilse Weinberger: Herr Major, was haben Sie in Romantik auf Lager?
    Major Glenn Miller: You mean romance?
    Ilse Weinberger: Gerade das meine ich.
    Major Glenn Miller: Ich habe da something special.
    Ilse Weinberger: Sie meinen etwas Spezielles.
    Major Glenn Miller: Good. Was Spezielles? Here ist das Spezielle und zwar der
      romantische Sergeant Johnny Desmond. Er sieht gar nicht so aus, aber er ist
      romantisch. He will sing "Now I Know."
    Ilse Weinberger: Feldwebel Johnny Desmond singt jetzt den Schlager "Now I Know." Auf
      deutsch "Ich Verstehe."
    Major Glenn Miller: Sie versteht, ich versteh', er versteht.
    NOW I KNOW
      Vocal refrain by Sergeant Johnny Desmond (in German)
    Ilse Weinberger: Jetzt verstehe auch ich, warum Sie so beliebt sind, Feldwebel Desmond.
      Vielen Dank für das schöne Lied.
    Sergeant Johnny Desmond: Bitte schön.
    Ilse Weinberger: Soeben ist unser Berichterstatter mit einer interesanten Nachricht
      gekommen, die er uns übermitteln will.

Translation:

    Ilse Weinberger: Major, what have you in store in romance.
    Major Glenn Miller: You mean romance?
    Ilse Weinberger: I mean that exactly.
    Major Glenn Miller: I have something special.
    Ilse Weinberger: You mean something special.
    Major Glenn Miller: Good. Something special? Here's that special and it is the
      romantic Sergeant Johnny Desmond. He does not look it but he is romantic. He will
      sing "Now I Know."
    Ilse Weinberger: Sergeant Johnny Desmond now sings the hit "Now I Know." In German "I
      Understand."
    Major Glenn Miller: She understands, I understand, he understands.
    NOW I KNOW
      Vocal refrain by Sergeant Johnny Desmond (in German)
    Ilse Weinberger: Now I too understand why you are so popular, Sergeant Desmond. Many
      thanks for the beautiful song.
    Sergeant Johnny Desmond: You're welcome.
    Ilse Weinberger: Just now our reporter came with an interesting message, which he wants
      to give us.

CTPX-12766-1 **BEGIN THE BEGUINE**   Program 2, Record 5

Ilse Weinberger: Herr Major, was bringen Sie uns jetzt?
Major Glenn Miller: Ilse, do you know what a beguine is?
Ilse Weinberger: Ein Beginn ist ein Anfang, Herr Major, oder nicht?
Major Glenn Miller: Sorry, nein, diesmal muss ich Sie unterrichten. Beguine, nicht
    Beginn, is a Latin dance.
Ilse Weinberger: Aha, ein südamerikanischer Reigen. Bitte sehr, dann lass uns
    beginnen.
Major Glenn Miller: The beguine.
BEGIN THE BEGUINE
Ilse Weinberger: Eine kleine Ruhepause, Herr Major, für Sie und Ihre Soldaten?
Major Glenn Miller: Well, it couldn't do any harm.
Ilse Weinberger: Sie meinen, es könnte nicht schaden. Bitte sehr. Da kommt gerade
    unser Berichterstatter in den Senderaum. Er hat immer etwas Interesantes auf Lager.
    Hören wir uns ihn mal an.

Translation:

Ilse Weinberger: Major, what do you present now?
Major Glenn Miller: Ilse, do you know what a beguine is?
Ilse Weinberger: A beginning is a start, Major, or not?
Major Glenn Miller: Sorry, no, this time I must instruct you. Beguine, not beginning,
    is a Latin dance.
Ilse Weinberger: Aha, a South American square dance, please, then let's begin.
Major Glenn Miller: The beguine.
BEGIN THE BEGUINE
Ilse Weinberger: A little intermission, Major, for you and your soldiers?
Major Glenn Miller: Well, it couldn't do any harm.
Ilse Weinberger: You mean, it could not harm. Very good. Just now our reporter comes
    into the studio. He has something interesting in store. Let's listen to him.

CTPX-12767-1 **ANVIL CHORUS**   Program 2, Record 6

Ilse Weinberger: Herr Major, interessieren Sie sich auch für klassische Musik?
Major Glenn Miller: Ich liebe alle Musik.
Ilse Weinberger: Auch Opern?
Major Glenn Miller: Of course I like operas, no matter whether they are composed by
  Germans, Italians or Frenchmen. In fact we've arranged some of the most popular
  operatic melodies for our orchestra.
Ilse Weinberger: Major Miller sagte soeben, er interessiert sich für jede Musik,
  gleichgültig welche Nationalität der Komponist ist. Er hat sogar einige bekannte
  Opernmelodien, die volkstümlich geworden sind, in modernen Rhythmus für sein Orchester
  arrangiert. Wie wäre es Herr Major, wenn Sie uns eines dieser Arrangements vorspielen
  würden?
Major Glenn Miller: Gern, hier ist unser Arrangement von Verdi's "Ambows Chor" aus "Dem
  Troubador" and Sergeant Ray McKinley bedient die Trommel.
Ilse Weinberger: Also, schlagen Sie los.
ANVIL CHORUS
Ilse Weinberger: Bei Ihrer Musik vergisst man Zeit und Raum, Herr Major. Unsere halbe
  Stunde ist leider schon wieder um. Aber Auf Wiedersehen nächste Woche um dieselbe
  Zeit.
Major Glenn Miller: Von meinetwegen, mein liebes Fräulein.
Ilse Weinberger: Danke sehr. Das diese Musiker immer so gallant sind. Auf
  Wiedersehen.
Major Glenn Miller: Und Auf Wiederhören, deutsche Soldaten.

Translation:

Ilse Weinberger: Major, are you also interested in classical music?
Major Glenn Miller: I love all music.
Ilse Weinberger: Even operas?
Major Glenn Miller: Of course I like operas, no matter whether they are composed by
  Germans, Italians or Frenchmen. In fact we've arranged some of the most popular
  operatic melodies for our orchestra.
Ilse Weinberger: Major Miller said just now, he is interested in all music, no matter
  which nationality the composer is. He even has arranged a few of the most popular
  operatic melodies in modern rhythms for his orchestra. Major, how about playing one
  of your arrangements?
Major Glenn Miller: With pleasure, here is our arrangement of Verdi's "Anvil Chorus"
  from "Il Trovatore" and Sergeant Ray McKinley beats the drums.
Ilse Weinberger: Well, then pound away.
ANVIL CHORUS
Ilse Weinberger: Listening to your music one forgets time and space, Major. Our half
  hour is up again much to my regret. But until we meet again next week at the same
  time.
Major Glenn Miller: If you so wish, my dear Miss.
Ilse Weinberger: Thank you very much. These musicians are always so gallant. Good
  bye.
Major Glenn Miller: And until we hear again, German soldiers.

CTPX-12768-1 **MOONLIGHT SERENADE** (opening theme)   Program 3, Record 1

Ilse Weinberger: Deutsche Soldaten, heute lade ich Sie wieder zu einem Rendezvous ein,
  das ich mit zweiundfüfzig strammen amerikanischen Soldaten habe, nämlich mit den
  Musikern des Orchesters der Alliierten Expeditionsstreitkräfte und ihrem schneidigen
  Dirigenten Major Glenn Miller. Bevor der Krieg ausbrach war Glenn Miller einer der
  beliebtesten Dirigenten amerikanischer Tanzmusik. Er meldete sich zum Militär und
  wurde zum Leiter dieser Soldatenkapelle ernannt, die sich aus ehemaligen Mitgliedern
  verschiedener amerikanischer Konzert-, Symphonie- und Tanzorchester zusammensetzt.
  Eine fidele Gruppe, die täglich die amerikanischen Soldaten in ihren freien Stunden
  unterhält.

MOONLIGHT SERENADE (opening theme)
Ilse Weinberger: "Mondscheinserenade" heisst diese romantische Melodie und denen, die
  heute zum erstenmal zuhören, möchte ich kurz wiederholen, dass dies die Sendezeichen
  Musik Major Glenn Millers ist. Es ist seine eigene Komposition.
Ilse Weinberger: Deutsche Soldaten, vor das Mikrofon tritt jetzt persönlich Major Glenn
  Miller.
Major Glenn Miller: How do you do, Ilse? Here we are again for our short rendezvous
  and I wish to thank you for the nice things you said about the members of our
  orchestra. I'd like to add that you find all nationalities among them. There're even
  quite a number of boys whose parents came from Germany, Russia, Italy and many other
  countries. But today they are true Americans sitting side by side with their buddies,
  no matter who they are or where they came from. This is a true picture of the great
  melting pot, America, and a symbol of unity in the fight for freedom and peace.
Ilse Weinberger: Ja. Das war sehr schön gesprochen, Herr Major, und ich hoffe, dass es
  recht viele verstanden haben.
Major Glenn Miller: Why don't you repeat in German what I just said?
Ilse Weinberger: Kurz zusammengefasst sagte Major Miller, dass sich unter den
  zweiundfüfzig Musikern seines Orchesters auch Söhne von Deutschen, Italienern und
  anderen Nationalitäten befinden. Ein wahres Symbol Amerikas, wo jeder dieselben
  Rechte hat, ganz gleich welcher Rasse, Herkunft und Religion er ist. Major Glenn
  Miller, der Dirigent des Orchesters der Alliierten Expeditionsstreitkräfte, erhebt
  jetzt den Taktstock und bringt Ihnen als erstes "Here We Go Again," "Wir Marschieren
  Wieder."

Translation:

Ilse Weinberger: German soldiers, today I invite you again to a rendezvous that I have with 52 tough American soldiers that are the musicians with the Band of the Allied Expeditionary Forces and their gallant conductor Major Glenn Miller. Before the war broke out Glenn Miller was one of the most popular conductors of American dance music. Then he enlisted in the military and was named the leader of this military orchestra that is composed of former members of different American concert, symphony and dance orchestras. A happy group that daily entertains the American soldiers in their free time.

MOONLIGHT SERENADE (opening theme)

Ilse Weinberger: "Moonlight Serenade" is the name of this romantic melody and for those who listen today for the first time, I would like to repeat briefly that this is the theme song of Major Glenn Miller. It is his own composition.

Ilse Weinberger: German soldiers, now Major Glenn Miller personally steps up to the microphone.

Major Glenn Miller: How do you do, Ilse? Here we are again for our short rendezvous and I wish to thank you for the nice things you said about the members of our orchestra. I'd like to add that you find all nationalities among them. There're even quite a number of boys whose parents came from Germany, Russia, Italy and many other countries. But today they are true Americans sitting side by side with their buddies, no matter who they are or where they came from. This is a true picture of the great melting pot, America, and a symbol of unity in the fight for freedom and peace.

Ilse Weinberger: Yes. That was beautifully spoken, Major, and I hope that many people have understood it.

Major Glenn Miller: Why don't you repeat in German what I just said?

Ilse Weinberger: In short, Major Miller said that among the 52 musicians of his orchestra you will find even sons of German, Italian and other nationalities. A true symbol of America, where everybody has the same rights, it is all equal regardless of race, color and religion. Major Glenn Miller, the conductor of the Band of the Allied Expeditionary Forces, now raises his baton and brings you first of all "Here We Go Again," "We March Again."

CTPX-12770-1 **MY HEART TELL ME (Should I Believe My Heart?)** (JD-German)   Prog. 3, Record 3

Ilse Weinberger: Das war ein schmissiger Anfang, Herr Major. Recht vielen Dank.
  Übrigens, wie steht es mit Ihren Fortschritten in der deutschen Sprache?
Major Glenn Miller: Mit der deutschen Sprache geht es wie mit meiner Frau, ich liebe
  sie, aber ich beherrsche sie nicht.
Ilse Weinberger: Na, es geht ja ausgezeichnet. Und ich bin sicher, Sie können Ihr
  zweites Konzertstück selbst ansagen.
Major Glenn Miller: No, we reserve this pleasure for the good Sergeant Johnny Desmond.
  Sergeant Johnny Desmond, report to Ilse.
Sergeant Johnny Desmond: Yes, sir. Ah, yes, ma'm.
Ilse Weinberger: Herr Feldwebel Desmond, was darf ich für Sie ansagen?
Sergeant Johnny Desmond: Ah, "My Heart Tells Me" and I'll sing it in German.
Major Glenn Miller: You should announce it in German too, John. It's simple to say
  "Mein Herz Sagt Mir."
Sergeant Johnny Desmond: Yes, sir. "Mein Hertz meldet sich zur Stelle."
MY HEART TELLS ME (Should I Believe My Heart?)
  Vocal refrain by Sergeant Johnny Desmond (in German)
Major Glenn Miller: Mein Herz sagt mir, dein Herz sagt dir, sein Herz sagt ihm. How'm
  I doin', Ilse?
Ilse Weinberger: Grammatik ausgezeichnet, Aussprache sehr romantisch. Herr Major, Sie
  sprechen immer besser. Wie wär's mit einer kleinen Rede in deutscher Sprache?
Major Glenn Miller: Das kann ihr Reporter viel besser. Listen to him.
Ilse Weinberger: Einverstanden.

Translation:

  Ilse Weinberger: That was an exciting beginning, Major. Many thanks. By the way, how
    is your progress in the German language coming along?
  Major Glenn Miller: With the German language it is the same as with my wife, I love
    her, but I am not in command of her.
  Ilse Weinberger: Well, it is going very well. And I am sure you can announce your
    second concert piece yourself.
  Major Glenn Miller: No, we reserve this pleasure for the good Sergeant Johnny Desmond.
    Sergeant Johnny Desmond, report to Ilse.
  Sergeant Johnny Desmond: Yes, sir. Ah, yes, ma'm.
  Ilse Weinberger: Sergeant Desmond, what may I announce for you?
  Sergeant Johnny Desmond: Ah, "My Heart Tells Me" and I'll sing it in German.
  Major Glenn Miller: You should announce it in German too, John. It's simple to say "My
    Heart Tells Me."
  Sergeant Johnny Desmond: Yes, sir. "My Heart Reports For Duty."
  MY HEART TELLS ME (Should I Believe My Heart?)
    Vocal refrain by Sergeant Johnny Desmond (in German)
  Major Glenn Miller: My heart tells me, your heart tells you, his heart tells him.
    How'm I doin', Ilse?
  Ilse Weinberger: Grammer excellent, pronunciation very romantic. Major, you speak
    better every time. How about a little speech in the German language?
  Major Glenn Miller: That your reporter can do much better. Listen to him.
  Ilse Weinberger: Agreed.

CTPX-12771-1 **A STRING OF PEARLS**   Program 3, Record 4

  Ilse Weinberger: Nun wieder zurück zum Orchester der Allierten Expeditionsstreitkräfte
  und Ihrem Dirigenten Glenn Miller. Herr Major, die musikalischen Schätze, die Sie aus
  Amerika mitgebracht haben, dürften wohl unerschöpflich sein.
  Major Glenn Miller: Right, Ilse. For, believe it or not, our next selection is called
  "String of Pearls." How would you say that in German?
  Ilse Weinberger: Das is sehr einfach, "String of Pearls" heisst "Perlenkette." Und
  "Perlenkette" ist "String of Pearls," der Titel, des folgenden Schlagers.
  A STRING OF PEARLS

Translation:

  Ilse Weinberger: Now back again to the Orchestra of the Allied Expeditionary Forces and
  your conductor Glenn Miller. Major, the musical treasures that you brought with you
  from America are seemingly inexhaustible.
  Major Glenn Miller: Right, Ilse. For, believe it or not, our next selection is called
  "String of Pearls." How would you say that in German?
  Ilse Weinberger: That is very easy, "String of Pearls" is called "String of Pearls."
  And "String of Pearls" is "String of Pearls," the title of the following song.
  A STRING OF PEARLS

CTPX-12772-1 **STORMY WEATHER (Keeps Rainin' All the Time)**   Program 3, Record 5

  Ilse Weinberger: Was dürfen wir jetzt ankündigen?
  Major Glenn Miller: Well, here's one of our favorite tunes, "Stormy Weather."
  Ilse Weinberger: Abermals erhebt Major Miller den Taktstock und bringt Ihnen einen der
  bekanntesten amerikanischen Schlager "Stormy Weather," auf deutsch "Stürmisches
  Wetter."
  STORMY WEATHER (Keeps Rainin' All the Time)

Translation:

  Ilse Weinberger: What may we now announce?
  Major Glenn Miller: Well, here's one of our favorite tunes, "Stormy Weather."
  Ilse Weinberger: And again Major Miller lifts his baton and brings to you one of the
  most familiar American songs "Stormy Weather," in German "Stormy Weather."
  STORMY WEATHER (Keeps Rainin' All the Time)

CTPX-12773-1 **DIALOGUE** verbal introduction to "Poinciana (Song of the Tree)" and closing
          to program after "Poinciana (Song of the Tree)"   Program 3, Record 6

[Dialogue preceding "Poinciana (Song of the Tree)"]
Ilse Weinberger: Wir gönnen unseren fleissigen Musikern eine kleine Rastpause und
  übergeben abermals das Mikrofon unseren Berichterstatter.
Major Glenn Miller: Yesterday I spoke to a German prisoner who's a faithful listener to
  your programs, Ilse.
Ilse Weinberger: Das sollte mich nicht wundern, denn wie ich höre haben alle
  Befangenenlager in England und Amerika Radioempfangsgeräte und die deutschen
  Gefangenen können jede Station einschalten, sogar den Deutschlandsender.
Major Glenn Miller: So ist es auch in Amerika, jeder Amerikaner kann Deutschland, oder
  wenn er will, Japan hören. I hope the day will soon come when German soldiers will be
  able to return to their homes and families to be happy and listen to whatever they may
  please, especially to the Voice of America, the voice of freedom and liberty.
Ilse Weinberger: Major Miller gab der Hoffnung Ausdruck, dass die deutschen Soldaten
  recht bald bei Ihren Lieben daheim sein werden, vom Nazijoch erlöst, und das sie bald
  den Radiostationen aller Welt lauschen werden, insbesondere der Stimme Amerikas, der
  Stimme der Freiheit und Gleichberechtigung.
Major Glenn Miller: Now how 'bout some more music?
Ilse Weinberger: Einverstanden, was wird es diesmal sein?
Major Glenn Miller: The name of the next tune, "Poinciana."

[Dialogue following "Poinciana (Song of the Tree)"]
Ilse Weinberger: Wieder ist die Zeit wie im Flug vergangen, und abermals heisst es
  Abschied nehmen von Glenn Miller und dem Orchester der Allierten
  Expeditionsstreitkräfte. Vielen Dank allerseits, besonders Ihnen Herr Major.
Major Glenn Miller: To you, too, many thanks and Auf Wiedersehen.

Translation:

[Dialogue preceding "Poinciana (Song of the Tree)"]
Ilse Weinberger: We allow our busy musicians a little break and we again hand over the
  microphone to our reporter.
Major Glenn Miller: Yesterday I spoke to a German prisoner who's a faithful listener to
  your program, Ilse.
Ilse Weinberger: That shouldn't surprise me because as I hear, all prisoner camps in
  England and America have radio receiving sets and the German prisoners can tune in any
  station, even the Deutschlandsender.
Major Glenn Miller: So it is also in America, every American can hear Germany or, if he
  wants, Japan. I hope the day will soon come when German soldiers will be able to
  return to their homes and families to be happy and listen to whatever they may please,
  especially to the Voice of America, the voice of freedom and liberty.
Ilse Weinberger: Major Glenn Miller gave the sincere hope that the German soldiers will
  be home with their loved ones very soon, freed from the Nazi yoke, and that they soon
  can listen to the radio stations of the entire world, mainly the Voice of America, the
  voice of freedom and equal rights.
Major Glenn Miller: Now how 'bout some more music?
Ilse Weinberger: Agreed, what will it be this time?
Major Glenn Miller: The name of the next tune, "Poinciana."

[Dialogue following "Poinciana (Song of the Tree)"]
Ilse Weinberger: Again the time has flown, and again we must take our leave from Glenn
  Miller and the orchestra of the Allied Expeditionary Forces. Many thanks to
  everybody, especially to you, Major.
Major Glenn Miller: To you, too, many thanks and good bye.

06Nov44 (Mon) 7:15-7:30PM BBC Maida Vale studio, London, England
STRINGS WITH WINGS broadcast   Script

Announcer: This is a feature of the American Band of the A.E.F.
I SUSTAIN THE WINGS (opening theme)
   Corporal Paul Dubov: "Strings with Wings," a program of music for you of the Allied
     Liberation Forces, presented by the string section of the American Band of the A.E.F.,
     featuring Sergeant George Ockner and his violin.
Corporal Paul Dubov: Hello there, folks, welcome to another program of "Strings with
   Wings." If you were here in the studio tonight you'd see the boys polishing up their
   fiddles as they've never been polished before, rosining their bows, and tuning each
   violin string to perfect pitch. Just watching 'em you'd probably guess there was
   something big on the fire for this evening. And you'd be right. Because tonight we are
   privileged to have as our guest Sir Adrian Boult, distinguished conductor of the B.B.C.
   Symphony Orchestra. Sir Adrian is here now, ready to guide the boys through the
   fortissimos and diminuendos of tonight's program. And appropriately enough, he's chosen
   as his opening number a composition by an eminent British composer, the First Movement
   of Sir Edward Elgar's "Serenade Suite for Strings."
SERENADE SUITE FOR STRINGS (First Movement)
Corporal Paul Dubov: Looking over the boys' music library the other day, Sir Adrian
   happened on a brand new arrangement, fresh from the pen of Sergeant George Ockner. And
   he liked it so much that he immediately scheduled it for this program. Here it is now,
   Sergeant Ockner's arrangement of Debussy's beautiful nocturne, "Clouds."
"CLOUDS" NOCTURNE
Corporal Paul Dubov: For his closing number tonight, Sir Adrian has chosen one of the
   world's great favorites, a simple tune that has sung its way into the hearts of
   millions. It's Corporal Eugene Bergen's arrangement, conducted by Sir Adrian and played
   by the string orchestra. "Annie Laurie."
ANNIE LAURIE
Corporal Paul Dubov: And with the last notes of "Annie Laurie" we end another program of
   "Strings with Wings." Our thanks to Sir Adrian Boult for taking time off from his many
   duties with the B.B.C. Symphony to give us the pleasure of his presence here tonight.
   And I only hope that you folks enjoyed it as much as the boys did themselves. We'll be
   back with another program Wednesday evening. So don't forget to be listening.
   Meanwhile, this is Corporal Paul Dubov saying, "So long, and good luck to you."
I SUSTAIN THE WINGS (closing theme)
   Corporal Paul Dubov: You've been listening to music by the string section of the
     American Band of the A.E.F., featuring Sergeant George Ockner and his violin, and
     conducted tonight by Sir Adrian Boult of the B.B.C. Symphony Orchestra. Don't forget
     to join us Wednesday evening when we again present "Strings with Wings."

08Nov44 (Wed) 6:15-6:30PM Co-Partners Hall, Bedford, England
  THE UPTOWN HALL broadcast   Script

Announcer: This is a feature of the American Band of the A.E.F.
MY GUY'S COME BACK (opening theme)
  Corporal Paul Dubov: Good evening, all, it's "The Uptown Hall," music for you of the
    Allied Liberation Forces, presented by members of the American Band of the A.E.F.,
    featuring Sergeant Mel Powell at the piano.
Corporal Paul Dubov: Welcome to "The Uptown Hall," fellow members. The boys,
  masterminded by brother Mel, are back again to do right by you with a spot of music.
  They've tatted up a fancy set of tunes for tonight's meeting. So if you folks will just
  check your sidearms, dog tags, and troubles at the door, and come in and take a seat,
  we'll get the rhythm rolling. The kick-off number this evening, Sergeant Carmen
  Mastren's swell arrangement of "Song of the Wanderer."
SONG OF THE WANDERER (Where Shall I Go?)
Corporal Paul Dubov: Not content with writing peachy arrangements for other people's
  tunes, Sergeant Carmen Mastren can also shake together a nice original of his own on
  occasion. We're bending an ear to one of 'em tonight, a little thing made up of two
  parts mild and one part prussic acid called "Shandy."
SHANDY
Corporal Paul Dubov: Now we're gonna put the touch on Sergeant Mel himself for a few
  words of introduction to this next one. Brother, can you spare the time?
S/Sgt. Mel Powell: I've always got the time, Paul, to put in a good word for our "Band
  within a Band." This is the spot, folks, where three of the boys in the group peel off
  and the rest of us deal ourselves a little four-handed hand of harmony. It's Sergeant
  Ray McKinley at the drums; Sergeant Trigger Alpert, string bass; Sergeant Michael Hucko,
  clarinet; and yours truly back at the piano. Which is where I better get to, before
  they take off without me. It's "One, Two, Button Your Shoe" and, boys, here's the one,
  two.
ONE, TWO, BUTTON YOUR SHOE (quartet: Hucko, Powell, Alpert, McKinley)
Corporal Paul Dubov: We tried to get a temple bell or two for this next number to give it
  that hundred-proof oriental flavor. It's a little tune that takes us down to Limehouse,
  London. And we deliver it complete with dark, foggy streets, stealthy figures, and Fu
  Manchu. Here it is, arranged by Sergeant Norman Leyden and featuring Sergeant Mel
  Powell at the piano, "Limehouse Blues."
LIMEHOUSE BLUES
Corporal Paul Dubov: Well, if we want to stay around here any longer we gotta put another
  shilling in the gas meter. And being fresh out of shillings, I guess we better button
  things up for tonight. But we'll be back this coming Friday evening with more of that
  soft but oh so solid music. Until then, this is Corporal Paul Dubov saying, "So long,
  and good luck to you."
MY GUY'S COME BACK (closing theme)
  Corporal Paul Dubov: You've been listening to music by members of the American Band of
    the A.E.F. Don't forget to join us Friday night for another musical meeting in "The
    Uptown Hall."

08Nov44 (Wed) 7:45-8:00PM Co-Partners Hall, Bedford, England
  STRINGS WITH WINGS broadcast   Script

Announcer: This is a feature of the American Band of the A.E.F.
I SUSTAIN THE WINGS (opening theme)
  Corporal Paul Dubov: "Strings with Wings." "Strings with Wings," a program of music
    for you of the Allied Liberation Forces, presented by the string section of the
    American Band of the A.E.F., featuring Sergeant George Ockner and his violin.
Corporal Paul Dubov: Hello there, folks, welcome to another program of "Strings with
  Wings." Sergeant Ockner and the boys are here tonight, 21 violins with but a single
  idea, to help you pass the time this evening with a quiet tune 'er two. What's more,
  we've got some special listening on hand for us. The boys have added four brand new
  numbers to their list of arrangements. And tonight they're gonna play 'em for us. So
  get as comfortable as you can while we open the program with new arrangement number one.
  It's by Sergeant Norman Leyden and it's called "Spring Will Be a Little Late This Year."
SPRING WILL BE A LITTLE LATE THIS YEAR
Corporal Paul Dubov: Sergeant Harry Katzman, who sits up front here in the "A" violin
  section, did a little doubling this week with the pen and manuscript paper. The result
  is a fancy new arrangement of an old Duke Ellington favorite. It's in the key of blue
  and it bears the familiar title of "Mood Indigo."
MOOD INDIGO
Corporal Paul Dubov: Credit for some of the best listening on this program belongs to
  arranger Sergeant Ralph Wilkinson. He's just written a few more pages for our music
  book. And from the title we guess that this time it's a love story. Here it is,
  Sergeant Ralph Wilkinson's sugar-coated arrangement of "My Romance."
MY ROMANCE
Corporal Paul Dubov: That's all for tonight, folks. But Sergeant Ockner and the violins
  will be back next Monday night with another one of these sack time serenades. So don't
  get too far away from that radio. Meanwhile this is Corporal Paul Dubov saying, "So
  long, and good luck to you."
I SUSTAIN THE WINGS (closing theme)
  Corporal Paul Dubov: You've been listening to music by the string section of the
    American Band of the A.E.F., featuring Sergeant George Ockner and his violin. Don't
    forget to join us again next Monday evening when we present another program of
    "Strings with Wings."

10Nov44 (Fri) 6:15-6:30PM Co-Partners Hall, Bedford, England
  THE UPTOWN HALL broadcast   Script

Announcer: This is a feature of the American Band of the A.E.F.
MY GUY'S COME BACK (opening theme)
  Corporal Paul Dubov: Good evening, all, it's "The Uptown Hall," music for you of the
    Allied Liberation Forces, presented by members of the American Band of the A.E.F.,
    featuring Sergeant Mel Powell at the piano.
Corporal Paul Dubov: Welcome to "The Uptown Hall," fellow members. Another evening,
    another round-up of rhythm for you guys and gals in the Hall. Brother Mel has brought
    his little aggregation around to serve up the syncopation for us and we've got a full
    schedule of swell listening ahead for us. So come on in, pick out a seat, and get ready
    to split a tune or two with the assembled members. There's the green light, Mel gives
    me the downbeat, and we're away in a cloud of eighth notes with "Flying Home."
FLYING HOME
Corporal Paul Dubov: Nice goin', boys. And now we follow that first one right into
    number two. Here's one straight out of the dream department called "What Is There to
    Say."
WHAT IS THERE TO SAY
Corporal Paul Dubov: Just about every day when Sergeant Mel Powell trots into the Hall,
    he finds somebody's gone in an' dropped a note into the piano, and it always reads,
    quote, "I must have that song.," unquote. So here's the "Band within a Band" bringing a
    repeat of the tune in question. It's Sergeant Mel Powell, piano; Sergeant Ray McKinley,
    drums; Sergeant Trigger Alpert, string bass; and Sergeant Michael Hucko playin' one
    especially for those folks who must have that song. It's called "I Must Have That Man."
I MUST HAVE THAT MAN (quartet: Hucko, Powell, Alpert, McKinley)
Corporal Paul Dubov: "I Must Have That Man." And I refer, of course, to Sergeant Mel
    Powell. Mel, say something to the folks.
S/Sgt. Mel Powell: Along with those requests in the piano we've been getting, there's a
    couple of mailbags of letters around here from folks who want to hear our theme song in
    full. Well, tonight we're gonna oblige. The boys and I cooked up this little theme
    during our first meeting here in the Hall. Everybody put in two bars worth but nobody
    got around to giving it a title. Paul, got any ideas?
Corporal Paul Dubov: Have I got any ideas? He's asking me if I've got any ideas! Well,
    no, matter of fact, I haven't. What ya say we just send it out the way she is? Mel,
    take a four and lead on the boys.
MY GUY'S COME BACK
Corporal Paul Dubov: And there you have the theme, folks. But since the old clock is
    getting around here, we might as well just let the theme get going again. That's all
    for tonight, but we'll be back tomorrow P.M. with more of that music that's soft but
    solid. Until that happy time, this is Corporal Paul Dubov saying, "So long, and good
    luck to you."
MY GUY'S COME BACK (closing theme)
  Corporal Paul Dubov: You've been listening to music by members of the American Band of
    the A.E.F. And remember to join us again for our next musical meeting in "The Uptown
    Hall."

11Nov44 (Sat) 11:45AM-Noon Co-Partners Hall, Bedford, England
PIANO PARADE broadcast   Script

Announcer: This is a feature of the American Band of the A.E.F.
CHOPSTICKS (opening theme)
   Announcer: "Piano Parade," a daily quarter-hour of piano music that today brings you
      Private First Class Jack Rusin in a medley of memory melodies.
Announcer: And here's Jack back with a noontime, tune-time serenade of popular piano
   favorites. Opening the show we hear a request number, "Serenade in Blue," followed by
   "Going My Way," "It Had to Be You," "Stars in My Eyes," an original by Jack himself
   called "Sequence," and "After You're Gone." So let's all gather around the piano and
   listen while Jack turns these six titles into some mighty tuneful music.
SERENADE IN BLUE
GOING MY WAY
IT HAD TO BE YOU
STARS IN MY EYES
SEQUENCE
AFTER YOU'VE GONE
CHOPSTICKS (closing theme)
   Announcer: You've been listening to "Piano Parade," fifteen minutes of piano melodies,
      with P.F.C. Jack Rusin at the keyboard. Heard today were "Serenade in Blue," "Going
      My Way," "It Had to Be You," "Stars in My Eyes," Jack's own tune entitled "Sequence,"
      and "After You're Gone." That's all for now. But don't forget to be along the line
      of march when we come this way again with "Piano Parade."

11Nov44 6:15-6:30PM Co-Partners Hall, Bedford, England
  THE UPTOWN HALL broadcast   Script

Announcer: This is a feature of the American Band of the A.E.F.
MY GUY'S COME BACK (opening theme)
    Corporal Paul Dubov: Good evening, all, it's "The Uptown Hall," music for you of the
    Allied Liberation Forces, presented by members of the American Band of the A.E.F.,
    featuring Sergeant Mel Powell at the piano.
Corporal Paul Dubov: Welcome to "The Uptown Hall," fellow members. Sergeant Powell has
    pushed me out here in front to say hello to you folks and hand out an invitation to
    crowd on into the Hall for a spot of music this evening. We've got plenty of it, so
    don't be afraid of imposing. Now if the Sergeant at Arms will close and bolt the doors
    of the Hall, we'll get on with the business at hand. And the first item on tonight's
    agenda is a swingy little thing called "Little White Lies."
LITTLE WHITE LIES
Corporal Paul Dubov: Now Mel sprinkles a little dream-dust on the keys and comes out with
    a little number on the smooth and easy side. It's "Stars Fell on Alabama."
STARS FELL ON ALABAMA
Corporal Paul Dubov: Mel, if you tear yourself away from that piano for a minute, how
    about comin' over here and tossin' the folks an introduction to this next one.
S/Sgt. Mel Powell: Gladly, Paul, gladly, 'cause it gives me another chance to bring on
    the "Band within a Band." When we get real cozy here in the Hall, folks, we give three
    of the boys a chance to drop out and cop a smoke. And we knuckle down to a few choruses
    with our intimate little quartet. Reading from East to West, we have Sergeant Ray
    McKinley on the drums; Sergeant Trigger Alpert, string bass; Sergeant Michael Hucko,
    clarinet; and one other one. Let's see --- it's --- oh, it's me. Hey, I gotta get back
    to the piano. Paul, say something.
Corporal Paul Dubov: All right then, Mel. Here it is, "Pennies from Heaven."
PENNIES FROM HEAVEN (quartet: Hucko, Powell, Alpert, McKinley)
Corporal Paul Dubov: Vocal boy makes good. It's Sergeant Johnny Desmond handling the
    vocal assignment on our next number, "Once in a While."
ONCE IN A WHILE
    Vocal refrain by Sergeant Johnny Desmond
Corporal Paul Dubov: And as we swing into the last few minutes of the meeting, we hear
    Mel and the boys knockin' down the rafter and breaking up the furniture with "Blue
    Room."
THE BLUE ROOM
Corporal Paul Dubov: Well, that really does it, folks. And before the bobbies get here
    we'd better take it on the lam. But don't forget, we'll assemble here next Wednesday
    night, under the cover of darkness, for another session of swing. So make it a point to
    be on hand. Until then this is Corporal Paul Dubov saying, "So long, and good luck to
    you."
MY GUY'S COME BACK (closing theme)
    Corporal Paul Dubov: You've been listening to music by members of the American Band of
    the A.E.F. Don't forget to join us next Wednesday night for another musical meeting
    in "The Uptown Hall."

13Nov44 (Mon) 7:01-7:15PM BBC Maida Vale studio, London, England
SONGS BY SGT. JOHNNY DESMOND broadcast   Script

Corporal Paul Dubov: This is a feature of the American Band of the A.E.F.
TIME ON MY HANDS (opening theme)
  Corporal Paul Dubov: "Songs by Sergeant Johnny Desmond."
  Vocal refrain by Sergeant Johnny Desmond
  Corporal Paul Dubov: Three songs by a three-striper. The type of tunes that keep
    runnin' 'round in your head and runnin' 'round in your heart.
Corporal Paul Dubov: And here he is, the singin' Sarge. John, you're on.
Sergeant Johnny Desmond: You're right on the ball, Paul. And hello there, everybody.
  First out of the startin' gate for this session is the kind of tune that parts your
  heart right in the middle. So, if Sergeant Norm Leyden will give it the windup and
  pitch, I'll give ya "Long Ago and Far Away."
LONG AGO (And Far Away)
  Vocal refrain by Sergeant Johnny Desmond
Sergeant Johnny Desmond: Some songs have a habit of sorta leadin' your voice along. They
  make mighty easy singin', which makes 'em mighty handy for a guy like me. Here's where
  I hitch myself a free ride on a sweet song, "Sweet Lorraine."
SWEET LORRAINE
  Vocal refrain by Sergeant Johnny Desmond
Sergeant Johnny Desmond: Now, if Sergeant Norm Leyden will lay a beat on the band, we'll
  help ourselves to a little basin-full of music without words. "Get Happy."
GET HAPPY
Sergeant Johnny Desmond: Time now for me to go back to work. But, believe me, work's fun
  when the job at hand is singin' a song like this next one. I don't know how it's doin'
  back home, but over on this side it's getting plenty of well-deserved action, especially
  in the heart department. "Spring Will Be a Little Late This Year."
SPRING WILL BE A LITTLE LATE THIS YEAR
  Vocal refrain by Sergeant Johnny Desmond
Sergeant Johnny Desmond: Now, this is Sergeant Johnny Desmond sayin' thanks for listenin'
  along. I'll be back next week at this same time. Hope you can make it then.
TIME ON MY HANDS (closing theme)
  Corporal Paul Dubov: You have been listening to three songs by a three-striper, "Songs
    by Sergeant Johnny Desmond."
  Vocal refrain by Sergeant Johnny Desmond

13Nov44 (Mon) 7:15-7:30PM BBC Maida Vale studio, London, England
  STRINGS WITH WINGS broadcast   Script

I SUSTAIN THE WINGS (opening theme)
  Corporal Paul Dubov: "Strings with Wings." "Strings with Wings," a program of music
    for you of the Allied Liberation Forces, presented by the string section of the
    American Band of the A.E.F., featuring Sergeant George Ockner and his violin.
Corporal Paul Dubov: Hello there, folks. Welcome to another program of "Strings with
  Wings." Looks as though you got here just in time to tune in on some more tunes. We've
  readied a little sack time serenade for your evening pleasure, and Sergeant Ockner and
  the boys are here to give out with the sweet music. So cozy up to that radio and lend a
  listen while we start things going with "How Deep Is the Ocean."
HOW DEEP IN THE OCEAN (How High Is the Sky)
Corporal Paul Dubov: Now some soft light, please, for the sweet music that follows. It's
  Sergeant Ockner and the violins playing us a Mexican love song called "Estrellita,"
  "Little Star."
ESTRELLITA
Corporal Paul Dubov: No one over here in the E.T.O. has to look at the calendar to know
  that old man winter is upon us. There's a real chill in the air. But if you'll just
  move in a wee bit closer, you can warm your ears with a few musical memories of a warmer
  season as the boys play "Indian Summer."
INDIAN SUMMER
Corporal Paul Dubov: Composer Jerome Kern has inked in a lot of scores in his time, but
  few better than this recent hit of his. You heard Rita Hayward and Gene Kelly sing it
  in "Cover Girl." Now you're gonna hear how it sounds as arranged for violins, "Sure
  Thing."
SURE THING
Corporal Paul Dubov: And there you have it, all signed, sealed and delivered, fifteen
  minutes of your favorites, set to strings by Sergeant Ockner and the boys. Don't forget
  to get in touch with us again this coming Wednesday night when we take to the air with
  some more music for you. Until then, this is Corporal Paul Dubov saying, "So long, and
  good luck to you."
I SUSTAIN THE WINGS (closing theme)
  Corporal Paul Dubov: You've been listening to music by the string section of the
    American Band of the A.E.F., featuring Sergeant George Ockner and his violin. Be sure
    to be listening Wednesday night for another program of "Strings with Wings."

14Nov44 (Tue) 8:30-9:00PM Queensbury All-Services Club, London, England   SWN-19601
MOONLIGHT SERENADE broadcast   Attendance: 2500

Corporal Paul Dubov: This is a feature of the American Band of the A.E.F., originating at
   the Queensbury All-Services Club in London.
MOONLIGHT SERENADE (opening theme)
   Corporal Paul Dubov: This is the music of the Moonlight Serenader, presenting the
      American Band of the A.E.F. in thirty minutes of friendly melody.
Sergeant Keith Jameson: This is Sergeant Keith Jameson. This show finds its regular
   proprietor away on military duties. It is my pleasure to pinch-hit in the "words
   department" for Major Glenn Miller, while Sergeant Jerry Gray waves the big stick over
   the music. And first over the hurdles is one of Jerry's own high-jumpers, "Here We Go
   Again."
HERE WE GO AGAIN
Sergeant Keith Jameson: On with your "Moonlight Serenade." This time, sweet and mellow,
   "Body and Soul."
BODY AND SOUL
Sergeant Keith Jameson: Up firing the big guns in the drum department for the American
   Band of the A.E.F. sits Sergeant Ray McKinley. Back in "the big 48" Sergeant Mac made
   big fame and a big name as co-author and top singer of the southpaw song he's about to
   saddle and ride for you right now. "Beat Me Daddy, Eight to the Bar."
BEAT ME DADDY, EIGHT TO THE BAR
   Vocal refrain by Technical Sergeant Ray McKinley

   ...

MY BUDDY (Old tune)
   Sergeant Keith Jameson: For somethin' new, somethin' romantic. Sergeant Johnny Desmond
      sings ...
NOW I KNOW (New tune)
   Vocal refrain by Sergeant Johnny Desmond
   Sergeant Keith Jameson: We put the bite on Harry James for the borrowed tune and up
      jumps "Music Makers."
MUSIC MAKERS (Borrowed tune)
   Sergeant Keith Jameson: Somethin' blue, shaded in whisperin' jazz. "Farewell Blues."
FAREWELL BLUES (Blue tune)
Sergeant Keith Jameson: Comin' up now a new ballad born of the pen of America's
   deep-South songwriter, Willard Robison, entrusted here to the lovin' care of Sergeant
   Johnny Desmond. "Deep Summer Music."
DEEP SUMMER MUSIC
   Vocal refrain by Sergeant Johnny Desmond
Sergeant Keith Jameson: Up with the bright lights as the American Band of the A.E.F.
   turns on the juice for a one-hundred-and-ten-jolt hunk o' jazz. "I Hear You Screamin'."
I HEAR YOU SCREAMIN'
Sergeant Keith Jameson: This is Sergeant Keith Jameson hangin' out the welcome sign for
   the next show by the American Band of the A.E.F. You'll be hearing Major Glenn Miller
   and company Friday night at twenty-twenty. For now, it's good luck and good night.
MOONLIGHT SERENADE (closing theme)
   Corporal Paul Dubov: You have heard the music of the Moonlight Serenader, Major Glenn
      Miller's American Band of the A.E.F.

15Nov44 (Wed) 7:45-8:00PM Co-Partners Hall, Bedford, England
STRINGS WITH WINGS broadcast   Script

Announcer: This is a feature of the American Band of the A.E.F.
I SUSTAIN THE WINGS (opening theme)
   Corporal Paul Dubov: "Strings with Wings." "Strings with Wings," a program of music
     for you of the Allied Liberation Forces, presented by the string section of the
     American Band of the A.E.F., featuring Sergeant George Ockner and his violin.
Corporal Paul Dubov: Hello there, folks. Welcome to another program of "Strings with
   Wings." Sergeant Ockner and the boys are back here tonight to give the once over
   lightly, but brightly, to some of your favorite tunes. It's a few songs of yesterday
   and today, fashioned for fiddles, music sweet and slow to help you guys and gals pass
   the evening a little more pleasantly. But I see that Sergeant Ockner and the lads are
   all ready. So what ya say we do something about that first tune. Here's our romance
   special for today, "Sweet and Lovely."
SWEET AND LOVELY
Corporal Paul Dubov: For their next number the boys in the string orchestra bring you
   something that oughta be just the thing for that end-of-the-day feeling. It's a sure
   cure for lagging spirits, the old spiritual "Deep River."
DEEP RIVER
Corporal Paul Dubov: Still time for one more tune. And for their closing number tonight,
   the boys dream one your way in three-four time, the string section of the American Band
   of the A.E.F. playing "Our Waltz."
OUR WALTZ
Corporal Paul Dubov: That's all for now, folks. But we'll be back knocking at your radio
   door next Monday night with another sack-time serenade of tunes old and new, played as
   only violins can play them. So if you get a chance, be sure to give us a listen. Until
   then, this is Corporal Paul Dubov saying, "So long, and good luck to you."
I SUSTAIN THE WINGS (closing theme)
   Corporal Paul Dubov: You've been listening to music by the string section of the
     American Band of the A.E.F., featuring Sergeant George Ockner and his violin. Don't
     forget to join us next Monday evening when we again present another program of
     "Strings with Wings."

17Nov44 (Thu) 8:30-9:00PM Queensbury All-Services Club, London, England   SLO-65370
  MOONLIGHT SERENADE broadcast   Attendance: 2500

Corporal Paul Dubov: ... Band of the A.E.F., originating at the Queensbury All-Services
  Club in London.
MOONLIGHT SERENADE (closing theme)
  Corporal Paul Dubov: This is the music of the Moonlight Serenader, Major Glenn Miller,
    presenting the American Band of the A.E.F. in one-half hour of easy listening.
Sergeant Keith Jameson: This is Sergeant Keith Jameson. I've been detailed to fill in
  the open spaces between tunes in the absence of Major Glenn Miller, away on military
  duty. Arranger Sergeant Jerry Gray is riding pilot on the music. First down the
  runway, hitting on all brass, "7-0-5."
7-0-5
Sergeant Keith Jameson: Corporal Artie Malvin now with a tune that reads like a letter to
  the gal you left behind. A sweet song, "Sweet Lorraine."
SWEET LORRAINE
  Vocal refrain by Corporal Artie Malvin
Sergeant Keith Jameson: The letters keep calling for, the American Band of the A.E.F.
  keeps playing it, "Tuxedo Junction."
TUXEDO JUNCTION
Sergeant Keith Jameson: Now it's medley time, saluting the mothers, wives, sweethearts
  and sisters of the Allied Forces with something old, something new, something borrowed
  and something blue. The old song, fragrant as a breath of heather, "Loch Lomond."
JEANIE WITH THE LIGHT BROWN HAIR (Old tune)
  Sergeant Keith Jameson: Following "Jeanie" a new song in heartbeat tempo, Corporal
    Artie Malvin sings ...
AMOR (New tune)
  Vocal refrain by Corporal Artie Malvin

  ...

BEGIN THE BEGUINE (Borrowed tune)
  Sergeant Keith Jameson: For something blue, "Blue Rain."
BLUE RAIN (Blue tune)
Sergeant Keith Jameson: Sergeant Ray McKinley divides his time and talents on the next
  tune, hitting the first half with his voice and the second half with his drumsticks.
  Here's the old Sarge in a good mood, struttin' "Down the Road a Piece."
(That Place) DOWN THE ROAD A PIECE
  Vocal refrain by Technical Sergeant Ray McKinley
Sergeant Keith Jameson: Ah, mighty fancy, Sergeant Mac. And now set up at the other end
  of the alley, waiting to be bowled over by the American Band of the A.E.F. is a Sergeant
  Jerry Gray arrangement. Here lighting up the hall with some bright and shiny brass is
  "Great Day."
GREAT DAY

  ...

18Nov44 (Sat) 3:01-3:30PM Co-Partners Hall, Bedford, England   SLO-65292
  THE SWING SHIFT broadcast   Script

Announcer: This is a feature of the American Band of the A.E.F.
Corporal Paul Dubov: Presenting "The Swing Shift," featuring Sergeant Ray McKinley and
  his music.
SONG AND DANCE (opening theme)
  Vocal refrain by Technical Sergeant Ray McKinley
Corporal Paul Dubov: Well, what say, Mac?
T/Sgt. Ray McKinley: Quite a bit, Paul, quite a bit.
Corporal Paul Dubov: Well, that's an original retort. The usual answer is "Nothin'
  much."
T/Sgt. Ray McKinley: The usual has no place in my colorful life.
Corporal Paul Dubov: Ha!
T/Sgt. Ray McKinley: (Imitating W. C. Fields) Ah, yes. It all began in a little ranch
  house on the flat lands of Texas. There was Jim, Slim, Slam, "Wham, Re-Bop-Boom-Bam" --
  - lemme see, where was I? Ah, yes, a little house, small place, 'bout eight thousand
  acres. Well, one day ...
Corporal Paul Dubov: Oh, Ray! There's a man outside from the A.E.F. network.
T/Sgt. Ray McKinley: Out of my hair, funny man. I go on.
Corporal Paul Dubov: Yeah, yeah. What about some music?
T/Sgt. Ray McKinley: I'm getting there, maggot. There's always a little guy stuck way
  back in the last ship of the bomber formations and he rarely makes headlines.
Corporal Paul Dubov: So?
T/Sgt. Ray McKinley: So that's where the music comes in 'cause we're takin' off with a
  salute to a number one, gun-totin' rough-rider, ol' "Tail End Charlie." Hold on now,
  one, two.
TAIL END CHARLIE
Corporal Paul Dubov: A songwriter's lot at best is not a happy one, particularly when
  he's forced to compete with standards like this next one. You just can't do much better
  than Gershwin, and here's the proof, "Lady Be Good!"
OH, LADY BE GOOD!
Corporal Paul Dubov: Corporal Artie Malvin, the advance man for a famine, hasn't left the
  studio since last Thursday. From the glass-eyed stare he's wearing, there must be quite
  a story to tell, something about a gal that's crazy for him 'cause "She's Funny That
  Way." Spill it, sad eyes.
(I Got a Woman Crazy for Me) SHE'S FUNNY THAT WAY
  Vocal refrain by Corporal Artie Malvin
Corporal Paul Dubov: Very touching, Art. And while you're drying your eyes, I want to
  check on a rumor. It seems that Sergeant Mastren, our git-box quonker, claims fame as
  an arranger. We'll be happy if this next work keeps him silent for two minutes. Here
  goes with Carmen's "Spanish Shawl."
SPANISH SHAWL
Corporal Paul Dubov: "The Swing Shifters" never bothered giving the next arrangement a
  name. They just dig down to the back of the library and come up with "7-0-5." What's
  in a name anyway.
7-0-5
Corporal Paul Dubov: Our good-will spot follows. Sort of lowers the blood pressure after
  all that heat. Corporal Artie Malvin, everyman's Mr. Anthony, warns all listeners that
  "It Could Happen to You."
IT COULD HAPPEN TO YOU
  Vocal refrain by Corporal Artie Malvin
Corporal Paul Dubov: Just what this tune is supposed to signify escapes me. We know the
  title, "The Big Ones Are Eatin' the Little Ones," and it's weird, I tell you, weird!
THE BIG ONES ARE EATIN' THE LITTLE ONES
Corporal Paul Dubov: There's a half hour that seemed like thirty seconds to us. However,
  we've got to go for now. Remember that we'll be back at 1930 hours on Thursday with a
  special Thanksgiving show, featuring Sergeant Ray McKinley and his music. This is
  Corporal Paul Dubov saying so long and turning you over to Sergeant Mac.

SONG AND DANCE (closing theme)
  Vocal refrain by Technical Sergeant Ray McKinley
Corporal Paul Dubov: See you Thursday at 1930 hours. "The Swing Shift" is a presentation
  of the American BAnd of the A.E.F.

20Nov44 (Mon) EMI studio, St. John's Wood, Abbey Road, London, England
 OWI RECORDING SESSION for ABSIE Network
 Program 4 aired 29Nov44; Program 5 aired 06Dec44

CTPX-12792-1 **MOONLIGHT SERENADE (opening theme)/CARIBBEAN CLIPPER**   Program 4, Record 1

  Ilse Weinberger: Deutsche Soldaten, hier spricht Ilse. Ich freue mich Ihnen heute
    wieder einen musikalischen Genuss bereiten zu können. Ich bringe Ihnen das
    Amerikanische Orchester der Alliierten Expeditionsstreitkräfte, unter der Leitung von
    Major Glenn Miller. Zweiundfünfzig stramme amerikanische Jungens spielen wie immer am
    Anfang und am Ende ihrer Konzerte Glenn Miller's Sendezeichenmusik.
  MOONLIGHT SERENADE (opening theme)
    Ilse Weinberger: Major Glenn Miller begrüsst Sie mit dieser romantischen Serenade.
      Sein Tackstock wirkt wie ein Zauberstab, denn seine Musik macht auch die trübsten
      Stunden unbeschwert und froh. Die ganze Woche habe ich mich auf diese halbe Stunde
      gefreut, auf mein Rendezvous mit Major Glenn Miller und seinem Orchester. Doch hier
      ist der Meister selbst, Major Glenn Miller.
  Major Glenn Miller: Danke schön, Ilse, and hello to everybody. We're gonna get off
    right away with a high powered tune called "Caribbean Clipper."
  Ilse Weinberger: Major Miller bringt Ihnen als erstes eine besondere beschwingte
    amerikanische Nummer, betitelt "Caribbean Clipper."
  CARIBBEAN CLIPPER

Translation:

  Ilse Weinberger: German soldiers, here speaks Ilse. I'm happy that today I can again
    serve you a musical delight. I bring you the American Orchestra of the Allied
    Expeditionary Forces under the direction of Major Glenn Miller. 52 sharp-looking
    American boys playing, like always, at the beginning and end of their concerts Glenn
    Miller's theme song.
  MOONLIGHT SERENADE (opening theme)
    Ilse Weinberger: Major Glenn Miller greets you with this romantic serenade. His
      baton works like a magic wand, because his music makes your weary hours light and
      happy. The whole week I have looked forward to this half hour for my rendezvous
      with Major Glenn Miller and his orchestra. Here is the master himself, Major Glenn
      Miller.
  Major Glenn Miller: Thank you very much, Ilse, and hello to everybody. We're gonna get
    off right away with a high powered tune called "Caribbean Clipper."
  Ilse Weinberger: Major Glenn Miller brings you first an extra fast American number
    titled "Caribbean Clipper."
  CARIBBEAN CLIPPER

CTPX-12793-1   (When Your Heart's on Fire) SMOKE GETS IN YOUR EYES   Program 4, Record 2

Ilse Weinberger: Das war wirklich Tempo und Rhythmus Herr Major.
Major Glenn Miller: Glad you liked it, Ilse. And what would you like now?
Ilse Weinberger: Ach, Herr Major, jetzt hätte ich gerne etwas Süsses.
Major Glenn Miller: "Süsses," does it mean sweet?
Ilse Weinberger: Ja, Herr Major, süss heisst sweet.
Major Glenn Miller: Sorry, Ilse, but we haven't any chocolate.
Ilse Weinberger: Aber Herr Major, das will ich ja garnicht. Ihre Musik ist süsser als
    Schokolade, ich wollte etwas zartes, etwas romantisches.
Major Glenn Miller: Oh, you mean romantic. Well, what about "Smoke Gets in Your Eyes?"
Ilse Weinberger: Ja, Herr Major. "Smoke Gets in Your Eyes" ist gerade das richtige für
    meine Stimmung. Das erinnert mich an ein galantes deutsches Sprichwort, "Eine schöne
    Kerze lädt dich ein, sie anzuzünden." Sie hören jetzt "Smoke Gets in Your Eyes" auf
    Deutsch "Rauch Trübt deinen Blick."
(When Your Heart's on Fire) SMOKE GETS IN YOUR EYES
Ilse Weinberger: Herr Major, das war wunderbar, diese Musik kann eine Frau verrückt
    machen.
Major Glenn Miller: Ich weiss noch ein Mittel, eine Frau verrückt zu machen.
Ilse Weinberger: So was für eines?
Major Glenn Miller: Man sperrt eine Frau in ein Zimmer mit hundert neuen Hüten.
Ilse Weinberger: Hüten?
Major Glenn Miller: Und ohne Spiegel, da wird sie verrückt.
(Laughter from the band)
Ilse Weinberger: Und nun benützen wir eine kleine Musikpause, um unseren
    Berichterstatter ans Mikrofon zu bitten.

Translation:

Ilse Weinberger: That was really tempo and rhythm, Major.
Major Glenn Miller: Glad you liked it, Ilse. And what would you like now?
Ilse Weinberger: Oh, Major, now I would like something sweet.
Major Glenn Miller: Sweet, does it mean sweet?
Ilse Weinberger: Yes, Major, sweet means sweet.
Major Glenn Miller: Sorry, Ilse, but we haven't any chocolate.
Ilse Weinberger: But, Major, that's not what I want, your music is sweeter than
    chocolate, I would like something tender, something romantic.
Major Glenn Miller: Oh, you mean romantic. Well, what about "Smoke Gets in Your Eyes?"
Ilse Weinberger: Yes, Major. "Smoke Gets in Your Eyes" is just right for my mood.
    That reminds me of a gallant German saying, "A lovely candle invites you to light it."
    You hear now "Smoke Gets in Your Eyes," in German "Smoke Blurs Your Eyesight."
(When Your Heart's on Fire) SMOKE GETS IN YOUR EYES
Ilse Weinberger: Major, that was wonderful, this music can drive a woman crazy.
Major Glenn Miller: I know another formula to drive a woman crazy.
Ilse Weinberger: So, which one?
Major Glenn Miller: Lock a woman in a room with a hundred new hats.
Ilse Weinberger: Hats?
Major Glenn Miller: And without a mirror, that will drive her crazy.
(Laughter from the band)
Ilse Weinberger: And now we take a little break from the music to ask our reporter to
    the microphone.

CTPX-12794-1 **LITTLE BROWN JUG**   Program 4, Record 3

   Ilse Weinberger: Als nächstes bringt Ihnen Major Glenn Miller und sein Orchester sein
      Arragement des amerikanischen Volkliedes "Little Brown Jug."
   LITTLE BROWN JUG

Translation:

   Ilse Weinberger: Next Major Glenn Miller and his orchestra brings to you his
      arrangement of the American folk song "Little Brown Jug."
   LITTLE BROWN JUG

CTPX-12795-1 **WHERE OR WHEN** (AM-German)   Program 4, Record 4

   Ilse Weinberger: Herr Major, wo ist denn heute Feldwebel Desmond?
   Major Glenn Miller: Sergeant Desmond's unable to be here today but Corporal Malvin is
      over there in the corner puttin' his tonsils through open order drill. He'll sing any
      minute now.
   Ilse Weinberger: Der Herr Major sagte, Feldwebel Desmond ist heute nicht hier, aber
      dort in der Ecke steht sein Singender Gefreiter, der gerade seinen Kehlkopf
      Probeexerzieren lässt. Er wird zleich singen.
   Major Glenn Miller: Corporal Malvin.
   Corporal Artie Malvin: Yes, sir.
   Major Glenn Miller: How 'bout singin' "Wo Oder Wann?"
   Ilse Weinberger: Bravo, Herr Major, Ihr Deutsch wird immer besser. Glenn Millers
      Orchester spielt jetzt "Where or When," "Wo Oder Wann," und Gefreiter Malvin singt das
      Lied auf deutsch.
   Major Glenn Miller: Corporal, sehen Sie besser mehr in die Noten und weniger auf Ilse.
   WHERE OR WHEN
      Vocal refrain by Corporal Artie Malvin (in German)
   Ilse Weinberger: Das war sehr schön, vielen Dank Gefreiter Malvin.

Translation:

   Ilse Weinberger: Major, where is Sergeant Desmond today?
   Major Glenn Miller: Sergeant Desmond's unable to be here today but Corporal Malvin is
      over there in the corner puttin' his tonsils through open order drill. He'll sing any
      minute now.
   Ilse Weinberger: The Major said Sergeant Desmond is not here today, but there in the
      corner stands his singing Corporal, who is just now warming up his tonsils. Soon he
      will sing.
   Major Glenn Miller: Corporal Malvin.
   Corporal Artie Malvin: Yes, sir.
   Major Glenn Miller: How 'bout singin' "Where or When?"
   Ilse Weinberger: Bravo, Major, your German is continually getting better. Glenn
      Miller's orchestra now plays "Where or When," "Where or When," and Corporal Malvin
      sings the song in German.
   Major Glenn Miller: Corporal, you better look more at your music and less at Ilse.
   WHERE OR WHEN
      Vocal refrain by Corporal Artie Malvin (in German)
   Ilse Weinberger: That was very beautiful, many thanks Corporal Malvin

CTPX-12796-1 **COW-COW BOOGIE** (RM)   Program 4, Record 5

> Ilse Weinberger: Und nun ...
> **COW-COW BOOGIE**
>   Ilse Weinberger: ... zurück zu Major Miller's schneidigem Orchester, Feldwebel Ray
>   McKinley tritt jetzt vor das Mikrofon. Was werden Sie singen, Herr Feldwebel?
>   T/Sgt. Ray McKinley: I'm gonna sing the American hit "Cow-Cow Boogie."
>   Ilse Weinberger: Sie hören gesungen von Feldwebel Ray McKinley den Amerikanischen
>   Schlager "Cow-Cow Boogie."
>   Vocal refrain by Technical Sergeant Ray McKinley

Translation:

> Ilse Weinberger: And now ...
> **COW-COW BOOGIE**
>   Ilse Weinberger: ... back to Major Glenn Miller's sharp looking orchestra, Sergeant
>   Ray McKinley now steps up to the microphone. What will you sing, Sergeant?
>   Sergeant Ray McKinley: I'm gonna sing the American hit "Cow-Cow Boogie."
>   Ilse Weinberger: You will hear the American hit "Cow-Cow Boogie" sung by Sergeant Ray
>   McKinley.
>   Vocal refrain by Technical Sergeant Ray McKinley

CTPX-12797-1 **HOLIDAY FOR STRINGS**   Program 4, Record 6

> Ilse Weinberger: Leider geht unser musikalisches Rendezvous schon wieder seinem Ende
> entgegen. Wie wär es mit einer schmissigen Abschiedsnummer, Herr Major?
> Major Glenn Miller: All right, then let's play "Holiday for Strings."
> Ilse Weinberger: Glenn Millers Amerikanisches Orchester der Allierten
> Expeditionsstreitkräfte spielt zum Abschluss "Holiday for Strings."
> **HOLIDAY FOR STRINGS**
> Ilse Weinberger: Jetzt heisst es leider wieder Abschied nehmen, Herr Major, und bis
> nächste Woche Auf Wiederhören.
> Major Glenn Miller: Und ich sage in meinem perfekten Deutsch, "Auf Wiedersehen."

Translation:

> Ilse Weinberger: Sorry to say our musical rendezvous again is coming to an end. How
> about an up tempo closing number, Major?
> Major Glenn Miller: All right, then let's play "Holiday for Strings."
> Ilse Weinberger: Glenn Miller's American Orchestra of the Allied Expeditionary Forces
> plays in closing "Holiday for Strings."
> **HOLIDAY FOR STRINGS**
> Ilse Weinberger: Now it's time to say farewell again, Major, and until next week 'til
> we hear again.
> Major Glenn Miller: And I say in my perfect German, 'til we meet again.

CTPX-12798-1 **MOONLIGHT SERENADE** (opening theme)/**TAIL END CHARLIE**   Program 5, Record 1

Ilse Weinberger: Deutsche Soldaten, hier spricht Ilse. Ich freue mich, dass ich Euch
    heute wieder Major Glenn Miller mit seinem Amerikanischen Orchester der Allierten
    Expeditionsstreitkräfte ankündigen kann. Ich hoffe, dass Euch unser Programm gefallen
    wird, zumal wir Euch später mit einer besonderen Attraktion aufwarten können.
MOONLIGHT SERENADE (opening theme)
Ilse Weinberger: Glenn Miller's romantische Sendezeichenmusik, seine
    "Mondscheinserenade," wird Euch sicherlich schon vertraut klingen. Im Frieden hat
    Glenn Miller sämtliche Tanzbeine Amerikas rebellisch gemacht. Jetzt dient er der
    Armee seines Landes und bringt Millionen allierter Soldaten Musik, Freude, Stimmung
    und Begeisterung. Hier ist er selbst, Major Glenn Miller!
Major Glenn Miller: Guten Tag, Ilse. And hello, everybody. Wie geht es?
Ilse Weinberger: Danke, sehr gut, Herr Major. Sie scheinen ja heute besonders gut
    aufgelegt zu sein. Sicher haben Sie wieder ein schönes Programm für uns vorbereitet.
Major Glenn Miller: Jawohl, and a big surprise, Musik und ein Gast.
Ilse Weinberger: Fein, was bringen Sie zuerst?
Major Glenn Miller: Musik, we're gonna play "Tail End Charlie."
Ilse Weinberger: Glenn Miller spielt "Tail End Charlie."
TAIL END CHARLIE

Translation:

Ilse Weinberger: German soldiers, here speaks Ilse. I am happy that I can again
    present to you today Major Glenn Miller with his American Orchestra of the Allied
    Expeditionary Forces. I hope that you will enjoy our program. Especially because we
    can expect a special attraction for you later.
MOONLIGHT SERENADE (opening theme)
Ilse Weinberger: Glenn Miller's romantic theme song, his "Moonlight Serenade," which
    is certainly already familiar to you. In peacetime Glenn Miller made all dance legs
    of America rebellious. Now he serves the army of his country and brings to millions
    of Allied soldiers music, pleasure, good spirits and inspiration. Here he is
    himself, Major Glenn Miller!
Major Glenn Miller: Hello, Ilse. And hello, everybody. How are you?
Ilse Weinberger: Thank you, very well, Major. You seem to be in especially good humor
    today. Surely you have prepared a nice program for us again?
Major Glenn Miller: Yes indeed, and a big surprise, music and a guest.
Ilse Weinberger: Fine, what are you presenting first?
Major Glenn Miller: Music, we're gonna play "Tail End Charlie."
Ilse Weinberger: Glenn Miller plays "Tail End Charlie."
TAIL END CHARLIE

CTPX-12799-1 **EVERYBODY LOVES MY BABY (But My Baby Don't Love Nobody but Me)**

Program 5, Record 5

Ilse Weinberger: Mit diesem Lied haben Sie sicherlich allen Anwesenden Ihren grossen Tonfilmerfolg "Yankee Doodle Dandy" lebhaft in Erinnerung gebracht. Irene Manning, und es ist eine schöne Erinnerung. Herr Major, was kommt denn jetzt?

Major Glenn Miller: Ilse, the next selection we would like to dedicate to our guest of honor, Irene Manning. It's going to be "Everybody Loves My Baby."

Ilse Weinberger: Das nächste Musikstück, das Glenn Miller und sein Orchester der Allierten Expeditionsstreitkräfte zum Vortrag bringen wird ist unserem heutigen Ehrengast Irene Manning gewidmet. Es ist das populäre amerikanische Schlagerlied "Everybody Loves My Baby," auf deutsch "Jeder Hat Mein Liebchen gern."

EVERYBODY LOVES MY BABY (But My Baby Don't Love Nobody but Me)

Translation:

Ilse Weinberger: With this song you have surely brought back memories to all present here of your great film success "Yankee Doodle Dandy," Irene Manning, and it is a beautiful memory. Major, what comes now?

Major Glenn Miller: Ilse, the next selection we would like to dedicate to our guest of honor, Irene Manning. It's going to be "Everybody Loves My Baby."

Ilse Weinberger: The next musical selection that Glenn Miller and his Orchestra of the Allied Expeditionary Forces presents is dedicated to our guest of honor Irene Manning. It is the popular American hit "Everybody Loves My Baby," in German "Everybody Likes My Sweetheart."

EVERYBODY LOVES MY BABY (But My Baby Don't Love Nobody but Me)

20Nov44 (Mon) 7:15-7:30PM Co-Partners Hall, Bedford, England
  STRINGS WITH WINGS broadcast   Script

Announcer: This is a feature of the American Band of the A.E.F.
I SUSTAIN THE WINGS (opening theme)
  Corporal Paul Dubov: "Strings with Wings." "Strings with Wings," a program of music
    for you of the Allied Liberation Forces, presented by the string section of the
    American Band of the A.E.F., featuring Sergeant George Ockner and his violin.
Corporal Paul Dubov: Hello there, folks. Welcome to another program of "Strings with
  Wings." Twice each week, Monday and Wednesday, we hang out the "Reserved" sign on this
  parcel of air waves. And here we are, ready to use 'em to bring you some more music for
  your end-of-the-day listening. It's soft music, slow music, played on the violins, just
  the kind of tunes we think you folks are lookin' for around this time of an evening. So
  leave that radio dial right where it is and make yourself comfortable while we bring you
  tonight's first tune, as arranged by Sergeant Dave Herman. It's called "Please."
PLEASE
Corporal Paul Dubov: We've been tryin' for the past three programs to get that last
  number in and we finally did it. Sergeant Herman, who must have thought we'd never play
  it, is probably taking bows all over the hospital where he is taking a little rest these
  days. And while he's busy with that, what ya say we bow in with the next number. "What
  Is There to Say."
WHAT IS THERE TO SAY
Corporal Paul Dubov: Now turn back the clock and let's make ourselves cozy with some
  musical memories of a happier season. It's "Memories of You."
MEMORIES OF YOU
Corporal Paul Dubov: This is your program of the Allied Expeditionary Forces network.
  And here's the string section of the American Band of the A.E.F. to continue the program
  with another tune. The boys tell me this has been a real good year for ballads and
  they've picked one of the best of the crop for their next number. "I'll Remember
  April."
I'LL REMEMBER APRIL
Corporal Paul Dubov: Well, folks, that winds up our miniature musicale for tonight.
  There's another program waitin' to take over our lease on this spot of air, so we'll
  remind you to look for us again on Wednesday night, and take off. Until then this is
  Corporal Paul Dubov saying, "So long, and good luck to you."
I SUSTAIN THE WINGS (closing theme)
  Corporal Paul Dubov: You have been listening to a program of music by the string
    section of the American Band of the A.E.F., featuring George Ockner and his violin.
    Don't forget to join us this coming Wednesday night when we again present "Strings
    with Wings."

24Nov44 (Fri) 8:30-9:00PM Queensbury All-Services Club, London, England   SLO-65321
  MOONLIGHT SERENADE broadcast   Script   Attendance: 2500

Corporal Paul Dubov: This is a program produced for the A.E.F.P. by the American Band of
  the A.E.F., originating at the Queensbury All-Services Club in London.
MOONLIGHT SERENADE (opening theme)
  Corporal Paul Dubov: Thirty minutes with the Moonlight Serenader, presenting the
    American Band of the A.E.F., under the direction of Major Glenn Miller, music for and
    by members of the Allied Expeditionary Forces. And here is Major Glenn Miller.
Major Glenn Miller: Thank you, Corporal Paul Dubov, and hello, everybody. A bit of a
  cold has the words comin' straight from the cellar, so we'll give your ear a break and
  keep 'em few and far between. First target on our musical firing-line is Sergeant Jerry
  Gray's "Sun Valley Jump."
SUN VALLEY JUMP
Major Glenn Miller: We call on a lad with a heart-shaped voice, Corporal Art Malvin, for
  a song, and the tune is "Long Ago and Far Away."
LONG AGO (And Far Away)
  Vocal refrain by Corporal Artie Malvin
Major Glenn Miller: Our one-man trio, composer, arranger and pianist Sergeant Mel Powell
  is sole proprietor of the next tune on the show inasmuch as he composed it, arranged it
  and plays it. "Mission to Moscow."
MISSION TO MOSCOW
Major Glenn Miller: And now it's medley time, salutin' the mothers, wives, sweethearts
  and sisters of the Allied Forces with somethin' old, somethin' new, somethin' borrowed
  and somethin' blue. The old song, "Mighty Lak' a Rose."
MIGHTY LAK A ROSE (Old tune)
  Major Glenn Miller: In the new department Corporal Art Malvin gives romance the
    Latin-American treatment singin' ...
AMOR (New tune)
  Vocal refrain by Corporal Artie Malvin
  Major Glenn Miller: From the back of our own book we borrow a tune that's been mighty
    nice to us, all aboard the "Chattanooga Choo Choo."
CHATTANOOGA CHOO CHOO (Borrowed tune)
  Vocal refrain by Technical Sergeant Ray McKinley and the Crew Chiefs
  Major Glenn Miller: Into the blue spotlight moves a melody shaded in whisperin' jazz,
    "Bye Bye Blues."
BYE BYE BLUES (Blue tune)
Major Glenn Miller: Answerin' a long string of letters requestin' it, here comes "String
  of Pearls."
A STRING OF PEARLS
Major Glenn Miller: Once again it's a great pleasure to announce that big-league arranger
  Sergeant Jerry Gray has socked himself another musical home-run. And this time the
  Sarge has poured his talents into a big, all-out arrangement of the tune that identifies
  the A.E.F.P. between each program. "Oranges and Lemons."
ORANGES AND LEMONS
  Vocal refrain by Corporal Artie Malvin and the Crew Chiefs
Major Glenn Miller: This is Major Glenn Miller remindin' you that playin' your kind of
  music is our kind of pleasure. Keep an eye on the newspapers and an ear on the radio.
  Hope to have you back for more real soon. Until then it's good luck and good bye.
MOONLIGHT SERENADE (closing theme)
  Corporal Paul Dubov: You have heard thirty minutes with the Moonlight Serenader,
    presenting the American Band of the A.E.F. under the direction of Major Glenn Miller,
    music for and by members of the Allied Expeditionary Forces.

25Nov44 (Sat) 5:15-5:45PM Co-Partners Hall, Bedford, England   SLO-65810
  STRINGS WITH WINGS recording   Script   Aired 01Jan45

Announcer: This is a feature of the American Band of the A.E.F.
I SUSTAIN THE WINGS (opening theme)
  Corporal Paul Dubov: "Strings with Wings." "Strings with Wings," a program of music
    for you of the Allied Liberation Forces, presented by the string section of the
    American Band of the A.E.F., featuring Sergeant George Ockner and his violin.
Corporal Paul Dubov: Hello there, folks. You know, it's usually quite a shuffle here
    every Monday and Wednesday nights before the broadcast. Some of the boys like to
    practice and tune their violins right up to the last second before we go on the air.
    Others are grabbing a last cigarette. And still others are just wandering around the
    studio, looking lost. But tonight we used whips. And at this moment they're all in
    their proper places, ready to play. So while we've got 'em there, let's get on with the
    first tune and open our little sack time serenade tonight with "My Heart Stood Still."
MY HEART STOOD STILL
Corporal Paul Dubov: There was a time when we thought we'd have to put this next tune
    away in the moth balls for a good long time. But the way things are going these days,
    it looks as though it's due to make a fast come-back. An old tune with a new meaning,
    "April in Paris."
APRIL IN PARIS
Corporal Paul Dubov: Every once in a while a song comes along that seems to say just what
    everybody's thinking at the moment. And here's one that fits that description to a "T."
    It's a perfect carbon copy of what a whole lot of folks today have got on their minds.
    "I'll See You Again."
I'LL SEE YOU AGAIN
Corporal Paul Dubov: You're listening to a program of the Allied Expeditionary Forces
    network. And here's the string section of the American Band of the A.E.F. to carry on
    with the next number. "September Song."
SEPTEMBER SONG
Corporal Paul Dubov: Well, folks, while we've been tossin' off the tunes for you tonight,
    the old clock on the wall's been tickin' off the minutes. And here it is time to go.
    But don't forget, we're back here every Monday and Wednesday evenings. So remember to
    catch us the next time 'round. Until then, this is Corporal Paul Dubov saying, "So
    long, and good luck to you."
I SUSTAIN THE WINGS (closing theme)

25Nov44 (Sat) 5:45-6:15PM Co-Partners Hall, Bedford, England   SLO-65811
  STRINGS WITH WINGS recording   Aired 03Jan45

Announcer: This is an A.E.F.P. production, a feature of the American Band of the A.E.F.
I SUSTAIN THE WINGS (opening theme)
  Corporal Paul Dubov: "Strings with Wings." "Strings with Wings," a program of music
    for you of the Allied Liberation Forces, presented by the string section of the
    American Band of the A.E.F., featuring Sergeant George Ockner and his violin.
  Corporal Paul Dubov: Hello there, folks. Welcome to another program of "Strings with
    Wings." Radio, you know, is a sort of funny thing. You get up here in front of the
    microphone, play some tunes and never know whether there's anybody listening or not.
    But we kind of figure there must be because the kind of music we put out is just what we
    think you guys and gals like around this time of an evening. It's violin music played
    soft and slow. And whether you're out there or not, here we go, the first tune, "Spring
    Will Be a Little Late This Year."
SPRING WILL BE A LITTLE LATE THIS YEAR
Corporal Paul Dubov: There's hardly a one of us here who doesn't carry around with him a
    picture of the girl he left behind. But if you don't happen to have one, here's a
    musical shnapshot (sic) that might fill the bill, "Jeanie with the Light Brown Hair."
JEANIE WITH THE LIGHT BROWN HAIR
Corporal Paul Dubov: If you folks are still out there listening at the other end of this
    A.E.F. network, we'll keep the music moving with tune number three. Here it is, that
    old bittersweet ballad "Lover, Come Back to Me!"
LOVER, COME BACK TO ME!
Corporal Paul Dubov: Love seems to be getting a big play in the program tonight. It's
    amor and still more amor as the boys in the string orchestra play "I'm in the Mood for
    Love."
I'M IN THE MOOD FOR LOVE
Corporal Paul Dubov: Well, folks, it's time to give the boys in the orchestra "at ease"
    and say, "That's all for tonight." We hope you folks out there have enjoyed these
    violin versions of your old favorites and we're counting on you being out there
    listening every Monday and Wednesday night for more of the same. Meanwhile this is
    Corporal Paul Dubov passing along the best wishes of the boys and saying, "So long, and
    good luck to you."
I SUSTAIN THE WINGS (closing theme)

25Nov44 (Sat) 6:15-6:30PM Co-Partners Hall, Bedford, England
THE UPTOWN HALL broadcast   Script

Announcer: This is a feature of the American Band of the A.E.F.
MY GUY'S COME BACK (opening theme)
   Corporal Paul Dubov: Good evening, all, it's "The Uptown Hall." Music for you of the
      Allied Liberation Forces, presented by members of the American Band of the A.E.F.,
      featuring Sergeant Mel Powell at the piano.
Corporal Paul Dubov: Welcome to "The Uptown Hall," fellow members. And you folks over
   there by the door, move in and find yourself a nice comfortable seat. It's open house
   here in the Hall every Wednesday, Thursday and Saturday evening. And all you music
   lovers have a standing invitation. There's no charge, no tipping, no buckin' the line.
   Everything is free and easy. And just to show you what we mean, here's Mel and the lads
   giving the free and easy treatment to one of your old swing favorites, "Emaline."
EMALINE

   ...

Corporal Paul Dubov: From time to time, here in the Hall, we introduce some of your old
   swing sweethearts. There's been "Louise" and "Sweet Sue" and tonight we're saying,
   "Pleased t' meetcha," to another one of our musical gal friends, "Charmaine."
CHARMAINE
Corporal Paul Dubov: Now the folks start collecting their hats and coats, pushing back
   the chairs and headin' for the door. We've just brought down the gavel on another
   meeting here in "Uptown Hall." But we're keepin' that gavel handy 'cause there'll be
   another session of soft but solid music on these premises next Wednesday night. Don't
   miss it! Until then, this is Downtown Paul of "The Uptown Hall" saying, "So long, and
   good luck to you."
MY GUY'S COME BACK (closing theme)
   Corporal Paul Dubov: You've been listening to music by members of the American Band of
      the A.E.F. Don't forget to join us next Wednesday evening for another Allied
      Expeditionary Forces program from "The Uptown Hall."

25Nov44 (Sat) 9:00-10:00PM Co-Partners Hall, Bedford, England   SLO-65813
MOONLIGHT SERENADE recording   Script   Aired 22Dec44

Announcer: This is a program produced for the A.E.F.P. by the American Band of the A.E.F.
MOONLIGHT SERENADE (opening theme)
  Corporal Paul Dubov: Thirty minutes with the Moonlight Serenader, music by the American
    Band of the A.E.F. under the direction of Major Glenn Miller. Music for and by
    members of the Allied Expeditionary Forces. And here is Major Glenn Miller.
Major Glenn Miller: Thank you, Corporal Paul Dubov, and hello, everybody. We're here
  again to try to cover all the musical bases in thirty minutes. That means there isn't
  much room for talk. So first, for those who like their music sprinkled with hot-sauce,
  here's a real ear-scorcher, "I Hear You Screamin'"
I HEAR YOU SCREAMIN'
Corporal Paul Dubov: Time now for Sergeant Johnny Desmond to throw another log on the
  heart fires and the Sarge lets his voice go a'strollin' through "Spring Will Be a Little
  Late This Year."
SPRING WILL BE A LITTLE LATE THIS YEAR
  Vocal refrain by Sergeant Johnny Desmond
Major Glenn Miller: The Crew Chiefs become the "Chew" Chiefs just long enough to unload
  the lyrics of Corporal Murray Kane's canteen cantata "Have Ya Got Any Gum, Chum?"
HAVE YA GOT ANY GUM, CHUM?
  Vocal refrain by the Crew Chiefs
Major Glenn Miller: It's medley time for the American Band of the A.E.F., salutin' the
  mothers, wives, sweethearts and sisters of the Allied Forces with somethin' old,
  somethin' new, somethin' borrowed and somethin' blue. The old song, "Caprice Viennois."
CAPRICE VIENNOIS (Old tune)
  Major Glenn Miller: For somethin' new, somethin' in heartbeat tempo. Sergeant Johnny
    Desmond sings ...
I'LL WALK ALONE (New tune)
  Vocal refrain by Sergeant Johnny Desmond
  Major Glenn Miller: From Phil Spitalny we borrow "Isle of Golden Dreams."
MY ISLE OF GOLDEN DREAMS (Borrowed tune)
  Major Glenn Miller: For somethin' blue, the "Birth of the Blues."
BIRTH OF THE BLUES (Blue tune)
Major Glenn Miller: The American band of the A.E.F. presents a few chips off the old
  block, Sergeants Powell, McKinley, Alpert and Hucko, gathered 'round a tune that would
  have been better off untitled, "E.T.O. What a Horrible Morning Blues."
E.T.O. WHAT A HORRIBLE MORNING BLUES
  (quartet: Hucko, Powell, Alpert, McKinley)
Major Glenn Miller: And now that we've had a shot of Hot Club informality, we go
  legitimate again with the American Band of the A.E.F.'s big Sunday-go-to-meetin' tune.
  Sergeant Jerry Gray's arrangement of "Holiday for Strings."
HOLIDAY FOR STRINGS
Major Glenn Miller: This is Major Glenn Miller remindin' you that we'll be back right
  soon with some more music by the American Band of the A.E.F. Keep an eye on the
  newspapers and an ear on the radio and you'll know exactly when and where. Hope to have
  you with us for our next show. Until then, it's good luck and good bye.
MOONLIGHT SERENADE (closing theme)

25Nov44 (Sat) 11:00PM-Midnight   Co-Partners Hall, Bedford, England   SLO-65911
** MOONLIGHT SERENADE** recording   Script   Edited and aired 02Jan45

Announcer: This is a program produced for the A.E.F.P. by the American Band of the A.E.F.
MOONLIGHT SERENADE (opening theme)
    Corporal Paul Dubov: Thirty minutes with the Moonlight Serenader, music by the American
      Band of the A.E.F. under the direction of Major Glenn Miller. Music for and by
      members of the Allied Expeditionary Forces. And here is Major Glenn Miller.
Major Glenn Miller: Thank you, Corporal Paul Dubov, and hello, everybody. We're here
    again to see what we can do about making the next thirty minutes a listening pleasure
    for you Tommies and Yanks and Johnny Canucks. And our first shot at that target is a
    smile-a-minute arrangement hot off the mind of Sergeant Jerry Gray, "Get Happy."
GET HAPPY
Major Glenn Miller: The big heart-throb man around the American Band of the A.E.F. is a
    lad named Sergeant Johnny Desmond. And right now John is on singin' "I'll Be Seeing
    You."
I'LL BE SEEING YOU
    Vocal refrain by Sergeant Johnny Desmond
Major Glenn Miller: Now a tune for the gallant guys who are fightin' the good fight all
    over the embattled oceans, a salute to the salt-water toughies of the U.S. Navy,
    "Anchors Aweigh."
ANCHORS AWEIGH
Major Glenn Miller: And now we turn to medley time, saluting the mothers, wives,
    sweethearts and sisters of the Allied Forces with somethin' old, something new,
    somethin' borrowed and somethin' blue. Our old, old song, "Long, Long Ago."
LONG, LONG AGO (Old tune)
    Major Glenn Miller: Squirin' our new song is Sergeant Johnny Desmond singin' "The Music
      Stopped."
THE MUSIC STOPPED (New tune)
    Vocal refrain by Sergeant Johnny Desmond
    Major Glenn Miller: From friend and Army team-mate Lieutenant Larry Clinton we borrow
      "The Dipsy Doodle."
THE DIPSY DOODLE (Borrowed tune)
    Major Glenn Miller: And holdin' down the blue spot, good old "Blues in My Heart."
BLUES IN MY HEART (Blue tune)
Major Glenn Miller: Sergeant Ray McKinley and the Crew Chiefs swing along with that old
    army spirit, singin' their way around the words that decorate the music of "G.I. Jive."
G.I. JIVE
    Vocal refrain by Technical Sergeant Ray McKinley and the Crew Chiefs
Major Glenn Miller: And now we'd like to give you a sample of the kind of music you'll
    find kicking around the day room at the quarters of the American Band of the A.E.F. when
    the boys get together for some after-work fun. Sergeants Powell, McKinley, Hucko and
    Alpert play you some home-cookin' jazz they call "Jerry's Aachen Back."
JERRY'S AACHEN BACK (quartet: Hucko, Powell, Alpert, McKinley)
Major Glenn Miller: Now, for the anchor-tune of our show, an all-out salute to the
    magnificent Red Army that has the Eastern Front Jerries singin' the blues. To our
    fightin' Russian Allies we pay tribute with the "Song of the Volga Boatmen."
SONG OF THE VOLGA BOATMEN
Major Glenn Miller: Now, this is Major Glenn Miller hangin' out the latchstring to the
    American Band of the A.E.F. During the next few days we'll be sprinkled around the air
    lanes with programs by Sergeants Ray McKinley, Mel Powell and George Ockner and, of
    course, we'll be back with more music by the big band. If you'd care for another
    basin-full of the same, help yourself. For now, it's good luck and good night.
MOONLIGHT SERENADE (closing theme)

The preceding program was aired after Major Glenn Miller's disappearance was announced.
To "salvage" the program, Glenn Miller's announcements were edited out of the recording
and announcements by Sgt. Keith Jameson were substituted. The program was aired as
follows.

BBC announcer: We'll now hear a recording of the American Band of the A.E.F., under the direction of Major Glenn Miller, made especially for the A.E.F. program before the band went to France.

Sergeant Keith Jameson: This is a program produced for the A.E.F.P. by the American Band of the A.E.F.

MOONLIGHT SERENADE (opening theme)

Sergeant Keith Jameson: Hi, gang. This is Sergeant Keith Jameson making with the words for the American Band of the A.E.F. We're here again to see what we can do about making the next thirty minutes a listening pleasure for you Tommies and Yanks and Johnny Canucks. And our first shot at that target is a smile-a-minute arrangement hot off the mind of Sergeant Jerry Gray, "Get Happy."

GET HAPPY

[Sergeant Keith Jameson: The big heart-throb man around the American Band of the A.E.F. is a lad named Sergeant Johnny Desmond. And right now John is on singin' "I'll Be Seeing You."

I'LL BE SEEING YOU

Vocal refrain by Sergeant Johnny Desmond

Sergeant Keith Jameson: Now a tune for the gallant guys who are fightin' the good fight all over the embattled oceans,] a salute to the salt-water toughies of the U.S. Navy, "Anchors Aweigh."

ANCHORS AWEIGH

Sergeant Keith Jameson: And now we turn to medley time, saluting the mothers, wives, sweethearts and sisters of the Allied Forces with somethin' old, something new, somethin' borrowed and somethin' blue. [Our old, old song, "Long, Long Ago."

LONG, LONG AGO (Old tune)

Sergeant Keith Jameson: Squirin' our new song is Sergeant Johnny Desmond singin' "The Music Stopped."

THE MUSIC STOPPED (New tune)

Vocal refrain by Sergeant Johnny Desmond

Sergeant Keith Jameson: From friend and Army team-mate Lieutenant Larry Clinton we borrow "The Dipsy Doodle."

THE DIPSY DOODLE (Borrowed tune)

Sergeant Keith Jameson: And holdin' down the blue spot, good old "Blues in My Heart."

BLUES IN MY HEART (Blue tune)

Sergeant Keith Jameson: Sergeant Ray McKinley and the Crew Chiefs swing along with that old army spirit, singin' their way around the words that decorate the music of] "G.I. Jive."

G.I. JIVE

Vocal refrain by Technical Sergeant Ray McKinley and the Crew Chiefs

Sergeant Keith Jameson: And now we'd like to give you a sample of the kind of music you'll find kicking around the day room of the quarters of the American Band of the A.E.F. when the boys get together for some after-work fun. Sergeants Powell, McKinley, Hucko and Alpert play you some home-cookin' jazz they call "Jerry's Aachen Back."

JERRY'S AACHEN BACK (quartet: Hucko, Powell, Alpert, McKinley)

Sergeant Keith Jameson: And now, for the anchor-tune of our show, an all-out salute to the magnificent Red Army that has the Eastern Front Jerries singin' the blues. To our fightin' Russian Allies we pay tribute with the "Song of the Volga Boatmen."

SONG OF THE VOLGA BOATMEN

Sergeant Keith Jameson: And now, this is Sergeant Keith Jameson hangin' up the latchstring to the American Band of the A.E.F. During the next few days we'll be sprinkled around the air lanes with programs by Sergeants Ray McKinley, Mel Powell and George Ockner and, of course, we'll be back with more music by the big band. If you'd care for another basin-full of the same, just help yourself. For now, it's so long and all the best, gang.

MOONLIGHT SERENADE (closing theme)

26Nov44 (Sun) 3:50-4:10PM Co-Partners Hall, Bedford, England   SLO-65815
  SONGS BY SGT. JOHNNY DESMOND recording   Script   Aired 18Dec44

Corporal Paul Dubov: This is a program produced for the A.E.F.P. by the American Band of
   the A.E.F.
TIME ON MY HANDS (opening theme)
   Corporal Paul Dubov: "Songs by Sergeant Johnny Desmond."
   Vocal refrain by Sergeant Johnny Desmond
   Corporal Paul Dubov: Three songs by a three-striper, with music by the American Band of
   the A.E.F.
Sergeant Johnny Desmond: Hello there. This is Sergeant Johnny Desmond. There's nothin'
   I can say that forty musicians can't make sound better. So I'll just get to singin'
   with a tune that recently did about three months flagpole sittin' way up on top of the
   Hit Parade."
I'LL WALK ALONE
   Vocal refrain by Sergeant Johnny Desmond
Sergeant Johnny Desmond: And now here's a tune that's mighty soothin' to tired tonsils.
   The lyric is simple as a nursery rhyme, the music's as sweet as the frostin' on one of
   mom's cakes. If you'd like to cut yourself a piece, why sing right along, here's the
   song.

   . . .

Sergeant Johnny Desmond: Sergeant Norman Leyden is the lad who swings the big stick over
   the American Band of the A.E.F. for this show. And now I'm gonna step aside to make
   room for Sergeant Norm while he directs some slow-movin' musical traffic over the smooth
   melodic road marked "Blue Is the Night."
BLUE IS THE NIGHT
Sergeant Johnny Desmond: Mighty fancy, Norm. And 'long about here I'd like to jump back
   on the bandwagon 'n' give my voice a free ride along with a song for the gals we left
   behind. It goes like this.
I'LL BE SEEING YOU
   Vocal refrain by Sergeant Johnny Desmond
Sergeant Johnny Desmond: This is Sergeant Johnny Desmond sayin' thanks for the loan of
   the hall and hopin' we meet again next time I hit the air with ...
Corporal Paul Dubov: ... three songs by a three-striper, "Songs by Sergeant Johnny
   Desmond," a program of the American Band of the A.E.F.
TIME ON MY HANDS (closing theme)
   Vocal refrain by Sergeant Johnny Desmond

26Nov44 (Sun) 4:10-4:25PM Co-Partners Hall, Bedford, England   SLO-65816
SONGS BY SGT. JOHNNY DESMOND recording   Edited but not used

The dialogue on this recording was edited out and new dialogue, recorded at a later date
(probably during the 23-31Dec44 period; see under c.23-31Dec44), was substituted,
apparently in an attempt to "convert" the program from a "Songs by Sgt. Johnny Desmond"
program to a "A Soldier and a Song" program. The six announcements shown below were the
ones recorded at the later date.

   ...

TIME ALONE WILL TELL (opening theme)
   Vocal refrain by Sergeant Johnny Desmond
   Corporal Paul Dubov: Presenting "A Soldier and a Song," the voice of Sergeant Johnny
      Desmond, vocalist with the American Band of the A.E.F., and the songs old and new.
Corporal Paul Dubov: From the hit musical "Oklahoma," Sergeant Johnny Desmond takes his
   first song, "Oh, What a Beautiful Mornin'."
OH, WHAT A BEAUTIFUL MORNIN'
   Vocal refrain by Sergeant Johnny Desmond
Corporal Paul Dubov: The mail we get from you guys here in the E.T.O. ...
LONG AGO (And Far Away)
   Corporal Paul Dubov: ... makes this next song one of our most requested, Jerome Kern's
      "Long Ago and Far Away."
   Vocal refrain by Sergeant Johnny Desmond
Corporal Paul Dubov: So now we give the vocal department a rest and call upon the
   orchestra who return our call with "Enlisted Men's Mess."
ENLISTED MEN'S MESS
Corporal Paul Dubov: Now our Sergeant Johnny Desmond returns to close this week's show
   with "I Only Have Eyes for You."
I ONLY HAVE EYES FOR YOU
   Vocal refrain by Sergeant Johnny Desmond
Corporal Paul Dubov: "A Soldier and a Song" has presented the voice of Sergeant Johnny
   Desmond, vocalist with the American Band of the A.E.F. We'll be back again soon, so for
   now, good bye and good luck.
TIME ALONE WILL TELL (closing theme)
   Vocal refrain by Sergeant Johnny Desmond

26Nov44 (Sun) 4:25-4:40PM Co-Partners Hall, Bedford, England   SLO-65914
  SONGS BY SGT. JOHNNY DESMOND recording   Script   Aired 08Jan45

Corporal Paul Dubov: This is a program produced for the A.E.F.P. by the American Band of
  the A.E.F.
TIME ALONE WILL TELL (opening theme)
  Corporal Paul Dubov: "Songs by Sergeant Johnny Desmond."
  Vocal refrain Sergeant Johnny Desmond
  Corporal Paul Dubov: Three songs by a three-striper, with music by the American Band of
    the A.E.F.
Sergeant Johnny Desmond: Hello there. This is Sergeant Johnny Desmond. There's music to
  do, so let's get with it. First an old thought warmly wrapped in a new song. The
  thought is "love stuff," the song, "It Could Happen to You."
IT COULD HAPPEN TO YOU
  Vocal refrain by Sergeant Johnny Desmond
Sergeant Johnny Desmond: Now for a tune on a three-day pass. Of course, it's easier to
  get the tune than it is the pass, but it's a pretty piece o' music anyway. "Fellow on a
  Furlough."
A FELLOW ON A FURLOUGH
  Vocal refrain by Sergeant Johnny Desmond
Sergeant Johnny Desmond: Sergeant Norm Leyden, directin' the American Band of the A.E.F.
  through a few of its prettier paces, now gives us a mild 'n' mellow tune in a
  once-over-politely arrangement of "All the Things You Are."
ALL THE THINGS YOU ARE

  ...

26Nov44 (Sun) 4:40-5:00PM Co-Partners Hall, Bedford, England   SLO-65915
SONGS BY SGT. JOHNNY DESMOND recording   Script   Aired 15Jan45

Corporal Paul Dubov: This is a program produced for the A.E.F.P. by the American Band of the A.E.F.

TIME ON MY HANDS (opening theme)
    Corporal Paul Dubov: "Songs by Sergeant Johnny Desmond."
    Vocal refrain by Sergeant Johnny Desmond
    Corporal Paul Dubov: Four songs by a three-striper, with music by the American Band of the A.E.F.

Sergeant Johnny Desmond: Hello there. This is Sergeant Johnny Desmond. First thing to do, I suppose, is to warm up the voice and the hall and there's no better way to do that musically than to reach for a Latin-American tune. Here's a beauty, "Amor, Amor."

AMOR
    Vocal refrain by Sergeant Johnny Desmond

Sergeant Johnny Desmond: When you sit down to write a letter to the gal back home, it would be mighty nice to have one of those boys who write the lyrics to love-songs around to help you get your thoughts on paper. Here, just listen to what those lads can do with a simple thought about romance, the kind of thought every one of us must have had at some time or other. Norm, set up the music 'n' I'll rattle off the words.

NOW I KNOW
    Vocal refrain by Sergeant Johnny Desmond

Sergeant Johnny Desmond: There's nothin' like a real warm, comfortable arrangement to make a singer feel right at home and do his best. And Sergeant Norm Leyden sure put me in the musical easy-chair with his easy-to-sing score for this next tune. "The Music Stopped."

THE MUSIC STOPPED
    Vocal refrain by Sergeant Johnny Desmond

Sergeant Johnny Desmond: These days, with a lot of song-writers in uniform, we find the supply of new things runnin' rather low. However, sometimes it's a big kick retracin' a few musical footsteps and makin' a new tune out of an old one. So here, in it's well-deserved second childhood, is an oldie that's a goodie, "I Only Have Eyes for You."

I ONLY HAVE EYES FOR YOU
    Vocal refrain by Sergeant Johnny Desmond

Sergeant Johnny Desmond: This is Sergeant Johnny Desmond 'n' in just a moment we'll be latchin' along but not before I say thanks for listenin' 'n' join us the next time it's handy thing to do for ...

Corporal Paul Dubov: ... more songs by a three-striper, "Songs by Sergeant Johnny Desmond," with music by the American Band of the A.E.F.

TIME ON MY HANDS (closing theme)
    Vocal refrain by Sergeant Johnny Desmond

27Nov44 (Mon) EMI studio, St. John's Wood, Abbey Road, London, England
  OWI RECORDING SESSION for ABSIE Network
  Program 6 aired 13Dec44; Program 7 was scheduled to air 20Dec44

CTPX-12806-1 **MOONLIGHT SERENADE (opening theme)/JEEP JOCKEY JUMP**   Program 6, Record 1

  Ilse Weinberger: Deutsche Soldaten, hier spricht Ilse, die Ansagerin, die allwöchentlich
    um diese Zeit ein Rendezvous mit zweiundfünfzig Soldaten hat. Das ist kein Geheimnis,
    handelt es sich doch um das musikalische Rendezvous mit den schneidigen Musikern des
    Orchesters der Alliierten Expeditionsstreitkräfte und ihren berühmten Dirigenten Major
    Glenn Miller.
  MOONLIGHT SERENADE (opening theme)
    Ilse Weinberger: Diese bezaubernde Melodie ist die wohlbekannte "Mondscheinserenade,"
      Glenn Miller's Sendezeichenmusik. Sie eröffnet auch diesmal wieder ein Konzert
      beschwingter amerikanischer Musik, das Glenn Miller und seine fleissigen Musiker nun
      zum Besten geben werden. Doch hier ist der Meister selbst, Major Glenn Miller.
  Major Glenn Miller: Danke, Ilse. Here we are again, wir sind schon wieder da. What do
    you say to my progress in the German language, Ilse?
  Ilse Weinberger: Ihre Fortschritte in der deutschen Sprache sind ausgezeichnet. Aber
    Herr Major ich habe Sie ein bisschen in Verdacht, dass Sie Privatstunden nehmen.
  Major Glenn Miller: Nein, aber in der Armee lernt man alles.
  Ilse Weinberger: Schade, dass ich kein Soldat bin.
  Major Glenn Miller: Warum?
  Ilse Weinberger: Oh, ich würde gerne fliegen lernen und auch autofahren.
  Major Glenn Miller: Autofahren? How would you like to have me as your teacher?
  Ilse Weinberger: Das wäre ja grossartig.
  Major Glenn Miller: Well then, let's get goin' and with music, for our first tune,
    "Jeep Jockey Jump."
  Ilse Weinberger: Das ist ein guter Anfang. Glenn Miller und sein Orchester bringen als
    erstes einen typisch amerikanischen Schlager, "Jeep Jockey Jump." Ein "Jeep" ist das
    kleine amerikanische Soldatenauto, was ein "Jockey" ist, wissen wohl alle, und "Jump"
    heisst so viel wie Sprung; also, "Jeep Jockey Jump."
  JEEP JOCKEY JUMP

Translation:

Ilse Weinberger: German soldiers, this is Ilse speaking, the announcer who weekly at this time has a rendezvous with 52 soldiers. That is no secret, it concerns the musical rendezvous with those good looking musicians of the Orchestra of the Allied Expeditionary Forces and their famous director Glenn Miller.

MOONLIGHT SERENADE (opening theme)

Ilse Weinberger: This bewitching melody is the well known "Moonlight Serenade," Glenn Miller's theme song. At this time it again opens a concert of lively American music, that of Glenn Miller and his busy musicians now present. Here is the master himself, Major Glenn Miller.

Major Glenn Miller: Thanks, Ilse. Here we are again, we are here again. What do you say to my progress in the German language, Ilse?

Ilse Weinberger: Your progress in the German language is excellent. But, Major, I am a little bit suspicious that you take private lessons.

Major Glenn Miller: No, but in the army one learns everything.

Ilse Weinberger: Too bad that I am not a soldier.

Major Glenn Miller: Why?

Ilse Weinberger: Oh, I would like to learn how to fly and also to drive a car.

Major Glenn Miller: Drive a car? How would you like to have me as your teacher?

Ilse Weinberger: That would be wonderful.

Major Glenn Miller: Well then, let's get goin' and with music, for our first tune, "Jeep Jockey Jump."

Ilse Weinberger: That is a real good start. Glenn Miller and his orchestra present as the first selection a typical American hit, "Jeep Jockey Jump." A "jeep" is a small American soldier's car, what a "jockey" is everybody knows, and "jump" means jump. And now "Jeep Jockey Jump."

JEEP JOCKEY JUMP

CTPX-12807-1 **ALL THE THINGS YOU ARE** (JD-German)   Program 6, Record 2

Ilse Weinberger: Jawohl, Herr Major, das war ein schmissiger Anfang. Da bekommt man
   direkt Lust in so einem Soldatenauto "Jeep" genannt, über Stock und Stein zu fahren.
Major Glenn Miller: This pleasure you may have, Ilse, und ich gebe Ihnen Sergeant
   Desmond als Chauffeur.
Ilse Weinberger: Feldwebel Desmond mit der romantischen Stimme? Den höre ich lieber
   singen.
Major Glenn Miller: Well, I don't blame you. Sergeant Desmond.
Sergeant Johnny Desmond: Here I am, sir.
Ilse Weinberger: Herr Feldwebel, mit welchen Liede werden Sie uns heute erfreuen?
Sergeant Johnny Desmond: Ich singe "All the Things You Are."
Major Glenn Miller: Ah, you better sing it in German, John.
Sergeant Johnny Desmond: Yes, sir. Und ich singe das Lied für Miss Ilse, denn es
   heisst in deutsch "Alles Was Du Mir Bist."
ALL THE THINGS YOU ARE
   Vocal refrain by Sergeant Johnny Desmond (in German)
Ilse Weinberger: Ach, das war so schön. Vielen Dank Feldwebel Desmond.
Major Glenn Miller: Don't get sentimental, Ilse. That's bad for your heart. I mean,
   das ist nicht gut für das Herz.
Ilse Weinberger: Sie haben recht, Herr Major. Gönnen wir meinem Herzen und Ihren
   tüchtigen Musikern eine kleine Pause und übergeben wir das Mikrofon unserem
   Berichterstatter.

Translation:

Ilse Weinberger: Yes, Major, that was a fast beginning. One gets in the mood to ride
   over sticks and stones in that soldier's car called a jeep.
Major Glenn Miller: This pleasure you may have, Ilse, and I give you Sergeant Desmond
   as chauffeur.
Ilse Weinberger: Sergeant Desmond with the romantic voice? I'd rather hear him sing.
Major Glenn Miller: Well, I don't blame you. Sergeant Desmond.
Sergeant Johnny Desmond: Here I am, sir.
Ilse Weinberger: Sergeant, with what song will you make us happy today?
Sergeant Johnny Desmond: I sing "All the Things You Are."
Major Glenn Miller: Ah, you better sing it in German, John.
Sergeant Johnny Desmond: Yes, sir. And I sing that song for Miss Ilse because it is
   called in German "All What You Are To Me."
ALL THE THINGS YOU ARE
   Vocal refrain by Sergeant Johnny Desmond (in German)
Ilse Weinberger: Ah, that was so beautiful. Many thanks, Sergeant Desmond.
Major Glenn Miller: Don't get sentimental, Ilse. That's bad for your heart. I mean,
   that is not good for the heart.
Ilse Weinberger: You are right, Major. Give my heart and your hard working musicians a
   little break and we hand over the microphone to our reporter.

CTPX-12808-1 **SWING LOW, SWEET CHARIOT**   Program 4, Record 3

Ilse Weinberger: Und nun zurück zu Major Glenn Miller und seinem Orchester. Wir hören wiederum einen echt amerikanischen Tanzschlager, der den Titel trägt "Swing Low, Sweet Chariot."
SWING LOW, SWEET CHARIOT

Translation:

Ilse Weinberger: And now back to Major Glenn Miller and his orchestra. We are going to hear a real American dance tune, which carries the title "Swing Low, Sweet Chariot."
SWING LOW, SWEET CHARIOT

CTPX-12809-1 **BODY AND SOUL**   Program 6, Record 4

Ilse Weinberger: Das klang typisch amerikanisch, so beschwingt, so heiter, und so frei.
Major Glenn Miller: Right you are, Ilse. Love of freedom and love of carefree life, Lebensfreude, are two vital American characteristics and I hope the time will soon be here when we will completely wipe out all Nazi gangsterism so that not only the people of Europe but also the Germans may enjoy home life and happiness. The Allies will see to that.
Ilse Weinberger: Das war sehr schön gesprochen. Major Miller sagte gerade Lebensfreude und Freiheit sind typisch für Amerika. Die Alliierten werden dafür sorgen, dass nach Vernichtung der Nazis, nicht nur alle Völker Europas, sondern auch die Deutschen selbst Lebensfreude und Freiheitsliebe würdigen werden.
Major Glenn Miller: Thank you, Ilse. Our next tune's entitled "Body and Soul"
Ilse Weinberger: Und nun spielt Major Millers Orchester den populären Schlager "Body and Soul," "Mit Leib und Seele."
BODY AND SOUL

Translation:

Ilse Weinberger: That sounded typically American, so loose, so happy and so free.
Major Glenn Miller: Right you are, Ilse. Love of freedom and love of carefree life, happiness of life, are two vital American characteristics and I hope the time will soon be here when we will completely wipe out all Nazi gangsterism so that not only the people of Europe but also the Germans may enjoy home life and happiness. The Allies will see to that.
Ilse Weinberger: That was very well spoken. Major Miller just said love of life and freedom are typical for America. The Allies will make sure that after wiping out the Nazis not only all European countries but also the Germans themselves will enjoy freedom and love of life.
Major Glenn Miller: Thank you, Ilse. Our next tune's entitled "Body and Soul."
Ilse Weinberger: And now Major Miller's orchestra plays the popular hit "Body and Soul."
BODY AND SOUL

CTPX-12810-1 **BEAT ME DADDY, EIGHT TO THE BAR** (RM)   Program 6, Record 5

Major Glenn Miller: Ilse, we now call on Sergeant Ray McKinley who has more rhythm than a cat on a hot brick. He is our popular drummer and what a dancer. Would you like to hear him sing?
Ilse Weinberger: Einverstanden. Feldwebel Ray McKinley, der temperamentvolle Trommler des Orchesters tritt jetzt vor das Mikrofon. Womit werden Sie uns heute erfreuen, Herr Feldwebel?
T/Sgt. Ray McKinley: Ein Lied.
Ilse Weinberger: Oh, Sie werden singen?
T/Sgt. Ray McKinley: Ah, yes, Ma'am. I shall, ah, sing "Beat Me Daddy, Eight to the Bar."
Major Glenn Miller: How would you say that in German, Ilse?
Ilse Weinberger: Das ist nicht leicht, aber der Sinn des Liedes ist sehr lustig. Es handelt sich um einen Pianospieler in Texas, der so temperamentvoll spielt, dass die Zuhörer aufhören zu tanzen und im Chor mitsingen, "Schlag zu, Vati, acht Takte im Rhythmus."
BEAT ME DADDY, EIGHT TO THE BAR
  Vocal refrain by Technical Sergeant Ray McKinley
Ilse Weinberger: Feldwebel McKinley, Sie sind wirklich ein Meister des Rhythmus. Nun übergeben wir das Mikrofon dem Berichterstatter.

Translation:

Major Glenn Miller: Ilse, we now call on Sergeant Ray McKinley who has more rhythm than a cat on a hot brick. He is our popular drummer and what a dancer. Would you like to hear him sing?
Ilse Weinberger: Agreed. Sergeant Ray McKinley, the lively drummer of the orchestra, now steps up to the microphone. With what will you make us happy today, Sergeant?
T/Sgt. Ray McKinley: A song.
Ilse Weinberger: Oh, you will sing?
T/Sgt. Ray McKinley: Ah, yes, Ma'am. I shall, ah, sing "Beat Me Daddy, Eight to the Bar."
Major Glenn Miller: How would you say that in German, Ilse?
Ilse Weinberger: That is not easy but the meaning of the song is very funny. It is about a piano player in Texas who plays so lively that the audience stops dancing and sings along with him, "Hit It Daddy, Eight Bars in Rhythm."
BEAT ME DADDY, EIGHT TO THE BAR
  Vocal refrain by Technical Sergeant Ray McKinley
Ilse Weinberger: Sergeant McKinley, you are really a master of rhythm. Now we hand over the microphone to the reporter.

27Nov44 (Mon) 3:30-4:15PM Co-Partners Hall, Bedford, England   **SLO-65817**
MOONLIGHT SERENADE recording Script   Not used, remade 01Dec44 (SLO-65831A)

Corporal Paul Dubov: This is a program produced for the A.E.F.P. by the American Band of
   the A.E.F.
MOONLIGHT SERENADE (opening theme)
   Corporal Paul Dubov: Thirty minutes with the Moonlight Serenader, music by the American
      Band of the A.E.F. under the direction of Major Glenn Miller. Music for and by
      members of the Allied Expeditionary Forces. And here is Major Glenn Miller.
Major Glenn Miller: Thank you, Corporal Paul Dubov, and hello, everybody. Once again the
   American Band of the A.E.F. gets a chance to swing down the air lanes in a column of
   tunes. And leadin' the big parade is a piece of marchin' music with a hop on it,
   "American Patrol."
AMERICAN PATROL
Major Glenn Miller: And here's a tune that always sounds like a letter from the gal back
   home. Here, in real heartbeat tempo, "Star Dust."
STAR DUST
Major Glenn Miller: Anything from home, so long as it is from the big forty-eight,
   quickens the pulse and gives a real lift to any Yank over here. So, here special
   delivery, from the very heart of the U.S.A., a high-spirited piece of sportin' music,
   "On Wisconsin!"
ON WISCONSIN!
Major Glenn Miller: Now for medley time, salutin' the mothers, wives, sweethearts and
   sisters of the Allied Forces with somethin' old, somethin' new, somethin' borrowed and
   somethin' blue. Our old song, "Old Refrain."
THE OLD REFRAIN (Old tune)
   Major Glenn Miller: Sergeant Johnny Desmond sings our new tune, "The Same Old Love."
THE SAME OLD LOVE (New tune)
   Vocal refrain by Sergeant Johnny Desmond
   Major Glenn Miller: From Jerome Kern's long list of hits we borrow "Smoke Gets in Your
      Eyes."
(When Your Heart's on Fire) SMOKE GETS IN YOUR EYES (Borrowed tune)
   Major Glenn Miller: Strollin' into the blue spot, here comes "Blue Again."
BLUE AGAIN (Blue tune)
Major Glenn Miller: Some of the best jazz ever written has been shot straight off the
   cuff of musicians playing something that just happened to strike their fancy at the
   moment. So, right now, we're going on a little musical huntin' trip with Sergeants
   Powell, McKinley, Hucko and Alpert. The title, "If Dreams Come True."
IF DREAMS COME TRUE (quartet: Hucko, Powell, Alpert, McKinley)
Major Glenn Miller: For the closing slot on these shows by the American Band of the
   A.E.F., we always like to give some tune the "full treatment." So, again, we call on
   music-doctor Sergeant Jerry Gray who prescribes a variety of rejuvenating exercises to
   revitalize an old timer. Here's his all-out version of an all-American tune, "You Are
   My Sunshine."
YOU ARE MY SUNSHINE
   Vocal refrain by Sergeant Johnny Desmond and the Crew Chiefs
Major Glenn Miller: This is Major Glenn Miller, invitin' you back for the next big
   go-'round of the American Band of the A.E.F. Keep an eye on the papers and an ear on
   the radio and you're sure to find us playin' around. Until we get together again, it's
   good luck and good bye.
MOONLIGHT SERENADE (closing theme)

27Nov44 (Mon) 7:15-7:30PM Co-Partners Hall, Bedford, England
  STRINGS WITH WINGS broadcast   Script

Announcer: This is a feature of the American Band of the A.E.F.
I SUSTAIN THE WINGS (opening theme)
  Corporal Paul Dubov: "Strings with Wings." "Strings with Wings," a program of music
    for you of the Allied Liberation Forces, presented by the string section of the
    American Band of the A.E.F., featuring Sergeant George Ockner.
Corporal Paul Dubov: Hello there, folks. We're saying good evening again at the
  beginning of another program of "Strings with Wings." And we hope that good evening
  stands for some good music and good listening. Sergeant Ockner and the boys have
  bundled up some of your old favorites and brought 'em along to play for you. So while
  they're getting ready to go, why don't you folks pick the softest spot on that bunk and
  take it easy. All set? O.K. then here's the first one, "Make-Believe."
MAKE-BELIEVE
Corporal Paul Dubov: If any of you folks are feeling a little E.T.O. happy tonight, I
  think we've got something here that'll banish those blues in a jiffy. It's a little
  hair of the dog that bit ya, a blues tune by old doctor Duke Ellington, "Mood Indigo."
MOOD INDIGO
Corporal Paul Dubov: I don't know what we'd do on this program if songwriters stopped
  writing love songs. Probably have to play "Mairzy Doats." But don't worry, the boys
  still have plenty of the sentimental stuff on hand. Here's one of 'em, one of your very
  favorite torch songs, "Lover, Come Back to Me!"
LOVER, COME BACK TO ME!
Corporal Paul Dubov: You folks out there on the other end of this Allied Expeditionary
  Forces network are listening to the string section of the American Band of the A.E.F.
  And here are the boys to ease another one your way. This time it's "Dancing in the
  Dark."
DANCING IN THE DARK
Corporal Paul Dubov: Well, we started at the top and played right to the bottom. So I
  guess that's all 'til next time. We'll be back with more violin versions of your old
  favorites this coming Wednesday. And you'll make us real happy if you're out there
  listening. Until then, this is Corporal Paul Dubov saying, "So long, and good luck to
  you."
I SUSTAIN THE WINGS (closing theme)
  Corporal Paul Dubov: You've been listening to music by the string section of the
    American Band of the A.E.F., featuring Sergeant George Ockner. Don't forget to join
    us this coming Wednesday night when we again present "Strings with Wings."

28Nov44 (Tue) 11:00AM-Noon Co-Partners Hall, Bedford, England   SLO-65820
  MOONLIGHT SERENADE recording   Script   Aired 12Jan45

Corporal Paul Dubov: This is a program produced for the A.E.F.P. by the American Band of
  the A.E.F.
MOONLIGHT SERENADE (opening theme)
  Corporal Paul Dubov: Thirty minutes with the Moonlight Serenader, music by the American
    Band of the A.E.F., under the direction of Major Glenn Miller. Music for and by
    members of the Allied Expeditionary Forces. And here is Major Glenn Miller.
Major Glenn Miller: All during this past week we've again been enjoying ourselves playing
  some hand-to-hand engagements with you Tommies and Yanks scattered around the U.K. Not
  only that, but we've also been enjoying the good news which is the payoff for the
  teamwork you fightin' guys have been putting into winning this war. Tonight again, it's
  radio-meetin' time. The music's all yours and the pleasure's all ours. The first tune
  blowin' right outa your barracks bag into our brass section, "Snafu Jump."
SNAFU JUMP
Major Glenn Miller: This radio show, like every radio show on this radio network, is
  aimed especially at you guys who make up the all-Allied team. And, whether your old
  home town is Manchester, England or Manchester, New Hampshire back U.S.A. way, we think
  maybe it'll do when it comes to stirring up a few pleasant memories. So, just step
  right up and help yourself to "Body and Soul."
BODY AND SOUL
Major Glenn Miller: Here's an old timer that you keep askin' for so we keep playin' it,
  "Tuxedo Junction."
TUXEDO JUNCTION
Major Glenn Miller: And now it's medley time, salutin' the mothers, wives, sweethearts
  and sisters of you Tommies and Yanks with somethin' old, somethin' new, somethin'
  borrowed and somethin' blue. Our old song, "Songs My Mother Taught Me."
SONGS MY MOTHER TAUGHT ME (Old tune)
  Major Glenn Miller: For our new tune here come the Crew Chiefs singin' "It's Love,
    Love, Love!"
IT'S LOVE, LOVE, LOVE! (New tune)
  Vocal refrain by the Crew Chiefs
  Major Glenn Miller: For our borrowed tune we pay a visit to our musical antique dealer,
    pickin' up a fine old piece designed by Mozart, refinished by Raymond Scott and
    polished up by Sergeant Mel Powell. "Eighteenth Century Drawing Room."
IN AN EIGHTEENTH CENTURY DRAWING ROOM (Borrowed tune)
  Major Glenn Miller: Sergeant Johnny Desmond turns the heat on our blue song singin'
    "Blue Orchids."
BLUE ORCHIDS (Blue tune)
  Vocal refrain by Sergeant Johnny Desmond
Major Glenn Miller: Now here's sort of a Reader's Digest version of the music of the
  American Band of the A.E.F. Stepping outa formation come Sergeants Powell, McKinley,
  Hucko and Alpert. The title of the tune? "I Must Have That Man."
I MUST HAVE THAT MAN (quartet: Hucko, Powell, Alpert, McKinley)
Major Glenn Miller: What do we do when we need a bright windup for a radio show? "What
Do We Do in the Infantry."
WHAT DO YOU DO IN THE INFANTRY
  Vocal refrain by Corporal Artie Malvin and the Crew Chiefs
Major Glenn Miller: That's the run-down for now. And this is Major Glenn Miller,
  thankin' you for stoppin' by and remindin' you all that we'll be back in a few days to
  deliver another half-hour along these same lines. If this is your kind of music we'll
  be here right soon to play for you. For now it's good luck and good bye.
MOONLIGHT SERENADE (closing theme)

28Nov44 (Tue) 8:30-9:00PM Queensbury All-Services Club, Bedford, England   SLO-64971
  AMERICAN BAND OF THE AEF broadcast   Script   Attendance: 2500

Corporal Paul Dubov: This is a program produced for the A.E.F.P. by the American Band of
  the A.E.F., originating in the Queensbury All-Services Club in London.
MOONLIGHT SERENADE (opening theme)
  Corporal Paul Dubov: Thirty minutes with Moonlight Serenader, presenting the American
    Band of the A.E.F., under the direction of Major Glenn Miller. Music for and by
    members of the Allied Expeditionary Forces. And here is Major Glenn Miller.
Major Glenn Miller: Thank you, Corporal Paul Dubov, and hello, everybody. Once again the
  American Band of the A.E.F. grabs a good hold on your radio and promises not to let go
  for a full half-hour. First thing to do is to heat up the hall. 'N' seeing as how
  there's nothin' makes you feel warmer than meetin' an old friend, here's "In the Mood."
  IN THE MOOD
Major Glenn Miller: After meetin' a couple of hundred thousand of 'em, there doesn't seem
  to be a Yank over here who isn't proud of some little snapshot he carries around in his
  wallet. And we're no different than the rest. Here, to all our "only gals in the
  world" Sergeant Johnny Desmond sings for us "Sweet and Lovely."
SWEET AND LOVELY
  Vocal refrain by Sergeant Johnny Desmond
Major Glenn Miller: Back home by droppin' a nickel in a slot you can either get a cup of
  coffee, a ride on the subway or a listen to America's greatest bands. And here come the
  Crew Chiefs and Sergeant Bobby Nichols to put in their five cents on "Juke Box Saturday
  Night."
JUKE BOX SATURDAY NIGHT
  Vocal refrain by the Crew Chiefs
Major Glenn Miller: And now it's medley time as the American Band of the A.E.F. salutes
  the mothers, wives, sweethearts and sisters of the Allied Forces with somethin' old,
  somethin' new, somethin' borrowed and somethin' blue. The old song, "Flow Gently Sweet
  Afton."
FLOW GENTLY SWEET AFTON (Old tune)
  Major Glenn Miller: Heart-warmer Sergeant Johnny Desmond joins the Crew Chiefs singin'
    our new song, "Moon Dreams."
MOON DREAMS (New tune)
  Vocal refrain by Sergeant Johnny Desmond and the Crew Chiefs
  Major Glenn Miller: From Benny Goodman, who beats beauty into music with a big, black
    stick, we borrow "Don't Be That Way."
DON'T BE THAT WAY (Borrowed tune)
  Major Glenn Miller: Toastin' our blue department with some sparklin' fizz-music comes
    "Blue Champagne."
BLUE CHAMPAGNE (Blue tune)
Major Glenn Miller: And now we pull a little inspection on our brass, just to make sure
  it's shinin', with a high-jumpin' version of "Everybody Loves My Baby."
EVERYBODY LOVES MY BABY (But My Baby Don't Love Nobody but Me)
Major Glenn Miller: For the big, last go-'round on the show we have chosen a tune that
  sat for its portrait on arranger Sergeant Jerry Gray's music-rack. The Sarge, being an
  artist of the modern school, used a lot of bright colors in his arrangement, which
  includes some singin' by Sergeant Johnny Desmond and the Crew Chiefs. "Poinciana."
POINCIANA (Song of the Tree)
  Vocal refrain by Sergeant Johnny Desmond and the Crew Chiefs
Major Glenn Miller: This is Major Glenn Miller sayin' keep an eye on the papers and an
  ear on the radio for the American Band of the A.E.F., 'cause we want to see you again
  right soon. For now it's good luck and good bye.
MOONLIGHT SERENADE (closing theme)
  Corporal Paul Dubov: You have been listening to one half hour with the Moonlight
    Serenader. Presenting the American Band of the A.E.F., under the direction of Major
    Glenn Miller. Music for and by members of the Allied Expeditionary Forces.

29Nov44 (Wed) 7:45-8:00PM Co-Partners Hall, Bedford, England
STRINGS WITH WINGS broadcast   Script

Announcer: This is a program produced for the A.E.F.P. by the American Band of the A.E.F.
I SUSTAIN THE WINGS (opening theme)
    Corporal Paul Dubov: "Strings with Wings." "Strings with Wings," a program of music
    for you of the Allied Liberation Forces, presented by the string section of the
    American Band of the A.E.F., featuring Sergeant George Ockner and his violin.
Corporal Paul Dubov: Hello there, folks. Seein' as how it's about that time in the
    evening when a spot of soft music always seems to be in order, we thought we'd drop
    around with the violins and see what we could do about it. If you've got a few minutes
    to spare, just hand 'em over and we'll fill 'em up with some tunes. There's a promise,
    and here's Sergeant Ockner and the boys to keep it. It's "Strings with Wings" takin'
    off in your direction and lighting up the runway with our first tune of the evening,
    "With a Song in My Heart."
WITH A SONG IN MY HEART
Corporal Paul Dubov: Well, that first one seemed to put a song in everybody's heart.
    Even the boys themselves seem to be glowing with sudden optimism. I don't know who
    they're looking for, but they seem in a mighty hopeful mood as they say "Someday I'll
    Find You."
SOMEDAY I'LL FIND YOU
Corporal Paul Dubov: We reached right up and took this next one off the top shelf where
    it's been gathering dust for too long. Maybe you haven't heard it for quite a while,
    but ten gets you five you'll be glad to hear it again. "They Didn't Believe Me."
THEY DIDN'T BELIEVE ME
Corporal Paul Dubov: When we say this is a program of the Allied Expeditionary Forces you
    can take it for a fact. You can also count on this being the string section of the
    American Band of the A.E.F. In fact, we're even positive about the title of the next
    tune. It's a "Sure Thing."
SURE THING
Corporal Paul Dubov: Now it's about time to say, "Thanks, guys and gals, for listening."
    We hope it's been fun for you and if it has, just remember we'll be back next Monday
    evening with more of same. But until that happy time, this is Corporal Paul Dubov
    saying, "So long, and good luck to you."
I SUSTAIN THE WINGS (closing theme)
    Corporal Paul Dubov: You've been listening to music by the string section of the
    American Band of the A.E.F., featuring Sergeant George Ockner and his violin. Don't
    forget to join us next Monday night when we again present "Strings with Wings."

30Nov44 (Thu) 5:55-6:30PM Co-Partners Hall, Bedford, England   SLO-66424
  THE SWING SHIFT recording   Script   Aired 28Dec44

Announcer: This is a feature of the American Band of the A.E.F.
Corporal Paul Dubov: Presenting "The Swing Shift," featuring Sergeant Ray McKinley and
  his music.
SONG AND DANCE (opening theme)
  Vocal refrain by Technical Sergeant Ray McKinley
Corporal Paul Dubov: Hi'ya, Mac.
T/Sgt. Ray McKinley: Good evenin', Paul.
Corporal Paul Dubov: Say, Mac, how many people do you think we play to each broadcast?
T/Sgt. Ray McKinley: Astronomical figures are not my fancy, son. However, I do know
  we've got fans in Kwibeyshev, Upper Rhodesia and a small but thickly populated prairie
  called Flatbush!
Corporal Paul Dubov: Gee, gosh!
T/Sgt. Ray McKinley: What sparkling repartee. Isn't it stimulating when great minds
  meet?
Corporal Paul Dubov: I mean it makes you feel that maybe radio isn't a fad.
T/Sgt. Ray McKinley: I think it's safe to say that, Paul. But enough of this nonsense.
  Stop hangin' on my words right quick before we lose a few customers. We've got a
  showcase packed with music and we're ready for business with "Get Happy." Ready, boys.
  One, two.
GET HAPPY
Corporal Paul Dubov: Here's an item that would be a buy at any price, but you steady
  listeners can have it just for the askin'. Settle back while "The Swing Shifters"
  spotlight Sergeant Bernie Privin playing "You Go to My Head."
YOU GO TO MY HEAD
Corporal Paul Dubov: The blockhouse gate opens and six characters in fatigues emerge
  after a strenuous afternoon spent polishing Sergeant Mac's cowbells. The Crew Chiefs
  and Sergeant Johnny Desmond, overflowing with new-found vitality, caress the microphone
  with "Sweet and Lovely."
SWEET AND LOVELY
  Vocal refrain by Sergeant Johnny Desmond and the Crew Chiefs
Corporal Paul Dubov: "The Swing Shifters" roll up their sleeves in preparation for a bout
  with a mess of notes. Sergeant Mac steps on the (gas) and we're off in a burst of
  smoke, as he steps down to ask "Is You Is or Is You Ain't My Baby?"
IS YOU IS OR IS YOU AIN'T MY BABY?
  Vocal refrain by Technical Sergeant Ray McKinley
Corporal Paul Dubov: Our soldier with the bag full of songs pulls one right off the top
  and offers it for your approval. Sergeant Johnny Desmond sings "Time Waits for No One."
TIME WAITS FOR NO ONE
  Vocal refrain by Sergeant Johnny Desmond
Corporal Paul Dubov: I'll take that, Johnny! The spice for these programs you hear over
  A.E.F. comes from Sergeants Hucko, Powell and McKinley who form the trio responsible for
  the small band jazz you like so well. Here they are playing "Spam What Am."
SPAM WHAT AM (trio: Hucko, Powell, McKinley)
Corporal Paul Dubov: Lock that door, guard! Sergeant Desmond, date or no date, your
  contract calls for an occasional slice of romance on this "Swing Shift." Come right
  over here and tonsilize, Johnny, 'cause we're ready for "She's Funny That Way."
(I Got a Woman Crazy for Me) SHE'S FUNNY THAT WAY
  Vocal refrain by Sergeant Johnny Desmond
Corporal Paul Dubov: We're almost sold out, fellas. In fact, there's only one thing left
  on the shelves and when that's gone, we'll be gone. Don't rush the counter, 'cause
  we're comin' at you with "Nine Twenty Special."
NINE TWENTY SPECIAL

Corporal Paul Dubov: You've heard another "Swing Shift," featuring Sergeant Ray McKinley
  and his music. Keep your dial set for A.E.F. and we'll be back Saturday afternoon at
  1501 hours. 'Til then, this is Corporal Paul Dubov saying, "So long," and turning you
  over to Sergeant Ray McKinley.
SONG AND DANCE (closing theme)
  Vocal refrain by Technical Sergeant Ray McKinley

01Dec44 (Fri) 10:00-10:40AM Co-Partners Hall, Bedford, England   **DLO-66425A**
   MOONLIGHT SERENADE recording   Script   Edited and aired 26Jan45

Corporal Paul Dubov: This is a program produced for the A.E.F.P. by the American Band of the A.E.F.
MOONLIGHT SERENADE (opening theme)
   Corporal Paul Dubov: Thirty minutes with the Moonlight Serenader, music by the American Band of the A.E.F. under the direction of Major Glenn Miller, music for and by members of the Allied Expeditionary Forces. And here is Major Glenn Miller.
Major Glenn Miller: Thank you, Corporal Paul Dubov, and hello, everybody. Once again the American Band of the A.E.F. takes off on a half-hour mission through the air lanes, to cruise in a wide musical circle 'round your radio. Our first bit of navigatin' takes us over about three minutes and fifteen seconds of familiar territory, "In the Mood."
IN THE MOOD
Major Glenn Miller: After meetin' a couple of hundred thousand of 'em, there doesn't seem to be a Yank over here who isn't proud of some little snapshot he carries around in his wallet, and we're no different than the rest. Here, to all our "only gals in the world" Sergeant Johnny Desmond sings for us "Sweet and Lovely."
SWEET AND LOVELY
   Vocal refrain by Sergeant Johnny Desmond
Major Glenn Miller: Back home by droppin' a nickel in a slot you can either get a cup of coffee, a ride on the subway or a listen to America's greatest bands. And here come the Crew Chiefs and Sergeant Bobby Nichols to put in their five cents worth on "Juke Box Saturday Night."
JUKE BOX SATURDAY NIGHT
   Vocal refrain by the Crew Chiefs
Major Glenn Miller: And now it's medley time as the American Band of the A.E.F. salutes the mothers, wives, sweethearts and sisters of the Allied Forces with somethin' old, somethin' new, somethin' borrowed and somethin' blue. The old song, "Flow Gently Sweet Afton."
FLOW GENTLY SWEET AFTON (Old tune)
   Major Glenn Miller: Heart-warmer Sergeant Johnny Desmond joins the Crew Chiefs singin' our new song, "Moon Dreams."
MOON DREAMS (New tune)
   Vocal refrain by Sergeant Johnny Desmond and the Crew Chiefs
   Major Glenn Miller: From Benny Goodman, who beats beauty into music with a big, black stick, we borrow "Don't Be That Way."
DON'T BE THAT WAY (Borrowed tune)
   Major Glenn Miller: Toastin' our blue department with some sparklin' fizz-music comes "Blue Champagne."
BLUE CHAMPAGNE (Blue tune)
Major Glenn Miller: Applying the principle that good things come in small packages, we now call upon Sergeants Powell, McKinley, Hucko and Alpert to wrap up their gift of musical small-talk in four or five rounds of "You Turned the Tables on Me." Start turnin', boys.
YOU TURNED THE TABLES ON ME (quartet: Hucko, Powell, Alpert, McKinley)
Major Glenn Miller: For the big, last go-'round on the show we have chosen a tune that sat for its portrait on arranger Sergeant Jerry Gray's music-rack. The Sarge, being an artist of the modern school, used a lot of bright colors in his arrangement, which includes some singin' by Sergeant Johnny Desmond and the Crew Chiefs. "Poinciana."
POINCIANA (Song of the Tree)
   Vocal refrain by Sergeant Johnny Desmond and the Crew Chiefs
Major Glenn Miller: This is Major Glenn Miller sayin' keep an eye on the papers and an ear to the radio for the American Band of the A.E.F., 'cause we want to see you again right soon. For now it's good luck and good bye.
MOONLIGHT SERENADE (closing theme)

The preceding program was aired after Major Glenn Miller's disappearance was announced. To "salvage" the program, Paul Dubov's and Glenn Miller's announcements were edited out of the recording and announcements by T/Sgt. Dick Dudley were substituted. The program was aired as follows.

[T/Sgt. Dick Dudley: This is a program produced for the A.E.F.P. by the American Band of the A.E.F.
MOONLIGHT SERENADE (opening theme)
   T/Sgt. Dick Dudley: Thirty minutes with the Moonlight Serenader, music by the American Band of the A.E.F. under the direction of Major Glenn Miller, music for and by members of the Allied Expeditionary Forces.
T/Sgt. Dick Dudley: This is Sergeant Dick Dudley. Once again the American Band of the A.E.F. takes off on a half-hour mission through the air lanes, to cruise in a wide] musical circle around your radio. Our first bit of navigatin' takes us over about three minutes and fifteen seconds of familiar territory. It's "In the Mood."
[IN THE MOOD
T/Sgt. Dick Dudley: After meetin' a couple of hundred thousand of 'em,] there doesn't seem to be a Yank over here who isn't proud of some little snapshot he carries around in his wallet, and we're no different from the rest. Here, to all our "only gals in the world" Sergeant Johnny Desmond sings for us "Sweet and Lovely."
[SWEET AND LOVELY
   Vocal refrain by Sergeant Johnny Desmond
T/Sgt. Dick Dudley: Back home by droppin' a nickel in a slot you can either get a cup of coffee, a ride on the subway or you can listen to America's greatest bands. And here come the Crew Chiefs and Sergeant Bobby Nichols to put in their five cents worth on "Juke Box Saturday Night."
JUKE BOX SATURDAY NIGHT
   Vocal refrain by the Crew Chiefs
T/Sgt. Dick Dudley: And now it's medley time as the American Band of the A.E.F. salutes the mothers, wives, sweethearts and sisters of the Allied Forces with somethin' old, somethin' new, somethin' borrowed and somethin' blue. The old song, "Flow Gently Sweet Afton."
FLOW GENTLY SWEET AFTON (Old tune)
   T/Sgt. Dick Dudley: Heart-warmer Sergeant Johnny Desmond joins the Crew Chiefs singin' our new song, "Moon Dreams."
MOON DREAMS (New tune)
   Vocal refrain by Sergeant Johnny Desmond and the Crew Chiefs
   T/Sgt. Dick Dudley: From Benny Goodman, who beats beauty into music with a big, black stick, we borrow "Don't Be That Way."
DON'T BE THAT WAY (Borrowed tune)
   T/Sgt. Dick Dudley: Toastin' our blue department with some sparklin' fizz-music comes "Blue Champagne."
BLUE CHAMPAGNE (Blue tune)
T/Sgt. Dick Dudley: Applying the principle that good things come] in small packages, we now call upon Sergeants Powell, McKinley, Hucko and Alpert to wrap up their gift of musical small-talk in four or five rounds of "You Turned the Tables on Me." Start turnin', boys.
YOU TURNED THE TABLES ON ME (quartet: Hucko, Powell, Alpert, McKinley)
T/Sgt. Dick Dudley: For the big, last go-around on this show [we have chosen a tune that sat for its portrait on arranger Sergeant Jerry Gray's music-rack. The Sarge, being an artist of the modern school, used a lot of bright colors in his arrangement, which includes some singin' by Sergeant Johnny Desmond and the Crew Chiefs. "Poinciana."
POINCIANA (Song of the Tree)
   Vocal refrain by Sergeant Johnny Desmond and the Crew Chiefs
T/Sgt. Dick Dudley: And so we come to the close of another program by the American Band of the A.E.F. This is Sergeant Dick Dudley saying keep an eye on the papers and an ear to the radio because we want to see you again right soon. For now it's good luck and good bye.
MOONLIGHT SERENADE (closing theme)]

01Dec44 (Fri) 10:40-11:20AM Co-Partners Hall, Bedford, England   DLO-65918A
  MOONLIGHT SERENADE recording   Edited and aired 13Feb45

This program was aired after Major Glenn Miller's disappearance was announced. To
"salvage" the program, Paul Dubov's and Glenn Miller's announcements were edited out of
the recording and announcements by T/Sgt. Dick Dudley were substituted. The program was
aired as follows.

  ...

T/Sgt. Dick Dudley: Like every show on this hook-up, this one is cut to measure and
  especially tailored to fit the ears of Tommy and G.I. Joe and Johnny Canuck. The
  get-away tune calls for some high altitude flying by the brass section and it gets
  around under the title "Caribbean Clipper."
CARIBBEAN CLIPPER

  ...

T/Sgt. Dick Dudley: We've set one of our fanciest mental pleasures to music. Sergeant
  Ray McKinley and the Crew Chiefs sing the praises of "I'm Headin' for California."
I'M HEADIN' FOR CALIFORNIA
  Vocal refrain by Technical Sergeant Ray McKinley and the Crew Chiefs

  ...

IRRESISTIBLE YOU (New tune)
  Vocal refrain by Sergeant Johnny Desmond and the Crew Chiefs
  T/Sgt. Dick Dudley: And from our own musical past we borrow "Little Brown Jug."
LITTLE BROWN JUG

  ...

T/Sgt. Dick Dudley: ... and Sergeant Mac's Sunday punch calls on a still smaller
  combination from within the band which gets around the town under the title "The Boogie
  Woogie Quartet." Sergeants McKinley, drums; Powell, piano; Hucko, clarinet; and Alpert,
  bass. They're pulling off a triple play for you now to the tune of the jumpin'
  something known as the "Parachute Jump."
PARACHUTE JUMP (quartet: Hucko, Powell, Alpert, McKinley)
T/Sgt. Dick Dudley: In certain sections the booming of the Liberty Guns has put a
  surprised look on the face of Europe. Some ill-informed person once said we'd never get
  where we are going. And the fact that we're on our way is the biggest tribute to you
  members of the all Allied fighting team. However, right here and now we'd like to add a
  musical salute to what the rest of the free world is saying about you guys up on the
  fighting fronts by playing a song you boys and gals are helping the folks back home to
  sing. Here's the "Vict'ry Polka."
VICT'RY POLKA
  Vocal refrain by the Crew Chiefs and Ensemble

  ...

01Dec44 (Fri) 8:30-9:00PM Co-Partners Hall, Bedford, England   SLO-65322
MOONLIGHT SERENADE broadcast   Script

Corporal Paul Dubov: This is a program produced for the A.E.F.P. by the American Band of the A.E.F.

MOONLIGHT SERENADE (opening theme)

Corporal Paul Dubov: Thirty minutes with the Moonlight Serenader, music by the American Band of the A.E.F. under the direction of Major Glenn Miller. Music for and by members of the Allied Expeditionary Forces. And here is Major Glenn Miller.

Major Glenn Miller: Thank you, Corporal Paul Dubov, and hello, everybody. By the looks of the scenery, this should be a great show. The A.E.F.P., great network. You Tommies and Yanks and Johnny Canucks, great audience. Opening tune, "Great Day."

GREAT DAY

Major Glenn Miller: A couple of Christmas presents arrived in the mail today, a little beat up by the journey, but plenty welcome. And they gave us the cue to pull a song outa the books and Sergeant Johnny Desmond up to the microphone for "White Christmas."

WHITE CHRISTMAS

Vocal refrain by Sergeant Johnny Desmond

Major Glenn Miller: Mighty fancy, Sarge. And now for you Yanks from the cotton country, we knock you a tune that should rest easy on your ears. Here's our Southern-fried version of "Swing Low, Sweet Chariot."

SWING LOW, SWEET CHARIOT

Major Glenn Miller: Medley time sends all our best to the mothers, wives, sweethearts and sisters of the Allied Forces with somethin' old, somethin' new, somethin' borrowed and somethin' blue. Our old song, "All through the Night."

ALL THROUGH THE NIGHT (Old tune)

Major Glenn Miller: The lad with the heart-shaped voice, Sergeant Johnny Desmond, decorates our new song, "Time Waits for No One."

TIME WAITS FOR NO ONE (New tune)

Vocal refrain by Sergeant Johnny Desmond

Major Glenn Miller: The Crew Chiefs put the tap on Guy Lombardo for a borrowed tune and up pops "Take It Easy."

TAKE IT EASY (Borrowed tune)

Vocal refrain by the Crew Chiefs

Major Glenn Miller: For somethin' blue, here's "Blue Hawaii."

BLUE HAWAII (Blue tune)

Major Glenn Miller: The American Band of the A.E.F. calls on a foursome of musical individualists, who are about to shoot nine holes in a "hop" tune. Sergeants Powell, McKinley, Hucko and Alpert swing down the fairway with "Tea for Four."

TEA FOR FOUR (actually "Tea for Two")

(quartet: Hucko, Powell, Alpert, McKinley)

Major Glenn Miller: And here's the tune that gets the big applause of the evenin' whenever we play it, Sergeant Jerry Gray's sure-fire hand-getter all over the E.T.O., "Holiday for Strings."

HOLIDAY FOR STRINGS

Major Glenn Miller: This is Major Glenn Miller, hangin' out the welcome sign that invites you back for more music by the American Band of the A.E.F. Keep an eye on the papers and an ear on the radio for the time and place. Until then, it's good luck and good bye.

MOONLIGHT SERENADE (closing theme)

Corporal Paul Dubov: You've been listening to the American Band of the A.E.F. under the direction of Major Glenn Miller. Music for and by members of the Allied Expeditionary Forces.

01Dec44 (Fri) Co-Partners Hall, Bedford, England   SLO-65831A
  MOONLIGHT SERENADE recording Remake of SLO-65817 (27Nov44)   Script   Aired 05Jan44

Corporal Paul Dubov: This is a program produced for the A.E.F.P. by the American Band of
  the A.E.F.
MOONLIGHT SERENADE (opening theme)
  Corporal Paul Dubov: Thirty minutes with the Moonlight Serenader, music by the American
    Band of the A.E.F. under the direction of Major Glenn Miller. Music for and by
    members of the Allied Expeditionary Forces. And here is Major Glenn Miller.
Major Glenn Miller: Thank you, Corporal Paul Dubov, and hello, everybody. Once again the
  American Band of the A.E.F. gets a chance to swing down the air lanes in a column of
  tunes. And leadin' the big parade is a piece of marchin' music with a hop on it,
  "American Patrol."
AMERICAN PATROL
Major Glenn Miller: And here's a tune that always sounds like a letter from the gal back
  home. Here, in real heartbeat tempo, "Star Dust."
STAR DUST
Major Glenn Miller: Anything from home, so long as it is from the big forty-eight,
  quickens the pulse and gives a real lift to any Yank over here. So, here special
  delivery, from the very heart of the U.S.A., a high-spirited piece of sportin' music,
  "On Wisconsin!"
ON WISCONSIN!
Major Glenn Miller: Now for medley time, salutin' the mothers, wives, sweethearts and
  sisters of the Allied Forces with somethin' old, somethin' new, somethin' borrowed and
  somethin' blue. Our old song, "Old Refrain."
THE OLD REFRAIN (Old tune)
  Major Glenn Miller: Sergeant Johnny Desmond sings our new tune, "The Same Old Love."
THE SAME OLD LOVE (New tune)
  Vocal refrain by Sergeant Johnny Desmond
  Major Glenn Miller: From Jerome Kern's long list of hits we borrow "Smoke Gets in Your
    Eyes."
(When Your Heart's on Fire) SMOKE GETS IN YOUR EYES (Borrowed tune)
  Major Glenn Miller: Strollin' into the blue spot, here comes "Blue Again."
BLUE AGAIN (Blue tune)
Major Glenn Miller: Some of the best jazz ever written has been shot straight off the
  cuff of musicians playing something that just happened to strike their fancy at the
  moment. So, right now, we're going on a little musical huntin' trip with Sergeants
  Powell, McKinley, Hucko and Alpert. The title, "If Dreams Come True."
IF DREAMS COME TRUE (quartet: Hucko, Powell, Alpert, McKinley)
Major Glenn Miller: For the closing slot on these shows by the American Band of the
  A.E.F., we always like to give some tune the "full treatment." So, again, we call on
  music-doctor Sergeant Jerry Gray who prescribes a variety of rejuvenating exercises to
  revitalize an old timer. Here's his all-out version of an all-American tune, "You Are
  My Sunshine."
YOU ARE MY SUNSHINE
  Vocal refrain by Sergeant Johnny Desmond and the Crew Chiefs
Major Glenn Miller: This is Major Glenn Miller, invitin' you back for the next big
  go-'round of the American Band of the A.E.F. Keep an eye on the papers and an ear on
  the radio and you're sure to find us playin' around. Until we get together again, it's
  good luck and good bye.
MOONLIGHT SERENADE (closing theme)

02Dec44 (Sat) 11:45AM-Noon Co-Partners Hall, Bedford, England
PIANO PARADE broadcast
Script

Announcer: This is a program produced for the A.E.F.P. by the American Band of the A.E.F.
CHOPSTICKS (opening theme)
  Announcer: "Piano Parade," a daily quarter hour of piano music that today brings you
    Private First Class Jack Rusin in a medley of memory melodies.
Announcer: Jack's little session of midday music brings us today some of your all-time,
    old time favorites. There's "I've Got the World on a String," I Concentrate on You,"
    "Makin' Whoopee!," "Besame Mucho," "I Guess I'll Have to Change My Plan" and "Blue
    Skies." That's the line-up for today, and here's Jack to play.
I'VE GOT THE WORLD ON A STRING
I CONCENTRATE OF YOU
MAKIN' WHOOPEE!
BESAME MUCH (Kiss Me Much)
I GUESS I'LL HAVE TO CHANGE MY PLAN
BLUE SKIES
CHOPSTICKS (closing theme)
  Announcer: You've been listening to the A.E.F. program "Piano Parade," fifteen minutes
    of piano melodies with P.F.C. Jack Rusin at the keyboard, heard today with "I've Got
    the World on a String," I Concentrate on You," "Makin' Whoopee!," "Besame Mucho," "I
    Guess I'll Have to Change My Plan" and "Blue Skies." That's all for now, folks. But
    don't forget to be listening when we come your way again with "Piano Parade."

02Dec44 (Sat) 5:45-6:10PM Co-Partners Hall, Bedford, England   SLO-65835
  STRINGS WITH WINGS recording   Script   Aired 29Jan45

Announcer: This is a program produced for the A.E.F.P. by the American Band of the A.E.F.
I SUSTAIN THE WINGS (opening theme)
  Corporal Paul Dubov: "Strings with Wings." "Strings with Wings," a program of music
    for you of the Allied Liberation Forces, presented by the string section of the
    American Band of the A.E.F., featuring Sergeant George Ockner and his violin.
Corporal Paul Dubov: Hello there, folks. Welcome to another program of "Strings with
  Wings." Those violins you heard in the background just then probably told all you
  steady customers that it's sweet music time again. And right you are! It's Sergeant
  Ockner and the lads comin' your way with another (batch) of tunes, fashioned for fiddles
  and easy listening. So get as comfortable as you can and we'll take care of everything
  else. Here's tonight's first tune, "Stairway to the Stars."
STAIRWAY TO THE STARS
Corporal Paul Dubov: Now the boys make you a present of another picture for that pin-up
  collection of yours above the bunch. She's a little girl who's been around quite a
  while and she's gettin' lovelier every day. "Sophisticated Lady."
SOPHISTICATED LADY
Corporal Paul Dubov: You can talk about your red-heads and your blonds and brunettes.
  But after you take one listen to this next musical pin-up the boys are handin' out, it's
  shillings to crumpets you'll say, "That's for me." It's the "Maid with the Flaxen
  Hair."
MAID WITH THE FLAXEN HAIR
Corporal Paul Dubov: To top off their tunes tonight, Sergeant Ockner and the boys pick
  one of your favorites from the musical stage hit "Show Boat." It's one of those tunes
  folks never get tired of, it just keeps rollin' along, "Ol' Man River."
OL' MAN RIVER
Corporal Paul Dubov: Which brings us right down to the bottom of tonight's program,
  folks. Sorry we can't stay and play, but don't forget, we're right here on your radio
  every Monday and Wednesday evening. So if you feel in the mood for some music, just
  give that dial a twist. Until the next time, then, this is Corporal Paul Dubov saying,
  "So long, and good luck to you."
I SUSTAIN THE WINGS (closing theme)

02Dec44 (Sat) 6:35-7:00PM Co-Partners Hall, Bedford, England   SLO-66436
STRINGS WITH WINGS recording   Script   Aired 05Feb44

Announcer: This is a program produced for the A.E.F.P. by the American Band of the A.E.F.
I SUSTAIN THE WINGS (opening theme)
   Corporal Paul Dubov: "Strings with Wings." "Strings with Wings," a program of music
      for you of the Allied Liberation Forces, presented by the string section of the
      American Band of the A.E.F., featuring Sergeant George Ockner and his violin.
Corporal Paul Dubov: Hello there, folks, and welcome to another program of "Strings with
   Wings." Just about this time in the studio, the folks back home are probably sitting
   down by the radio to enjoy a bit of music. And if you've got a few minutes to spare
   tonight, why don't you folks join 'em? Sergeant Ockner and the boys have got some swell
   tunes on hand, just the kind we think you guys and gals really go for. So, while the
   violins take over, let's you and I just lean back and listen. Here's the first one
   coming up, "You and the Night and the Music."
YOU AND THE NIGHT AND THE MUSIC
Corporal Paul Dubov: A few years back composer Hoagy Carmichael hit the best seller list
   with a tune that's been one of your favorites ever since. Here it is in a violin
   version, as played by the string section of the American Band of the A.E.F., "Star
   Dust."
STAR DUST
Corporal Paul Dubov: For their next number the violins take you on a little trip down
   South America way. It's Sergeant Jerry Gray's arrangement of that popular Brazilian
   samba "Tico-Tico."
TICO-TICO
Corporal Paul Dubov: Our "Strings with Wings" take off again. And it's Sergeant Ockner
   and the boys completing their missions for tonight with a little musical high-flying
   "Over the Rainbow."
OVER THE RAINBOW
Corporal Paul Dubov: Well, we've got more tunes, but no more time. So I guess that's all
   for tonight. But don't forget, we're waitin' for you here every Monday and Wednesday
   night with more of that soft, sweet music played by the violins. And here's hopin' you
   can join us the next time. Until then, this is Corporal Paul Dubov saying, "So long,
   and good luck to you."
I SUSTAIN THE WINGS (closing theme)

03Dec44 (Sun) 3:30-4:00PM Co-Partners Hall, Bedford, England   SLO-65840
   SONGS BY SGT. JOHNNY DESMOND recording   Script   Aired 22Jan45

Announcer: This is a program produced for the A.E.F.P. by the American Band of the A.E.F.
TIME ON MY HANDS (opening theme)
   Corporal Paul Dubov: "Songs by Sergeant Johnny Desmond."
   Vocal refrain by Sergeant Johnny Desmond
   Corporal Paul Dubov: Three songs by a three-striper, with music by the American Band of
      the A.E.F.
Sergeant Johnny Desmond: Hello there. This is Sergeant Johnny Desmond. Our lead-off
   song for this session is real "easy singin'." It rolls along smooth as a baby's cheek,
   flavored with words tellin' a love-letter story.
SPRING WILL BE A LITTLE LATE THIS YEAR
   Vocal refrain by Sergeant Johnny Desmond
Sergeant Johnny Desmond: And now if Sergeant Norm Leyden will shoot me another of those
   handsome musical picture-frames he creates, I'll try paintin' ya a portrait of a tune
   that's more beautiful than it is young, "The Lamp Is Low."
THE LAMP IS LOW
   Vocal refrain by Sergeant Johnny Desmond
Sergeant Johnny Desmond: Back home, 'way down South, where the honeysuckle is on the vine
   and the fried chicken is on the dinner-plate, we have a song-writin' son-of-a-gun who
   really gets a heart-beat into his music. The writer, Willard Robison. His latest tune,
   "Deep Summer Music."
DEEP SUMMER MUSIC
   Vocal refrain by Sergeant Johnny Desmond
Sergeant Johnny Desmond: This is Sergeant Johnny Desmond sayin' thanks for listenin' to
   this show and hope you'll be back for the next one. We'll all be back in just about a
   week with ...
Corporal Paul Dubov: ... three songs by a three-striper, "Songs by Sergeant Johnny
   Desmond," with music by the American Band of the A.E.F.
TIME ON MY HANDS (closing theme)
   Vocal refrain by Sergeant Johnny Desmond

03Dec44 (Sun) 4:00-4:30PM Co-Partners Hall, Bedford, England   SLO-65841
   SONGS BY SGT. JOHNNY DESMOND recording   Script   Aired 29Jan45
                                 OR
08Oct44 (Sun) 12:45-1:00PM Co-Partners Hall, Bedford, England
   A SOLDIER AND A SONG broadcast   Script

   ...

Sergeant Johnny Desmond: A few years ago on Broadway, a show opened titled "Very Warm for
   May." Well, it wasn't very hot for the critics, because they turned their typewriter
   thumbs down on the production, and the show didn't last very long. However, one of its
   songs seems to be standing the test of time and I'd like to sing it for ya now, "All the
   Things You Are."
ALL THE THINGS YOU ARE
   Vocal refrain by Sergeant Johnny Desmond

   ...

03Dec44 (Sun) 4:30-5:00PM Co-Partners Hall, Bedford, England   SLO-65842
SONGS BY SGT. JOHNNY DESMOND recording   Script   Aired 05Feb45

Announcer: This is a program produced for the A.E.F.P. by the American Band of the A.E.F.
TIME ON MY HANDS (opening theme)
  Corporal Paul Dubov: "Songs by Sergeant Johnny Desmond."
  Vocal refrain by Sergeant Johnny Desmond
  Corporal Paul Dubov: Three songs by a three-striper, with music by the American Band of
    the A.E.F.
Sergeant Johnny Desmond: Hello there. This is Sergeant Johnny Desmond. Sergeant Norm
  Leyden opines as how the best way to get you in the right mood for the show is to
  sprinkle a little musical stardust in your eyes. Then when you can't see what you're
  hearin', let you have it one-two-three with a brace of romantic songs. So, look out,
  here comes the stardust, in a few well-measured bars of "Where or When."
WHERE OR WHEN
  Vocal refrain by Sergeant Johnny Desmond
Sergeant Johnny Desmond: First in our own particular heart and second on this particular
  program, a real seven-o'clock song, "In the Blue of Evening."
IN THE BLUE OF EVENING
  Vocal refrain by Sergeant Johnny Desmond
Sergeant Johnny Desmond: Back about six years ago, before I got a chance to do any
  singin' with bands, I wrote in a request to a big band askin' 'em to play a certain
  song. Well, up until now they haven't played it. So, I'm takin' opportunity while it's
  hot and askin' the American Band of the A.E.F. to knock me a chorus of "Deep Purple."
DEEP PURPLE
Sergeant Johnny Desmond: Thank you, Norm Leyden. And 'long about now I'd like to chime
  in with a few words singin' the praises of "Sweet Lorraine." Serenade me, Sarge.
SWEET LORRAINE
  Vocal refrain by Sergeant Johnny Desmond
Sergeant Johnny Desmond: This is Sergeant Johnny Desmond sayin' thanks for listenin' to
  this show and hope you'll be back for the next one. We'll all be back in just about a
  week with ...
Corporal Paul Dubov: ... three songs by a three-striper, "Songs by Sergeant Johnny
  Desmond," with music by the American Band of the A.E.F.
TIME ON MY HANDS (closing theme)
  Vocal refrain by Sergeant Johnny Desmond

03Dec44 (Sun) 10:20-10:40PM   Co-Partners Hall, Bedford, England   SLO-65844
   THE UPTOWN HALL recording   Aired 11Jan45

Announcer: This is a program produced for the A.E.F.P. by the American Band of the A.E.F.
MY GUY'S COME BACK (opening theme)
   Corporal Paul Dubov: Good evening, all, it's "The Uptown Hall," music for you of the
      Allied Liberation Forces, presented by members of the American Band of the A.E.F.,
      featuring Sergeant Mel Powell at the piano.
   Corporal Paul Dubov: Hi there and welcome to "The Uptown Hall," meeting place of those
      who like their music soft but solid. You know, here in the Hall we don't waltz around
      much before we get started, there's no formality, no delay. We say, "Take a seat and
      get under way." And that's just what we're gonna do right now with Mel and the lads
      building a fire under one of your old favorites, "Hallelujah!"
HALLELUJAH!
   Corporal Paul Dubov: Very pretty, boys, very pretty. Before we go on, we've got a little
      piece of unfinished business to take up. Mel tells me that last meeting he had a word
      for you folks but couldn't get it in. So tonight we're giving him another chance.
      O.K., Mel, what was the word? "Louise?" Well, why didn't you say so?
LOUISE
   Corporal Paul Dubov: Yes, sir. And now the rhythm really gets rambunctious. It's our
      "Band within a Band," a pear-shaped little outfit that's really peachy. It's Pri -
      P.F.C. Frank Ippolito, pum, at the drums; Sergeant Trigger Alpert, string bass; getting
      a little on me; Sergeant Michael Hucko, clarinet; and that mellow fellow Sergeant Powell
      at the piano. Their target for tonight, "If Dreams Come True."
IF DREAMS COME TRUE (quartet: Hucko, Powell, Alpert, Ippolito)
   Corporal Paul Dubov: Yes, sir, we've got a million of 'em. But right now it's time for a
      song by Sergeant Johnny Desmond. And tonight he's putting the vocal frosting on that
      little white lie called "I'm thru with Love."
I'M THRU WITH LOVE
   Vocal refrain by Sergeant Johnny Desmond
   Corporal Paul Dubov: In this little aggregation of our's there a man who plays the French
      horn with a Shreveport accent. He's Corporal Addison S. Collins, Junior. And among his
      many accomplishments he'll also turn out an arrangement now and then if we use whips.
      We've penciled in one of his arrangements tonight for our closing number and here it is,
      "Night in Tunisia."
NIGHT IN TUNISIA
   Corporal Paul Dubov: Well, fellow members, that just about buttons things up for now.
      But we're not taking in that welcome mat, no, sir, 'cause we're gonna be needing it
      again every Wednesday, Thursday and Saturday night when Mel and his lads from the
      American Band of the A.E.F. bring you more of that soft but oh so solid music. Here's
      hoping you can join the merry throng next time. Until then, so long and good luck to
      you.
MY GUY'S COME BACK (closing theme)

04Dec44 (Mon) 3:30-4:15PM Co-Partners Hall, Bedford, England   SLO-66381
  THE SWING SHIFT recording   Aired 20Jan45

[Announcer: This is a feature of the American Band of the A.E.F.
Corporal Paul Dubov: Presenting "The Swing Shift" with Sergeant Ray McKinley and his
  music.]
SONG AND DANCE (opening theme)
  Vocal refrain by Technical Sergeant Ray McKinley:
    This is Sergeant Ray McKinley saying howdya do,
    And all the boys in the band saying howdy too.
    So get yourself settled 'round the radio,
    While I tell you what's cooking on this evening's show.
    Because a whole lot of folks like the first one hot,
    We call on the brass for our opening shot.
    On hand are the Crew Chiefs who will harmonize,
    On a tune I'm sure that most of you will recognize.
    Then Sergeant Johnny Desmond's gonna have his say,
    On a couple of pretties from the U.S.A.
    Since I have to justify my presence here,
    Why somewhere along the line I'll probably interfere.
    But the band is a'staying, which without a doubt,
    Should get most of the credit, so from here on out,
    I'll go and give the drums a little wear and tear.
    Dubov, my boy, you're on the air.
Corporal Paul Dubov: Hi, Mac. What's new with our drum-chum?
T/Sgt. Ray McKinley: Ah, nothing except for this tasty little menu I've prepared for
  today's song feast.
Corporal Paul Dubov: Musical home-cooking, huh, Mac?
T/Sgt. Ray McKinley: Exactly, Paul. Same sort of stuff our G.I.s used to stomp at at the
  Palladium, Roseland, and Ritz back home.
Corporal Paul Dubov: I'll bet our listeners are rarin' to sample some of that brew.
T/Sgt. Ray McKinley: Well, we won't keep them waiting another minute. We're lighting up
  the parlor with some real big mouth music called "Snafu Jump." It's fast, boys, one,
  two.
SNAFU JUMP
Corporal Paul Dubov: And now "The Swing Shifters" shift right into a quiet mood with some
  real rumble-seat music, "Star Dust."
STAR DUST
Corporal Paul Dubov: Sergeant McKinley and the Crew Chiefs carry the mail in this next
  hunk o' wishful thinkin'. Here they are, tickets in hand, shoutin' "I'm Headin' for
  California."
I'M HEADIN' FOR CALIFORNIA
  Vocal refrain by Technical Sergeant Ray McKinley and the Crew Chiefs
Corporal Paul Dubov: Here's Ray and the boys rambling cross country in a toe-tapping
  special called "Another One of Them Things."
ANOTHER ONE OF THEM THINGS
[Corporal Paul Dubov: Now it's front and center for Sergeant] Johnny Desmond, who has a
  few well-chosen notes on the subject of love. Johnny sings "Now I Know."
NOW I KNOW
  Vocal refrain by Sergeant Johnny Desmond
[Corporal Paul Dubov: Sergeant Michael Hucko joins Sergeants Powell and McKinley] in the
  kitchen. And here's the trio whipping up a hunk of pastry they call "Cheesecake."
CHEESECAKE [trio: Hucko (tenor saxophone), Powell, McKinley]
Corporal Paul Dubov: Back comes [Sergeant Johnny Desmond to say it with another song.
  And this time it's "Time Alone Will Tell."
TIME ALONE WILL TELL
  Vocal refrain by Sergeant Johnny Desmond
Corporal Paul Dubov: Sergeant Steve Steck added a] few notes to "The Swing Shift" slogan
  and we're all looking forward to that day when we'll be "Flying Home."
FLYING HOME

[Corporal Paul Dubov: Now we swing over to the package wrappin' department where Sergeant
   Ray McKinley is ready to tie up this session. Keep tuned to A.E.F. and we'll see you
   soon.
SONG AND DANCE (closing theme)
   Vocal refrain by Technical Sergeant Ray McKinley]

BBC female announcer: This program was recorded by the American Dance Band before the
   American Band of the A.E.F. left for the Continent. In just a moment all your A.E.F.
   stations will identify themselves. This is the Allied Expeditionary Forces Program of
   the B.B.C.

04Dec44 (Mon) 7:01-7:15PM Co-Partners Hall, Bedford, England
SONGS BY SGT. JOHNNY DESMOND broadcast   Script

Announcer: This is a program produced for the A.E.F.P. by the American Band of the A.E.F.
TIME ON MY HANDS (opening theme)
   Corporal Paul Dubov: "Songs by Sergeant Johnny Desmond."
   Vocal refrain by Sergeant Johnny Desmond
   Corporal Paul Dubov: Four songs by a three-striper, "Songs by Sergeant Johnny Desmond,"
      with music by the American Band of the A.E.F.
Sergeant Johnny Desmond: Hello there. This is Sergeant Johnny Desmond. Maybe you'll
   think what's good enough for Frank Sinatra is too good for me, but I'll take a chance
   anyway, in leadin' off with a song into which "The Voice" has injected a bit of new
   life, "Without a Song."
WITHOUT A SONG
   Vocal refrain by Sergeant Johnny Desmond
Sergeant Johnny Desmond: And now that we've got "The Voice's" choice out of our system,
   we'll lay a little selection of our own choosin' on ya. 'Tain't new but it sure is
   good. "It Had to Be You."
IT HAD TO BE YOU
   Vocal refrain by Sergeant Johnny Desmond
Sergeant Johnny Desmond: Sergeant Norm Leyden, directin' the American Band of the A.E.F.,
   won't let me up for a minute. Already his baton is describin' the slow easy beat that
   paves the way for soft and sentimental "Sweet and Lovely."
SWEET AND LOVELY
   Vocal refrain by Sergeant Johnny Desmond
Sergeant Johnny Desmond: And here's a listener's idea of what the windup song on our
   quarter-hour should be. Requested by a P.F.C., which apparently in this case mean a
   "Plenty Fine Chooser," here's "Time Waits for No One."
TIME WAITS FOR NO ONE
   Vocal refrain by Sergeant Johnny Desmond
Sergeant Johnny Desmond: This is Sergeant Johnny Desmond, and before we mosey along, I'd
   like to pin a thank-you note on the ear that listened today, and a "Welcome" sign on the
   other ear which we hope'll be listenin' next week for ...
Corporal Paul Dubov: ... three songs by a three-striper, "Songs by Sergeant Johnny
   Desmond," with music by the American Band of the A.E.F.
TIME ON MY HANDS (closing theme)
   Vocal refrain by Sergeant Johnny Desmond
   Corporal Paul Dubov: Next Monday, same time, same place is the time and place for next
      week's edition of "Songs by Sergeant Johnny Desmond," with music by the American Band
      of the A.E.F.

04Dec44 (Mon) 7:15-7:29PM Co-Partners Hall, Bedford, England
STRINGS WITH WINGS broadcast   Script

I SUSTAIN THE WINGS (opening theme)
   Corporal Paul Dubov: "Strings with Wings." "Strings with Wings," a program of music
      for you of the Allied Liberation Forces, presented by the string section of the
      American Band of the A.E.F., featuring Sergeant George Ockner and his violin.
   Corporal Paul Dubov: Hello there, folks, and welcome to another program of "Strings with
     Wings." Just about this time in the studio, the folks back home are probably sitting
     down by the radio to enjoy a bit of music. And if you've got a few minutes to spare
     tonight, why don't you folks join 'em? Sergeant Ockner and the boys have got some swell
     tunes on hand this evening, just the kind we think you guys and gals really go for. So,
     while the violins take over, let's you and I just lean back and listen. Here's the
     first one coming up, "You and the Night and the Music."
YOU AND THE NIGHT AND THE MUSIC
   Corporal Paul Dubov: A few years back composer Hoagy Carmichael hit the best seller list
     with a tune that's been one of your favorites ever since. Here it is in a violin
     version, as played by the string section of the American Band of the A.E.F., "Star
     Dust."
STAR DUST
   Corporal Paul Dubov: For their next number the violins take you on a little trip down
     South America way. It's Sergeant Jerry Gray's arrangement of that popular Brazilian
     samba "Tico-Tico."
TICO-TICO
   Corporal Paul Dubov: Our "Strings with Wings" take off again. And it's Sergeant Ockner
     and the boys completing their missions for tonight with a little musical high-flying
     "Over the Rainbow."
OVER THE RAINBOW
   Corporal Paul Dubov: Well, we've got more tunes, but no more time. So I guess that's all
     for tonight. Come Wednesday, we'll be back with some more of your popular favorites
     played by the violins. And here's hopin' you'll be around to listen. Until then, this
     is Corporal Paul Dubov saying, "So long, and good luck to you."
I SUSTAIN THE WINGS (closing theme)
   Corporal Paul Dubov: You've been listening to a program of music by the string section
     of the American Band of the A.E.F., featuring Sergeant George Ockner and his violin.
     Don't forget to join us this coming Wednesday night when we again present "Strings
     with Wings."

06Dec44 (Wed)   EMI studio, St. John's Wood, Abbey Road, London, England
CHRISTMAS GREETINGS FROM DON HAYNES
Lt. Don Haynes recorded a Christmas message for his wife, Polly Davis   Haynes.

Merry Christmas. I can't be with you this Christmas, that is, I can't be with you in person. But, sweetheart, I'm certainly with you in spirit and my thoughts are only of you today and every day. So here's a little scheme thought up by that fast-thinkin' Mr. Joy Hodges that will enable me to tell you how much I love you and miss you.

Though we're some three thousand some odd miles away (it brings us) a little closer together (and) I'm all for it. As I sit here with my mustache resting comfortably on this microphone, talking to the sweetest gal that ever drew a breath, I can't help but do a little day dreaming, or wishful thinking might be the better term for it. I can picture you in our cosy little apartment this Christmas day in 1944 devoid of any stockings --- there just ain't any fireplace. If I were there I would probably be getting our breakfast, fixing the grapefruit, making the coffee, setting the table, and burning the toast. Waking you out of that sound slumber you seem to be enjoying so much would come next and that was always a pleasure, dear, 'cause it enabled me to kneel down beside your bed and kiss you until you became sufficiently awake to know that it was time to get up. You'd always open your pretty blue eyes, you know I mean brown, smile and put your arms around me. It was always so wonderful and will be again, darling, but I'd better stop day dreaming right now 'cause I'm not really in New York but 'way over here looking out on the Eiffel Tower and the Rue de la Paix. There'll come a day, sweetie, and I don't think that it is so far off, when the little one-act drama referred to earlier will be reenacted over and over again. And that's what I'm looking forward to, darling, believe me.

Glenn, Paul, McKinley, Trigger, Jerry Gray and all the boys have been doing a wonderful job over here, honey, and the stories of our experiences over here will make awful good listening when we return.

I imagine you'll be talking long distance to Cleveland today so be sure and wish mother, Andy, Bob and Lucille a Merry Christmas for me. You'll no doubt spend the day in Tenafly, so give Helen, Steven and Jonnie Dee a big Christmas hug for me. The same to Fritzy, Joel and Steven Spivak. If you talk to Charlie, wish him a Merry Christmas and a most prosperous New Year. Tell Tommy not to lose faith in Notre Dame; this just wasn't their year. Give George Effenbach and Bea Brown my best also. And tell the youngest they don't say "Merry Christmas" over here but "Joyous Noel," but that I wish her the same and lots of it. Same to Joy and Kay and Sally too.

See you, precious. A Merry Christmas and a happy New Year. And it will be a happy one, darling, 'cause we're sure to be together some time in 1945. I love you more than anything in this world, honey, and I thank god every day that I have you to go home to. Good bye for now, sweetheart. I'll be seeing you.

06Dec44 (Wed) EMI studio, St. John's Wood, Abbey Road, London, England
CHRISTMAS GREETINGS FROM GLENN MILLER
Major Glenn Miller recorded a Christmas message for his wife, Helen Miller.

Hello, Helen, dear. Merry Christmas. I beat you to the punch on that one. You won't get a chance to answer. I'm following a pretty tough routine because Don and Paul were just here and made records to send to Joy and Polly and they had their's all written out, but I thought I'd rather just sit down and talk a little while. Course, you can't answer but I can imagine what the answers'd be. Ah, don't know when we're gonna get home. Looks like it's gonna be quite a little while yet, but if this makes Christmas any better for you then that'll be such a great pleasure for me.

Sure dyin' to see Steve. Got the pictures. He sure has grown. Great little guy. Ah. Tell him Merry Christmas for me. And Jonnie Dee, course she won't understand but I'm tickled to death that she's there and I-I'm dyin' to see the pictures and get letters from you tellin' me about her.

Ah, Paul and Don send their greetings and, ah, oh, there's not an awful lot to say when you're so far away on Christmas, you know. Well, this is a couple of 'em that we've missed together, the next few will make up for all the time that we've wasted and we'll have our family with us, really have a wonderful time. Ah, a million sweet kisses and god bless you and keep you and the kids 'til we come home. Merry Christmas, dear.

06Dec44 (Wed) 6:15-6:30PM Co-Partners Hall, Bedford, England
THE UPTOWN HALL broadcast
Script

Announcer: This is a program produced for the A.E.F.P. by the American Band of the A.E.F.
MY GUY'S COME BACK (opening theme)
Corporal Paul Dubov: Good evening, all, it's "The Uptown Hall," music for you of the Allied Liberation Forces, presented by members of the American Band of the A.E.F., featuring Sergeant Mel Powell at the piano.
Corporal Paul Dubov: Hi there, and welcome to "The Uptown Hall," fellow members. As you know, one of the by-laws of the Hall reads as follows, quote, "Whereas these meetings are only fifteen minutes long, and inasmuch as the members want to hear as much music as possible in the aforementioned time, be it resolved that each meetin' shall get goin' without any verbal schmaltzing around." So following the rules to the letter, here's tonight's first tune, "Charmaine."
CHARMAINE
Corporal Paul Dubov: Well, that musical encounter with "Charmaine" left the boys feeling a little mellow. So suitin' the music to their mood, they're coming back with something on the dreamy side, "Stars Fell on Alabama."
STARS FELL ON ALABAMA
Corporal Paul Dubov: And before any of the more unruly element here can stand up and yell "More," we're takin' the play away from 'em with our little "Band within a Band." It's Sergeant Ray McKinley at the drums; Sergeant Trigger Alpert, string bass; Sergeant Michael Hucko, clarinet; and the man himself, Sergeant Mel Powell at the piano. Tonight they're giving you folks a few directions for locating "The Uptown Hall." They say, go two blocks up Harmony Highway, turn left on Rhythm Road and you'll see it straight ahead "On the Sunny Side of the Street."
ON THE SUNNY SIDE OF THE STREET (quartet: Hucko, Powell, Alpert, McKinley)
Corporal Paul Dubov: Gather 'round now for a little session of words and music. It's music by Mel and company, words by Sergeant Johnny Desmond. Put 'em together and you get "What a Diff'rence a Day Made."
WHAT A DIFF'RENCE A DAY MADE
Vocal refrain by Sergeant Johnny Desmond
Corporal Paul Dubov: For their last number this evening, Mel and the lads tie a few fancy ribbons on an old swing favorite, "Somebody Loves Me."
SOMEBODY LOVES ME
Corporal Paul Dubov: And that's all from "Uptown Hall." Sorry we gotta cut out like this. But no tears now because remember we'll be back again tomorrow night with more of that soft but oh so solid music that features Sergeant Mel Powell at the piano. So don't forget to be listening. Until then, this is Corporal Paul Dubov saying, "So long, and good luck to you."
MY GUY'S COME BACK (closing theme)
Corporal Paul Dubov: You've been listening to music by members of the American Band of the A.E.F. Don't forget to join us tomorrow night for another musical meeting in "The Uptown Hall."

06Dec44 (Wed) 7:45-8:00PM Co-Partners Hall, Bedford, England
STRINGS WITH WINGS broadcast
Script

Announcer: This is a program produced for the A.E.F.P. by the American Band of the A.E.F.
I SUSTAIN THE WINGS (opening theme)
    Corporal Paul Dubov: "Strings with Wings." "Strings with Wings," a program of music
        for you of the Allied Liberation Forces, presented by the string section of the
        American Band of the A.E.F., featuring Sergeant George Ockner and his violin.
Corporal Paul Dubov: Hello there, folks. Welcome to another program of "Strings with
    Wings." Well, Sergeant Ockner blew the whistle and we're falling out here in front of
    your radio, to make with the music again. The boys have brought along their violins,
    and a lot of mighty fine tunes. So it looks as though we've got a real pleasant
    quarter-hour ahead of us. So light up a cigarette, if you've got one, and take it easy
    for a few minutes, while we get the show under way with our opening tune tonight, "I
    Surrender, Dear."
I SURRENDER, DEAR
Corporal Paul Dubov: We clipped this next one from the song book of composer Duke
    Ellington. There's a gentleman who's been responsible for a lot of mighty swell
    numbers. But number one in everybody's list of favorites seems to be "Sophisticated
    Lady."
SOPHISTICATED LADY
Corporal Paul Dubov: Sergeant Ockner passes out the music for the next one, tosses the
    boys a down-beat, and tucks his violin back under his chin, all in one graceful gesture.
    And we hear the string orchestra playing "Sweet and Low."
SWEET AND LOW
Corporal Paul Dubov: The boys bring the program to a close with a question mark. Just
    why they're asking this question, I wouldn't know. But here they are trying to find the
    answer to "How Deep Is the Ocean?"
HOW DEEP IS THE OCEAN (How High Is the Sky)
Corporal Paul Dubov: And that winds up our miniature musicale for tonight, folks. But
    don't go too far away, because we're back here every Monday and Wednesday night,
    bringing you more tunes by Sergeant Ockner and the string section of the American Band
    of the A.E.F. Listen in again, won't you? Until the next time, this is Corporal Paul
    Dubov saying, "So long, and good luck to you."
I SUSTAIN THE WINGS (closing theme)

06Dec44 (Wed) 11:00-11:25PM Co-Partners Hall, Bedford, England   SLO-65855
   THE UPTOWN HALL recording   Aired 26Jan45

Oranges and Lemons (BBC theme --- not by Miller group)
BBC announcer: The American Band of the A.E.F. is now on the Continent entertaining
   Allied troops. The program you are about to hear was specially recorded for you under
   the direction of Major Glenn Miller before the band left.

[Announcer: This is a program produced for the A.E.F.P. by the American Band of the
   A.E.F.]
MY GUY'S COME BACK (opening theme)
   Corporal Paul Dubov: Good evening, all, it's "The Uptown Hall," music for you of the
      Allied Liberation Forces, presented by members of the American Band of the A.E.F.,
      featuring Sergeant Mel Powell at the piano.
   Corporal Paul Dubov: Hi there and welcome to "The Uptown Hall," fellow members. As you
      know, one of the by-laws of the Hall reads as follows, quote, "Whereas these meetings
      are only fifteen minutes long, and inasmuch as the members want to hear as much music as
      possible in the aforementioned time, be it resolved that each meetin' shall get going
      without any verbal schmaltzing around," unquote. So, following the rules to the letter,
      here's tonight's first tune, "Charmaine."
CHARMAINE
Corporal Paul Dubov: Well, that little encounter with "Charmaine" left the boys feeling a
   bit mellow. So suitin' the music to their mood, they're coming right back with
   something on the dreamy side, "Stars Fell on Alabama."
STARS FELL ON ALABAMA
Corporal Paul Dubov: Now before any of the more unruly elements here can stand up and
   yell "More," we're takin' the play away from 'em with our little "Band within a Band,"
   Sergeant Ray McKinley at the drums; Sergeant Trigger Alpert, string bass; Sergeant
   Michael Hucko, clarinet; and the man himself, Sergeant Mel Powell at the piano. Tonight
   they're giving you folks a few directions for locating "The Uptown Hall." They say, go
   two blocks up Harmony Highway, turn left on Rhythm Road and you'll see it straight ahead
   "On the Sunny Side of the Street."
ON THE SUNNY SIDE OF THE STREET (quartet: Hucko, Powell, Alpert, McKinley)
Corporal Paul Dubov: Gather 'round now [for a little session of words and music. It's
   music by Mel and company, words by Sergeant Johnny Desmond. Put 'em together and you
   get "What a Diff'rence a Day Made."
WHAT A DIFF'RENCE A DAY MADE
   Vocal refrain by Sergeant Johnny Desmond
Corporal Paul Dubov: For their last number this evening, Mel and the lads tie a few fancy
   ribbons on an old swing favorite, "Somebody Loves Me."]
SOMEBODY LOVES ME
Corporal Paul Dubov: And that's all from "Uptown Hall." I'm sorry we gotta cut out like
   this. But huh, huh, huh, huh, no tears now because remember we'll be back here every
   Wednesday, Thursday and Saturday night with more of that soft but oh so solid music that
   features Sergeant Mel Powell at the piano. So drop around and cut yourself a ration of
   rhythm. Until the next time then, so long, and good luck to you.
MY GUY'S COME BACK (closing theme)

BBC announcer: The program you have just heard ...

06Dec44 (Wed) 11:50PM - 07Dec44 (Thu) 12:15AM Co-Partners Hall, Bedford, England
SLO-65857
THE UPTOWN HALL recording
Aired 31Jan45

[Announcer: This is a program produced for the A.E.F.P. by the American Band of the A.E.F.

MY GUY'S COME BACK (opening theme)

Corporal Paul Dubov: Good evening, all, it's "The Uptown Hall," music for you of the Allied Liberation Forces, presented by members of the American Band of the A.E.F., featuring Sergeant Mel Powell at the piano.

Corporal Paul Dubov: Hi there] and welcome to "The Uptown Hall," fellow members. That little theme you just heard tells all the steady customers that the stuff is here and it's mellow. Yes, sir, we're back in harmony headquarters at the Hall, ready to serve up another helping of sweet music to you folks who like your music soft but solid. I see the audience is still troopin' in. So just by way of a processional, get out that first number, Mel, and play 'em to their seats. "O.K.," says Mel and here it comes, "Lady Be Good!"

OH, LADY BE GOOD!

Corporal Paul Dubov: Now let's have a little soft light for some sweet music. It's our romance special for tonight featuring Sergeant Bernie Privin and his trumpet playing "You Go to My Head."

YOU GO TO MY HEAD

Corporal Paul Dubov: O.K., fellows, you got the folks real happy. And we're going to keep 'em that way by bringing on Sergeant [Johnny Desmond for a song. Here he is now to tell us all about why "She's Funny That Way."

(I Got a Woman Crazy for Me) SHE'S FUNNY THAT WAY

Vocal refrain by Sergeant Johnny Desmond

Corporal Paul Dubov: Here to answer "Present" when her name's called] tonight is a little lady who's done a lot to make these meetings really enjoyable. Fellow members, I give you "Emaline."

EMALINE

Corporal Paul Dubov: And that's all from "The Uptown Hall." Well, as you file out quietly, the ushers will pass among you and pick up your promise to be back for our next little musical meeting. Remember, we gather here every Wednesday, Thursday and Saturday night. [So don't forget to drop around and give us a listen. Until the next time then, "So long, and good luck to you."

MY GUYS COME BACK (closing theme)]

07Dec44 (Thu) 12:15-12:40AM Co-Partners Hall, Bedford, England   **SLO-65858**
  THE UPTOWN HALL recording   Script   Aired 02Feb45

Announcer: This is a program produced for the A.E.F.P. by the American Band of the A.E.F.
MY GUY'S COME BACK (opening theme)
  Corporal Paul Dubov: Good evening, all, it's "The Uptown Hall," music for you of the
    Allied Liberation Forces, presented by members of the American Band of the A.E.F.,
    featuring Sergeant Mel Powell at the piano.
  Corporal Paul Dubov: Hi there and welcome to "The Uptown Hall," fellow members. Come
    right in and make yourself at home. Back in New York, U.S.A. when you get up above 52nd
    Street you hear a kind of music that swing fans call the "Uptown" style. And here in
    the Hall we've transplanted a big quarter-hour of that same music for you folks who like
    it soft but solid. That's what this little rhythm review really adds up to. But to
    give you a better idea of what I mean, here's Mel and the lads with "You're Driving Me
    Crazy!"
YOU'RE DRIVING ME CRAZY! (What Did I Do?)
  Corporal Paul Dubov: Now that we've explained what we mean by "Uptown," we can carry on
    with the business of the evening. The agenda calls next for something in a lazier
    cadence. So, Mel, take it slow and easy while the folks and I lean back and listen to
    "Dream a Little Dream of Me."
DREAM A LITTLE DREAM OF ME
  Corporal Paul Dubov: Every time the program calls for a tune like this next one, we send
    in a rush order for our little "Band within a Band." It's a tune just suited to their
    capabilities, and they're here on hand to deal with it. There's Sergeant Ray McKinley
    at the drums; Sergeant Trigger Alpert, string bass; Sergeant Michael Hucko, clarinet;
    and Sergeant Mel Powell, piano. Here they are soundin' off with "I'll Do Most Anything
    for You."
(I Would Do) ANYTHING FOR YOU (quartet: Hucko, Powell, Alpert, McKinley)
  Corporal Paul Dubov: Walking across the stage now comes Sergeant Johnny Desmond, blind-
    folded and carrying a white flag. Being a master of musical charades, I'd say you can
    be pretty sure the title of his song tonight is "I Surrender, Dear."
I SURRENDER, DEAR
  Vocal refrain by Sergeant Johnny Desmond
  Corporal Paul Dubov: With brother Mel officiating at the black and whites, the lads break
    up our little meeting tonight with their V-1 version of "Struttin' with Some Barbecue,"
    featuring Sergeant Bernie Privin and his trumpet.
STRUTTIN' WITH SOME BARBECUE
  Corporal Paul Dubov: Well, it looks as though we're fresh out of downbeats tonight,
    folks. But we're gonna get a new supply in right away, and you'll be hearin' from us as
    usual every Wednesday, Thursday and Saturday evening. So don't get lost. In the
    meantime, we're lockin' up the Hall and sayin', "So long, and good luck to you."
MY GUY'S COME BACK (closing theme)

07Dec44 (Thu) 1:05-1:30AM Co-Partners Hall, Bedford, England   SL0-65860
  THE UPTOWN HALL recording   Aired 07Feb45

[Announcer: This is a program produced for the A.E.F.P. by the American Band of the
   A.E.F.
MY GUY'S COME BACK (opening theme)
  Corporal Paul Dubov: Good evening, all, it's "The Uptown Hall," music for you of the
     Allied Liberation Forces, presented by members of the American Band of the A.E.F.,
     featuring Sergeant Mel Powell at the piano.
  Corporal Paul Dubov: Hi there and welcome to "The Uptown Hall," fellow members. Well,
     we're back here in the Hall to deal out some more music to you guys and gals. It's our
     own special style of music. And the only way you can describe] it is to say it occupies
     a groove about half way between sweet and swing. But now that we've got Sergeant Mel
     and the boys here, why maybe we ought to follow up that explanation by passing out a few
     samples. First sample coming up, Mel gives me the nod, and I give you the title, it's
     "Shandy."
SHANDY
Corporal Paul Dubov: Refreshment time in the Hall. And for this occasion Sergeant Powell
   has fixed up a little serving of some Dixieland jazz. Here it is, sprinkled with a
   touch of hot trumpet by Sergeant Bernie Privin, "Please Don't Talk about Me When I'm
   Gone."
PLEASE DON'T TALK ABOUT ME WHEN I'M GONE
Corporal Paul Dubov: Here comes the "Band within a Band," featuring guess who and guess
   who playing "I Must Have That Man."
I MUST HAVE THAT MAN (quartet: Hucko, Powell, Alpert, McKinley)
Corporal Paul Dubov: For their closing number tonight the lads rub two notes together and
   build a fire under one of Sergeant Powell's latest. Here it is, "Triple-X."
TRIPLE-X
Corporal Paul Dubov: Sue me if I'm wrong but I'm afraid that just about takes care of the
   business for tonight. Don't forget, we're here at the Hall every Wednesday, Thursday
   and Saturday night with more music by members of the American Band of the A.E.F.,
   featuring Sergeant Mel Powell at the piano. So don't forget to drop around. Until the
   next time then, so long and good luck to you.
MY GUY'S COME BACK (closing theme)

07Dec44 (Thu) 1:30-2:00AM Co-Partner's Hall, Bedford, England   SLO-66654
THE UPTOWN HALL recording   Script   Aired 09Feb45

Announcer: This is a program produced for the A.E.F.P. by the American Band of the A.E.F.
MY GUY'S COME BACK (opening theme)
  Corporal Paul Dubov: Good evening, all, it's "The Uptown Hall," music for you of the
    Allied Liberation Forces, presented by members of the American Band of the A.E.F.,
    featuring Sergeant Mel Powell at the piano.
Corporal Paul Dubov: Hi there and welcome to "The Uptown Hall," fellow members. Park
  your troubles at the door and walk right in. Admission is free and the music is free
  and easy. So grab a chair and make yourself right at home, while Mel and the lads start
  givin' out with the good stuff. All set? O.K., men, the folks are ready and waitin'.
  So let's have that little bash from the band called "I'm Coming Virginia."
I'M COMING VIRGINIA
Corporal Paul Dubov: Well played, old chap! And now, Mel, if you please, a few well-
  chosen notes about an old glamour-girl of ours that I'm sure we all remember, "Louise."
LOUISE
Corporal Paul Dubov: Falling out in formation now is our little "Band within a Band."
  It's Sergeant Ray McKinley at the drums; Sergeant Trigger Alpert, string bass; Sergeant
  Michael Hucko, clarinet; and that old rajah of the rippling arpeggio, Sergeant Mel
  himself. They open their sealed orders, look at one another in amazement, and take off
  in all directions with "What Is This Thing Called Love?"
WHAT IS THIS THING CALLED LOVE? (quartet: Hucko, Powell, Alpert, McKinley)
Corporal Paul Dubov: There's not a dry eye in the Hall now, as Sergeant Johnny Desmond
  comes forward with a little bitter-sweet ballad called "I'll Walk Alone."
I'LL WALK ALONE
  Vocal refrain by Sergeant Johnny Desmond
Corporal Paul Dubov: It's "All hands 'round" for the final tune of the evening. It's
  brother Mel at the piano, and his little swing group from the American Band of the
  A.E.F., closing tonight's meeting with "You're Lucky to Me."
YOU'RE LUCKY TO ME
Corporal Paul Dubov: Well, fellow members, looks like our lease is up on the Hall for
  tonight. But don't forget, we've got the old place rented again every Wednesday,
  Thursday and Saturday night. So drop around and give the band a hand. Here's hopin' we
  see you here next time. But until then, "So long, and good luck to you."
MY GUY'S COME BACK (closing theme)

07Dec44 (Thu) 5:50-6:30PM Co-Partners Hall, Bedford, England   SLO-66555
  THE SWING SHIFT recording   Aired 27Jan45

[Announcer: This is a feature of the American Band of the A.E.F.
Corporal Paul Dubov: Presenting "The Swing Shift" with Sergeant Ray McKinley and his
  music.
SONG AND DANCE (opening theme)
  Vocal refrain by Technical Sergeant Ray McKinley
Corporal Paul Dubov: Welcome, Mac. You're lookin' well-padded these days.
T/Sgt. Ray McKinley: It's the fault of the mess hall, son. If I have difficulty getting
  close to the A.E.F. microphone, it's because I've been putting away doubles of
  everything.
Corporal Paul Dubov: Boy, you skinny guys really massacre those rations.
T/Sgt. Ray McKinley: Speak for yourself. I sat opposite you at chow and the last time I
  saw a mouth open like yours, there was a fish-hook in it.
Corporal Paul Dubov: Touche. Nevertheless, I'll bet you're ready for pipe, slippers and
  a copy of Yank.
T/Sgt. Ray McKinley: Far from it, Paul. That food is gonna be turned into energy right
  here and now. Watch those calories go up in smoke as we] burn our way through "Stealin'
  Apples." One, two.
STEALIN' APPLES
Corporal Paul Dubov: Now that we've got our kettle boilin', we'll add a large hunk of
  sugar in an ear-fillin' arrangement of George Gershwin's "Rhapsody in Blue."
RHAPSODY IN BLUE
Corporal Paul Dubov: Time for the Crew Chiefs to join voices in a sure-fire aid to
  digestion. [Here they are singing Corporal Murray Kane's original ditty "Have Ya Got
  Any Gum, Chum?"
HAVE YA GOT ANY GUM, CHUM?
  Vocal refrain by the Crew Chiefs
Corporal Paul Dubov: Sergeant Mel Powell insists that while he] may not always be right,
  he's never wrong. His latest arrangement helps his case because you'll be forced to
  agree, after hearing it, that Mel is right and "Somebody's Wrong."
SOMEBODY'S WRONG
Corporal Paul Dubov: The next tune to falter through the air-waves is along romantic
  lines, a ballad escorted by Sergeant Johnny Desmond called "Going My Way."
GOING MY WAY
  Vocal refrain by Sergeant Johnny Desmond
[Corporal Paul Dubov: "The Shift's" Chamber Music Society,] featuring Sergeants Hucko,
  Powell and McKinley, hop into our kitchen to mix a batter of happy melody called "Fruit
  Cake."
FRUIT CAKE (trio: Hucko, Powell, McKinley)
Corporal Paul Dubov: From the sublime to the sublimer as Sergeant Johnny Desmond soothes
  an aching heart with "I Dream of You."
I DREAM OF YOU (More Than You Dream I Do)
  Vocal refrain by Sergeant Johnny Desmond
[Corporal Paul Dubov: The man who really puts boogie]-woogie on the map, steps down to
  answer those requests from you G.I.s who do your beatin' "Eight to the Bar." Sergeant
  Mac, "Beat Me Daddy."
BEAT ME DADDY, EIGHT TO THE BAR
  Vocal refrain by Technical Sergeant Ray McKinley and Ensemble
Corporal Paul Dubov: The big guns up in the brass section load their horns with a stick
  of musical dynamite and here they are smack on the target with "Snafu Jump."
SNAFU JUMP
Corporal Paul Dubov: You've been listening to "The Swing Shift," featuring Sergeant Ray
  McKinley and his music. Keep your dial set for A.E.F. and we'll see you soon. [This is
  Corporal Paul Dubov sayin', "So Long," and turning you over to Sergeant McKinley.
SONG AND DANCE (closing theme)
  Vocal refrain by Technical Sergeant Ray McKinley
Corporal Paul Dubov: "The Swing Shift" is a feature of the American Band of the A.E.F.]

07Dec44 (Thu) 7:30-8:00PM Co-Partners Hall, Bedford, England   SLO-64996
  THE SWING SHIFT broadcast   Script

Announcer: This is a feature of the American Band of the A.E.F.
Corporal Paul Dubov: Presenting "The Swing Shift" with Sergeant Ray McKinley and his
  music.
SONG AND DANCE (opening theme)
  Vocal refrain by Technical Sergeant Ray McKinley
Corporal Paul Dubov: Welcome, Mac. You're lookin' well-padded these days.
T/Sgt. Ray McKinley: It's the fault of the mess hall, son. If I have difficulty getting
  close to the A.E.F. microphone, it's because I've been putting away doubles of
  everything.
Corporal Paul Dubov: Boy, you skinny guys really massacre those rations.
T/Sgt. Ray McKinley: Speak for yourself. I sat opposite you at chow and the last time I
  saw a mouth open like yours, there was a fish-hook in it.
Corporal Paul Dubov: Touche. Nevertheless, I'll bet you're ready for pipe, slippers and
  a copy of Yank.
T/Sgt. Ray McKinley: Far from it, Paul. That food is gonna be turned into energy right
  here and now. Watch those calories go up in smoke as we burn our way through "Stealin'
  Apples." Ready, boys. One, two.
STEALIN' APPLES
Corporal Paul Dubov: Now that we've got our kettle boilin', we'll add a large hunk of
  sugar in an ear-fillin' arrangement of George Gershwin's "Rhapsody in Blue."
RHAPSODY IN BLUE
Corporal Paul Dubov: Sweet sounds fill the night as Sergeant McKinley and the boys fill
  the air with their ear-pleasing version of "Sweet and Slow."
SWEET AND SLOW
Corporal Paul Dubov: Sergeant Mel Powell insists that while he may not always be right,
  he's never wrong. His latest arrangement helps his case because you'll be forced to
  agree, after hearing it, that Mel is right and "Somebody's Wrong."
SOMEBODY'S WRONG
Corporal Paul Dubov: The next tune to falter through the air-waves is along romantic
  lines, a ballad escorted by Sergeant Johnny Desmond called "Going My Way."
GOING MY WAY
  Vocal refrain by Sergeant Johnny Desmond
Corporal Paul Dubov: "The Swing Shift's" Chamber Music Society, featuring Sergeants
  Hucko, Powell and McKinley, hop into our kitchen to mix a batter of happy melody called
  "Fruit Cake."
FRUIT CAKE (trio: Hucko, Powell, McKinley)
Corporal Paul Dubov: From the sublime to the sublimer as Sergeant Johnny Desmond soothes
  an aching heart with "I Dream of You."
I DREAM OF YOU (More Than You Dream I Do)
  Vocal refrain by Sergeant Johnny Desmond
Corporal Paul Dubov: The man who really puts boogie-woogie on the map, steps down to
  answer those requests from you G.I.s who do your beatin' "Eight to the Bar." Sergeant
  Mac, "Beat Me Daddy."
BEAT ME DADDY, EIGHT TO THE BAR
  Vocal refrain by Technical Sergeant Ray McKinley and Ensemble
Corporal Paul Dubov: The big guns up in the brass section load their horns with a stick
  of musical dynamite and here they are smack on the target with "Snafu Jump."
SNAFU JUMP
Corporal Paul Dubov: You've been listening to "The Swing Shift," featuring Sergeant Ray
  McKinley and his music. We'll be back again with more music at 1501 hours Saturday.
  This is Corporal Paul Dubov sayin', "So Long," and turning you over to Sergeant
  McKinley.
SONG AND DANCE (closing theme)
  Vocal refrain by Technical Sergeant Ray McKinley
Corporal Paul Dubov: "The Swing Shift" is a feature of the American Band of the A.E.F.

07Dec44 (Thu) 9:15-9:30PM Co-Partners Hall, Bedford, England
THE UPTOWN HALL broadcast   Script

Announcer: This is a program produced for the A.E.F.P. by the American Band of the A.E.F.
MY GUY'S COME BACK (opening theme)
   Corporal Paul Dubov: Good evening, all, it's "The Uptown Hall," music for you of the
      Allied Liberation Forces, presented by members of the American Band of the A.E.F.,
      featuring Sergeant Mel Powell at the piano.
Corporal Paul Dubov: Hi there and welcome to "The Uptown Hall," fellow members. As
   secretary to this here now meeting, it's my duty to ready the minutes of the last
   session. But figurin' you folks don't care two K-ration biscuits about what happened
   last time, we'll just file those minutes in the wastebasket under "M" and get on with
   the music. All of which brings us right up to the first bar of tonight's opening tune,
   "Rosetta."
ROSETTA
Corporal Paul Dubov: Now romance raises it's lovely head, and lo and take hold, it's
   Sergeant Johnny Desmond coming up front and center with a love song. Sing ahead,
   Johnny, and make it "East of the Sun."
EAST OF THE SUN
   Vocal refrain by Sergeant Johnny Desmond
Corporal Paul Dubov: I got rhythm, you got rhythm, we all got rhythm here in the Hall.
   And coming up now to add an exclamation point to that statement is our little "Band
   within a Band." It's Sergeant Ray McKinley at the drums; Sergeant Trigger Alpert,
   string bass; Sergeant Michael Hucko, clarinet; and at the keyboard, Sergeant Mel Powell.
   Here they are, glowin' and goin' with "I'm Gonna Sit Right Down and Write Myself a
   Letter."
I'M GONNA SIT RIGHT DOWN AND WRITE MYSELF A LETTER
   (quartet: Hucko, Powell, Alpert, McKinley)

   ...

08Dec44 (Fri) 4:00-5:00PM Co-Partners Hall, Bedford, England   SAL-17833
  SONGS BY SGT. JOHNNY DESMOND recordings   Script   Aired 01Jan45

Corporal Paul Dubov: This is a program produced for the A.E.F.P. by the American Band of
  the A.E.F.
TIME ON MY HANDS (opening theme)
  Corporal Paul Dubov: "Songs by Sergeant Johnny Desmond."
  Vocal refrain by Sergeant Johnny Desmond
  Corporal Paul Dubov: Three songs by a three-striper, with music by the American Band of
    the A.E.F.
Sergeant Johnny Desmond: Hello there. This is Sergeant Johnny Desmond. When it comes to
  pickin' sure-fire tunes, all a singer has to do is listen to the advice of the man who
  ran a trained frog in his voice up to a couple o' million dollars, Bing Crosby. And,
  from the greatest of 'em all comes the O.K. for this song.
GOING MY WAY
  Vocal refrain by Sergeant Johnny Desmond
Sergeant Johnny Desmond: Now for a soft-hearted song hallmarked "Hit" by the popular
  bandleaders of the U.S.A. They play it over the air every time they see a microphone in
  front of 'em, "Time Waits for No One."
TIME WAITS FOR NO ONE
  Vocal refrain by Sergeant Johnny Desmond
Sergeant Johnny Desmond: Now for a small saucer-full of music without words. I'm sittin'
  this next one out and listenin' along with ya, while the American Band of the A.E.F.
  blends a bright and happy mixture for you, "Cherokee."
CHEROKEE (Indian Love Song)
Sergeant Johnny Desmond: Here I go again. I feel another song comin' on. And again it's
  one of the 1944 bumper crop of Hit-Parade-busters. You'll remember this one, "I'll
  Remember April."
I'LL REMEMBER APRIL
  Vocal refrain by Sergeant Johnny Desmond
Sergeant Johnny Desmond: This is Sergeant Johnny Desmond.
TIME ON MY HANDS (closing theme)
  Sergeant Johnny Desmond: Blackout time for this session. But before we pull the
    curtain, here's an invite to join us again next time it's handy for ...
  Corporal Paul Dubov: ... three songs by a three-striper. "Songs by Sergeant Johnny
    Desmond," a program of the American Band of the A.E.F.
  Vocal refrain by Sergeant Johnny Desmond

08Dec44 (Fri) 11:30PM-Midnight Co-Partners Hall, Bedford, England   SLO-66682
  THE SWING SHIFT recording   Script   Aired 14Dec44

Announcer: This is a feature of the American Band of the A.E.F.
Corporal Paul Dubov: Presenting "The Swing Shift" with Sergeant Ray McKinley and his
  music.
SONG AND DANCE (opening theme)
  Vocal refrain by Technical Sergeant Ray McKinley
Corporal Paul Dubov: Hi'ya, Mac. Say, I've got something important to ask you.
T/Sgt. Ray McKinley: You mean you want to brush up on your ignorance?
Corporal Paul Dubov: No kiddin', this is a serious affair!
T/Sgt. Ray McKinley: O.K., I'm listenin'.
Corporal Paul Dubov: Well, lately I have more trouble with females, they're always
  chasing me. They keep hollerin', "He's so cute, so skinny and weak." I'm gettin' tired
  of runnin' and I wanna know what to do.
T/Sgt. Ray McKinley: This poses quite a problem, Paul. I can't understand it at all.
  You know you're not exactly the romantic type. In fact I have it on reasonable
  authority that when snakes get high, they see you.
Corporal Paul Dubov: Well, what is it?
T/Sgt. Ray McKinley: Off hand, I'd say it was the way you introduce people on these
  "Swing Shift" shows. That charming, gay manner you have of saying things.
Corporal Paul Dubov: Yeah! That gets 'em - it kills 'em! I suppose I was born to suffer
  for my art.
T/Sgt. Ray McKinley: Listen, balloon-head, the customers on the other end have suffered
  through enough of this hogwash, and we're gonna cut it short right now. Got on those
  readin' specs, boys, it's time for some music. The take off tune, with Trigger Alpert
  at the controls, is "Swing Low, Sweet Chariot."
SWING LOW, SWEET CHARIOT
Corporal Paul Dubov: Now "The Swing Shifters" toss a handful of dream dust into your eyes
  and we're off on a lazy trip aboard the "Sleepy Town Train."
SLEEPY TOWN TRAIN
Corporal Paul Dubov: Sergeant McKinley downs a quick shot of three-in-one oil and arrives
  at our side with song on his lips. Listen to Mac's advice as he sings "Sweet and Slow."
SWEET AND SLOW
  Vocal refrain by Technical Sergeant Ray McKinley
Corporal Paul Dubov: A top drawer ballad delivered in tip-top shape by our "Soldier with
  a Song." The song, "My Shining Hour," the singer, Sergeant Johnny Desmond.
MY SHINING HOUR
  Vocal refrain by Sergeant Johnny Desmond
Corporal Paul Dubov: Time to heat the studio with a slice of music delivered downtown
  style by that combustible little combo we call the "Boogie Woogie Trio." Here are
  Sergeants Hucko, Powell and McKinley with tonight's tidbit, "Fry Me Cookie, with a Can
  of Lard."
FRY ME COOKIE, WITH A CAN OF LARD (trio: Hucko, Powell, McKinley)
Corporal Paul Dubov: Back to the counter marked romance, and time for chief clerk Desmond
  to do a little selling again, Here is Johnny singing "Time Waits for No One."
TIME WAITS FOR NO ONE
  Vocal refrain by Sergeant Johnny Desmond
Corporal Paul Dubov: There's a guy headin' this way totin' a built-in voice filled with
  choice notes. Yep, it's time for Sergeant McKinley and he's "Waitin' For the Evenin'
  Mail."
WAITIN' FOR THE EVENIN' MAIL (Sittin' on the Inside Lookin' at the Outside)
  Vocal refrain by Technical Sergeant Ray McKinley
Corporal Paul Dubov: In the clean-up spot we're tossin' away all the mutes and giving the
  brass a chance to make some real big noise. Hang on to the roof. We're comin' at you
  with the "King Porter Stomp."
KING PORTER STOMP

Corporal Paul Dubov: Keep your eyes on the papers and your ears tuned to A.E.F., and
   we'll be back soon with another "Swing Shift" featuring Sergeant Ray McKinley and his
   music. This is Corporal Paul Dubov saying "So long" and turning you over to Sergeant
   Ray McKinley.
SONG AND DANCE (closing theme)
   Vocal refrain by Technical Sergeant Ray McKinley

09Dec44 (Sat) 11:45AM-Noon   Co-Partners Hall, Bedford, England
PIANO PARADE broadcast   Script

Announcer: This is a program produced for the A.E.F.P. by the American Band of the A.E.F.
CHOPSTICKS (opening theme)
   Announcer: "Piano Parade," a daily quarter-hour of piano music that today brings you
      Private First Class Jack Rusin in a medley of memory melodies.
Announcer: Jack just handed me the program for today. And as I glance down the list I
   see "Over the Rainbow;" a request number, "The Lady Is a Tramp;" "Body and Soul;" a
   waltz, "Sympathy;" another request, "Sweet Lorraine;" and "I Know That You Know." O.K.,
   Jack, carry on.
OVER THE RAINBOW
THE LADY IS A TRAMP
BODY AND SOUL
SYMPATHY
SWEET LORRAINE
I KNOW THAT YOU KNOW
CHOPSTICKS (closing theme)
   Announcer: You've been listening to "Piano Parade," fifteen minutes of piano music by
      P.F.C. Jack Rusin. Heard today were "Over the Rainbow," "The Lady Is a Tramp," "Body
      and Soul," "Sympathy," "Sweet Lorraine" and "I Know That You Know." That's all for
      now. But don't forget to be listening the next time we come marching down the air
      lanes with "Piano Parade."

09Dec44 (Sat) Co-Partners Hall, Bedford, England   SLO-65867
THE UPTOWN HALL recording   Aired 13Dec44

BBC Announcer: ... and recorded by a unit of the American Band of the Allied
Expeditionary Forces. The program is introduced by Corporal Paul Dubov.

[Announcer: This is a program produced for the A.E.F.P. by the American Band of the
A.E.F.
MY GUY'S COME BACK (opening theme)
    Corporal Paul Dubov: Good evening, all, it's "The Uptown Hall," music for you of the
        Allied Liberation Forces, presented by members of the American Band of the A.E.F.,
        featuring Sergeant Mel Powell at the piano.]
Corporal Paul Dubov: Hi there and welcome to "The Uptown Hall," fellow members.
    Greetings, salutations, how'd you do, and all that sort of thing. We convene here in
    the Hall tonight to run through some more rhythm for you. The minutes of the last
    meeting have been read and Mel's passing out the music for the first number. So, if
    everybody's ready, let's be at it. And we open the meeting with "Blue Skies."
BLUE SKIES
Corporal Paul Dubov: Make way now for our vice-president in charge of vocals, Sergeant
    Johnny Desmond. And here he is to give out with a little lyrical lament called "Don't
    Blame Me."
DON'T BLAME ME
    Vocal refrain by Sergeant Johnny Desmond
Corporal Paul Dubov: Right nice, John. Introducing now the lads who put wham in jam.
    It's our little "Band within a Band." Sergeant Ray McKinley at the drums; Sergeant
    Trigger Alpert, string bass; Sergeant Michael Hucko, clarinet; and top man on this totem
    pole, Sergeant Mel Powell at the piano. They're coming right at you now with "One, Two,
    Button Your Shoe."
ONE, TWO, BUTTON YOUR SHOE (quartet: Hucko, Powell, Alpert, McKinley)
Corporal Paul Dubov: And that unquestionably was "One, Two, Button Your Shoe" but you
    won't need either shoes or socks for the next few minutes. Yes, sir, we're in the
    barefoot department now with some down home, bottom land, riverboat music. Which means
    that Sergeant Bernie Privin, a Brooklyn bugler with a Mississippi manner, is back here
    in the Hall tonight. And as Mel releases that soft pedal, there's a Dixieland
    procession headin' for "'Way Down Yonder in New Orleans."
'WAY DOWN YONDER IN NEW ORLEANS
Corporal Paul Dubov: Why it's Satchmo. I'll buy that. Come back here. You ain't
    leavin' now. How's about some of that raucous music you were dishing out before we
    opened the doors?
S/Sgt. Mel Powell: Oh no, Paul. We've got a future date set for the world's premiere of
    that prestigious opus.
Corporal Paul Dubov: Oh well, Mel, just a preview.
S/Sgt. Mel Powell: Oh well, I - I guess it'll be O.K. It's no sense getting exclusive at
    this late date.
Corporal Paul Dubov: Well fine, that's what I'm talking about. Get your trumpet ready,
    Bernie. Here we go again and it's a secret showing of Mel Powell's newest concoction,
    "Triple-X."
TRIPLE-X
Corporal Paul Dubov: Well, the folks next door have just called up the M.P.s so I guess
    we'd better cut and run. But don't run too far because we want you back here again.
MY GUY'S COME BACK (closing theme)

BBC female announcer: There'll be another program by the Swing Sextet next Friday evening
    at 7:15.

[On another broadcast of this program, all the dialogue after "Triple-X" was deleted and a
BBC announcer said: There'll be another program of the Swing Sextet next week at the same
time.]

09Dec44 (Sat) Co-Partners Hall, Bedford, England   SLO-65868
  THE UPTOWN HALL recording   Aired 14Dec44

  ...

Corporal Paul Dubov: ... another session of that music that's soft but oh so solid.
  You're all invited to stick around and join in the jive. But enough of this talk, let's
  get right on to the music. And here's tonight's first tune, "I'll Remember April."
I'LL REMEMBER APRIL
Corporal Paul Dubov: For tonight's song Sergeant Johnny Desmond went right out in the
  ballad garden and picked one of the best of 'em.

  ...

Corporal Paul Dubov: It's Sergeant Ray McKinley at the drums; Sergeant Trigger Alpert,
  string bass; Sergeant Michael Hucko, clarinet; and on the piano detail, Sergeant Mel
  Powell himself. Here they are giving the complete treatment to "'S Wonderful."
'S WONDERFUL (quartet: Hucko, Powell, Alpert, McKinley)
Corporal Paul Dubov: The man who came to dinner had nothing on Sergeant Bernie Privin.
  When he's invited to do a guest shot on "Uptown Hall" he really settles down and gets
  comfortable. And right now he's itching to join in the proceedings. So make way for a
  great big chunk of "Sweet Georgia Brown."
SWEET GEORGIA BROWN
Corporal Paul Dubov: Yes, indeed. Bernie, you've just sold us all on the idea of an
  encore. So keep the tape on the windows and hold tight for a little taste of "Please
  Don't Talk about Me When I'm Gone."
PLEASE DON'T TALK ABOUT ME WHEN I'M GONE
Corporal Paul Dubov: Ah hah, now it's time to turn off the lights and light out
  ourselves.

BBC female announcer: There'll be another program of the Swing Sextet ...

09Dec44 (Sat) 7:45-8:00PM Co-Partners Hall, Bedford, England   SLO-65864
STRINGS WITH WINGS recording   Script   Aired 13Dec44

Announcer: This is a program produced for the A.E.F.P. by the American Band of the A.E.F.
I SUSTAIN THE WINGS (opening theme)
  Corporal Paul Dubov: "Strings with Wings." "Strings with Wings," a program of music
    for you of the Allied Liberation Forces, presented by the string section of the
    American Band of the A.E.F., featuring Sergeant George Ockner and his violin.
Corporal Paul Dubov: Hello there, folks. Welcome to another program of "Strings with
  Wings." Here we are again, back with some more tunes to help you pass the time of
  evening. Sergeant Ockner tells me he's got some real nice numbers lined up tonight.
  So, if you'll just give us your divided or undivided attention, we'll start the music
  right about here, with our first tune, "Flamingo."
FLAMINGO
Corporal Paul Dubov: Amor, amor, seems like that old devil amor keeps gettin' into every
  program. But when it comes in the shape of a love tune like this next one, we can stand
  a lot of it. O.K., boys, let's hear "Sweet and Lovely."
SWEET AND LOVELY
Corporal Paul Dubov: Accordin' to this next tune, all the stars aren't up in heaven or
  out in Hollywood. Here's Sergeant Ockner and the boys rhapsodizing about some different
  stars altogether. It's the ever-lovely "Stars in Your Eyes."
STARS IN YOUR EYES
Corporal Paul Dubov: Comes the string orchestra now to add a postscript to that next
  V-Mail letter of yours. P.S. "I'll Be Seeing You."
I'LL BE SEEING YOU
Corporal Paul Dubov: Sorry, folks, but that's about all we'll have time for tonight.
  Don't forget, we're back here knockin' at your radio door every Monday and Wednesday
  evening. So if you feel in the mood for a little soft, sweet music, just give us a
  listen. Until the next time then, this is Corporal Paul Dubov saying, "So long, and
  good luck to you."
I SUSTAIN THE WINGS (closing theme)

11Dec44 (Mon) 7:01-7:15PM Co-Partners Hall, Bedford, England
SONGS BY SGT. JOHNNY DESMOND broadcast   Script

Announcer: This is a program produced for the A.E.F.P. by the American Band of the A.E.F.
TIME ON MY HANDS (opening theme)
  Vocal refrain by Sgt. Johnny Desmond
  Corporal Paul Dubov: "Songs by Sgt. Johnny Desmond." Three songs by a three-striper.
    "Songs by Sgt. Johnny Desmond," with music by the American Band of the A.E.F.
Sgt. Johnny Desmond: Hello there. This is Sergeant Johnny Desmond. Once again the music
  is on and the spirit is willing, so reachin' for a heavyweight hit to get things started
  right, we lay a few lyrics on ya that are doing big business back home. Here's "Now I
  Know."
NOW I KNOW
  Vocal refrain by Sgt. Johnny Desmond
Sgt. Johnny Desmond: Now, for a real three-minute song, soft-boiled and right tasty,
  enjoying it's second trip to the heights of popularity, and its third trip to this
  program. We hope you'll enjoy listening along as we musically escort our old gal friend
  "Louise."
LOUISE
  Vocal refrain by Sgt. Johnny Desmond
Sgt. Johnny Desmond: Sergeants Steve Steck and Harry Hartwick of the American Band of the
  A.E.F. unloaded a big romantic thought and a lot of talent onto paper, and here's the
  world premiere of their new song. Sorry we haven't got a bottle of champagne to bust
  over its nose, fellas, but I'll try not to let my voice bust over its notes. The song,
  "Alone."
ALONE (Till the Day)
  Vocal refrain by Sgt. Johnny Desmond
Sgt. Johnny Desmond: This is Sergeant Johnny Desmond. I've only got a few seconds of our
  quarter-hour left in m' pocket and I'm gonna spend them inviting you back for the next
  session of ...
Corporal Paul Dubov: ... three songs by a three-striper, "Songs by Sergeant Johnny
  Desmond," with music by the American Band of the A.E.F.
TIME ON MY HANDS (closing theme)

11Dec44 (Mon) 7:15-7:30PM Co-Partners Hall, Bedford, England
STRINGS WITH WINGS broadcast   Script

I SUSTAIN THE WINGS (opening theme)
　Corporal Paul Dubov: "Strings with Wings." "Strings with Wings," a program of music
　　for you of the Allied Liberation Forces, presented by the string section of the
　　American Band of the A.E.F., featuring Sergeant George Ockner and his violin.
Corporal Paul Dubov: Hello there, folks. Welcome to another program of "Strings with
　Wings." Every Monday and Wednesday night we reserve these air lanes for Sergeant Ockner
　and the boys, in order to bring you this late evening serenade, played by the violins.
　This being Monday, here we are, all ready to go with a few of your old favorites. So
　get as comfortable as you can and we'll start things off tonight with "More Than You
　Know."
MORE THAN YOU KNOW
Corporal Paul Dubov: For their second number this evening, the violins pick a tune of
　mighty pleasant memory. Here they are, adding their own special magic to Sergeant
　Norman Leyden's arrangement of "Yesterdays."
YESTERDAYS
Corporal Paul Dubov: When composer Jerome Kern wrote this next one he really had it
　zeroed in! It's that bull's-eye ballad "Smoke Gets in Your Eyes."
(When Your Heart's on Fire) SMOKE GETS IN YOUR EYES
Corporal Paul Dubov: Our closing tune tonight sums up the sentiments of just about
　everybody these days. Here's the string section of the American Band of the A.E.F. and
　"The World Is Waiting for the Sunrise."
THE WORLD IS WAITING FOR THE SUNRISE
Corporal Paul Dubov: Well, that's all for now, folks. But don't forget to be back with
　me this coming Wednesday, for more music by the violins. Until then this is Corporal
　Paul Dubov saying, "So long and good luck to you."
I SUSTAIN THE WINGS (closing theme)
　Corporal Paul Dubov: You've been listening to music by the string section of the
　　American Band of the A.E.F., featuring Sergeant George Ockner and his violin. Join us
　　again this coming Wednesday when we again present "Strings with Wings."

12Dec44 (Tue) 4:00-5:00PM Queensbury All-Services Club, London, England
  MOONLIGHT SERENADE recording   Script

SLO-65879
Aired 15Dec44

Corporal Paul Dubov: This is a program produced for the A.E.F.P. by the American Band of the A.E.F.
MOONLIGHT SERENADE (opening theme)
  Corporal Paul Dubov: Thirty minutes with the Moonlight Serenader, music by the American Band of the A.E.F. under the direction of Major Glenn Miller. Music for and by members of the Allied Expeditionary Forces. And here is Major Glenn Miller.
Major Glenn Miller: Thank you, Corporal Paul Dubov, and hello, everybody. Puttin' the finger on a bunch of guys who deserve a big, healthy salute, we throw a musical high-ball to the boys realizing their life's Spam-bitions here in the E.T.O. To the cooks and bakers who get "A" for effort with C-rations, here's "Enlisted Men's Mess."
ENLISTED MEN'S MESS
Major Glenn Miller: Old Mister Heartthrob himself, Sergeant Johnny Desmond, turns on the heat now and up comes smooth and velvety "Sweet and Lovely."
SWEET AND LOVELY
  Vocal refrain by Sergeant Johnny Desmond
Major Glenn Miller: Back home, the biggest state of 'em all, Texas, is noted for its cattle, its cotton and its Sergeant Ray McKinley. And Sergeant Mac is noted for his drummin' and his singin', the latter goin' on display now as the Fort Worth troubadour sings you a slow-rollin' rondelet titled "Sittin' on the Inside Lookin' on the Outside Waitin' for the Evenin' Mail."
WAITIN' FOR THE EVENIN' MAIL (Sittin' on the Inside Lookin' at the Outside)
  Vocal refrain by Technical Sergeant Ray McKinley
Major Glenn Miller: Now for medley time, salutin' the mothers, wives, sweethearts and sisters of the Allied Forces with somethin' old, somethin' new, somethin' borrowed and somethin' blue. Our old song, "Sweet and Low."
SWEET AND LOW (Old tune)
  Major Glenn Miller: For somethin' new, Sergeant Johnny Desmond sings somethin' romantic.
SPRING WILL BE A LITTLE LATE THIS YEAR (New tune)
  Vocal refrain by Sergeant Johnny Desmond
  Major Glenn Miller: For something borrowed we put the bite on friend Duke Ellington. The good Duke says "Things Ain't What They Used to Be."
THINGS AIN'T WHAT THEY USED TO BE (Borrowed tune)
  Major Glenn Miller: Our somethin' blue spot calls for a softie and straight outa the bayou comes "Blues Serenade."
A BLUES SERENADE (Blue tune)
Major Glenn Miller: We give a three-minute pass to Sergeants Powell, McKinley, Hucko, Privin and Alpert, lettin' them go where they want and do what they please with a little tune titled "Good Enough to Keep." Ready, boys? One, two.
GOOD ENOUGH TO KEEP (quintet: Privin, Hucko, Powell, Alpert, McKinley)
Major Glenn Miller: A few weeks ago we gave Sergeant Jerry Gray a big assignment and he carried it through in a big way. The Sarge's job was to make an arrangement based upon the little theme you hear runnin' around the A.E.F.P. between programs. How about a demonstration, Sergeant Powell?
ORANGES AND LEMONS (S/Sgt. Mel Powell, piano)
Major Glenn Miller: That's what it sounds like, the way the A.E.F.P. uses it and this is what it sounds like the way the American Band of the A.E.F. uses it. "Oranges and Lemons."
ORANGES AND LEMONS
Major Glenn Miller: This is Major Glenn Miller hangin' a word of welcome on you, invitin' you to join us next time we're playin' around your wireless. Keep an eye on the papers and an ear on the radio for the time and place. Until we meet again, then, it's good luck and good bye.
MOONLIGHT SERENADE (closing theme)

12Dec44 (Tue) 8:30-9:00PM Queensbury All-Services Club, London, England   SLO-65569
  MOONLIGHT SERENADE broadcast   Script   Attendance: 2500

Corporal Paul Dubov: This is a program produced for the A.E.F.P. by the American Band of
  the A.E.F., originating at the Queensbury All-Services Club in London.
MOONLIGHT SERENADE (opening theme)
  Corporal Paul Dubov: Thirty minutes with the Moonlight Serenader. Presenting the
    American Band of the A.E.F. under the direction of Major Glenn Miller. Music for and
    by members of the Allied Expeditionary Forces. And here is Major Glenn Miller.
Major Glenn Miller: Thank you, Corporal Paul Dubov, and hello, everybody. We've got a
  surprise and eight tunes up our sleeve for ya and we're gonna start by putting the
  surprise on ice and the first tune on the air. Just by way of warmin' up the hall, we
  turn on our solid brass plumbin' and out pours "Everybody Loves My Baby."
EVERYBODY LOVES MY BABY (But My Baby Don't Love Nobody but Me)
Major Glenn Miller: And here's where we spend three minutes with a three-striper,
  Sergeant Johnny Desmond, wrappin' his voice warmly around "It Had to Be You."
IT HAD TO BE YOU
  Vocal refrain by Sergeant Johnny Desmond
Major Glenn Miller: Now for medley time, sendin' love and kisses to the gals we left
  behind. For the mothers, wives, sweethearts and sisters of the Allied Forces, somethin'
  old, somethin' new, somethin' borrowed and somethin' blue. Our old, old song, "Long,
  Long Ago."
LONG, LONG AGO (Old tune)
  Major Glenn Miller: Somethin' new finds Sergeant Johnny Desmond modelin' a tune that's
    a right nice fit for his right nice voice.
THE MUSIC STOPPED (New tune)
  Vocal refrain by Sergeant Johnny Desmond
  Major Glenn Miller: From friend and Army teammate Larry Clinton comes our borrowed
    tune, which gives us the pleasure of playin' "The Dipsy Doodle."
THE DIPSY DOODLE (Borrowed tune)
  Major Glenn Miller: Sergeant Hank Freeman's Southern-fried saxophone wails out the
    beginning of our blue tune and the whole band falls in with "Blues in My Heart."
BLUES IN MY HEART (Blue tune)
Major Glenn Miller: Back on the top end of the show we promised you a surprise. U.S.O.
  Camp Shows delivered him here just a few days ago and we're not keeping you from hearin'
  him one minute longer. So, here he is, with a song in his heart and a smile on his
  face, Morton Downey!
Morton Downey: Thank you, Glenn.
Major Glenn Miller: Welcome to the hall, Mort. Make yourself right at home. You'll find
  all the Allied guys and gals right friendly and glad to see you.
Morton Downey: Bing Crosby told me that's the way it would be, and it looks like he's
  more than right.
Major Glenn Miller: You'll be up there singin' for the boys on the far shore in just a
  few days now. So, how about givin' 'em a little preview of what they're gonna hear?
Morton Downey: Play me a tune, Major Miller, and I'll hop myself a ride.
Major Glenn Miller: Okay, and we're gonna knock you out, "I'll Get By."
Morton Downey: Then I'll get singin'.
I'LL GET BY (As Long As I Have You)
  Vocal refrain by Morton Downey
Major Glenn Miller: Nice goin', Morton Downey, you get more altitude out of your voice
  than a B-17. And now we're windin' up for the big last pitch. And Sergeant Jerry Gray
  has gone and done it again. The ink's still wet on the music paper carryin' the Sarge's
  newest arrangement, a somewhat zoot salute respectfully tendered to our gallant Russian
  Allies. Here's "The Red Cavalry March."
THE RED CAVALRY MARCH
Major Glenn Miller: This is Major Glenn Miller closin' the show and openin' the door for
  our next one. You're always welcome, so, keep an eye on the papers and an ear on the
  radio for the time and place. Until we meet again, then, it's good luck and good bye.

MOONLIGHT SERENADE (closing theme)
  Corporal Paul Dubov: You have heard thirty minutes with the Moonlight Serenader.
    Presenting the American Band of the A.E.F. under the direction of Major Glenn Miller.
    Music for and by members of the Allied Expeditionary Forces.

---

c.23-31Dec44 Co-Partners Hall, Bedford, England
  Recording of new announcements by Corporal Paul Dubov

Announcements for SLO-65816 (26Nov44 "A Soldier and a Song"):

  1. Corporal Paul Dubov: Presenting "A Soldier and a Song," the voice of Sergeant
        Johnny Desmond, vocalist with the American Band of the A.E.F., and the songs old
        and new.

  2. Corporal Paul Dubov: From the hit musical "Oklahoma," Sergeant Johnny Desmond
        takes his first song, "Oh, What a Beautiful Mornin'."

  3. Corporal Paul Dubov: The mail we get from you guys here in the E.T.O. makes this
        next song one of our most requested, Jerome Kern's "Long Ago and Far Away."

  4. Corporal Paul Dubov: So now we give the vocal department a rest and call upon the
        orchestra who return our call with "Enlisted Men's Mess."

  5. Corporal Paul Dubov: Now our Sergeant Johnny Desmond returns to close this week's
        show with "I Only Have Eyes for You."

  6. Corporal Paul Dubov: "A Soldier and a Song" has presented the voice of Sergeant
        Johnny Desmond, vocalist with the American Band of the A.E.F. We'll be back
        again soon, so for now, good bye and good luck.

Announcements for a medley (American Band of the AEF):

  7. Corporal Paul Dubov: Now it's something old, something new, something borrowed and
        something blue. And our old tune, it's "Carry Me Back to Old Virginny.

  8. Corporal Paul Dubov: Something new, "I'll Walk Alone."

  9. Corporal Paul Dubov: Borrowed from all the kids around us, "Any Gum, Chum?"

  10. Corporal Paul Dubov: And finally it's something blue, Sergeant Jerry Gray's fine
        arrangement of the "St. Louis Blues March."

Miscellaneous:

  11. Corporal Paul Dubov: This is the Armed Forces Radio Service, the voice of
        information and education.

24Dec44 (Sun)
NEWS ANNOUNCEMENTS

Edward R. Murrow
This is London. Major Glenn Miller, director of the U.S. Air Force Band, is missing on a flight from England to Paris, it was announced today. No trace of the plane has been found.

BBC newscaster
Supreme Headquarters Allied Expeditionary Forces announced that an aircraft, in which Major Glenn Miller was a passenger, disappeared on December the 15th on a routine flight to Paris. No trace of the missing aircraft has yet been found.

9:00PM BBC News broadcast, BBC newscaster
This is the first time that Northern England has been mentioned in these reports since the flying bomb attacks started last June.
Major Glenn Miller, the well-known American band leader, is reported missing. He left England by air for Paris nine days ago. Major Glenn Miller came over from the States early this year to direct the American Band of the A.E.F., which has often been heard playing in the Allied Expeditionary Program of the B.B.C.

25Dec44 (Mon) 8:00-8:15AM   NBC, New York, New York
WAR WORLD NEWS ROUNDUP

James Stevenson
American headquarters in Paris announced today that Major Glenn Miller, director of the American Army Air Forces Band and a former popular orchestra leader in the United States, is missing on a flight from England to Paris. Miller left England on December 15th as a passenger aboard a plane. No trace of the plane has been found since. His Air Force band had been playing in Paris, but no member of the band was with him on the flight.

25Dec44 (Mon) 4:00-4:05PM Olympia Theatre, Paris France   SLO-67216
  GRAND ROUNDUP recording   Aired 7:52PM 25Dec44   Audience: 1500

Ronald Waldman: And so we come to the final item in our "Roundup."
Gerry Wilmott: From the Queensbury All-Services Club in London we take you to hear a
  recording made earlier this Christmas Day at an Allied Troop Theater in Paris. There,
  before an audience composed of members of the Allied Expeditionary Forces, was the
  American Band of the A.E.F., conducted by Sergeant Jerry Gray, substituting for Major
  Glenn Miller. Come in, American Band of the A.E.F.

Lieutenant Don Haynes: Here we are in France on Christmas Day 1944.
Warrant Officer Paul Dudley: Thank you, Lieutenant Don Haynes, and hello, everybody.
  This is Warrant Officer Paul Dudley sayin' "Merry Christmas" to all of you in France, in
  England, and back home in the big 48, for Major Glenn Miller's American Band of the
  A.E.F. Between shows on the A.E.F. Program there's a little jingle taken from a
  traditional English nursery rhyme. Sergeant Mel Powell will let you hear how it sounds.
ORANGES AND LEMONS (S/Sgt. Mel Powell, celeste)
Warrant Officer Paul Dudley: Well, that's the way the A.E.F.P. uses it. And here's how
  our chief arranger and pinch-hitting conductor, Sergeant Jerry Gray, uses it in the
  American Band of the A.E.F. arrangement of "Oranges and Lemons."
ORANGES AND LEMONS
  Vocal refrain by Corporal Artie Malvin and the Crew Chiefs
Gerry Wilmott: And so we come to the end of this A.E.F.P. Christmas Show. During the
  course of this two-hour program, A.E.F. listeners have heard the American Band of the
  A.E.F. conducted by Sergeant Jerry Gray substituting for Major Glenn Miller, the
  Canadian Band of the A.E.F. directed by Captain Robert Farnon, and the British Army
  Radio Orchestra directed by Sergeant Eric Robinson.
Ronald Waldman: With them were Gwen Catley, Berle Davis, Teddy Brown, Jackie Hunter and
  Phil Fletcher.
Gerry Wilmott: Your Masters of Ceremonies were Warrant Officer Paul Dudley from Paris and
  Ronald Waldman and Gerry Wilmott from London.
Ronald Waldman: And now the Allied Expeditionary Forces Program invites listeners in the
  A.E.F. and listeners at home, in the United States, Canada, and the United Kingdom to
  join our combined orchestras and sing us on our way.
AULD LANG SYNE (Combined three orchestras)
  Vocal refrain by the audiences
  WOR, New York, announcer 1: WOR, in connection with the British Broadcasting
    Corporation, has presented from England and France on this Christmas day the Canadian
    Band with the A.E.F.; the 3rd British Band with the A.E.F.; and the American Band with
    the A.E.F., lead by Sergeant Jerry Gray, but which is ordinarily conducted by Major
    Glenn Miller, who has been reported within the past 24 hours as missing. This was a
    special program of the type of entertainment that our fighting men are now seeing this
    wartime Christmas in the field.

  WOR, New York, announcer 2: This ...

15Jan45 (Mon) 3:30-4:00PM Olympia Theatre, Paris, France   SLO-68223
  AMERICAN BAND OF THE AEF recording   Aired 16Jan45   Attendance: 1400

  ...

YOU ARE MY SUNSHINE
  Vocal refrain by Sergeant Johnny Desmond and the Crew Chiefs
Warrant Officer Paul Dudley: Medley time salutes the mothers, wives, sweethearts and
  sisters of the Allied Forces with something old, something new, something borrowed and
  something blue. The old song, "In the Gloaming."
IN THE GLOAMING (Old tune)

  ...

THE RED CAVALRY MARCH
Warrant Officer Paul Dudley: This has been music by Major Glenn Miller's American Band of
  the A.E.F. on the Continent, directed by chief arranger Sergeant Jerry Gray. Music for
  and by members of the Allied Expeditionary Forces. For now it's good bye and good luck
  to you.
MOONLIGHT SERENADE

15Jan45 (Mon) 8:30-9:00PM Olympia Theatre, Paris, France   SLO-67959
  AMERICAN BAND OF THE AEF recording   Aired 19Jan45   Attendance: 1800

  ...

Warrant Officer Paul Dudley: Here's a listener's digest version of the American Band of
  the A.E.F. You'll hear a slight concerto played by a small group here picked from the
  large combination. Sergeants Mel Powell, Michael Hucko, Trigger Alpert and Ray McKinley
  gather around a tune titled "Jubilee."
JUBILEE

  ...

22Jan45 (Mon) 5:30-6:00PM Olympia Theatre, Paris, France   SLO-67948
AMERICAN BAND OF THE AEF recording   Aired 23Jan45   Attendance: 1500

MOONLIGHT SERENADE (opening theme)
    Warrant Officer Paul Dudley: This is the music of Major Glenn Miller's American Band of
      the A.E.F. on the Continent, directed by chief arranger Sergeant Jerry Gray. Music
      for and by members of the Allied Expeditionary Forces.
Warrant Officer Paul Dudley: Hello, everybody, this is Warrant Officer Paul Dudley. The
    American Band of the A.E.F. is standing by the big switch all set and ready to light up
    the hall. Here's the first shot of juice, bright and brassy, "Here We Go Again."
HERE WE GO AGAIN
Warrant Officer Paul Dudley: And now Sergeant Johnny Desmond racks up a heart beat and
    packs it into a song. Here's "I'll Be Seeing You."
I'LL BE SEEING YOU
    Vocal refrain by Sergeant Johnny Desmond
Warrant Officer Paul Dudley: The American Band of the A.E.F. gets to rockin' and rollin'
    with a Southern accent cutting into the measures of "Swing Low, Sweet Chariot."
SWING LOW, SWEET CHARIOT

   ...

Warrant Officer Paul Dudley: One leisure lyric with a long distance title, "Sittin' on
    the Inside Lookin' on the Outside, Waitin' for the Evenin' Mail."
WAITIN' FOR THE EVENIN' MAIL (Sittin' on the Inside Lookin' at the Outside)
    Vocal refrain by Technical Sergeant Ray McKinley

   ...

Warrant Officer Paul Dudley: ... "Poinciana."
POINCIANA (Song of the Tree)
    Vocal refrain by Sergeant Johnny Desmond and the Crew Chiefs
Warrant Officer Paul Dudley: This has been the music of Major Glenn Miller's American
    Band of the A.E.F. on the Continent, directed by chief arranger Sergeant Jerry Gray.
    Music for and by members of the Allied Expeditionary Forces. Until next time we meet
    it's good luck and good bye.
MOONLIGHT SERENADE (closing theme)

29Jan45 (Mon) 5:30-6:00PM Olympia Theatre, Paris, France   SLO-69208
AMERICAN BAND OF THE AEF recording   Aired 30Jan45   Attendance: 1500

MOONLIGHT SERENADE (opening theme)
   Warrant Officer Paul Dudley: This is the music of Major Glenn Miller's American Band of
      the A.E.F. on the Continent, directed by chief arranger Sergeant Jerry Gray. Music
      for and by members of the Allied Expeditionary Forces.
   Warrant Officer Paul Dudley: Hello, everybody, this is Warrant Officer Paul Dudley.
      Going into the windup of the merc --- first musical pitch, which happens to be a
      snowball of fire which melted out of Sergeant Jerry Gray's own composing pen, "Sun
      Valley Jump."
SUN VALLEY JUMP
Warrant Officer Paul Dudley: Time now for a little romantic jazz. So here comes Sergeant
   Johnny Desmond, wearing his heart on his voice and singing "Long Ago and Far Away."
LONG AGO (And Far Away)
   Vocal refrain by Sergeant Johnny Desmond
Warrant Officer Paul Dudley: The American Band of the A.E.F. makes a grandstand play as
   Sergeant Jerry Gray borrows a football song from a great American university and gives
   it the full uptown treatment, "On Wisconsin!"
ON WISCONSIN!

   ...

Warrant Officer Paul Dudley: ... Ray McKinley and the Crew Chiefs and "Chattanooga Choo
   Choo."
CHATTANOOGA CHOO CHOO
   Vocal refrain by Technical Sergeant Ray McKinley and the Crew Chiefs
Warrant Officer Paul Dudley: It's just been announced back home that Sergeant Mel Powell,
   our big piano man, has been chosen in a nation-wide poll as the most popular American
   jazz musician in the Armed Forces. So just by way of taking a bow, we call upon the
   good Sarge and his good musical friends Sergeants McKinley, Hucko and Alpert to whip up
   a little piece of jazz titled "After You're Gone."
AFTER YOU'VE GONE (quartet: Hucko, Powell, Alpert, McKinley)
Warrant Officer Paul Dudley: And now on to the air with a song that the lads who carry on
   their part of the big fight into the air. Sergeant Johnny Desmond and the Crew Chiefs
   spark the singing in Sergeant Jerry Gray's arrangement of "The Army Air Corps" song.
THE ARMY AIR CORPS
   Vocal refrain by Sergeant Johnny Desmond and the Crew Chiefs
Warrant Officer Paul Dudley: This has been the music of Major Glenn Miller's American
   Band of the A.E.F. on the Continent, directed by chief arranger Sergeant Jerry Gray.
   Music for and by members of the Allied Expeditionary Forces. Until next time we meet
   it's good bye and good luck to you.
MOONLIGHT SERENADE (closing theme)

05Feb45 (Mon) 5:30-6:15PM Olympia Theatre, Paris, France   SLO-68716
    AMERICAN BAND OF THE AEF recording   Aired 06Feb45   Attendance: 1500

MOONLIGHT SERENADE (opening theme)
   Warrant Officer Paul Dudley: This is the music of Major Glenn Miller's American Band of
     the A.E.F. on the Continent, directed by chief arranger Sergeant Jerry Gray. Music
     for and by members of the Allied Expeditionary Forces.
Warrant Officer Paul Dudley: Hello, everybody, this is Warrant Officer Paul Dudley.
   Music's big job in the world is to help make people happy. So we might as well light up
   the hall with a smile, "It Must Be Jelly 'cause Jam Don't Shake Like That."
IT MUST BE JELLY ('Cause Jam Don't Shake Like That)
Warrant Officer Paul Dudley: Time now for Sergeant Johnny Desmond to start lovin' up that
   microphone with a fine old tune aged in the heart, "I Only Have Eyes for You."
I ONLY HAVE EYES FOR YOU
   Vocal refrain by Sergeant Johnny Desmond
Warrant Officer Paul Dudley: And now it's medley time, saluting the mothers, wives,
   sweethearts and sisters of the Allied Forces with something old, something new,
   something borrowed and something blue. The old song, "Silver Threads among the Gold."
SILVER THREADS AMONG THE GOLD (Old tune)
   Warrant Officer Paul Dudley: Our something new tune pops to attention to salute the Red
     Cross as Sergeant Johnny Desmond and the Crew Chiefs sing ...
AT THE RAINBOW CORNER (New tune)
   Vocal refrain by Sergeant Johnny Desmond and the Crew Chiefs
   Warrant Officer Paul Dudley: We borrow the theme tune from Mel Powell's "Uptown Hall"
     program, which soon we'll be humming around town under the title "My Guy's Come Back."
MY GUY'S COME BACK (Borrowed tune)

   ...

Warrant Officer Paul Dudley: And here's an all out high ball to those all out fighting
   men, "The Red Cavalry March."
THE RED CAVALRY MARCH
Warrant Officer Paul Dudley: This has been the music of Major Glenn Miller's American
   Band of the A.E.F. on the Continent, directed by chief arranger Sergeant Jerry Gray.
   Music for and by members of the Allied Expeditionary Forces. Until next time we meet
   it's good bye and good luck to you.
MOONLIGHT SERENADE (closing theme)

05Feb45 (Mon) 8:30-9:15PM Olympia Theatre, Paris, France   SLO-69094
  AMERICAN BAND OF THE AEF recording   Aired 09Feb45   Attendance: 2000

  ...

TAIL END CHARLIE
Warrant Officer Paul Dudley: If you've got some dreamin' to do, here's a good chance to
  do it. Just the right music for just the right memories, mellow and sweet, "Body and
  Soul."
BODY AND SOUL
Warrant Officer Paul Dudley: Up come the bright light and with 'em come the voices of
  Sergeant Johnny Desmond and the Crew Chiefs singin' "I've Got a Heart Filled with Love."
I'VE GOT A HEART FILLED WITH LOVE (For You Dear)
  Vocal refrain by Sergeant Johnny Desmond and the Crew Chiefs

  ...

I'M MAKING BELIEVE (New tune)
  Vocal refrain by Sergeant Johnny Desmond
  Warrant Officer Paul Dudley: For the borrowed spot Mike Hucko and Bernie Privin borrow
    the vocal and trumpet mannerisms of Louis Armstrong. Are you ready, Pops?
I CAN'T GIVE YOU ANYTHING BUT LOVE (Baby) (Borrowed tune)
  Vocal refrain by Private Michael (Peanuts) A. Hucko

  ...

Warrant Officer Paul Dudley: ... Sergeant Jerry Gray's arrangement of "Holiday For
  Strings."
HOLIDAY FOR STRINGS
Warrant Officer Paul Dudley: This has been the music of Major Glenn Miller's American
  Band of the A.E.F. on the Continent, directed by chief arranger Sergeant Jerry Gray.
  Music for and by members of the Allied Expeditionary Forces. Until next time we meet
  it's good bye and good luck to you.
MOONLIGHT SERENADE (closing theme)

06Feb45 (Tue) 5:30-6:00PM Olympia Theatre, Paris, France   SLO-68994
  THE SWING SHIFT recording   Aired 17Feb45   Attendance: 1500

...

T/Sgt. Ray McKinley: ... "Boogie Woogie Trio," that's Mel Powell at the piano, Michael
  Hucko on clarinet and, at the drums, your obedient servant. We're getting in our licks
  tonight on a little thing labeled "With Malice and No Thought." Take it away, Mel.
WITH MALICE AND NO THOUGHT (trio: Hucko, Powell, McKinley)

...

T/Sgt. Ray McKinley: ... from the last war, featuring Zeke Zarchy on the trumpet with "My
  Buddy."
MY BUDDY
T/Sgt. Ray McKinley: Well, every now and then Mel Powell deserts the piano and grabs a
  pen and turns out a tune of his own. We're playing one of Mel's originals tonight.
  Here it 'tis with hot and cold runnin' rhythm, "Bubble Bath."
BUBBLE BATH
T/Sgt. Ray McKinley: Well, back in the good old blue serge suit days we used to hear this
  next tune every time we saw a Paramount newsreel. Just for old time's sake, here it is
  again with Michael Hucko taking the top notes on the clarinet. Wrap up the party boys
  with "Eyes and Ears and the World."
THE EYES AND EARS OF THE WORLD

...

12Feb45 (Mon) 6:30-8:00PM Olympia Theatre, Paris, France   SBU-59233
  AMERICAN BAND OF THE AEF recording   Aired 16Feb45   Attendance: 1800

...

MOON DREAMS (New tune)
  Vocal refrain by Sergeant Johnny Desmond and the Crew Chiefs
  Warrant Officer Paul Dudley: Our borrowed tune, the lead off batter on Irving Berlin's
    personal hit parade, "Alexander's Ragtime Band."
ALEXANDER'S RAGTIME BAND (Borrowed tune)
  Warrant Officer Paul Dudley: And for something blue, "Blue Is the Night."
BLUE IS THE NIGHT (Blue tune)

...

Warrant Officer Paul Dudley: ... and we go on to say that he's the composer, arranger and
  featured soloist in this next selection played by the American Band of the A.E.F.,
  "Pearls on Velvet."
PEARLS ON VELVET
Warrant Officer Paul Dudley: As many of you know, this outfit was born and brought up in
  the U.S. Army Air Forces. And here's where the band gets together with a song that
  started out the very same way. It's goin' to be like singin' over old times with this
  tune, "With My Head in the Clouds."
WITH MY HEAD IN THE CLOUDS
  Vocal refrain by the Crew Chiefs

...

15Feb45 (Thu) 11:20PM-Midnight Olympia Theatre, Paris, France   SLO-69668
  THE SWING SHIFT recording   Aired 24Feb45

      ...

Announcer: ... for the Joes who insist that "parle vous Francais" meant all sorts of ...
    obstacle towards themselves, here's the premier airing of "No Compris."
NO COMPRIS

      ...

18Feb45 (Sun) 8:30-10:45PM Paris Opera House, Paris, France
  CONCERT For benefit of French War Prisoners   Script   Attendance: 2200

Bravig Imbs: Nous sommes a l'Opera, a Paris. Dans un instant, le lourd rideau de velours
  rouge se levera sur les quarante sept soldats musiciens de l'Orchestre Americain du
  Major Glenn Miller du Corps Expeditionnaire Allie. Aussitot, ils commenceront de jouer
  le morceau d'ouverture de l'orchestre dont Glenn Miller a regle lui-mene l'arrangement
  et l'adaptation: "Moonlight Serenade" - "La Serenade au Clair de Lune." Le chef n'est
  pas la au pupitre, mais sa presence est toujours vivante dans l'esprit et dans le coeur
  de chaque musicien, et ils joueront comme s'il etait a sa place habituelle. Ils
  joueront avec la foi que leur communiquait la direction du Glenn Miller et pour rendre
  hommage a cette presence invisible, les trois premiers morceaux se succederont sans
  announces, sans que soit troublee la pensee de chacun. Vous entendrez ainsi: "In the
  Mood," "Dans l'Ambiance;" "Stormy Weather," "Temps d'Orage;" et "Song of the Volga
  Boatmen," "La Chanson de Batelier de la Volga." C'est grace a l'initiative du Mouvement
  de Liberation Nationale que vous avez ce soir le plaisir d'entendre ce concert, le seul
  qui sera donne en France par l'Orchestre Americain du Major Glenn Miller. Ce Concert
  est donne avec la gracieuse autorisation du Special Service (Seine Section) de l'armee
  americaine au profit des oeuvres sociales du Mouvement de Liberation Nationale -
  Prisonniers, Refugies, Deportes. L'Orchestre Americain du Major Glenn Miller est
  beureux de cette occasion qui lui est donnes de faire un geste fraternal en faveur de
  tous ces francais qui souffrent si durement pour la liberte des peuples. Et c'est bien
  dans cet esprit d'amitie qu'ils vous offrent, mesdames et messieurs, cette soiree de
  musique americaine. Acceuillez la, s'il vous plaint, d'un meme elan. Voila, le rideau
  s'est leve. L'Orchestre Americain du Major Glenn Miller du Corps Expeditionnaire Allie
  apparait sur la scene, la celebre scene de l'Opera a Paris.
Bravig Imbs: L'Orchestre Americain du Major Glenn Miller du Corps Expeditionnaire Allie.
MOONLIGHT SERENADE (opening theme)
IN THE MOOD
STORMY WEATHER (Keeps Rainin' All the Time)
SONG OF THE VOLGA BOATMEN
Bravig Imbs: Voici maintenant le soliste de l'Orchestre, le Sergent Johnny Desmond. Aux
  Etats Unis, Johnny Desmond a chante avec Bob Crosby et Gene Krupa, avant son
  incorporation dans l'Armee Americaine. C'est un chanteur qui interprete avec gout et
  avec delicatesse, la melancolie de certaines chansons contemporaines. En voici une des
  plus jolies: "I'll Walk Alone" - "Je me promenerai tout seul."
Bravig Imbs: Johnny Desmond, feature soloist of Major Glenn Miller's American Band of the
  Allied Expeditionary Forces, gives you "I'll Walk Alone."
I'LL WALK ALONE
  Vocal refrain by Sergeant Johnny Desmond
Bravig Imbs: L'atmosphere de tendresse que vous avez sentie dans cette chanson, vous la
  trouverez egalement dans, "I'll Be Seeing You" - "Je te verrai" - que le Sergent Johnny
  Desmond vous chante maintenant.
Bravig Imbs: Sergeant Johnny Desmond continues with "I'll Be Seeing You."
I'LL BE SEEING YOU
  Vocal refrain by Sergeant Johnny Desmond
Bravig Imbs: Chez nous, comme en France, il est convenu que le Samedi deit etre gai.
  Dans la "Juke Box Saturday Night" - "Quand On Guinche le Samedi Soir" - vous entendrez
  des imitations du celebre Harry James, jouant de la trompette. L'imitateur est un autre
  virtuose de la trompette, le Sergent Bobby Nichols. D'autre part, le fameux quatuor
  noir, "The Ink Spots" - "Les Taches d'Encre" - chantera pour vous.
Bravig Imbs: "Juke Box Saturday Night." In this number you hear Sergeant Bobby Nichols
  in a sparkling imitation of Harry James playing the trumpet, and the singing of the
  famous negro quartet, "The Ink Spots."
JUKE BOX SATURDAY NIGHT
  Vocal refrain by the Crew Chiefs
Bravig Imbs: Dans chaque avion de l'armee de l'air americain, il y a des Crew Chiefs -
  des chefs d'equipage. Comme l'orchestre du Major Glenn Miller etait attache a cette
  armee de l'air, il possede egalement ses Crew Chiefs - ses Chefs d'Equipage. Ce sont
  eux qui chanteront maintenant la delicieux "Shoo-Shoo Baby."

Bravig Imbs: The Crew Chiefs of Major Glenn Miller's American Band sing "Shoo-Shoo Baby."
SHOO-SHOO BABY
  Vocal refrain by the Crew Chiefs
Bravig Imbs: L'Orchestre du Major Glenn Miller a presque l'importance d'un orchestre
  symphonique. Et chaque section de cet orchestre est composee de musiciens de premier
  ordre. Vous remarquerez les instrument a cordes, diriges par le Sergent George Ockner,
  dans le morceau qui suit: "Estrellita."
Bravig Imbs: The next number, "Estrellita," features the string section, directed by
  Sergeant George Ockner.
ESTRELLITA (string section)
Bravig Imbs: Le Sergent George Ockner faisait partie avant la guerre de l'Orchestre
  Philharmonique de New York. Il etait egalemant vedette de la Radio Americaine. Le
  Sergent Ockner, virtuose extraordinaire, joue en solo: "Le Vol de l'Abeille."
Bravig Imbs: Listen now to "Flight of the Bumble-Bee" with a violin solo by Sergeant
  George Ockner.
FLIGHT OF THE BUMBLE-BEE (string section)
Bravig Imbs: Voici maintenant: "It Must Be Jelly 'Cause Jam Don't Shake Like That," qui
  traduit litteralement en Francais, donne ce titre surprenant: "C'est Surement de la
  Gelee, Car la Confiture ne Tremble Pas Comme Ca."
Bravig Imbs: The "Flight of the Bumble-Bee" takes us straight to a sweet spot, "It Must
  Be Jelly 'cause Jam Don't Shake Like That."
IT MUST BE JELLY ('Cause Jam Don't Shake Like That)
Bravig Imbs: Et maintenant je voudrais vous parler tout specialement d'un des musiciens
  de l'Orchestre qui merite des eloges particuliers. C'est le Sergent Jerry Gray, celui
  qui a fait l'arrangement de "Begin the Beguinne" pour Artie Shaw et tous les
  arrangements des plus grands succes du Major Glenn Miller. Pour s'amuser, il a aussi
  fait des arrangements pour Andre Kostelanetz. Le Sergent Jerry Gray va diriger
  maintenant l'Orchestre dans une de ses propres oeuvres, qu'on peut appeler un chef
  d'oeuvre: "Poinciana."
Bravig Imbs: The chief arranger of Major Glenn Miller's American Band, Sergeant Jerry
  Gray, leads the orchestra in his own arrangement of "Poinciana."
POINCIANA (Song of the Tree)
  Vocal refrain by Sergeant Johnny Desmond and the Crew Chiefs
Bravig Imbs: Peut-etre avez vous deja entendu l'indicatif que l'Orchestre du Major Glenn
  Miller emploie a la radio. C'est le theme miniscule d'une chanson d'enfance anglaise:
  "Oranges and Lemons" - "Oranges et Citrons." Le Sergent Mel Powell va vous le jouer au
  piano, et ensuite, vous entendrez - avec etonnement - comment ce theme est developpe par
  le Sergent Jerry Gray.
Bravig Imbs: Perhaps you've heard the English nursery jingle "Oranges and Lemons" that
  Major Glenn Miller's American Band uses as a theme on the A.E.F.P. radio network.
  Sergeant Mel Powell will demonstrate it on the piano. It's just a tiny acorn of a theme
  but in the hands of Sergeant Jerry Gray it soon sprouts and grows into a mighty piece,
  "Oranges and Lemons."
ORANGES AND LEMONS (Pfc. Mel Powell, piano)
ORANGES AND LEMONS

INTERMISSION

(Start of broadcast, 9:30PM)
Bravig Imbs: L'Orchestre du Major Glenn Miller continue avec une marche, la marche des
  jousurs de football a West Point - le Saint Cyr d'Amerique. Vous verrez que c'est une
  chanson qui peut s'appeler une marche. Elle a pour titre: "En Avant la Bonne Vieille
  Equipe de l'Armee," et elle est transposee en jazz.
Bravig Imbs: A West Point football song provides the theme for the next number, "On,
  Brave Old Army Team."
ON, BRAVE OLD ARMY TEAM
Bravig Imbs: Voici maintenant le chef d'oeuvre de Gershwin: "Rhapsody in Blue."
RHAPSODY IN BLUE

Bravig Imbs: "Chatanooga Choo choo." Gette chanson celebre du film "Sun Valley Serenade"
  a battu tous les records de vente du disque aux Etats Unis. Plus d'un million cinq cent
  mille enregistrements de "Chatanooga Choo Choo" ont ete vendu. C'est Ray McKinley qui
  vous chante les paroles.
Bravig Imbs: Here's Major Glenn Miller's famous arrangement of "Chattanooga Choo Choo,"
  sung by Ray McKinley.
CHATTANOOGA CHOO CHOO
  Vocal refrain by Technical Sergeant Ray McKinley and the Crew Chiefs
Bravig Imbs: La musique de jazz n'est pas aussi eloignee qu'on le pense de la musique
  classique, vous en conviendrez quand vous aurez entendu: "Les Violens en Vacances" -
  "Holiday for Strings."
HOLIDAY FOR STRINGS
Bravig Imbs: "Tuxedo Junction" est le nom d'une gare de triage dans l'Alabama - une gare
  que les musiciens en tournee connaissent bien.
Bravig Imbs: Here's another Glenn Miller hit, "Tuxedo Junction."
TUXEDO JUNCTION
Bravig Imbs: Une des chansons americaines qui ont le plus seduit les francais est: "Long
  Ago and Far Away" - "Il y a Longtemps, C'est Bien Loin." En hommage aux prisonniers
  francais pour qui ce concert est donne, le Sergent Johnny Desmond chantera les paroles
  en francais.
Bravig Imbs: As a tribute to the French prisoners, for whom this concert is given,
  Sergeant Johnny Desmond sings "Long Ago (And Far Away)" in French.
LONG AGO (And Far Away)
  Vocal refrain by Sergeant Johnny Desmond (French and English)
Bravig Imbs: Le Sergent Mel Powell, pianiste de l'Orchestre du Major Glenn Miller, est
  bien connu des francais fervente de jazz. Accompagne de l'orchestre, il joue maintenant
  une de ses compositions: "Les Perles sur Velours."
Bravig Imbs: The next number is "Pearls on Velvet," featuring the composer himself,
  Sergeant Mel Powell, at the piano.
PEARLS ON VELVET
Bravig Imbs: Avec "Les Perles sur Velours," l'Orchestre Americain du Major Glenn Miller
  du Corps Expeditionnaire Allie termine son programme de ce soir. Ce concert a ete donne
  a l'Opera de Paris au profit des oeuvres sociales du Mouvement de Liberation Nationale.
  Ici Bravig Imbs, du Service d'Information des Etats Unis qui vous dit: Bon Soir.
(End of broadcast, 10:00PM)

Bravig Imbs: Voici "Trois Minutes Avec Mel" - un solo de piano par le Sergent Mel Powell
  lui-meme.
Bravig Imbs: We don't know what Sergeant Mel Powell has got up his sleeve, so we've
  called the next number, a piano solo, "Three Minutes with Mel."
THREE MINUTES WITH MEL
Bravig Imbs: "Je ne peux rien te donner que l'amour" - "I Can't Give You Anything But
  Love" - joue a la maniere de Louis Armstrong. Mais Louis Armstrong est un musicien
  tellement formidable qu'll faut deux hommes pour l'imiter. Alors, le Sergent Michael
  Hucko chante les paroles et le Sergent Bernie Privin jous le solo de trompette.
Bravig Imbs: "I Can't Give You Anything but Love," played in the manner of Louis
  Armstrong, with Sergeant Michael Hucko singing and Sergeant Bernie Privin playing the
  trumpet. Are you ready?
I CAN'T GIVE YOU ANYTHING BUT LOVE (Baby)
  Vocal refrain by Private Michael (Peanuts) A. Hucko
Bravig Imbs: Le Caporal Phil Marino est un violiniste de swing extraordinaire qui joue
  dans le style des boites de la cinquante deuxieme rue a New York. Ecoutez le dans:
  "Lady Be Good!"
Bravig Imbs: Corporal Phil Marino plays the violin solo in the old time favorite "Lady Be
  Good!"
OH, LADY BE GOOD! (trio: Marino, Mastren, Alpert)
Bravig Imbs: Le Caporal Phil Marino joue encore pour vous: "Deux Comme l'Aurore" - une
  chanson viellotte et sentimentale rajeunie dans sa version de jazz.
Bravig Imbs: Corporal Phil Marino gives you another violin solo in "Softly As in a
  Morning Sunrise."

SOFTLY AS IN A MORNING SUNRISE (trio: Marino, Mastren, Alpert)
Bravig Imbs: Voici de nouveau le Sergent Jerry Gray que je vous ai presente deja dans la premiere partie du programme. Le Sergent Jerry Gray voulant rendre hommage a nos camarades de l'armee rouge, a arrange une de leurs marches: "La Marche de la Cavalerie Rouge."
Bravig Imbs: As a tribute to our gallant Russian Allies, Sergeant Jerry Gray has arranged "The Red Cavalry March," which he conducts now.
THE RED CAVALRY MARCH
Bravig Imbs: Il y a actuellement aux Etats Unis une chanson qui s'annonce aussi populaire que: "Yes, We Have No Bananas." C'est: "Ac-cent-tchu-ate the Positive" - "Insistez Sur Le Positive." C'est une chanson qui exprime bien l'attitude observee aujourd'hul par le peuple americain. Voici les paroles du refrain:

> Insistez sur le positif,
> Eliminez le negatif,
> Attrapez bien l'affirmatif,
> Et ne vous mouillez pas
> Avec Monsieur Ni-Chair-Hi-Poisson.

Ces paroles seront chante par le Sergent Ray McKinley et les Chefs d'Equipage. Mais avant de jouer cette chanson sensationelle, nous voulons exprimer tonte notre gratitude enver la Section, La Seine, de l'Armee Americaine qui a aimablement autoise ce concert. En principe, nos musiciens doivent jouer pour les soldats seulement mais la Section, La Seine, de l'Armee Americaine a bien voulu nous accorder cette soiree afin que nous puissions avoir le plaisir de jouer pour vous. De tout notre coeur, nouslui disons: merci.
Bravig Imbs: Here's the newest American hit, "Ac-cent-tchu-ate the Positive," sung by Sergeant Ray McKinley and the Crew Chiefs.
AC-CENT-TCHU-ATE THE POSITIVE (Mister In-Between)
Vocal refrain by Technical Sergeant Ray McKinley and the Crew Chiefs
Bravig Imbs: L'Orchestre americain du Major Glenn Miller du Corps Expeditionnaire Allie termine son programme ce soir avec: "Au Long de la Route" - chante par le Sergent Ray McKinley et avec un solo de base joue per le Sergent Trigger Alpert qui a fait partie de l'Orchestre originale de Glenn Miller.
Bravig Imbs: Major Glenn Miller's American Band of the Allied Expeditionary Forces end the program of this evening with "Down the Road a Piece," sung by Sergeant Ray McKinley and featuring a bass solo by Sergeant Trigger Alpert.
(That Place) DOWN THE ROAD A PIECE
ANVIL CHORUS
LA MARSEILLAISE (The French National Anthem)
GOD SAVE THE KING (British National Anthem)
GOSUDARSTVENY GIMN SOVETSKOGO SOYUSA (Russian National Anthem)
THE STAR-SPANGLED BANNER (USA National Anthem)

Translation:

Bravig Imbs: We are at the Paris Opera. In a moment, the heavy red velvet curtain will
  rise to reveal forty-seven soldiers, musicians of Major Glenn Miller's American
  Orchestra of the Allied Expeditionary Forces. For the overture they will play the
  orchestra's theme song, composed and arranged by Glenn Miller, "Moonlight Serenade," "La
  Serenade au Clair de Lune." Unfortunately the leader is not at the podium, but his
  presence is very much alive and his spirit is in the heart of each musician. They will
  play exactly as if Glenn Miller were directing the orchestra and will pay tribute to his
  invisible presence. The first three numbers will be played without interruption. You
  will hear: "In the Mood," "Dans l'Ambiance;" "Stormy Weather," "Temps d'Orage;" and
  "Song of the Volga Boatmen," "La Chanson de Batelier de la Volga." It is because of the
  kindness and grace of the "National Liberation Movement" that tonight you have the
  pleasure of hearing this concert, the only concert that will be played in France by the
  American Orchestra of Glenn Miller. This concert is given with the kind permission of
  the Special Service (Seine Section) of the American Army to help the work of the
  National Liberation Movement, i.e. prisoners, refugees and deported people. The
  American Orchestra of Major Glenn Miller is very happy for the opportunity to take part
  in this fraternal gesture in favor of all the French people who have suffered so much
  for the liberation of France. And it is in this spirit of friendship, ladies and
  gentlemen, that you'll hear an evening of American music. Welcome them, if you will, in
  this same spirit. The curtain is going up. The Major Glenn Miller American Orchestra
  of the Allied Expeditionary Forces appears on the stage of the famous Paris Opera.
Bravig Imbs: The Major Glenn Miller American Orchestra of the Allied Expeditionary
  Forces.
MOONLIGHT SERENADE (opening theme)
IN THE MOOD
STORMY WEATHER (Keeps Rainin' All the Time)
SONG OF THE VOLGA BOATMEN
Bravig Imbs: Here now is the soloist of the orchestra, Sergeant Johnny Desmond. In the
  United States Johnny Desmond sang with Bob Crosby and Gene Krupa before joining the
  American Army. He is a singer who performs with taste and delicacy certain modern,
  melancholy tunes. And here is one of the most lovely, "I'll Walk Alone," "Je me
  promenerai tout seul."
Bravig Imbs: Johnny Desmond, feature soloist of Major Glenn Miller's American Band of the
  Allied Expeditionary Forces, gives you "I'll Walk Alone."
I'LL WALK ALONE
  Vocal refrain by Sergeant Johnny Desmond
Bravig Imbs: The atmosphere of tenderness that you felt in this song you will also feel
  in "I'll Be Seeing You," "Je te verrai," which Sergeant Johnny Desmond now sings.
Bravig Imbs: Sergeant Johnny Desmond continues with "I'll Be Seeing You."
I'LL BE SEEING YOU
  Vocal refrain by Sergeant Johnny Desmond
Bravig Imbs: At home, as in France, it is customary that Saturday night be festive. In
  "Juke Box Saturday Night," "Quand On Guinche le Samedi Soir," you will hear the
  imitation of the famous Harry James, playing trumpet. The imitator is another virtuoso
  of the trumpet, Sergeant Bobby Nichols. Also, the famous quartet, "The Ink Spots," "Les
  Taches d'Encre," will sing for us.
Bravig Imbs: "Juke Box Saturday Night." In this number you hear Sergeant Bobby Nichols
  in a sparkling imitation of Harry James playing the trumpet, and the singing of the
  famous negro quartet, "The Ink Spots."
JUKE BOX SATURDAY NIGHT
  Vocal refrain by the Crew Chiefs
Bravig Imbs: In each American Air Force airplane there are Crew Chiefs, those who are in
  charge of the equipment. Seeing as the Major Glenn Miller Orchestra was attached to the
  Air Force, it also has its own Crew Chiefs, in charge of equipment crew. They will now
  sing for us the lovely "Shoo-Shoo Baby."
Bravig Imbs: The Crew Chiefs of Major Glenn Miller's American Band sing "Shoo-Shoo Baby."
SHOO-SHOO BABY
  Vocal refrain by the Crew Chiefs

Bravig Imbs: The Major Glenn Miller Orchestra has just about the same importance as a symphony orchestra. And each section of this orchestra is composed of first class musicians. You will observe the string instruments, lead by Sergeant George Ockner, in the next number, "Estrellita."
Bravig Imbs: The next number, "Estrellita," features the string section, directed by Sergeant George Ockner.
ESTRELLITA (string section)
Bravig Imbs: Sergeant George Ockner was a member of the New York Philharmonic Orchestra. He was also a star of American radio. Sergeant Ockner, vituoso extraordinary, will play a solo, "Flight of the Bumble-Bee."
Bravig Imbs: Listen now to "Flight of the Bumble-Bee" with a violin solo by Sergeant George Ockner.
FLIGHT OF THE BUMBLE-BEE (string section)
Bravig Imbs: Here now "It Must Be Jelly 'Cause Jam Don't Shake Like That," which, translated literally in French, a sweet title, "C'est Surement de la Gelee, Car la Confiture ne Tremble Pas Comme Ca."
Bravig Imbs: The "Flight of the Bumble-Bee" takes us straight to a sweet spot, "It Must Be Jelly 'cause Jam Don't Shake Like That."
IT MUST BE JELLY ('Cause Jam Don't Shake Like That)
Bravig Imbs: And now I would like to talk to you especially about one of the musicians of the orchestra who deserves special attention. It is Sergeant Jerry Gray, the one who made the arrangement of "Begin the Beguine" for Artie Shaw and was the chief arranger of the biggest hits for Major Glenn Miller. For his own amusement, without being paid he also arranged for Andre Kostelanetz. Sergeant Jerry Gray will now lead the orchestra in his own arrangement of "Poinciana."
Bravig Imbs: The chief arranger of Major Glenn Miller's American Band, Sergeant Jerry Gray, leads the orchestra in his own arrangement of "Poinciana."
POINCIANA (Song of the Tree)
  Vocal refrain by Sergeant Johnny Desmond and the Crew Chiefs
Bravig Imbs: Perhaps you've heard the identification theme Major Glenn Miller's Orchestra uses on radio. It is the tiny theme from an English nursery rhyme, "Oranges and Lemons," "Oranges et Citrons." Sergeant Mel Powell will demonstrate it on the piano, and following that you'll hear the remarkable development of the theme by Sergeant Jerry Gray.
Bravig Imbs: Perhaps you've heard the English nursery jingle "Oranges and Lemons" that Major Glenn Miller's American Band uses as a theme on the A.E.F.P. radio network. Sergeant Mel Powell will demonstrate it on the piano. It's just a tiny acorn of a theme but in the hands of Sergeant Jerry Gray it soon sprouts and grows into a mighty piece, "Oranges and Lemons."
ORANGES AND LEMONS (Pfc. Mel Powell, piano)
ORANGES AND LEMONS

INTERMISSION

(Start of broadcast, 9:30PM)
Bravig Imbs: The Major Glenn Miller Orchestra continues now with a march, the football song at West Point, the Saint Cyr of America. You'll understand that a march is a song of special appeal. It's title, "On Brave Old Army Team," and it is transposed into jazz.
Bravig Imbs: A West Point football song provides the theme for the next number, "On, Brave Old Army Team."
ON, BRAVE OLD ARMY TEAM
Bravig Imbs: We continue with Gershwin's masterpiece, "Rhapsody in Blue."
RHAPSODY IN BLUE
Bravig Imbs: "Chattanooga Choo Choo." This famous song of the film "Sun Valley Serenade" beat all records for record sales in the United States. More than one million five hundred thousand recordings of "Chattanooga Choo Choo" were sold. Here is Ray McKinley, who will sing the lyrics for you.
Bravig Imbs: Here's Major Glenn Miller's famous arrangement of "Chattanooga Choo Choo," sung by Ray McKinley.

CHATTANOOGA CHOO CHOO
Vocal refrain by Technical Sergeant Ray McKinley and the Crew Chiefs
Bravig Imbs: The music of jazz is not as far from classical music as one would think; you will be convinced of this when you hear "Les Violens en Vacances," "Holiday for Strings."
HOLIDAY FOR STRINGS
Bravig Imbs: "Tuxedo Junction" is the name of a switch yard in Alabama, a yard that these musicians, who travel so much, know well.
Bravig Imbs: Here's another Glenn Miller hit, "Tuxedo Junction."
TUXEDO JUNCTION
Bravig Imbs: One of the American songs that played the most on the French heart strings is "Long Ago (And Far Away)," "Il y a Longtemps, C'est Bien Loin." In tribute to the French prisoners, for whom this concert is given. Sergeant Johnny Desmond will sing the words in French.
Bravig Imbs: As a tribute to the French prisoners, for whom this concert is given, Sergeant Johnny Desmond sings "Long Ago (And Far Away)" in French.
LONG AGO (And Far Away)
Vocal refrain by Sergeant Johnny Desmond (French and English)
Bravig Imbs: Sergeant Mel Powell, pianist for the Orchestra of Major Glenn Miller, is well known among the French who love jazz. Accompanied by the orchestra, he will now play one of his compositions, "Pearls on Velvet."
Bravig Imbs: The next number is "Pearls on Velvet," featuring the composer himself, Sergeant Mel Powell, at the piano.
PEARLS ON VELVET
Bravig Imbs: With "Pearls on Velvet," the Major Glenn Miller American Orchestra of the Allied Expeditionary Forces brings this concert to an end this evening. This concert was given by the Paris Opera for the benefit of social work by the National Liberation Movement. This is Bravig Imbs, of the Information Service of the United States, bidding you good night.
(End of broadcast, 10:00PM)

Bravig Imbs: Here is "Three Minutes with Mel," a piano solo by Sergeant Mel Powell himself.
Bravig Imbs: We don't know what Sergeant Mel Powell has got up his sleeve, so we've called the next number, a piano solo, "Three Minutes with Mel."
THREE MINUTES WITH MEL
Bravig Imbs: "Je ne peux rien te donner que l'amour," "I Can't Give You Anything But Love" played in the style of Louis Armstrong. But Louis Armstrong is a musician of such formidable talent that it takes two men to imitate him. Sergeant Michael Hucko sings the lyrics and Sergeant Bernie Privin plays the trumpet solo.
Bravig Imbs: "I Can't Give You Anything But Love," played in the manner of Louis Armstrong, with Sergeant Michael Hucko singing and Sergeant Bernie Privin playing the trumpet. Are you ready?
I CAN'T GIVE YOU ANYTHING BUT LOVE (Baby)
Vocal refrain by Private Michael (Peanuts) A. Hucko
Bravig Imbs: Corporal Phil Marino is an extraordinary swing violinist who plays in the style of the night clubs on 52nd Street in New York. Listen to him in "Lady Be Good."
Bravig Imbs: Corporal Phil Marino plays the violin solo in the old time favorite "Lady Be Good!"
OH, LADY BE GOOD! (trio: Marino, Mastren, Alpert)
Bravig Imbs: Corporal Phil Marino plays an encore, "Softly As in a Morning Sunrise," an old-fashioned and sentimental song, redone in his jazz version.
Bravig Imbs: Corporal Phil Marino gives you another violin solo in "Softly As in a Morning Sunrise."
SOFTLY AS IN A MORNING SUNRISE (trio: Marino, Mastren, Alpert)
Bravig Imbs: Here again is Sergeant Jerry Gray, whom I have already presented in the first part of the program. Sergeant Jerry Gray wanted to pay tribute to our comrades of the Red Army with an arrangement of one of their marches, "The Red Cavalry March."
Bravig Imbs: As a tribute to our gallant Russian Allies, Sergeant Jerry Gray has arranged "The Red Cavalry March," which he conducts now.

THE RED CAVALRY MARCH
Bravig Imbs: There is now in the United States a song that appears to be as popular as "Yes, We Have No Bananas." It is "Ac-cent-tchu-ate the Positive," "Insistez Sur Le Positive." It is a song that expresses very well the attitude adopted by the American people today. Here are the lyrics:

> Ac-cent-tchu-ate the Positive,
> Eliminate the negative,
> Latch on to the affirmative,
> And don't mess with Mister In-Between.

These lyrics are to be sung by Sergeant Ray McKinley and the Crew Chiefs. But before singing this sensational song, we would like to express all our gratitude to the Seine Section of the American Army, who graciously authorized this concert. In principle, our musicians must play only for soldiers of the Seine Section of the American Army, however these three groups agreed to this evening's performance in order that we have the pleasure to have them play for us. With all out heart we say thank you.
Bravig Imbs: Here's the newest American hit, "Ac-cent-tchu-ate the Positive," sung by Sergeant Ray McKinley and the Crew Chiefs.
AC-CENT-TCHU-ATE THE POSITIVE (Mister In-Between)
   Vocal refrain by Technical Sergeant Ray McKinley and the Crew Chiefs
Bravig Imbs: Major Glenn Miller's American Orchestra of the Allied Expeditionary Forces ends the program of this evening with "Down the Road a Piece," sung by Sergeant Ray McKinley and featuring a bass solo by Sergeant Trigger Alpert, who was a member of the original Glenn Miller Orchestra.
Bravig Imbs: Major Glenn Miller's American Band of the Allied Expeditionary Forces ends the program of this evening with "Down the Road a Piece," sung by Sergeant Ray McKinley and featuring a bass solo by Sergeant Trigger Alpert.
(That Place) DOWN THE ROAD A PIECE
ANVIL CHORUS
LA MARSEILLAISE (The French National Anthem)
GOD SAVE THE KING (British National Anthem)
GOSUDARSTVENY GIMN SOVETSKOGO SOYUSA (Russian National Anthem)
THE STAR-SPANGLED BANNER (USA National Anthem)

19Feb45 (Mon) 3:15-4:00PM Olympia Theatre, Paris, France   SLO-69971
AMERICAN BAND OF THE AEF recording   Aired 20Feb45   Attendance: 1200

MOONLIGHT SERENADE (opening theme)
  Warrant Officer Paul Dudley: ... A.E.F. on the Continent, conducted by Sergeant Jerry
  Gray. Music for and by members of the Allied Expeditionary Forces.
  Warrant Officer Paul Dudley: Hello, everybody. This is Warrant Officer Paul Dudley.
  Nine tunes in thirty minutes, that's the line-up and here's the pitch, first ball across
  the plate, Mel Powell's "Mission to Moscow."
MISSION TO MOSCOW
  Warrant Officer Paul Dudley: When it comes to writin' songs with a Southern flavor,
  Willard Robison's our number one choice. And when it comes to singin' 'em, Sergeant
  Johnny Desmond is our number one vote. Here's the combination in "Deep Summer Music."
DEEP SUMMER MUSIC
  Vocal refrain by Sergeant Johnny Desmond

  ...

AMOR (New tune)
  Vocal refrain by Sergeant Johnny Desmond
  Warrant Officer Paul Dudley: We borrow the big boss's big hit, "Chattanooga Choo Choo."
CHATTANOOGA CHOO CHOO (Borrowed tune)
  Vocal refrain by Technical Sergeant Ray McKinley and the Crew Chiefs

  ...

Warrant Officer Paul Dudley: Musical small talk's their specialty as demonstrated now in
  a little tete-a-tete between piano and drums and clarinet, "Sweet Georgia Brown."
SWEET GEORGIA BROWN (trio: Hucko, Powell, McKinley)
Warrant Officer Paul Dudley: You've all heard the little theme jingle that tinkles around
  the A.E.F.P. network and many of you have heard our chief arranger's adaptation of that
  tiny bit of music. Anyway it's time for an encore ...

  ...

20Feb45 (Tue) 3:30-4:00PM Olympia Theatre, Paris, France   SLO-69784/SLO-69974
  THE SWING SHIFT recording   Aired 03Mar45   Attendance: 1400

...

T/Sgt. Ray McKinley: ... "The Swing Shift." As usual, we're set to give out with a variety of danceable "dysarrands" designed to please a variety of you guys and gals of the A.E.F. To break the ice we're goin' to break it up with a Fletcher Henderson arrangement of "Breakin' in a New Pair of Shoes." Start walking, boys. It's one, two.
BREAKIN' IN A PAIR OF SHOES
T/Sgt. Ray McKinley: Time now for a stroll through the moon and June department. Arm in arm we find Johnny Desmond and "I'll Walk Alone."
I'LL WALK ALONE
  Vocal refrain by Sergeant Johnny Desmond

...

T/Sgt. Ray McKinley: ... the theme song of Mel Powell's "Uptown Hall," it's called "My Guy's Come Back."
MY GUY'S COME BACK

...

OH, LADY BE GOOD! (trio: Marino, Mastren, Alpert)
T/Sgt. Ray McKinley: Well, sir, we are diggin' deep for one now that fits right nicely into the remember spot. It's a shot of downtown music I sort of put the fresh diaper on and it's called "Beat Me Daddy, Eight to the Bar."
BEAT ME DADDY, EIGHT TO THE BAR
  Vocal refrain by Technical Sergeant Ray McKinley and Ensemble
T/Sgt. Ray McKinley: There's some tunes that just simply good enough to take any kind of treatment, sweet, hot or sort of in between. Such a one, we think, is "Harvest Moon."
SHINE ON, HARVEST MOON
T/Sgt. Ray McKinley: Not since the arrival of that timeless phrase, "A woman is two-faced," have we met a more confusing little gal than this next one. Johnny Desmond sings all about her.
(I Got a Woman Crazy for Me) SHE'S FUNNY THAT WAY
  Vocal refrain by Sergeant Johnny Desmond

...

T/Sgt. Ray McKinley: ... pleasure when it's the "King Porter Stomp." I'm giving you two, boys, so look out now. One, two.
KING PORTER STOMP
Corporal Paul Dubov: Well, fellows, it's so long for now but ...

...

26Feb45 (Mon) 3:15-3:45PM Olympia Theatre, Paris, France   SLO-69690
   AMERICAN BAND OF THE AEF recording   Aired 02Mar45   Attendance: 1500

  ...

Warrant Officer Paul Dudley: ... with us with one of the soft, sweet songs, "All the
  Things You Are."
ALL THE THINGS YOU ARE
  Vocal refrain by Sergeant Johnny Desmond

  ...

Warrant Officer Paul Dudley: ... American accent. The American Band of the A.E.F. says
  howdy to "Adios."
ADIOS

  ...

  Warrant Officer Paul Dudley: ... the borrowed tune and up jumps "Cherokee."
CHEROKEE (Indian Love Song) (Borrowed tune)

  ...

Warrant Officer Paul Dudley: And now the whole band uncorks a killer for the last big go
  around, a large basin full of brass polish labeled "Flying Home."
FLYING HOME

  ...

26Feb45 (Mon) 8:30-9:00PM Olympia Theatre, Paris, France   **SLO-69194**
  AMERICAN BAND OF THE AEF recording   Aired 06Mar45   **Attendance: 2000**

Female BBC announcer: We now present the recording of a program given by the American Band
  of the A.E.F. before an audience in an Allied Troop Theatre somewhere on the Continent.
MOONLIGHT SERENADE (opening theme)
  Warrant Officer Paul Dudley: This is the music of Major Glenn Miller's American Band of
    the A.E.F. on the Continent, conducted by chief arranger Sergeant Jerry Gray. Music
    for and by members of the Allied Expeditionary Forces.
Warrant Officer Paul Dudley: Hello, everybody. This is Warrant Officer Paul Dudley.
  Gangway for the take off tune. Here she comes barrelling into the air, "Caribbean
  Clipper."
CARIBBEAN CLIPPER
Warrant Officer Paul Dudley: Now right from the bottom of his heart and the top of his
  voice, Sergeant Johnny Desmond singing a song, "Together."
TOGETHER
  Vocal refrain by Sergeant Johnny Desmond
Warrant Officer Paul Dudley: And from the long string of Glenn Miller hit records,
  "String of Pearls."
A STRING OF PEARLS
Warrant Officer Paul Dudley: And now for medley time, saluting the mothers, wives,
  sweethearts and sisters of the Allied Forces with something old, something new,
  something borrowed and something blue. The old song, "Killarney."
KILLARNEY (Old tune)

  ...

AT THE RAINBOW CORNER (New tune)
  Vocal refrain by Sergeant Johnny Desmond and the Crew Chiefs
  Warrant Officer Paul Dudley: We borrow our band in playing the full treatment of our
    theme, "Moonlight Serenade."
MOONLIGHT SERENADE (Borrowed tune)
  Warrant Officer Paul Dudley: And for something blue here's a whispering jazz
    arrangement of good old "Wabash Blues."
WABASH BLUES (Blue tune)
Warrant Officer Paul Dudley: Fort Worth, Texas gave us Sergeant Ray McKinley, and
  Sergeant Ray McKinley gives us "Is You Is or Is You Ain't (Ma' Baby)."
IS YOU IS OR IS YOU AIN'T (Ma' Baby)
  Vocal refrain by Technical Sergeant Ray McKinley
Warrant Officer Paul Dudley: And here's where Mel Powell, Ray McKinley and Mike Hucko
  deal themselves a little three-handed music. Strictly on the informal side, "'S
  Wonderful."
'S WONDERFUL (trio: Hucko, Powell, McKinley)
Warrant Officer Paul Dudley: You combat guys are writing your names in history from D-Day
  to V-Day. And we'd like to snap you a salute in music as the whole gang gathers around
  Jerry Gray's hard hitting arrangement of the "Vict'ry Polka."
VICT'RY POLKA
  Vocal refrain by Sergeant Johnny Desmond, the Crew Chiefs and Ensemble
Warrant Officer Paul Dudley: This has been the music of Major Glenn Miller's American
  Band of the A.E.F. on the Continent, conducted by chief arranger Sergeant Jerry Gray.
  Music for and by members of the Allied Expeditionary Forces. Until next time we meet,
  it's good bye and good luck to you.
MOONLIGHT SERENADE (closing theme)

27Feb45 (Tue) 3:15-3:45PM Olympia Theatre, Paris, France   SLO-69691
  THE SWING SHIFT recording   Aired 10Mar45   Attendance: 1400

  . . .

T/Sgt. Ray McKinley: Many things can happen in the next half hour and probably will. So
  hang with us you guys and gals of the A.E.F. while we plant the motive for what we hope
  will be some happy listening with "Get Happy." Look out, boys. One, two.
GET HAPPY
T/Sgt. Ray McKinley: Having declared our weight we can afford to soften down and slow it
  down nice and easy, "Swing Low, Sweet Chariot."
SWING LOW, SWEET CHARIOT

  . . .

T/Sgt. Ray McKinley: . . . tells us why as he sings "I Dream of You."
I DREAM OF YOU (More Than You Dream I Do)
  Vocal refrain by Sergeant Johnny Desmond
T/Sgt. Ray McKinley: Here's Mel Powell original now, light and frothy, it's aptly titled
  "Bubble Bath."
BUBBLE BATH
T/Sgt. Ray McKinley: Johnny Mercer wrote it, Jerry Gray arranged it, the band, the Crew
  Chifs, Chiefs, Chefs, Chufs, ah, Crew Chiefs and I go to work on it now. It's
  "Ac-cent-tchu-ate the Positive."
AC-CENT-TCHU-ATE THE POSITIVE (Mister In-Between)
  Vocal refrain by Technical Sergeant Ray McKinley and the Crew Chiefs

  . . .

T/Sgt. Ray McKinley: Time to wrap it up now, which is always a pleasure when it's
  Fletcher Henderson's arrangement of "Stealin' Apples." Let's have a solid start now,
  you boys, with one, two.
STEALIN' APPLES

  . . .

06Mar45 (Tue) 3:15-3:45PM Olympia Theatre, Paris, France   SLO-70421
  THE SWING SHIFT recording   Aired 17Mar45   Attendance: 1400

  ...

T/Sgt. Ray McKinley: Howdy, folks, and welcome to another go around with "The Swing
  Shift." Once again it's our privilege to play for you guys and gals of the A.E.F. So
  we'll get about that instanter by pulling the lanyard on the big guns in the brass.
  It's "I Hear You Screamin'." Look out, boys, one, two.
I HEAR YOU SCREAMIN'
T/Sgt. Ray McKinley: Some what has. The boys in Tin Pan Alley have turned out a sizeable
  load of mighty fine songs during this man's war. Here's one of the latest with Johnny
  Desmond to sing it, "Some Other Time."
SOME OTHER TIME
  Vocal refrain by Sergeant Johnny Desmond
T/Sgt. Ray McKinley: Our boss, Major Miller, booted up to the 52nd story, it's "Tuxedo
  Junction."
TUXEDO JUNCTION
T/Sgt. Ray McKinley: Blues time is boogie time and boogie time is trio time. So, Mel, if
  you'll just lay a little of your time on us, Mike and me'll join in due time and by that
  time we oughta have the right time on "Train Number 88."
TRAIN NO. 88 (trio: Hucko, Powell, McKinley)
T/Sgt. Ray McKinley: Here's Johnny Desmond to sing us another lovely. This time it's
  "The Day after Forever."
THE DAY AFTER FOREVER
  Vocal refrain by Sergeant Johnny Desmond

  ...

T/Sgt. Ray McKinley: ... play me one of those down yonder introductions, I'll join in on
  the chorus of "Waitin' for the Evenin' Mail."
WAITIN' FOR THE EVENIN' MAIL (Sittin' on the Inside Lookin' at the Outside)
  Vocal refrain by Technical Sergeant Ray McKinley
Warrant Officer Paul Dudley: Sergeant Ray McKinley has cooked up a rowdy little rondelet
  that features Sergeant Ray McKinley and his drums. Here it is now in it's premier
  showing, "The Big Beat."
THE BIG BEAT (Drums Away)

  ...

08Mar45 (Thu) 10:45-11:15PM Olympia Theatre, Paris, France   SLO-70422
  THE SWING SHIFT recording   Aired 22Mar45

BBC female announcer: Next comes a recording of a performance given by a unit of the
  American Band of the A.E.F. on the Continent.
Corporal Paul Dubov: Presenting "The Swing Shift," featuring Sergeant Ray McKinley and
  his music.
SONG AND DANCE (opening theme)
  Vocal refrain by Technical Sergeant Ray McKinley:
    This is Sergeant Ray McKinley saying how do ya do,
    And all the boys in the band say howdy too.
    So get yourself settled 'round the radio,
    While I tell you what's cooking on this evening's show.
    Because most everybody likes a version hot,
    We call on the brass for our opening shot.
    Then to equalize the pressure of so much strain,
    Why we slow it down to a quieter vein.
    So Sergeant Johnny Desmond's gonna have his say,
    About romance and blue skies and et cetera.
    Tunes there's gonna be one by your own trio,
    Composed of drums, a clarinet and a pie-an-o.
    And the Crew Chiefs are back and will harmonize,
    A brand new number which we kind of prize.
    That's the end of the song and it's our intent,
    That the next thirty minutes will see you sent.
T/Sgt. Ray McKinley: Howdy, friends, and welcome to another go around with "The Swing
  Shift." Once again we've lined up a half hour of oldies and newies, fasties and fluties
  for you guys and gals of the A.E.F. To get it going we pick one of the all time daddies
  of jazz, it's the "King Porter Stomp" with two beats, gents. Look out now, one, two.
KING PORTER STOMP
T/Sgt. Ray McKinley: Yes, yes. Here's a Bill Finegan arrangement now of one of George
  Gershwin's best, "Lady Be Good!"
OH, LADY BE GOOD!
T/Sgt. Ray McKinley: Night time is lover's time and I'm sure Johnny Desmond echoes one of
  those meaningless sentiments which somehow means everything when he sings "How Blue the
  Night."
HOW BLUE THE NIGHT
  Vocal refrain by Sergeant Johnny Desmond
T/Sgt. Ray McKinley: You know, a lot of people claim there's just four cities in the U.S.
  What say we take now to one that's always included and go "'Way Down Yonder in New
  Orleans" with two beats, boys? Look out now, one, two.
'WAY DOWN YONDER IN NEW ORLEANS
Corporal Paul Dubov: Comes the trio Powell, Hucko and McKinley to burn a little bathroom
  incense known in impolite circles as "Shoemaker's Apron."
SHOEMAKER'S APRON (trio: Hucko, Powell, McKinley)
T/Sgt. Ray McKinley: Well, the customers are always right and it seems as our customers
  want a repeat on Johnny Desmond's singing of "As Long As There's Music."
AS LONG AS THERE'S MUSIC
  Vocal refrain by Sergeant Johnny Desmond
T/Sgt. Ray McKinley: Well, that's enough temporizing so right here and now the Crew
  Chiefs and I are gonna lay down the law with "Ac-cent-tchu-ate the Positive."
AC-CENT-TCHU-ATE THE POSITIVE (Mister In-Between)
  Vocal refrain by Technical Sergeant Ray McKinley and the Crew Chiefs
T/Sgt. Ray McKinley: Here's the last one now, a fast flying clipper known as the
  "Caribbean Clipper."
CARIBBEAN CLIPPER
Corporal Paul Dubov: That's all for tonight, fellows. "The Swing Shift," featuring
  Sergeant Ray McKinley and his drums, will be back again soon. So try to be around your
  radio if you can. And now here's Sergeant Mac and his "Git Along Song."

SONG AND DANCE (closing theme)
  Vocal refrain by Technical Sergeant Ray McKinley:
    Well, so long, everybody, I guess that's enough,
    And we certainly hope you liked our stuff.
    It was indeed quite a pleasure to play for you all,
    Now here are a few of the boys to take a curtain call.
  Vocal refrain by Sergeant Johnny Desmond:
    This is Sergeant Johnny Desmond wishing you well.
  Vocal refrain by Technical Sergeant Ray McKinley:
    Well, thank you, Johnny, for helping us to gel.
  Vocal refrain by the Crew Chiefs:
    This is the Crew Chiefs saying we've been ill.
  Vocal refrain by Technical Sergeant Ray McKinley:
    Well, I'll have to give each one of you boys a vitamin pill.

12Mar45 (Mon) 8:30-9:00PM Olympia Theatre, Paris, France   SLO-70222
AMERICAN BAND OF THE AEF recording   Aired 16Mar45   Attendance: 2000

  ...

Warrant Officer Paul Dudley: Starting things the band goes over the bars for a high jump
  "Measure for Measure."
MEASURE FOR MEASURE
Warrant Officer Paul Dudley: And now cuddle your ear up to something soft and warm,
  Sergeant Johnny Desmond sings "As Long As There's Music."
AS LONG AS THERE'S MUSIC
  Vocal refrain by Sergeant Johnny Desmond

  ...

Warrant Officer Paul Dudley: ... this fight song we're singin' and playin', the "Notre
  Dame Victory March."
NOTRE DAME VICTORY MARCH

  ...

DANCE WITH A DOLLY (With a Hole in Her Stockin') (New tune)
  Vocal refrain by Corporal Artie Malvin
  Warrant Officer Paul Dudley: For something borrowed, Ray Noble owns this one, "The Very
    Thought of You."
THE VERY THOUGHT OF YOU (Borrowed tune)

  ...

Warrant Officer Paul Dudley: ... "Swing Low, Sweet Chariot."
SWING LOW, SWEET CHARIOT
Warrant Officer Paul Dudley: Here Sergeant Jerry Gray has gone and done it again. He's
  taken a tune that's plenty big among the hits back home and proceeded to make it even
  bigger. This time Jerry's given the all out treatment to "The Trolley Song."
THE TROLLEY SONG
  Vocal refrain by Sergeant Johnny Desmond and Ensemble

  ...

13Mar45 (Tue) 3:15-3:45PM Olympia Theatre, Paris, France   SLO-70336
  THE SWING SHIFT recording   Aired 24Mar45   Attendance: 1400

  . . .

T/Sgt. Ray McKinley: We've got the boys in the band behind us and lots of guys and gals
  of the A.E.F. seated out here before us. So without further ado we'll go to work on Mel
  Powell's "Mission to Moscow." Look out you Montmartre hilly-billies, here we go. One,
  two.
MISSION TO MOSCOW
T/Sgt. Ray McKinley: What say we sneak a long, cool pull now from that "Little Brown
  Jug?"
LITTLE BROWN JUG
T/Sgt. Ray McKinley: It's at the top of the song heap both here and at home. Hence we
  call on Sergeant Johnny Desmond ...

  . . .

I DREAM OF YOU (More Than You Dream I Do)
  Vocal refrain by Sergeant Johnny Desmond
T/Sgt. Ray McKinley: We're gonna pass amongst you now with some slight samples of
  Sergeant Hucko's music called culinary dexterity. It's trio time and some "Fruit Cake."
FRUIT CAKE (trio: Hucko, Powell, McKinley)
T/Sgt. Ray McKinley: Well, sir, the boys in the brass look a little rested after that but
  we'll take care of that right now. Gentlemen, one chorus to get it set and I'll expect
  you all to sink your valves in "Wham
  Re-Bop-Boom-Bam." And it's one, two.
WHAM (Re-Bop-Boom-Bam)
  Vocal refrain by Technical Sergeant Ray McKinley and Ensemble
T/Sgt. Ray McKinley: Again Johnny Desmond comes out singing. This time ...

  . . .

T/Sgt. Ray McKinley: ... lately. Bernie Privin's trumpet, the singing of the Crew
  Chiefs, and my own cactus cured cupidity combined to comply with "G.I. Jive."
G.I. JIVE
  Vocal refrain by Technical Sergeant Ray McKinley and the Crew Chiefs
Corporal Paul Dubov: Wrappin' up time is goin' home time, a tune that promises a great
  day for us all, "Flying Home."
FLYING HOME

  . . .

15Mar45 (Thu) 10:40-11:10PM Olympia Theatre, Paris, France   SLO-70268
  THE SWING SHIFT recording   Aired 29Mar45

  ...

T/Sgt. Ray McKinley: Once again the dance band is set to throw its weight around in a
  manner refe-reminiscent, or reminiscent of all those places that stretch from the
  Hollywood's Palladium to New York's Glen Island Casino. Comin' at you first tune is one
  that's part of every band's library, the "King Porter Stomp."
KING PORTER STOMP
T/Sgt. Ray McKinley: Well, if that one was a little fast for you and the girl friend,
  here's a sample that's slower and softer, it's still full of starch, "Sleepy Town
  Train."
SLEEPY TOWN TRAIN

  ...

T/Sgt. Ray McKinley: ... "Some Other Time."
SOME OTHER TIME
  Vocal refrain by Sergeant Johnny Desmond

  ...

T/Sgt. Ray McKinley: ... boy we borrowed from one Phil Marino by name who, aided by
  Carmen Mastren's guitar and by Trigger Alpert's bass, is gonna take a cut at "I've Found
  a New Baby."
I'VE FOUND A NEW BABY (trio: Marino, Mastren, Alpert)
T/Sgt. Ray McKinley: Well, sir, besides playing an accomplished guitar, Carmen Mastren
  rates a high seat in the American academy of swing arrangers. Here's a sample of his
  work, albeit an old one, on "Spanish Shawl."
SPANISH SHAWL
T/Sgt. Ray McKinley: A ballad which ranks high in Johnny Desmond's adenoidal catalog and
  about to be delivered to you now, "It Could Happen to You."
IT COULD HAPPEN TO YOU
  Vocal refrain by Sergeant Johnny Desmond

  ...

T/Sgt. Ray McKinley: ... which goes by so fast it's not easy to take it all in in one
  hearing. Here then is a repeat-peat, repeat of "No Compris."
NO COMPRIS
T/Sgt. Ray McKinley: Thank you, Mel. We've of(ten) ...

  ...

SOMEBODY'S WRONG
Corporal Paul Dubov: Well, it's so long for now, fellows, but don't forget "The Swing
  Shift" with Sergeant Ray McKinley will be back again soon. And now here's Sergeant Mac
  and his "Git Along Song."
SONG AND DANCE (closing theme)
  Vocal refrain by Technical Sergeant Ray McKinley:
    Well, so long, everybody, guess that's enough,
    And we certainly hope that you like our stuff.
    It was indeed quite a pleasure to play for you all.
    Now here are two of the boys to take a curtain call.
  Vocal refrain by Sergeant Johnny Desmond:
    This is Sergeant Johnny Desmond wishing you well.
  Vocal refrain by Technical Sergeant Ray McKinley:
    Well, thank you, Johnny, for helping this to gel.

Vocal refrain by Corporal Paul Dubov:
  This is Paul staff Dubov sayin' I'm bein' told.
Vocal refrain by Technical Sergeant Ray McKinley:
  You can stay, bub, but that's - ah - gotta go.
  So if you leave your dial right where it is now,
  The chances are we'll - ah - keep a rendezvow.
  Here's the last two bars of our crazy tune,
  Which give me a chance to say adioose.

19Mar45 (Mon) 3:15-3:45PM Olympia Theatre, Paris, France   SLO-70285
  AMERICAN BAND OF THE AEF recording   Aired 20Mar45   Attendance: 1400

  ...

Warrant Officer Paul Dudley: ... start the music. Well, then you'd better take cover
  because it's comin' at you right here and now. Out of the starting gate comes
  "Limehouse Blues."
LIMEHOUSE BLUES

  ...

Warrant Officer Paul Dudley: ... (manuscript), composing, arranging and playing, it's
  name, "Pearls on Velvet."
PEARLS ON VELVET

26Mar45 (Mon) 2:40-3:20PM Olympia Theatre, Paris, France   SLO-70759
  AMERICAN BAND OF THE AEF recording   Aired 27Mar45   Attendance: 1400

  ...

ALOUETTE (Borrowed tune)
  Warrant Officer Paul Dudley: And rounding out the medley with something blue, here's
    "Blue Moon."
BLUE MOON (Blue tune)

  ...

02Apr45 (Mon) 3:20-3:55PM Olympia Theatre, Paris, France   SLO-71948
    AMERICAN BAND OF THE AEF recording   Aired 17Apr45   Attendance: 1500

    ...

WAITIN' FOR THE EVENIN' MAIL (Sittin' on the Inside Lookin' at the Outside)
    Vocal refrain by Technical Sergeant Ray McKinley
Warrant Officer Paul Dudley: Just about the nicest thing that could happen to any piano
    is to have Mel Powell play it. Here's where Mel gets the best out of his French 88,
    joining up with Mike Hucko and Ray McKinley in "After You've Gone."
AFTER YOU'VE GONE (trio: Hucko, Powell, McKinley)

    ...

03Apr45 (Tue) 2:45-3:20PM Olympia Theatre, Paris, France   SAL-19920
    AMERICAN BAND OF THE AEF recording   Aired 24Apr45   Attendance: 1400

    ...

THE SAME OLD LOVE (New tune)
    Vocal refrain by Sergeant Johnny Desmond
    Warrant Officer Paul Dudley: We put the bit on Harry James for our borrowed tune and up
    jumps the "Music Makers."
MUSIC MAKERS (Borrowed tune)
    Warrant Officer Paul Dudley: A whispering jazz arrangement moves into the blues
    spotlight, "Farewell Blues."
FAREWELL BLUES (Blue tune)
Warrant Officer Paul Dudley: When Major Glenn Miller formed this outfit, he scoured the
    whole U.S. Army to find the men he wanted to bring over here. Men like Ray McKinley,
    who led his own band in civilian days; Mel Powell, pianist and arranger for Benny
    Goodman; Bernie Privin, Hank Freeman from Artie Shaw's band; and the string section,
    headed by George Ockner, from all the leading symphonies. And as chief arranger he
    choose the lad who did all Artie Shaw's hit arranging as well as plenty of fine work for
    the Major's own civilian band, Sergeant Jerry Gray. Here's a fine example of Jerry's
    arranging talents, a zoot salute to our Russian Allies, "The Red Cavalry March."
THE RED CAVALRY MARCH
Warrant Officer Paul Dudley: This has been the music of Major Glenn Miller's American
    Band of the A.E.F. on the Continent, conducted by chief arranger Sergeant Jerry Gray.
    Music for and by members of the Allied Expeditionary Forces. 'Til next time we meet
    it's good bye and good luck to you.
MOONLIGHT SERENADE (closing theme)

05Apr45 (Thu) 10:35-11:10PM Olympia Theatre, Paris, France   SAL-20115
  THE SWING SHIFT recording   Aired 25Apr45

BBC female announcer: A.E.F.P. brings you a recording made by a unit of the American Band
  of the A.E.F. now on the Continent.

Corporal Paul Dubov: Presenting "The Swing Shift," featuring Sergeant Ray McKinley and
  his music.
SONG AND DANCE (opening theme)
  Vocal refrain by Technical Sergeant Ray McKinley:
    This is Sergeant Ray McKinley saying hiya sport,
    And for "The Swing Shift" program I oodle a forth.
    We're glad to see you out there, happy and beamin',
    And we'll answer your smile with "I Hear You Screamin'."
    The second tune running on our chemin de fer,
    Is "Sleepy Town Train" I do declare.
    And then you'll hear a song that's a real warm dreamer,
    Sung by Sergeant Johnny Desmond, whom _Time_ calls The Creamer.
    After which the trio makes a fast triple play,
    Shooting you a rooting, tooting rondelet.
    The "Nine Twenty Special," with its title mathematic,
    Will swing from the rafters with the music acrobatic.
    A tune from the newsreels will wind up the show,
    We've told you our story so now you're in the know.
    Without addenda the program begins,
    You beat your hands and I'll beat the skins.
T/Sgt. Ray McKinley: Howdy, neighbors. Pull up an ear and make yourselves at home.
  We're scheduled to do eight tunes in thirty minutes. Eight into thirty comes out three
  point seven-five, which is slightly stronger than that three point two we used to get
  back in the PX, and therefore should be slightly more stimulating. And first from out
  of the tap comes a boilermaker. It's "I Hear You Screamin'." Look out, you cats, the
  beat is all on you with a one, two.
I HEAR YOU SCREAMIN'
T/Sgt. Ray McKinley: You'll find this next arrangement spinning around the phonograph in
  your day room, this is if you have a day room and your day room has a phonograph. This
  one is on a V-Disc that we made back you know where, it's "Sleepy Town Train."
SLEEPY TOWN TRAIN
T/Sgt. Ray McKinley: We hear that Frankie Sinatra is all but on his way over here to do
  some entertaining. Well, while we do our breathless awaiting for Frankie to do his
  breathless singing, we'll just have to struggle along with our own Sergeant Johnny
  Desmond, who's had to do all his warbling for the past year in the key of C-ration.
  Johnny's on now singing "You, Fascinating You."
YOU, FASCINATING YOU
  Vocal refrain by Sergeant Johnny Desmond
Corporal Paul Dubov: Three's the lucky number for the next spot. Three minutes filled by
  three big operators in the small combination of piano, clarinet and drums, Mel Powell,
  Mike Hucko and Ray McKinley in "'S Wonderful."
'S WONDERFUL (trio: Hucko, Powell, McKinley)
T/Sgt. Ray McKinley: Yes, indeed. All Right. You have to hurry to get up here. Now for
  all you _Downbeat_ subscribers in our audience, here's a little score exhibiting some of
  the subtler implications of the formal school of the La Jazz Hot, "Nine Twenty Special."
NINE TWENTY SPECIAL
T/Sgt. Ray McKinley: Encore time for Sergeant Johnny Desmond, who's going to unleash - ah
  - another romantic ballad out our way right now and this time Johnny's wearing his heart
  on his voice to the tune of "She's Funny That Way."
(I Got a Woman Crazy for Me) SHE'S FUNNY THAT WAY
  Vocal refrain by Sergeant Johnny Desmond

T/Sgt. Ray McKinley: Now I'm not trying to steal any of young John's thunder or anything
   like that, I'd like to wrap my own Texas tremolo around a tune, parting a longhorn
   larynx right in the middle with "Sittin' on the Inside Lookin' at the Outside, Waitin'
   for the Evenin' Mail."
WAITIN' FOR THE EVENIN' MAIL (Sittin' on the Inside Lookin' at the Outside)
   Vocal refrain by Technical Sergeant Ray McKinley
Corporal Paul Dubov: Now Sergeant Mac is back behind the drum pile all set and ready to
   pull the lanyard on a barrage of clarinet solos by Michael Hucko and shower the airways
   with some mixed light and heavy flak entitled "The Eyes and Ears of the World."
THE EYES AND EARS OF THE WORLD
Corporal Paul Dubov: You have been lending your ear abandon to "The Swing Shift" program,
   featuring Sergeant Ray McKinley and his music. You'll be hearing this show again soon.
   And now here comes Sergeant Mac singing his "Git Along Song."
SONG AND DANCE (closing theme)
   Vocal refrain by Technical Sergeant Ray McKinley:
      Well, so long, everybody, I guess that's enough.
      We certainly hope you liked our stuff.
      It was indeed quite a pleasure to play for you all.
      Now here's a couple of the boys to take a curtain call.
   Vocal refrain by Sergeant Johnny Desmond:
      This is Sergeant Johnny Desmond wishing you well.
   Vocal refrain by Technical Sergeant Ray McKinley:
      Thank you, Johnny, for making it gel.
   Vocal refrain by Corporal Paul Dubov:
      This is Paul staff Dubov saying thanks indeedy.
   Vocal refrain by Technical Sergeant Ray McKinley:
      Well, I guess on that point we're all agreedy.
      And if you've nothing to do of a Wed. or a Sat.,
      We'll be comin' at you right where you're at.
      It's time for our chow and that's thought for food,
      So we'll bid you farewell and hit the route.

BBC female announcer: You're been listening to a recording made by a unit of the American
   Band of the A.E.F., now on the Continent. This is the Allied Expeditionary Forces
   Program.

05Apr45 (Thu) 11:10-11:45PM Olympia Theatre, Paris, France   SAL-20116
  THE SWING SHIFT recording   Aired 28Apr45

BBC female announcer: A.E.F.P. brings you a recording by - made by the unit of the
  American Band of the A.E.F. now on the Continent.

Corporal Paul Dubov: Presenting "The Swing Shift," featuring Sergeant Ray McKinley and
  his music.
SONG AND DANCE (opening theme)
  Vocal refrain by Technical Sergeant Ray McKinley:
    This is Sergeant Ray McKinley saying howdya do,
    And all the boys in the band saying howdy too.
    So light up a smoke and flip out an ear,
    Here's a blues to raise a may of what you're gonna hear.
    Because it's tradition, sort of start out strong,
    We always pick a screamer for our opening song.
    But then to equalize the pressure of so much strain,
    We slow down the next one in a quieter vein.
    Course, Sergeant Johnny Desmond's gonna have his say,
    About romance and heartaches and et cetera.
    Tonight we'll have a number by your old trio,
    Composed of drums, a clarinet and a piano.
    Yep, some of it's old and some of it's new,
    And some tunes are happy and some of 'em blue.
    But whichever you prefer, It's our intent,
    That the next thirty minutes will see you sent.
T/Sgt. Ray McKinley: Howdy, guys. Time to plant your Eustachian tubes this way and
  funnel in another avalanche of hot licks, sweet songs, delayed bucks and maybe even a
  well intended clinker or two from out of the old "Swing Shift." If you think we're
  gonna swing down the opening stretch with a starchy stride, you're right, even if the
  title of this opening opus is "Somebody's Wrong." Lay it on me, boys, one, two.
SOMEBODY'S WRONG
T/Sgt. Ray McKinley: Here's an oldie that ought to take you back to almost any night
  about 1939 or '40 with a prefatory apology to the Joes over here whose know-how on the
  Western front is plenty plain to see. I'll go along with the lyric of "Whatcha Know
  Joe."
WHATCHA KNOW JOE
  Vocal refrain by Technical Sergeant Ray McKinley and Ensemble
T/Sgt. Ray McKinley: Time for Sergeant Johnny Desmond to sing us a song. Tonight
  Johnny's chosen a subject that's mighty close to all of us, to wit, "I Dream of You."
I DREAM OF YOU (More Than You Dream I Do)
  Vocal refrain by Sergeant Johnny Desmond
Corporal Paul Dubov: You know the blues is in itself a pretty exciting form of jazz. And
  when you add not only a boogie beat from Mel Powell's left hand but some clarinetic
  legerdemain from Mike Hucko and some of Ray McKinley's pulsating drum thumpin', well,
  and here I might add another well, the result has got to be "Plain and Fancy Blues."
PLAIN AND FANCY BLUES (Train No. 88) (trio: Hucko, Powell, McKinley)
T/Sgt. Ray McKinley: The boys in the Navy asked for this next one, so here it 'tis, the
  Crew Chiefs, all of 'em singin' "Shoo-Shoo Baby."
SHOO-SHOO BABY
  Vocal refrain by the Crew Chiefs
T/Sgt. Ray McKinley: Now it's encore time for Johnny Desmond. Time for the modest
  Sergeant all set for singin' "Time Alone Will Tell."
TIME ALONE WILL TELL
  Vocal refrain by Sergeant Johnny Desmond
T/Sgt. Ray McKinley: Which brings us to a tune that seems to be catching on in this neck
  of the woods. It all started when Mel Powell whipped up "My Guy's Come Back." One,
  two.
MY GUY'S COME BACK

T/Sgt. Ray McKinley: Well, sir, when Jerry Gray made our arrangement of "Everybody Loves My Baby" he must have been in one of those happy moods that all arrangers pray for, because that kind of mood pays off to the guys that play it because from start to finish it jumps, and I don't mean maybe, it just jumps. So judge for yourselves. Look out now, boys, here we go, ready, one, two.

EVERYBODY LOVES MY BABY (But My Baby Don't Love Nobody but Me)

Corporal Paul Dubov: You have been lending your ear abandon to "The Swing Shift" program, featuring Sergeant Ray McKinley and his music. You'll be hearing this show again soon. And now here comes Sergeant Mac a singing his "Git Along Song."

SONG AND DANCE

Vocal refrain by Technical Sergeant Ray McKinley:
Well, so long, everybody, I guess that's enough.
We certainly hope that you liked our stuff.
It was indeed quite a pleasure to play for you all.
Now here's a couple of the boys to take a curtain call.
Vocal refrain by Sergeant Johnny Desmond:
This is Sergeant Johnny Desmond ...

BBC female announcer: You've been listening to a recording made on the Continent by a unit of the American Band of the A.E.F. In just a moment all your A.E.F. stations will identify themselves. This is the Allied Expeditionary Forces Program.

09Apr45 (Mon) 2:45-3:20PM   Olympia Theatre, Paris, France   SLO-71256
AMERICAN BAND OF THE AEF recording   Aired 27Apr45   Attendance: 1500

BBC female announcer: 20:30 Friday night. Time for music and one of your three main
  A.E.F. orchestras. This is a recording of a performance given by the American Band of
  the A.E.F. on the Continent.

MOONLIGHT SERENADE (opening theme)
  Warrant Officer Paul Dudley: This is the music of Major Glenn Miller's American Band of
    the A.E.F. on the Continent, conducted by chief arranger Sergeant Jerry Gray. Music
    for and by members of the Allied Expeditionary Forces.
  Warrant Officer Paul Dudley: Hello, everybody, this is Warrant Officer Paul Dudley.
    Well, once again we're ready to come swinging past your radio in a thirty minute revue.
    And struttin' proudly along at the head of the parade comes a sharp and successful
    musical citizen, "In the Mood."
IN THE MOOD
Warrant Officer Paul Dudley: And now sounding mighty handsome and wearing a brand new
  made-to-measure tune here's the voice of Sergeant Johnny Desmond in "More and More."
MORE AND MORE
  Vocal refrain by Sergeant Johnny Desmond
Warrant Officer Paul Dudley: We're heading back to the brass works and an all out
  stampede over a racy little steeplechase called "Get Happy."
GET HAPPY
Warrant Officer Paul Dudley: And now comes medley time, saluting your mothers, wives,
  sweethearts and sisters with something old, something new, something borrowed and
  something blue. The old song, "Old Black Joe."
OLD BLACK JOE (Old tune)
  Warrant Officer Paul Dudley: Sergeant Johnny Desmond brings on our something new song
    singing ...
SOMEONE TO LOVE (I've Got the Blues) (New tune)
  Vocal refrain by Sergeant Johnny Desmond
  Warrant Officer Paul Dudley: From our British teammates comes our borrowed tune, Artie
    Malvin and the whole gang sing "I've Got Sixpence."
I'VE GOT SIXPENCE (As We Go Rolling Home) (Borrowed tune)
  Vocal refrain by Corporal Artie Malvin and Ensemble
  Warrant Officer Paul Dudley: And here's the very greatest of the something blue tunes,
    "Rhapsody in Blue."
RHAPSODY IN BLUE (Blue tune)
Warrant Officer Paul Dudley: And here's this show's Miller thriller. From our big boss's
  big string of hit recordings, "String of Pearls."
A STRING OF PEARLS
Warrant Officer Paul Dudley: We know that many an epic has been written in a dusty garret
  but we'll guarantee that this is the first big time musical arrangement ever made in the
  bathtub. That's the only space Sergeant Jerry Gray could find to set up his arranging
  desk to produce the hot and cold running rhythm of "The Trolley Song."
THE TROLLEY SONG
  Vocal refrain by Sergeant Johnny Desmond, Technical Sergeant Ray McKinley, the Crew
    Chiefs and Ensemble
Warrant Officer Paul Dudley: This has been the music of Major Glenn Miller's American
  Band of the A.E.F. on the Continent, conducted by chief arranger Sergeant Jerry Gray.
  Music for and by members of the Allied Expeditionary Forces. Until next time we meet
  it's good bye and good luck to you.
MOONLIGHT SERENADE (closing theme)

09Apr45 (Mon) 3:20-3:55PM Olympia Theatre, Paris, France   SLO-71954
   AMERICAN BAND OF THE AEF recording   Aired 01May45   Attendance: 1500

BBC chimes
BBC female announcer: 20:30 hours, Tuesday night. Time for one of your three main A.E.F.
   orchestras. This is a recording of a performance given by the American Band of the
   A.E.F. in an Allied troop theatre somewhere on the Continent.

MOONLIGHT SERENADE (opening theme)
   Warrant Officer Paul Dudley: This is the music of Major Glenn Miller's American Band of
      the A.E.F. on the Continent, conducted by chief arranger Sergeant Jerry Gray. Music
      for and by members of the Allied Expeditionary Forces.
   Warrant Officer Paul Dudley: Hello, everybody. This is Warrant Officer Paul Dudley. Our
      problem is to - to divide thirty minutes by ten tunes and try to make the answer your
      listening pleasure. Top on the list comes a real Miller thriller, "Here We Go Again."
HERE WE GO AGAIN
Warrant Officer Paul Dudley: And here's the voice of Sergeant Johnny Desmond romancing
   its way through "My Prayer."
MY PRAYER
   Vocal refrain by Sergeant Johnny Desmond
Warrant Officer Paul Dudley: Sergeant Ray McKinley from Fort Worth, Texas is our number
   one exponent of the cactus country calypso and here he comes a singing "And Her Tears
   Flowed Like Wine."
AND HER TEARS FLOWED LIKE WINE
   Vocal refrain by Technical Sergeant Ray McKinley and Ensemble
Warrant Officer Paul Dudley: Medley time salutes your mothers, wives, sweethearts and
   sisters with something old, something new, something borrowed and something blue. The
   old song, "Schubert's Serenade."
SCHUBERT'S SERENADE (Old tune)
   Warrant Officer Paul Dudley: For something new here's Sergeant Johnny Desmond singing
      . . .
SOME OTHER TIME (New tune)
   Vocal refrain by Sergeant Johnny Desmond
   Warrant Officer Paul Dudley: A famous Glenn Miller recording lends us our borrowed tune
      and it's "Little Brown Jug."
LITTLE BROWN JUG (Borrowed tune)
   Warrant Officer Paul Dudley: And to play the last quarter of this medley game, coach
      Jerry Gray sends in something blue, "Under a Blanket of Blue."
UNDER A BLANKET OF BLUE (Blue tune)
Warrant Officer Paul Dudley: Despite having been in the Army for two years and over here
   for nearly one, Mel Powell is still winning the American championship as the nation's
   finest popular pianist. And here Mel puts his talents on display with his newest
   composition, "No Compris."
NO COMPRIS
Warrant Officer Paul Dudley: Major Glenn Miller's American Band of the A.E.F. was born
   and brought up in the U.S. Army Air Forces. And now a salute to General H. H. Arnold
   and the old alma mammy, "With My Head in the Clouds."
WITH MY HEAD IN THE CLOUDS
   Vocal refrain by Sergeant Johnny Desmond, the Crew Chiefs and Ensemble
Warrant Officer Paul Dudley: This has been the music of Major Glenn Miller's American
   Band of the A.E.F. on the Continent, conducted by chief arranger Sergeant Jerry Gray.
   Music for and by members of the Allied Expeditionary Forces. Until next time we meet
   it's good bye and good luck to you
MOONLIGHT SERENADE (closing theme)

   BBC female announcer: The program you've just heard was a recording of a performance
      given by the American Band of the A.E.F. somewhere on the Continent.

10Apr45 (Tue) 3:20-3:55PM Olympia Theatre, Paris, France   SLO-71510
  THE SWING SHIFT recording   Aired 05May45   Attendance: 1600

  . . .

DRUMS AWAY (The Big Beat)
  Corporal Paul Dubov: Go on, Ray.
  Corporal Paul Dubov: Wonderful, Ray.
T/Sgt. Ray McKinley: Yeah.
Corporal Paul Dubov: That's all for now, fellows, but "The Swing Shift," featuring
  Sergeant Ray McKinley and his music, will be back again soon. And now here's Sergeant
  Mac and his "Git Along Song."
SONG AND DANCE (closing theme)
  Vocal refrain by Technical Sergeant Ray McKinley

  . . .

11Apr45 (Wed) 10:20-10:55PM Olympia Theatre, Paris, France   SLO-71956
  THE SWING SHIFT recording   Aired 02May45

  . . .

BREAKIN' IN A PAIR OF SHOES
T/Sgt. Ray McKinley: Well, it's encore time now for the lad with the porcupine hairdo,
  the olive complexion, and the Mediterranean eyes. This, by way of an aside to our
  sister's norms, for out of the golden depths, the vocal depths of this velvet visage,
  comes now the strains of "How Blue the Night."
HOW BLUE THE NIGHT
  Vocal refrain by Sergeant Johnny Desmond

  . . .

FLYING HOME
Corporal Paul Dubov: You've been listening to "The Swing Shift" program, featuring
  Sergeant Ray McKinley and his music. We'll be back again soon, so keep an eye on the
  Stars and Stripes and an ear on the radio. For now it's so long and good luck to you.
SONG AND DANCE (closing theme)
  Vocal refrain by Technical Sergeant Ray McKinley

Announcer: You've been listening to a recording made by a unit of the American Band of
  the A.E.F. on the Continent.

16Apr45 (Mon) 8:30-9:00PM Olympia Theatre, Paris, France   SLO-71881
  AMERICAN BAND OF THE AEF recording   Aired 18May45   Attendance: 2000

MOONLIGHT SERENADE (opening theme)
  Warrant Officer Paul Dudley: This is the music of Major Glenn Miller's American Band of
    the AEF on the Continent, conducted by chief arranger Sergeant Jerry Gray. Music for
    and by members of the Allied Expeditionary Forces.

  . . .

20Apr45 (Fri) 10:30-11:00PM Olympia Theatre, Paris, France   SLO-72005
THE SWING SHIFT recording   Aired 19May45

Corporal Paul Dubov: Presenting "The Swing Shift," featuring Sergeant Ray McKinley and
   his music.
SONG AND DANCE (opening theme)
   Vocal refrain by Technical Sergeant Ray McKinley:
      This is Sergeant Ray McKinley calling order in the meetin',
      While I read you the minutes of this next repeatin'.
      We'll open up shop with the business unfinished,
      Which is "Tail End Charlie" full of chords undiminished.
      We'll take some water and soap and really stay with 'em,
      For a swing "Bubble Bath," hot and cold running rhythm.
      Then Sergeant Johnny Desmond, whom <u>Time</u> calls the Creamer,
      Will sing a love song for each listening dreamer.
      Time for jazz on tee, we'll slip you a sermon,
      Which includes a word or two about the Nazi vermin.
      Then a little more blues and a lot more jazz,
      And Sergeant Johnny Desmond's romance razzmatazz.
      We'll come down the stretch with some music that spins,
      As it cuts through the air, why I'll hammer the skins.
      You relax and we'll do the labor,
      Of mowing the brass for each radio neighbor.
T/Sgt. Ray McKinley: Howdy, neighbors. The music is on and we're off to the races with
   "Tail End Charlie." Look out, Latin quarterbacks, the beat is reet, so toody-root now
   with a one, two.
TAIL END CHARLIE
T/Sgt. Ray McKinley: Mel Powell lubricated his talents with midnight oil and the result
   is a composition that's a real listening pleasure. We now have the pleasure of playing
   "Bubble Bath."
BUBBLE BATH
T/Sgt. Ray McKinley: Time now for Sergeant Johnny Desmond to sing you a romantic softy,
   some music that'll melt in your ears, "Embraceable You."
EMBRACEABLE YOU
   Vocal refrain by Sergeant Johnny Desmond
T/Sgt. Ray McKinley: Johnny Mercer wrote this next one in the original and we rewrote it
   in the E.T.O. Here now is our field kitchen version of "Ac-cent-tchu-ate the Positive."
AC-CENT-TCHU-ATE THE POSITIVE (Mister In-Between)
   Vocal refrain by Technical Sergeant Ray McKinley and the Crew Chiefs

   . . .

(I Got a Woman Crazy for Me) SHE'S FUNNY THAT WAY
   Vocal refrain by Sergeant Johnny Desmond
Corporal Paul Dubov: Here's the chief of the show, the man who sang his way from rodeos
   to radios, it's Texas Ray McKinley singin' "Sittin' on the Inside Lookin' on the
   Outside, Waitin' for the Evenin' Mail."
WAITIN' FOR THE EVENIN' MAIL (Sittin' on the Inside Lookin' at the Outside)
   Vocal refrain by Technical Sergeant Ray McKinley
Corporal Paul Dubov: The wonder of it all is that they can build drums strong enough to
   take the smackin' that Sergeant Ray McKinley gives them. And here again he does his
   best to bust his battery wide open playing his own composition, "Drums Away."
DRUMS AWAY (The Big Beat)
Corporal Paul Dubov: This has been "The Swing Shift" program and there'll be another
   along soon, so keep an eye on the <u>Stars</u> <u>and</u> <u>Stripes</u> and an ear on the radio for the time
   and place. For now, here comes Sergeant Mac singin' his "Git Along Song."

SONG AND DANCE (closing theme)
  Vocal refrain by Technical Sergeant Ray McKinley:
    Well, so long, everybody, I guess that's enough.
    We certainly hope that you liked our stuff.
    It was indeed quite a pleasure to play for you all.
    Now here are a couple of the boys to take a curtain call.
  Vocal refrain by Sergeant Johnny Desmond:
    This is Sergeant Johnny Desmond wishing you well.
  Vocal refrain by Technical Sergeant Ray McKinley:
    Well, thank you, Johnny, for helping it to gel.
  Vocal refrain by the Crew Chiefs:
    Here's the Crew Chiefs sayin' thanks indeed.
  Vocal refrain by Technical Sergeant Ray McKinley:
    So I guess I'll point out "boyn" we're all agreed.
    And if you keep your dial right where it is now,
    Why I reckon we'll keep a rondezvow.
    So we'll mosey along, we're out of the mood,
    We'll just pack it in and hit the road.

07May45 (Mon) 8:45-9:15PM Olympia Theatre, Paris, France   SLO-73128
AMERICAN BAND OF THE AEF recording   Aired 05Jun45   Attendance: 2100

MOONLIGHT SERENADE (opening theme)
  Sergeant Broderick Crawford: This is the music of Major Glenn Miller's American Band of
    the A.E.F. on the Continent, conducted by chief arranger Sergeant Jerry Gary. Music
    for and by members of the Allied Expeditionary Forces.
  Sergeant Broderick Crawford: Hello, everybody. This is Sergeant Broderick Crawford.
  We're going to fill the next thirty minutes with some music for you. We got nine swell
  tunes all bottled and labeled and we're pullin' the cork on the first one right now,
  "American Patrol."
AMERICAN PATROL

  ...

Sergeant Broderick Crawford: ... will lift you on your way, "Swing Low, Sweet Chariot."
  SWING LOW, SWEET CHARIOT

  ...

10May45 (Thu) 10:30-11:10PM Olympia Theatre, Paris, France   SLO-74256
THE SWING SHIFT recording   Aired 16Jun45

...

ANCHORS AWEIGH
Sergeant Broderick Crawford: That's it. You've had it, folks. A full half hour of "The
   Swing Shift," featuring Sergeant Ray McKinley and his music. They'll be coming your way
   again soon with another bandwagon load of music and here he is, Sergeant Mac with his
   "Git Along Song."
SONG AND DANCE (closing theme)
   Vocal refrain by Technical Sergeant Ray McKinley:
      Well, so long, everybody, I guess that's enough.
      We certainly hope you liked our stuff.
      It was indeed quite a pleasure to play for you all.
      Now here's a couple of the boys to take a curtain call.
   Vocal refrain by Sergeant Johnny Desmond:
      This is Sergeant Johnny Desmond wishing you well.
   Vocal refrain by Technical Sergeant Ray McKinley:
      Well, thank you, Johnny, for makin' it gel.
   Vocal refrain by the Crew Chiefs:
      And here's the Crew Chiefs saying thanks indeed.
   Vocal refrain by Technical Sergeant Ray McKinley:
      Well, I guess on that point we're all agreed.
      And if you set your dial right where it is now,
      The chances are we'll all keep a rendezvow.
      Here's wishing you the best, all the boys and me,
      Good old A.F.N. and the B.B.C.

   Announcer: You've been listening to a recording made on the Continent by a unit of the
      American Band of the A.E.F.
   Announcer: In just a moment all your A.E.F. stations will identify themselves.
   Announcer: This is the Allied Expeditionary Forces Program. You're listening to the
      A.E.F. Program on five-fifteen meters, five-eighty-three kilocycles and on the shortwave
      length of forty point nine-eight meters, seven point three-two megacycles.
Oranges and Lemons (theme --- not the Miller band)

14May45 (Mon) 2:45-3:20PM Olympia Theatre, Paris, France   SLO-74270
  AMERICAN BAND OF THE AEF recording   Aired 12Jun45   Attendance: 1400

...

(When Your Heart's on Fire) SMOKE GETS IN YOUR EYES (Borrowed tune)
  Sergeant Broderick Crawford: We put our blue chips on "Blue Again."
BLUE AGAIN (Blue tune)
Sergeant Broderick Crawford: The good Sergeant Jerry Gray up there in front of the band
  just handed me our travel orders for the next one. So let's get goin'. Get aboard
  "Sleepy Town Train."
SLEEPY TOWN TRAIN

...

VICT'RY POLKA
  Vocal refrain by the Crew Chiefs and Ensemble
Sergeant Broderick Crawford: This has been the music of Major Glenn Miller's American
  Band of the A.E.F. on the Continent, conducted by chief arranger Sergeant Jerry Gray.
  Music for and by members of the American Expeditionary Forces. Until next time we meet
  it's good bye and good luck to you.
MOONLIGHT SERENADE (closing theme)

14May45 (Mon) 3:20-3:55PM Olympia Theatre, Paris, France   SLO-74365
  AMERICAN BAND OF THE AEF recording   Aired 15Jun45   Attendance: 1400

...

STOMPIN' AT THE SAVOY (Borrowed tune)
  Sergeant Broderick Crawford: And bluer than blue, our blue tune, "Deep Purple."
DEEP PURPLE (Blue tune)

...

15May45 (Tue) 10:40-11:00PM Olympia Theatre, Paris, France   SLO-74541
STRINGS WITH WINGS recording   Aired 08Jun45

Teddy Gower: I'm sorry. Recording is somewhat --- interruptions again. So it's safe.

I SUSTAIN THE WINGS (opening theme)
  Corporal Paul Dubov: "Strings with Wings." "Strings with Wings," a program of music
    for you of the Allied Liberation Forces, presented by the string section of the
    American Band of the A.E.F., featuring Sergeant George Ockner and his violin.
Corporal Paul Dubov: Greetings, folks, and welcome to another program of "Strings with
  Wings." We sorta thought you'd be there by the radio lookin' for something to listen to
  so we dropped around to help you pass the next few moments very pleasantly with more of
  your favorite tunes played soft and sweet by the violins. Starting right up at the top
  of the list we hear "I'll See You Again."
I'LL SEE YOU AGAIN
Corporal Paul Dubov: Still in the soft mood, a real oldie that's still around makin' new
  friends, here's Sergeant Ockner, the violins and "Londonderry Air."
LONDONDERRY AIR
Corporal Paul Dubov: This next one was plenty lovely when it was first written, but
  Sergeant Dave Herman tied some more ribbons on it with a new arrangement. And just as
  if that wasn't enough, we're gonna add another touch of glamour to it by having Sergeant
  Johnny Desmond sing it. The title, "Just the Way You Look To-night."
THE WAY YOU LOOK TO-NIGHT
  Vocal refrain by Sergeant Johnny Desmond
Corporal Paul Dubov: For our closing tune Sergeant Ockner has gone and picked out one of
  your favorites. Here it is, easier to listen to than ever, "I'll Be Seeing You."
I'LL BE SEEING YOU
Corporal Paul Dubov: Which brings us right down to the bottom of the program. Time to
  say so long for now. But don't forget, we'll be back again real soon with more violin
  versions by Sergeant Ockner and the string section of the American Band of the A.E.F.
  So keep in touch with us. 'Til we meet again, good listenin', good night and good luck
  to you.
I SUSTAIN THE WINGS (closing theme)

21May45 (Mon) 3:25-4:00PM Olympia Theatre, Paris, France   SLO-74073
THE SWING SHIFT recording   Aired 30Jun45   Attendance: 1900

    ...

EMBRACEABLE YOU
  Vocal refrain by Sergeant Johnny Desmond
Corporal Paul Dubov: Originally a tenor sax man, Mike Hucko reverts to form on this next
  tune, aided by Mel Powell's piano and Ray McKinley's drums, to play one of his own
  compositions which serves a home front ...

    ...

21May45 (Mon) 8:50-9:20PM Olympia Theatre, Paris, France   SLO-74075
  AMERICAN BAND OF THE AEF recording   Aired 22Jun45   Attendance: 2100

...

UNCLE TOM (Get with It)
Sergeant Broderick Crawford: Sergeant Jerry Gray took that bit of medley which identifies
  the A.E.F. theme between programs and arranged it right into a full-sized tune. Give us
  an ear now as the boys bring down the curtain with "Oranges and Lemons."
ORANGES AND LEMONS
  Vocal refrain by Corporal Artie Malvin and the Crew Chiefs

...

24May45 (Thu) 10:30-11:10PM Olympia Theatre, Paris, France   SLO-74785
  THE SWING SHIFT recording   Not used

...

(I Got a Woman Crazy for Me) SHE'S FUNNY THAT WAY
  Vocal refrain by Sergeant Johnny Desmond
T/Sgt. Ray McKinley: One newie deserves an oldie and since nobody's here to stop me,
  well, here's one from the 1939 vintage, "Wham Re-Bop-Boom-Bam." And it's one, ah two,
  ah.
WHAM (Re-Bop-Boom-Bam)
  Vocal refrain by Technical Sergeant Ray McKinley and Ensemble
Sergeant Broderick Crawford: Well, time to wrap it up now, which always finds us ready,
  specially when it's Mel Powell's fast steppin' salute to the Soviets, "Mission to
  Moscow."
MISSION TO MOSCOW
Sergeant Broderick Crawford: There it 'tis, as nifty an assortment of harmonic and
  contrapuntal legerdemain as could be squeezed into an allotted half hour. "The Swing
  Shift" with Sergeant Ray McKinley will be preparing another batch o' tunes for your next
  listenin'. Meanwhile, here's Sergeant two-gun Ray McKinley with his "Git Along Song."
SONG AND DANCE (closing theme)
  Vocal refrain by Technical Sergeant Ray McKinley:
    Well, so long, everybody, I guess that's enough.
    We certainly hoped you liked our stuff.
    It was indeed quite a pleasure to play for you all.
    Now here are a couple of the boys to take a curtain call.
  Vocal refrain by Sergeant Johnny Desmond:
    This is Sergeant Johnny Desmond goin' with the fun.
  Vocal refrain by Technical Sergeant Ray McKinley:
    What kind of rhyme is that sign?
  Vocal refrain by Sergeant Broderick Crawford:
    This is Sergeant Crawford sayin' au revoir.
  Vocal refrain by Technical Sergeant Ray McKinley:
    Well, bud, you really got me thar,
    So if you leave your dial right where it is now,
    Well, chances are we'll keep a rendezvow.
    Here's wishin' you the best, the boys and me,
    Good old A.F.N. and the B.B.C.

28May45 (Mon) 2:50-3:35PM Olympia Theatre, Paris, France   SLO-74528
   AMERICAN BAND OF THE AEF recording   Aired 03Jul45   Attendance: 2000

   . . .

Sergeant Broderick Crawford: ... "American Patrol."
AMERICAN PATROL

   . . .

BLUE MOON (Blue tune)
Sergeant Broderick Crawford: Up come the bright lights, up goes the tempo and there goes
   the band takin' off like a scared jeep with a little thing called "The Spirit Is
   Willing."
THE SPIRIT IS WILLING

   . . .

_____

28May45 (Mon) 3:35-4:20PM Olympia Theatre, Paris, France   SLO-75136
   AMERICAN BAND OF THE AEF recording   Aired 10Jul45   Attendance: 2000

   . . .

Sergeant Broderick Crawford: ... Mel arranged it. Here's Mel at the piano to take off
   with the other characters on "Mission to Moscow."
MISSION TO MOSCOW

   . . .

31May45 (Thu) 10:30-10:50PM Olympia Theatre, Paris, France   SLO-74642
  STRINGS WITH WINGS recording   Aired 20Jul45

I SUSTAIN THE WINGS (opening theme)
  Corporal Paul Dubov: "Strings with Wings." "Strings with Wings," a program of music
    for you of the Allied Liberation Forces, presented by the string section of the
    American Band of the A.E.F., featuring Sergeant George Ockner and his violin.
  Corporal Paul Dubov: Greetings, everybody, and welcome to another program of "Strings
    with Wings." We've had this date with you on your radio dial ever since the last time
    we dropped around and here we are back to keep it. Better yet, we've toted along some
    tunes, some of your favorites played soft and sweet by the violins. Well, I see the
    violins are ready so let's ease ourselves right into the program with our number one
    number, "The Song Is You."
THE SONG IS YOU
  Corporal Paul Dubov: The strings take wing again and this time the violins turn for
    inspiration to the French composer Ravel. Here's one of his best known tunes, the
    tender, graceful "Pavane."
PAVANE POUR UNE INFANTE DEFUNTE
  Corporal Paul Dubov: Signing the guest book on the program is Sergeant Johnny Desmond
    here to sing us another song. As usual it's one of those ballads that'll bring back a
    million memories. So just relax and reminisce as Johnny and the violins give you
    "Indian Summer."
INDIAN SUMMER
  Vocal refrain by Sergeant Johnny Desmond
  Corporal Paul Dubov: Here's a tune that's bound to be a big hit when this whole thing is
    over and the boys come sailing home. It's been the theme music of a lot of weddings
    already because it's a tune that spells pure romance, "I Love You Truly."
I LOVE YOU TRULY

(No closing theme on this recording)

04Jun45 (Mon) 8:45-9:15PM Olympia Theatre, Paris, France   **SLO-75684**
AMERICAN BAND OF THE AEF recording   Aired 24Jul45   Attendance: 2100

MOONLIGHT SERENADE (opening theme)
  Sergeant Broderick Crawford: This is the music of Major Glenn Miller's American Band of
    the A.E.F. on the Continent, conducted by chief arranger Sergeant Jerry Gray. Music
    for and by members of the Allied Expeditionary Forces.
Sergeant Broderick Crawford: Hello, everybody. This is Sergeant Broderick Crawford.
  Once again we're ready to come swinging past your radio in a thirty minute review of
  your favorite tunes. And right up there in front of the parade is the brass section to
  take it away with "Song of the Volga Boatmen."
SONG OF THE VOLGA BOATMEN
Sergeant Broderick Crawford: Coming up now Sergeant Johnny Desmond with a song in his
  heart and his heart in his voice. Here he is going romantic on us with a new ballad
  called "Laura."
LAURA
  Vocal refrain by Sergeant Johnny Desmond
Sergeant Broderick Crawford: That was mighty sweet, Johnny, but swinging back over to
  swing let's listen now to a couple of words of wisdom from Sergeant Jerry Gray. He sums
  it all up in his mile-a-minute arrangement of "Get Happy."
GET HAPPY
Sergeant Broderick Crawford: Medley time salutes your mothers, wives, sweethearts and
  sisters with something old, something new, something borrowed and something blue. The
  old song, "Think of Me Only with Thine Eyes."
DRINK TO ME ONLY WITH THINE EYES (Old tune)
  Sergeant Broderick Crawford: Sergeant Johnny Desmond unwraps our something new tune.
THERE GOES THAT SONG AGAIN (New tune)
  Vocal refrain by Sergeant Johnny Desmond
  Sergeant Broderick Crawford: For our borrowed tune we pick one out of the library of
    Ray Noble, "The Very Thought of You."
THE VERY THOUGHT OF YOU (Borrowed tune)

   ...

21Jul45 (Sat) early evening SHAEF Headquarters, Frankfurt, Germany
  CONCERT outdoors (Frankfurt B area)   Attendance: 10,000

IT MUST BE JELLY ('Cause Jam Don't Shake Like That)
T/Sgt. Ray McKinley: Thank you very much. That was Sergeant Bernie Privin tooting the
  trumpet on that one, I thought you might like to know that. Now by way of contrast, I'd
  like to call your attention to our string section up here. Might find it of interest to
  know that these boys with the violins, before the lad with the beard put the snag on
  them, used to play with the various symphony orchestras back home. I think we have
  representatives here in the violin section of all the great symphonies at home; Boston,
  Cleveland, New York and, of course, Stokowski's old bunch down in Philadelphia. Here
  they're headed by Sergeant George Ockner and have chosen to play for you this evening
  "Over the Rainbow."
OVER THE RAINBOW (string section)
T/Sgt. Ray McKinley: George Ockner is going to play us a favorite of mine on the very
  difficult Rimsky-Korsakoff's "The Flight of the Bumble-Bee." Play it good, George, Jack
  Benny's around here.
THE FLIGHT OF THE BUMBLE-BEE (string section)
T/Sgt. Ray McKinley: Time now for the Crew Chiefs, Bobby Nichols, "Juke Box Saturday
  Night."
JUKE BOX SATURDAY NIGHT
  Vocal refrain by the Crew Chiefs
HAVE YA GOT ANY GUM, CHUM?
  Vocal refrain by the Crew Chiefs
T/Sgt. Ray McKinley: The fighting man on my right happens to be the author of that last
  number, both words and music, Corporal Murray Kane. Murray, I think the fellows might
  like to hear a few words from you, something about your past, how you happened to write
  such an important contribution to American music as that number. All right?
Corporal Murray Kane: All right.
T/Sgt. Ray McKinley: Not nervous or anything?
Corporal Murray Kane: Nope.
T/Sgt. Ray McKinley: O.K. You're on your own.
Corporal Murray Kane: Are you?
T/Sgt. Ray McKinley: Nervous?
Corporal Murray Kane: I, ah, think that was a very nice introduction that Mac gave me
  but, ah, he did forget to tell you one thing that's very important, that is that my job
  here besides singing with the Crew Chiefs is that of chief arranger. I arrange the
  stands, the chairs. Also, if I may add just a little bit about a biography for a couple
  of minutes, I'd like to, ah, I don't know, I'd like to tell you how I did get to write
  the song but in order to do that I've got to go back to the days during which I was a
  civilian. That's a very difficult word to pronounce. Especially when you've only got
  36 points. Just about enough to buy a pound of butter. But it was during those days
  that I recall having been with Fred Waring and his Pennsylvanians and my job at the time
  was, ah, was a part of a vocal trio known as the "Two Bees and a Honey." It's a funny
  thing, though, whenever I tell anybody that I used to be with the "Two Bees and a Honey"
  there's always some wise guy who pops up and says ...
Band member: Were you the Honey?
Corporal Murray Kane: Were you the wise guy? Well, that's what I want to clear up right
  here and now. I wanna have it known that I wasn't the Honey, it was my brother. Also,
  I remember that we used to do five programs a week for a firm known as Chesterfield.
  That's a cigarette. I smoked marijuana myself. It's much easier to get. But then all
  of a sudden one day I get one of those letters from a group of my friends and neighbors
  which informed me that I could join --- that I could have my choice of branches in the
  Armed Forces. Matter of fact the letter said I could join the Navy and see the world or
  join the Army and C-rations. I asked to join the WAC to see what I could see. But you
  know when I --- when I finally did get in I --- I didn't go directly into this
  organization. It so happens that before I joined this outfit I was a pretty big man
  with a pretty big job in the Army. I used to be a P.F.C. in an induction center.
  Remember? For those that don't quite understand the, ah, the very unique rank of a
  P.F.C. in an induction center I might explain that he's just a little bit above a

Private and a little bit below a Second Lieutenant. But I never will forget the day I
got that one big stripe. I sewed it on my arm, walked into the barracks --- see, I was
in command of a division at the time. 23 men, it wasn't up to strength, of course. But
as I walked in through the door, you know, the --- the guys just jumped right up to
attention, you know. I was going to tell them they didn't have to but I figured what
the hell, what they don't know won't hurt them. And they sort of gathered around with
that look of awe and admiration that you have for a fellow that makes good. And I could
tell that they wanted me to address them. So I did. I said, "Men." No, ah, first I
gave them, "At ease." Then I said, "Men, I want you to feel free to come and see me at
any time. I want you to remember that I came up through the ranks just the way you're
doing now." Of course, all that took place a very long time ago, so it seems, and
unfortunately, when I joined this outfit seated on the stage, I was busted from the rank
of P.F.C. to that of Corporal. In a fit of dejection and despondency over the whole
thing I wrote "Have Ya Got Any Gum, Chum?" That's the way it all started. You know,
ah, I've been trying, while we were in France recently, I tried to get the --- the kids
over there to sort of pick up the phrases the way they did back in England. You know,
stop the soldiers and all that, but somehow that language there is sort of a barrier.
Oh, I think the time that I was there I did pretty well with the language. I learned a
--- a very important phrase in French, you know. It's not the one you think it is.
There are others, you know. But this one is "an te vu." "An te vu." I might pass it
along to you, it still might come in handy to you. Now, let's say that you're hungry,
you want something to eat. It's very simple, all you have to say is "an te vu yum, yum,
yum, yum, yum, yum, yum." You want something to drink, you're thirsty, it's "an te vu
woooooooooooooooooooooooooo." Of course there's "an te vu (makes the shape of a girl with
his hands)" -- ah. That's a bottle of Coca-Cola. Also, it may interest you to know
that I sent this, ah, "Gum, Chum?" song back to the States where it was published and
Deems Taylor, the very famous music critic, heard it on the air one day and he wrote a
little article about it in the paper. Ah, it so happens that, ah, I brought that
article with me today. I, ah, don't usually carry it around. He, he starts by saying,
"I believe that Murray Kane," that's me. "I believe that Murray Kane is a young song
writer who I predict will some day be an old song writer." Isn't that nice? Then he
says, "If this song were sung throughout the world, I shutter to think what would happen
to the goodwill in those countries." Well, he's wrong about the good will in the
countries because I've been in a lot of countries and I've found out that the good
won't.
Well, I think it's time to turn you back over to Mac and the boys for some more music.
So I'd like to remain yours truly, Murray Kane, who wishes every day that he could meet
a --- a nice young widow with three children, object: 85 points.

...

AMERICAN PATROL
T/Sgt. Ray McKinley: I'd like to bring out one of our small units now within the band.
  This one's composed of the violin of Phil Marino, who hails from up around NBC way in
  New York; Carmen Mastren and his guitar, out of Tommy Dorsey's band; Trigger Alpert and
  his bass, out of Fox-Hole Nathan's band. The three of them now are gonna take us on a
  little tour uptown.
OH, LADY BE GOOD! (trio: Marino, Mastren, Alpert)
PARDON ME PRETTY BABY (Don't I Look Familiar to You)
  (trio: Marino, Mastren, Alpert)
T/Sgt. Ray McKinley: We've had a request for one of Jerry Gray's arrangements and this
  one is on the famous Russian "Red Cavalry March."
THE RED CAVALRY MARCH
T/Sgt. Ray McKinley: I'd like now to call a halt to the musical festivities and introduce
  a gentleman to you, Colonel A. H. Rosenfeld, Acting Headquarters Commander, U.S. Armed
  Forces European Theater. Colonel.
Colonel A. H. Rosenfeld: Tonight, men, it's a distinct pleasure to present an award to
  the band on their last appearance in the European Theater. We've known them for a long
  time, through England, Scotland, Ireland, France, Belgium, Holland, Austria, and now
  Germany. It's a pleasure to read the citation as awarded by General Eisenhower:

Headquarters, U.S. Forces European Theater, dated 21 July 1945, Meritorial Service Unit 5. On provisional of section 1, circular number 3-4-5, War Department, dated 23 August 1944, as amended. The Meritorial Service Unit 5 is awarded to the Army Air Forces Band Special for superior performance of duty in the accomplishment of an exceptionally difficult task during the period from 13 July 1944 to 30 June 1945. All personnel of this unit illustrated outstanding efficiency and great professional skill in providing entertainment for the troops of the Allied Expeditionary Force in radio broadcasts and personal appearances in camps and bases throughout the European Theater. Their exemplary performance of duty is in keeping with the highest tradition of the Armed Forces of the United States. As Commanding General Eisenhower, signed, W. C. Smith, General, Lieutenant General U.S.A., Chief of Staff.

T/Sgt. Ray McKinley: Yes, sir.
Colonel A. H. Rosenfeld: Captain Haynes, members of the Glenn Miller Band, it's an honor and pleasure to present this plaque to you. I know you happen to be the most traveled organization in the Theater, you've traveled further, you've played before more people, you've played more concerts than any organization in the Theater. We also know that no matter what the weather was, no matter under what conditions, foxholes or anything else, you're always willing and ready to play. It's because of that the Supreme Commander has recognized your merit and it's an honor to present this plaque to you and to members of the band.
Colonel Sterns: General Order 1-4-9, Headquarters U.S. Forces European Theater, 12 July 1945, Bronze Star Medal, First Lieutenant Don W. Haynes, Air Corps, United States Army, 22 June 1944 to 8 May 1945, Citation. First Lieutenant Don W. Haynes, Air Corps, United States Army for meritorial service with connection of military operation from 20 June 1944 to 8 May 1945. Initially as administrative assistant and later as commanding officer of the Army Air Force Band Special, First Lieutenant Haynes directed the administration, planned the move, and arranged the broadcraft --- broadcast programs and performances of the band. The Army Air Force Band has contributed greatly to the morale of the Allied troops on the Continent and much of the credit for its success is due to the outstanding service of First Lieutenant Haynes, which reflects high credit upon himself and the United States Army. Entered military service in New York.
Captain Don W. Haynes: Thank you very much.

. . .

T/Sgt. Ray McKinley: Well, we're going to play all of those. Right now --- right now, the boys in the brass section, being just a little bit whipped from, ah, playing a great deal, I think I'll give them a rest and bring out a brand new kind of music for you. That is, I think it's a brand new kind of music. At any rate, ah. Oh well, I don't count that, Jim. Hah. Carmen Mastren, our guitar player here, happens to have been the lad that, ah, made arrangements for Tommy Dorsey --- "Marie" and "Song of India" and a number of others. He's getting his own post-war band together, I think from within this band, I'm not too sure. At any rate we hear some very strange noises coming out from behind locked doors. And I think if we put a little bit of that special pressure on them we can get Carmen and his new orchestra out here now and from then on anything can happen. What do you say, huh? You're up, Carmen.
(General commotion as band members make their way to front of stage --- a cymbal crash.)
S/Sgt. Carmen Mastren: I should like to introduce my soloist. I wish you'd give him a big hand because he's very temperamental. Ladis Hall. Come out here, Laddy, take a bow. La, la, la, la.
I'M GETTIN' SENTIMENTAL OVER YOU (Few bars by trombone section --- sickening sweet)
MAIRZY DOATS (First chord, trombone section)
S/Sgt. Carmen Mastren: What a band!
MAIRZY DOATS (trombone section)
  S/Sgt. Carmen Mastren: I love this. I could do it all day.
  S/Sgt. Carmen Mastren: Larry!

T/Sgt. Ray McKinley: Mel Powell's going to work right now. For those of you haven't already recognized him because his back's to you tonight, I might remind you that he used to be with Benny Goodman and moreover he's the winner of this year's <u>Down</u> <u>Beat</u> Poll in the piano department despite the fact that he was over here at the time and has been in the Army more than two years and therefore not in the public eye. Nevertheless the vote in this poll for the most popular pianist in America today went to Mel Powell. Mellie, take a bow.

Pfc. Mel Powell: Thank you. Ah, if, as Mac said, most of you recognize me in the particular position in which I'm in, ah, you've been seeing some very unflattering pictures of me. Ah, I'd like to play a composition for you which, ah, I've just written and dedicated to sidetracks in this Army. It's entitled "Little Brown Nose."

LITTLE BROWN NOSE (No Compris)

Pfc. Mel Powell: Ah, usually at this time "Peanuts" Hucko and I and Mac play a tune and, ah. "Peanuts" Hucko plays clarinet, you know. I'm gonna call for a substitute, this kind of sets a precedent, you should never do this, but special occasion. And I have someone I haven't seen since the time when most of you wore tweeds and most of us wearing bow ties. Ah, this fellow used to come around dance sessions. And he was an oddity there because he does two things very well. Let's see, I have to humor him. Two things he says, ah, namely one, he plays the clarinet very well and two, he is a very, very local surgeon. When he joined the Army he found out that clarinet players wind up playing in a cheap dive and a surgeon is a Captain at least. So, of course, he chose to operate with a scalpel instead of a clarinet. Anyway he's here now and I'd like to get back to Phil Scovack. Captain Scovack now, come up and play clarinet with us. He said he hasn't played now in a year and a half but let's give him a big hand and get him up here. All right, sir. The boys think this is very unusual. We don't permit enlisted officers to play with enlisted men. What do you want to play?

Captain Phil Scovack: How about "Sugar?"

Pfc. Mel Powell: "Sugar." O.K. What key?

SUGAR (trio: Scovack, Powell, McKinley)

...

29Sep45 (Sat) 11:30PM-Midnight   NBC Radio City, New York, New York
  I SUSTAIN THE WINGS broadcast

THE ARMY AIR CORPS (opening fanfare)
  Private John Conti: Your Army Air Forces present "I Sustain the Wings."
I SUSTAIN THE WINGS (opening theme)
  Private John Conti: "I Sustain the Wings," welcoming home tonight Major Glenn Miller's
    Army Air Forces Overseas Orchestra, directed by chief arranger Sergeant Jerry Gray,
    and presenting a message from General of the Army H. H. Arnold, Commanding General of
    the Army Air Forces.
Private John Conti: And here's Sergeant Tom Hudson.
Sergeant Tom Hudson: Major Glenn Miller is not with us tonight. Since December 1944 he's
  been officially listed as "missing in action." This evening, after fourteen months
  overseas, Major Miller's Orchestra returns to the American air waves and to you with his
  kind of music for your kind of pleasure. We head off with a tune for the men in the
  world circling Globester, and for all the Air Transport Command men, for bringing our
  troops "Flying Home."
FLYING HOME
Sergeant Tom Hudson: All during the time when the 8th, 9th and 15th Air Forces were
  flying their thousands of raids over Europe, Major Glenn Miller's Army Air Forces
  Overseas Orchestra flew around to the bases to play a total of four hundred and
  thirty-five concerts for the boys. However back in February, the outfit, with Sergeant
  Ray McKinley pinch hitting at the controls, took time out to play at the Paris Opera
  House and raised not only the roof but also two and one-half million francs for the
  benefit of French war prisoners. One of the top features of the evening was the voice
  of Sergeant Johnny Desmond, who made the little ma'moiselles swoon to the tune of "Long
  Ago and Far Away."
LONG AGO (And Far Away)
  Vocal refrain by Sergeant Johnny Desmond (French and English)
Private John Conti: On Air Force Day the Commanding General of the Army Air Forces had
  some things to say that we think bear repeating. We quote the words of General of the
  Army H. H. Arnold.
Sergeant Tom Hudson: We think it axiomatic that in any future encounter with an enemy
  the Air Force must be an impregnable line of defense. Our country tried 25 years ago
  and tried with its whole heart to make a workable democratic world by throwing away our
  armament, our policing power. It did not work. I repeat, it did not work.
Private John Conti: Does that mean we're never going to have world peace?
Sergeant Tom Hudson: It means nothing of the sort. It merely means that we must go about
  creating world peace in a different way. The force at the disposal of peace loving
  peoples must be an instrument for peace. The instrument must be effective, it's not
  based on satisfied, complacent, apparent power. No men anywhere can longer be blind to
  the meaning and use of air power. The case is stated simply and clearly in the 45th
  Article of the Charter adopted by the United Nations. "In order to enable the United
  Nations to take urgent military measures, members shall hold immediately available
  national air force contingents." There it is. There is a plan for the ...
I Sustain the Wings (Incidental music)
  Sergeant Tom Hudson: ... vital part that our aviation must play in the great new
    endeavor to end war. We must concentrate our air strength and our contribution must
    be not the air strength of the past but the air strength of the future.
Sergeant Tom Hudson: And now it's medley time, saluting the mothers, wives, sweethearts
  and sisters of the boys in the Army Air Forces with something old, something new,
  something borrowed and something blue. The old song, "Long, Long Ago."
LONG, LONG AGO (Old tune)
  Sergeant Tom Hudson: For something new Sergeant Johnny Desmond sings ...
LAURA (New tune)
  Vocal refrain by Sergeant Johnny Desmond
  Sergeant Tom Hudson: We put the bite on Charlie Barnet for our borrowed tune and come
    up jumpin' with "Cherokee."
CHEROKEE (Indian Love Song) (Borrowed tune)
  Sergeant Tom Hudson: And for something blue here's good, old "Blue Rain."

BLUE RAIN (Blue tune)
The Army Air Corps (Incidental music)
   Sergeant Tom Hudson: Since June 1944 the Army Air Forces Orchestra, organized and
      directed by Major Glenn Miller, has been overseas playing for the men in the fight.
      It was back in December that Major Miller returned to his quarters in England after a
      long day to find two young AAF pilots waiting to see him.
   Sergeant Tom Hudson: They had a story to tell.
   Harry: You see, the thing is, Major Miller, that maybe we wouldn't be back here if it
      wasn't for you and the band so we thought we ought to come around and say thanks. You
      see, we'd caught a piece of flak over Germany and Jim here and I got together after we
      bailed out and decided we'd try to walk it back to our lines. Well, I don't want to
      build this up any. Boy, it was rugged. We'd walk all night, keeping off the main
      roads, and days we'd hide in haystacks and barns and in culverts to try to catch some
      sleep. You know, they didn't build us fly boys for walking so our feet were pretty
      shot. We were so hungry we were about ready to give up. Well, that's the way we were
      after two hundred and fifty miles when we spotted this farmhouse and it looked deserted.
   Jim: How's it look, Harry? O.K.?
   Harry: Well, I don't know. Well, let's take a break anyway, I'm about done in.
   Jim: Stretch out in those bushes here. We can case the house, get a little rest.
   Harry: O.K. Only we'd better get some chow pretty quick. I'm telling you I'm hungry.
      We crawled into the bushes and kept an eye on that farmhouse. We figured there ought to
      be some scraps of food around even if nobody lived there. We lay in those bushes a
      couple of hours watching, only we didn't rest much because we were so hungry. It's all
      we could think of. Finally we were about ready to take a chance on the place when...
   Jim: Harry! Harry, look! Down by the corner of the farmhouse.
   Harry: Oh, where? Oh, yeah, yeah.
   Jim: Three of 'em. Jerries. Hey, they're goin' in the front door.
   Harry: Oh, that's wonderful. That's great. Now what?
   Jim: Look! But they stacked their rifles outside. Listen, Harry.
   Harry: Yeah?
   Jim: Are you as hungry as I am?
   Harry: Are you kidding?
   Jim: Well now it's twenty to one those Krauts got food in there.
   Harry: Yeah, what do we do? Knock on the door and ask for a handout?
   Jim: There are only three of 'em, Harry. We got our 45s. We can take 'em easy.
   Harry: Oh, yeah.
   Jim: Listen, you said you were hungry.
   Harry: Well, O.K., only let's go easy.
      We went easy, all right, on our bellies all the way. We crawled around to the back door
      and eased our way into a little sort of a pantry they had right off the kitchen. We
      could hear the Krauts inside the kitchen and we were ready.
   Jim: Listen to 'em. They're stuffin' their fat bellies in there. O.K., Harry, now look.
      I'll kick in the door; it's part way open anyway.
   Harry: Yeah.
   Jim: And we give it to the first guy that makes a move.
   Harry: O.K., good enough. Let's go.
   Jim: O.K., but keep it quiet until you hear me kick that door.
   Harry: Yeah.
   Jim: Easy now.
   Harry: O.K., I'm right in back of you.
   Jim: O.K. I'm going to...
   Harry: Let's let 'em have it.
   Jim: Hold it! Harry, get back!
   Harry: What's the matter. Come on, kick it!
   Jim: Shut up! Holy smokes!
   Harry: For cryin' out loud. What's the matter with you? We were almost in there.
   Jim: I just got a quick look in there, Harry. There are at least eight Krauts in that
      room.
   Harry: Eight?
   Jim: Yeah, there must have been some in there all the time.

Harry: Oh, that's great. What do we do now?

Jim: Suppose you tell me.

Harry: I tell you, Major Miller, we really felt sick. We could have handled three, but eight? Heh. I mean we were weak from all that walking and we didn't have a pipe dream of a chance of taking on eight so we just sat there. I don't know why we didn't clear right out, maybe we were too tired, or maybe it was just to torture ourselves listenin' to those pigs stuffin' themselves.

Jim: Yeah, would you listen to 'em? I bet it's like Thanksgiving in there.

Harry: Aw, maybe they'll get ptomaine poisoning.

Jim: Harry, listen.

Harry: Yeah.

Jim: They must have a radio in there.

Harry: Even they can't listen to that stuff. Come on, let's get out of here, Jim.

Jim: What for? Maybe they'll go away.

Harry: Maybe they'll come out here too.

Moonlight Serenade (Incidental music)

Jim: What? He-hey!

Harry: What's the matter now? Hey!

Jim: Harry, that's Glenn ...

Harry: Yeah.

Jim: Where did they get Glenn Miller?

Harry: Well, I'll be darned. Oh, sure, he's playing on the shortwave out of London.

Jim: Well, for the love of ...

Harry: Oh, that really takes you back. Aw, how do you like that?

Jim: Listen, Harry. You know what I think?

Harry: What?

Jim: I think we're in. You know what I mean?

Harry: Yeah, yeah, you know what they're playin', aw "Moonlight Serenade."

Jim: That's right. What do you say, Harry?

Harry: Oh, how can we miss? We're home. Oh, boy, let's take 'em.

Jim: That's what I mean. Are you ready?

Harry: I'll never be readier.

Jim: Then here we go.

Jim: All right, Krauts, reach! Get 'em in the air! Come on, move!

(Gunshots)

Harry: Anybody else? Now move over in that corner and keep 'em high.

Jim: Come on, you heard him. Quick, over there.

Harry: O.K. and let's keep it that way and nobody will get hurt.
Yeah, we took 'em, the whole eight of 'em. And we had a good meal. And we listened to the rest of the program. Now, maybe it sounds a little screwy to you, Major Miller, I mean just hearing your program and then diving right in. I don't know how to explain it exactly but, well, it was home. You know, we both got the same feeling. We suddenly felt that it was home and, and we were in. And we made up our minds if we did get back we ought to tell you how it happened, Major. And that's why we're telling you now so you'll know and so we can both say thanks. You know you, you really did us a favor. Thanks.

Incidental Music

Sergeant Tom Hudson: And that's a true story, the way it was told to Major Glenn Miller in England back in December 1944. It's just one of the countless heartwarming expressions the orchestra heard overseas, appreciation from the men in the fight who heard in the orchestra the sound of home. And now here's the biggest tune in the books, arrangement by Sergeant Jerry Gray, rendition by Major Glenn Miller's Air Forces Overseas Orchestra, "Russian Patrol."

RUSSIAN PATROL

Sergeant Tom Hudson: This has been the welcome home broadcast of Major Glenn Miller's Army Air Forces Overseas Orchestra, under the direction of chief arranger Sergeant Jerry Gray. Next week we'll be back with more music and other stories ...

MOONLIGHT SERENADE (closing theme)

Sergeant Tom Hudson: ... from the A.A.F. files. Until then, same time, same station, let's keep 'em flying to keep the peace.

Private John Conti: "I Sustain the Wings" is an all-soldier presentation of your Army
   Air Forces, came to you from New York.
NBC Announcer: This is the National Broadcasting Company.
NBC chimes

06Oct45 (Sat) NBC Radio City, New York, New York
 I SUSTAIN THE WINGS dress rehearsal

THE ARMY AIR CORPS (opening fanfare)
   Private John Conti: Your Army Air Forces present "I Sustain the Wings."
I SUSTAIN THE WINGS (opening theme)
   Private John Conti: "I Sustain the Wings" with our special guest Major Jack Best and
      the music of Major Glenn Miller's Army Air Forces Overseas Orchestra conducted by
      Sergeant Jerry Gray.
Private John Conti: And here is Sergeant Tom Hudson.
Sergeant Tom Hudson: Over in Paris the subway is known as the Metro and from one of the
   many signs which confuse American soldiers during their trips on the Metro, Sergeant
   Jerry Gray borrows the title for his newest original tune, "Passage Interdit."
PASSAGE INTERDIT
Sergeant Tom Hudson: Carrying the ball now, the voice of Sergeant Johnny Desmond, in the
   backfield Major Glenn Miller's Army Air Forces Overseas Orchestra playin' "The More I
   See You."
THE MORE I SEE YOU
   Vocal refrain by Sergeant Johnny Desmond
Sergeant Tom Hudson: Well, there's hardly a man in the Air Forces who isn't sweating out
   that day when he's tapped by the point system and can grab that paper and get on home.
   Isn't that right, Major John Best?
Major John Best: No, that's wrong, Sergeant.
Sergeant Tom Hudson: Well, now, wait a minute, sir. You mean you don't want to go home?
Major John Best: Of course I do. But that doesn't mean I'm getting out of the outfit.
Sergeant Tom Hudson: Well, that's Major John Best, A.A.F. of Riverside, California and
   he's wearing a nice array of fruit salad on his chest; Distinguished Flying Cross and
   Air Medal and they're topped off with a pair of Silver Pilot's Wings. You fly fighters,
   isn't that right, Major?
Major John Best: We flew P-40s in China, Sergeant. I was with the 23rd Fighter Group.
Sergeant Tom Hudson: And what was your job, sir?
Major John Best: Oh, the usual, strafing, dive bombing, air fighting. We did about sixty
   missions.
Sergeant Tom Hudson: Well, you make it sound easy, Major, but it wasn't for just the
   usual that the Chinese people gave your flight that scroll at Lanling.
Major John Best: Oh, that. That wasn't much. When the American volunteer group was
   disbanded around Lanling the Japs announced that they'd push us right out of the
   country.
Sergeant Tom Hudson: And did they?
Major John Best: Well, not exactly. We only had about fifteen fighters at the time.
   When the Japs quit trying we still had fifteen and the Japs were minus quite a few.
Sergeant Tom Hudson: I see, and that's when you got the scroll, eh?
Major John Best: That's right. The people of Lanling thought we'd done O.K. The Jap
   Shanghai radio was saying we had three hundred planes around then, so the people gave us
   this silk scroll. And that's about all.
Sergeant Tom Hudson: Well, I'm sure that the Japs felt that was quite enough. Now, you
   say you're staying in the Air Forces, sir. How come? Because you like to fly?
Major John Best: Well, I suppose one reason is because I'm a little crazy about fighter
   planes and you don't see them outside of the Air Forces. But it's more than that. I
   like planes, I like flying, and I like the guys I work with. Where else can you find a
   setup like that?
Sergeant Tom Hudson: Well, you've got me, sir.
Major John Best: And anyway I have it figured out that we're going to need some good
   planes and some good men to keep them in the air if we want to keep the country out of
   trouble. Doesn't that make sense?
Sergeant Tom Hudson: Good enough, Major John Best. And many thanks for dropping in on
   us.

Private John Conti: Major John Best of Riverside, California is just one of the many Air Forces officers and enlisted men who are signing back on with the outfit. And his reasons are sound. The future peace and the future strength of our nation will rest on the wings of the air power. The men with the know-how are in the Air Forces now and America will need their continuing services. A.A.F. men and their families are invited to examine the many advantages to be derived from service with the peacetime Air Forces.

Incidental Music

Sergeant Tom Hudson: It's medley time. Major Glenn Miller's Army Air Forces Overseas Orchestra with something old, something new, something borrowed and something blue. The old song, "Danny Boy."

DANNY BOY (Old tune)

Sergeant Tom Hudson: For something new Sergeant Johnny Desmond sings ...

I DON'T WANT TO BE LOVED (New tune)

Vocal refrain by Sergeant Johnny Desmond

Sergeant Tom Hudson: We put the bite on Benny Goodman for our borrowed tune, "Stompin' at the Savoy."

STOMPIN' AT THE SAVOY (Borrowed tune)

Sergeant Tom Hudson: And for something bluer than blue here's "Deep Purple."

DEEP PURPLE (Blue tune)

Sergeant Tom Hudson: It works both ways. Trained men without the proper modern instruments of war are ineffective but the instruments are useless unless they are in the hands of trained men. It is for that reason that the Air Forces invite the careful attention of its personnel and the families of Air Forces men to the opportunity of service in the Air Corps Reserve now being formed. By serving in the Air Corps Reserve officers and men of the Air Forces, retaining their attained rank, grade and rating, will be able to keep their special skills abreast of the advancing developments of science, will form the firm foundation of America's best insurance against future wars. Until full details are made available on future broadcasts, we simply call your attention to the Air Corps Reserve and invite your continued participation in the active service of your country now that peace has come.

AMERICAN PATROL

Sergeant Tom Hudson: And now Major Glenn Miller's Army Air Forces Overseas Orchestra and "American Patrol."

Sergeant Tom Hudson: Back in December 1944, when Major Glenn Miller was reported missing in flight, Sergeant Jerry Gray was sent in to pinch hit for the Major, conducting the full orchestra on the radio, while Sergeant Ray McKinley continued to head his own radio show heard twice weekly in the ETO, the "Swing Shift" program, which came on the air something like this.

SONG AND DANCE ("Swing Shift" theme song)

Vocal refrain by Sergeant Ray McKinley

This is Sergeant Ray McKinley saying howdy, boys,
Spreadin' several minutes of "Swing Shift" joys.
It's really quite delightful for the gang and me,
To be back home on the N.B.C.
We'll be singin' and playin' a tune they know,
From the C.B.I to the E.T.O.
So flip out an ear and keep it bent,
And the next couple o' minutes will see you sent.

Sergeant Tom Hudson: And that's but a brief sample of the theme song with Sergeant Ray McKinley's "Swing Shift" program back in the E.T.O. And comin' right up is a tune with some special lyrics written and sung by Sergeant Mac as the Crew Chiefs and Major Glenn Miller's Army Air Forces Overseas Orchestra join in on "Ac-cent-tchu-ate the Positive."

AC-CENT-TCHU-ATE THE POSITIVE (Mister In-Between)

Vocal refrain by Technical Sergeant Ray McKinley and the Crew Chiefs

Sergeant Tom Hudson: Well, that's all for now but we'll be back with more of the same next week. Major Glenn Miller's Air Forces Overseas Orchestra, conducted by Sergeant Jerry Gray. Until next week, same time, same station, this is Sergeant Tom Hudson saying keep 'em flyin' to keep the peace.

MOONLIGHT SERENADE (closing theme)
Private John Conti: "I Sustain the Wings," an all-soldier presentation of your Army Air
Forces, came to you from New York.
This is the National Broadcasting Company.
NBC chimes

13Oct45 (Sat) NBC Radio City, New York, New York
  I SUSTAIN THE WINGS dress rehearsal

THE ARMY AIR CORPS (opening fanfare)
  Announcer: Your Army Air Forces present "I Sustain the Wings."
I SUSTAIN THE WINGS (opening theme)
  Announcer: "I Sustain the Wings," featuring the all-soldier music of Major Glenn
    Miller's Army Air Forces Overseas Orchestra, conducted by Sergeant Jerry Gray.
  Announcer: And here's Corporal Paul Dubov.
  Corporal Paul Dubov: The first play of the evening salutes the guys who flew the tailback
    position in the Army Air Forces' T-N-T formations over Germany and Japan. Here's "Tail
    End Charlie."
TAIL END CHARLIE
  Corporal Paul Dubov: During its fourteen months overseas Major Glenn Miller's Army Air
    Forces Orchestra piled up over 500 flying hours. Three and a half of those flying hours
    were spent traveling to the French Riviera where the band helped a big bunch of battle
    weary G.I.s celebrate V-E Day. One night in a little French cafe overlooking that big,
    beautiful Mediterranean, Sergeant Johnny Desmond heard a little mademoiselle singing a
    real heart written song. He brought it back to the U.S. with him and now it looks like
    it's gonna be one of the big hits, Sergeant Johnny Desmond singing "Symphony."
SYMPHONY
  Vocal refrain by Sergeant Johnny Desmond (French and English)
  Announcer: And now...
  Corporal Paul Dubov: And now, well done, men of the 58th Bombardment Wing, 20th Air
    Force.
The Army Air Corps (Incidental music)
  Announcer: Home this week after circling the globe to hit the Japs are the men and
    planes of the 58th Bombardment Wing, 20th Air Forces, the men and their B-29s. First
    land-based unit to drop its bombs on the Japanese homeland, the 58th has been honored
    by being recalled to the United States as an intact fighting force. Japan, Formosa,
    Manchuria, Sumatra, Mai Lai Peninsula, Singapore, China, Thailand, Burma, Indochina,
    all of these felt the force of the 58th's attack wherever the Japs held out in their
    far flung inland empire. Seven thousand, one hundred and forty-five bombing sorties
    were flown by the Wing's Super Forts, among them the longest bombing mission on
    record. For their pioneer work and the realization of the Super Fort as a mighty
    battle wagon, each group of the 58th Wing was awarded the Distinguished Unit Citation
    and five Battle Participation Stars. Each service group in the Wing was awarded the
    Distinguished Service Unit Plaque. Their mission accomplished, we salute the men of
    the 58th Bombardment Wing, 20th Air Force and say, "Welcome home and well done."
  Corporal Paul Dubov: Now it's medley time for Major Glenn Miller's Army Air Forces
    Overseas Orchestra with somethin' old, somethin' new, somethin' borrowed and somethin'
    blue. The old song, "In the Gloaming."
IN THE GLOAMING (Old tune)
  Corporal Paul Dubov: Sergeant Johnny Desmond sings the new tune, "Homesick."
HOMESICK - THAT'S ALL (New tune)
  Vocal refrain by Sergeant Johnny Desmond
  Corporal Paul Dubov: We take our borrowed tune from old Satchmo Louie Armstrong.
    Private Mike Hucko makes like Louie on the vocal; Private Bernie Privin does likewise
    on the trumpet; "I Can't Give You Anything but Love."
I CAN'T GIVE YOU ANYTHING BUT LOVE (Baby) (Borrowed tune)
  Vocal refrain by Private Michael (Peanuts) A. Hucko
  Corporal Paul Dubov: And now something blue, the greatest of them all, "Rhapsody in
    Blue."
RHAPSODY IN BLUE (Blue tune)
  Announcer: Here's a thought for you. The nation that controls the air can certainly
    control its own fate. Those are the words of Commanding General of the Air Forces H. H.
    Arnold and they lead to a second thought, that the best aircraft in the world are
    useless to a nation without the men with the know-how to maintain and fly them. There
    are opportunities now for officers and enlisted men of the A.A.F. to sign up for a hitch
    with the peacetime Air Forces. Here's a future that's essentially tied to the future of

our country. Here's a thought for the men of the Air Forces and their families, consider it carefully and sign on with the greatest flying team in the world, the United States Army Air Forces.

Incidental Music

Corporal Paul Dubov: Now here's one that'll take you back, way back and well worth the trip. Major Glenn Miller's Army Air Forces Overseas Orchestra, Sergeant Jerry Gray at the throttle, pulling in to "Tuxedo Junction."

TUXEDO JUNCTION

Corporal Paul Dubov: Overseas Major Glenn Miller's Army Air Forces Orchestra played a total of five hundred and twenty-eight programs over the Allied Expeditionary Forces radio network. That network identified itself to listeners with a tiny, tinkling jingle that sounded like this.

ORANGES AND LEMONS (piano)

Corporal Paul Dubov: That little seed planted itself in Sergeant Jerry Gray's fertile imagination and the good Sarge came up with a good arrangement sung now by the Crew Chiefs as the all-soldier orchestra offers "Oranges and Lemons."

ORANGES AND LEMONS

   Vocal refrain by the Crew Chiefs

Corporal Paul Dubov: That's all for now but we'll all be back next week for more music by Major Glenn Miller's Army Air Forces Overseas Orchestra, conducted by Sergeant Jerry Gray, with Sergeant Johnny Desmond and the Crew Chiefs. This is Corporal Paul Dubov saying good night and keep 'em flying to keep the peace.

MOONLIGHT SERENADE (closing theme)

   Announcer: This program came to you from New York. This is the National Broadcasting Company.

20Oct45 (Sat) NBC Radio City, New York, New York
  I SUSTAIN THE WINGS dress rehearsal

THE ARMY AIR CORPS (opening fanfare)
  Announcer: Your Army Air Forces present "I Sustain the Wings."
I SUSTAIN THE WINGS (opening theme)
  Announcer: "I Sustain the Wings," featuring the all soldier music of Major Glenn
    Miller's Army Air Forces Overseas Orchestra, conducted by Sergeant Jerry Gray.
Announcer: And here is Private John Conti.
Private John Conti: Here's a real 1945 battle song. This one helped spark the First,
  Third, Ninth and Seventh Armies as they listened to the radio on the way up to the front
  during last winter's big drives, "Here We Go Again."
HERE WE GO AGAIN
Private John Conti: Sergeant Johnny Desmond now singin' a heart warming song as Major
  Glenn Miller's Army Air Forces Overseas Orchestra plays "I Only Have Eyes for You."
I ONLY HAVE EYES FOR YOU
  Vocal refrain by Sergeant Johnny Desmond
Private John Conti: And now, welcome home to the Red Tails of the Fifteenth Air Force.
Incidental music
  Announcer: Home this week from the Mediterranean Theater of Operations are the Red
    Tails of the Twelfth and Fifteenth Air Forces, one of the fightin'est fighter units in
    the E.T.O. The all negro officers and men of the Red Tails group are credited with
    knocking one hundred eleven enemy planes out of the air and wiping one hundred fifty
    out on the ground. 57 enemy locomotives were demolished by their guns and bombs, 68
    more were damaged. The Red Tails even sank an Italian destroyer and they did that the
    hard way, with machine gun fire. Well, they're home today to hang up their impressive
    record in the A.A.F. files. To Lieutenant George Roberts and his men of the fighting
    Red Tails we say, "Welcome home, well done."
Private John Conti: It's medley time with Major Glenn Miller's Army Air Forces Overseas
  Orchestra playing something old, something new, something borrowed and something blue.
  The old song, "Goin' Home."
GOIN' HOME (Old tune)
  Private John Conti: The Crew Chiefs and Sergeant Johnny Desmond hitch a ride on the new
  tune.
IN THE MIDDLE OF MAY (New tune)
  Vocal refrain by Sergeant Johnny Desmond and the Crew Chiefs
  Private John Conti: The borrowed tune comes from our big boss's big list of big hits,
  "Little Brown Jug."
LITTLE BROWN JUG (Borrowed tune)
  Private John Conti: And for the something blue song, "Blue Is the Night."
BLUE IS THE NIGHT (Blue tune)
Announcer: As we stand on the threshold of the air age we become increasingly aware of
  one simple fact, the future of America's defense will rest on the wings of air power.
  It is with this thought in mind that we invite the attentions of the officers and men of
  the Army Air Forces and their families to the opportunities now open for service with
  the peacetime Air Forces. America will need the strong reservoir of know-how that has
  made the A.A.F. the greatest Air Force in the world. In the hands of the men who have
  served with the A.A.F. in war rests the future of the A.A.F. in peace. Get the facts.
  Study them carefully and then sign on for another hitch with the Army Air Forces in
  peace as in war, first in the air.
Incidental music
Private John Conti: For 14 months in England , France, Germany, Austria, Belgium, Holland
  there was always a rip-roaring reaction whenever Major Glenn Miller's Army Air Forces
  Overseas Orchestra played "Swing Low, Sweet Chariot."
SWING LOW, SWEET CHARIOT
Private John Conti: Last December along about the time of the Battle of the Bulge,
  Sergeant Jerry Gray decided to write an arrangement to give the combat boys on leave a
  few much needed smiles. Artie Malvin contributed some lyrics saluting the Paris subway
  system, the Metro, and the Crew Chiefs and Sergeant Johnny Desmond did the vocalizing in
  the vive l'France version of "The Trolley Song."

THE TROLLEY SONG
   Vocal refrain by Sergeant Johnny Desmond, the Crew Chiefs and Ensemble
Private John Conti: That's all for now but we'll all be back next week for more music by
   Major Glenn Miller's Army Air Forces Overseas Orchestra, conducted by Sergeant Jerry
   Gray, with Sergeant Johnny Desmond and the Crew Chiefs. This is Private John Conti
   saying goodnight and "Keep 'Em Flyin'."
MOONLIGHT SERENADE (closing theme)
   Private John Conti: This program came to you from New York. This is the National
   Broadcasting Company
NBC chimes

03Nov45 (Sat) 11:30PM-Midnight NBC Radio City, New York, New York
   I SUSTAIN THE WINGS broadcast

THE ARMY AIR CORPS (opening fanfare)
   Announcer: Your Army Air Forces present "I Sustain the Wings."
I SUSTAIN THE WINGS (opening theme)
   Announcer: "I Sustain the Wings," featuring the all-soldier music of Major Glenn
      Miller's Army Air Forces Overseas Orchestra, conducted by Sergeant Jerry Gray.
Announcer: And here is Tom Hudson.
Sergeant Tom Hudson: The band has swung from peace to war and back to peace again. But
   the real tunes, the solid tunes, remain unchanged, as witness this original
   Miller-thriller, "Sun Valley Jump."
SUN VALLEY JUMP
Sergeant Tom Hudson: The biggest name in a soldier singing for World War Two is without a
   doubt Sergeant Johnny Desmond. And tonight the good Sarge lends his good voice to the
   words and music of "Autumn Serenade."
AUTUMN SERENADE
   Vocal refrain by Sergeant Johnny Desmond
Announcer: And now, welcome home men of the 6th Air Force.
Incidental music
   Announcer: As the men come back from overseas in ever increasing numbers, you'll see
      more of the gallant patch of the 6th Air Force. You never read of them bombing the
      Nazis or stopping the Japs because they were stationed in the Caribbean and their work
      wasn't headline stuff. But since a year before Pearl Harbor the 6th Air Force has
      been on 24-hour alert in some of the hottest, most rugged terrain in the world. In
      '42 and '43 the men of the 6th slugged it out with the U-boats, suffering losses but
      giving far better than they took. The enemy would have given much to slip just one
      plane through our defenses to get a crack at the Panama Canal, our transportation life
      line, but they didn't get through, high tribute to the skill and determination of the
      men of the 6th Air Force to whom in increasing numbers America is proud to say,
      "Welcome home, well done."
Sergeant Tom Hudson: It's medley time with Major Glenn Miller's Army Air Forces Overseas
   Orchestra playing something old, something new, something borrowed and something blue.
   The old song, "Songs My Mother Taught Me."
SONGS MY MOTHER TAUGHT ME (Old tune)
   Sergeant Tom Hudson: For something new, Sergeant Johnny Desmond sings...
I DON'T WANT TO BE LOVED (New tune)
   Vocal refrain by Sergeant Johnny Desmond
   Sergeant Tom Hudson: Raymond Scott borrowed it from Mozart and Sergeant Jerry Gray puts
      the bite on Scott for a triple play on our borrowed tune, "Eighteenth Century Drawing
      Room."
IN AN EIGHTEENTH CENTURY DRAWING ROOM (Borrowed tune)
   Sergeant Tom Hudson: Now something blue, "Blue Rain."
BLUE RAIN (Blue tune)
Sergeant Tom Hudson: More and more men of the Army Air Forces returning from arduous duty
   overseas are signing on again for service in the peacetime Air Forces. And there are
   good reasons for their action. There are unlimited opportunities open now for young,
   alert men to grow with aviation by serving in the peacetime A.A.F. A good job with full
   security and opportunities for advancement is the first reward of service in the A.A.F.
   But beyond that is the knowledge that in that service A.A.F. men will keep America
   strong in the air, the greatest insurance we can have of America's future peace and
   security. Men of the A.A.F. and their families are asked to consider carefully this
   call. Fly with peacetime Army Air Forces, the greatest flying team in the world.
Incidental music
Sergeant Tom Hudson: Back in England and in France the boys in Major Glenn Miller's Army
   Air Forces Overseas Orchestra came to know the local kids, and to know that their tastes
   didn't differ much from the tastes of the kids back here in the States. They liked the
   band's music, sure. What they wanted was chewing gum, good American chewing gum and
   they let the boys know about it at every opportunity. Well, Corporal Murray Kane jotted

their cries down and whipped them into a song for his singing group, the Crew Chiefs. And here it 'tis, "Have Ya Got Any Gum, Chum?"

HAVE YA GOT ANY GUM, CHUM?
  Vocal refrain by Corporal Murray Kane and the Crew Chiefs
Sergeant Tom Hudson: During its fourteen months overseas Major Glenn Miller's Army Air Forces Overseas Orchestra presented many famous American performers on its broadcasts and on personal appearances. Two were Bing Crosby and Dinah Shore. Another gal who appeared with the band is here tonight. She sang her songs before 45,000 cheering G.I.s in the great Nuremberg Stadium. One other occasion was when she appeared on the band's 500th broadcast over the American Forces Network. And here she is to tell you all about it, Joy Hodges. Joy.
Joy Hodges: Thank you, Tom. Well, there's nothing much to tell except that I was invited to appear with Major Miller's band for that broadcast.
Sergeant Tom Hudson: Uh huh.
Joy Hodges: What a thrill that was. So I jumped in a jeep and the jeep jumped all over the road all the way to Paris from Compiegne, France. Well, when I arrived at the Olympia Theatre where the broadcast was taking place Captain Don Haynes informed me that I had just about eight minutes to get into makeup and on the air.
Sergeant Tom Hudson: Wow!
Joy Hodges: Well, I rushed backstage to my dressing room, but, ah, just as I was, ah, ready to change I heard what sounded like a new Jerry Gray arrangement. Well, I became quite interested.
Sergeant Tom Hudson: Why, naturally.
Joy Hodges: In fact, so interested in what Fiddlin' Phil Marino and the band were playing and what Carmen Mastren and the Crew Chiefs were singing that I wound up doing my share of the show in street makeup, sporting one false eyelash in place of the customary two. Well, Tom, no kidding, I defy anyone to keep their mind on what they're doing when they hear this Jerry Gray arrangement for the first time.
Sergeant Tom Hudson: Agreed, Joy, agreed.

HOW YA GONNA KEEP 'EM DOWN ON THE FARM (After They've Seen Paree?)
  Vocal refrain by S/Sgt. Carmen Mastren, the Crew Chiefs and M/Sgt. Zeke   Zarchy
Sergeant Tom Hudson: Well, that's all for now but we'll all be back next week with more music by Major Glenn Miller's Army Air Forces Overseas Orchestra, conducted by Sergeant Jerry Gray, and the voices of Sergeant Johnny Desmond and the Crew Chiefs. This is Tom Hudson saying good night and keep 'em flying to keep the peace.

MOONLIGHT SERENADE (closing theme)
  Sergeant Tom Hudson: "I Sustain the Wings" has come to you from our Radio
    City studios in New York. This is the National Broadcasting Company.
NBC Chimes

10Nov45 (Sat) NBC Radio City, New York, New York
 I SUSTAIN THE WINGS dress rehearsal

THE ARMY AIR CORPS (opening fanfare)
 Announcer: Your Army Air Forces present "I Sustain the Wings."
I SUSTAIN THE WINGS (opening theme)
 Announcer: "I Sustain the Wings," featuring the all-soldier music of Major Glenn
  Miller's Army Air Forces Overseas Orchestra, conducted by Sergeant Jerry Gray.
Announcer: And here is Tom Hudson.
Sergeant Tom Hudson: The brass puts on the big blast for tonight's starter as the program
 doors swing open with "7-0-5."
7-0-5
Sergeant Tom Hudson: In the long months over there in England, France and in Germany the
 boys in Major Glenn Miller's Army Air Forces Overseas Orchestra played a lot of shows
 for a lot of guys who seemed to like what they heard. And one of the things they best
 liked to hear was Sergeant Johnny Desmond singing "The More I See You."
THE MORE I SEE YOU
 Vocal refrain by Sergeant Johnny Desmond
Announcer: And now a welcome home, men of the 7th Air Force.
Incidental music
 Announcer: This week in ever increasing numbers men of the 7th Air Force are passing
  through separation centers and coming on home. Based in Hawaii, the 7th found its
  nucleus in the men who first met the enemy in the air over Pearl Harbor, men who knew
  our first bitter taste of defeat and the hard days that followed. Short of men and
  equipment, the 7th struck back early in 1943 in the Battle of Midway and the emblem of
  the 7th A.A.F. was in the skies over the Solomons at Guadalcanal. Hawaii based, sure,
  but they did their fighting a long way from home in the Gilberts, the Marshalls and
  the Marianas and they did a job. And right up to the last days it was the 7th of
  Hawaii in there, blasting out a pattern of irresistible triumph. So this week, as
  they come home from the distant wars, we say, "Welcome home, men of the 7th Air Force,
  well done."
Sergeant Tom Hudson: And now it's medley time for Major Glenn Miller's Army Air Forces
 Overseas Orchestra with something old, something new, something borrowed and something
 blue. The old tune, "Flow Gently, Sweet Afton."
FLOW GENTLY, SWEET AFTON (Old tune)
 Sergeant Tom Hudson: For something new here's Sergeant Johnny Desmond to unveil a new
  ballad by Sergeant Steve Steck and Harry Hartwick.
WHY DREAM? (New tune)
 Vocal refrain by Sergeant Johnny Desmond
 Sergeant Tom Hudson: We turn to Duke Ellington for our borrowed tune and come up with
  "Things Ain't What They Used to Be."
THINGS AIN'T WHAT THEY USED TO BE (Borrowed tune)
 Sergeant Tom Hudson: And finally something blue, "A Blues Serenade."
A BLUES SERENADE (Blue tune)
Sergeant Tom Hudson: Service in the peacetime Air Force is an honorable and patriotic
 calling and it has definite job advantages which we invite young Americans to consider.
 For enlisted men pay scales range as high as $207 a month in addition to food, lodging,
 clothing and medical care. Peacetime service in the Air Forces carries with it the
 added opportunity for specialized study and training in the many branches of aviation
 and Allied occupation. After 20 years of honorable service a man may retire on part
 pay, after 30 years on a full 75% of his pay, pay which, incidentally, automatically
 increases 5% every three years of service. There is a fine future for fine young men in
 the peacetime Air Forces. Think about it then sign up for the greatest flying team in
 the world, the United States Army Air Forces.
Incidental music
Sergeant Tom Hudson: In the days before V-E Day over there, there was a strong feeling of
 comradeship between our fighting G.I.s and the men of the Red Army battling in from the
 East to join us. And to honor our Russian Allies the boys polished up an old
 Miller-thriller. Here it is once more, "The Volga Boatmen."
SONG OF THE VOLGA BOATMEN

Sergeant Tom Hudson: Major Glenn Miller's Army Air Forces Overseas Orchestra spotlights a
  Sergeant Jerry Gray super production. Sergeant Johnny Desmond lines up with the Crew
  Chiefs and what comes out is "Poinciana."
POINCIANA (Song of the Tree)
  Vocal refrain by Sergeant Johnny Desmond and the Crew Chiefs
Sergeant Tom Hudson: Whether it's on the war scarred battle fields of the world or on the
  cleat torn turf of the gridiron, the greatest team of all is that khaki clad team of
  dough boys who do business under our Star-Spangled Banner. And to them a 21-gun salute
  from Sergeant Jerry Gray and the band with "On, Brave Old Army Team."
ON, BRAVE OLD ARMY TEAM
Sergeant Tom Hudson: Well, that's all for now but we'll be back with you next week, same
  time, same station, with the Crew Chiefs, Sergeant Johnny Desmond and the music of Major
  Glenn Miller's Army Air Forces Overseas Orchestra, conducted by Sergeant Jerry Gray.
  Until then this is Tom Hudson saying, " Keep 'Em Flying to keep the peace."
MOONLIGHT SERENADE (closing theme)
  Sergeant Tom Hudson: "I Sustain the Wings" originates in New York's Radio City. This
  is the National Broadcasting Company.
NBC Chimes

17Nov45 (Sat) 11:30PM-Midnight Bolling Field, Washington, D.C.
  I SUSTAIN THE WINGS broadcast in barracks and transmitted to NBC

THE ARMY AIR CORPS (opening fanfare)
  Announcer: From the nation's capitol, Washington, D.C., your Army Air Forces present "I Sustain the Wings."
I SUSTAIN THE WINGS (opening theme)
  Announcer: "I Sustain the Wings," the farewell performance of Major Glenn Miller's Army Air Forces Overseas Orchestra, conducted by Sergeant Jerry Gray and coming to you tonight from Bolling Field.
Announcer: And here is Sergeant Vern Wilson.
Sergeant Vern Wilson: We're winding up tonight, playing the last tunes, calling the last roll. And there's a name at the top of the roster to which the answer is "Missing in Flight," Major Glenn Miller. We called him the big boss. We started out with him, back in the early days, to do the job that he set, to tell the story of the Air Forces, to get the men for the job ahead, to go over there to the fighting men to bring them a breath of home with our music. We got to know the big boss as a fine musician, a great guy. When he was lost to us back in December, we carried on the way that we knew he's want us to, the way he'd showed us and taught us, the way we're playing this one, because it's his tune. The Miller-thriller, "In the Mood."
IN THE MOOD
Sergeant Vern Wilson: We started "I Sustain the Wings" two and a half years ago, telling America about its Air Forces, inviting young men to join the greatest flying team in the world. We went over with the men and we found that a bunch of soldiers with a tune to play and a song to sing got a high priority in the hearts of the war-weary G.I.s in the E.T.O. We remember them now and we're grateful to them, to the high-ranking officers, Generals Spaatz and Eaker, Doolittle, Giles, and to the wonderful guys who served in their commands. High on the lists of favorites that they asked to hear over there because it wrapped up a memory of home was an American song that they all knew and loved, "Star Dust."
STAR DUST
Sergeant Vern Wilson: You're in the market for a job and somebody makes you an offer like this.
Announcer: Work, interesting, with maybe some travel thrown in. Take home pay that really adds up because food, quarters and clothing are free. Thirty days vacation a year with full pay. Opportunity? Lots of it. With the chance to train in one of the most famous technical schools in the world and to put this training into practice. Security? No job could offer you more. And there's a twenty year retirement plan now in operation. What would you say? Thousands of American fighting men have already said yes to this offer by re-enlisting in the peacetime Air Forces of the regular Army. How about you? You know there's real news in the fact that you'll be given a regular Army rating in your present grade if you sign on before February first. And you can enlist for one, two or three years or for 18 months, the choice is yours. Think it over. Figure it out for yourself. Compare the security and opportunity offered by the peacetime Army Air Forces with the uncertainties of a civilian job. Then visit your nearest Army Recruiting Station tomorrow.
Incidental music
Sergeant Vern Wilson: Now it's medley time for Major Glenn Miller's A.A.F. Overseas Orchestra, a farewell medley time which we're dedicating to General of the Army Dwight D. Eisenhower and to all the guys we knew and played for over there and to the wives, mothers and sweethearts that they're coming home to now. Here's something old, something new, something borrowed and something blue. The old tune, "My Buddy."
MY BUDDY (Old tune)
  Sergeant Vern Wilson: Something new now and Sergeant Johnny Desmond joins the Crew Chiefs and we hear ...
IN THE MIDDLE OF MAY (New tune)
  Vocal refrain by Sergeant Johnny Desmond and the Crew Chiefs
  Sergeant Vern Wilson: We reach deep in our hearts and take our borrowed tune from a guy it will always belong to, Major Glenn Miller, and we play it in the way he showed us, "Moonlight Serenade."

MOONLIGHT SERENADE (Borrowed tune)
  Sergeant Vern Wilson: Something blue with a touch of silver lining, "My Blue Heaven."
MY BLUE HEAVEN (Blue tune)
Sergeant Vern Wilson: This is the last broadcast of "I Sustain the Wings" and it's the
  last of many broadcasts from your Army Air Forces. We've brought you the Air Forces'
  story from headquarters over the major networks, from posts and airfields and the
  smaller stations, from overseas direct by wire recorder. At home and overseas we
  reported on the lives of your fighting men in the Army Air Forces, a great bunch of men
  and a great fighting team. Our mission's ended now and this is our thanks to you who
  have been with us all the way. We're grateful for the opportunity to do the job and
  proud of the organization with which we served, the United States Army Air Forces.
SYMPHONY
  Sergeant Vern Wilson: We pulled a bit of reverse lend-lease over there and brought back
    a song that you seemed to like. So here's Sergeant Johnny Desmond for a reprise of
    "Symphony."
  Vocal refrain by Sergeant Johnny Desmond
Sergeant Vern Wilson: And now here's Lieutenant Colonel Frederick Brisson, Chief of Army
  Air Forces Radio, who has inspired and led the operation all the way. Colonel Brisson.
Lt. Col. Frederick Brisson: Winning the war took better men, better planes, and better
  weapons than our enemy could produce. But it also took words, millions of words, to
  explain an entirely new type of warfare to the men and women of America, words to
  explain the new meaning of air power, for General of the Army H. H. Arnold has felt that
  in a people's war and a people's peace the people must be fully informed of the mighty
  weapon they hold in their Army Air Forces. This has been our primary objective during
  the war and during the months of peace that have followed. Through our wartime radio
  mission we were able to achieve our planned objectives and, as General Arnold has said,
  quote:

  Announcer: I have always regarded our Air Force radio broadcasts as a strictly military
    operation whose objective of public understanding and support is just as vital as a
    mission in a theater of war. Now it enables us to write "Mission accomplished" in the
    log of our radio programs.

Lt. Col. Frederick Brisson: Unquote. The necessity for all-out radio activity has
  passed. It is hoped that the vital stories and messages that were carried will continue
  to live in the consciousness of America as the A.A.F., symbol of America's air power,
  continues as a guardian of the peace and protector of the rights of liberty-loving
  nations throughout the world.
Sergeant Vern Wilson: Thank you, Colonel Brisson.
THE ARMY AIR CORPS
  Sergeant Vern Wilson: Now, for General of the Army H. H. Arnold, for the officers and
    men of the Army Air Forces, from Sergeant Jerry Gray and Major Glenn Miller's A.A.F.
    Overseas Orchestra, "The Air Corps Song."
  Vocal refrain by Sergeant Johnny Desmond and Ensemble
Sergeant Vern Wilson: That's it. That's finale for your A.A.F. on the air, except for
  one thing. Our sincere thanks to the National Broadcasting Company and the other major
  networks for their unstinting cooperation, to the civilian artists who have from time to
  time given us a hand with our mission, and to all those people in and out of service who
  have given us help and encouragement in a thousand ways. And now from Washington, D.C.
  this is Sergeant Vern Wilson saying just once more to all Americans, "Keep 'Em Flying to
  keep the peace."
MOONLIGHT SERENADE (closing theme)
  Announcer: This series was written by Sergeant Irving Nyman and produced by Sergeant
    George Voutsas.
NBC announcer: This is the National Broadcasting Company.
NBC chimes

UNKNOWN DATES

T/Sgt. Ray McKinley: ... we've got one of them here in Mike Hucko. And we're gonna turn
   him loose on "The Eyes and Ear of the World."
THE EYES AND EARS OF THE WORLD

From "The Swing Shift" program. Possible dates: 18Jul44, 04Aug44, 25Aug44, 23Sep44,
20Oct44, 16Nov44, 02Dec44, 08Dec44, 15Feb45, 27Mar45, 12Apr45, or 23May45. I suspect that
it is from one of the 1945 dates since there is no mention of rank for Mike Hucko.

Cpl. Paul A. Dubov: .. Jerry Gray's arrangement of "Holiday for Strings."
HOLIDAY FOR STRINGS

Warrant Officer Paul Dudley: ... "Long Tall Mama."
LONG TALL MAMA

From "American Band of the AEF" program. Possible dates: 26Mar45, 2Apr45, 16Apr45, or
24Apr45.

BBC announcer: ... "Measure for Measure."
MEASURE FOR MEASURE

16Apr45 or 14May45 "American Band of the AEF."

    Issues:
       12" 33s: Magic (England) AWE-11-test, AWE-11
       Cassette: Magic (England) CAWE-11

Warrant Officer Paul Dudley: ... over at Pagliacci's place of business and we'd like to
   see what you think of it now. Here's Mel and the tune he composed, arranged and plays,
   "No Compris."
NO COMPRIS

19Feb45 or 12Mar45 "American Band of the AEF."

Warrant Officer Paul Dudley: The tall, blond man back there, Mel Powell by name, is composer, arranger and pianist by choice. And Mel now plays his latest composition, dedicated to the many American soldiers facing the pitfalls of the French language, "No Compris."
NO COMPRIS

12Mar45 or 19Feb45 "American Band of the AEF."

T/Sgt. Ray McKinley: Well, for the windup tune tonight the lads swing down the field and right over the goal line with "On, Brave Old Army Team." Look out, boys, one, two.
ON, BRAVE OLD ARMY TEAM

From "The Swing Shift" program. Possible dates: 30Jan45, 20Mar45, or 03Apr45.

Warrant Officer Paul Dudley: Sergeant Jerry Gray directs now as we listen to the exciting Miller classic "Meadowlands."
THE RED CAVALRY MARCH

25Dec44 or 19Feb45 "American Band of the AEF."

Warrant Officer Paul Dudley: The American Band of the A.E.F. invites you all aboard the "Sleepy Town Train."
SLEEPY TOWN TRAIN

From an "American Band of the AEF" program. Possible dates: 15Jan45, 26Mar45, or 16Apr45.

T/Sgt. Ray McKinley: ... we're all out of some of that fine jewelry, so we're selling a bright little gem that just keeps ... Get set for "String of Pearls."
A STRING OF PEARLS

From a "The Swing Shift" program. Possible dates: 17Oct44, 02Dec44, 15Feb45, or 01Mar45.

Warrant Officer Paul Dudley: Here's a tune that should make your heart beat faster. Sergeant Ray McKinley and the Crew Chiefs do the vocalizing, and "When Johnny Comes Marching Home."
WHEN JOHNNY COMES MARCHING HOME
  Vocal refrain by Technical Sergeant Ray McKinley and the Crew Chiefs

26Mar45 or 16Apr45 "American Band of the AEF."

APPENDIX II

GLENN MILLER ARMY AIR FORCE BAND

SIDEMEN SESSIONS

This section covers the sessions made by members of Glenn Miller's Army Air Force Band while they were members of or still attached to the band. The organization of this Appendix is the same as for the main body of the discography.

ABBREVIATIONS

33	33-1/3 rpm
45	45 rpm
78	78 rpm
ABO	Arthur Briggs and His Orchestra
AFRS	Armed Forces Radio Service
AFRTS	Armed Forces Radio-Television Service
ALT	Alternate take
AM	Ante Meridiem
AUG	August
BF	Bud Freeman
BG	Benny Goodman
BML	Basic Musical Library
BR	Buddy Rich
BS	Bill Stegmeyer
C.	Circa
CBS	Columbia Broadcasting System
CH	Chorus
CM	Composer(s)
CPL.	Corporal
CSP	Columbia Special Products
DRB	Delta Rhythm Boys
EBO	Eddie Barclay and His Orchestra
EF	Ella Fitzgerald
EP	Extended Play (45 rpm)
F	France
FDMS	Five De Marco Sisters
FEB	February
FRI	Friday
G.I.	General Issue
II	Second
JAN	January
JD	Johnny Desmond
JL	Jack Leonard
LM	Liza Morrow
LP	Long Play (33-1/3 rpm)
LYR	Lyricist(s)
MAR	March
ML	Monica Lewis
MON	Monday
MP	Mel Powell
MS	Muggsy Spanier
MT	Martha Tilton
MUS. 2/C	Musician Second Class
NOV	November
OCT	October
PFC.	Private First Class
PIANO	Piano Forte
PM	Post Meridiem
PVT.	Private
RB	Red Barber
RCA	Radio Corporation of America
RE	Roy Eldridge
RM	Ray McKinley
RPM	Revolutions per Minute

SEP	September
SGT.	Sergeant
S/SGT.	Staff Sergeant
SUN	Sunday
TC	Thelma Carpenter
THU	Thursday
T/SGT.	Technical (Tech) Sergeant
TY	Trummy Young
UH	Uptown Hall
USA	United States of America
VOL.	Volume
WED	Wednesday

Dates are shown in the following format:

    xxyyyzz   xx = day of the month; yyy = month; zz = year (preceded by 19)

**25Jan45 (Thu) 10:30AM-2:00PM Jazz Club Francais, Rue de Ranelagh, Paris, France
RECORDING SESSION**

"JAZZ CLUB MYSTERY HOT BAND" (Jazz Club Francais)
JAZZ CLUB MYSTERY JIVERS (Victory)
GLENN MILLER'S UPTOWN HALL GANG led by Mel Powell (Esquire)
DJANGO REINHARDT WITH GLENN MILLER'S ALL STARS (CBS)
DJANGO REINHARDT & THE GLENN MILLER ALL STARS (Affinity)
Trumpet: **Pvt. Bernie Privin**; Tenor saxophone: **Pvt. "Peanuts" Hucko**; Piano: **Pfc. Mel
Powell**; Guitar: Django Reinhardt; String bass: **Cpl. Joe Shulman**; Drums: **T/Sgt. Ray
McKinley**

ST-1227-1 **HOW HIGH THE MOON**

ST-1227-2 **HOW HIGH THE MOON**
  Issues:
    10" 78s: Esquire (England) 10-043
           Jazz Club Francais (France) ST-1227/1232
    12" 33s: Affinity (England) Box 107-13/14
           Avan-Guard Music (Australia) BVL 046
           CBS (France) 63052
           CBS (The Netherlands) 63052
           Esquire (England) ESQ-302

ST-1228-1 **IF DREAMS COME TRUE**
  Issues:
    10" 78s: Esquire (England) 10-087
           Jazz Club Francais (France) ST-1228/F-1235 (wrong label), ST-1228/1235,
             JC-121
    12" 33s: Affinity (England) Box 107-13/14
           Avan-Guard Music (Australia) BVL 046
           CBS (Brazil) 159024/25 (159025)
           CBS (England) 88225 (M-CBS-81827)
           CBS (France) 63052
           CBS (The Netherlands) 63052
           Columbia (USA) CG-33566 (C33568), CG-33566-DJ (C33568)
           Esquire (England) ESQ-302
           Reader's Digest (France) LSP-13308
    Cassette: Columbia (USA) CGT-33566

ST-1229-1 **HALLELUJAH!**

ST-1229-2 **HALLELUJAH!**
  Issues:
    10" 78s: Esquire (England) 10-243
           Jazz Club Francais (France) ST-1229/1231, JC-122
           Victory (Belgium) 9032
    12" 33s: Affinity (England) Box 107-13/14
           Avan-Guard Music (Australia) BVL 046
           CBS (France) 63052
           CBS (The Netherlands) 63052
           Esquire (England) ESQ-302

ST-1230 **STOMPIN' AT THE SAVOY**
  Issues:
    10" 78s: Esquire (England) 10-043
           Jazz Club Francais (France) ST-1230/1233, JC-123
    12" 33s: Affinity (England) Box 107-13/14
           Avan-Guard Music (Australia) BVL 046
           CBS (France) 63052

                    CBS (The Netherlands) 63052
                    Esquire (England) ESQ-302

28Jan45 (Sun) Jazz Club Francais, Rue de Ranelagh, Paris, France
RECORDING SESSION

"JAZZ CLUB MYSTERY HOT BAND" (Jazz Club Francais)
JAZZ CLUB MYSTERY JIVERS (Victory)
GLENN MILLER'S UPTOWN HALL GANG led by Mel Powell (Esquire)
JAZZ MEN IN UNIFORM (CBS and Harmony)
Trumpet: **Pvt. Bernie Privin**; Clarinet: **Pvt. "Peanuts" Hucko**; Piano: **Pfc. Mel Powell**;
Guitar: **Sgt. Carmen Mastren**: String bass: **Cpl. Joe Shulman**; Drums: **T/Sgt. Ray McKinley**

ST-1231   **I MUST HAVE THAT MAN**
    Issues:
      10" 78s: Esquire (England) 10-097
                    Jazz Club Francais (France) ST-1229/1231, JC-122
                    Victory (Belgium) 9044
      12" 33s: CBS (France) 63130
                    Esquire (England) ESQ-302
                    Harmony (Canada) HEL-6004

ST-1232-1 **PLEASE DON'T TALK ABOUT ME WHEN I'M GONE**
    Issues:
      10" 78s: Esquire (England) 10-053
                    Jazz Club Francais (France) ST-1227/1232, JC-120
                    Victory (Belgium) 9032
      12" 33s: CBS (France) 63130
                    Esquire (England) ESQ-302
                    Harmony (Canada) HEL-6004

ST-1233   **'S WONDERFUL**
    Issues:
      10" 78s: Esquire (England) 10-097
                    Jazz Club Francais (France) ST-1230/1233, JC-123
      12" 33s: CBS (France) 63130 (mislabeled as "You're Driving Me Crazy")
                    Esquire (England) ESQ-302
                    Harmony (Canada) HEL-6004

ST-1234-1 **SOMEDAY SWEETHEART**
    Issues:
      10" 78s: Esquire (England) 10-053
                    Jazz Club Francais (France) JC-120
      12" 33s: CBS (France) 63130
                    Esquire (England) ESQ-302
                    Harmony (Canada) HEL-6004

ST-1235   **BLUE SKIES**
    Issues:
      10" 78s: Esquire (England) 10-087
                    Jazz Club Francais (France) ST-1228/F-1235 (wrong label), ST-1228/1235,
                      JC-121
                    Victory (Belgium) 9044
      12" 33s: CBS (France) 63130
                    Esquire (England) ESQ-302
                    Harmony (Canada) HEL-6004

01Feb45 (Thu) Studio Technisonor, Paris, France
RECORDING SESSION

EDDIE BARCLAY AND HIS ORCHESTRA
Director and arranger: Eddie Barclay; Trumpet: Arthur Briggs; Clarinet: Hubert Rostaing;
Alto saxophones: Andre Ekyan, Charles Lisee; Tenor saxophones: Max Hugot, Chico
Christobal; Piano: Jack Dieval; Guitar: Pierre Gergardot; String bass: Lucien Simoens;
Drums: Jerry Mengo; Vocalist: **Sgt. Johnny Desmond**

ST-1236-1 **PAPER DOLL** (JD)

ST-1236-2 **PAPER DOLL** (JD)
  Issue:
    10" 78:   Blue Star (France) 14

ST-1237-1 **A LOVELY WAY TO SPEND AN EVENING** (JD)

ST-1237-2 **A LOVELY WAY TO SPEND AN EVENING** (JD)
  Issue:
    10" 78:   Blue Star (France) 13

ST-1238-1 **I'LL WALK ALONE** (JD)
  Issue:
    10" 78:   Blue Star (France) 13

ST-1239-1 **GOOD NIGHT, WHEREVER YOU ARE** (JD)

ST-1239-2 **GOOD NIGHT, WHEREVER YOU ARE** (JD)
  Issue:
    10" 78:   Blue Star (France) 14

11Mar45 (Sun) Jazz Club Francais, Rue de Ranelagh, Paris, France
RECORDING SESSION

ARTHUR BRIGGS AND HIS ORCHESTRA
Leader and trumpet: Arthur Briggs; Clarinet: **Pvt. "Peanuts" Hucko**; Tenor saxophone: Alix
Combelle; Piano: **Pfc. Mel Powell**; Guitar: Pierre Gergardot; String Bass: **Cpl. Joe
Shulman**; Drums: Jerry Mengo

ST-1263   **IT HAD TO BE YOU**

ST-1264   **BLUE LOU**

ST-1265   **BRIGGS BOOGIE**
  Issue:
    10" 78:   Blue Star (France) 11

ST-1266   **WHEN THE SAINTS GO MARCHIN' IN**
  ISsue:
    10" 78:   Blue Star (France) 11

19Mar45 (Mon) Jazz Club Francais, Rue de Ranelagh, Paris, France
RECORDING SESSION

EDDIE BARCLAY AND HIS ORCHESTRA
Director and arranger: Eddie Barclay; Trumpet: **Sgt. Bobby Nichols**; Clarinet and
arrangements: Hubert Rostaing; Alto saxophones: Andre Ekyan, Charles Lisee; Tenor
saxophones: Alex Gaija, Gaston Rahier; Piano: Jack Dieval; Guitar: Roger Chaput; String
bass: Emmanuel Soudieux; Drums: Jerry Mengo

ST-1276-1 **YOU BELONG TO ME**

ST-1276-2 **YOU BELONG TO ME**
    Issue:
        10" 78:   Blue Star (France) 1

ST-1277-1 **BODY AND SOUL**
    Issue:
        10" 78:   Blue Star (France) 1

ST-1278 **ROSETTA**
    Issues:
        10" 78:   Blue Star (France) 2
        12" 33:   Barclay (France) 81.004

ST-1279 **ONE O'CLOCK JUMP**
    Issues:
        10" 78:   Blue Star (France) 2
        12" 33:   Barclay (France) 81.004

ST-1280 **I GOT RHYTHM**
    Issue:
        10" 78:   Blue Star (France) 3 (as by Blue Star Swing Band)

**12May45 (Sat) Jazz Club Francais, Rue de Ranelagh, Paris, France
RECORDING SESSION**

JAZZ CLUB AMERICAN HOT BAND (Jazz Club Francais)
ALL STAR AMERICAN ORK. (Victory)
GLENN MILLER'S UP-TOWN HALL GANG led by Mel Powell (Esquire)
JAZZMEN IN UNIFORM (CBS and Harmony)
Trumpet: **Pvt. Bernie Privin**; Clarinet (ST-1359) and Alto saxophone (ST-1356/7/8): **Pvt. "Peanuts" Hucko**; Piano: **Pfc. Mel Powell**; Guitar: **Sgt. Carmen Mastren**; String bass: **Cpl. Joe Shulman**; Drums: **T/Sgt. Ray McKinley**

ST-1356-1 **RED LIGHT** (actually "I've Found a New Baby")
    Issues:
        10" 78s: Esquire (England) 10-243
                   Jazz Club Francais (France) JC-132
                   Victory (Belgium) 9045
        12" 33s: CBS (France) 63130
                   Esquire (England) ESQ-302
                   Harmony (Canada) HEL-6004

ST-1357-1 **YOU'RE DRIVING ME CRAZY!** (What Did I Do?)

ST-1357-2 **YOU'RE DRIVING ME CRAZY!** (What Did I Do?)

ST-1357-3 **YOU'RE DRIVING ME CRAZY!** (What Did I Do?)
    Issues:
        10" 78s: Jazz Club Francais (France) JC-132
                   Victory (Belgium) 9059
        12" 33s: CBS (France) 63130 (as "S'Wonderful")
                   Harmony (Canada) HEL-6004

ST-1358-1 **YOU'RE DRIVING ME CRAZY!** (What Did I Do?)

ST-1358-2 **YOU'RE DRIVING ME CRAZY!** (What Did I Do?)
    Issues:
       10" 78s: Esquire (England) 10-209
                   Jazz Club Francais (France) JC-133 (as "Indiana")
                   Victory (Belgium) 9045
       12" 33:   Esquire (England) ESQ-302

ST-1359-1 **ON THE SUNNY SIDE OF THE STREET**

ST-1359-2 **ON THE SUNNY SIDE OF THE STREET**
    Issues:
       10" 78s: Esquire (England) 10-209
                   Jazz Club Francais (France) JC-133
       12" 33s: CBS (France) 63130
                   Esquire (England) ESQ-302
                   Harmony (Canada) HEL-6004

19May45 (Sat) Jazz Club Francais, Rue de Ranelaugh, Paris, France
RECORDING SESSION

MEL POWELL (piano solos)

ST-1368-1 **HOMMAGE A FATS WALLER**

ST-1368-2 **HOMMAGE A FATS WALLER**
    Issues:
       10" 78s: Esquire (England) 10-199
                   Jazz Club Francais (France) JC-140
                   Victory (Belgium) 9046
        7" EP: Esquire (England) EP-199
       12" 33s: Avan-Guard Music (Australia) BVL 046
                   CBS (France) 63052
                   CBS (The Netherlands) 63052
                   Esquire (England) ESQ-304

ST-1369-1 **HOMMAGE A DEBUSSY**

ST-1369-2 **HOMMAGE A DEBUSSY**
    Issues:
       10" 78s: Esquire (England) 10-199
                   Jazz Club Francais (France) JC-140
                   Victory (Belgium) 9046
        7" EP: Esquire (England) EP-199
       12" 33s: Avan-Guard Music (Australia) BVL 046
                   CBS (France) 63052
                   CBS (The Netherlands) 63052
                   Esquire (England) ESQ-304

ST-1370-1 **POUR MME BLANC**

ST-1370-2 **POUR MME BLANC**

ST-1370-3 **POUR MME BLANC**
    Issues:
       10" 78s: Esquire (England) 10-086 (as "For Miss Black")
                   Jazz Club Francais (France) JC-141 (as "For 'Miss Black'")
                   Victory (Belgium) 9047 (as "For Miss Black")
        7" EP: Esquire (England) EP-199 (as "For Miss Black")
       12" 33s: Avan-Guard Music (Australia) BVL 046
                   CBS (England) 88061 (M-80244)

CBS (France) 63052, 67257 (64946) (both as "For Miss Black")
CBS (The Netherlands) 63052, S 67257 (64946) (both as "For Miss Black")
Columbia (Canada) KG-32355
Columbia (USA) KG-32355 (C-32356), PG-32355 (C-32356)
Esquire (England) ESQ-304

ST-1371-1 DON'T BLAME ME

ST-1371-2 DON'T BLAME ME
Issues:
  10" 78s: Esquire (England) 10-086
                Jazz Club Francais (France) JC-141
                Victory (Belgium) 9047
   7" EP: Esquire (England) EP-199
  12" 33s: Avan-Guard Music (Australia) BVL 046
                CBS (France) 63052
                CBS (The Netherlands) 63052
                Esquire (England) ESQ-304

"Pour Mme Blanc" is a tribute to Yvonne Blanc, who was responsible for this
recording session

**20May45 (Sun) AM Jazz Club Francais, Rue de Ranelaugh, Paris, France
RECORDING SESSION**

JAZZ CLUB AMERICAN HOT BAND (Jazz Club Francais)
ALL STAR AMERICAN ORK. (Victory)
GLENN MILLER'S UPTOWN HALL GANG led by Mel Powell (Esquire)
JAZZMEN IN UNIFORM (CBS and Harmony)
Trumpet: **Pvt. Bernie Privin**; Clarinet: **Pvt. "Peanuts" Hucko**; Piano: **Pfc. Mel Powell**;
Guitar: **Sgt. Carmen Mastren**; String bass: **Cpl. Joe Shulman**; Drums: **T/Sgt. Ray McKinley**

ST-1372-1 PENNIES FROM HEAVEN

ST-1372-2 PENNIES FROM HEAVEN
Issues:
  10" 78s: Esquire (England) 10-149
                Jazz Club Francais (France) 134-test, 134
  12" 33s: CBS (France) 63130
                Esquire (England) ESQ-302
                Harmony (Canada) HEL-6004

ST-1373-1 ONE, TWO, BUTTON YOUR SHOE

ST-1373-2 ONE, TWO, BUTTON YOUR SHOE
Issues:
  10" 78s: Esquire (England) 10-240
                Jazz Club Francais (France) 135
  12" 33s: CBS (France) 63130
                Esquire (England) ESQ-302
                Harmony (Canada) HEL-6004

ST-1374-1 AT SUNDOWN (Love Is Calling Me Home)
Issues:
  12" 33s: CBS (France) 63130
                Harmony (Canada) HEL-6004

ST-1374-2 **AT SUNDOWN (Love Is Calling Me Home)**
  Issues:
    10" 78s: Esquire (England) 10-149
              Jazz Club Francais (France) 134-test, 134
              Victory (Belgium) 9059
    12" 33:   Esquire (England) ESQ-302

ST-1375-1 **STEALIN' SMACK'S APPLES** (Actually "Stealin' Apples")

ST-1375-2 **STEALIN' SMACK'S APPLES** (Actually "Stealin' Apples")
  Issues:
    10" 78s: Esquire (England) 10-240
              Jazz Club Francais (France) 135
    12" 33s: CBS (France) 63130
              Esquire (England) ESQ-302
              Harmony (Canada) HEL-6004

**20May45 (Sun) PM Jazz Club Francais, Rue de Ranelagh, Paris, France
RECORDING SESSION**

HOT TRIO RAY MAC KINLEY (Cupol, Jazz Club Francais, Victory)
RAY McKINLEY TRIO (Esquire)
THE RAY McKINLEY TRIO (CBS)
Clarinet: **Pvt. "Peanuts" Hucko**; Piano: **Pfc. Mel Powell**; Drums: **T/Sgt. Ray McKinley**

ST-1376-1 **SUGAR (That Sugar Baby o' Mine)**

ST-1376-2 **SUGAR (That Sugar Baby o' Mine)**

ST-1376-3 **SUGAR (That Sugar Baby o' Mine)**
  Issues:
    10" 78s: Esquire (England) 10-070
              Jazz Club Francais (France) JC-130
              Victory (Belgium) 9057
     7" EP: Esquire (England) EP-180
    12" 33s: Avan-Guard Music (Australia) BVL 046
              CBS (France) 63052
              CBS (The Netherlands) 63052

ST-1377-1 **AFTER YOU'VE GONE**

ST-1377-2 **AFTER YOU'VE GONE**

ST-1377-3 **AFTER YOU'VE GONE**
  Issues:
    10" 78s: Cupol (Sweden) 4063
              Esquire (England) 10-070
              Jazz Club Francais (France) JC-130
              Victory (Belgium) 9057
     7" EP: Esquire (England) EP-180
    12" 33s: Avan-Guard Music (Australia) BVL 046
              CBS (France) 63052
              CBS (The Netherlands) 63052

ST-1378-1 **SHOEMAKER'S APRON**

ST-1378-2 **SHOEMAKER'S APRON**
  Issues:
    10" 78s: Esquire (England) 10-150
               Jazz Club Francais (France) JC-131

<pre>
                       Victory (Belgium) 9058
        7" EP: Esquire (England) EP-180
        12" 33s: Avan-Guard Music (Australia) BVL 046
                       CBS (France) 63052
                       CBS (The Netherlands) 63052
</pre>

ST-1379-1 **CHINA BOY**

ST-1379-2 **CHINA BOY**

ST-1379-3 **CHINA BOY**
<pre>
   Issues:
        10" 78s: Cupol (Sweden) 4063
                       Esquire (England) 10-150
                       Jazz Club Francais (France) JC-131
                       Victory (Belgium) 9058
        7" EP: Esquire (England) EP-180
        12" 33s: Avan-Guard Music (Australia) BVL 046
                       CBS (France) 63052
                       CBS (The Netherlands) 63052
</pre>

29Aug45 (Wed) Columbia studio, New York, New York
COLUMBIA RECORDING SESSION

BENNY GOODMAN SEXTET
Clarinet: Benny Goodman; Vibraphone: Red Norvo (Kenneth Norville); Piano: **Pfc. Mel Powell**; Guitar: Mike Bryan; String bass: Slam Stewart; Drums: Morey Feld

CO-35143   **TIGER RAG (Hold That Tiger!)**

CO-35143   **TIGER RAG (Hold That Tiger!)**

CO-35143-breakdown **TIGER RAG (Hold That Tiger!)**

CO-35143-breakdown **TIGER RAG (Hold That Tiger!)**

CO-35143-breakdown **TIGER RAG (Hold That Tiger!)**

CO-35143   **TIGER RAG (Hold That Tiger!)**
<pre>
   Issue:
        7" 33:   Phontastic (Sweden) MX-EPH84
</pre>

CO-35143-1 **TIGER RAG (Hold That Tiger!)**
<pre>
   Issues:
        10" 78s: Columbia (Brazil) 30-1302; CB-2.122
                       Columbia (Canada) A-31 (C6625)
                       Columbia (Japan) L3020, M555
                       Columbia (USA) C-113 (36922)
                       Odeon (France) 281786
                       Odeon (West Germany) O-28343
                       Parlophone (England) R-3022
                       Parlophone (Switzerland) PZ11155
        12" 78:   V-Disc (USA) 556
        7" 45:   Columbia (USA) 4-36922
        7" EP: Columbia (USA) B-113 (5-1200)
        10" 33s: Columbia (England) 33S1048
                       Columbia (France) FP1031
                       Columbia (USA) CL-2564, CL-6052
                       Fontana (England) TFR-6006, 662003TR
</pre>

```
        12" 33s:   CBS (The Netherlands) 52965
                   Columbia (USA) CJ-44292
                   Sunbeam (USA) SB-142-44, SB-143
        16" 33s:   AFRS (USA) BML P-? (SSL-2433); EN-12-2252, EN-12-2273
                   Department of State (USA) Notes On Jazz Program 11
     Compact Disc: Columbia (USA) CK-44292
     Cassettes: Columbia (USA) CJT-44292
                   Sunbeam (USA) SBC-143
```

CO-35143-breakdown **TIGER RAG (Hold That Tiger!)**

CO-35143-2 **TIGER RAG (Hold That Tiger!)**
  Issues:
```
     10" 78:    Columbia (USA) Test pressing
     12" 33s:   Blu-Disc (USA) T-1004
                Phontastic (Sweden) LV-50, NOST-7652
                Sony (Japan) 20AP-1810
```

CO-35144   **S-H-I-N-E**

CO-35144   **S-H-I-N-E**

CO-35144-breakdown **S-H-I-N-E**

CO-35144   **S-H-I-N-E**
  Issues:
```
      7" 33:    Phontastic (Sweden) XMAS MIX 1986
     12" 33:    Phontastic (Sweden) NOST-7661
```

CO-35144-1 **S-H-I-N-E**
  Issues:
```
     10" 78s:   Columbia (Argentina) 291726
                Columbia (Canada) A-31 (C6228)
                Columbia (USA) C-113 (36925)
                Parlophone (England) R-3002
                Parlophone (Finland) DPY1019
                Parlophone (Switzerland) PZ11099
     12" 78:    V-Disc (USA) 556
      7" 45:    Columbia (USA) 4-36925
      7" EPs:   Columbia (USA) B-113 (5-1200)
                Fontana (England) TFE-17184
     10" 33s:   Columbia (England) 33S1048
                Columbia (France) FP1031
                Columbia (USA) CL-2564, CL-6052
                Fontana (England) TFR-6006, 662003TR
     12" 33s:   CBS (The Netherlands) 52965
                Columbia (USA) CJ-44292, P4M-5678
                Phontastic (Sweden) NOST-7661
                Sony (Japan) 20AP-1810
                Sunbeam (USA) SB-142-44, SB-143
     16" 33s:   AFRS (USA) BML P-? (SSL-2433); EN-12-2252
                Department of State (USA) Notes On Jazz Program 11
     Compact Discs: Columbia (USA) CK-44292
                Phontastic (Sweden) PHONT-CD-7660
     Cassettes: Columbia (USA) CJT-44292
                Sunbeam (USA) SBC-143
```

CO-35144-breakdown **S-H-I-N-E**

CO-35144-2 **S-H-I-N-E**
   Issues:
     10" 78s: Columbia (Australia) DO-3142
                Columbia (USA) Test pressing
     12" 33s: Blu-Disc (USA) T-1004
                Phontastic (Sweden) NOST-7652

15Aug-13Sep45 Majestic studio, New York, New York
MAJESTIC RECORDING SESSION

BUD FREEMAN and his ORCHESTRA
Trumpet: Yank Lawson (John Lausen); Trombone: Mus. 2/C Louis McGarity; Clarinet: **Pvt. Michael (Peanuts) Hucko**; Tenor saxophone: Lawrence (Bud) Freeman; Piano: Gene Schroeder; **Guitar: S/Sgt. Carmen Mastren**; String Bass: Bob Haggart; Drums: Specs Powell; Vocalists: Thelma Carpenter, Delta Rhythm Boys

T555   **MY GUY'S COME BACK** (TC/DRB)
   Issue:
     10" 78:   Majestic (USA) 1017 (top billing "Thelma Carpenter")

T556   **THESE FOOLISH THINGS (Remind Me of You)** (TC)
   Issue:
     10" 78:   Majestic (USA) 1017 (top billing "Thelma Carpenter")

T557   **HURRY HOME** (TC/DRB)
   Issue:
     10" 78:   Majestic (USA) 1023 (top billing "Thelma Carpenter")

T558   **JUST A-SITTIN' AND A-ROCKIN'** (TC)
   Issue:
     10" 78:   Majestic (USA) 1023 (as "THELMA CARPENTER With Orchestra
                   Directed by Earl Sheldon")

15Aug-13Sep45 Majestic studio, New York, New York
MAJESTIC RECORDING SESSION

BUD FREEMAN and his ORCHESTRA
Trumpet: Yank Lawson (John Lausen); Trombone: Mus. 2/C Louis McGarity; Clarinet: Edmond Hall; Tenor saxophone: Lawrence (Bud) Freeman; Piano: Gene Schroeder; Guitar: **S/Sgt. Carmen Mastren**; String bass: Bob Haggart; Drums: **T/Sgt. Ray McKinley**

T559   **I'M JUST WILD ABOUT HARRY**
   Issues:
     10" 78:   Majestic (USA) 1031
     10" 33:   Allegro (USA) 4047
     12" 33:   Halo (USA) 50275

T560   **I GOT RHYTHM**
   Issue:
     10" 78:   Majestic (USA) 1018

T560-alt **I GOT RHYTHM**
   Issues:
     10" 33:   Allegro (USA) 4047
     12" 33:   Halo (USA) 50275

T561   **WHERE HAVE YOU BEEN?**
   Issues:
     10" 78:   Majestic (USA) 1018
     10" 33:   Allegro (USA) 4047

```
        12" 33:    Halo (USA) 50275

T562      OL' MAN RIVER
     Issues:
        10" 78:    Majestic (USA) Test pressing
        10" 33:    Allegro (USA) 4047
        12" 33:    Halo (USA) 50275
```

06Sep45 (Thu) 9:00-9:30PM   NBC, New York, New York
KRAFT MUSIC HALL broadcast Bing Crosby program
Guest artist: Sgt. Johnny Desmond

12Sep45 (Wed) Columbia studio, New York, New York
COLUMBIA RECORDING SESSION

BENNY GOODMAN AND HIS ORCHESTRA
Trumpets: Vince Badale, Gordon (Chris) Griffin, Tony Faso, Frank LePinto; Trombones: Sy
Shaeffer, Eddie Aulino, Chauncey Welsch; Clarinet: Benny Goodman; Alto saxophones: Hymie
Schertzer, Gerald (Jerry) Sanfino; Tenor saxophones: Bill Shine, Al Epstein; Baritone
saxophone: Danny Bank; Piano: **Pfc. Mel Powell**; Guitar: Mike Bryan; String bass: Clyde
Lombardi; Drums: Morey Feld; Vocalist: Liza Morrow

CO-35190-breakdown **MY GUY'S COME BACK** (LM)   (Mel Powell arrangement)

```
CO-35190-1  MY GUY'S COME BACK (LM)   (Mel Powell arrangement)
     Issues:
        12" 78:    V-Disc (USA) 585
        12" 33s:   CSP (USA) P5-15536 (P-15541)
                   Dan Records (Japan) VC-5022
                   Sunbeam (USA) SB-142-44, SB-143
        16" 33:    AFRS (USA) BML P-493
        Cassette:  Sunbeam (USA) SBC-143

CO-35190-2  MY GUY'S COME BACK (LM)   (Mel Powell arrangement)
     Issues:
        10" 78s:   Columbia (Brazil) 30-1184
                   Columbia (Canada) 766
                   Columbia (USA) 36874
                   Odeon (Spain) 204359
                   Parlophone (England) R-3000
                   Parlophone (Switzerland) PZ11097
                   Time-Life (USA) STBB-28-2
        12" 33s:   Franklin Mint (USA) FMRS-SOWW-2
                   History in Sound (USA) 1941
        Cassettes: Franklin Mint (USA) SOWW
                   Time-Life (USA) 4TBB-28
```

CO-35191   **THAT'S ALL THAT MATTERS TO ME** (LM)   (possibly Mel Powell arrangement)

CO-35191-breakdown **THAT'S ALL THAT MATTERS TO ME** (LM) (possibly Mel Powell arrangement)

CO-35191-breakdown **THAT'S ALL THAT MATTERS TO ME** (LM) (possibly Mel Powell arrangement)

```
CO-35191-1  THAT'S ALL THAT MATTERS TO ME (LM)   (possibly Mel Powell arrangement)
     Issues:
        10" 78:    Columbia (USA) Test pressing
        12" 33:    Nostalgia Book Club (USA) 1004 [CSP P3-13618 (CSP P-13615)]
```

CO-35191-2 **THAT'S ALL THAT MATTERS TO ME** (LM)   (possibly Mel Powell arrangement)
    Issues:
      10" 78:   Columbia (USA) Test pressing
      12" 33:   Phontastic (Sweden) NOST-7652

Prior to 15Sep45 Churchill Downs, Louisville, Kentucky
    POPS CONCERT
    Benny Goodman appeared as a classical soloist and jazz man. With him for the jazz
    portion of the program was **Pfc. Mel Powell**. The two staged a jam session that lasted
    far into the night. This was the largest crowd of the five weeks of concerts.

18Sep45 (Wed) New York, New York
    V-DISC RECORDING SESSION

MONICA LEWIS AND HER V-DISC FRIENDS
Trumpet and Director: Yank Lawson (John Lausen); Trombone: Vernon Brown; Clarinet: Bill
Stegmeyer; Tenor saxophone: Lawrence (Bud) Freeman; Piano: Howard Smith; Guitar: **S/Sgt.
Carmen Mastren**; String bass: Sam Fidel; Drums: Bob Dickerson; Vocalist: Monica Lewis

Unissued **MY HEART STOOD STILL** (ML)

Unissued **I'M AN OLD COWHAND** (From the Rio Grande) (ML)

Unissued **I'M AN OLD COWHAND** (From the Rio Grande) (ML)

VP-1565   **Spoken Introduction**
           MY HEART STOOD STILL (ML)
           I'M AN OLD COWHAND (From the Rio Grande) (ML)
    Issues:
      Spoken Introduction/MY HEART STOOD STILL
        12" 78:   V-Disc (USA) 560
        12" 33:   Elec (Japan) KV-111
      I'M AN OLD COWHAND (From the Rio Grande)
        12" 78:   V-Disc (USA) 560
        12" 33s: Dan Records (Japan) VC-5017
                    Elec (Japan) KV-111
                    Swing House (England) SWH-32

Unissued **WHEN DAY IS DONE** (ML)

Unissued **WHEN DAY IS DONE** (ML)

Unissued **WHEN DAY IS DONE** (ML)

18Sep45 (Wed) Columbia studio, New York, New York
    COLUMBIA RECORDING SESSION

BENNY GOODMAN SEXTET
Clarinet: Benny Goodman; Vibraphone: Red Norvo (Kenneth Norville); Piano: **Pfc. Mel
Powell**; Guitar: Mike Bryan; String bass: Slam Stewart; Drums: Morey Feld

CO-35206-1 **AIN'T MISBEHAVIN'**
    Issues:
      10" 78s: Columbia (Argentina) 291726
                   Columbia (Australia) DO-3142
                   Columbia (Brazil) 30-1276
                   Columbia (Canada) A-31 (C6225)
                   Columbia (USA) C-113 (36922)
                   Odeon (France) 281785
                   Odeon (Spain) 204344

```
                  Parlophone (England) R-3014
                  Parlophone (Switzerland) PZ11111
    7" 45:        Columbia (USA) 4-36922
    7" EP:        Columbia (USA) B-113 (5-1200)
   10" 33s:       Columbia (England) 33S1048
                  Columbia (France) FP1031
                  Columbia (Italy) QS6033
                  Columbia (USA) CL-2564, CL-6052
                  Fontana (England) TFR-6006, 662003TR
   12" 33s:       CBS (The Netherlands) 52965
                  Columbia (USA) CJ-44292, P4M-5678
                  Sony (Japan) 20AP-1810
   16" 33s:       AFRS (USA) EN-12-2273
                  Department of State (USA) Notes On Jazz Program 11
Compact Disc: Columbia (USA) CK-44292
Cassette:  Columbia (USA) CJT-44292
```

CO-35206-6 AIN'T MISBEHAVIN'
Issues:
```
    7" EP:     Phontastic (Sweden) BG NOST 86
    7" 33:     Phontastic (Sweden) MX-EPH85
```

CO-35207 I GOT RHYTHM
Issue:
```
    7" 33:     Phontastic (Sweden) MXEPH 87
```

CO-35207-1 I GOT RHYTHM
Issue:
```
   12" 33:     Phontastic (Sweden) NOST-7652
```

CO-35207-2 I GOT RHYTHM
Issues:
```
   10" 78s:    Columbia (Argentina) 291697
               Columbia (Australia) DO-3155
               Columbia (Canada) A-31 (C6226)
               Columbia (USA) C-113 (36923)
               Odeon (Spain) 184889
               Odeon (West Germany) O-28398
               Parlophone (England) R-3007
               Parlophone (Finland) DPY1070
               Parlophone (Switzerland) PZ11106
    7" 45:     Columbia (USA) 4-36923
    7" EP:     Columbia (USA) B-113 (5-1201)
   10" 33s:    Columbia (England) 33S1048
               Columbia (France) FP1031
               Columbia (Italy) QS6033
               Columbia (USA) CL-6052
               Fontana (England) TFR-6006, 662003TR
   12" 33s:    AFRS (USA) END-708-199
               Columbia (USA) CJ-44292
               Heritage (Japan) MFPL-82801-810 (MFPL-82804)
   16" 33:     AFRS (USA) EN-12-2273
Compact Discs: Columbia (USA) CK-44292
               Wave (Japan) MFPC-85634
Cassettes: ARC (Japan) SPC-23
               Columbia (USA) CJT-44292
```

XCO-35208-1 **I GOT RHYTHM**
  Issues:
    12" 78s: Columbia (Canada) 20511
                Columbia (Japan) SW282
                Columbia (USA) 55038
                V-Disc (USA) 601
    12" 33s: CBS (The Netherlands) 52965, CBS-21064
                CSP (USA) P5-15536 (P-15541)
                Columbia (USA) CJ-44292
                Sony (Japan) 20AP-1810
                Sunbeam (USA) SB-142-44, SB-143
    16" 33:   AFRS (USA) BML P-? (SSL-2433)
  Compact Disc: Columbia (USA) CK-44292
  Cassettes: CBS (The Netherlands) 40-21064
                Columbia (USA) CJT-44292
                Diskport (Japan) Unknown #
                Sunbeam (USA) SBC-143

24Sep45 (Mon) Columbia studio, New York, New York
COLUMBIA RECORDING SESSION

BENNY GOODMAN QUINTET
Clarinet: Benny Goodman; Vibraphone: Red Norvo (Kenneth Norville); Piano: **Pfc. Mel Powell**; Guitar: Mike Bryan; Drums: Morey Feld

CO-35234   **LIZA (All the Clouds'll Roll Away)**
  Issue:
    12" 33:   Blu-Disc (USA) T-1012

CO-35234   **LIZA (All the Clouds'll Roll Away)**
  Issue:
    12" 33:   Blu-Disc (USA) T-1012

CO-35234-1 **LIZA (All the Clouds'll Roll Away)**
  Issues:
    10" 78s: Columbia (England) DB-2287
                Columbia (Japan) M205
                Columbia (Norway) GNS-5082
                Columbia (Switzerland) DZ461
                Fontana (England) JAZ107
                Regal (Spain) C8787
    12" 78:   V-Disc (USA) 627
     7" 45s: Columbia (USA) G4-2 (4-14-G)
                Philips (England) 322212BF, JAZ 107 (362013)
     7" EPs: Columbia B-350 (5-1652)
                Philips (England) 429410BE, BBE12189
    12" 33s: CBS (England) 67268 (S-65039)
                CBS (The Netherlands) 52965, CBS-21064
                CBS Coronet (Australia) KLP675
                Columbia (England) 33SX1035
                Columbia (France) FPX-112
                Columbia (Japan) PL5004
                Columbia (USA) CJ-44292, GL-500, KG-31547 (C-31549), PG-31547 (C-31549),
                  P4M-5678
                Philips (England) B07225L, BBL7178
                Regal (Spain) 33LS1009
                RTB (Yugoslavia) LPV4316
                Sony (Japan) SOPM-162
                Sunbeam (USA) SB-142-44, SB-143
  Compact Disc: Columbia (USA) CK-44292

Cassettes: CBS (The Netherlands) 40-21064
          Columbia (USA) CJT-44292, GT-31547
          Diskport (Japan) Unknown #
          Sunbeam (USA) SBC-143

CO-35234-2 **LIZA (All the Clouds'll Roll Away)**
  Issues:
    10" 78:   Columbia (USA) DJ issue
    12" 33:   Phontastic (Sweden) NOST-7652

BENNY GOODMAN SEXTET
Clarinet: Benny Goodman; Vibraphone: Red Norvo (Kenneth Norville); Piano: **Pfc. Mel Powell**; Guitar: Mike Bryan; String bass: Slam Stewart; Drums: Morey Feld

CO-35234-breakdown **LIZA (All the Clouds'll Roll Away)**
  Issue:
    12" 33:   Blu-Disc (USA) T-1012

CO-35234 **LIZA (All the Clouds'll Roll Away)**
  Issue:
    12" 33:   Blu-Disc (USA) T-1012

CO-35234 **LIZA (All the Clouds'll Roll Away)**
  Issue:
    12" 33:   Blu-Disc (USA) T-1012

CO-35234-breakdown **LIZA (All the Clouds'll Roll Away)**
  Issue:
    12" 33:   Blu-Disc (USA) T-1012

CO-35234 **LIZA (All the Clouds'll Roll Away)**
  Issue:
    12" 33:   Blu-Disc (USA) T-1012

No matrix **MY DADDY ROCKS ME**

No matrix **MY DADDY ROCKS ME**
  Issues:
    12" 33:   Columbia (USA) CJ-44292
    Compact Disc: Columbia (USA) CK-44292
    Cassette: Columbia (USA) CJT-44292

CO-35235-1 **CHINA BOY**
  Issues:
    10" 78s: Columbia (Argentina) 291697
              Columbia (Brazil) 30-1302; CB-2.122
              Columbia (Canada) A-31 (C6227)
              Columbia (Japan) M555
              Columbia (USA) C-113 (36924)
              Odeon (France) 281785
              Odeon (Spain) 204344
              Parlophone (England) R-3014
              Parlophone (Finland) DPY1019
              Parlophone (Switzerland) PZ11111
    12" 78:   V-Disc 627 (vinyl)
    7" 45:   Columbia (USA) 4-36924
    7" EPs: Columbia (USA) B-113 (5-1201)
              Fontana (England) TFE-17184
    10" 33s: Columbia (England) 33S1048
              Columbia (France) FP1031

```
                    Columbia (USA) CL-2564, CL-6052
                    Fontana (England) TFR-6006, 662003TR
        12" 33s:    CBS (The Netherlands) 52965
                    Columbia (USA) CJ-44292, J2C-45037 (C-45038), P4M-5678
                    Sony (Japan) 20AP-1810
                    Sunbeam (USA) SB-142-44, SB-143
        16" 33:     AFRS (USA) EN-12-2252
        Compact Discs: Columbia (USA) CK-44292, G2K-45037 (CK-45038)
        Cassettes: Columbia (USA) CJT-44292, J2T-45037 (CT-45038)
                    Sunbeam (USA) SBC-143
```

CO-35235-2 **CHINA BOY**
   Issues:
```
        12" 78:     V-Disc (USA) 627 (shellac)
        12" 33:     Phontastic (Sweden) NOST-7652
```

BENNY GOODMAN AND HIS ORCHESTRA
Trumpets: Vince Badale, **Pvt. Bernie Privin**, Tony Faso, Frank LePinto; Trombones: Sy Shaeffer, Eddie Aulino, Tommy Reo; Clarinet: Benny Goodman; Alto saxophones: Hymie Schertzer, Gerald (Jerry) Sanfino; Tenor saxophones: Bill Shine, Al Epstein; Baritone saxophone: Danny Bank; Piano: **Pfc. Mel Powell**; Guitar: Mike Bryan; String bass: Clyde Lombardi; Drums: Morey Feld; Vocalist: Liza Morrow

CO-35236-1 **SYMPHONY** (LM)
   Issues:
```
        10" 78s:    Columbia (Brazil) 30-1184
                    Columbia (Canada) 766
                    Columbia (Mexico) 2071
                    Columbia (USA) 36874
        12" 78:     V-Disc 574
        12" 33s:    CSP (USA) 2P6264, 6P6465, P6-14954 (P-14955), PM-16932
                    Dan Records (Japan) VC-5022
                    Festival (England) 214
                    Heritage (Japan) MFPL-82801-810 (MFPL-82809)
                    Realm Records (USA) 2V-8065 (V2-8065)
                    Sunbeam (USA) SB-142-44, SB-143
        16" 33:     AFRS (USA) H-12-1184, H-12-2016
        Compact Disc:  Wave (Japan) MFPC-85639
        8-track:    CSP (USA) PA-14955
        Cassettes: ARC (Japan) SPC-26
                    CSP (USA) BMT-16932, BT-15899, BT-16932, PT-14955
                    Sunbeam (USA) SBC-143
```

CO-35236-2 **SYMPHONY** (LM)
   Issue:
```
        10" 78:     Columbia (USA) Test pressing
```

No matrix-breakdown **KING PORTER STOMP**

No matrix **KING PORTER STOMP**

No matrix **KING PORTER STOMP**

CO-35237 **LUCKY (You're Right - I'm Wrong)** (Eddie Sauter arrangement)

CO-35237 **LUCKY (You're Right - I'm Wrong)** (Eddie Sauter arrangement)

CO-35237 **LUCKY (You're Right - I'm Wrong)** (Eddie Sauter arrangement)

CO-35237-breakdown **LUCKY (You're Right - I'm Wrong)** (Eddie Sauter arrangement)

CO-35237-1 **LUCKY (You're Right - I'm Wrong)** (Eddie Sauter arrangement)
    Issues:
        10" 78:   Columbia (USA) Test pressing
        12" 33:   Nostalgia Book Club (USA) 1004 [CSP P3-13618 (CSP P-13615)]

CO-35237-2 **LUCKY (You're Right - I'm Wrong)** (Eddie Sauter arrangement)
    Issues:
        10" 78:   Columbia (USA) Test pressing
        12" 33:   Phontastic (Sweden) NOST-7652

29Sep45 (Sat) N.B.C., New York, New York
    Occasionally **Sgt. John M. Ferrier** and **Pvt. Michael (Peanuts) A. Hucko** and **the Miller string section** augmented the Slatkin reed and string sections on some of the Slatkin band's N.B.C. broadcasts. The Slatkin band was doing two (possibly three) broadcast series at this time:

        Possibly "AAF Scrapbook" 5:00-5:30PM CBS Friday broadcasts
            This series started on 18May45 and may have ended before 14Sep45.

        "Return to Duty" Tuesday broadcasts 18Sep-06Nov45

        "Your AAF" 1:30-2:00PM ABC Saturday broadcasts 15Sep-03Nov45

    It is not known on exactly which of the Slatkin broadcasts Sgt. Ferrier, Pvt. Hucko and the Miller string section performed.

29Sep-11Nov45 New York, New York
V-DISC RECORDING SESSION

    M/Sgt. Felix Slatkin and the 39th Army Air Forces Base Unit (Second Radio Unit) (AAFTC Orchestra)

    Unissued **WHEN JOHNNY COMES MARCHING HOME (The Crew Chiefs** and the Matt Dennis Quintet)
            (Matt Dennis arrangement)

c.Oct45 Paramount Theatre, New York, New York
Vic Schoen Band with the Andrews Sisters
    M/Sgt. Rubin (Zeke) Zarchy played (in uniform) in the Vic Schoen band for this two-week engagement.

Oct-Nov45 New York, New York
    CONCERT Paul Whiteman conducted an All-Soldier Band in a concert. Many of the musicians from the Glenn Miller Band, including **M/Sgt. Rubin (Zeke) Zarchy**, played in this concert.

c.Oct45 Majestic studio, New York, New York
MAJESTIC RECORDING SESSION

BUD FREEMAN and his ORCHESTRA
Trumpet: Yank Lawson (John Lausen); Trombone: Mus. 2/C Louis McGarity; Clarinet: Edmond Hall; Tenor saxophone: Lawrence (Bud) Freeman; Piano: Gene Schroeder; Guitar: S/Sgt. **Carmen Mastren**; String bass: Bob Haggart; Drums: **T/Sgt. Ray McKinley**, Vocalists: Five De Marco Sisters

T576   **FLAT RIVER, MISSOURI** (FDMS)
    Issue:
        10" 78:   Majestic (USA) 7160 (top billing "Five De Marco Sisters")

T577   **IT'S BEEN A LONG, LONG TIME** (FDMS)
  Issue:
    10" 78:   Majestic (USA) 7157 (top billing "The Five De Marco Sisters")

T579   **CHICO, CHICO (From Porto Rico)** (FDMS)
  Issues:
    10" 78:   Majestic (USA) 7157 (top billing "The Five De Marco Sisters")
    12" 33:   Halo (USA) 50275

BUD FREEMAN and RAY McKINLEY
Tenor saxophone: Lawrence (Bud) Freeman; Drums: **T/Sgt. Ray McKinley**

T580   **THE ATOMIC ERA**
  Issues:
    10" 78:   Majestic (USA) 1031
    10" 33:   Allegro (USA) 4047
    12" 33:   Savoy (USA) MG-12024

T580-alt **THE ATOMIC ERA**
  Issue:
    12" 33:   Halo (USA) 50275

04Oct45 (Thu) RCA Victor studio, New York, New York
V-DISC RECORDING SESSION

BUD FREEMAN AND THE V-DISC JUMPERS
Trumpet: Yank Lawson (John Lausen); Trombone: Cpl. Bill Mustarde; Clarinet: **Pvt. Michael (Peanuts) Hucko**; Tenor saxophone: Lawrence (Bud) Freeman; Piano: Sgt. Harold "Buddy" Weed; Guitar: **S/Sgt. Carmen Mastren**; String bass: **S/Sgt. Herman Trigger Alpert**; Drums: **T/Sgt. Ray McKinley**

VP-1550 XP-35170   **"THE LATEST THING IN HOT JAZZ"**
  Issues:
    12" 78:   V-Disc (USA) 555 (as "Eight Squares and a Critic")
    12" 33:   Bandstand (USA) 7106

VP-1595 D5TC-1428 **FOR MUSICIANS ONLY (A Musical Treatise on Jazz)**
  Issues:
    12" 78:   V-Disc (USA) 564
    12" 33s: Bandstand (USA) 7106
               Dan Records (Japan) VC-5028
               Swing House (England) SWH-32
    16" 33:   AFRS (USA) H-7-270
    Compact Disc: Jazz Road (Japan) BY28-12

NVP-1611 D5TC-1440 **LOVE IS JUST AROUND THE CORNER**
  Issues:
    12" 78:   V-Disc (USA) 588 (as "The V-Disc Jumpers")
    12" 33s: Dan Records (Japan) VC-5010
               Fonit Cetra (Italy) VDL-1005
               Jazz Society (Sweden) AA-511
               Swing House (England) SWH-32
    Compact Disc: Jazz Road (Japan) BY28-9

JDB-VP-1683 D5TC-1512 **COQUETTE**
  Issues:
    12" 78s: V-Disc (USA) VP-1683 test pressing, 740 (as "Bud Freeman and his Boys")
    12" 33s: Dan Records (Japan) VC-5010
               Swing House (England) SWH-32

12Oct45 (Fri) Columbia studio, 799 Seventh Avenue, New York, New York
 V-DISC RECORDING SESSION

BUDDY RICH AND HIS SPEED DEMONS
Trumpet: Charlie Shavers; Trombone: Robert Louis (Lou) McGarity; Clarinet: **Pvt. Michael
(Peanuts) Hucko**; Tenor saxophone: Al Sears; Piano: Harold (Buddy) Weed; Guitar: Remo
Palmieri; String bass: **S/Sgt. Herman Trigger Alpert**; Drums: Bernard (Buddy) Rich;
Vocalist: Ella Fitzgerald

Unissued   **I'LL SEE YOU IN MY DREAMS** (EF)

Unissued   **I'LL SEE YOU IN MY DREAMS** (EF)   (Breakdown)

Unissued   **I'LL SEE YOU IN MY DREAMS** (EF)

VP-1661 D5TC-1489 **I'LL SEE YOU IN MY DREAMS** (EF)
     Issues:
       12" 78:   V-Disc (USA) 730 (as "Ella Fitzgerald and her V-Disc Boys")
       12" 33s: Dan Records (Japan) VC-5014
                   Elec (Japan) KV-111
                   Fonit Cetra (Italy) VDL-1003
                   Jazz Society (Sweden) AA-511

VP-1599 D5TC-1430 **I'LL ALWAYS BE IN LOVE WITH YOU** (EF)
     Issues:
       12" 78:   V-Disc (USA) 569 (as "Ella Fitzgerald and her V-Disc Special Servers")
       12" 33s: Caracol (France) 423
                   Dan Records (Japan) VC-5014
                   Elec (Japan) KV-111
                   Fonit Cetra (Italy) VDL-1005
       16" 33:   AFRS (USA) H-7-270

VP-1596 D5TC-1422 **THAT'S RICH** (EF)
     Issues:
       12" 78:   V-Disc (USA) 603
       12" 33s: Black Jack (West Germany) LP-3008
                   Caracol (France) 423
                   Dan Records (Japan) VC-5014
                   Elec (Japan) KV-111
                   Hep (United Kingdom) HEP.12
                   Jazz Society (Sweden) AA-511
                   Redwood (Canada) 1001

Unissued   **OH, LADY BE GOOD!** (EF)

Mid-Oct45 RCA Victor studio, New York, New York
 V-DISC RECORDING SESSION

TRUMMY YOUNG AND HIS SPECIAL SERVERS
Trumpet: David (Roy) Eldridge; Trombone: James (Trummy) Young; Clarinet: Bill Stegmeyer;
Tenor saxophone: Nick Caiazza; Piano: Henry (Billy) Rowland; Guitar: Allan Hanlon;
String bass: **S/Sgt. Herman Trigger Alpert**; Drums: Gordon (Specs) Powell; Vocalists:
Martha Tilton, Jack Leonard

VP-1665 D5TC-1493 **TWO SLEEPY PEOPLE** (MT/JL)
     Issues:
       12" 78:   V-Disc (USA) 582
       12" 33:   Elec (Japan) KV-122

VP-1666 D5TC-1494 **TEA FOR TWO**
  Issues:
    12" 78:   V-Disc (USA) 603 (as "Bill Stegmeyer and his Hot Eight")
    12" 33s: Caracol (France) 426
               Dan Records (Japan) VC-5010
               Elec (Japan) KV-114
               Fonit Cetra (Italy) VDL 1008
               Jazz Society (Sweden) AA-511
               Swing House (England) SWH-34

VP-1667 D5TC-1495 **THANKS FOR THE MEMORY** (MT/JL)
  Issues:
    12" 78:   V-Disc (USA) 629
    12" 33s: Elec (Japan) KV-122
               Fonit Cetra (Italy) VDL-1003
               Swing House (England) SWH-34
  Compact Disc: Jazz Road (Japan) BY28-13

19Oct45 (Fri) New York, New York
RED BARBER'S PROGRAM broadcast
Guest artist: **Sgt. Johnny Desmond**
Autumn Serenade (JD)/It's Only a Paper Moon (JD)

22Oct45 (Mon) RCA Victor studio, New York, New York
V-DISC RECORDING SESSION

MUGGSY SPANIER AND HIS V-DISC JAZZ BAND
Cornet: Muggsy Spanier; Trombone: Mus. 2/C Louis McGarity; Clarinet: **Pvt. Michael
(Peanuts) Hucko**; Tenor saxophone: Lawrence (Bud) Freeman; Piano: Dave Bowman; Guitar: Hy
White; String bass: **S/Sgt. Herman Trigger Alpert**; Drums: George Wettling

NVP-1627 D5TC-1453 **TIN ROOF BLUES**
  Issues:
    12" 78:   V-Disc (USA) 588
    12" 33s: Connoisseur (England) CR-522
               Dan Records (Japan) VC-5008
               Elec (Japan) KV-121
               Everybody's (Sweden) 1020
               Fonit Cetra (Italy) CT.7197, VDL-1005
               Joker (Italy) SM-3575
               Saga (England) SAGA 6917
               Spook Jazz (England) 6603
               Swing House (England) SWH-32

NVP-1627 D5TC-1453 **CHERRY**
  Issues:
    12" 78:   V-Disc (USA) 588
    12" 33s: Connoisseur (England) CR-522
               Dan Records (Japan) VC-5008
               Elec (Japan) KV-121
               Everybody's (Sweden) 1020
               Fonit Cetra (Italy) VDL-1005
               Joker (Italy) SM-3575
               Saga (England) SAGA 6917
               Spook Jazz (England) 6603
               Swing House (England) SWH-32

Unissued   **ROYAL GARDEN BLUES** (Breakdown)

JDB-7   D6TC-5008   **ROYAL GARDEN BLUES**
   Issues:
     12" 78:   V-Disc (USA) 730
     12" 33s: Connoisseur (England) CR-522
                Dan Records (Japan) VC-5028
                Elec (Japan) KV-121
                Everybody's (Sweden) 1020
                Swing House (England) SWH-32

Unissued   **YOU TOOK ADVANTAGE OF ME** (Breakdown)

                     YOU TOOK ADVANTAGE OF ME
   Issue:
     12" 33:   IAJRC (USA) 51

JDB-295   D6TC-6465   **YOU TOOK ADVANTAGE OF ME**
   Issues:
     12" 78:   V-Disc (USA) 753
     12" 33s: Connoisseur (England) CR-522
                Elec (Japan) KV-121
                Everybody's (Sweden) 1020
                Swing House (England) SWH-32

Unissued   **CHINA BOY** (Breakdown)

Unissued   **CHINA BOY** (Breakdown)

                     CHINA BOY (Breakdown)
   Issue:
     12" 33:   IAJRC (USA) 51

JDB-VP-1668   D6TC-5053   **CHINA BOY**
   Issues:
     12: 78:   V-Disc (USA) 611
     12" 33s: Connoisseur (England) CR-522
                Dan Records (Japan) VC-5008
                Elec (Japan) KV-121
                Everybody's (Sweden) 1020
                Fonit Cetra (Italy) VDL-1008
                Redwood (Canada) 1001
                Sandy Hook (USA) SH-2072
                Sunbeam (USA) SB-231
                Swing House (England) SWH-32
     Compact Disc: Jazz Road (Japan) BY28-9
     Cassette: Sandy Hook (USA) CSH-2072

c.Oct-Nov45 New York, New York
MAJESTIC RECORDING SESSIONS

BUD FREEMAN and his ORCHESTRA
Trumpet: Yank Lawson (John Lausen); Trombone: Mus. 2/C Louis McGarity; Clarinet: Edmond Hall; Tenor saxophone: Lawrence (Bud) Freeman; Piano: Gene Schroeder; Guitar: **S/Sgt. Carmen Mastren**; String bass: Bob Haggart; Drums: **T/Sgt. Ray McKinley**, Vocalists: Five De Marco Sisters, Thelma Carpenter

T587   **HOP, SKIP AND JUMP!** (FDMS)
   Issues:
     10" 78s: Majestic (USA) Test pressing, 7160 (top billing "Five De Marco Sisters")
     12" 33:   Halo (USA) 50275

T588   **I DON'T KNOW WHY (I Just Do)** (FDMS)
    Issues:
       10" 78:   Majestic (USA) 7194 (top billing "The Five De Marco Sisters")
       12" 33:   Halo (USA) 50275

       I'LL TELL YOU HOW I FEEL (FDMS)
    Issues:
       10" 33:   Allegro (USA) 4047 (As "I'll Tell You")
       12" 33:   Halo (USA) 50275

       LOVE IS SUCH A CRAZY THING (FDMS)
    Issue:
       12" 33:   Halo (USA) 50275

T595   **BILL** (TC)
    Issue:
       10" 78:   Majestic (USA) 1028 (as "THELMA CARPENTER With Orchestra Directed by Earl
               Sheldon")

T597   **CAN'T HELP LOVIN' DAT MAN** (TC)
    Issue:
       10" 78:   Majestic (USA) 1028 (as "THELMA CARPENTER With Orchestra Directed by Earl
               Sheldon")

T630   **SWEET I'VE GOTTEN ON YOU (The Pennsylvania Dutch Song)** (FDMS)
    Issue:
       10" 78:   Majestic (USA) 7166 (top billing "The Five De Marco Sisters")

T631   **BLUE** (FDMS)
    Issue:
       10" 78:   Majestic (USA) 7166 (top billing "The Five De Marco Sisters")

T632   **HER MAJESTY'S DANCE**
    Issues:
       10" 78:   Majestic (USA) Test pressing
       10" 33:   Allegro (USA) 4047

Late-Oct45 NBC studio, New York, New York
V-DISC RECORDING SESSION

ROY ELDRIDGE AND HIS V-DISC LITTLE JAZZ BAND
Trumpet: David (Roy) Eldridge; Trombone: Mort Bullman; Clarinet: Ernesto (Ernie)
Caceres; Tenor saxophone: Nick Caiazza; Piano: Henry (Billy) Rowland; Guitar: Allan
Hanlon; String bass: **S/Sgt. Herman Trigger Alpert**; Drums: Gordon (Specs) Powell

JDB-VP-1703 D5TC-1536 **ROY MEETS HORN**
    Issues:
       12" 78:   V-Disc (USA) 612
       12" 33s: Caracol (France) 426
                Dan Records (Japan) VC-5028
                Elec (Japan) KV-114
                Joker (Italy) SM-3119

VP-1706 B-44515 **OLD ROB ROY**
    Issues:
       12" 78:   V-Disc (USA) 605
       12" 33s: Caracol (France) 426
                Dan Records (Japan) VC-5028
                Elec (Japan) KV-114
                Fonit Cetra (Italy) VDL-1007

Jazz Society (Sweden) AA-511
Joker (Italy) SM-3119

JDB-187 D6TC-6031 **I'VE FOUND A NEW BABY**
    Issues:
      12" 78:   V-Disc (USA) 713
      12" 33s: Dan Records (Japan) VC-5010
                   Elec (Japan) KV-114
                   Fonit Cetra (Italy) VDL-1007

  J-610 USS-1040 **TEA FOR TWO**
  Unissued

04Nov45 (Sun) 4:30-5:00PM **WEAF NBC,** New York, New York
THE RCA VICTOR PROGRAM broadcast
Jay Blackton and his orchestra and chorus
Host: Tommy Dorsey
Guest artists: **Sgt. Johnny Desmond** and the Phil Moore Four
I'VE GOT YOU UNDER MY SKIN (JD/Chorus) (Jay Blackton Orchestra)/SYMPHONY (JD-French and English) (Jay Blackton Orchestra)/HOW DEEP IS THE OCEAN (How High Is the Sky) (JD/Phil Moore Four/Tommy Dorsey trombone solo/chorus) (Jay Blackton Orchestra)

    Issues:
      I'VE GOT YOU UNDER MY SKIN
        16" 33:   AFRS (USA) Music America Loves Best 74-Part 1
      SYMPHONY
        16" 33:   AFRS (USA) Music America Loves Best 74-Part 2
      HOW DEEP IS THE OCEAN (How High Is the Sky)
        16" 33:   AFRS (USA) Music America Loves Best 74-Part 2

18Nov45 (Sun) 4:30-5:00PM **WEAF NBC,** New York, New York
THE RCA VICTOR PROGRAM broadcast
Jay Blackton and his orchestra and chorus
Host: Tommy Dorsey
Guest artist: Sgt. Johnny Desmond

GLENN MILLER ARMY AIR FORCE BAND

SIDEMEN RECORDS AND TAPES

This section is a listing of the recordings made by members of Glenn Miller's Army Air Force Band while they were members of or still attached to the band.

ORGANIZATION

This listing is arranged alphabetically by label name. Each label is segregated by type of issue (e.g. 10" 78s, 12" 33s, etc.). The first column is the issue number. A non-bold first column issue number indicates that I have that issue. A **bold** first column issue number indicates that I do not have that particular issue.

If a record (or tape) is part of a set and the individual record (or tape) issue number is not an extension of the set number, the set number follows the record (or tape) issue number and the set number is printed in **bold**. If a record (or tape) is part of a set and the individual record (or tape) number is an extension of the set number, the set number is shown in the issue number column and the individual record (or tape) issue numbers are indented beneath the set number.

For abbreviations see the abbreviations listing at the beginning of this Appendix.

AFFINITY   England   12" 33s
  BOX 107   DJANGO DJANGO REINHARDT 8LP set
    BOX 107-13/14 DJANGO REINHARDT & THE GLENN MILLER ALL STARS: If Dreams Come True;
        Stompin' at the Savoy; Hallelujah; How High the Moon

AFRTS   USA   12" 33
  END-708-198/199 THE SWINGIN' YEARS Chuck Cecil
    END-708-199 BENNY GOODMAN SEXTET: I Got Rhythm

AFRS   USA   16" 33s

  BASIC MUSICAL LIBRARY Series P-
    P-493   BENNY GOODMAN AND HIS ORCHESTRA: My Guy's Come Back
    P-? (SSL-2433) BENNY GOODMAN SEXTET: Tiger Rag; Shine; I Got Rhythm

  DOWNBEAT   Series H-7
    H-7-270   BUD FREEMAN AND THE V-DISC JUMPERS: For Musicians Only (A Musical Treatise
        on Jazz); ELLA FITZGERALD AND HER V-DISC SPECIAL SERVERS: I'll Always Be in
        Love with You

  G.I. JIVE Series H-12 (EN-12)
    H-12-1183/1184 1184 BENNY GOODMAN AND HIS ORCHESTRA: Symphony
    H-12-2015/2016 2016 BENNY GOODMAN AND HIS ORCHESTRA: Symphony
    EN-12-2252 BENNY GOODMAN SEXTET: Tiger Rag; Shine; China Boy
    EN-12-2273 BENNY GOODMAN SEXTET: Tiger Rag; Ain't Misbehavin'; I Got Rhythm

  MUSIC AMERICA LOVES BEST   No series number   Single-sided pressings
    74-Part 1 I've Got You under My Skin (4Nov45) (Johnny Desmond with Jay Blackton
        Orchestra)
    74-Part 2 Symphony (4Nov45) (Johnny Desmond with Jay Blackton Orchestra); How Deep Is
        the Ocean? (4Nov45) (Johnny Desmond with Jay Blackton Orchestra, Phil Moore
        Four and Tommy Dorsey)

ALLEGRO   USA   10" 33
  4047   BUD FREEMAN --- TENOR SAX AND ORCHESTRA
    I Got Rhythm; Ol' Man River; I'm Just Wild about Harry; Where Have You
    Been. The Atomic Era; Her Majesty's Dance; I'll Tell You

ARC   Japan   Cassettes
  SPC-23   BIG BAND HIT SERIES 23   BENNY GOODMAN: I Got Rhythm
  SPC-26   BIG BAND HIT SERIES 26   BENNY GOODMAN: Symphony

AVAN-GUARD MUSIC   Australia   12" 33
  BVL 046   "PARIS 1945" DJANGO REINHARDT WITH THE GLENN MILLER'S ALL STARS
    THE RAY McKINLEY TRIO - MEL POWELL   = CBS (France) 63052

BANDSTAND RECORDS   USA   12" 33
  7106   SCREWBALLS IN SWINGTIME
    BUD FREEMAN'S V-DISCERS: For Musicians Only;
    EIGHT SQUARES & A CRITIC: Latest Thing in Hot Jazz

BARCLAY   France   12" 33s
  81.004/05 LE JAZZ PARISIEN.....LIBERE
    81.004   EDDIE BARCLAY: Rosetta; One O'Clock Jump

BLACK JACK   West Germany   12" 33
  LP-3008   THAT'S RICH BUDDY RICH AND HIS ORCHESTRA
    That's Rich

BLU-DISC   **USA**   **12" 33s**
T-1004   THE UN-HEARD BENNY GOODMAN VOLUME TWO   Tiger Rag; Shine
T-1012   BENNY GOODMAN QUINTET: Liza; Liza; BENNY GOODMAN SEXTET: Liza-breakdown;
            Liza; Liza; Liza-breakdown; Liza

BLUE STAR   **France**   **10" 78s**
  1   EDDIE BARCLAY: You Belong to Me; Body and Soul
  2   EDDIE BARCLAY: Rosetta; One O'Clock Jump
  3   BLUE STAR SWING BAND: (Blues for Sale); I Got Rhythm
 11   ARTHUR BRIGGS: Briggs Boogie; When the Saints Go Marching in
 13   EDDIE BARCLAY: I'll Walk Alone; A Lovely Way to Spend an Evening
 14   EDDIE BARCLAY: Goodnight wherever You Are; Paper Doll

CARACOL   **France**   **12" 33s**
 423   ALL STAR JAM SESSIONS - VOLUME 1 1944/1945
              BUDDY RICH: That's Rich; I'll Always Be in Love with You
 426   JAM SESSIONS - VOLUME 2 1943/1945
              ROY ELDRIDGE: Roy Meets Horn; BILL STEGMEYER: Tea for Two; ROY ELDRIDGE:
              Old Rob Roy

CBS   **Brazil**   **12" 33s**
 159024/25 50 YEARS OF JAZZ GUITAR   2LP set
  159025   JAZZ CLUB MYSTERY HOT BAND: If Dreams Come True

CBS   **England**   **12" 33s**
 67268   ALL-TIME GREATEST HITS - BENNY GOODMAN   2LP set   (S-65039)
 88061   A JAZZ PIANO ANTHOLOGY   2LP set   (M-80244)
 88225   50 YEARS OF JAZZ GUITAR   2LP set   (M-CBS-81827)
 M-80244   **88061** MEL POWELL: For Miss Black
 M-CBS-81827 **88225** JAZZ CLUB MYSTERY HOT BAND: If Dreams Come True
 S-65039   **67268** Benny Goodman Quintet: Liza (All the Clouds'll Roll Away)

CBS   **France**   **12" 33s**
 63052   "PARIS 1945" DJANGO REINHARDT WITH THE GLENN MILLER'S ALL STARS
            THE RAY McKINLEY TRIO - MEL POWELL
              If Dreams Come True; Stompin' at the Savoy; Hallelujah; How High the
              Moon; Hommage A Fats Waller; Hommage A Debussy. After You've Gone;
              Shoemaker's Apron; China Boy; Sugar; Don't Blame Me; Poor Miss Black
 63130   JAZZMEN IN UNIFORM PARIS 1945
              Please Don't Talk about Me; Pennies from Heaven; Blue Skies; One, Two,
              Button Your Shoe; On the Sunny Side of the Street; Red Light. Somedays
              Sweetheart; S'Wonderful [actually "You're Driving Me Crazy! (What Did I
              Do?)"]; I Must Have that Man; At Sundown; Stealin' Apples; You're Driving
              Me Crazy (actually "'S Wonderful")
 64946   **67257** MEL POWELL: For Miss Black
 67257   A JAZZ PIANO ANTHOLOGY 2LP set   (64946)

CBS   **The Netherlands**   **12" 33s**
 52965   BENNY GOODMAN 1945 SEXTET, QUINTET & TRIO JAZZ PARTY 21
              Tiger Rag; Shine; Ain't Misbehavin'; I Got Rhythm; Liza; China Boy
 63052   "PARIS 1945" DJANGO REINHARDT WITH THE GLENN MILLER'S ALL STARS
            THE RAY McKINLEY TRIO - MEL POWELL   = CBS (France) 63052
 64946   **S 67257** MEL POWELL: For Miss Black
 CBS-21064 BENNY GOODMAN PLAYS GERSHWIN   I Got Rhythm (1); Liza (1)
 S 67257   A JAZZ PIANO ANTHOLOGY 2LP set   (64946)

CBS   **The Netherlands**   **Cassette**
 40-21064   BENNY GOODMAN PLAYS GERSHWIN   = CBS-21064 (12" 33)

CBS CORONET	Australia	12" 33
KLP675	BENNY GOODMAN QUINTET: Liza	

COLUMBIA	Argentina	10" 78s
291697	SEXTETO BENNY GOODMAN: Tengo Ritmo (I Got Rhythm);	
	Muchacho Chino (China Boy)	
291726	BENNY GOODMAN SEXTET: Shine; Ain't Misbehavin'	

COLUMBIA	Australia	10" 78s
DO-3142	BENNY GOODMAN SEXTET: Shine; Ain't Misbehavin'	
DO-3155	BENNY GOODMAN SEXTET: I Got Rhythm	

COLUMBIA	Brazil	10" 78s
30-1184	BENNY GOODMAN AND HIS ORCHESTRA: Symphony; My Guy's Come Back	
30-1276	BENNY GOODMAN SEXTET: Ain't Misbehavin'	
30-1302	SEXTETO BENNY GOODMAN: O Passo do Tigre (Tiger Rag);	
	Menino de Porcelana (China Boy)	
CB-2.122	BENNY GOODMAN SEXTET: Tiger Rag; China Boy	

COLUMBIA	Canada	10" 78s
766	BENNY GOODMAN SEXTET: My Guy's Come Back;	
	BENNY GOODMAN AND HIS ORCHESTRA: Symphony	
A-31	BENNY GOODMAN SEXTET SESSION 4-record set	C6225/6/7/8
C6225	A-31 BENNY GOODMAN SEXTET: Tiger Rag; Ain't Misbehavin'	
C6226	A-31 BENNY GOODMAN SEXTET: I Got Rhythm	
C6227	A-31 BENNY GOODMAN SEXTET: China Boy	
C6228	A-31 BENNY GOODMAN SEXTET: Shine	

COLUMBIA	Canada	12" 78
20511	BENNY GOODMAN SEXTET: I Got rhythm	

COLUMBIA	Canada		12" 33s
KG-32355	A JAZZ PIANO ANTHOLOGY	2LP set	MEL POWELL: For Miss Black

COLUMBIA	England	10" 78
DB-2287	BENNY GOODMAN SEXTET: Liza	

COLUMBIA	England	10" 33
33S1048	SESSION FOR SEXTET BENNY GOODMAN SEXTET	
	Tiger Rag; Ain't Misbehavin'; I Got Rhythm. China Boy; Shine	

COLUMBIA (EPIC)	England	12" 33
33SX1035	BENNY GOODMAN QUINTET: Liza	

COLUMBIA	France	10" 33
FP1031	BENNY GOODMAN SEXTET	
	Tiger Rag; Ain't Misbehavin'; I Got Rhythm. China Boy; Shine	

COLUMBIA	France	12" 33
FPX-112	BENNY GOODMAN QUINTET: Liza	

COLUMBIA	Italy	10" 33
QS6033	BENNY GOODMAN SEXTET: Ain't Misbehavin'; I Got Rhythm	

COLUMBIA	Japan	10" 78s
L3020	BENNY GOODMAN SEXTET: Tiger Rag	
M205	BENNY GOODMAN QUINTET: Liza (All the Clouds'll Roll Away)	
M555	BENNY GOODMAN SEXTET: Tiger Rag; China Boy	

COLUMBIA   Japan   12" 78
  SW282   BENNY GOODMAN SEXTET: I Got Rhythm

COLUMBIA   Japan   12" 33
  PL5004   BENNY GOODMAN QUINTET: Liza (All the Clouds'll Roll Away)

COLUMBIA   Mexico   10" 78
  2071   BENNY GOODMAN AND HIS ORCHESTRA: Symphony

COLUMBIA   Norway   10" 78
  GNS-5082   BENNY GOODMAN'S SEKTETT: Liza

COLUMBIA   Switzerland   10" 78
  DZ461   BENNY GOODMAN QUINTET: Liza

COLUMBIA   USA   10" 78s
  36874   BENNY GOODMAN AND HIS ORCHESTRA: My Guy's Come Back; Symphony
  36922   C-113   BENNY GOODMAN SEXTET: Tiger Rag; Ain't Misbehavin'
  36923   C-113   BENNY GOODMAN SEXTET: I Got Rhythm
  36924   C-113   BENNY GOODMAN SEXTET: China Boy
  36925   C-113   BENNY GOODMAN SEXTET: Shine
  C-113   BENNY GOODMAN SEXTET SESSION 4-record set   36922/3/4/5
  CO-35143-2 BENNY GOODMAN SEXTET: Tiger Rag   Single-sided test pressing
  CO-35144-2 BENNY GOODMAN SEXTET: Shine   Single-sided test pressing
  CO-35191-1 BENNY GOODMAN AND HIS ORCHESTRA: That's All that Matters
                                                        Single-sided test pressing
  CO-35191-2 BENNY GOODMAN AND HIS ORCHESTRA: That's All that Matters
                                                        Single-sided test pressing
  CO-35234-2 DJ issue BENNY GOODMAN QUINTET: Liza (All the Clouds'll Roll Away);
             (Slipped Disc)
  CO-35236-2 BENNY GOODMAN AND HIS ORCHESTRA: Symphony Single-sided test pressing
  CO-35237-1 BENNY GOODMAN AND HIS ORCHESTRA:
             Lucky (You're Right - I'm Wrong)   Single-sided test pressing
  CO-35237-2 BENNY GOODMAN AND HIS ORCHESTRA:
             Lucky (You're Right - I'm Wrong)   Single-sided test pressing

COLUMBIA   USA   12" 78
  55038   BENNY GOODMAN SEXTET: I Got Rhythm

COLUMBIA   USA   7" 45s
  4-14-G   G 4-2   BENNY GOODMAN QUINTET: Liza (All the Clouds'll Roll Away)
  4-36922   BENNY GOODMAN SEXTET: Tiger Rag; Ain't Misbehavin'
  4-36923   BENNY GOODMAN SEXTET: I Got Rhythm
  4-36924   BENNY GOODMAN SEXTET: China Boy
  4-36925   BENNY GOODMAN SEXTET: Shine
  G 4-2   BENNY GOODMAN COMBOS Set, includes 4-14-G

COLUMBIA   USA   7" 45s (EPs)
  5-1200   B-113 BENNY GOODMAN SEXTET: Tiger Rag; Ain't Misbehavin'. Shine
  5-1201   B-113 BENNY GOODMAN SEXTET: I Got Rhythm. China Boy
  5-1652   B-350 BENNY GOODMAN SEXTET: Liza
  B-113   BENNY GOODMAN SEXTET SESSION 2EP set   5-1200, 5-1201
  B-350   THE GOLDEN ERA SERIES PRESENTS BENNY GOODMAN COMBOS 3EP set   5-1652

COLUMBIA   USA   10" 33s
  CL-2564   THE B.G. SIX   BENNY GOODMAN SEXTET
             Tiger Rag; Ain't Misbehavin'. China Boy; Shine
  CL-6052   BENNY GOODMAN SEXTET
             Tiger Rag; Ain't Misbehavin'; I Got Rhythm. China Boy; Shine

```
COLUMBIA                              USA                                    12" 33s
  2P6264      BENNY GOODMAN: Symphony
  6P6465      BENNY GOODMAN: Symphony
  C-31549     KG-31547 and PG-31547              BENNY GOODMAN QUINTET: Liza
  C-32356     KG-32355 and PG-32355                  MEL POWELL: For Miss Black
  C-33568     CG-33566             JAZZ CLUB MYSTERY HOT BAND: If Dreams Come True
  CG-33566    50 YEARS OF JAZZ GUITAR   2LP set                          (C-33568)
  CG-33566-DJ 50 YEARS OF JAZZ GUITAR   2LP set                          (C-33568)
  CJ-44292    BENNY GOODMAN SEXTET  SLIPPED DISC, 1945-1946
                Tiger Rag (-1); Shine (-1).  Ain't Misbehavin' (-1); I Got Rhythm
                (CO.35207-2); I Got Rhythm (XCO.35208-1); Liza (-1); My Daddy Rocks Me;
                China Boy (-1)
  GL-500      THE GOLDEN ERA SERIES PRESENTS BENNY GOODMAN COMBOS
                BENNY GOODMAN SEXTET: Liza
  J2C-45037   THE JAZZ MASTERS  2LP set
   C-45038     Sides 1/2                    BENNY GOODMAN SEXTET: China Boy (-1)
  KG-31547    ALL-TIME GREATEST HITS  BENNY GOODMAN  2LP set              (C-31549)
  KG-32355    A JAZZ PIANO ANTHOLOGY    2LP set                          (C-32356)
  P4M-5678    4LP set
                BENNY GOODMAN SEXTET: Shine; Ain't Misbehavin'; Liza; China Boy
  P3-13618 (P-13615/6/7)  See: NOSTALGIA BOOK CLUB (USA) 1004  3LP set
  P6-14954 (CSP)  BIG BAND BASH  6LP set
   P-14955     BENNY GOODMAN AND HIS ORCHESTRA: Symphony
  P5-15536 (CSP)  THE LEGENDARY BENNY GOODMAN  5LP set  (Publishers Central Bureau)
   P-15541     BENNY GOODMAN AND HIS ORCHESTRA: My Guy's Come Back;
                BENNY GOODMAN SEXTET: I Got Rhythm
  PG-31547    ALL-TIME GREATEST HITS  BENNY GOODMAN  2LP set              (C-31549)
  PG-32355    A JAZZ PIANO ANTHOLOGY    2LP set                          (C-32356)
  PM-16932 (CSP)  THE "MUSIC OF YOUR LIFE"  BENNY GOODMAN & HIS ORCHESTRA   Symphony

COLUMBIA                              USA                              Compact Discs
  CK-44292    BENNY GOODMAN SEXTET  SLIPPED DISC, 1945-1946    = CJ-44292 (12" 33)
  G2K-45037   THE JAZZ MASTERS  2CD set
   CK-45038    Disc 1                       BENNY GOODMAN SEXTET: China Boy (-1)

COLUMBIA                              USA                                    8-tracks
  PA-14955/6/7 (CSP)  BIG BAND BASH  3 8-track set
   PA-14955 (Volume One)  BENNY GOODMAN AND HIS ORCHESTRA: Symphony

COLUMBIA                              USA                                    Cassettes
  BMT-16932 (CSP)  THE "MUSIC OF YOUR LIFE"  BENNY GOODMAN & HIS ORCHESTRA   Symphony
  BT-15899 (CSP)  BENNY GOODMAN  "CLARINET A LA KING"                      Symphony
  BT-16932 (CSP)  BENNY GOODMAN & HIS ORCHESTRA                            Symphony
  CGT-33566    50 YEARS OF JAZZ GUITAR      JAZZ CLUB MYSTERY HOT BAND: If Dreams Come True
  CJT-44292    BENNY GOODMAN SEXTET  SLIPPED DISC, 1945-1946    = CJ-44292 (12" 33)
  GT-31547    ALL-TIME GREATEST HITS  BENNY GOODMAN
                BENNY GOODMAN QUINTET: Liza (All the Clouds'll Roll Away)
  J2T-45037   THE JAZZ MASTERS  2-Cassette set
   CT-45038     Cassette 1                   BENNY GOODMAN SEXTET: China Boy (-1)
  PT-14955/6/7 (CSP)  BIG BAND BASH  3-Cassette set
   PT-14955 (Volume One)  BENNY GOODMAN AND HIS ORCHESTRA: Symphony

CONNOISSEUR                          England                                  12" 33
  CR-522      MUGGSY SPANIER  THE V-DISCS
                Royal Garden Blues; You Took Advantage of Me; China Boy; Tin Roof Blues.
                Cherry

CUPOL                                Sweden                                   10" 78
  4063        HOT TRIO RAY MacKINLEY: After You've Gone; China Boy
```

DAN RECORDS	Japan	12" 33s

VC-5008   TRADITIONAL JAZZ ON V-DISC
      MUGGSY SPANIER: China Boy; Tin Roof Blues; Cherry
VC-5010   52nd STREET SCENE 1943-47 V-DISC ALL STAR JAZZ SESSIONS Vol.1
      BILL STEGMEYER & HIS HOT EIGHT: Tea for Two;
      ROY ELDRIDGE AND HIS ORCH.: I've Found a New Baby;
      BUD FREEMAN AND THE V-DISC JUMPERS: Coquette;
      THE V-DISC JUMPERS: Love Is Just Around the Corner
VC-5014   BILLIE HOLIDAY ELLA FITZGERALD SARAH VAUGHAN
      THE GREAT LADIES ON V-DISC, Vol. 1
      ELLA FITZGERALD: I'll Always Be in Love with You; I'll See You in My
      Dreams; That's Rich
VC-5017   THE FAVORITE POP SONGS OF THE '40's   MONICA LEWIS: I'm an Old Cow-Hand
VC-5022   BENNY GOODMAN ON V-DISC, Vol. 2   Symphony; My Guy's Come Back
VC-5028   V-DISC CATS PARTY V-DISC ALL-STAR JAM SESSIONS Vol.5
      ROY ELDRIDGE & HIS V-DISCATTERS: Old Rob Roy;
      ROY ELDRIDGE & HIS V-DISC LITTLE JAZZ BAND: Roy Meets Horn.
      BUD FREEMAN & THE V-DISC JUMPERS: For Musicians Only;
      MUGGSY SPANIER & HIS BAND: Royal Garden Blues

DEPARTMENT OF STATE	USA	16" 33

NOTES ON JAZZ Program 11 BENNY GOODMAN SEXTET: Tiger Rag; Shine; Ain't Misbehavin'

DISKPORT	Japan	Cassettes

Unknown #   MUSIC BLEND BENNY GOODMAN SP COLLECTION 4-Cassette set
   Volume 3   Liza (CO-35234-1)
   Volume 4   I Got Rhythm (XCO-35208-1)

ELEC	Japan	12" 33s

KV-111   BUDDY RICH: That's Rich; I'll Always Be in Love with You; I'll See You in
      My Dreams; MONICA LEWIS: Spoken Introduction/My Heart Stood Still/I'm an
      Old Cowhand
KV-114   V-DISC JAZZ SESSIONS VOL. 2
      BILL STEGMEYER & HIS HOT EIGHT: Tea for Two;
      ROY ELDRIDGE & HIS V-DISCATTERS: Old Rob Roy;
      ROY ELDRIDGE & HIS ORCH.: I've Found a New Baby;
      ROY ELDRIDGE & HIS V-DISC LITTLE JAZZ BAND: Roy Meets Horn
KV-121   DIXIELAND HORN/MUGGSY SPANIER
      China Boy; You Took Advantage of Me; Tin Roof Blues; Cherry; Royal Garden
      Blues
KV-122   MARTHA TILTON: Two Sleepy People; Thanks for the Memory

ESQUIRE	England	10" 78s

10-043   GLENN MILLER'S UPTOWN HALL GANG: How High the Moon; Stomping at the Savoy
      Two copies, different printing
10-053   GLENN MILLER'S UPTOWN HALL GANG:
      Please Don't Talk about Me When I'm Gone; Someday Sweetheart
10-070   RAY McKINLEY TRIO: Sugar; After You've Gone
10-086   MEL POWELL: For Miss Black; Don't Blame Me
10-087   GLENN MILLER'S UPTOWN HALL GANG: If Dreams Come True; Blue Skies
10-097   GLENN MILLER'S UPTOWN HALL GANG: I Must Have that Man; S'Wonderful
10-149   GLENN MILLER'S UPTOWN HALL GANG: Pennies from Heaven; At Sundown
10-150   RAY McKINLEY TRIO: Shoemaker's Apron; China Boy
10-199   MEL POWELL: Homage to 'Fats' Waller; Homage to Debussy
10-209   GLENN MILLER'S UP-TOWN HALL GANG:
      You're Driving Me Crazy; On the Sunny Side of the Street
10-240   GLENN MILLER'S UP-TOWN HALL GANG:
      One, Two, Button Your Shoe; Stealin' Smack's Apples
10-243   GLENN MILLER'S UP-TOWN HALL GANG: Hallelujah; Red Light

ESQUIRE   England   7" 45s (EPs)
  EP-180   MILLERMEN IN TOWN! RAY McKINLEY TRIO
              After You've Gone; Sugar. Shoemaker's Apron; China Boy
  EP-199   THE IMPECCABLE   MEL POWELL
              Homage to Fats; Homage to Debussy. Don't Blame Me; For Miss Black

ESQUIRE   England   12" 33s
  ESQ-302   GLENN MILLER UP TOWN HALL GANG
              How High the Moon; If Dreams Come True; Beatin' Those Hallelujah Drums;
              Stompin' at the Savoy; I Must Have That Man; Please Don't Talk about Me
              When I'm Gone; 'Swonderful; Someday Sweetheart. Blue Skies; Red Light;
              You're Driving Me Crazy; On the Sunny Side of the Street; Pennies from
              Heaven; One, Two, Button Your Shoe; At Sundown; Stealin' Smack's Apples
  ESQ-304   I LOVE A PIANO
              MEL POWELL: Homage to Fats; Homage to Debussy; For Miss Blanc; Don't
              Blame Me

EVERYBODY'S   Sweden   12" 33
  1020   MUGGSY SPANIER ON V-DISC 1944-45
              Tin Roof Blues; Cherry; China Boy; Royal Garden Blues; You Took Advantage
              of Me

FESTIVAL   England   12" 33
  214   BENNY GOODMAN AND HIS ORCHESTRA: Symphony

FONIT CETRA (V-DISC)   Italy   12" 33s
  CT-7196   GLI ANNI D'ORO DELLA MUSICA AMERICANA
              MUGGSY SPANIER AND HIS V-DISC DIXIELANDERS: Tin Roof Blues
  VDL-1003 LE VOCI INDIMENTICABILI VOL. 1
              MARTHA TILTON & JACK LEONARD WITH THEIR SPECIAL SERVICERS FEATURING
              TRUMMY YOUNG: Thanks for the Memory; ELLA FITZGERALD AND HER V-DISC BOYS:
              I'll See You in My Dreams
  VDL-1005 LE STELLE DEL JAZZ VOL. 1
              ELLA FITZGERALD ACC. BY ELLA FITZGERALD V-DISC JUMPERS: I'll Always Be in
              Love with You; THE V-DISC JUMPERS: Love Is Just Around the Corner; MUGGSY
              SPANIER AND HIS V-DISC DIXIELANDERS: Tin Roof Blues; Cherry
  VDL-1007 GRANDI SOLISTI VOL. 1
              ROY ELDRIDGE AND HIS DISCATTERS: Old Rob Roy;
              ROY ELDRIDGE AND HIS ORCHESTRA: I've Found a New Baby
  VDL-1008 GRANDI SOLISTI VOL. 2
              MUGGSY SPANIER AND HIS V-DISC JAZZ BAND: China Boy.
              BILL STEGMEYER AND HIS HOT EIGHT: Tea for Two

FONTANA   England   10" 78
  JAZ107   BENNY GOODMAN QUINTET: Liza

FONTANA   England   7" 45 (EP)
  TFE-17184 BENNY GOODMAN SEXTET: Shine; China Boy

FONTANA   England   10" 33
  TFR-6006 BENNY GOODMAN SEXTET
              Tiger Rag; Ain't Misbehavin'; I Got Rhythm. China Boy; Shine
  662003TR (Continental) BENNY GOODMAN SEXTET
              Tiger Rag; Ain't Misbehavin'; I Got Rhythm. China Boy; Shine

THE FRANKLIN MINT RECORD SOCIETY   USA   12" 33s
  FMRS-SOWW   SONGS TO REMEMBER FROM WW2 2LP set
    FMRS-SOWW-2 BENNY GOODMAN: My Guy's Come Back (2)

THE FRANKLIN MINT RECORD SOCIETY   **USA**   Cassette
   SOWW   SONGS TO REMEMBER FROM WW2
                 BENNY GOODMAN: My Guy's Come Back (2)

HALO   **USA**   12" 33
   50275   JAZZ BUD FREEMAN, TENOR SAX AND ORCHESTRA
                 BUD FREEMAN, TENOR SAX WITH VOCALS BY THE DEMARCO SISTERS
                 I Got Rhythm; Ol' Man River; I'm Just Wild about Harry; The Atomic Age;
                 Where Have You Been. I Don't Know Why; Hop, Skip and Jump; Love Is Such
                 a Crazy Thing; Chico Chico; I'll Tell You How I Feel; [Gay Melody]

HARMONY   **Canada**   12" 33
   HEL-6004   JAZZMEN IN UNIFORM PARIS 1945   = CBS (France) 63130

HEP   **United Kingdom**   12" 33
   HEP.12   BUDDY RICH '47'48   That's Rich

HERITAGE   **Japan**   12" 33s
   MFPL-82801-810 ALL HIT SONGS FROM 1001 10LP set
     MFPL-82804   BENNY GOODMAN SEXTET: I Got Rhythm
     MFPL-82809   BENNY GOODMAN AND HIS ORCHESTRA: Symphony

HISTORY IN SOUND   **USA**   12" 33
   1941   BENNY GOODMAN: My Guy's Come Back (2)

IAJRC   **USA**   12" 33
   51   V-DISC STOMP
                 MUGGSY SPANIER: China Boy (3); You Took Advantage of Me (2).

JAZZ CLUB FRANCAIS   **France**   10" 78s
   ST1227/1232   JAZZ CLUB MYSTERY HOT BAND:
                 How High the Moon; Please Don't Talk About Me When I'm Gone
   ST1228/1235   JAZZ CLUB MYSTERY HOT BAND: If Dreams Come True; Blue Skies
                 Mislabeled on "Blue Skies" side with a label for F1235 (instead of
                 ST1235) as JACK BURROWS AND THE "DIVISIONAIRS": Shick Of Araby
   ST1228/1235   JAZZ CLUB MYSTERY HOT BAND: If Dreams Come True; Blue Skies
   ST1229/1231   JAZZ CLUB MYSTERY HOT BAND: Hallelujah; I Must Have That Man
   ST1230/1233   JAZZ CLUB MYSTERY HOT BAND: Stompin at the "Savoy"; S'Wonderful
   JC-120   JAZZ CLUB MYSTERY HOT BAND:
                 Please Don't Talk About Me When I'm Gone; Some Days Sweetheart
   JC-121   JAZZ CLUB MYSTERY HOT BAND: If Dreams Come True; Blue Skies
   JC-122   JAZZ CLUB MYSTERY HOT BAND:
                 Beatin the Hallelujah Drums; I Must Have That Man
   JC-123   JAZZ CLUB MYSTERY HOT BAND: Stompin at the "Savoy"; S'Wonderful
   JC-130   HOT TRIO RAY Mac KINLEY: Sugar; After You've Gone
   JC-131   HOT TRIO RAY Mac KINLEY: Shoemaker's Apron; China Boy
   JC-132   JAZZ CLUB AMERICAN HOT BAND: Red Light; You, You're Driving Me Crazy
   JC-133   JAZZ CLUB AMERICAN HOT BAND: Indiana [actually "You're Driving Me Crazy!
                 (What Did I Do?)"]; On the Sunny Side of the Street
      134   JAZZ CLUB AMERICAN HOT BAND: Pennies From Heaven; At Sundawn
   134-test   JAZZ CLUB AMERICAN HOT BAND: Pennies From Heaven; At Sundawn
      135   JAZZ CLUB AMERICAN HOT BAND:
                 One, Two, Button Your Shoe; Stealin' Smack's Apples
   JC-140   MEL POWELL: Hommage A Fatts Waller; Hommage A Debussy
   JC-141   MEL POWELL: For "Miss Black"; Don't Blame Me
   (F1235/1236   JACK BURROWS AND THE "DIVISIONAIRS": Shick of Araby; It's a Sin to Tell a
                 Lie   This item has the label for ST1235 (Blue Skies) used in place
                 of the correct label for F1235. The correct label is pasted over the
                 incorrect label.)

JAZZ ROAD   Japan   Compact Discs
BY28-9   V-DISCS ON CD   VOLUME THREE   "SMALL GROUPS OF THE 40s" TRAD TO SWING
            MUGGSY SPANIER: China Boy; BUD FREEMAN: Love Is Just Around the Corner
BY28-12   V-DISCS ON CD   VOLUME SIX   "JAZZ AND POPS OF THE 40s"   FOR MUSICIANS ONLY
            BUD FREEMAN: For Musicians Only
BY28-13   V-DISCS ON CD   VOLUME SEVEN   "JAZZ AND POPS OF THE 40s"
            JUKEBOX SATURDAY NIGHT   TRUMMY YOUNG: Thanks for the Memory

JAZZ SOCIETY   Sweden   12" 33
AA-511   TRUMPET TIME
            THE V-DISC JUMPERS: Love Is Just Around the Corner.
            BILL STEGMEYER AND HIS HOT EIGHT: Tea for Two;
            ROY ELDRIDGE AND HIS V-DISCATTERS: Old Rob Roy;
            ELLA FITZGERALD AND HER V-DISC BOYS: I'll See You in My Dreams; BUDDY
            RICH AND HIS SPEED DEMONS, FEATURING ELLA FITZGERALD: That's Rich

JOKER   Italy   12" 33s
SM-3119   JAM SESSION 1944-1946   ROY ELDRIDGE: Roy Meets Horn; Old Rob Roy
SM-3575   MUGGSY SPANIER AND HIS ALL STARS   Tin Roof Blues; Cherry

MAJESTIC   USA   10" 78s
1017   THELMA CARPENTER/BUD FREEMAN AND HIS ORCHESTRA:
            My Guy's Come Back; These Foolish Things (Remind Me of You)
1018   BUD FREEMAN AND HIS ORCHESTRA I Got Rhythm; Where Have You Been?
1023   THELMA CARPENTER WITH ORCHESTRA DIRECTED BY EARL SHELDON:
            Just A-Sittin' and A-Rockin';
            THELMA CARPENTER/BUD FREEMAN AND HIS ORCHESTRA: Hurry Home
1028   THELMA CARPENTER WITH ORCHESTRA DIRECTED BY EARL SHELDON:
            Bill; Can't Help Lovin' Dat Man
1031   BUD FREEMAN and RAY McKINLEY: The Atomic Era;
            BUD FREEMAN AND HIS ALL-STAR ORCHESTRA: I'm Just Wild about Harry
7157   THE FIVE DE MARCO SISTERS/BUD FREEMAN AND HIS ORCHESTRA:
            It's Been a Long, Long Time; Chico, Chico (From Porto Rico)
7160   FIVE DE MARCO SISTERS/BUD FREEMAN AND HIS ORCHESTRA:
            Hop, Skip and Jump!; Flat River, Missouri
7166   THE FIVE DE MARCO SISTERS/BUD FREEMAN AND HIS ORCHESTRA:
            Blue; Sweet I've Gotten on You (The Pennsylvania Dutch Song)
7194   THE FIVE DE MARCO SISTERS/BUD FREEMAN AND HIS ORCHESTRA:
            [Chiquita Banana (The Banana Song)]; I Don't Know Why (I Just Do)
Test pressing BUD FREEMAN: Ol' Man River   Single-sided
Test pressing DE MARCO SISTERS & BUD FREEMAN: Hop, Skip and Jump!;
            BUD FREEMAN: Her Majesty's Dance

NOSTALGIA BOOK CLUB   USA   12" 33
1004 (CSP P3-13618) RARE BIG BAND GEMS 1932-1947 3LP set
   CSP P-13615 BENNY GOODMAN AND HIS ORCHESTRA: That's All That Matters to Me (1); Lucky
            (You're Right - I'm Wrong) (1)

ODEON   France   10" 78s
281785   BENNY GOODMAN SEXTET: Ain't Misbehavin'; China Boy
281786   BENNY GOODMAN SEXTET: Tiger Rag

ODEON   Spain   10" 78s
184889   BENNY GOODMAN SEXTET: I Got Rhythm
204344   BENNY GOODMAN SEXTET: Ain't Misbehavin'; China Boy
204359   BENNY GOODMAN SEXTET: My Guy's Come Back

ODEON   West Germany   10" 78s
0-28343   BENNY GOODMAN SEXTET: Tiger Rag
0-28398   BENNY GOODMAN SEXTET: I Got Rhythm

PARLOPHONE   England   10" 78s
R-3000   BENNY GOODMAN AND HIS ORCH.: My Guy's Come Back
R-3002   BENNY GOODMAN SEXTET: Shine
R-3007   BENNY GOODMAN SEXTET: I Got Rhythm
R-3014   BENNY GOODMAN SEXTET: China Boy; Ain't Misbehavin'
R-3022   BENNY GOODMAN SEXTET: Tiger Rag

PARLOPHONE   Finland   10" 78s
DPY1019   BENNY GOODMAN SEXTET: Shine; China Boy
DPY1070   BENNY GOODMAN SEXTET: I Got Rhythm

PARLOPHONE   Switzerland   10" 78s
PZ11097   BENNY GOODMAN SEXTET: My Guy's Come Back
PZ11099   BENNY GOODMAN SEXTET: Shine
PZ11106   BENNY GOODMAN SEXTET: I Got Rhythm
PZ11111   BENNY GOODMAN SEXTET: Ain't Misbehavin'; China Boy
PZ11155   BENNY GOODMAN SEXTET: Tiger Rag

PHILIPS   England   7" 45s
322212BF (Continental) BENNY GOODMAN QUINTET: Liza
JAZ 107 (362013) JUNIOR JAZZ GALLERY BENNY GOODMAN
          BENNY GOODMAN QUINTET: Liza (All the Clouds'll Roll Away)

PHILIPS   England   7" 45s (EPs)
429410BE (Continental) BENNY GOODMAN QUINTET: Liza
BBE12189   BENNY GOODMAN QUINTET: Liza

PHILIPS   England   12" 33s
BO7225L (Continental) BENNY GOODMAN QUINTET: Liza
BBL7178   BENNY GOODMAN QUINTET: Liza

PHONTASTIC   Sweden   7" 45 (EP)
BG NOST 86   BENNY GOODMAN SEXTET: Ain't Misbehavin' (6)

PHONTASTIC   Sweden   7" 33s
MX-EPH84   XMAS MIX 1984 FROM PHONTASTIC ARTEMIS NOSTALGIA
            BENNY GOODMAN SEXTET: Tiger Rag
MX-EPH85   XMAS MIX 1985 FROM PHONTASTIC ARTEMIS NOSTALGIA
            BENNY GOODMAN SEXTET: Ain't Misbehavin' (6)
XMAS MIX 1986 XMAS MIX 1986 FROM PHONTASTIC ARTEMIS NOSTALGIA
            BENNY GOODMAN SEXTET: Shine
MXEPH 87   XMAS MIX 1987 FROM PHONTASTIC ARTEMIS NOSTALGIA
            BENNY GOODMAN SEXTET: I Got Rhythm

PHONTASTIC   Sweden   12" 33s
LV-50   LELIO 50 TRIBUTE IN SOUND (35 copies pressed)
            BENNY GOODMAN SEXTET: Tiger Rag (2)
NOST-7652   THE ALTERNATE GOODMAN Vol. XI
            BENNY GOODMAN SEXTET: Tiger Rag (2); Shine (2); BENNY GOODMAN AND HIS
            ORCHESTRA: That's All That Matters to Me (2); BENNY GOODMAN SEXTET: I Got
            Rhythm (1); BENNY GOODMAN QUINTET: Liza (All the Clouds'll Roll Away)
            (2). BENNY GOODMAN SEXTET: China Boy (2); BENNY GOODMAN AND HIS
            ORCHESTRA: Lucky (You're Right - I'm Wrong) (2)
NOST-7659-61 THE PERMANENT GOODMAN 3LP set
  NOST-7661   BENNY GOODMAN SEXTET: Shine (CO-35144); Shine (CO-35144-1)

PHONTASTIC   Sweden   Compact Disc
PHONT-CD-7660 THE PERMANENT GOODMAN Vol. II   BENNY GOODMAN SEXTET: Shine (CO-35144-1)

READER'S DIGEST   France   12" 33s
  LSP-13302-8 JAZZ STARS JAZZ CLASSICS 7LP set
    LSP-13308   THE UNIQUE HISTORICAL JAZZ DUOS Django Reinhardt with the Glenn Miller's
      All Stars: If Dreams Come True

REALM RECORDS   USA   12" 33s
  2V-8065   BIG BANDS FOREVER! FOUR KINGS OF SWING VOLUME 2 2LP SET
   V2-8065   BENNY GOODMAN LET'S DANCE   BENNY GOODMAN AND HIS ORCHESTRA: Symphony

REDWOOD   Canada   12" 33
  1001   BUDDY RICH: That's Rich; MUGGSY SPANIER: China Boy

REGAL   Spain   10" 78
  C8787   BENNY GOODMAN QUINTET: Liza

REGAL   Spain   12" 33
  33LS1009   BENNY GOODMAN QUINTET: Liza

RTB   Yugoslavia   12" 33
  LPV4316   BENNY GOODMAN QUINTET: Liza

SAGA   England   12" 33
  SAGA 6917   A MUGGSY SPANIER MEMORIAL   Tin Roof Blues; Cherry

SANDY HOOK   USA   12" 33
  SH-2072   "G.I. JIVE" VOLUME 1 THE BEST OF THE V-DISCS
    MUGGSY SPANIER AND HIS V-DISC JAZZ BAND: China Boy

SANDY HOOK   USA   Cassette
  CSH-2072   "G.I. JIVE" VOLUME 1 THE BEST OF THE V-DISCS
    MUGGSY SPANIER AND HIS V-DISC JAZZ BAND: China Boy

SAVOY   USA   12" 33
  MG-12024   RAY McKINLEY "BORDERLINE"
    BUD FREEMAN AND HIS ORCHESTRA: The Atomic Era

SONY   Japan   12" 33s
  20AP-1810   BENNY GOODMAN SEXTET
    Tiger Rag (2); Shine; Ain't Misbehavin'; I Got Rhythm; China Boy
   SOPM-162   BENNY GOODMAN COMBOS   Liza

SPOOK JAZZ   England   12" 33
  6603   MUGGSY SPANIER AND HIS ALL STARS   Tin Roof Blues; Cherry

SUNBEAM   USA   12" 33s
  SB-142-44   BENNY GOODMAN ON V-DISC 1939-48 3LP set   includes SB-143
  SB-143   BENNY GOODMAN ON V-DISC VOLUME 2 1945-46
    Shine; Tiger Rag; Symphony; My Guy's Come Back. I Got Rhythm; Liza;
    China Boy
  SB-231   EDDIE CONDON 1946 JAZZ CONCERT WITH GUEST SOLOIST TOMMY DORSEY
    MUGGSY SPANIER: China Boy

SUNBEAM   USA   Cassette
  SBC-143   BENNY GOODMAN ON V-DISC VOLUME 2 1945-46   = SB-143 (12" 33)

SWING HOUSE   England   12" 33s
SWH-32   BUD FREEMAN ALL STARS
          BUD FREEMAN: Coquette; For Musicians Only; MUGGSY SPANIER: Royal Garden
          Blues; Tin Roof Blues; Cherry; MONICA LEWIS: I'm an Old Cowhand. MUGGSY
          SPANIER: You Took Advantage of Me; V-DISC JUMPERS: Love Is Just Around
          the Corner; MUGGSY SPANIER: China Boy
SWH-34   ALL STARS "THANKS (FOR THE MEMORY)"
          BILL STEGMEYER AND HIS HOT EIGHT: Tea for Two;
          TRUMMY YOUNG AND HIS SPECIAL SERVERS: Thanks for the Memory

TIME-LIFE   USA   12" 33
STBB-28   BIG BANDS WORLD WAR II 2LP set
   STBB-28-2   VISIONS OF PEACE: BENNY GOODMAN: My Guy's Come Back (2)

TIME-LIFE   USA   Cassette
4TBB-28   BIG BANDS WORLD WAR II   = STBB-28 (2 12" 33s)

V-DISC   USA   12" 78s
555   EIGHT SQUARES AND A CRITIC: "The Latest Thing in Hot Jazz"
556   BENNY GOODMAN SEXTET: Shine; Tiger Rag
560   MONICA LEWIS AND HER V-DISC FRIENDS
          My Heart Stood Still; I'm an Old Cow-Hand
564   BUD FREEMAN AND THE V-DISC JUMPERS:
          For Musicians Only (A Musical Treatise on Jazz)
569   ELLA FITZGERALD AND HER SPECIAL SERVERS: I'll Always Be in Love with You
574   BENNY GOODMAN AND HIS ORCHESTRA: Symphony
582   MARTHA TILTON AND JACK LEONARD WITH THEIR SPECIAL SERVERS FEATURING TRUMMY
          YOUNG: Two Sleepy People
585   BENNY GOODMAN AND HIS ORCHESTRA: My Guy's Come Back
588   THE V-DISC JUMPERS: Love Is Just Around the Corner.
          MUGGSY SPANIER AND HIS V-DISC DIXIELANDERS: Tin Roof Blues; Cherry
601   THE BENNY GOODMAN SEXTET: I Got Rhythm
603   BUDDY RICH AND HIS V-DISC SPEED DEMONS FEATURING ELLA FITZGERALD: That's
          Rich. BILL STEGMEYER AND HIS HOT EIGHT: Tea for Two
605   ROY ELDRIDGE AND HIS V-DISCATTERS: Old Rob Roy
611   MUGGSY SPANIER AND HIS V-DISC JAZZ BAND: China Boy
612   ROY ELDRIDGE AND HIS V-DISC LITTLE JAZZ BAND: Roy Meets Horn
627 (vinyl) BENNY GOODMAN AND HIS SEXTET: Liza; China Boy (1)
627 (shellac) BENNY GOODMAN AND HIS SEXTET: Liza; China Boy (2)
629   MARTHA TILTON AND JACK LEONARD WITH TRUMMY YOUNG AND HIS SPECIAL SERVERS:
          Thanks for the Memory
713   ROY ELDRIDGE AND HIS ORCHESTRA: I've Found a New Baby
730   ELLA FITZGERALD (And her V-DISC Boys): I'll See You in My Dreams.
          MUGGSY SPANIER AND HIS BAND: Royal Garden Blues
740   BUD FREEMAN AND HIS BOYS: Coquette
753   MUGGSY SPANIER AND HIS V-DISC DIXIELANDERS: You Took Advantage of Me
VP-1683   BED FREEMAN AND HIS BOYS: Coquette   Single-sided test pressing

VICTORY   Belgium   10" 78s
9032   JAZZ CLUB MYSTERY JIVERS: Beatin' The Hallelujah Drums;
          Please Don't Talk about Me   1, 2, 3
9044   JAZZ CLUB MYSTERY JIVERS: I Must Have That Man; Blue Skies   2, 3
9045   ALL STAR AMERICAN ORCHESTRA: Red Light; Indiana [actually "You're Driving
          Me Crazy! (What Did I Do?)"]   1
9046   MEL POWELL: Hommage A Fats Waller; Hommage A Debussy   1, 3
          Some copies of 9046 presumably as by ALL STAR AMERICAN ORCH.
9047   MEL POWELL: For Miss Black; Don't Blame Me   1, 3
9057   HOT TRIO RAY Mac KINLEY: Sugar; After You've Gone   1
9058   HOT TRIO RAY Mac KINLEY: Shoemaker's Apron; China Boy
9059   ALL STAR AMERICAN ORK.: You, You're Driving Me Crazy; At Sundown   2

Label variations:
  1. White label with blue and black print
  2. White label with red and black print
  3. Blue label with gold print

WAVE   Japan   **Compact Discs**
  MFPC-85634   ALL HIT SONGS FROM 1001 Volume 4
                  BENNY GOODMAN SEXTET: I Got Rhythm
  MFPC-85639   ALL HIT SONGS FROM 1001 Volume 9
                  BENNY GOODMAN AND HIS ORCHESTRA: Symphony

GLENN MILLER ARMY AIR FORCE BAND

SIDEMEN TUNE TITLES/PERFORMANCES

ORGANIZATION

This listing is arranged alphabetically by tune title. If a specific performance has been issued, one of the release numbers is shown.

In this section "Columbia" means "Columbia (USA)."

AFTER YOU'VE GONE
  Turner Layton (cm); Henry Creamer (lyr) 1918
  20May45 RM trio ST-1377-1
  20May45 RM trio ST-1377-2
  20May45 RM trio ST-1377-3   CBS (F) 63052, etc.

AIN'T MISBEHAVIN' (From the 1929 revue "Connie's Hot Chocolates")
  Thomas Wright (Fats) Waller, Harry Brooks (cm); Andy Razaf (lyr)
  18Sep45 BG CO-35206-1   Columbia CL-6052, etc.
  18Sep45 BG CO-35206-6   Phontastic MX-EPH85, etc.

At Sundawn See "At Sundown (Love Is Calling Me Home)"

AT SUNDOWN (Love Is Calling Me Home)
  Walter Donaldson 1927   CBS (F) 63130, etc.
  20May45 UH ST-1374-1
  20May45 UH ST-1374-2   Esquire ESQ-302, etc.

THE ATOMIC ERA
  (An Improvisation by Bud Freeman and Ray McKinley)
  c.Oct45 BF/RM T580   Savoy MG-12024, etc.
  c.Oct45 BF/RM T580-alt   Halo 50275, etc.

AUTUMN SERENADE
  Peter DeRose (cm); Sammy Gallop (lyr) 1945
  Ralph Wilkinson arrangement
  19Oct45 RB JD

BILL (From the 1927 musical comedy "Show Boat")
  Jerome D. Kern (cm); P. G. Wodehouse, Oscar Hammerstein II (lyr)
  c.Oct-Nov45 TC TC T595   Majestic 1028

BLUE
  Charles Kenny, Abner Silver (cm); Nick Kenny (lyr)
  c.Oct-Nov45 FDMS FDMS T631   Majestic 7166

BLUE LOU
  Edgar Sampson 1933
  11Mar45 ABO ST-1264

BLUE SKIES (From the 1926 musical comedy "Betsy")
  Irving Berlin (Israel Baline)
  28Jan45 UH ST-1235   Esquire ESQ-302, etc.

BODY AND SOUL (From the 1930 revue "Three's a Crowd")
  John (Johnny) W. Green (cm); Edward Heyman, Robert Sour, Frank Eyton (lyr)
  19Mar45 EBO ST-1277-1   Blue Star 1

BRIGGS BOOGIE
  Arthur Briggs
  11Mar45 ABO ST-1265   Blue Star 11

CAN'T HELP LOVIN' DAT MAN (From the 1927 musical comedy "Show Boat")
  Jerome D. Kern (cm); Oscar Hammerstein II (lyr)
  c.Oct-Nov45 TC TC T597   Majestic 1028

CHERRY
  Donald (Don) Redman (cm); Ray Gilbert (lyr) 1928
  22Oct45 MS NVP-1627 D5TC-1453   Everybody's 1020, etc.

CHICO, CHICO (From Porto Rico) (From the 1945 film "Doll Face")
Jimmy McHugh (cm); Harold Adamson (lyr)
c.Oct45 FDMS FDMS T579   Halo 50275, etc.

CHINA BOY
Dick Winfree, Phil Boutelje 1922
20May45 RM trio   ST-1379-1
20May45 RM trio   ST-1379-2
20May45 RM trio   ST-1379-3   CBS (F) 63052, etc.
24Sep45 BG sextet CO-35235-1   Sunbeam SB-143, etc.
24Sep45 BG sextet CO-35235-2   Phontastic NOST-7652, etc.
22Oct45 MS   Unissued (Breakdown)
22Oct45 MS   Unissued (Breakdown)
22Oct45 MS   (Breakdown)   IAJRC 51
22Oct45 MS   JDB-VP-1668   Sunbeam SB-231, etc.

COQUETTE
Carmen Lombardo, John (Johnny) W. Green (cm); Gus Kahn (lyr) 1928
4Oct45 BF JDB-VP-1683 D5TC-1512   Dan Records VC-5010, etc.

DON'T BLAME ME
Jimmy McHugh cm; Dorothy Fields (lyr) 1933
19May45 MP ST-1371-1
19May45 MP ST-1371-2   Esquire ESQ-304, etc.

FLAT RIVER, MISSOURI
Grace Shannon 1945
c.Oct45 FDMS FDMS T576   Majestic 7160

For "Miss Black" See "Pour Mme Blanc"

For Miss Blanc See "Pour Mme Blanc"

FOR MUSICIANS ONLY (A Musical Treatise on Jazz)
Traditional
4Oct45 BF VP-1595 D5TC-1428   Bandstand 7106, etc.

GOOD NIGHT, WHEREVER YOU ARE
Dick Robertson, Al Hoffman, Frank Weldon 1944
1Feb45 EBO JD ST-1239-1
1Feb45 EBO JD ST-1239-2   Blue Star 14

HALLELUJAH! (From the 1927 musical comedy "Hit the Deck")
Vincent Youmans (cm); Leo Robin, Clifford Grey (lyr)
25Jan45 UH ST-1229-1
25Jan45 UH ST-1229-2   Esquire ESQ-302, etc.

HER MAJESTY'S DANCE

c.Oct-Nov45 BF T632   Allegro 4047, etc.

Homage to Debussy See "Hommage a Debussy"

Homage to Fats Waller See "Hommage a Fats Waller"

HOMMAGE A DEBUSSY
Mel Powell 1945
19May45 MP ST-1369-1
19May45 MP ST-1369-2   Esquire ESQ-304, etc.

HOMMAGE A FATS WALLER
Mel Powell 1945
19May45 MP ST-1368-1
19May45 MP ST-1368-2   Esquire ESQ-304, etc.

HOP, SKIP AND JUMP!
Keller, Livingston, Hoffman, Drake
c.Oct-Nov45 FDMS FDMS T587   Halo 50275, etc.

HOW DEEP IS THE OCEAN (How High Is the Sky)
Irving Berlin (Israel Baline) 1932
4Nov45 RCA JD   AFRS Music America Loves Best 74-Part 2

HOW HIGH THE MOON (From the 1940 revue "Two for the Show")
Morgan Lewis (cm); Nancy Hamilton (lyr)
25Jan45 UH ST-1227-1
25Jan45 UH ST-1227-2   Esquire ESQ-302, etc.

HURRY HOME
Joseph Meyer (cm); Buddy Bernier, Bob Emmerich (lyr) 1938
15Aug-13Sep45 TC TC/DRB T557   Majestic 1023

I DON'T KNOW WHY (I Just Do)
Fred E. Ahlert (cm); Roy Turk (lyr)
c.Oct-Nov45 BF FDMS T588   Halo 50275

I GOT RHYTHM (From the 1930 musical comedy "Girl Crazy")
George Gershwin (cm); Ira Gershwin (lyr)
19Mar45   EBO ST-1280   Blue Star 3
15Aug-13Sep45 BF   T560   Majestic 1018
15Aug-13Sep45 BF   T560-alt   Halo 50275, etc.
18Sep45   BG   CO-35207   Phontastic MXEPH 87
18Sep45   BG   CO-35207-1   Phontastic NOST-7652
18Sep45   BG   CO-35207-2   Columbia CL-6052, etc.
18Sep45   BG   XCO-35208-1   Sunbeam SB-143, etc.

I MUST HAVE THAT MAN (From the 1928 revue "Lew Leslie's Blackbirds of 1928")
Jimmy McHugh (cm); Dorothy Fields (lyr)
28Jan45 UH ST-1231   Esquire ESQ-302, etc.

IF DREAMS COME TRUE
Edgar Sampson, Benjamin (Benny) David Goodman (cm); Irving Mills (lyr) 1937
25Jan45 UH ST-1228-1   Esquire ESQ-302, etc.

I'LL ALWAYS BE IN LOVE WITH YOU (From the 1927 Film Booking Office film "Stepping High")
Sam H. Stept (cm); Bud Green, Herman Ruby (lyr)
12Oct45 EF EF VP-1599 D5TC-1430   Fonit Cetra VDL-1005, etc.

I'LL SEE YOU IN MY DREAMS
Isham Jones (cm); Gus Kahn (lyr) 1924
12Oct45 EF EF Unissued
12Oct45 EF EF Unissued (Breakdown)
12Oct45 EF EF Unissued
12Oct45 EF EF VP-1661 D5TC-1489   Jazz Society AA-511, etc.

I'LL TELL YOU HOW I FEEL

c.Oct-Nov45 BF FDMS   Halo 50275, etc.

I'LL WALK ALONE (From the 1944 film "Follow the Boys")
  Jule Styne (Jules Stein) (cm); Sammy Cahn (lyr)
  1Feb45 EBO JD ST-1238-1   Blue Star 13

I'M AN OLD COWHAND (From the Rio Grande)
  (From the 1936 Paramount film "Rhythm on the Range")
  Johnny Mercer
  18Sep45 ML ML Unissued
  18Sep45 ML ML Unissued
  18Sep45 ML ML VP-1565   Dan Records VC-5017, etc.

I'M JUST WILD ABOUT HARRY (From the 1921 revue "Shuffle Along")
  Eubie Blake (cm); Noble Sissle (lyr)
  15Aug-13Sep45 BF T559   Halo 50275, etc.

Indiana See "You're Driving Me Crazy! (What Did I Do?)"

IT HAD TO BE YOU
  Isham Jones (cm); Gus Kahn (lyr) 1924
  11Mar45 ABO ST-1263

IT'S BEEN A LONG, LONG TIME
  Jule Styne (Jules Stein) (cm); Sammy Cahn (lyr) 1945
  c.Oct45 FDMS FDMS T577   Majestic 7157

IT'S ONLY A PAPER MOON (From the 1933 Paramount film "Take a Chance")
  Harold Arlen (Hymie Arluck) (cm); William (Billy) Rose, E. Y. (Yip) Harburg (lyr)
  19Oct45 RB JD

I'VE FOUND A NEW BABY Also see "Red Light"
  Spencer Williams, Jack Palmer 1926
  Late Oct45 RE JDB-187 D6TC-6031   Fonit Cetra VDL-1007, etc.

I'VE GOT YOU UNDER MY SKIN (From the 1936 MGM film "Born to Dance")
  Cole Porter
  4Nov45 RCA JD/Ch   AFRS Music American Loves Best 74-Part 1

JUST A-SITTIN' AND A-ROCKIN'
  Edward Kennedy (Duke) Ellington, Billy Strayhorn (cm); Lee Gaines (lyr) 1945
  15Aug-13Sep45 TC TC T558   Majestic 1023

KING PORTER STOMP
  Ferdinand (Jelly-Roll) Morton 1925
  24Sep45   BG Breakdown
  24Sep45   BG
  24Sep45   BG

"THE LATEST THING IN HOT JAZZ"
  Traditional
  4Oct45 BF VP-1550 XP-35170   Bandstand 7106, etc.

LIZA (All the Clouds'll Roll Away) (From the 1929 musical comedy "Show Girl")
   George Gershwin (cm); Gus Kahn, Ira Gershwin (lyr)
   24Sep45 BG quintet CO-35234   Blu-Disc T-1012
   24Sep45 BG quintet CO-35234   Blu-Disc T-1012
   24Sep45 BG quintet CO-35234-1   Sunbeam SB-143, etc.
   24Sep45 BG quintet CO-35234-2   Phontastic NOST-7652, etc.
   24Sep45 BG sextet   CO-35234-breakdown   Blu-Disc T-1012
   24Sep45 BG sextet   CO-35234   Blu-Disc T-1012
   24Sep45 BG sextet   CO-35234   Blu-Disc T-1012
   24Sep45 BG sextet   CO-35234-breakdown   Blu-Disc T-1012
   24Sep45 BG sextet   CO-35234   Blu-Disc T-1012

LOVE IS JUST AROUND THE CORNER (From the 1934 Paramount film "Here Is My Heart")
   Lewis E. Gensler (cm); Leo Robin (lyr)
   4Oct45 BF NVP-1611 D5TC-1440   Jazz Society AA-511, etc.

LOVE IS SUCH A CRAZY THING

   c.Oct-Nov45 BF FDMS   Halo 50275

A LOVELY WAY TO SPEND AN EVENING (From the 1943 RKO film "Higher and Higher")
   Jimmy McHugh (cm); Harold Adamson (lyr)
   1Feb45 EBO JD ST-1237-1
   1Feb45 EBO JD ST-1237-2   Blue Star 13

LUCKY (You're Right - I'm Wrong)
   Edgar Sampson, Benjamin (Benny) David Goodman, Jack Palmer
   Eddie Sauter arrangement
   24Sep45   BG CO-35237
   24Sep45   BG CO-35237
   24Sep45   BG CO-35237
   24Sep45   BG CO-35237-breakdown
   24Sep45   BG CO-35237-1   Nostalgia Book Club 1004, etc.
   24Sep45   BG CO-35237-2   Phontastic NOST-7652, etc.

MY DADDY ROCKS ME

   24Sep45   BG No matrix
   24Sep45   BG No matrix   Columbia CJ-44292, etc.

MY GUY'S COME BACK
   Mel Powell (cm); Ray McKinley (lyr) 1944
   Mel Powell arrangement for 12Sep45
   15Aug-13Sep45 TC TC/DRB T555   Majestic 1017
   12Sep45   BG LM   CO-35190-breakdown
   12Sep45   BG LM   CO-35190-1   Sunbeam SB-143, etc.
   12Sep45   BG LM   CO-35190-2   Franklin Mint FMRS-SOWW-2, etc.

MY HEART STOOD STILL (From the 1927 musical production "A Connecticut Yankee")
   Richard Rodgers (cm); Lorenz Hart (lyr)
   18Sep45 ML ML Unissued
   18Sep45 ML ML VP-1565   Elec KV-111, etc.

OH, LADY BE GOOD! (From the 1924 musical comedy "Lady, Be Good!")
   George Gershwin (cm); Ira Gershwin (lyr)
   12Oct45 BR EF Unissued

OL' MAN RIVER (From the 1927 musical production "Show Boat")
   Jerome D. Kern (cm); Oscar Hammerstein II (lyr)
   15Aug-13Sep45 BF T562   Halo 50275, etc.

OLD ROB ROY
  Dolan (cm); Johnny Mercer (lyr)
  Late Oct45 RE VP-1706 B-44515   Fonit Cetra VDL-1007, etc.

ON THE SUNNY SIDE OF THE STREET (From Lew Leslie's 1930 revue "International Revue")
  Jimmy McHugh (cm); Dorothy Fields (lyr)
  12May45 UH ST-1259-1
  12May45 UH ST-1259-2   Esquire ESQ-302, etc.

ONE O'CLOCK JUMP
  William (Bill, Count) Basie, Lee Gaines 1937
  19Mar45   EBO ST-1279   Blue Star 2, etc.

ONE, TWO, BUTTON YOUR SHOE (From the 1936 Columbia film "Pennies from Heaven")
  Arthur Johnston (cm); John (Johnny) Burke (lyr)
  20May45 UH ST-1373-1
  20May45 UH ST-1373-2   Esquire ESQ-302, etc.

PAPER DOLL
  Johnny S. Black
   1Feb45 EBO JD ST-1236-1
   1Feb45 EBO JD ST-1236-2   Blue Star 14

PENNIES FROM HEAVEN (From the 1936 Columbia film "Pennies from Heaven")
  Arthur Johnston (cm); John (Johnny) Burke (lyr)
  20May45 UH ST-1372-1
  20May45 UH ST-1372-2   Esquire ESQ-302, etc.

PLEASE DON'T TALK ABOUT ME WHEN I'M GONE
  Sam H. Stept (cm); Sidney Clare (lyr) 1930
  28Jan45 UH ST-1232-1   Esquire ESQ-302, etc.

Poor "Miss Black" See "Pour Mme Blanc"

POUR MME BLANC
  Mel Powell
  19May45 MP ST-1370-1
  19May45 MP ST-1370-2
  19May45 MP ST-1370-3   Esquire ESQ-304, etc.

RED LIGHT (Actually "I've Found a New Baby")
  Mel Powell 1945
  12May45 UH ST-1356-1   Esquire ESQ-302, etc.

ROSETTA
  Earl (Fatha) Hines, Henri Woode 1933
  19Mar45 EBO ST-1278   Blue Star 2, etc.

ROY MEETS HORN
  Roy Eldridge
  Late Oct45 RE JDB-VP-1703 D5TC-1536   Joker SM-3119, etc.

ROYAL GARDEN BLUES
  Clarence Williams, Spencer Williams 1921
  22Oct45 MS Unissued (Breakdown)
  22Oct45 MS JDB-7 D6TC-5008   Everybody's 1020, etc.

'S WONDERFUL (From the 1927 musical comedy "Funny Face")
  George Gershwin (cm); Ira Gershwin (lyr)
  28Jan45 UH ST-1233   Esquire ESQ-302, etc.

S-H-I-N-E
Ford Dabney (cm); Cecil Mack, Lew Brown (lyr) 1924
29Aug45 BG CO-35144
29Aug45 BG CO-35144
29Aug45 BG CO-35144-breakdown
29Aug45 BG CO-35144   Phontastic XMAS MIX 1986, etc.
29Aug45 BG CO-35144-1   Sunbeam SB-143, etc.
29Aug45 BG CO-35144-breakdown
29Aug45 BG CO-35144-2   Blu-Disc T-1004, etc.

SHOEMAKER'S APRON
Michael Hucko 1945
20May45 RM trio ST-1378-1
20May45 RM trio ST-1378-2   CBS (F) 63052, etc.

SOMEDAY SWEETHEART
John Spikes, Benjamin Spikes 1919
28Jan45 UH ST-1234-1   Esquire ESQ-302, etc.

STEALIN' APPLES
Thomas Wright (Fats) Waller (cm); Andy Razaf (lyr) 1936
20May45 UH ST-1375-1
20May45 UH ST-1375-2   Esquire ESQ-302, etc.

Stealin' Smack's Apples See "Stealin' Apples"

STOMPIN' AT THE SAVOY
Benjamin (Benny) David Goodman, Edgar Sampson, Chick Webb (cm); Andy Razaf (lyr) 1935
25Jan45   UH ST-1230   Esquire ESQ-302, etc.

SUGAR (That Sugar Baby o' Mine)
Maceo Pinkard (cm); Sidney D. Mitchell, Edna Alexander (lyr) 1926
20May45 RM trio ST-1376-1
20May45 RM trio ST-1376-2
20May45 RM trio ST-1376-3   CBS (F) 63052, etc.

SWEET I'VE GOTTEN ON YOU
(The Pennsylvania Dutch Song)
Brad Reynolds, Willard Robison 1945
c.Oct-Nov45 FDMS FDMS T630   Majestic 7166

Symphonie See "Symphony"

SYMPHONY
(Original French title "C'est Fini," changed by American soldiers to "Symphony;"
published in France as "Symphonie")
Alex Alstone (cm); Andre Tabet, Roger Bernstein (lyr); Jack Lawrence (English lyr) 1945
24Sep45 BG   LM   CO-35236-1   Sunbeam SB-143, etc.
24Sep45 BG   LM   CO-35236-2   Columbia test pressing
 4Nov45 RCA JD (French)   AFRS Music American Loves Best 74-Part 2

TEA FOR TWO (From the 1925 musical comedy "No, No, Nanette")
Vincent Youmans (cm); Irving Caesar (lyr)
Mid-Oct45 BS VP-1666 D5TC-1494   Jazz Society AA-511, etc.
Late Oct45 RE J-610   USS-1040

THANKS FOR THE MEMORY (From the 1937 Paramount film "The Big Broadcast of 1938")
Ralph Rainger (cm); Leo Robin (lyr)
Mid-Oct45 TY MT/JL VP-1667 D5TC-1495   Fonit Cetra VDL-1003, etc.

THAT'S ALL THAT MATTERS TO ME
Jacobson, Roberts
Possibly Mel Powell arrangment
12Sep45 BG LM CO-35191
12Sep45 BG LM CO-35191-breakdown
12Sep45 BG LM CO-35191-breakdown
12Sep45 BG LM CO-35191-1   Nostalgia Book Club 1004, etc.
12Sep45 BG LM CO-35191-2   Phontastic NOST-7652

THAT'S RICH
Melvin James (Sy) Oliver
12Oct45 BR EF VP-1596 D5TC-1422   Jazz Society AA-511, etc.

THESE FOOLISH THINGS (From the 1936 London revue "Spread It Abroad")
Jack Strachey, Harry Link (cm); Holt Marvell (lyr)
15Aug-13Sep45 TC TC T556   Majestic 1017

TIGER RAG (Hold That Tiger!)
Tony Sbarbaro, Eddie Edwards, Henry Ragas, Larry Shields, Nick LaRocca (Original
   Dixieland Jazz Band) (cm); Harry DeCosta (lyr) 1917
29Aug45 BG CO-35143
29Aug45 BG CO-35143
29Aug45 BG CO-35143-breakdown
29Aug45 BG CO-35143-breakdown
29Aug45 BG CO-35143-breakdown
29Aug45 BG CO-35143   Phontastic MX-EPH84
29Aug45 BG CO-35143-1   Sunbeam SB-143, etc.
29Aug45 BG CO-35143-breakdown
29Aug45 BG CO-35143-2   Blu-Disc T-1004, etc.

TIN ROOF BLUES
New Orleans Rhythm Kings (Paul Mares, George Brunies, Leon Roppolo, Mel Stitzel, Ben
   Pollack) (cm); Walter Melrose (lyr) 1923
22Oct45 MS NVP-1627 D5TC-1453   Everybody's 1020, etc.

TWO SLEEPY PEOPLE (From the 1938 film "Thanks for the Memory")
Hoagland (Hoagy) Howard Carmichael (cm); Frank Loesser (lyr)
Mid-Oct45 TY MT/JL VP-1665 D5TC-1493   V-Disc 582, etc.

WHEN DAY IS DONE
Robert Katscher (cm); Buddy G. DeSylva (lyr) 1924
18Sep45 ML ML Unissued
18Sep45 ML ML Unissued
18Sep45 ML ML Unissued

WHEN JOHNNY COMES MARCHING HOME
Patrick Sarsfield Gilmore (cm); Harold (Hal) Dickinson, William (Bill) George (nee
   Gidley) Conway, William (Bill) J. Finegan (lyr and adaptation)
Matt Dennis arrangement
29Sep-11Nov45 V-Disc session CC/Matt Dennis Quintet Unissued

WHEN THE SAINTS GO MARCHIN' IN
Traditional
11Mar45 ABO ST-1266   Blue Star 11

WHERE HAVE YOU BEEN? (From the 1930 musical production "The New Yorkers")
Cole Porter
15Aug-13Sep45 BF T561   Halo 50275, etc.

YOU BELONG TO ME
  Eddie Barclay
  Hubert Rostaing arrangement
  19Mar45 EBO ST-1276-1
  19Mar45 EBO ST-1276-2   Blue Star 1

YOU TOOK ADVANTAGE OF ME   (From the 1928 musical comedy "Present Arms!")
  Richard Rodgers (cm); Lorenz Hart (lyr)
  22Oct45 MS Unissued (Breakdown)
  22Oct45 MS   IAJRC 51
  22Oct45 MS JDB-295 D6TC-6465   Everybody's 1020, etc.

You, You're Driving Me Crazy See "You're Driving Me Crazy! (What Did I Do?)"

YOU'RE DRIVING ME CRAZY! (What Did I Do?)   (From the 1930 musical production "Smiles")
  Walter Donaldson
  12May45 UH ST-1357-1
  12May45 UH ST-1357-2
  12May45 UH ST-1357-3   CBS (F) 63130, etc.
  12May45 UH ST-1358-1
  12May45 UH ST-1358-2   Esquire Esq-302, etc.

BANDS/UNIT NAMES/PROGRAM NAMES

AAF SCRAPBOOK 29Sep45
ALL STAR AMERICAN ORK. 12May45; 20May45
EDDIE BARCLAY AND HIS ORCHESTRA 1Feb45; 19Mar45
JAY BLACKTON AND HIS ORCHESTRA AND CHORUS 4Nov45
BLUE STAR SWING BAND 1Feb45; 19Mar45
ARTHUR BRIGGS AND HIS ORCHESTRA 11Mar45
[JACK BURROWS AND THE "DIVISIONAIRS" 28Jan45]
THELMA CARPENTER 15Aug-13Sep45; c.Oct-Nov45
EIGHT SQUARES AND A CRITIC 4Oct45
ROY ELDRIDGE AND HIS V-DISC LITTLE JAZZ BAND Late-Oct45
ELLA FITZGERALD AND HER V-DISC BOYS 12Oct45
ELLA FITZGERALD AND HER V-DISC SPECIAL SERVERS 12Oct45
(THE) FIVE DE MARCO SISTERS c.Oct45; c.Oct-Nov45
BUD FREEMAN AND HIS BOYS 4Oct45
BUD FREEMAN AND HIS ORCHESTRA 15Aug-13Sep45; c.Oct45; c.Oct-Nov45
BUD FREEMAN AND RAY McKINLEY c.Oct45
BUD FREEMAN AND THE V-DISC JUMPERS 4Oct45
BENNY GOODMAN Prior to 15Sep45
BENNY GOODMAN AND HIS ORCHESTRA 12Sep45; 24Sep45
BENNY GOODMAN QUINTET 24Sep45
BENNY GOODMAN SEXTET 29Aug45; 18Sep45; 24Sep45
HOT TRIO RAY MAC KINLEY 20May45
JAZZ CLUB AMERICAN HOT BAND 12May45; 20May45
JAZZ CLUB MYSTERY HOT BAND 25Jan45; 28Jan45
JAZZ CLUB MYSTERY JIVERS 25Jan45; 28Jan45
JAZZ MEN IN UNIFORM 28Jan45; 12May45; 20May45
KRAFT MUSIC HALL (Bing Crosby) 6Sep45
MONICA LEWIS AND HER V-DISC FRIENDS 18Sep45
(THE) RAY McKINLEY TRIO 20May45
GLENN MILLER'S UPTOWN (UP-TOWN) HALL GANG led by Mel Powell 25Jan45; 28Jan45; 12May45;
   20May45
PHIL MOORE FOUR 4Nov45
THE RCA VICTOR PROGRAM 4Nov45
DJANGO REINHARDT WITH GLENN MILLER'S ALL STARS 25Jan45
RETURN TO DUTY 29Sep45
BUDDY RICH AND HIS SPEED DEMONS 12Oct45
VIC SCHOEN BAND WITH THE ANDREWS SISTERS c.Oct45
EARL SHELDON 15Aug-13Sep45; c.Oct-Nov45
M/SGT. FELIX SLATKIN AND THE 39th ARMY AIR FORCES BASE UNIT (SECOND RADIO UNIT) (AAFTC
   ORCHESTRA) 29Sep-11Nov45
MUGGSY SPANIER AND HIS V-DISC JAZZ BAND 22Oct45
BILL STEGMEYER AND HIS HOT EIGHT Mid-Oct45
THE V-DISC JUMPERS 4Oct45
PAUL WHITEMAN AND ALL-SOLDIER BAND Oct-Nov45
TRUMMY YOUNG AND HIS SPECIAL SERVERS Mid-Oct45
YOUR AAF 29Sep45

PERSONNEL

S/SGT. HERMAN TRIGGER ALPERT (string bass) 4Oct45; 12Oct45; Mid-Oct45; 22Oct45;
  Late-Oct45
Andrews Sisters Vocal trio c.Oct45
Eddie Aulino Trombone 12Sep45; 24Sep45
Vince Badale Trumpet 12Sep45; 24Sep45
Danny Bank Baritone saxophone 12Sep45; 24Sep45
Eddie Barclay Director and arranger 1Feb45; 19Mar45
Jay Blackton Director 4Nov45
Yvonne Blanc 19May45
Dave Bowman Piano 22Oct45
Arthur Briggs Trumpet and leader 1Feb45; 11Mar45
Vernon Brown Trombone 18Sep45
Mike Bryan Guitar 29Aug45; 12Sep45; 18Sep45; 24Sep45
Mort Bullman Trombone Late-Oct45
Ernesto (Ernie) Caceres Clarinet Late-Oct45
Nick Caiazza Tenor saxophone Mid-Oct45; Late-Oct45
Thelma Carpenter Vocal 15Aug-13Sep45; c.Oct-Nov45
Roger Chaput Tenor saxophone 19Mar45
Chico Christobal Tenor saxophone 1Feb45
CREW CHIEFS Vocal quintet 29Sep-11Nov45
Alix Combelle Tenor saxophone 11Mar45
Bing Crosby Vocal 6Sep45
Delta Rhythm Boys Vocal 15Aug-13Sep45
Matt Dennis Vocal, arranger 29Sep-11Nov45
SGT. JOHNNY A. DESEMONE (Desmond) 1Feb45; 6sep45; 4Nov45
Johnny Desmond See: Johnny A. Desemone
Bob Dickerson Drums 18Sep45
Jack Dieval Piano 1Feb45; 19Mar45
Tommy Dorsey Host, trombone 4Nov45
Andre Ekyan Alto saxophone 1Feb45; 19Mar45
David (Roy) Eldridge Trumpet Mid-Oct45; Late-Oct45
Al Epstein Tenor saxophone 12Sep45; 24Sep45
Tony Faso Trumpet 12Sep45; 24Sep45
Morey Feld Drums 29Aug45; 12Sep45; 18Sep45; 24Sep45
SGT. JOHN (Jack) MELTON FERRIER Tenor saxophone, reeds 29Sep45
Sam Fidel String bass 18Sep45
Ella Fitzgerald Vocal 12Oct45
(The) Five De Marco Sisters Vocal c.Oct45; c.Oct-Nov45
Lawrence (Bud) Freeman Tenor saxophone 15-13Sep45; 18Sep45; c.Oct45; 4Oct45; 22Oct45;
  c.Oct-Nov45
Alex Gaija Tenor saxophone 19Mar45
Pierre Gergardot Guitar 1Feb45; 11Mar45
Benjamin (Benny) David Goodman Clarinet 29Aug45; 12Sep45; Prior to 15Sep45; 18Sep45;
  24Sep45
Gordon (Chris) Griffin Trumpet 12Sep45
Bob Haggart String bass 15Aug-13Sep45; c.Oct45; c.Oct-Nov45
Edmond Hall Clarinet 15Aug-13Sep45; c.Oct45; c.Oct-Nov45
Allan Hanlon Guitar Mid-Oct45; Late-Oct45
PVT. MICHAEL (Peanuts) A. HUCKO Tenor saxophone, alto saxophone, clarinet 25Jan45;
  28Jan45; 11Mar45; 12May45; 20May45; 15Aug-13Sep45; 29Sep45; 4Oct45; 12Oct45; 22Oct45
Max Hugot Tenor saxophone 1Feb45
John Lausen See: Yank Lawson
Yank Lawson (John Lausen) Trumpet, director 15Aug-13Sep45; 18Sep45; c.Oct45; 4Oct45;
  c.Oct-Nov45
Jack Leonard Vocal Mid-Oct45
Frank LePinto Trumpet 12Sep45; 24Sep45
Monica Lewis Vocal 18Sep45
Charles Lisee Alto saxophone 1Feb45; 19Mar45

Clyde Lombardi   String bass   12Sep45; 24Sep45
Mus. 2/C Robert Louis (Lou) McGarity   Trombone   15Aug-13Sep45; c.Oct45; 12Oct45; 22Oct45;
   c.Oct-Nov45
T/SGT. RAYMOND (Ray, Mac) F. McKINLEY   Drums   25Jan45; 28Jan45; 12May45; 20May45;
   15Aug-13Sep45; c.Oct45; 4Oct45; c.Oct-Nov45
SGT. (S/SGT.) CARMEN NICHOLAS MASTANDREA (Mastren)   Guitar   28Jan45; 12May45; 20May45;
   15Aug-13Sep45; 18Sep45; c.Oct45; 4Oct45; c.Oct-Nov45
Carmen Mastren   See: Carmen Nicholas Mastandrea
Jerry Mengo   Drums   1Feb45; 11Mar45; 19Mar45
Phil Moore   Piano, vocal   4Nov45
Liza Morrow   Vocal   12Sep45; 24Sep45
Cpl. Bill Mustarde   Trombone   4Oct45
SGT. ROBERT (Bobby) JOSEPH NICHOLS   Trumpet   19Mar45
Kenneth Norville   See: Red Norvo
Red Norvo (Kenneth Norville)   Vibraphone   29Aug45; 18Sep45; 24Sep45
Remo Palmieri   Guitar   12Oct45
PFC. MEL POWELL   Piano   25Jan45; 28Jan45; 11Mar45; 12May45; 19May45; 20May45; 29Aug45;
   12Sep45; Prior to 15Sep45; 18Sep45; 24Sep45
Gordon (Specs) Powell   Drums   15Aug-13Sep45; Mid-Oct45; Late-Oct45
PVT. BERNARD (Bernie) PRIVIN   Trumpet   25Jan45; 28Jan45; 12May45; 20May45; 24Sep45
Gaston Rahier   Tenor saxophone   19Mar45
Django Reinhardt   Guitar   25Jan45
Tommy Reo   Trombone   24Sep45
Bernard (Buddy) Rich   Drums   12Oct45
Hubert Rostaing   Clarinet, Alto saxophone and Arranger   1Feb45; 19Mar45
Henry (Billy) Rowland   Piano   Mid-Oct45; Late-Oct45
Gerald (Jerry) Sanfino   Alto saxophone   12Sep45; 24Sep45
Eddie Sauter   Arranger   24Sep45
Hymie Schertzer   Alto saxophone   12Sep45; 24Sep45
Vic Schoen   Conductor, arranger   c.Oct45
Gene Schroeder   Piano   15Aug-13Sep45; c.Oct45; c.Oct-Nov45
Al Sears   Tenor saxophone   12Oct45
Sy Shaeffer   Trombone   12Sep45; 24Sep45
Charlie Shavers   Trumpet   12Oct45
Bill Shine   Tenor and alto saxophones   12Sep45; 24Sep45
CPL. JOSEPH (Joe) SHULMAN   String bass   25Jan45; 28Jan45; 11Mar45; 12May45; 20May45
Lucien Simoens   String bass   1Feb45
M/Sgt. Felix Slatkin   Conductor, violin   29Sep-11Nov45
Howard Smith   Piano   18Sep45
Emmanuel Soudieux   String bass   19Mar45
Muggsy Spanier   Cornet   22Oct45
Bill Stegmeyer   Clarinet   18Sep45; Mid-Oct45
Slam Stewart   String bass   29Aug45; 18Sep45; 24Sep45
Martha Tilton   Vocal   Mid-Oct45
Sgt. Harold (Buddy) Weed   Piano   4Oct45; 12Oct45
Chauncey Welsch   Trombone   12Sep45
George Wettling   Drums   22Oct45
Hy White   Guitar   22Oct45
Paul Whiteman   Conductor, violin   Oct-Nov45
James (Trummy) Young   Mid-Oct45

LOCATIONS

Paris, France 25Jan45; 28Jan45; 1Feb45; 11Mar45; 19Mar45; 12May45; 19May45; 20May45
New York, New York, USA 29Aug-4Nov45

GLENN MILLER ARMY AIR FORCE BAND

SIDEMEN SCRIPTS

This section is comprised of a spoken introduction and comments at a V-Disc recording session attended by S/Sgt. Carmen Mastren, a comment at a V-Disc recording session attended by Pvt. Michael (Peanuts) Hucko and S/Sgt. Herman Trigger Alpert, and a sample of a script of one of the broadcasts that was done by Sergeant Johnny Desmond, while they were still members of the Glenn Miller Army Air Force Band.

An indented name of a speaker signifies that the speaking was taking place while the music listed before it was being played. The script material that follows was transcribed from recordings.

18Sep45 (Wed) New York, New York
  V-DISC RECORDING SESSION

  MONICA LEWIS AND HER V-DISC FRIENDS

Monica Lewis: Hiya, fellows. This is Monica Lewis speaking. I'm very happy to be here
    today to make this V-Disc for you, with Yank Lawson's jazz band. I hope you're gonna
    like these two tunes. One is "My Heart Stood Still," by Rodgers and Hart, and the other
    is Johnny Mercer's "I'm an Old Cowhand."

WHEN DAY IS DONE (Unissued first take)
  Vocal refrain by Monica Lewis
  Monica Lewis: I'm sorry.
Monica Lewis: I love that trumpet happening in that.

12Oct45 (Fri) Columbia studio, 799 Seventh Avenue, New York, New York
  V-DISC RECORDING SESSION

  BUDDY RICH AND HIS SPEED DEMONS

I'LL SEE YOU IN MY DREAMS (Unissued breakdown)
  Voice: Hold it.

04Nov45 (Sun) 4:30-5:00PM WEAF NBC, New York, New York
  THE RCA VICTOR PROGRAM broadcast

Announcer (Dick): Tommy Dorsey, Johnny Desmond, the Phil Moore Four, Jay Blackton and his orchestra and chorus, "The RCA Victor Program."
Theme
  Announcer: RCA Victor, world acknowledged leader in radio, television, phonographs and records, presents Johnny Desmond, the Phil Moore Four, Jay Blackton, his orchestra and chorus and your host for RCA Victor, Tommy Dorsey.
Tommy Dorsey: How do you do? This is Tommy Dorsey coming around to your house to talk about music and musicians. Our musician guests are Phil Moore and his group of Victor swing artists, who are responsible for the popularity of such tunes as "Shoo-Shoo Baby." Phil Moore wrote that one himself. Our singing guest is a young fellow in the United States Air Corps who has traveled all over the European Theater entertaining our troops. His special assignment was singing vocals with the famous Glenn Miller Band. He's Johnny Desmond and here he is with one of Cole Porter's best, "I've Got You under My Skin."
I'VE GOT YOU UNDER MY SKIN
  Vocal refrain by Sergeant Johnny Desmond and chorus
Tommy Dorsey: Thank you, Johnny Desmond. That was but good.
Sergeant Johnny Desmond: Thanks, Tommy.
Tommy Dorsey: Say, while you were touring Europe with the band, what songs did you find the boys liked best?
Sergeant Johnny Desmond: Well, they liked the fa..., the old familiar ones, Tommy, like "I've Got You Under My Skin." But they're always waiting to hear the latest hit from the States.
Tommy Dorsey: Well, that would include the tune that Phil Moore has lined up for us. It's Phil's newest composition and it's headed for the top.
Phil Moore: I hope that those are prophetic words, Tommy.
Tommy Dorsey: Well, just sound off, Phil, and let my prophesy come true.
I Want a Little Doggie (Phil Moore Four)
  Tommy Dorsey: I hear you, Philip. Make it jump.
  Phil Moore: All right.
  Tommy Dorsey: Here's Phil Moore and his fabulous four playing "I Want a Little Doggie."
  Vocal refrain by the Phil Moore Four
Tommy Dorsey: To the millions who know and enjoy the romantic tenor voice of Alan Jones, here's Dick to feed us with news about his very newest record.
Announcer: It's an RCA Victor record, of course. It's been called a bouquet of tender sentiment from the celebrated screen, musical comedy, concert and radio star Alan Jones. "When I Grow Too Old to Dream," he sings, "I'll have you to remember." Here is one of the loveliest lines of all lyrics, one of Romberg's loveliest melodies, sung with sincerity and sentiment that are as romantic as a love letter. RCA Victor has recorded Alan Jones' voice with such clarity and such naturalness that he seems to be there in the room with you, singing it to you and you only. On the reverse side of this RCA Victor record Alan Jones sings "Who Are We to Say?," another of your Romberg favorites, sings it with a delightful lilt and a deep feeling. See your RCA Victor dealer tomorrow. Take home to that record library you prize so much this newest and exclusively RCA Victor record by Alan Jones. Ask for "When I Grow Too Old to Dream" at your dealers tomorrow.
Poor Little Rhode Island (Full orchestra)
  Tommy Dorsey: Here's an extra special Jay Blackton arrangement that highlights the orchestra and chorus, "Poor Little Rhode Island."
  Vocal refrain by the chorus
Tommy Dorsey: Johnny Desmond has been singing with name bands ever since he left high school. He was with Gene Krupa and Bob Crosby. When he joined the Air Corps he sang with the famous Glenn Miller Band. That kind of work gets you around, doesn't it, Johnny?
Sergeant Johnny Desmond: Sure does, Tommy. I've been all over England, Ireland, Europe and as far south as the French Riviera. Now there's the place, the Riviera.
Tommy Dorsey: I know what you mean. Ah, do you like that, John?

Sergeant Johnny Desmond: Yes, all the G.I.s like it, Tommy. It's a rest center for the boys, with million dollar scenery. When I was there I went to a small cafe with some of the boys in the band and heard a little French gal singin' a song that sounded mighty good.

Tommy Dorsey: I know, but how was the girl?

Sergeant Johnny Desmond: Mighty good, too, Tommy. But we brought the song back with us and I'd like to sing it now.

Tommy Dorsey: Step right up, Johnny. The hall is yours.

Sergeant Johnny Desmond: The song, "Symphony."

SYMPHONY (Full orchestra)
  Vocal refrain by Sergeant Johnny Desmond (French and English)

Tommy Dorsey: Thank you, Johnny Desmond. That was in there. I'll buy that rendition. And as - as my contribution to your "RCA Victor Program" I'd like to play Jerome Kern's "Smoke Gets in Your Eyes" as a trombone solo.

Smoke Gets in Your Eyes (Full orchestra)

Announcer: Mr. Jenkins is out walking with his collie when he meets a stranger on the street.

Stranger: Mighty fine looking dog you got there, sir.

Mr. Jenkins: Oh, thank you. Know dogs, do you?

Stranger: No, no expert, but I'll bet you that dog's got a pedigree as long as your arm. Look at him. Handsome, aristocratic, got lots of poise.

Mr. Jenkins: Yes, I've won quite a bit of prizes with this fellow.

Stranger: Can't get away from it, sir. There's something about heredity.

Announcer: Yes, heredity counts in bringing you champion collies. Champion radio-phonographs, too. Your new radio-phonograph, whatever its name, will be the result of the background and experience of its makers. Can you think of a better engineering background in the field of radio and electronics than RCA? Or any name in the field of recorded music equal to Victor? Combine them and you have the secret of the world's most famous instrument of home entertainment, the Victrola. For only RCA Victor, RCA Victor makes the Victrola. Watch for the new post-war models, instruments that are brilliantly worthy of the 26-year engineering heritage of RCA, the 47-year musical heritage of Victor. So keep in touch with your RCA Victor dealer. For remember ...

Stranger: There's something in heredity.

HOW DEEP IS THE OCEAN (How High Is the Sky) (Full orchestra)
  Tommy Dorsey: Jay Blackton has made an arrangement of Irving Berlin's famous ballad "How Deep Is the Ocean," the best parts for our guests Johnny Desmond and the Phil Moore Four. I'll be there with my trombone. Here it is with the background filled in by the RCA Victor Orchestra and chorus.
  Vocal refrain by Sergeant Johnny Desmond (full orchestra)
  Phil Moore Four (with orchestra in background)
  Tommy Dorsey trombone solo (with orchestra and chorus in background)
  Vocal refrain by Sergeant Johnny Desmond and the chorus (full orchestra)

Theme
  Tommy Dorsey: Folks, we want to invite you to take part in a birthday celebration. Richard, will you cut the cake?
  Announcer: Friends, it's a very big cake. It has 25 candles on it, each one representing a year in the life and growth of radio broadcasting. This week has been designated as National Radio Week. RCA, the Radio Corporation of America, joins with millions of you folks to whom radio has become a part of everyday life, in paying tribute to the men in broadcasting who helped to build the foundations of a great American institution that has served us in peace and in war. 25 years is old in experience but young in enthusiasm. The Radio Corporation of America is proud of the contributions which it has been able to make towards furthering this new art and industry. Radio broadcasting will continue to grow and while we salute it in this week and its 25th milestone we look ahead with it to the years of service, entertainment and inspiration that we expect of it and that we are confident it will deliver. Tommy Dorsey, Johnny Desmond, the Phil Moore Four and Jay Blackton and his orchestra and chorus have been brought to you by RCA Victor, a division of the Radio Corporation of America, that's R

Announcer 2: Radio
Announcer: C
Announcer 2: Corporation
Announcer: A
Announcer 2: America
Announcer: and RCA Victor dealers everywhere.
Tommy Dorsey: Next week we'll all be back, Jay Blackton, his orchestra and chorus, and our special guest Thomas L. Thomas for another RCA Victor Program. Until then, this is Tommy Dorsey saying so long.
Announcer: This is the National Broadcasting Company.
NBC chimes